An Introduction to **PSYCHOLOGY**

An Introduction to
PSYCHOLOGY

by GARDNER MURPHY

WITH THE ASSISTANCE OF HERBERT SPOHN

HARPER & BROTHERS, NEW YORK

AN INTRODUCTION TO PSYCHOLOGY

Copyright, 1951, by Harper & Brothers
Printed in the United States of America

All rights in this book are reserved. No part of the book may be used or reproduced in any manner whatsoever without written permission except in the case of brief quotations embodied in critical articles and reviews. For information address Harper & Brothers, 49 East 33rd Street, New York 16, N. Y.

H-C

TO ALPEN AND MARGARET

CONTENTS

	Foreword	xv
1.	The Study of Persons	1
	Methods	
2.	The Biological Significance of Individuality	8
	Evolution and Individuality—Life and Adjustment	
3.	Heredity	16
	Genes and Temperament	
4.	Environment	27
5.	Individuality in Development	38
	The Nervous System	
6.	The Endocrine System	51
	Functions of the Thyroid—Sexual Development—Interdependence of Endocrine Organs	
7.	Some Elementary Motives	65
	The Physiology of Drives—The Maternal Drive—The Sex Motive—The Activity Drives—Sensory Drives	
8.	Emotions	86
	Fear—Rage—Emotion and the Autonomic Nervous System—The Interpretation of Emotional Expression—The Theory of the Emotions—Mood and Temperament—The Control of Emotion	
9.	Conflict	117
	Symbols—Frustration—Coping with Conflict—The Will	
10.	Sensing and Perceiving	137
	Thresholds—Attention—Four Aspects of Perceiving—The Development of Perception	

11.	Seeing	156
	Visual Quality—Past Experience—Set—Social Sharing of Visual Perception	
12.	Hearing	181
	Sensory Equipment—Auditory Qualities—Past Experience as Exemplified in the Localization of Sound—Set	
13.	Tasting, Smelling, and the General Senses	191
	Taste and Smell—Touch—Warm and Cold; Pain—Kinesthesis—Organic Sensitivity	
14.	Learning	205
	The Simplest Types of Learning—Competition Between Responses—The Acquisition of Skill—Transfer—Efficiency in Learning—The Theory of Learning	
15.	Remembering	249
	Association—Recall—Recognition	
16.	Imagining and Dreaming	270
	Imagining—Dreaming	
17.	Thinking	286
	Concepts—Individuality in Thinking	
18.	Creating	306
	Sensitiveness—Creative Skills—Factors Favorable to Creativeness—The Creator—The Education of Creativeness	
19.	Intelligence and Its Measurement	330
	Individual Testing—Group Testing—Performance Tests—The Distribution of Intelligence—Genetic and Environmental Background—The Theory of Intelligence	
20.	The Pattern of Abilities	365
	Some Statistical Terms and Ideas	
21.	The Self	388
	The Self and Social Perspective	
22.	Assertion of the Self	408
	The Means Used for Assertion of the Self	
23.	Defense of the Self	421
	Super-ego—Individual Differences in the Use of Psychoanalytic Mechanisms—Extroversion and Introversion—	

Compensation for Inferiority—Education and Therapy as Roads to Self-Knowledge

24. **Personality Measurement**   440
    Verbal Report Methods—Behavior Tests

25. **Projective Methods**   457
    Projective Tests with Children—Projective Tests with Adults—Picture Tests—Handwriting—The Interpretation of Projective Methods

26. **Social Attitudes and Their Testing**   480
    Attitude and Personality—Public Opinion Research

27. **Personality Patterns**   496
    "Sizing People Up"—The Continuity of Traits and Their Interrelations—Personality Types—Yet There Is a Place for Types

28. **Culture and the Individual: I. Ethnological Evidence**   518
    Social Roles

29. **Culture and the Individual: II. Our Own Tradition**   534
    The Psychological Results of Our History

30. **Oneself and Others**   555
    Mapping One's Own Education—Understanding Others

Index   565

ILLUSTRATIONS

1	Body Cells and Germ Cells	11
2	A Germ Cell	17
3	Trainability in Infants	21
4	Effect of City Environment on Intelligence Test Scores	29
5	Ape Reared in Human Environment	31
6	Individuality in Development	39
7	Expression of Emotions in a Ten-Month-Old Girl	42
8	Five Types of Connections Among Nerve Cells	46
9	A Case of Juvenile Myxedema	54
10	Pituitary Hormones Aiding the Reproductive Process	58
11	Chain of Reflex Activities	67
12	Depth of Sleep	73
13	Maternal Drive	75
14	The Autonomic Nervous System	*facing p.* 93
15	Bodily Changes Accompanying Emotion	96
16	Bodily Changes Accompanying Emotion	97
17	Section Through a Mammalian Brain	105
18	The Rosenzweig Picture-Frustration Test	125
19	An Act of Will	132
20	Threshold for Discrimination	139
21	The Köhler Cross	143
22	Cues to Distance	144
23	Individual Differences in Color Perception	*facing p.* 146
24	Double Color Cone	*facing p.* 157
25	Cross Section Through the Human Eye	160
26	A Monocular Cue	163
27	The Müller-Lyer Illusion	164

28	The Poggendorf Figure	165
29	Subject Viewing One of R. Levine's Figures	169
30	Average Scores in R. Levine's Experiment	170
31	Four Stimuli in R. Schafer's Experiment	171
32	Two Stimuli in R. Schafer's Post-Training Series	172
33	The Autokinetic Effect and Group Norms	175
34	Examples of Closure	179
35	Wave of Compression	182
36	The Ear	183
37	Organs of the Inner Ear	183
38	Timbre of a Violin	185
39	Chords and Vibration Rates	187
40	P. T. Young's Pseudophone	188
41	Touch Substituting for Sight	195
42	Elimination of Useless Movements	206
43	Learning to Write	207
44	Mirror Drawing	211
45	Individual Differences in the Ease of Conditioning	215
46	Competing Responses to the Same Stimulus	217
47	Salivary Conditioning in Human Subjects	219
48	A Stylus Maze	222
49	Practice Curve for Telegraphy	226
50	Effect of Motivation on Efficiency	238
51	Effect of Distributed Practice	239
52	Individual Differences in Remembering	250
53	The Effects of Labeling	257
54	Retention After Sleep and Waking	265
55	Recognition Memory	266
56	Effect of Physical Situation upon Dreaming	280
57	The Vigotsky Test	291
58	Thought Processes and Goals	303
59	Individuality in Creativeness	facing p. 310
60	Maze for Animals and Human Beings	334
61	The Wechsler-Bellevue Block Design Test	341
62	The Healy Pictorial Completion Test No. 2	344
63	The Normal Frequency Curve	345

ILLUSTRATIONS

64	The Normal Frequency Curve	351
65	The Minnesota Spatial Relations Test	370
66	The Bennett Mechanical Comprehension Test, Form AA	371
67	The Finger Dexterity Test	372
68	The Minnesota Rate of Manipulation Test	374
69	Data Yielding Positive, Zero, and Negative Correlations	378
70	Validation of Test Results	383
71	An Example of Empathy	391
72	Identification	414
73	Recognition Memory	433
74	Allport-Vernon Scale Profile of an Engineering Student	446
75	Allport-Vernon Scale Profile of a Liberal Arts Student	447
76	The Growth of Honesty	452
77	Patterns of Helpfulness in a Behavior Test	453
78	A Child's World Projected in Miniature Toys	458
79	Sensory Toys as Projective Materials	459
80	Brush Paintings by Two Boys	facing p. 460
81	Drawing by a Runaway Boy	462
82	Inkblots as Projective Materials	facing p. 464
83	Picture Test	470
84	"Complete the Drawing" Test	471
85	Posture and Attitude	481
86	The Social Situations Test	486
87	Rigidity and Ethnocentrism: Map 1	489
88	Rigidity and Ethnocentrism: Map 2	490
89	Rigidity and Ethnocentrism: Results	491
90	Diagram: An Interdependent, Dynamic System	499
91	Diagram: Self-View as Anchorage Point	500
92	Physical Types	511
93	The Individual and Society	523
94	Personality Development in Culture	528
95	Effect of Culture on Gesture: "Traditional" Jew	534
96	Effect of Culture on Gesture: "Traditional" Italian	535
97	Effect of Culture on Gesture: "Assimilated" Jew	536
98	Effect of Culture on Gesture: "Traditional" Italian	537
99	Personality; Ready-made or Potential?	561

FOREWORD

An interesting question facing the teacher of introductory psychology in recent years is the question whether a clear and consistent viewpoint can be combined with a genuine interest in all sorts of psychological facts. Can one give the student a way of looking at facts which he can use in his first systematization, and outgrow if he wishes? Can one give him an interest in the factual basis of the science offered by experimental, genetic, and clinical findings, without dogmatically forcing unwilling facts into a theoretical framework that squeezes them out of shape? Can one, on the other hand, provide plenty of facts without stuffing them into the student so fast that he can grasp neither interrelations nor implications?

Clearly the textbooks of the past half dozen years have marked a huge advance over their predecessors in these respects, and several very readable and appealing systematic presentations are available. Some of these are modern statements of classical association psychology; some are formulated in Gestalt terms; some are primarily physiological or broadly biological in their ultimate conception. I wish there were more of these systematic approaches. There is certainly a place for an introductory text viewing all psychology in terms of factor analysis; certainly a genuinely introductory psychology in Freudian or neo-Freudian terms would be warranted; certainly, likewise, the kind of general psychology which has been distilled in recent years from ethnology and sociology is ready for presentation in textbook form.

My own aim is quite different from all of these. My desire has been to try my hand at this task of systematic or unified presentation, utilizing a viewpoint developed primarily in the study of personality. The viewpoint shows obvious affinities to those of William Stern and Gordon W. Allport, and it could be called by Stern's term "personalistic." The conception is that every psychological act is the act of a whole person, and that the first task of psychology is to focus upon the nature of a person. Motives, percepts, thoughts, attitudes are activities of persons. Since biographers, novelists, dramatists are always concerned in the first instance with persons and their interactions, it becomes appropriate to draw upon their work to portray clearly and vividly what persons are. Another method of focusing attention upon persons is the use of photographs which make clear the relation of an individual human being to a goal object, a problem, or a challenge. Even more important in the development of such a viewpoint is the conception that each activity of a person can best be introduced not by describing the abstract process (e.g., perception, learning, thinking), but by describing *a person carrying out such an activity.* In some topics this has been easy to do, for good material is available. For example, it is not hard to describe emotion in terms of a concrete individual reacting emotionally (page 97), and it is not hard to show what intelligence tests (pages 340 ff.) or projective tests (pages 457 ff.) are like by showing how specific individuals react to them. In other chapters we have been less successful in finding material which completely satisfies this aim. But even when it has been necessary to fall back on abstractions about perception, learning, thinking, etc., with inadequate support from individual examples, it is hoped that the sense of individuality in the process has been conveyed.

It may properly be asked in this connection whether the book is therefore primarily a book about "individual differences." A glance through the pages will show that the answer is *no*. The book deals, to be sure, with individual differences somewhat more fully than is conventional in an introductory book. But the primary way in which it conceives of the nature of a *person* is in terms of what all persons have in common. It deals, therefore, not with "thinking" as such but with what a person is doing when he thinks; similarly, "conflict" is not a process to be investigated in its own right, but a process which occurs within and reflects a person. This means viewing each process both from *within* as the person sees it, and from *without,* as *other* persons see it. Here again I follow Stern.

As to the capacity of this viewpoint to give order and meaning to the facts of psychology, I can say only that to the one person who is doing the writing these facts have more luminous meaning, make deeper sense from this point of view than from any other. Whether this viewpoint will ultimately prevail will depend on the kinds of things which *persons* turn out to be, and nobody knows much about this today.

My obligation to the students who have assisted me in gathering data for this approach is greater than I can well express: Irving Dryman, Mark Grunes, Elliot Valenstein, Sheldon Waxenberg, and especially and always, Herbert Spohn. Miss Dorothy Thompson of Harper & Brothers gave extraordinarily valuable help in preparing the manuscript for the press.

G. M.

City College, New York
July, 1950

An Introduction to **PSYCHOLOGY**

1 THE STUDY OF PERSONS

When, during the first week of the introductory course, you ask students why they are taking psychology, you get such answers as these:

"The working of the human mind has always intrigued me and I thought if I could learn more about it and about people in general, I would be better able to understand them and be better equipped to mingle with them."

"I am majoring in a specialization which requires my contact with all kinds of people in everyday life. If I can understand myself, it will be much easier to understand them."

"I am interested in people. I chose psychology because I thought it was the logical choice to learn about the behavior and the reasons for the behavior of humans. I recently read a book on the psychology of the ape which I found interesting and amusing. If the study of human behavior is one half as interesting as that of the apes, I will be satisfied. Also, being human, I would like to be able to analyze my own behavior."

"With a basic course in psychology, people can be better understood. They just wouldn't look at a maladjusted person and laugh at him but there would be some sympathy for him since there would be a definite reason for his maladjustment."

Some students have more specific professional aims.

"I am very interested in social work and have been an adviser to a girls' group for a year. Many questions in relation to why the girls say and do certain things have confronted me, and I have not been able to give myself full explanations. This, I considered, was due to my lack of knowledge of human behavior."

"I have an interest in creative writing. I thought a more scientific study of human behavior would aid in my observation in the depicting of character."

"I took psychology because I am interested in law. The people that commit crimes and the profession itself probably would benefit greatly if they had a more intimate knowledge of the workings of the mind. The Judge in rendering a decision should be prepared to understand motivation and background leading to the crime. Psychology 1 being the introductory course naturally cannot make one a registered clinical analyst but still it is the necessary introduction to the field. . . ."

Psychology should be able to do a good deal to meet these needs and answer these reasonable questions, for the study of psychology is one of the roads to the understanding of oneself and of one's fellows. Psychology, as we shall define it, is the science that studies the responses which living individuals make to their environment. The field of psychology is, however, tremendously large, and there is no one single key to it all.

There are many legitimate ways of looking at our responses to our environment. Some psychologists are chiefly concerned with those responses which take the form of observed action or behavior. Some are most interested in those responses which enable us to become aware of our environment—responses like seeing, hearing, touching. Some are chiefly concerned with the world of our inner conflicts which make us blind both to outer realities and to our own weaknesses. *All* these ways of looking at psychology have something important to contribute. This textbook is one of many which aim to *combine* them.

But every approach involves some special emphasis, and the emphasis here is on the *wholeness of the individual: the psychology of the individual person*. It is possible to make constant use of the study of behavior, and of the ways in which we become aware of our environment, and of our conflicts, and still be chiefly interested in the way in which all these things fit into the whole going concern that is the individual. If we are told by laboratory investigators that we learn or forget at a certain rate (page 226) it is possible to put our emphasis upon the question why some individuals learn faster, others more slowly; and why some individuals display some areas in which they are more rapid learners than they are in others. It is possible to go beyond the many important general scientific laws which will lead to the way in which we learn and forget, and to ask what determines how each of us will differ from everyone else by virtue of the way in which he understands his task or the way in which he feels toward the things to be learned. Emphasis is not upon the *learning* considered solely in and for itself, but upon the individual as a learner, as a *person who is learning*.

In the same way, when it comes to the process of trying to understand ourselves, emphasis is given not only to the fact that we all indulge in a certain amount of self-deception ("kidding ourselves"), but to the fact that some people (for various reasons) do so more than others, and that some people (again for various reasons) can begin to outgrow or unlearn such self-deceptions more easily than others can. Without giving up the scientific laws or general principles, we shall seek to look for ways of particularizing them, so that they will relate most meaningfully to the individual personality.

Methods

Psychology uses many methods to gain understanding. One of them is the *social science* method—studying individuals in the community in order to see what our interaction with our fellows may be; what a man looks like to his friend, and what the latter looks like to him. A second method might be called the *biographical;* it gives the intimate story of individual development, including the pattern of growth and unfolding of the personality in home, neighborhood, and school, to see what resources and limitations the individual brings into each type of behavior. A third, the *biological* method, studies mankind, and therefore each one of us, as a living body that is an end result of the long series of biological changes which we know as evolution; it regards the individual as a system of life processes which have slowly evolved against a background of a vast development. The fourth, the *clinical* method, involves a study of those aspects of a person's psychological make-up on which his happiness and his effective adjustment to life's tasks depend; it studies his capacities and limitations, his successful or unsuccessful ways of meeting life's problems, the things which make or break a person's life. This leads to a fifth method, the *testing* method, the use of carefully prepared tests of human abilities and traits. Finally, there is a large place for the *experimental* method in psychology—the method of the psychological laboratory—in which trained observers with suitable instruments observe and measure human responses. Laboratory methods are available for the study of the emotions, learning, memory, thinking, imagination, and many other psychological processes.

In the light of these many useful approaches, the procedure to be followed here is one that synthesizes our knowledge of the individual by using all these methods. It will especially emphasize the experimental methods whenever experimental methods are available. The experimental method will be considered, for example, in relation to problems in perception, learning, and thinking. One can ask individuals to accept the working conditions of one's laboratory, or look at one's color charts, or listen to the musical tones or chords which one presents, or learn to find their arduous way through the mazes or to extricate themselves from the puzzle boxes which one has contrived or to think their way through one's specially designed problems. In this way, one may learn much about the nature of their basic processes of perceiving, learning, thinking. In recent years methods have also been devised for experimental study of motives and of emotions; one may, in the laboratory, gratify or frustrate the individual, and study his way of meeting sudden new opportunities or threats. One may experiment upon the individual's personal outlook on life and on his inner conflict, and in this way increase one's understanding of him and be more helpful to him. Every year some new aspect of human life becomes subject matter for experimental study.

Take the life history of Jerry Scott as an example of the ways in which the different methods can be combined. Jerry was born in Lynn, Massachusetts, in 1907, the son of a foreman in a tannery and a former school teacher. He had two younger brothers and one younger sister. Both parents were rather serious-minded hard-working people; Roman Catholics; usually voted Democratic; were known in the community as good citizens but rather withdrawn and socially inactive. (Here we are combining a social science method and a biographical method; cf. below, Chapters 24–27.)

Jerry was always wiry and full of bounce "from the cradle on up"; almost never sick, firm and muscular, he was always on the go, and wore his mother out—not through malicious mischief but through always getting into things. Moreover, he seemed to be more and more prone to worry and seemed to work off steam in ways that permitted him to forget his worries. For a nine-year-old to aim stones to see how near he can come to a window without hitting it, and then hit it, is not a heinous sin, but such episodes to the tune of thirty to forty a week were a good deal to "take." A "talking-to" never did any good. He seemed to have a deep need to win prestige in his gang, and did so with his escapades. His father, after talking to the priest and the school principal, but with no support from Jerry's mother, took him in to Boston one Saturday to "take some tests." Here a medical and psychological workout showed that he was overtense as well as far ahead of his years in strength, manual skills, and physical development; his intelligence was somewhat above average, but the personality test indicated nervousness and anxiety (testing and clinical methods; cf. especially Chapters 18–20 below). Recommendations were made about a boys' club in which Jerry could play basketball and gain social status from his peers under a tough young Canadian lad who had been wounded in Flanders in the winter of 1914–1915 and was quite a hero among the younger fellows. Jerry calmed down appreciably, partly through this experience, partly through sheer growing.

A true adolescent "growth spurt" began when he was 13 and carried him to 6 feet 1 by the time he was 16. His sex education had been scanty, but with very firm emphasis on right and wrong, and he had accepted without much inner protest his parents' strict and definite code. In the same way, though exposed to quite violent talk in the neighborhood regarding "Niggers" and "Kikes" and beginning to pick up this lingo, he heard his father say with emphasis that "good Catholics don't have to call other people dirty names," and it stopped him in his tracks.

At 16 began a series of very intense puppy-love affairs, actually very absorbing and enough to trouble his not very successful efforts to get interested in algebra and ancient history in high school. He kept up with basketball partly because it won him prestige with the ladies, partly because he felt more completely himself when he was doing something at which he was really good.

Shortly after this time as it happened he bumped into a man in the Lynn-to-Boston train who had given him psychological tests; he was cordially invited to come on a Sunday to the man's home and take some tests of *interests* and *values* (cf. Chapter 24). When he did so he was astonished to find himself showing many intellectual interests and values, and, though he could not tell why, a decline in response to things religious.

At 18 he asked a shy sensitive earnest young woman classmate to marry him; she thought it over very hard, decided she was not in love with him and said no. The sting hurt him deeply and it was two years before another girl interested him.

He had in the meantime buckled down, done well in biology, and, because he had heard there was good money in truck farming, gotten himself admitted to the Massachusetts Agricultural College. Here he did creditable though not brilliant work. In his sophomore year his teacher in animal husbandry, being puzzled about his lack of interest in farm matters, talked to him a couple of hours about his problems and showed him that he needed to understand himself better; in consequence, during Christmas vacation that year he went to a vocational counselor in Springfield. The counselor, after a long talk, administered tests of aptitude and interest, showed Jerry that he had more "academic intelligence" than he thought he had, and the fact "popped out"—Jerry had half-realized it—that he really wanted to be a historian, perhaps teach history in high school. With his parents' approval and a small financial lift from them, he transferred to Columbia University in New York, began to bury himself all too deeply in work in European history, while "working his way." He began to lose interest in athletics and social life.

At home at Christmas that year he happened to see his old flame at a party; they "sat out" a few dances and both discovered to their great surprise that they wanted to marry each other. The world somehow reversed itself; the girl was what counted, the history could go hang. He left Columbia, took "any old job" as insurance salesman. He and his new wife got a tiny apartment in White Plains, New York, and settled at once into an uneventful, highly conventional suburban life.

Jerry came to Columbia occasionally to see old friends. He was rapidly losing his self-consciousness. When a burly son appeared on the scene, he began to forget about his own childhood violence and his college shyness. When the little boy was 3, he seemed tense and worried, and Jerry took the little fellow for a psychological checkup, using the toys and games of the modern nursery school (cf. Chapter 25). The psychologist said artlessly that his daddy seemed to be pushing him into things that he himself had wanted to do but didn't do; in plain language he was "forcing" him intellectually. Jerry thought it over, talked it over with his wife. Just what *did* he want to do? His wife noticed that when he mentioned European history there was a wistful sound in his voice.

"Jerry, we've saved enough for you to finish college, and if you let me I'll teach while you do a year of graduate work for an M.A." He capitulated; did two years' work in eighteen months; and when last heard from had been teaching European history in Leonia, New Jersey, for some years.

He did an unusual thing. He came back to Columbia to do graduate work in psychology, and gladly lent himself as guinea pig for a number of *experiments,* partly for the sheer fun of understanding himself better, partly for direct practical help in deciding whether he ought to change direction again, this time becoming a psychologist. We shall leave him there; he has introduced us to a few of the problems and a few of the methods of psychology.

SUGGESTED READINGS

Allport, G., The use of personal documents in psychological science, *Soc. Sci. Res. Coun. Bull.,* No. 49, 1942.

Andrews, T. G. (ed.), *Methods of Psychology,* New York, Wiley, 1948, chaps. 1, 18.

Boring, E. G., *A History of Experimental Psychology,* New York, Appleton-Century-Crofts, 2nd ed., 1950.

Burton, A., and Harris, R. E. (eds.), *Case Histories in Clinical and Abnormal Psychology,* New York, Harper, 1947.

Dollard, J., *Criteria for the Life History,* New Haven, Yale Univ. Press, 1935.

Hunt, J. McV. (ed.), *Personality and the Behavior Disorders,* 2 vols., New York, Ronald Press, 1944, particularly Part 6.

Kluckhohn, C., and Murray, H. A. (eds.), *Personality in Nature, Society and Culture,* New York, Knopf, 1949.

Murphy, G., *Personality,* New York, Harper, 1947, particularly Part 6.

Murphy, G., *Historical Introduction to Modern Psychology,* New York, Harcourt, Brace, rev. ed., 1949.

2 THE BIOLOGICAL SIGNIFICANCE OF INDIVIDUALITY

Nature is always producing enormously more than can be used. A hundred thousand eggs may yield only two fishes which grow to maturity. English sparrows bring up in a season five broods of five fledglings each—if the individuals are lucky enough to grow up. Indeed the word *if* tells the story; for in the struggle for existence most individuals fail to achieve maturity. There is always much more given in potentiality than can be developed. This principle of the "prodigality of nature," the enormous wastefulness, constant tentative beginnings in one direction after another, is one of the primary clues that we need in studying the biological background from which humanity has sprung. Throughout the long millenniums of evolution there has been a premium upon those types of living organisms which were capable of rich and of constant *variation,* upon those forms of life which produce constantly varying offspring among which a few might be able to make the grade. Indeed, when considered in this light it is not really wastefulness; in the long run it is an asset to nature, or any of her works, to be capable of endless spontaneous variation. Life is always taking new directions, especially the new directions that appear when the young are produced, as the critical turn is made from one generation to the next.

Evolution and Individuality

Let us look more closely at these "new directions." The bodily parts of the animal parents—their claws, their feathers, their hair, their manes, their glossy coats, their eyes or ears or brains—are so well adapted to the environment in which they live that one asks how they ever developed such traits. How could the polar bear be more suitably decked out for its arctic hunting? How could the dark-green ovenbird be better protected for its life on the edge of the forest? Actually this extraordinary adaptation to environment did not come all at once; it was attained through the fact that at every phase in the history of the species there is much variation among the young. Some of the young in each generation are better fitted than the others to survive; and while these succeed in adapting to the environment, the others in each generation fall by the wayside before reaching the age of reproduction. In the long run, when those that are poorly adapted are eliminated, the remainder vary around a general type represented by their parents. Since those who survive are a selected group, and their descendants receive and transmit the favorable variations, there is a progressive shift in type.

There is always a place in nature for a new species, fitting into some nook or cranny, some new way of living, not already preëmpted by other forms of life. There is, moreover, always a place in nature for forms of life which develop new complex types of behavior that permit a better job of fitting into the environment than can be achieved at a simpler level. A swallow's wing, a hawk's eye, a monkey's brain permits complex activities which give their possessors a chance to make a new successful way of life for themselves. In particular, the gradual development of the *nervous system,* permitting a higher level of intelligence, enables a species to solve problems which at a lower level of blind brute stupidity could not be solved. The nervous system provides a system of communication between the various parts of the body and is also responsible for the individual's ability to make *new* responses, i.e., to *learn*. The more highly developed the nervous system, the more effective is the process of learning. There are great differences in the *nervous system* among the higher forms of life, differences closely correlated with the *ability to learn*. In a rather defenseless creature like man, the reproduction rate of which is low, brains are at a special premium.

If one sees this process on a large enough scale, he grasps why a species has been successful in its adaptation to gradually changing environments: because, instead of sticking to a narrow and fixed way of doing things, it was capable in every generation of producing individuals who differed considerably from one another, so that a few could take advantage of any new opening which nature offered; often a new complex organ could do a job better than an old simpler one. And the species in which there is plenty of variation among the young are those which have been capable of developing new organs. In other words, there has been a premium upon individuality, upon the tendency toward marked individual differences in ways of coping with difficulties. In species offering wide variations, a few may adapt to new problems and new threats.

We may summarize the discussion so far by saying that the evolutionary process results both in *increasing complexity* and in *increasing variability*. The nervous system, in particular, must be ready to vary in the direction of more effective integration of individual conduct. It is an advantage to have better eyes or better ears; but to have a better nervous system means being able to *learn* more quickly, or to *learn* more difficult things, so that in the long run there has been a premium upon the capacity to *learn*. The premium upon variability and the premium upon learning are two things which have been important in the background of mankind.

A serious danger confronts the student here (especially if he happens not to have had a course in biology), namely, the short cut of assuming that each generation inherits those traits which have been acquired by its ancestors during the ancestors' lifetimes. For example, it might be assumed that a chick runs from a moving shadow because its ancestors learned to run from the moving shadows of birds of prey. As far as we know, the habits learned by the chick's ancestors are not inherited by the chick. Rather, the chicks of today are descended from a biological strain which on the whole has a tendency to flee moving shadows. In each generation those with the greatest tendency of this sort will more likely be able to grow up. Those with the least tendency of this sort tend to get caught and eliminated. We are dealing with *biological variations* in attributes which are important for survival, not with the *transmission* of habits learned *in the lifetime* of each individual, and thus transmitted to its descendants. The matter can be explained by a diagram.

In Figure 1 we note the distinction between body cells and germ cells; the latter are the cells from which both the body and the germ of a new generation are derived. New tendencies arising in the germ cells from time to time give rise to new characteristics. As far as we know, these changes do not arise within the germ cells as a result of the accidents or new experiences or processes of learning undergone by the body material of the individual who carries them within him. We know that certain types of radiation, such as x-rays, can cause changes within

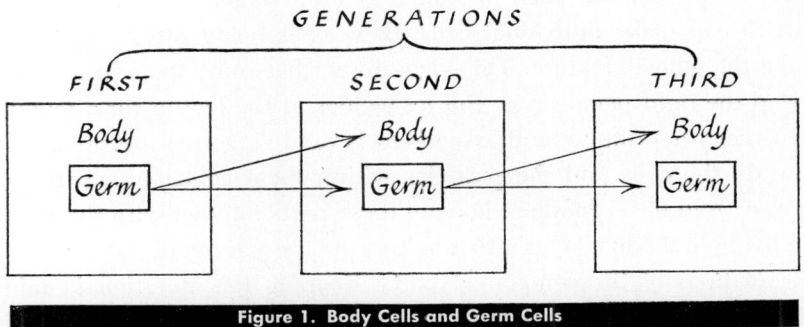

Figure 1. Body Cells and Germ Cells

Germ cells, while giving rise to both body and germ in the next generation, are independent of the body cells. It is what happens in the germ, not what happens in the body, that serves as the starting point for the next generation.

the germ cells; and it is possible that in the course of evolution various types of electrical phenomena in nature, such as the cosmic rays, may have had an effect upon the course of evolution in this way. The important point to stress is that when the change occurs in the germ it necessarily causes changes both in the new body which is to appear and also in the germs of the new individual, so that while the new individual gets the benefit of the change he is likewise able to transmit to his own descendants the new attributes which have appeared. The evolutionary process, then, as we understand it, involves the continuation of dispositions arising within the germs, not interference with such dispositions by the ordinary run of environmental effects happening to the individual in his lifetime. This is one reason why evolution takes so long. There are innovations, and they are of very fundamental importance, but they arise within the germ cells, not within the body cells.

Life and Adjustment

But we must look more closely at this process of adjusting to the environment, and ask ourselves how living things achieve such adjustments.

Our first answer to the problem of adjustment is that a living thing is a highly unified or integrated whole, not a loose assemblage of parts. We might be tempted to think of a living thing as made up of a great many little particles each of which is fitted together with the other particles to make individual cells, these cells being fitted together to make the whole creature. This view in fact has some truth in it, if it is put in the right perspective. But let us look at the matter for a moment the other way around, and ask: What is the living creature doing, and how do the cells and the particles within them contribute to the response? And in responding, how do these parts interact with the rest of the living individual? Our attention turns to the activity of the whole and the relations of the component parts. Keeping this question in mind, Wilson[1] flattened out a living sponge, squashed it, reduced it to pulp, rolled it into a thin layer, and then put it into a rapidly whirling centrifuge machine which separated its parts in accordance with their lightness or heaviness, so that nothing was left of the shape of the original sponge. He then allowed this material to stand. In the course of time it reorganized itself into the original sponge which it had been in the beginning. Sponges have been squeezed through fine bolting cloth, and found to reorganize themselves into their typical forms.[2]

There need be nothing particularly mysterious about this if our emphasis is upon the mutual attraction and interdependence of parts; in other words, if we allow ourselves to ask what the whole animal is doing, and understand this interaction that makes the whole. We should misunderstand evolution if we thought of parts as independent units, as if they could have evolved as single eyes or wings or muscles, rather than

---

[1] E. B. Wilson, *The Cell in Development and Heredity*, New York, Macmillan, 3rd ed., 1928.

[2] Ralph Buchsbaum, *Animals Without Backbones*, Chicago, University of Chicago Press, 1948.

evolving as aspects of whole living organisms. If particles were completely self-contained, with no chemical or other responses to other parts, they could never organize themselves into a functioning unity. An experiment like this shows that it is the interrelations between particles or between cells in the whole that gives us the first clue to the adaptation of organisms to their environment. One does not understand a living thing very well if he thinks of it as a juxtaposition of parts; he understands it much better if he realizes that the parts are attuned to one another in a basic physical and chemical sense. The individual is an integrated system, not a conglomeration.

Secondly, if an organism is to maintain its unity against threats, pressures, disturbances offered by the outer environment, its own inner organization must remain rather stable and constant. This clue to the extraordinary capacity which living things possess to maintain their unified existence was followed up by the French physiologist, Claude Bernard, who spoke of the "constancy of the inner environment." He pointed to the fact that in creatures built as we are, the temperature of the interior of the body, the amount of oxygen and water, the chemical balance of acids and bases, and indeed all the things upon which life depends, can vary only to a small degree without causing death. If your temperature varies a few degrees Fahrenheit as compared to the hundreds of degrees Fahrenheit measured from absolute zero, you are pretty sick. Experimentally, modern medicine elevates or depresses the temperature in order to achieve certain necessary results in special cases; but even with extreme safeguards, only a few degrees' deviation from the norm, amounting to 1 percent or so of the whole temperature measured from absolute zero, is permissible. The chemical and electrical states of the body are in the same way maintained at very nearly a constant level. The living individual might be regarded, then, as a little area of very high constancy in a sea of outer change. Outside of it, temperatures, air pressure, moisture, etc., are constantly changing. Inside, the organism must maintain itself at a level of great stability, for its life processes can go on only under very specific conditions.

If the stability of the inner environment is threatened, the living individual tends to do things which help to restore it. According to the process of evolution, methods for restoring such stability have been developed, and those forms of life which lack sufficient methods have not been able to survive. So far as we know, these methods of maintaining stability have arisen (like all other evolutionary products) through variations from generation to generation, and the continuation of those which are best adapted to the environmental requirements.

The delicate nervous system, in particular, can function only under certain specific inner conditions of the body; those specific conditions must be maintained inside the living individual, thus providing the immediate environment within which the nervous system can work. If the inner environment begins to change much from its normal, stable condition, the nervous system begins to respond. In the long run it responds in such a way as to restore the equilibrium in the inner environment. This conception helps us to formulate and answer the question: To what are the various activities of the living individual ultimately directed? If we answer this question in evolutionary terms, we may say that these activities are in a broad sense directed to the maintenance of the constancy of the inner environment; for they keep the individual alive and enable him to achieve the reproduction age. From this vantage point we may say that a large proportion of our human behavior (and a large proportion of animal behavior too) serves the end of maintaining inner stability.

This may at first sight appear paradoxical. Why does an Indian hunter make such a tremendous effort, get so hungry, thirsty, hot and tired, in his quest for food, or water, or shelter, or any other goal? Such behavior seems to upset his equilibrium, rather than to maintain a condition of inner constancy. If, however, we study over a long time the changes that go on inside the hunter which come under the general head of hunger, or thirst, or any other inner need, we find that his bodily state (for example, the state of the blood stream) has got further and further away from that balance which keeps the cells of his body in good working condition; and his nervous system, responding of course to a lifetime of experiences having to do with food and with food deprivation, is serving to bring about a change of conditions such that food will be put inside the body or its other needs met, and balance restored. A primary task of the life processes of the individual is this maintenance of a relatively constant inner state. The technical term for this inner constancy is *homeostasis*, literally, "standing the same." Each individual has the job of maintaining his own homeostasis; but since each individual differs in some respect from everyone else in the optimal conditions of internal balance, he will differ somewhat from everyone else in what he seeks. He will also differ in the way in which he seeks it—not only more food or less food, more exercise or less exercise, but also more even expenditure of energy in one case, more irregular expenditure of energy in another. The study of such individual differences will take us into the study of individual growth and learning.

SUGGESTED READINGS

Cannon, W. B., *The Wisdom of the Body*, New York, Norton, 1939.
Herrick, C. J., *An Introduction to Neurology*, Philadelphia, Saunders, 5th ed., 1931.
Hooton, E. A., *Up from the Ape*, New York, Macmillan, rev. ed., 1946.
Huxley, J., *The Uniqueness of Man*, London, Chatto & Windus, 1941.
Parker, G. H., *The Elementary Nervous System*, Philadelphia, Lippincott, 1919.
Warden, C. J., Jenkins, T. N., and Warner, L. H., *Introduction to Comparative Psychology*, New York, Ronald Press, 1934.
Young, C. W., and Stebbins, G. L., *The Human Organism and the World of Life*, New York, Harper, rev. ed., 1951.

3 HEREDITY

The understanding of the life processes requires an examination of heredity, and of the way in which heredity interacts with the environment as the individual grows. Nature has provided that we should all be essentially alike in the inner core that makes life possible, but very different in our ways of meeting day-by-day environmental changes. How does our hereditary make-up interact with our environment to make us what we are? This is the problem of "nature and nurture"; the problem of the relation between the individual's heredity and of the action of his environment upon him.

Well protected within the body, as shown in Figure 1 (page 11), are the germ cells containing the many particles, known as genes, which are the carriers of heredity. Figure 2 shows schematically (and with great simplification) a germ cell within which are small rodlike bodies known as chromosomes; arranged from one end to the other of each rod are small marks indicating the presence of the genes, the molecules (protein molecules) upon which heredity depends. When one germ cell from the father combines with one from the mother, the individual has his full complement of genes—thousands of them—and a unique combination of them, possessed by no one else (except that identical twins are individuals with the same genes; see page 19).

The genes can do their work only in a specific environment: first, the mother's body; later, the outer world. The recognition of this fact has caused a great change in our understanding of heredity in recent years. It was believed in the last century that heredity and environment were sharply contrasted forces, and that the individual owed some of his attributes simply to heredity, others simply to the environment. But it has become evident from recent experimental research that this sharp distinction between the effects of heredity and the effects of environment will not hold; even in the case of so obvious a hereditary attribute as the shape of the ears or the form and color of the hair, it has been found that the hereditary dispositions can do their work only by guiding the course of development along one rather than another line, while the environment of the mother's body maintains specific chemical conditions, supplying food and in other ways shaping the individual's growth. Before the time of birth, interaction between the body fluids of the mother's body and those of the body developing in the uterus goes on continuously; and as one looks closely at the embryo, the sharp separation of what is hereditary from what is environmental means less and less. After the time of birth it is the outer environment that guides, releases, and gives expression to hereditary potentialities.

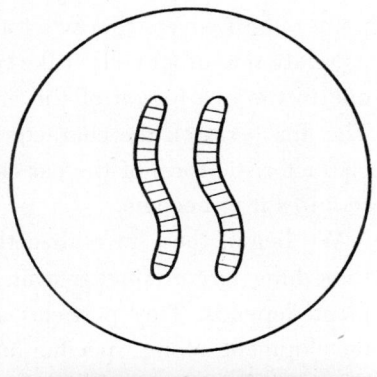

Figure 2. A Germ Cell

In this drawing of a hypothetical germ cell containing two chromosomes, the black bands indicate the location of the different genes. These are arranged along the length of the chromosomes.

Take this experiment with a species of white-furred arctic rabbit. About the inheritance of his white fur there can be no doubt, for the stock breeds true. Nevertheless, in this species of rabbit, it is necessary only to change the light in the room in which the animal is reared and his coat color turns out dark, rather than white. The potentiality for white can lead to an actual white coat color if and only if the environment permits it. In the same way some fish, like the flounder, which inherit a tendency to develop two eyes on the same side of the head, will if reared in water with a different salt content develop one eye on each side of the head like other fishes. Thus what is "inherited" in one environment is not "inherited" in another. The environment makes a difference in the appearance of the hereditary disposition.

The dependence of growth upon the environment is well brought out in studies of embryonic development. It is easy in animal experiments to interfere with the supposedly normal and universal processes of growth. One may tamper with the individual by transplanting tiny particles from one embryo to the body of another embryo, and in this way quickly convince oneself of the intimate interaction between the cells transplanted from the body of one embryo to the body of another, and of the intimate interaction between the cells transplanted and the other cells into whose region they are transplanted. From this viewpoint one discovers that what a cell is to become depends largely upon its relation to other cells. Take two similar bits of living matter and place one in the eye region of the embryo, and the other in the ear region. The first takes on the characteristic form of the eye cells, the latter the characteristic form of the ear cells. Each becomes what its environment requires it to become.

We begin, then, to realize that the term heredity does not refer to something foreordained within the tiny particles upon which development depends. Tiny particles are indeed essential, and they do guide development along specific lines. Indeed, only those which possess these predispositions can ever show the corresponding kinds of traits. But they can do so only when interacting with the environment in a particular way. This is to say that nature and nurture are aspects of a unitary developmental process. Pure nature is an abstraction; pure nurture is an abstraction. The terms may be necessary for certain purposes; but as we shall see later, the interaction of heredity and environment must be stressed even more in psychological traits than in anatomical traits of the sort which we have described. When the development of human personality is concerned, the conception of pure hereditary traits and pure environmental traits is as a rule not necessary, and indeed frequently confuses the issue. It is from the interacting effects of thousands of genes, together with the forces of food, oxygen, water, etc., made available to the growing body, that the architectural plan of the human individual is first constructed; after the time of birth this architectural plan interacts with the environment.

We might learn a great deal about heredity and environment by taking those individuals originally derived from two halves of the same growing individual—individuals known as identical twins—and seeing how their identical hereditary capacities interact with different kinds of training or environmental influence. In over 20 pairs of identical twins, Newman and his collaborators[1] studied the effect of contrasting environments. In every such pair the individuals had been separated in early infancy, and had grown up in very different environmental worlds. When after investigation and correspondence these cases had been identified, they were interviewed, given medical examinations, and put through a long series of psychological tests of intelligence and personality. Typical results are given in Burks' study of identical twin girls who had been separated in the early weeks of life, one of whom grew up as the daughter of a Marine officer stationed a large part of the time in Hawaii, the other as the daughter of a businessman traveling in New England.

. . . At 12 Adelaide and Beatrice were very similar and not far from average on individual intelligence tests, but Beatrice, the twin who had the more regular schooling, scored higher on a group intelligence test and on the Stanford Achievement Test, especially on the subtests most closely related to specific school content. . . . The twins were rather similar in play interests, both enjoying outdoor sports, scout activities, and reading, but B, unlike A, was interested in dolls and paper dolls. Interest patterns as revealed by The Strong Vocational Interest Blank appeared to be only slightly similar.

In certain aspects of temperament and social behavior, the twins showed some striking parallels in behavior. . . . They had similar histories with respect to nail biting, enuresis and early puberty; they were similar in observed expressive movements—gait, handshaking, writing tempo, . . . and in a group of traits (ratings) that appeared to rest on underlying physical vitality and non-adaptive irritability. Decided differences were noted, however, in a group of social-emotional traits, B, whose home situation was more free from pressure having a more cheerful mood level resulting in, or at least accompanied by, greater warmth and skill in the handling of social relationships. A "tendency to be dissatisfied," however, had been noted in both twins.[2]

The study of identical twins has also been carried out over the years at the Yale Psychological Clinic, under the directorship of Arnold

---

[1] H. H. Newman, F. N. Freeman, and K. J. Holzinger, *Twins: A Study of Heredity and Environment*, Chicago, University of Chicago Press, 1937.

[2] B. S. Burks, "A Study of Identical Twins Reared Apart Under Differing Types of Family Relationships," chapter 3 in *Studies in Personality*, Contributed in Honor of Lewis M. Terman, New York, McGraw-Hill, 1942, p. 67.

Gesell. The basic idea has been that when identical twins are tested at the same age, they should be very much alike, and that what they can learn will depend largely on their heredity and their age. In one of these investigations[3] twin infant girls served as subjects. One, Twin T, was trained at 46 weeks of age to climb stairs, and kept on practicing day by day for a matter of weeks. Her sister, Twin C, served as control at first, being given no such training. Of course her performance was inferior to that of her trained sister. Seven weeks later, however, she had her own turn with the training. Being now seven weeks older, she learned very much faster than Twin T had learned; and she soon caught up completely. Her quick catching up showed that the initial training of Twin T had made little or no difference in the long run; for Twin C, with a little practice at 53 weeks, was able to accomplish after two weeks what had required intensive practice for several weeks by Twin T, who had begun earlier. The effects of environmental opportunity depend upon the hereditary stuff present and the degree of development which it has achieved. Many such studies suggest strongly that the stuff of which the individual is made and the degree of its development provide the base line against which the effects of any specific training must be measured. It is naïve to brush off any question about the individual's attributes by saying that he "simply learned" them or "picked them up." The question is *how ready he was to learn* at the time that the particular occasion came along, and why it was that he *learned that particular attribute* while other individuals of a different constitution or at a different age, though exposed to it, showed very little response to it.

Another interesting study of the utilization of twins for comparisons of hereditary dispositions and training is the investigation by Myrtle McGraw.[4] Here the twin sons of a New York taxi driver were followed over a number of years. One of them was taught, while only a little over a year of age, to carry out such very complicated skills as roller skating and climbing a very steep slide (Figure 3), while the other went without such training. From the investigation there came a good deal of

---

[3] A. Gesell and H. Thompson, Learning and growth in identical infant twins: an experimental study by the method of co-twin control, *Genet. Psychol. Monog.*, 1929, 6, No. 1.

[4] M. B. McGraw, *Growth: A Study of Johnny and Jimmy*, New York, Appleton-Century, 1935.

Figure 3. Trainability in Infants

Johnny, one of the twins studied by McGraw, was given intensive training in a variety of activities. In 1 and 2, at about 8.5 months of age, he is beginning to learn to climb slopes. In 3, at 21 months, he has mastered a 70-degree slope. In 4 and 5, at the age of 13 months, he is walking up and down an incline of 32 degrees. (From M. B. McGraw, *Growth: A Study of Johnny and Jimmy*, New York, Appleton-Century, 1935.)

evidence as to the high degree of trainability which even a tiny infant possesses. This is of value even though it is likely that the twins in this instance were not identical, that is, did not have exactly the same genetic make-up. Another interesting result of McGraw's study is to show that what was accomplished with such spectacular success was not retained over a period of years. It takes steady practice to retain such skills as these. The body itself changes—the center of gravity, in the short-legged little child, is quite different from that in the older child—and other interests and habits have made the five-year-old individual quite a different person, so that it is scarcely surprising to find that the five-year-old was awkward and timid with the roller skates. Here again evidence as to the extraordinary effects of the environment must be seen in the perspective of the fact that rather little is retained even over a few years in this case if the practice is not kept going. There is really nothing in this study to contradict the proposition advanced by Gesell that fundamental importance attaches to the developmental level of the individual.

Even when heredity is constant, as it was in the studies of Twin T and Twin C described above, it is likely that many aspects of the environment are more important than is commonly recognized. Take the problem of the very first environment of the child, namely, the mother's body during her pregnancy. Some thoughts on this problem are suggested by the "five sisters of Quebec," the Dionne quints.[5] They were not only made of the same physical stuff—all being derived from one fertilized ovum, being in essence a pair of identical twins raised to the power of five—they were also subjected to an extremely uniform nursery environment in which the nurses supplied not only the same diet and regimen to all, but uniformity in treatment. The results were not reproductions or five carbon copies; on the contrary, the five individuals began to show distinctiveness in intelligence and in personality. They remind us that there are factors other than those which we ordinarily write down as heredity and environment; because in the usual formulation we forget many aspects of the environment. In this instance, five individuals growing inside the same uterus surely crowded upon each other; and some were crowded more than others. Just as ordinary twins crowd upon each other, and in some cases interfere with each other's growth, so the quints probably interfered with one another's growth a good deal. The effect upon the development of the brain is suggested by the very wide variations in intelligence which began to be evident among them as soon as tests could be given them. As far as their en-

---

[5] W. E. Blatz, *The Five Sisters, a Study of Child Psychology*, New York, Morrow, 1938.

vironment after birth is concerned, there must have been effects related to differential handling by the nurses. Nurses, like everyone else, have their human tendencies to make differences, to have favorites, to respond differently to different people. The little differences that emerged among the five individuals were undoubtedly magnified by their own interactions with one another in their own little community.

Genes and Temperament

Such studies of people with identical genes may serve as an introduction to the broad problem of the role of the genes in temperament. The problem is complicated. Yet there are good beginnings. We may begin with studies of animals, where the problem is simpler, and then turn to studies of human beings. For thousands of years men have bred animals not only for physical but for temperamental traits, and the dog fancier of today knows a great deal about the temperaments to be found in Chihuahuas, cockers, and Doberman pinschers. Research centers like the Roscoe B. Jackson Laboratories at Bar Harbor, Maine, have long known how to breed mice, rats, and other animals to produce specific physical attributes, and have found that it is feasible by a long series of inbreedings to produce stock which is absolutely uniform in terms of heredity; that is, every gene in one individual corresponds exactly with a gene in every other individual in the whole stock. In such pure strains, hereditary differences in temperament between one such strain and another strain appear in very striking form. There are savage and docile strains. The ancestry of the individual gives the clue to his temperament.

Sometimes a more ambitious attempt has been made over the years to determine the hereditary factors in the ability to learn to run a maze or the tendency to be timid or bold, or some other intellectual or emotional attribute. Calvin Hall[6] found it possible, by constantly selecting the bolder rats and the more timid rats, and breeding the bold only with the bold, the timid only with the timid, to accentuate these tendencies so as to produce a well-defined "bold strain" and a well-defined "timid strain"; animals reared in isolation in approximately identical

---

[6] C. S. Hall, The inheritance of emotionality, *Sigma Xi Quart.*, 1938, 26, 17–27; Temperament, a survey of animal studies, *J. comp. Psychol.*, 1948, 38, 909–943.

environments (and with no opportunity to learn from others) showed at the appropriate ages the boldness or the timidity which their ancestral predispositions called for. But here again we must emphasize the interaction of hereditary and environmental factors. One may alter the environment, and by rough or gentle handling make any individual animal bolder or more timid. There is an initial predisposition of the individual which is shown clearly by the behavior of animals coming from different strains, but what the animal actually does reflects likewise how it is reared.

Frequently it is possible to demonstrate that attributes owe much to heredity, although it remains impossible to specify what particular genes are involved. The whole matter is very complex and waits for far more investigation than has been done. Suppose we take as an example the demonstration by R. C. Tryon[7] that a particular kind of ability to learn to run a maze is clearly a product of heredity. He succeeded in the course of many years in producing from the same original ancestral stock of white rats two distinct strains; in each generation he selected those individuals that learned the maze with the fewest errors and those that took so many attempts to learn it that they piled up a huge error score. These bright and dull strains, as he called them, were gradually differentiated generation by generation until almost no individual in the dull strain was as bright as even the dullest individual in the bright strain. This would certainly appear on its face to be clear evidence for the inheritance of intelligence as such. Tryon pursued the problem, however, long enough to show that this solution was much too simple. He found that the capacity to solve this particular maze problem was not linked with the capacity to solve certain other problems; brightness and dullness were at least to a large degree relative to the task involved. We have therefore no right to say that general intelligence was the thing which the bright animals possessed and the duller ones lacked. Though Tryon certainly did show that there is a genetic basis for the animal's capacities in these tasks, it appears from his later studies that there were huge *temperamental* differences between the brights and the dulls; the brights were apparently the animals which were more strongly *motivated*

---

[7] R. C. Tryon, Genetic differences in maze-learning ability in rats, *39th Yearb. nat. Soc. Stud. Educ.*, 1940, Part 1, 111–119.

in this particular situation, and worked harder to solve the problem. Perhaps what was inherited was a certain disposition toward strong or weak motivation in relation to this kind of task. But again the role of the environment appeared; for motivation varied from one situation to another.

Regarding the inheritance of temperament in human beings, we have only fragments of evidence; however, these may be of interest. Mary Shirley[8] studied over a two-year period 25 children whose abilities and temperaments she observed every month. She and her assistant called at the home, showed the children some toys, made good contact with them, gave them some tests, and were able to evaluate their temperament and personality in many respects.

Shirley noted a great deal of continuity, or follow-through, from month to month during this two-year period, of a type which was probably related to heredity; it would be hard to explain it simply in terms of specific habits which had early been learned and been kept going as the child grew. Take, for example, the tendency to do "the unexpected." When any particular child is observed or given a test, he may do the things which are ordinarily typical of his age, or he may do something altogether unexpected, something so unusual that no place has been prepared for it on the observer's record chart. Now the children who do these unusual things at the age of six, nine, or twelve months tend to go on doing unusual things at later ages, although the specific unusual things that they do at each age are necessarily quite different from those done earlier. It is not a question of continuing to do at twelve months the same thing one has done at nine months. On the contrary, the general tendency to be "unusual" or unconventional seems somehow to run through the performance regardless of age. The child has perhaps a hereditary predisposition to a wide variety of action tendencies; is perhaps less simple, and therefore less predictable in his responses to the environment.

In an investigation by Ruth Washburn[9] which also bears on the question of hereditary tendencies, the temperaments of nearly 50 boys and

---

[8] M. Shirley, *The First Two Years*, Minneapolis, University of Minnesota Press, 3 vols., 1931–1933.

[9] R. W. Washburn, A study of the smiling and laughing of infants in the first year of life, *Genet. Psychol. Monog.*, 1929, 6, 397–537.

girls were followed through the first year of life. They were tested every four weeks with a series of twelve simple techniques similar to those which mothers have always used to bring out smiles and laughs from their children—things like peek-a-boo games, riding the baby on one's knee, holding him up by the ribs and jiggling him in the air above one's face. These experimental devices proved to give quite consistent results from month to month, in the sense that the children who were prone to smiles and laughs at one age level were on the whole prone to smiles and laughs at later age levels. Those who were nonresponsive when little continued to be nonresponsive when older. Those who were actually upset by the tests at an early age were likewise upset at a later age. The evidence, then, from continuity or follow-through, supports the view that temperamental differences between children have some deep basis. It must be emphasized that the evidence from such studies is only suggestive. It is, however, in harmony with the general evidence that certain tissues of the body (compare pages 93–100) are directly related to emotion and temperament, and with the fact that all tissues are derived from the individual's own personal assortment of genes and do not perfectly match the corresponding tissues from anyone else. But the tissues of the body have been acted upon throughout the individual's specific environment, and as we noted earlier his temperament really is a matter neither of his heredity alone nor of his environment alone but of the interaction appearing in his own life.

SUGGESTED READINGS

Glass, B., *Embryology and Genetics*, New York, Columbia Univ. Press, 1934.
Glass, B., *The Scientific Basis of Evolution*, New York, Norton, 2nd ed., 1935.
Glass, B., *Genes and the Man*, New York, Bureau of Publications, Teachers College, Columbia University, 1943.
Morgan, T. H., *The Theory of the Gene*, New Haven, Yale Univ. Press, 1928.
Newman, H. H., *Multiple Human Births*, New York, Doubleday, Doran, 1940.
Scheinfeld, A., *You and Heredity*, New York, Stokes, 1939.
Shull, A. F., *Heredity*, New York, McGraw-Hill, 4th ed., 1948.
Sinnot, E. W., and Dunn, L. C., *Principles of Genetics*, New York, Macmillan, 3rd ed., 1938.

4 ENVIRONMENT

Among the many environmental effects which are important for individual development, let us begin with factors of food and health. From chemistry today comes a variety of interesting leads showing the effects on intellectual growth of various sugars and acids, the administration of which may actually raise the intelligence level considerably. For example, in 1946 three investigators[1] offered preliminary data on the effect of glutamic acid:

Summary: The results here reported must be considered tentative because of the smallness of the group [nine subjects, 16 months to 17.5 years of age, seven patients with convulsive disorders and two mentally retarded without convulsions], but the consistent improvement reflected in the psychologic test scores under the conditions of our experiment [Stanford Binet, Form L, Wechsler-Bellevue, Kuhlman-Binet, Arthur Point Scale, Merrill-Palmer, Rorschach] suggests that glutamic acid may have a genuine facilitating effect on mental functioning in human subjects, as it does on maze learning in the white rat. (P. 501.)

For all subjects, sharp, positive increments in mental ages are apparent after treatment with glutamic acid, with the mental ages of the low grade subjects increasing at a rate faster than is expected in children of average intelligence. [Six-month experimental period.] (P. 498.)

On a follow-up study with much additional evidence the three investigators report:[2]

---

[1] F. T. Zimmerman, D. B. Burgemeister, and T. J. Putnam, Effect of glutamic acid on mental functioning in children and in adolescents, *Arch. Neurol. Psychiat.*, 1946, 56, 489–506.

[2] The ceiling effect of glutamic acid upon intelligence in children and adolescents, *Amer. J. Psychiat.*, 1947–1948, 104, 593–599.

Conclusions:
1. Glutamic acid accelerates mental functioning in human subjects.
2. The acceleration is general and is not restricted to segments of the intelligence and personality. . . .
3. The greatest improvement in intelligence and performance test scores occurs within the initial 6 months of treatment, after which the acceleration is diminished and appears to be approaching a ceiling after one year of therapy. (P. 598.)

And there is much evidence regarding the role of those glands which, by pouring complex chemical products into the blood stream, nourish and stimulate the nerve cells (cf. page 53). Limitation of diet to the traditional "hog and hominy" with no attention to minerals or vitamins may produce a loss of vitality and even perhaps also a certain amount of intellectual stunting (see page 54).

From biology and medicine come many clues regarding the role of health and disease in relation to bodily strength, endurance, speed of reaction, and the capacity to stand up under strain. (Later we shall note also the evidence that certain types of body build may be associated with certain types of temperament. Compare page 510.) Many investigations show the effect of early childhood diseases on the nervous and glandular systems, with permanent effects of various sorts on the personalities of some individuals. Medical data are important not only in relation to the occasional excessive deviations from the normal; the variations "within the normal limits" which may sometimes be overlooked or forgotten are nevertheless interesting and important for the psychologist. It is becoming customary today to look for clues to personality make-up not merely from hospital and clinic, but from day-by-day observations and physical examinations by those medical men and women who are interested not only in specific diseases, but in the nature of general health and physiological functioning, and the relation of the individual's whole physical situation to his whole personality.

From cultural anthropology—the study of human groups which have not developed written language—and from sociology—the study of more complex societies—a great deal has been discovered about the effects of environment upon intelligence and temperament. These tell us about the way in which the individual child is reared in the customs of his group, and learns not only to behave as is required by the system of local customs, but to take over the mental habits which characterize the group's way of life. His intellectual processes are seen to be molded by the social environment. In our own society, an example of such social effects in the development of the intellectual powers is the situation which characterizes the rural Negro child in the South.[3] Here about one-third as much is spent on the Negro school as is spent on the white school, and even these

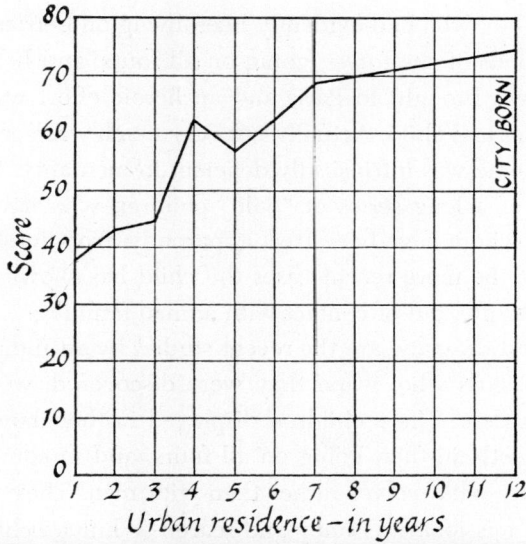

Figure 4. Effect of City Environment on Intelligence Test Scores

The National Intelligence Test was administered to 776 twelve-year-old Negro boys in three southern cities. Of these boys, only 359 were city-born; the rest came from a rural environment. When the boys are grouped on the basis of the length of time they have lived in the city (the city-born have lived in a city for 12 years) and the mean intelligence test scores are computed for these groups, there is a direct increase of intelligence with length of residence in the city. (From O. Klineberg, *Negro Intelligence and Selective Migration,* New York, Columbia University Press, 1935.)

rural white schools are grossly inferior to the general American school standard. Let these Negro children be brought early in life into contact with urban rather than rural Negro schools, and they make the gains shown in Figure 4. Let them be brought to northern cities, and one finds ordinarily no clear-cut and significant difference between them

---

[3] O. Klineberg, *Negro Intelligence and Selective Migration,* New York, Columbia University Press, 1935, p. 54.

and white children.[4] Thus one may say with some certainty that profound effects are exerted by the social environment.

Even more striking evidences of early social factors have been brought to light in the study of children who have from birth been reared (like the mythical Romulus and Remus) by wild animals; they are called *feral* children—from *fera*, a wild animal. We may begin with the story of the discovery, by some hunters, of a boy in the forests of eastern France over 100 years ago, a boy who had evidently been living on berries and other available wild foods of the forest, going on all fours, and behaving like an animal. He was brought to Paris and an heroic effort was made to turn him into a normal child. Actually not very much was accomplished, probably because he was intrinsically deficient in mentality. But he was merely the first of a long series of "wild" children who have been reported, many of whom have been free, apparently, from intellectual defects. In some of the more recent cases the child has shown the effects not simply of wild life, but of contact with animal families.

Among the most dramatic are the recent studies by an Indian missionary of two small girls who, when they were discovered, were actually living in a wolf's den.[5] These children displayed in their howls and the baring of their teeth, in their going on all fours, and in countless other ways, their affinity with wolves rather than with men. They were taken lovingly into the missionary's family and reared as human children. One of the little girls was in poor shape physically and did not live long. The other, however, was reared over a period of a dozen years with every attention and with every effort to make her human. It was hard going. She had originally shown the bodily postures and manners of a wolf. Her knees, for example, were calloused very heavily from her typical all-fours gait. She tore her food and jealously guarded scraps of it from others who might be nearby. When she was brought into a human home, she struggled long against discipline and against the acquisition of speech. Despite all this she gradually made progress during the dozen years that she lived.

The general picture is clear, then, that to be normally human depends

---

[4] J. Peterson, L. H. Lanier, and H. M. Walker, Comparisons of white and Negro children in certain ingenuity and speed tests, *J. comp. Psychol.*, 1925, 5, 271–283.
[5] A. Gesell, *Wolf Child and Human Child*, New York, Harper, 1941.

ENVIRONMENT

upon starting out with normal social upbringing, and that several years of a wild rather than a human environment can make a great initial difference, with enduring after-effects.

The reverse of the case of the feral children is the case in which a wild animal is reared in an essentially human way. It has long been noticed that domestic animals like dogs take over human ways of various sorts:

Figure 5. Ape Reared in Human Environment

Donald (13.5 months) and Gua (11 months) playing with blocks. The general reaction to blocks of this ape and child, who were reared together from birth, was "similar in that each will examine them, throw them, and put them in his mouth. Differences in manipulation and in the ability to build small towers are not observed until the later months." (From W. M. Kellogg and L. A. Kellogg, *Ape and Child*, New York, McGraw-Hill, 1933.)

for example, the tremendous craving for affection, and the development of intense personal loyalty, which are not found among the same animals in their wild state. Of course part of all this humanness may be due to breeding the dogs for such traits. But consider the case of animals adopted directly out of wild life and brought into human homes (fawns, bear cubs, falcons, etc.).

One of the most striking of these observations of what a human environment can do with an animal concerns a baby chimpanzee reared for about a year in a human home in which there was a child of about the same age.[6] In this study of the ape and the child there was a day-by-day record of the physical and social behavior of the two, and experiments and films showing the great readiness of the baby chimpanzee to take on human ways, not only in posture, in gesture, in the expression of affection, but also in habits and skills, up to a certain point (see Figure 5). The ape was practically on a sister-brother basis with the child. The ape's rate of development, especially physical and motor development, was at first so rapid that in many respects she was actually ahead of the child. The difference in growth tempo, however, was such that by the end of the first year she was plainly falling behind in many functions, and was obviously not going to make the grade in the matter of intellectual adaptation to human demands. This investigation showed that a great deal of human socialization can be accomplished in an animal which in the natural state is very different; but it also indicates very definite limits in what can be achieved by social pressure working against the limits set by biological make-up.

We have seen, then, what happens when heredity is held more or less constant and environment varies, and when environment is held more or less constant and heredity varies. The more typical everyday situation is one in which there is simultaneous variation in both stock and environment. Much that is popularly attributed to heredity or to environment is really due to the interaction of the two. Thus most people will tell you that the short stature of the Japanese is simply a hereditary trait. Actually Japanese reared on the western coast of North America average three inches taller than Japanese reared in Japan; but even among the American-born Japanese a relative shortness of stature prevails, with wide individual variability, of course, so that apparently both factors are involved.

A typical large-scale study in which the effects of varying stock and varying environment can both be seen is one by Myrtle Bruce[7] of chil-

---

[6] W. N. Kellogg and L. A. Kellogg, *The Ape and the Child*, New York, McGraw-Hill, 1933.

[7] M. Bruce, Factors affecting intelligence test performance of whites and Negroes in the rural South, *Arch. Psychol.*, 1940, No. 252.

dren growing up in Halifax County, Virginia. Here there is a very severe physical and social handicap. When their physical and economic status are measured on a scale which allows a certain amount for every comfort, convenience, or advantage—so much for running water, telephone, number of rooms per person, number of magazines, etc.—these children turn out to be at the very bottom among social groups investigated by such means in the United States; they are living in an extremely impoverished environment. Most of them have never seen or even heard of a motion picture. A poor diet and the narrow unstimulating nature of the daily life of these rural children would seem likely to produce a genuine dulling of their mentality. When given standard intelligence tests, their average score was far below the U. S. averages.

So one finds a striking relationship between their extreme economic handicap and their extreme intellectual handicap. Nevertheless, this does not tell the whole story. One finds also a very great individual variability despite the very limited world in which they live. The children range from mentally defective to a level of superior mental ability. Many of them are intellectually far beyond what normal children of their age could be expected to be even in a good environment. Studies of this sort, then, show that while environmental pressures can be credited with a great deal of gross effect on the group, they cannot iron out all the original individual differences. We are face to face here with an interaction between a varying stock and a varying (though on the whole remarkably limited) environment. (The white group and the Negro group both suffer from the environmental handicap and both show wide individual variability, child for child, in relation to the tests.)

When we get into the habit of assuming variation both in stock and in environment as the normal basis for the differences we see among people about us, we are perhaps less likely to be caught in some of the paradoxes or disturbed by the apparent "contradictions" among the research data. With a broad perspective it is doubtful whether science really gives us "contradictions." Some investigators do indeed take an extreme hereditarian position, and some take an extreme environmentalist position. And each seems to support his argument by a convincing array of data. Perhaps the problem really involves a recognition that both are right.

Let us look, for example, at the studies by Leahy[8] and by Wellman[9] dealing with the effects of environment on the intelligence of young children. Leahy carefully analyzed data from parents and their adopted children, and was able to show that even when the children are adopted very early there is little resemblance indeed between the intelligence of parents and that of children. In other words, even the whole growing-up period in the family did not make the children very much like those who had reared them. On the other hand, Wellman's studies indicate that the early exposure to good nursery schools and good elementary schools, as compared with the limited opportunities afforded by poor schools or by a narrow institutional life, makes large differences in the average level of intelligence. There are, moreover, many clinical studies of individual children whose intelligence quotients have climbed many points in consequence of friendly stimulating contacts with adults who understand the child's problems, draw him out emotionally, get him interested, and allow him to grow freely and vividly in his own way. One might, then, be tempted to conclude from Leahy's study that the environment cannot do much, and from these other studies that it can do almost everything. Really, however, each of these studies offers conclusive evidence of the importance of the particular kind of factor with which it is concerned; but since each one leaves out of account the close analysis of the various *other* factors with which other investigations are concerned, the paradox disappears.

It is, moreover, very clear from such studies that taking an average result from many children does not really tell the whole story. A given environment may be only slightly stimulating to one child; but to another child, with a different temperament, it may be very stimulating indeed. The interaction of hereditary predispositions and environmental opportunities remains in the last analysis an individual matter; the individual is a unique product of factors which are not exactly duplicated in other individuals.

A similar paradox appears with regard to the effects of heredity and environment in the matter of emotional and social development in early

---

[8] M. Leahy, Nature-nurture and intelligence, *Genet. Psychol. Monog.*, 1935, *17*, 235–308.

[9] B. L. Wellman, Iowa studies on the effects of schooling, *Yearb. nat. Soc. Stud. Educ.*, 1940, *39*, II, 377–399.

childhood. On the one hand, Dennis[10] has given us good evidence that the development of bodily functions, such as the ability to stand and to walk, is not much affected during the first year of life even by wide extremes of environment. Take, for example, the children of the Pueblo Indians of the Southwest, who are reared upon cradle boards. Thus they lie still most of the time, cannot even budge except for turning the head. Nevertheless, when these children are old enough to walk, they are ready to walk; when freed from the cradle board they can walk with very little practice. The implications are that the body goes on developing in its own way, grows like a flower under specified conditions of warmth, nourishment, and moisture, and that nothing much can be done by changing the environment. (This is like Gesell's emphasis; compare page 22.) Dennis has also offered evidence that many phases of social growth go on during the first year of life even among children who are not exposed to the ordinary presence of the human beings about them. Smiling, cooing, laughing, and so on do not appear to be retarded by their isolation. On the other hand, an equally dramatic series of studies from René Spitz[11] indicates, as Table 1 shows, that the presence and at-

TABLE 1

Type of Environment	Cultural-Social Background	Developmental Quotients	
		Average of First 4 Months	Average of Last 4 Months of First Year
Parental home	Professional	133	131
	Village population	107	108
Institution	Nursery	101.5	105
	Foundling home	124	72

titude of the mother make a huge difference in objectively observable developments in social characteristics as shown in a series of responses to standardized social situations. Desertion of the infant by the mother

---

[10] W. Dennis, Does culture appreciably affect patterns of infant behavior? *J. soc. Psychol.*, 1940, *12*, 305–317.

[11] B. Mittelmann's summary of the work of R. Spitz. See A. H. Maslow and B. Mittelmann, *Principles of Abnormal Psychology*, New York, Harper, rev. ed., 1951. See also R. Spitz, Anaclitic depression, *The Psychoanalytic Study of the Child*, 1946, *2*, 329.

often leads to social retardation. Attributes such as standing, clinging while standing, walking, and such social attributes as smiling, taking it on the chin, accepting life's frustrations with courage and persistence, and the ability to fit into social expectations appear clearly to be related to the child's amount of experience with intimate social comradeship. When a child of two or three months of age loses his mother and is reared for some months by other people who provide necessary nourishment and care but do not give steady mothering, we find a very marked change in the social development of the child. It is evident from the studies by Spitz that under these conditions social development not only may fail to progress during a certain period but may even go backward.

So, just as Leahy emphasizes heredity and Wellman environment, we find Spitz emphasizing environment and Dennis heredity. Does this mean that we face a hopeless contradiction in the facts? Not necessarily. Perhaps we have been like the three blind men who argued whether the elephant was trunk, legs, or tail; each has been grasping one aspect, and a perfectly good and real aspect of the problem, but leaving out other aspects which are also very vital. There is an inner dynamic growth process; and it is also shaped by the environment.

But perhaps the way in which heredity and environment interact varies with the process we are studying. It is not just a question of the "environment" in the abstract and "heredity" in the abstract; the kinds of environment that Wellman studied may have had effects which other environments could not have; the emotional shocks studied by Spitz may have had effects different from those which other environmental situations would have produced. It is always a question of what a particular pattern of genes will do when reacting with a particular environmental composite. It may well be that a group of children of a given stock will not on the average be affected more than a certain amount by a particular environment; but *some* children can take advantage of *some aspects* of that environment, while others can take advantage of other aspects. As earlier noted, the effect of a nature-nurture interaction is a highly individual matter. In the same way one can bring to bear a new environment, stimulating and helpful to some children, and get rather a meager result with other children. Some aspects of a given environment help some individuals in some specific ways, not necessarily in other ways.

The idea of a "good heredity" turns out, then, to be an abstraction which is not necessarily always helpful to us; nor is that of a "good environment," beyond a certain point. In the long run we find some stocks making better adjustments to life than others, and some environments more stimulating than others. But if you think back over your own life history, you will remember the way in which you responded with energy and enthusiasm to some particular new opportunity in childhood—a new ball team, a new playground, a new camp experience, a new teacher —though other children at the particular time were not able to see the value or importance of this. Yet they responded eagerly to other things which at the time meant little to you. It is only as a first approach to one's personal problems that one can advantageously use the abstract idea of "nature and nurture." Your actual make-up as a person is a question of how the particular predisposing factors were able to take hold of, assimilate, and exploit the particular stimulating opportunities provided by your environment. In other words, nature-nurture interaction is unique in the case of each individual person.

SUGGESTED READINGS

Day, C., *This Simian World,* New York, Knopf, 1920.
Itard, J., *The Wild Boy of Aveyron,* transl. by G. and M. Humphrey, New York, Century, 1932.
Kellogg, W. N., and Kellogg, L. A., *The Ape and the Child,* New York, McGraw-Hill, 1933.
Murphy, L. B., "Childhood Experience in Relation to Personality Development," in Hunt, J. McV. (ed.), *Personality and the Behavior Disorders,* New York, Ronald Press, 1944, chap. 21.
Ribble, M. A., "Infantile Experience in Relation to Personality Development," in Hunt, J. McV. (ed.), *Personality and the Behavior Disorders,* New York, Ronald Press, 1944, chap. 20.
Watson, J. B., *Behaviorism,* New York, Norton, 1925, chap. 5.
(*See also readings at the end of Chapter 5.*)

5   INDIVIDUALITY IN DEVELOPMENT

Most people who look at a newborn baby are not much impressed with the scrawny, struggling, helpless little object, more formless than formed, in some ways more animal than human. They know that they must say to the parents nothing that sounds just "nice"; they must say something that sounds reasonably individualized, appreciative, with respect to something that isn't true of all babies, and they find it hard. The child is not only unimpressive; he does not seem to be a person, according to ordinary standards, certainly not a "personality." Those, however, who know babies well, and who know how quickly the baby will fill out and take on the pattern of smiles and gestures which we think of as normally human, are able to see in him a certain humanness which is bound to appear; and likewise they see attributes which are distinctive of him and not of everybody in general. What they and the more skeptical people both see is that it takes time to become fully human and also time to become fully individualized. There must be a process of differentiation from the rather vague, diffuse mass of unformed behavior. As time goes on, the blurred, amorphous, foggy, indistinct, unclear, is replaced more and more by the specific, differentiated, sharply outlined, specifically human characteristics that you can depend upon. Month by month, as this process of differentiation goes on, the baby becomes capable of understanding, remembering, thinking, assuming responsibilities.

Along with this process of becoming more and more human there goes the process of becoming more and more different from other persons. If we may say that it is of the very nature of being human to be a person,

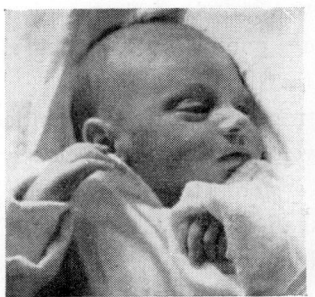
32 hours

1 month

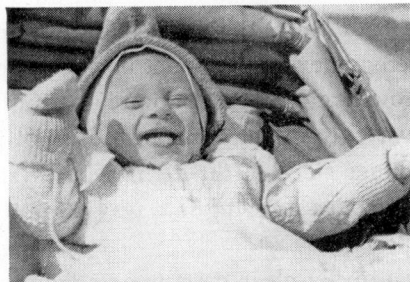
5 months

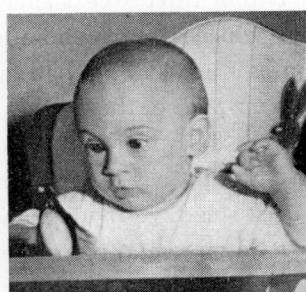
7 months

1 year

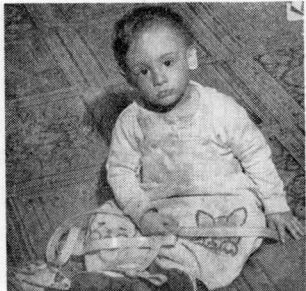
15 months

Figure 6. Individuality in Development

The newborn child cannot really be said to be an individual. In the early months the child shown in these photographs displays relatively few distinguishing expressions or characteristics. At 5 months the smile indicates the beginning of an awareness of others and with it the development of unique expressive qualities. At a year and also at 15 months it is evident from the features that individual patterns of reaction and expression have emerged and the child has become clearly recognizable.

we may also add that it is human to follow a growth pattern which differs from that of anyone else. One becomes oneself by traveling along one's own developmental route. (See Figure 6.)

We need to look more closely at this process of early differentiation and development. Some phases of the development are very closely related to the development of the nervous system (to phases which are more obviously related to the glands we shall refer in Chapter 6). During the period of growth before birth, and likewise after birth, the nervous system gradually undergoes changes which permit more and more kinds of specific well-differentiated response. A premature baby who is only two or three weeks short of his full nine-month term can do many things which a seven-and-a-half-month baby, that is, a baby a month-and-a-half less mature than the average newborn, cannot do. This shows the importance of the process of growth and differentiation in permitting readiness to respond in a specific way. An infant a month old is not just an infant who has learned some things since birth; his nervous system has been steadily growing, and it has been growing in a way permitting him to do more and more specific things.

On this point we have some beautifully clear experiments from animals; after considering these, we can make appropriate allowances for differences in growth between different species, and in the light of all the evidence we may begin to understand the process of growth in early childhood.

Avery did a very clean-cut experiment with the guinea pig, which develops so far during its prenatal growth that at the time of birth it is about ready to shift for itself.[1] Avery removed guinea pigs from the mother's uterus at various intervals before the normal time of birth. As compared with the normal 68-day period, some were removed at 66 days, some at 64, etc. He was then able to show that these premature individuals were lacking in some of the specific forms of behavior which are ordinarily found at birth; and the earlier they were removed, the more kinds of behavior were missing. As development had gone on during the period before birth, the nervous system had provided more and more ways of responding; it was laying down the appropriate machinery

---

[1] G. T. Avery, Responses of foetal guinea pigs prematurely delivered, *Genet. Psychol. Monog.*, 1928, 3, 247–331.

in an order which was more or less predictable from a general knowledge of a timetable of the species. In the same way kittens show for each day since birth certain new action patterns. At nine days, for example, they get up on their haunches. A study of the nervous system in connection with each new development indicates that kittens do each thing in their repertory of behavior as soon as the appropriate equipment in the nervous system is provided. As the biologist has formulated it, there appears to be a passing from diffuse responses or *mass* reactions, in which a touch upon the animal at any point causes slow massive responses of the body as a whole, to the capacity for specific, *localized* acts of one part of the body, each act being evoked by a particular type of stimulation. This conception of movement away from a diffuse mass response to a capacity for specific localized response has been described by Coghill[2] as a process of "individuation within the total mass." While there is some indication that the process of individuation is more complex than this phrase indicates, there is a good deal to suggest that the general trend is in the direction pointed out by Coghill.

Now to return to this process as it appears in man. Years ago a Swiss surgeon, Minkowski,[3] showed that this same general principle holds for human growth. He made an elaborate study of human embryos removed by Caesarian section at various periods before the completion of their normal nine-month growth because of the mother's medical condition. A great many of these embryos were only a few weeks old. He found a progression from mass action to specific response—from diffuse swaying, etc., of the whole body to well-defined responses of a specific member of the body. More recently Davenport Hooker[4] presented much material supporting this general view, by showing clearly the emergence of new behavior patterns at appropriate ages.

We find, then, elaborate bodily machinery ready at appropriate dates to exhibit each new type of response. While this general law of growth is subject to marked individual variation, there is nevertheless a fairly

---

[2] G. E. Coghill, *Anatomy and the Problem of Behavior*, Cambridge, University Press, 1929.
[3] M. Minkowski, *Rev. neurol.*, 1921, 37, 1105–1235.
[4] D. Hooker, "Reflex Activities in the Human Fetus," Chapter 2 of R. G. Barker, J. S. Kounin, and E. H. Wright, *Child Behavior and Development*, New York, McGraw-Hill, 1943.

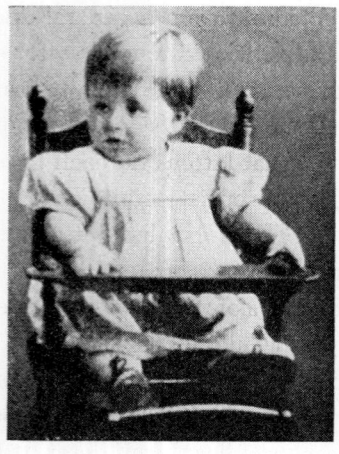 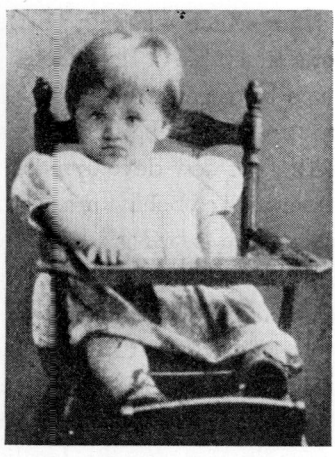
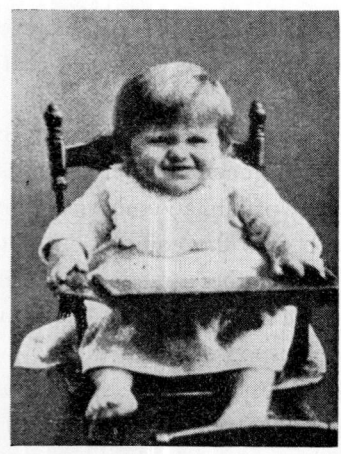 

Figure 7. Expression of Emotions in a Ten-Month-Old Girl

(From F. L. Goodenough and J. E. Anderson, *Experimental Child Study*, New York, Appleton-Century; after Büchner.) See page 44 for discussion of Figure 7.

characteristic sequence of activities in the first months of life of an average child, reflecting the growth of the nervous system. Shirley (cf. page 25) called this the "maturation sequence," the term maturation being the most general term for describing this process of movement from the mass response to the more specific localized response, as it depends on the growth of the nervous system.

An exceptionally interesting and important aspect of maturation is the

INDIVIDUALITY IN DEVELOPMENT   43

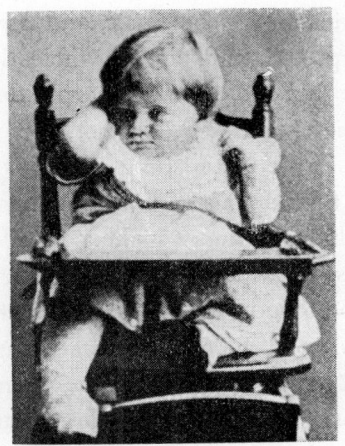

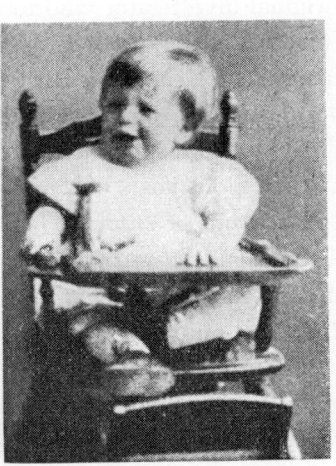

development of those complex patterns which will be known as the "facial expression of the emotions." It has been held by some that we innately exhibit facial patterns indicative of fear, surprise, scorn, amusement, etc., and maintained by others that these patterns are built up in experience or even that they are copied by the small child from the facial expressions of others. The study of the dynamics of maturation should throw some light on the question of these patterns of expression. Motion pictures of tiny infants taken by the Shermans[5] and presented to young

---

[5] M. Sherman and I. C. Sherman, *The Process of Human Behavior*, New York, Norton, 1929.

physicians, psychologists, and nurses were frequently very grossly misinterpreted, and on the whole the evidence supported the Shermans' view that there are no sharply defined facial expressions of emotion in the newborn. This does not, however, rule out the possibility that there may be characteristic expressions which are due to maturation, that is, that the nervous system may month by month provide more and more definite machinery making possible the specific patterns of fear, rage, and so on which we all recognize. Florence Goodenough[6] put this theory to the test. In the photographs of a ten-month-old girl there proved to be no great difficulty in identifying different emotional expressions (Figure 7). There was clear-cut agreement among the observers in a majority of instances, and the pictures which they designated as indicative of a particular emotion were mostly the pictures which had been offered by the original investigator who took them as samples of the kind of emotion involved.

This evidence shows at least that the patterns are distinctive at this age level. Also pertinent is Goodenough's study dealing with a little girl who had lost both sight and hearing during the first year of her life, and who, when eight years of age, was photographed displaying characteristic expressions of surprise, fear, rage, etc. A deaf-blind child studied by Thompson showed definite anger.[8] Thompson found, comparing blind and seeing children, that social imitation did have some effect on the laughing and smiling of seeing children, but not on their crying. These patterns turn out to be complicated in their origin; but they are evidently not dependent solely on learning by social intercourse in the case of children lacking both sight and hearing, whose social contacts are largely maintained by touching, grasping, and groping. In view of the fact that the newborn do not show well-defined emotional expressions, it appears that the distinctive elements (smiling, wide opening of the eyes, etc.) have arisen as different muscular activities combined into patterns through the growth of the nervous system.

---

[6] F. L. Goodenough, The expression of the emotions in infancy, *Child Develpm.*, 1931, 2, 96–101.

[7] F. L. Goodenough, Expression of the emotions in a blind-deaf child, *J. abnorm. soc. Psychol.*, 1932, 27, 328–333.

[8] J. Thompson, Development of facial expression of emotion in blind and seeing children, *Arch. Psychol.*, 1941, No. 264.

Maturation plays a large part not only in facial expression, but in motor development as a whole. At the Yale Psychological Clinic a great deal of research has been done on the age at which specific types of muscular coördination are possible. For example, one may try hard to get a child of six months to play pat-a-cake and yet fail completely; but at ten months the pattern is clear and easy to bring out. One might be tempted to think that it is only a question of learning; but the point is that at a particular level the game can be very quickly learned, though with practically no success at all at an earlier age despite huge and prolonged effort. (Compare the data on slide climbing mentioned above on page 21.) One might be tempted to think that whether a child can or cannot grasp and handle a cube is a question of his experience; but in point of fact if the nervous system is ready the fingers of the child quickly fold around the cube and grasp it and pull it in, whereas a little earlier nothing of the sort happens. Data of all the sorts given here show individual differences which are rather striking compared with the relative uniformities at a simpler animal level. It is likely, as we suggested earlier, that individual variability goes with increasing complexity of organization.

The Nervous System

If we are readily to understand the development of behavior, more must be said about the general layout and functioning of the nervous system. The nervous system is a coördinating system. While the simplest forms of life move toward or away from their environment without a specialized system of connections within the body, the more complex forms all contain a connecting system which leads from sense organs by inner circuit out to muscles. We may visualize this process best by thinking of nerve cells as connected with one another as shown in Figure 8.

Living matter is almost always divisible into cells or small particles of living substance. In the course of evolution, and also in the growth of the individual, cells become more and more differentiated from one another in function, and begin to show a division of labor. Some cells contract and serve as elements in the muscle tissues. Some form the skin or mucous membranes. Others, the nerve cells or neurons, are specialists in the

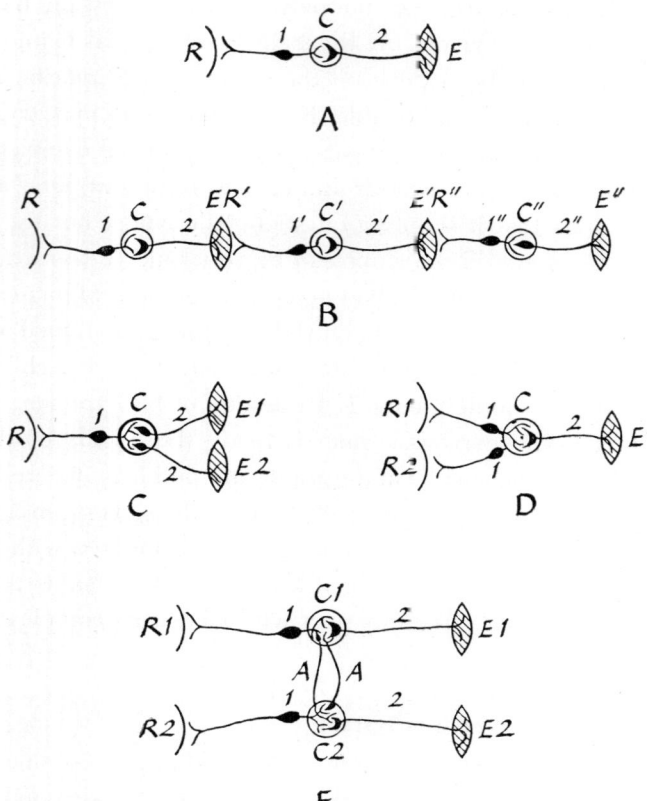

Figure 8. Five Types of Connections Among Nerve Cells

R is the *receptor* or receiving cell; E is the *effector* or responding cell. The incoming (afferent) nerve fibers which bring the impulse *in* to the center of the reaction are labeled 1. The outgoing (efferent) nerve fibers which carry the impulse *out* are labeled 2. Nerve fibers are called axons. Many nerve fibers run parallel inside of every nerve; hence in this way a nerve is like a cable. (From C. J. Herrick, *An Introduction to Neurology*, 5th ed., W. B. Saunders Company.)

A. A simple reflex involving only one receptor and one effector. A stimulus at R makes nerve fiber 1 active. At C, the next fiber in the chain, 2 becomes active and stimulates activity in E. The activity thus aroused is the response to the stimulus.

B. A chain reflex in which the activity of the first effector serves as the stimulus for another receptor, the reaction to which stimulates still another system.

C. A single stimulus at one receptor sets two effectors into action.

D. Stimulation of two receptors excites only one effector.

E. Two associated reflex arcs. Stimulation of either receptor may excite the activity of either or both effectors through the association neurons A.

conduction of impulses from one point to another. They are highly sensitive or irritable, and when once stimulated they transmit a message from one end of their extent to the other in a small fraction of a second. They always have a little concentrated mass or cell body and various fibers which reach out in various directions. In Figure 8, note particularly the distinction between three kinds of nerve cells: the sensory or afferent, the connector, and the motor or efferent. While it is possible theoretically to imagine an afferent and an efferent neuron connected directly with each other, there is practically always an intermediate. In fact, even this is a simplified abstraction from a very complex picture in which there may be many nerve cells of each of the three kinds. In a general way one can get an idea of how a simple automatic response to the environment is made by noting the kinds of reflex arc shown in the figure. Only a few junction points or synapses between the sensory and the central elements, and between the central and the motor elements are shown. As a rule, however, the branchings and interconnections are very numerous, and it is possible that the message might be routed along any one of many different lines. Consider E, the bottom drawing in Figure 8. From a given incoming impulse along the sensory neural paths, $R1$, it is possible that various central elements, $C1$, $C2$, etc., will receive excitement —indeed there may be many more than shown here—and possible that many different motor elements, $E1$, $E2$, and still others, will become excited and produce activity in their responding muscles. We begin to be able to see why the *same stimulation* may on different occasions lead to *different reactions*, and why the same muscular reaction may arise in different settings from different kinds of sensory stimulation.

Most of this increasing complexity is provided not by the lowest and simplest centers in the spinal cord, but in the brain. There are not only the simple reflex circuits at the spinal level, but ascending and descending nerve cells which make their connections in lower or higher brain centers. There are almost infinitely complicated possibilities for the rerouting of impulses in the brain. Injury to the brain produces all sorts of complications in the transmission of impulses, and the effects of surgery and of chemical disturbance of brain function bring out a variety of ways in which we are dependent for our higher mental life upon the normal possibility of rich connections between incoming and outgoing impulses.

Now as to the nomenclature of the nervous apparatus. The incoming and outgoing fibers are known as the *peripheral nervous system*. The nerve cells contained within the spinal column and the skull are known as the *central nervous system*. The great overarching cerebral hemispheres, together with the smaller hemispheres below and behind in the cerebellum, are known in general as the *higher centers;* while those parts which lie beneath and toward the base of the skull are usually called the *lower centers*. They merge into the centers of the spinal cord, the nervous material that is contained within the bony protection of the spinal column. The basic architecture of the central and peripheral systems is similar in all creatures having a bony protective covering—from the fishes up to and including man. Indeed, the lower centers remain essentially the same in all species as far as their gross anatomy and physiology are concerned; it is in the brain, the forward portion, that the enormous changes have occurred in the course of evolution. What has happened is that the old simple circuits providing swift and efficient reflex responses have been maintained; but that ever-increasing complexity of interconnections and the opportunity for infinitely diverse learning processes have been provided by increasing the space allocated to the higher centers, especially to the surface or *cortex* of the cerebral hemispheres.

Still a third system of neural structures remains to be mentioned. Lying outside of the bony covering in a series of bunches of nerve cells, shown in **Figure 14** (**facing** p. 93) arranged segment by segment parallel to the spinal cord, is the *autonomic nervous system*. It has to do with primitive involuntary vital responses connected with circulation, digestion, and, as we shall see, many emotional states. It is divided into three main portions—a middle or *sympathetic* portion which plays a large part in spurring the body onward in times of emergency, and the top and bottom portions, called the *parasympathetic*, which is continuously at work in "vegetative" activities such as growth, nutrition, self-repair. We shall return to the autonomic system in connection with the problem of emotion (pages 93–100).

Now it is very obvious that while the main phenomena of maturation are due to changes in the central nervous system which permit the development of specific *conduction from one point to another* (page 46), there are nevertheless important growth processes in the autonomic system, and also in the glandular system; to these we shall return later. The body is growing as a whole, and we now have to ask: Just what is it that is happening in the nervous system in these cases of maturation? We can say this much: At first the nervous system is a good deal like a network, in the sense that stimulation applied at one point spreads its energies through the system as a whole, and its effect can be detected at many other points within a short time. The conduction is diffuse; it is something not altogether unlike water seeping through the ground in many directions. As the nervous system develops, however, barriers are established here and there to the diffuse flow of energy, so that the effects are no longer diffuse but are directed into *specific channels.* This means that the network is replaced by a system of conduction within well-defined pathways. These pathways are actually the basis for the *individuation* mentioned by Coghill (page 41). After the specific individual parts have developed, integration makes possible definite back-and-forth effects between definite structures. The energy of stimulation, instead of spilling over diffusely, is conducted into particular regions; and from one region to another there is a specific, well-defined conduction so that real integration, not just a global "mass effect," is possible. Several specific activities may, for example, be aroused at once, all working together, as suggested in Figure 8. Note the difference between a sharply localized simple reflex and the *coördination* of several muscular units. These diagrams bring out general principles, but most coördination is much more complex than these figures can suggest. The integrating process involves the action of many parts simultaneously, a process sometimes called synergy, or "working together." Through synergy many parts of the body —hands, feet, trunk, etc.—are continuously interacting. The pattern of interaction is different in each person; it is this interaction which you recognize when you "size up" a person at a distance by his walk or his gestures. Ultimately, then, the way in which the nervous system grows and the way in which its parts interact are fundamental to personality. There is, however, still another kind of synergy, the *chemical* synergy provided by the glands. This will be our problem for consideration in the next chapter.

SUGGESTED READINGS

Carmichael, L. (ed.), *Manual of Child Psychology*, New York, Wiley, 1946, chaps. 2, 4, 5, 6, 7.

Gesell, A., *The Embryology of Behavior*, New York, Harper, 1945.

McGraw, M. B., *Growth: A Study of Johnny and Jimmy*, New York, Appleton-Century, 1935.

Morgan, C. T., and Stellar, E., *Physiological Psychology*, New York, McGraw-Hill, 2nd ed., 1950.

Munn, N. L., *Psychological Development*, Boston, Houghton Mifflin, 1938.

Shirley, M., *The First Two Years: A Study of Twenty-Five Babies*, 3 vols., Institute of Child Welfare Monograph Series, Minneapolis, 1931, 1933.

Spitz, R. A., Anaclitic depressions, *The Psychoanalytic Study of the Child*, 1946, 2, 313–342.

6   THE ENDOCRINE SYSTEM

As we have seen (Chapter 2), the body may be regarded from one viewpoint as a complicated chemical establishment. Life arose in the sea, and interaction with the salt water and with food substances gave the general ground plan for the chemical organization of life. With the development of animals with many cells, there developed a differentiation in chemical activity in various parts of the body. One part specialized in absorbing and utilizing food; another specialized in the matter of moving the organism about through the contraction of some of its tissues; a third specialized in pumping food and oxygen around through the medium of the blood.

Now certain parts of the body are made up of cells which have become specialized more and more as minute chemical factories, their task being confined to the production of certain specific chemical compounds. A gland is simply a group of cells which specialize in the task of manufacturing and distributing chemical compounds that are important in the nutrition or growth or stimulation of the parts of the body. In general, the glands are intimately related to the process of homeostasis mentioned earlier (page 15); that is, they help to maintain the constancy of the inner environment, protecting the individual against such extremes of heat or cold, acid or alkali, as would interfere with the carrying on of life functions.

Some of the glands are equipped with little tubes or ducts by means of which they can distribute their specialized chemical products to appropriate points. Thus the sweat glands, for example, squeeze the perspiration out through little ducts to the surface of the skin where rapid evaporation, and therefore cooling of the body, can occur. The tear ducts take care of the watery substance of the eye by a constant process of drainage into the nose.

The glands which are of the greatest importance for psychology, however, are ductless glands, glands which instead of squeezing out their product through ducts, simply spill them into the surrounding tissues where they are picked up and distributed by blood and lymph. In this way the effects of the ductless glands, or "endocrine" glands, are not local, but general. They reach the entire body. They are bound to influence all those tissues on which emotion, and action, and even thought, depend. They ultimately may be regarded as bathing the nervous system, including the brain, and all the organs of the body in their own appropriate chemical juices. One man has an attitude differing at this moment from that of another man partly because one of the men was angry earlier in the day, and the after-effects are still circulating in his blood long after his anger seemed to subside. The reactions to fresh annoyances, or to threats of danger, are different in such men. They are chemically different men.

In the same way, the changes in attitude and feeling during early childhood, adolescence, adulthood, and old age are related to the endocrine glands, which influence the nervous system in such a way as to make it relatively quick or relatively slow to respond to various types of stimulation. It is evident, then, that these glands of internal secretion are of fundamental importance in life activities. Each gland, moreover, acts through the blood stream to influence other glands, so that one must think not of separate glands working alone, but of an endocrine *system*. And since the system of endocrine glands is highly individualized, showing considerable variations from person to person, the glands are of great importance in the study of individual personality.

Within the normal adult range, for example, the weight of the thyroid gland may vary from 20 to 40 grams; and while the degree of action of an organ is not solely a result of its size, we regularly find in the endocrine glands a great variation in the range of function as well as in the range of size.[1] The endocrine glands may be identified in the embryo and

---

[1] W. Wolf, *Endocrinology in Modern Practice*, Philadelphia, Saunders, 2nd ed., 1939.

in the infant. They play a prominent part in the growth process both prior to and after the time of birth. But the glands do not all grow at an even pace, and the chemical effect of each gland depends upon its size and relative activity at any given time. There are therefore shifts of *endocrine balance,* or the systems of interrelations between endocrines, as life goes on. There are different kinds of endocrine balance in infancy, childhood, adolescence, maturity, old age. There are, moreover, differences from person to person in the rate of progression from one type of balance to another. There are also huge and relatively stable differences in the degree of prominence which a given gland represents in one person's total economy as compared with another person's.

At this point one might be inclined to think of the individual as beginning life with a particular type of endocrine balance, and trace this back to something in the interrelations between his genes. One might be inclined to give only a small place to the effect of the uterine environment and to the varying effects of food and of social stimulation. Actually, however, the endocrines are very sensitive to environmental pressures, and they respond vigorously to differences in the social arrangements under which a person lives. We shall find a number of examples below.

Functions of the Thyroid

Let us attempt a closer analysis of the various endocrine glands important for human personality. We might begin with the thyroid, a large mass on both sides of the windpipe, with a slender connecting strand between. The thyroid is important in connection with the utilization of oxygen. It plays a large role in controlling the rate at which body fuel is burned, that is, the process of oxidation of our food. If the physician decides to measure your "basal metabolic rate," he has you come to his office early in the morning without breakfast, lie down for half an hour, and then, while completely relaxed, breathe from his oxygen tank while he makes a careful tracing of the rate at which you use this oxygen. In general, this rate is a good reflection of the degree of activity of your thyroid. The results are, of course, considered in terms of body weight, area of the surface of the body, age, sex, and any complicating factors like a recent illness or worry. He wants to get the rate at which you utilize oxygen when the rate is at its lowest point.

Psychologists have long been interested in the thyroid because a serious defect in it is associated with inadequate development and function of the central nervous system. The individual thus affected is known as a cretin. He is mentally defective; his intellectual level never gets beyond that of a child a few years of age, and his physical development is greatly stunted. Oxidation is of course grossly below par. In recent years the medical profession has so fully understood the problem, and has

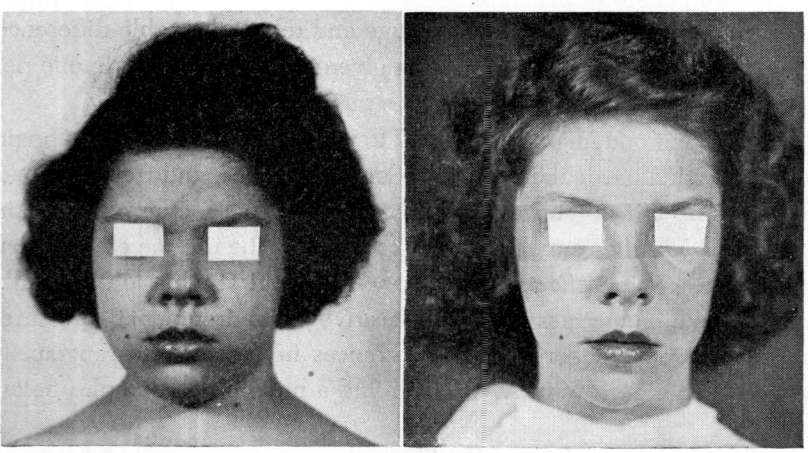

Figure 9. A Case of Juvenile Myxedema

Whereas cretinism develops prenatally as the result of the underactivity of the mother's thyroid, juvenile myxedema appears during childhood and is caused by an insufficient secretion of the child's thyroid gland which interferes with normal metabolism.

Left, the appearance of a patient, age 14 years, when thyroid treatment for myxedema was first begun. Note the bloated face and the dry, coarse quality of the skin. Right, the striking change in appearance after continued treatment for fifteen months. The face is no longer bloated and the skin is much lighter. The virtual disappearance of the symptoms was accompanied by a sudden spurt in growth, which had ceased almost entirely at the onset of the disease when the girl was 8 years old; her height increased from 4 feet 5 inches to 5 feet 1 in these fifteen months. (By courtesy of the Endocrine Department of The New York Hospital, Cornell University Medical College.)

learned so well to detect its early manifestations, that pure cretins are almost never seen today. The routine is the simple administration of sheep's thyroid as a dried powder, or the direct injection into the blood stream of thyroxin, one of the main active ingredients in the secretion of the thyroid gland. The result is to speed up the utilization of oxygen and to enable the central nervous system to develop normally. A condition similar in its consequences to cretinism is juvenile myxedema, which results from inadequate functioning of the thyroid during childhood. (See Figure 9.)

The thyroid, however, may be at times not underactive, but overactive. Thyroid activity gets out of control; oxidation is rapid, weight lost, eyeballs protruding ("exophthalmos"), and the patient restless and usually apprehensive. Such patients have taught us a great deal about the interrelations between personality and the endocrines, and have shown that personality not only is influenced by the endocrines but also influences them. The thyroid expresses to a degree the personality of the individual; it responds to his emotions and feelings. It used to be believed that the thyroid gland was the original cause of all the personality changes mentioned above, such as restlessness and apprehensiveness; it was believed that excess thyroid secretion in the blood stream simply served as an irritant to the central nervous system. But more recent evidence has shown that the thyroid, like other glands, bears a two-way relation to other organs of the body. The thyroid, unless defective, is not likely to initiate trouble elsewhere; rather, it responds to conditions elsewhere, and in turn influences them. It is therefore worth while to ask what other organs play a part in initiating hyperactivity of the thyroid. Perhaps the individual is up against a very difficult life situation. When a person is engaged in strenuous, restless, active intercourse with the environment, living in fear of failure, there may be a need to mobilize the energy requisite for his tasks; glandular activity must supply the cells of the nervous system with what they need, if they are not to be let down in their difficult assignment. From this viewpoint it is evident that the thyroid (and other glands concerned with mobilizing energy) may be keyed up not only to a normal but to an abnormal degree by a stressful or overintense attitude and style of activity.

As a matter of fact it began to be noticed after World War I that many of the cases of hyperthyroidism were appearing in people who were undergoing chronic anxiety. It occurred to one psychiatrist, Mittelmann,[2] to take 60 consecutive cases of hyperthyroidism—"run of the mill" cases—and go through their life histories and find what kind of

---

[2] B. Mittelmann, Psychogenic factors and psychotherapy in hyperthyreosis and rapid heart imbalance, *J. nerv. ment. Dis.*, 1933, 77, 465–488.

background there was. Actually, 56 out of these 60 individuals showed a long history of anxiety, and in particular a restlessness before the first indications of hyperthyroidism appeared. This suggests that the glands are responding to the strain shown elsewhere in the body—for example, in the brain—while of course they may in turn play a part in controlling the nervous system.

> Mrs. B., twenty-nine years old, has one child aged six years. Basal metabolic rate plus 33, pulse rate 110 per minute, tremor of both hands, beginning exophthalmos, more marked on the left side, slight enlargement of the thyroid. . . .
> This patient is the oldest daughter in the family and has always felt that her parents did not love her as much as the other children. She resented having to take care of the younger children and having to leave school to go to work contrary to her wishes at the age of thirteen years. She attempted suicide at the age of eighteen years because her parents objected to her keeping company with her future husband. She is dissatisfied with her life, is sexually frigid, and has a feeling of repulsion towards her sexual relations. She became disappointed with her husband soon after her marriage. She has often thought of leaving him but decided definitely to remain after her child was born.
> An interview with her husband revealed the following facts: As far back as he could remember the patient was subject to temper tantrums, especially with him and with the child. . . . About six months prior to the interview he had a difference with the janitor and in the patient's presence he was attacked by the janitor. . . . Ever since the patient's nervousness had been very marked and constant. Soon tremor, perspiration, loss of weight and eye signs followed. . . . As far back as she (the patient) could remember she had been periodically nervous although she recognized that the nervousness following the assault on her husband was different even subjectively and was associated with the tremor of the hands.[3]

Mittelmann concludes that the precipitating factor in this case was anxiety aroused by the assault upon the husband.

This kind of relation between a mental condition and bodily response to it is called a *psychosomatic* relation. Psychosomatic medicine is that branch of medicine which deals with the chronic influence of the patient's attitude or way of thinking or feeling upon his physiological activity.

Psychology as well as medical science is profoundly interested in the influence of strong feeling upon the physiological machinery of the body.

---

[3] *Ibid.*, pp. 472–473.

It is interested, for example, in the fact that chronic worry, apprehensiveness, or rage, whether the person is fully aware of his chronic emotional outlook or not, may operate to key up and overwork one part, or indeed many parts of his body, and ultimately force them to function abnormally. We shall return later to other instances of physiological derangements resulting from overstimulating certain regions of the body. We are mainly concerned here with showing the *two-way interrelations* between glands and personality. A defective thyroid may limit personality growth, and abnormal personality patterns like chronic anxiety may disturb the thyroid.

Sexual Development

Near the thyroid, in the upper breast, is the thymus gland, the "gland of childhood," especially important in early childhood growth. It is partly responsible for the development of characteristic proportions of limbs in the early years. It gradually begins to undergo relative reduction in the years just before adolescence; this is sometimes referred to as the atrophy of the thymus. This relative reduction of activity is one of the many factors which express the cycle of changes that we call puberty.

At nine or ten in a girl, and a year or two later in a boy, a shift of glandular balance begins to show itself; it takes several years to run its course and reach its full peak. Among the many glands which play their part, there is reason to emphasize especially the forwardly located branch of the pituitary gland, the anterior pituitary. There is likewise a posterior portion of the pituitary which has its own separate endocrine functions.

There is good evidence that the anterior pituitary begins to be more and more active in the period just preceding puberty; that it serves to stimulate rapid growth, including the "growth spurt" of adolescence; that it serves to energize some of the other endocrine glands; and that among other things it stimulates the rapid development of the *gonads*, or sex glands. These interact with various other glands in a complex system, as shown in Figure 10. Interaction, interdependence, rather than isolation, is the rule. During adolescence, the differentiation of male and female in glandular activity goes on. But this does not mean that male and female endocrines are utterly different. Indeed, male and female have in general most of the same endocrine substances; the male factors, or androgens, are simply somewhat more highly developed in the male than in the female, and the estrogens or female factors are somewhat more highly developed in the female than in the male.

Adolescence is ushered in by the *puberty changes.* Puberty involves the rapid development of the sex organs along with such "secondary sexual characteristics" as feminine development of breasts and masculine change of voice, based on the relative activity of estrogens and

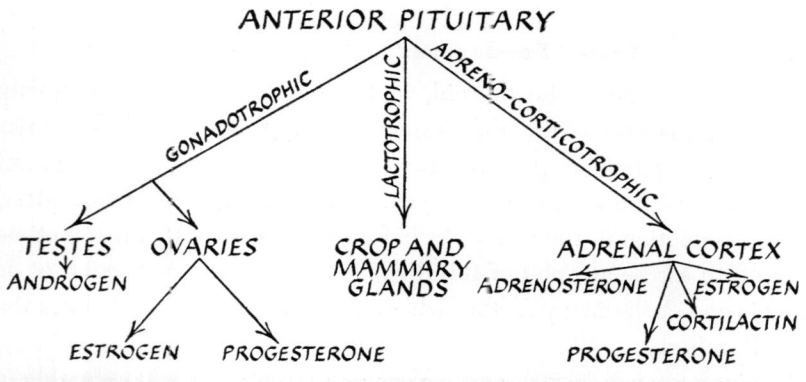

Figure 10. Pituitary Hormones Aiding the Reproductive Process

The effect of the pituitary hormones on the endocrine glands involved in the reproductive process is shown in this diagram. The trophic hormones secreted by the anterior pituitary gland stimulate the activity of those endocrine glands whose secretions play an important role in the reproductive process. The anterior pituitary is located in the floor of the skull. (From G. J. Seward, Sex and the Social Order, McGraw-Hill, 1946.)

androgens respectively. An increase in interest in the opposite sex usually appears at the same time.

The individual differences in the development of these systems among normal boys and among normal girls are so striking that one may expect to find in a group of 30 or 40 girls some who are as much as two or even three years ahead of some of the others with regard to any specific expression of endocrine activity. The average age of the first menstruation in a specific group shows variations over several years. It must be emphasized that these are normal, not abnormal variations. The boys are on the average about a year and a half behind the girls in the incidence of puberty if one uses the date of first menstruation and the appearance of mature spermatozoa as the basis for comparison. The lag of the boys behind the girls is a primary reason why at the beginning of the teens the girls tend to be not only taller than the boys, but interested in dancing and social dates, in trying out the new ways and attitudes that go with maturing femininity, while most of the boys are still absorbed in athletics, club or gang life, or masculine horseplay. No one who has ever given a party or a dance for thirteen-year-olds is likely to forget the wistful females waiting in the ballroom while the males alternate between roughhousing and soft drinks. By sixteen, however, the balance is reëstablished, and all is well. The practical importance of individuality in the process of growing up is never more conspicuous than in this transition which we call adolescence. Each child reaches adolescence at his own tempo and in his own way.

But it is not just a function of a different glandular balance for each individual. Whatever the many factors are which cause such individual differences (cf. pages 52–53), *their social consequences for the person* are tremendous. One girl reaches adolescence early, and is likely to find her attention drawn to her developing breasts and the sense of approaching womanhood; is likely for many reasons to begin to think of herself as further ahead than other girls; is likely, for both biological and social reasons, to become more interested in boys than the other girls are at that time; is likely to show a beginning of womanliness that appeals to the boys a few years older, however much or however little they understand of all that is going on. The physically precocious girl, ahead of her group, may be intellectually (and in other ways) less developed than she is physically, and may blunder much before she understands it all.

The boy who is ahead or behind his group—probably *especially* the boy who is behind—is likely also to have serious problems. Very human perception of what such a problem may mean appears in the California Adolescent Growth Study, in which we read of a number of boys who were slow in making the adolescent changes, did not respond at once to the new interests of the majority, and for a while felt isolated. The case of Lonnie illustrates some of the difficulties.

This boy belongs to a common type of body build, fairly well proportioned. His height and weight, however, are markedly below average. As a result of late maturing he gained in relative height in the last two years of the study, but still remained in the shortest 10 per cent of the group. In physical examinations he was repeatedly noted as being deficient in muscular development and muscle tone. Quick and agile, he was not as far below average in other aspects of motor performance as in strength.

During junior high school Lonnie reached a relatively high position in popularity and general prestige. He was quick-witted (above the 85th percentile in intelligence) and tended to dominate social situations by talkativeness and general activity. But if these were social assets in the ninth grade, they were not sufficiently supported by other prestige characteristics to enable him to maintain status at later ages.

In senior high school he began to drop into a relatively insignificant position in the social life of his group; his reaction to this was to show an increased aggressiveness, talkativeness, and attention-seeking. On the Reputation Test he was now judged "unpopular," and his former reputation for friendly, happy and jaunty behavior suffered a marked change.

Following are typical comments by observers made during a series of visits to the Institute. [Numbers refer to Lonnie's age.]

13.4: Lonnie is active and talkative . . . happy-go-lucky . . . facile with puns and pat remarks . . . directs barbed shots at others . . . has a remarkable capacity to hold attention and to influence the other boys, although he is somewhat mistrusted by them.

14.0: Lonnie demands the attention of everyone, adults as well as children, and obtains it, as usual, by continuous verbal activity.

14.4: Still a hearty, dynamic little boy, but seems immature in comparison with the others . . . as usual, he is very untidy with greasy hair and dirt smeared over his face . . . less confident than formerly . . . defensive about his poor ball-playing.

15.8: Full of activity, but not a leader. Lacks the assurance of the others . . . makes bids for attention by loud yells . . . he participates in physical activities started by the other boys, and is fairly well accepted by the group because of his apparently enthusiastic enjoyment of everything that is going on . . . his complexion is very pale, in sharp contrast to the other boys . . . his slender face seems drawn, eyes circled . . . looks inadequately nourished for such a tremendous output of energy.

16.8: Lonnie lives under such a pressure of ideas that he is virtually compelled to talk in a loud voice most of the time His short stature has so interfered with his athletic achievement that he is at a loss to know what to do when the other boys begin to play basketball . . . he smokes cigarettes continuously, perhaps a carry-over of earlier oral habits of fingering his lips, chewing a handkerchief, etc. . . . when anyone is watching, he assumes the role of a swaggering, arrogant somebody . . . refers to people and places in a tone meant to imply shadiness or deviltry . . . he is sensitive to criticism and shows his discomfort when Bob heckles him.

In his first year of senior high school his counselor noted:

Lonnie is very much on the defensive, highly emotional, rather easily goes into extreme rages. Very sensitive about his short stature. The larger girls in his own grade treat him like a pet Teddy bear. I am sure that he resents this, now that his own interest in girls is awakened. He came to a party when not invited; reproached for "horning in," he apologized profusely, and finally broke down and cried, but nevertheless stayed throughout the evening. He would not dance as he was too small for the girls. The other day he commented to me that fellows at school who aren't liked should go out for sports and try to get on. A few minutes later he said that he was playing with the *tallest* boys in the class. He likes football, but is too short to go out for the team. Gets bowled over when anyone hits him.

In Lonnie we have an example of a boy whose physical deficiencies in size and athletic prowess were a persistent source of tension and anxiety. There was little in his home life to give him aid and support in times of self-questioning, and as he entered the more mature adolescent culture of the later grades in school it was inevitable that he should feel increasingly underprivileged and excluded. This was clearly brought out in a personal-social inventory, in which he reported many indications of personal inferiority and resulting ego injury. A recurrent daydream serves to epitomize Lonnie's problem of adjustment: "I seem to be in a room which is awfully big, and keeps getting bigger and bigger, and I am very, very small."[4]

The effect of sexual development is not only to change the proportions of the body, but to *sensitize the individual to new feelings* which come from his body, and to make him more *responsive to elements in the outer world* which are connected directly or indirectly with the achievement of full manhood or womanhood. Consequently the social environment may profoundly affect the way in which the individual becomes aware of and responds to the fact that he is growing and changing. Some human societies—this would be true of parts of India—make the most of the early signs of mature masculinity and femininity, literally pushing the child forward into the acceptance and assertion of masculinity or femininity. Other human societies—like our own—are somewhat slower in such recognition of these signs, and insist on the individual's passing through nearly the full adolescent development before granting recognition of full manhood and womanhood. The individual is thus pushed ahead or held back in the development of *adult attitudes.* There are, moreover, variations from one society to another in the way the individual is supposed to feel toward members of the opposite sex—one society is more romantic, another more prosaic, etc. It would therefore be

---

[4] H. E. Jones, *Motor Performance and Growth,* Berkeley, University of California Press, 1949.

a mistake to ascribe the characteristic development of masculine or femnine attitudes solely to endocrine changes.

There is, furthermore, some evidence that not only *attitudes* but also physical sex development itself depends in some degree upon the environment. Just as the thyroid responds to environmental stimulation (page 55), so the other endocrines are probably sensitive in some degree to the ways of life of the group in which one grows up. This was brought out in a study of groups of girls in which both heredity and environment were considered.[5] Hundreds of girls growing up in Denmark were compared with girls of the same physical stock, the children of Danish parents, who were growing up in a Wisconsin city, but living under conditions of American culture, as contrasted with the conditions of Danish culture. In both groups only those girls were studied who were of "Nordic" type (light hair, light eyes). Under American conditions puberty came, on the average, six months earlier—13 years, 5 months, as against 13 years, 11 months in Denmark. We do not know what would happen in another generation, but at least we have sufficient evidence here that environment makes a considerable difference.

After the anterior pituitary has acted upon the sex glands in such a way as to start the typical adolescent development, the sex glands in turn seem to act back upon the anterior pituitary, and in this way slow down the growth spurt which has been set going. They act, as it were, as a brake upon the very organs which originally started their own development. Finally a balance is established; one ceases to grow taller; the sex glands maintain the adult level of activity which very slowly thereafter wanes with the years.

Reference was made above (page 55) to the fact that an extreme output of energy, as in struggling, or fighting, or escaping, may require extra activity of heart or lungs. Organs which are highly important in relation to such exertion and effort are the adrenal glands, just above the kidneys. The adrenals are shaped somewhat like acorns, the hull being called the adrenal cortex, and the kernel being called the adrenal medulla. While the cortex is important in maintaining muscle tone, the medulla is important in emergencies through the fact that its secretion,

---

[5] R. N. Franzblau, Race differences in mental and physical traits: studied in different environments, *Arch. Psychol.*, 1935, No. 177.

adrenin, plays a part in the acceleration of the heart, the constriction of the arteries in such a way as to increase blood pressure, and the activation of the liver to release sugars into the blood which are a primary source of energy for man or animal engaged in combat or struggle.

It is probably due partly to this fact that blood pressure and pulse tend to be high in an individualistic competitive environment like that of the United States, as contrasted with one less competitive, like that of China;[6] i.e., these contrasting environments act in different ways on the adrenals (and of course on other glands). We might think of our intensely competitive society as centering the endocrine activity of the individual to some degree more in those glands which have to do with increase in blood pressure, pulse, and a general steaming-up of the individual.

Interdependence of Endocrine Organs

The adrenals share with the thyroid the task of raising the level of activity; both the adrenals and the thyroid tend, for instance, to increase the pulse. This is an example of coöperation or mutual facilitation among endocrine glands; another example is the stimulation of the gonads by the anterior pituitary. There are likewise cases of *inhibition* of one gland by another and cases in which the activity of one gland produces bodily changes which are the opposites of those produced by another gland. An illustration appears in the case of the *parathyroids,* little glands near the thyroid. The parathyroids, in addition to controlling the rate at which the body uses the calcium taken in with the food in making the bones and teeth, appear to be related to the maintenance of normal emotional tone; at least, one occasionally finds, when the parathyroids are injured or defective, a jumpiness or incoördination sometimes called "emotional instability." There are, of course, a great many other things which cause emotional instability; but this particular function is of interest, in the sense that one notes a certain balance between thyroid and parathyroid in the maintenance of emotional tone. It will be remembered that *hyperthyroidism,* an excess of thyroid secretion, is likely to go with restlessness, but here we have restlessness in connection with a *defective* parathyroid; thus the result of too much

---

[6] O. Klineberg, *Race Differences,* New York, Harper, 1935.

of one is similar to the result of too little of the other. This suggests that the thyroid and parathyroid are opposed in some of their functions, and that health depends on the balance between them.

If one keeps in mind that there is constant interaction between the various endocrine glands, and that there is a constant give-and-take between the endocrine system and the nervous system, he will be less likely to make the mistake of assuming that any particular mode of behavior or any particular personality traits spring simply from the activity of some one endocrine gland. In the popular literature a good deal has been said about the man whose anxiety is said to be "due to his thyroid," or the man whose deficiency in sex development is "simply a question of gonads." Actually the personality pattern from which anxiety springs is frequently very complicated, and may prove to be one of the things that initiates the overactivity of the thyroid (page 56). A great many different endocrine glands affect sex development, and, as we have seen (page 58), the social environment may also be of some importance in determining the role of the endocrines.

SUGGESTED READINGS

Beach, F. A., *Hormones and Behavior*, New York, Hoeber, 1948.
Dashiell, J. F., *Fundamentals of General Psychology*, Boston, Houghton Mifflin, 3rd ed., 1949.
Hoskins, R. G., *The Tides of Life*, New York, Norton, 1933.
Hoskins, R. G., *Endocrinology*, New York, Norton, rev. ed., 1950.
Jones, H. E., *Development in Adolescence*, New York, Appleton-Century, 1943.
Jones, H. E., *Motor Performance and Growth*, Berkeley, Univ. of Calif. Press, 1949.
Mead, M., *Male and Female, A Study of the Sexes in a Changing World*, New York, Morrow, 1949.
Morgan, C. T., and Stellar, E., *Physiological Psychology*, New York, McGraw-Hill, 2nd ed., 1950, chaps. 5, 18, 20.

7 SOME ELEMENTARY MOTIVES

The pattern of our motives changes from hour to hour; but seldom, if ever, are we indifferent, or without motives. We want this or need that; or we are delighted at a new opportunity or miserable that an opportunity has been denied.

The degree to which our life is governed by a given motive is first of all a question of its intensity. When men were kept on a semi-starvation diet for a matter of months as part of an assignment in World War II, they began to think of food, dream of food, and be obsessed with problems of food.[1]

Food in all of its ramifications became the principal topic of the subjects' conversations, reading and day dreams. More dreams about food were reported as the stress continued. When subjects read books or attended the movies they were deeply impressed by the frequency with which food and eating were mentioned. Cook books, menus and information bulletins on food production became intensely interesting reading matter to many of the subjects who previously had little or no interest in dietetics or agriculture. Some men went so far as to replan their lives according to their newly acquired respect for food. For example: one man became impressed by the importance of developing efficient methods of food raising and decided to go into agriculture as a vocation.

Almost every psychological activity became colored by the question of food. A few men thought that this was debasing and inhuman, and hated themselves for being so dominated by food. But when a motive becomes

---

[1] Joseph C. Franklin, Burtrum C. Schiele, Josef Brozek, and Ancel Keys, Observations on human behavior in experimental semi-starvation and rehabilitation, *J. clin. Psychol.*, 1948, *4*, 28–45.

intense it affects the ways in which we perceive, learn, remember, and think.

The Physiology of Drives

Our problem in this chapter is to trace the relations between an inner state of tension, or need, and the kinds of things which people do when activated by these needs. We shall begin with some very simple and obvious needs like hunger and thirst. Later, as the book moves into more and more complex problems, we shall find ways in which these simpler principles may guide us in understanding even some of our very complex social needs, like the need to be accepted and the need to win prestige. The two things to be stressed are, first, that what we call *motives* spring (at least in these simpler instances) directly from the *needs* of the body: needs for food, water, oxygen, sleep, etc.; and secondly, that these needs, when they become acute, are expressed in the *restlessness* of some portion of the body, like the stomach, and that this restlessness may spread so that general bodily activity results. Thus in hunger, vigorous contractions of the muscles of the stomach occur. Other parts of the body may be affected; a strong stomach contraction may be accompanied by a gush of saliva.

Psychology uses the term *threshold* to denote the amount of stimulation required to elicit a response. The threshold is low when a response is easily called out; high, when it is called out only with difficulty. Armed with this concept, let us turn to the question: What is the hunger motive? How does it bring about the action which leads to the securing of food?

We begin with a newborn child who has awakened, is restless, evidently hungry, and whose stomach is active, in the form of activity which we know as hunger. The walls of the esophagus and upper stomach of the hungry child are vigorously moving. The intensity of hunger is reflected in the amount of bodily movement. Now in such a child, note that if the cheek is lightly touched, there is a quick turning of the head in the direction of the object which touches it. In the long run this will bring the lip into contact with the stimulating point. When the lips make contact with the object, sucking occurs. If the child is lucky, and if the object is the mother's breast, milk flows into the mouth, from which in turn follows the reflex act of swallowing. Figure 11 shows this chain of

SOME ELEMENTARY MOTIVES

reflex activities: first, turning the head; second, sucking; third, swallowing. All this can be rather easily brought out in a child who is hungry, for the reason that the thresholds for each of these three reflexes are very *low* while in a hungry state.

Try this same little experiment, however, on a child who has had his meal and is satiated; press upon the cheek quite vigorously and you will be lucky if you get any turning of the head at all. The threshold is now high. In the same way, it takes considerable stimulation of the lips to produce a sucking movement. If the mother presses the breast upon the

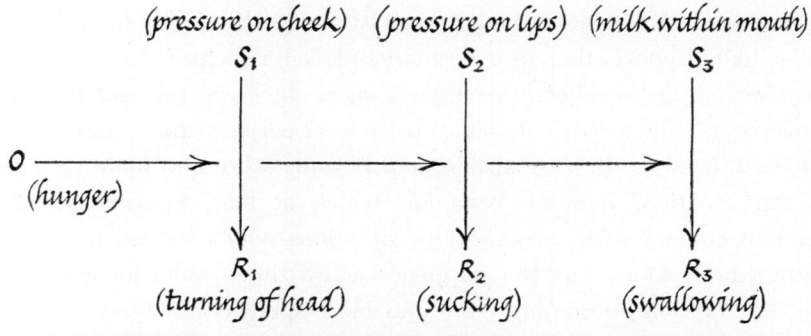

Figure 11. Chain of Reflex Activities

mouth of a satiated child, he may offer a slight amount of response, and then spew out the milk; swallowing is not likely to occur at all. Thus one may say that all three of the thresholds involved in this system of chain reflexes are low in a hungry child, high in a satiated child; thresholds are lowered or raised by the physiological conditions of hunger or satiation. And along with these activities which are relevant to the getting of food, many other activities, such as crying, are likewise more likely to occur in the hungry child; in other words, there is *general* restlessness.

Restlessness and hyperactivity appear in every state of acute deprivation, or deviation from homeostatic balance. Hunger, thirst, suffocation, cold, pain, and many other types of distress lower the thresholds for activity essentially as hunger does. Some of the activity is diffuse in the newborn, but some of it is specific to the situation. Thus while many of the restless activities are about the same from one type of distress to another, others, like the reflex responses of head turning, sucking, and swallowing, reflect to some degree the particular state of need which prevails. Interference with movements usually leads to tightening of muscles, thrashing, kicking, holding the breath, etc., but with large individual differences. Loud noises often lead to crying and twisting of the trunk in a form varying somewhat from child to child. Over and above the diffuse responses to sex stimulation which are often seen, the Kinsey Report[2] describes very specific male sexual responses observed in some very young babies. While these are not always present, they can probably be understood in terms of individual differences in maturation analogous to the great differences in age of walking, etc. (page 45).

Over and above these primitive variations in thresholds for reflex or reflex-like responses there is a very large place for the process of *learning* the thing to do to relieve the distress, as is shown in the fact that the movements which occur under distress soon cease to be as random or uncoördinated as they are at first, and become more and more relevant to the situation. Random behavior, which at first occurred blindly, brought contact with substances or situations which tended to put an end to the tension; after this happened a few times, behavior grew less and less random, becoming more and more specific and limited to the activity which was effective in relieving the tension. We find it worth while to differentiate, on the one hand, between the lowering of thresholds for specific reflexes appropriate to the drive (as in the hungry infant's responses) and, on the other, the learning of appropriate acts which lead to effective adjustment and the elimination of tensions. Sometimes part of the body, or all of it, is especially sensitive to a particular stimulus, more sensitive than it would be at other times. When a vigorous hunger pang is occurring, the salivary reflex is especially easily elicited. Or when the sprinter is crouching at the starting line, many of his taut muscles are ready to be released at the firing of the pistol. The starter may say, "*Get set.*" And the psychologist uses this same term. By *set* he means *readiness* to respond in a particular way. He does not, however, limit this to glandular or to muscular response; he uses the term set to comprise the general and fundamental tendency of the living individual to become especially predisposed at times to do a particular

---

[2] A. C. Kinsey, W. B. Pomeroy, and C. E. Martin, *Sexual Behavior in the Human Male,* Philadelphia, Saunders, 1948.

thing. From this viewpoint the drive or motive most active at any given time is just *one kind of set*. It is not of course the *only* kind of set; for you may simply become set to hear a given sound in a place where that sound has been heard before, or you may be set to carry out some habitual act when you find yourself in the familiar place where that act has often occurred before, without being at the time under the influence of a specific *drive* to do so. Nevertheless, present drive is a very common and important factor determining set.

We may summarize the findings on drive up to this point by saying that a deficit or other chemical change in the body which constitutes an interference with homeostasis alters thresholds for many responses, some specific, some diffuse and chaotic; and that with experience the diffuse responses become more specific. Food-seeking behavior follows more and more consistently from hunger pangs. These new specific reactions join with the original reflex reactions in producing the type of behavior which tends to put an end to the state of need. In general this same pattern applies to all the other drives which arise from the body's lack of something it needs.

This is far from saying that there is a cut and dried, uniform hunger pattern. Some children, though well fed, are frequently hungry and vociferous about it; others seem to live almost on air, and would rather have music or "This little pig went to market" than their bottles. Indeed, there are marked individual differences in the degree and type of hunger distress, and in the type of response made during such distress. When, moreover, we turn to the process of acquiring specific ways of satisfying hunger—that is, learning the appropriate ways of living with one's inner needs—we find individual differences even greater. These differences tend, in general, to take shape first in the kinds of things one seeks when one is hungry, and second, in the ways of seeking. Some of these differences are imposed by the social surroundings—the amount and form of one's breakfast, for instance. We shall give them much attention in the chapter on learning.

Deficits in water operate in about the same way as deficits in food. When the mucous membranes of the throat get dry, restlessness occurs, and this means restlessness and reflex "signals" (cries, etc.) which cause adults to minister to the child's needs. Later, when independent of adults, one acquires a specific way of getting the object needed; when one is working on a hot day, he gets up and moves about, perhaps even without especially thinking what he is doing. Random behavior is replaced by specific behavior as one *learns* where the water cooler is; the responses become more and more automatic.

Oxygen want has been studied intensively in recent years owing to the development of aviation. Here, as in the case of hunger, enough work has been done to show that just about everything in the individual is affected.

R. W. Schroeder writes: "When I reached 25000 I noticed the sun growing dim, I could hardly hear my motor run and I got very hungry. The trend of my thought was that it must be getting late for the sun was getting so dim and I went on talking to myself. I then turned on my oxygen and the sun grew bright again, the motor became so loud I thought there must be something wrong with it. I felt no longer hungry and felt like singing from sheer joy."

He kept on climbing until his oxygen began to give out at 29000 feet. The lack of oxygen soon affected him for he became very cross and the horizon seemed to him very much out of place. He assumed, however, that he was flying correctly and that the horizon was wrong. He then ran out of gas and began to descend in a spiral. At 20000 feet he felt more normal and made a safe landing.[3]

The incurring of an oxygen deficit involves first of all an inefficiency in the nerve cells. If, for example, the pilot begins to see poorly because of the development of many scattered blind spots in his eyes, this is due not to the eye tissue itself, but to the nervous elements in the retina which are no longer functioning at par. Oxygen deficit, as in the case of an infant half smothered by a blanket, shows itself first in restlessness which in the long run may tend to remove the danger. Many a mountain climber and many a flier become vaguely distressed when air shortage occurs.

At the beginning of oxygen deprivation, there is restlessness and distress; but as the condition continues, the individual may cease to experience strain; he becomes carefree and may even experience a sense of well-being. Thus some of the results of oxygen deprivation are like the results of alcoholic intoxication. It has long been noted that a slap-happy

---

[3] Ross A. McFarland, The psychological effect of oxygen deprivation (anoxemia) on human behaviour, *Arch. Psychol.*, 1932, No 145.

pilot who takes fantastic chances when at high elevations is in some ways like a person who is intoxicated. This proves to be more than just an analogy, for alcohol actually interferes with oxygen utilization. Yet it is not just a question of the sheer amount of oxygen deficit or the sheer amount of alcohol ingested, for there are big differences in individual tolerance for alcohol when one first uses it, and there is likewise the factor of habituation to it. The amount that one can handle before trouble begins to appear is dependent partly upon constitutional capacity, but partly upon the process of getting used to it. In the same way, there are constitutional differences in the ability to use oxygen efficiently and to stand up well against oxygen lack. The body also acquires the capacity to make good use of whatever oxygen is getting into the cells of the body. The Indians of the high Andes, working in the mines at an elevation of over 20,000 feet during the day, come down a few thousand feet at suppertime and play soccer in the evening. Their red blood corpuscles show an extraordinary capacity for carrying oxygen. Any man first adapting to such an elevation gradually develops a similar increase in capacity to make the most of whatever oxygen he gets.

There are very large individual differences in capacity to tolerate a deficit in oxygen. One of the most important aviation research problems has to do with the capacity of the individual to stand up under various types of oxygen deficit. The bodily tissues which play such a large part in our patterns of personal motivation appear here again to differentiate us a good deal from one another. One man crumples up in a chamber when oxygen is reduced till it is a little more than half the normal amount; another man keeps going. But just as we find that the endocrine glands not only tend to influence personality but are influenced by it, so we find here in the study of motives that the local physical condition can be affected by the personality as a whole. For when oxygen deprivation gets severe, whether or not a man can keep going is not just a question of his capacity to bear the deficit, but a question of his attitudes, his freedom from anxiety, his whole personality. Part of the problem is the capacity of our tissues to "take it," and part of it is the way we adjust to the fact that we find ourselves beginning to crumple up.

Here, as elsewhere, the results of a specific bodily need will depend upon the personality of the individual. Recent work has shown that there are specific personality traits which are very directly related to this ability to take an oxygen deficit. One can even predict from *personality tests* (Chapter 24) which people will lose their organization or crack up under certain conditions of reduced oxygen; one can even predict to some extent what types of behavior they will show as they go to pieces. This is probably because the extent of a person's general poise and capacity for coördination will determine how this state of discomfort or danger will be perceived and reacted to.

Another simple bodily need which may have much greater implications than are at first evident is the need to relieve the tensions of bladder and bowels. Indeed, some psychiatric studies indicate that the long struggles of adults to control the infant's elimination habits are of much greater importance to later personality development than the adult understands, because the strains and pressures experienced by the child are of huge importance to him, and the process of toilet training seems to be a much greater invasion of his personal freedom than is realized by the adult who undertakes the training process. It is believed by many psychiatrists that the attitude of *protest* which develops in many children in connection with the great effort to "keep dry" and "prevent accidents" has permanent effects on the tendency of the individual to resent all authoritative control of his life.

The need to rest and to sleep can certainly be considered very similar to the other needs so far considered. The accumulation of waste products in the muscles and the blood stream reaches a point where interference with the functioning of nerve cells occurs, and one feels listless or drowsy. Actually, to be awake or asleep is probably always a question of degree, rather than an absolute matter. It does not follow that because you are not sound asleep, you must be wide-awake. There are always some fatigue products in your blood. Drowsiness is not entirely a question of these waste products; it is partly a question of ventilation, food, and other things. Drowsiness is also a feeling which comes by association with certain familiar settings. Being in one's bed in a darkened room is itself part of a situation in which one goes to sleep; let a person be placed on a bed in a familiar, quiet room, and he has a strong predisposition to begin to sleep. At the same time there are other factors of habituation, such as monotonous voices, or the slow rhythms of distant sounds, which occasion no "alerting" of the individual to any specific task to be carried out. This is in general the situation in which sleep comes on; sleep is thus more easily precipitated.

Whatever the factors that go with sleepiness in the individual case, the depth of sleep varies with the individual, and from time to time in the same individual. The "curve of sleep" in Figure 12 shows that we fall asleep rapidly for an hour or so, and then gradually wake up during

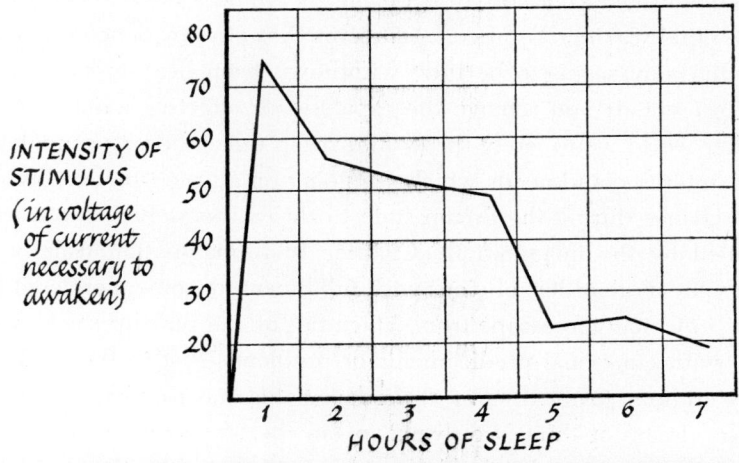

Figure 12. Depth of Sleep

At regular intervals during sleep, each of six male subjects was given an electric shock with currents of varying voltage. Points on the curve represent the average voltage required to awaken the subjects at successive hours during the night. The amount is at a peak during the first hour of sleep but decreases steadily during the night. (From J. Mullin, N. Kleitman, and N. R. Cooperman, *J. exp. Psychol.*, 1937, 21, 92.)

all the rest of the night. More strictly speaking, there is this general trend toward gradual waking up, but with fluctuations. The depth of sleep is measured by the loudness of a sound required to awaken the sleeper or by some other simple measure of his threshold of response to a physical stimulus. It is true that other methods, such as intensity of electric shock, do not give quite the same curves as those obtained by the use of sounds; but in general it is true that no matter what method of awakening a person is used, one finds that he sleeps more and more soundly during the first hour or hour and a half, and then begins to wake up, and wakes up slowly all the rest of the night.

Sleeping is a good example of a need that conflicts with other needs—the need to do or think about the many things to which you must say a temporary farewell when you go to sleep. The most direct evidence of this is the dream. In very sound sleep, your sleep may be dreamless. But your interests and wishes, your preoccupations and worries, are not really completely extinguished. Dreaming is most likely to occur as you sleep less deeply, especially as you come near to waking up. (Often if a person is waked up at any time during the night, a dream occurs during the rapid waking-up process.) Dreams thus offer evidence that even when the body seems to be fully withdrawn from life's tasks, activity is still present. If you remove the capacity for effective adjustment to the outer world, you merely throw into sharp relief the preoccupations, wishes, interests, and needs which are going on all the time, and which have a chance during the dream state to throw themselves into a form controlled by the imagination (Chapter 16). Imagination usually involves some more or less obvious wish fulfilment, or some more complex process in which you escape from difficulties or can play up the ways of coping with emotional predicaments or problems. Just as the cold and hungry arctic explorer dreams of verdant fields and tropical repasts, so you may dream of things you want, or, in the face of your embarrassments and difficulties, dream of renewed encounters with them and successful ways of conquering them. When two or more motives are at work at the same time—the motive to rest and the motive to meet your waking needs—the dream is a compromise. We shall come back to the problem of dreaming in Chapter 16.

The Maternal Drive

We have been considering examples of drives which directly depend upon simple bodily needs, especially the needs expressed in the activities of the vital organs. These are sometimes called the *visceral drives*. Many of these drives are evident in the opening weeks of life. Many others develop more slowly. Consider, for example, the development of the endocrine system, and take account of the reduction of thresholds for various kinds of responses which necessarily occurs with such growth. Of special importance are two late-maturing motives related to the endocrines, the maternal and the sexual drives.

SOME ELEMENTARY MOTIVES

By the maternal drive is meant a tendency to respond protectively to small living things—perhaps baby brothers and sisters, perhaps pets, perhaps other living things which can be loved, caressed, protected, fussed over, and enjoyed, and substitutes for living things, such as dolls, cuddly stuffed animals, etc. These tendencies usually appear late in the first year and are conspicuous in some children for the next few years,

Figure 13. Maternal Drive

Children differ markedly in their response to pets. Note the intense delight of this little girl as she holds the warm, furry, wriggling white mouse. Some studies suggest that the endocrine make-up of children determines, in part, the amount of play with pets and the interest in baby brothers and sisters.

or for life. (See Figure 13.) There is at first not much difference between boys and girls; cuddling, patting, protecting, making much of pets or dolls are equally conspicuous in the two groups, so that the term "maternal" may be a misnomer. But there is some evidence[4] that the endocrine make-up of a little girl predicts to some degree how much she will play with pets; how much she will enjoy baby brothers and sisters; how

---
[4] D. M. Levy, Psychosomatic studies of some aspects of maternal behavior, *Psychosom. Med.*, 1942, *4*, 223–227.

much the world of infants will mean to her as she roams the streets or parks. Will she ignore them, or will she—as David Levy puts it—become a "baby buggy peeker," one who makes the most of babies, enjoys them, or wants to be with them?

Concern for the immature is found among many animals, and in general appears so early that it can be called "constitutional," in the same broad sense as the other complex nature-nurture products which were mentioned on pages 32–36. The maternal drive can be regarded, then, as a late-maturing pattern. The maturing is, however, guided by social factors, as is true of all drives. Among some of the peoples of the Pacific, for example, there is almost no solicitude for babies and children; in others, an enormous amount of it is shown by men and women, boys and girls.[5] We come to the conclusion, then, that certain attitudes toward the immature are "standardized" within the culture; and these may, in many cultures such as our own, be encountered with much greater vigor in little girls and young women than in males. From this point of view it seems likely that the individual builds up an interest, a habit of solicitude for the young, which eventually looks as if it were a completely ready-made instinctive aspect of behavior. But like everything else, it has a more complex basis.

The Sex Motive

We have already considered some of the phases of the sexual maturing pattern. We need, however, to stress here the fact that what happens physiologically is in part a lowering of thresholds, a sensitization of the individual toward a variety of kinds of experiences involving primary and secondary sexual attributes, involving interest in and response to members of the other sex, and indeed also increased sensitiveness to one's own.[6]

This pattern is not just a question of glands, even if the whole endocrine system is considered; for sex is important in every human culture, and by the time one reaches puberty he has built up a rich world of experiences regarding it—excitement, romance, idealism, yearning, se-

---

[5] M. Mead, *Sex and Temperament*, New York, Morrow, 1936.

[6] C. L. Stone and R. G. Barker, The attitudes and interests of pre-menarcheal and post-menarcheal girls, *J. genet. Psychol.*, 1939, 54, 27–71.

crecy, fear of the unknown, uneasiness, embarrassment, disgust, moral disapproval, etc. He has observed in the faces and in the words of others a pattern of intense positive desire or of deep aversion, or of the two together in varying proportions, depending upon the group and the individual. As his own body changes, the intensity of its response is colored, for better or for worse, by these social attitudes, and the feelings from the sexual system of the body are blended with esthetic responses to line and color and tone of voice, and with the feelings of tenderness—or of conflict—which he had as a child toward his mother and father.

Since we all have both masculine and feminine endocrine secretions within us, it is not surprising that in many a tragic case, where there is no love object of the opposite sex, an intense attachment to a member of one's own sex (often acquired in the earlier years) may develop to a level of great intensity and interfere with the development of the relation which is general and normal within the culture. In addition to such acquired homosexual attachments, two other kinds of attachments often make for later unhappiness: (1) attachment to a person of the opposite sex who is so much like one's father or mother that one becomes a "clinging vine," without facing mature responsibilities; (2) accidental overstimulation from a person who offers no real basis for enduring affection, no foundation for a sound and satisfying day-in day-out sharing of one's life, but is considered on the basis of strong sex response alone to be a true "soul mate." We shall return to the themes of sex, love, marriage, and family in various other contexts later; from the present viewpoint the important thing is to show that falling in love, and indeed all the types of feeling and attitude between the sexes, are very complex events indeed, whether in terms of physiology or psychology. They depend upon the whole process of biological and social maturing and on many cultural forces. We are very far from being miraculously or infallibly guided by nature. Love can, like all other things related to our human motivational life, yield both great joy and great pain.

It is evident, then, that through the whole process of growing up the role of social forces in the development of the sex interest is just as great as it is in the case of the maternal interest. The essential thing is that the newly appearing energies (partly sexual, partly more general bodily energies) have got to be used, integrated, incorporated into life somehow; even when they are directed away from the paths which we think of as normal, they reflect an intense interest which cannot be handled constructively by just ignoring or condemning them. The idea, traditional in our culture, that one can simply "step upon" or "block off" or "repress" a drive if one believes that it interferes with other goals cannot be reconciled with the direct evidence from the patient study of individuals struggling for adjustment. The idea has taken such a beating that probably no responsible guide would any longer resort to this conception of attempting to extirpate a major component of human nature. Opinions may differ as to the forms of direction, redirection, or even misdirection which human energies, like the sexual, may take at different times and ages, and as to the wisest path along which to guide an individual who is psychologically or morally confused as to his own development; but there is agreement that denial of the reality of the problem or the attempt simply to squelch any human impulse by sheer fiat is often perilous.

It is of the utmost importance, however, to recognize that the huge fund of energy of the adolescent and young adult is due not simply to sexual development and indeed not simply to the endocrine system, but in part to an accentuation of the process of growth. This is connected with the fact that there is typically in mid-adolescence an enormous increase in activity in connection with almost everything from sports and horseplay to science and religion and philosophy, depending on the individual and the group. There is a deepening and a broadening of life. This is in some degree a direct or indirect expression of sex energy, but it is as profound and as extensive as personality development itself. Waiting only upon maturity and experience to give form and communicability to these impressions, much of the world's greatest lyric poetry and music has come from this first great gush of the creative powers in adolescence and early maturity. There is an activation and a sensitization of the whole living system; and whatever interests are already there, whatever skills already exist, whatever values have taken shape earlier as a result of growth and learning, are ready for intensification, fresh direction, in adolescence. Skills, values, outlooks toward life tend to achieve more definite form and to be stimulated, enriched, organized, enthusiastically cultivated, so that often the ground plan of life is laid in a relatively short time in this period of the first great accentuation of one's powers.

The Activity Drives

So far we have been looking at drives whose origin clearly lies to a large degree in the tensions of the vital organs. There are, however, many other drives the basis of which is a craving for activity as such; their physical basis appears to lie not in the vital organs, but in the central nervous system and the large muscles of arms, legs, neck, trunk. These muscles, which we can voluntarily control, are always getting restless if kept inactive, always contracting and relaxing in their own complex rhythms, partly through our volition, but also partly on a reflex basis. As we shift our position, as we turn over even in sleep, as most of us do every few minutes, we show how impossible it is to maintain a state of sheer inactivity. Few punishments are as terrible for a small child as to be kept perfectly still; few soldiers, however hardened, can stand at attention for more than a few minutes without misery. There is a continuous need to be active, a need to enter constantly upon new kinds of activity. Life may indeed be regarded as an *activity stream* in which the vital organs play their part, but a part subordinate in many ways to the perpetual complex pattern of shifting tensions within the life system as a whole, each part having its own tensions by turn and contributing to the tensions of other parts.

In the large muscles of trunk and limbs, since there is almost never a completely static condition, there is a constantly shifting tension system; and from these tensions, whether extreme or slight, a good deal of our behavior springs. Wenger[7] has studied the amount of general muscle tension which appears even when we are relaxed, and has shown that this tension is related to our total personality pattern. One person is, so to speak, really able to relax; another person is not.

We find, moreover, large differences in the output of energy, even among the newborn. Indeed, it is likely that energy level or activity level is one of the most basic and most important characteristics of children. The amount of energy and activity which characterizes a child may be a

---

[7] M. A. Wenger, An attempt to appraise individual differences in the level of muscular tension, *J. exp. Psychol.*, 1943, *32*, 213–225.

clue to many traits in his personality. In a large-scale study of sympathy, coöperation, and aggressiveness among children between two and four, there was found to be a very clear relationship between the tendency to be sympathetic and the tendency to be aggressive. This might appear paradoxical to anyone who approached small children with a simple, moralistic conception that sympathetic children are "good" children, and aggressive children "bad" children. Actually, many children, with their abundant energies, are all "steamed up" much of the time; and those who are the most steamed up, most intense, most active, are very frequently sympathetic and solicitous for others, but also frequently involved in quarrels, arguments, and fights. In the long run, the more active the child, the greater his score both on aggression and on sympathy. The result is that energy level or activity level proved to be a major guide to both forms of behavior, as it is indeed to many other types of behavior.

One experienced observer of children, when asked what she regarded as the most universal of all childhood traits, said simply, "Perpetual activity." We might, to be sure, add that perpetual activity may at times arise from worry, inability to relax, and other signs of trouble, but it also may arise from the most normal animal spirits or sheer abundance of energy; it is not in itself an indication of maladjustment. It means readiness to keep going; and in this sense the degree of readiness to keep going, or to act—the general fund of energy ready for disposal, the amount of activity that is going on all the time—influences the development of many psychological traits.

But at the same time each individual shows, in addition to his *general* activity level, a readiness to be active in *specific* ways. Most children are ready for rhythmical response, for example; one child sways, swings his arms, pushes his feet back and forth, as he sits on the edge of the bed listening to his mother's story; another follows the rhythm of verse or music by vigorously thumping or stamping out the time. Rhythms are regularly recurring patterns of muscular activity, and if they are interfered with, there is a mounting of tension and discomfort; but the characteristic direction of the expression of such tension varies with the individual child. One child does not mind stopping the music at the drop of a hat and turning to something else; for another child this kind of muscular rhythm, when initiated, has to be maintained, or there is a sense of gross frustration. Whatever their origin, these individual varying patterns of rhythm, whether they take the form of rolling over, pulling and pushing, swaying or drumming with the fingers, and so on, appear very early and become well organized and easily recognized personal traits. (Cf. page 162.)

Another type of response which could be called an activity drive is the tendency to keep on doing whatever we have started to do, just as a tune "runs in the head." We may find it hard to get going with our mathematics; yet when we get halfway through a problem and are nearing its solution, it may be very hard to leave it and to give an instant response to the call to dinner. When we "bury ourselves" in an activity, our eyes, or our hands, or our whole body may become keyed up, and the activity cannot be made to die down instantly. Such tensions are located chiefly in brain and muscular system, rather than in the vital organs.

Another type of activity drive, closely related to the foregoing, is the tendency to move forward to follow some stimulus which has a powerful effect upon us. When it first appears, it may just be a question of our eyes rolling in the direction of the object, as an infant's eyes may move in response to a flashlight; a little later it may be a question of a child's creeping or crawling on the floor toward the object, reaching out his hand and moving head and eyes in its direction. These activities of approach may be interrupted, or the object which is pursued may be withdrawn from sight, yet he keeps going. Thus Sonya at one year of age, pursuing a ball along the floor, follows it even after it has bounced out of sight down the hall, saying to herself, "Ball, ball!" This behavior could be regarded as a sort of inner response to a stimulus which keeps going even when the external response is removed; as we shall see at a later point, the stimulus may in a certain sense continue to be "present" to the individual even though it is no longer physically acting upon him (page 249). This could be called, if one likes, a primitive form of "curiosity"; at least it is a tendency to pursue that which is just beyond what is actually given to our observation.

In the case of the visceral drives we saw that the environment molds behavior in a specific form. Similarly we find in the activity drives that the form which they take is largely determined by the environment. The sports which the people of various countries undertake for amusement, the kinds of exercises which are satisfying to them, vary greatly. While the general form or need for activity is found everywhere, the specific direction it takes will depend upon social opportunities and training; and within a given cultural group, one child learns to ride, another to fence, another to play ball, depending partly upon personal choice and partly on what the environment offers.

Sensory Drives

But it is not only the muscles that have their own intrinsic tensions. Every part of the body has its own tensions, its own activities, and therefore contributes directly or indirectly to the ongoing flow of bodily response which we call motivation. One other group of needs within the tissues remains for special emphasis: the needs provided by the system of activities within our sense organs and the parts of the brain connected directly with them.

When the sense organs are stimulated and the brain is aroused, our response is frequently one of delight, excitement, interest. The tiny child and the tiny animal are strongly drawn toward certain sights, sounds, smells, touches, warm things, cold things. They snuggle up to, they sniff at, they push themselves into, they pursue with their eyes, they prick up their ears at many things. Such activities might be called sensory drives, arising from sensory tension systems. These are not, strictly speaking, located solely in the sense organs themselves, because a sense-organ activity dies down rather quickly when the sense organ itself is no longer under stimulation; but the sense organs are connected with the brain, which, when stimulated, is likely to keep going a considerable time.

Certainly the tendency to enjoy sensory stimulation like color, tone, taste, smell, must lie in the brain, not in the sense organs themselves. This delight in sensory values, this enjoyment of color or tone, is exploited by the arts. Even the two- or three-year-old makes a great deal of painting or crayoning, colored balls or beads, makes a great deal of the little music boxes that he can crank or whistles that he can blow, or may listen in rapt attention to the noise-making or music-making world about him. He combines activity drives and sensory drives whenever he can; few things are more satisfying than drums to beat, mouth organs to blow. It would be a mistake, however, to emphasize solely the behavior aspects of these responses to experiences given by the senses. There is sheer delight in tone and color itself; and though the response may be very vague and variable, one may say with confidence that the child loves music or that he loves rhythm, without being able to predict very closely what he will do about it at any particular moment. Children come into life equipped with a wide variety of eager and vivid responses to the things of the senses, and they exploit these to the utmost.

There are large individual differences in the different kinds of delight in and response to sensory stimulation.[8] One infant nods his head casually in response to music; another "comes to life" when the music starts, practically hibernates when it stops. One child hardly notices color; another "goes drunk" with it like a color-mad painter of the Turner type.

So far we have considered three classes of motives or tensions: those connected with the vital organs, those connected with the striped muscles, and those connected with the sensory systems. It must not be assumed, however, that we can regard all human motivation as a sort of jigsaw puzzle or mosaic pattern in which the motives at any given moment are like pieces to be fitted together. On the contrary, the various tensions tend to fuse or melt into one another. A motive, such as wanting a soda in good company after a tennis game, is a fresh creation in which it is no longer feasible to pick out what the separate elements are —how much of your satisfaction comes from the taste, how much from the relaxation, how much from the conversation. The social factors, like the pleasure in good company, are themselves likely to prove very complex; we shall give them attention later on.

Before leaving this topic, it may be worth while to glance ahead at some of the more complex motives. Let us begin with *self-love* and *love of power*. As we responded with pleasure during infancy to the faces and voices of others, and as we found ourselves responding with maternal or sexual feeling to other boys and girls during our years of growing up, we responded also to ourselves—to our own bodies, to our own voices, and to the picture which we developed of ourselves; we strove

---

[8] E. Lerner and L. B. Murphy (eds.), Methods for the study of personality in young children, *Monogr. Soc. Res. Child Develpm.*, 1941, 6, No. 4.

to make ourselves successful and lovable; we made this picture of ourselves into the best picture we knew how to make. Popular speech does not hesitate to call this response to ourselves "self-love." Part of this, of course, is the kind of self-love which means the enjoyment of *status*, as evidenced in prestige, or vanity—a system of motives very important for social life. At the same time we find among the various "activity drives" which can be noticed in childhood the delight in manipulation, the enjoyment in overcoming obstacles, getting things in order, lining them up, ruling out discord and interference; such activities might be described as manifestations of a *"power* motive."

Now the concern with *status* and the concern with *power* soon become closely tied together. Self-love, or the tendency to accept oneself as a pretty good person, becomes closely associated with this enjoyment in being a cause, being a power, getting things organized. The prestige motive and the power motive, both very important and vital, are developed and integrated very early in life. Likewise, the satisfactions from our senses that come from seeing, hearing, touching other people, and the satisfaction from using the muscles in playing with other children, while at first all very simple, become blended with our affections and develop in the direction of comradeship or friendship, or *esprit de corps*. At the same time the process of sharing in the activities of others, and the process of competing with others, are likely to tend more and more to *reinforcement of our own activity,* and may increase our sense of adequacy and therefore our own self-love. Florence Goodenough writes:

. . . Children were observed under two sets of circumstances:
1. The child was alone in a room with an adult observer who provided him with toys and picture-books but avoided direct verbal stimulation as far as was consistent with maintaining an easy, natural atmosphere.
2. The child was observed in play with other children during a free play hour in nursery school and kindergarten.
Pronouns of the first person singular (including the possessives) are used far more frequently during play with other children than when the child is alone with an adult. Both singular and plural pronouns of the third person with non-personal antecedents show the opposite trend in a very marked degree. . . .
Insofar as the use of these pronouns is indicative of something in the nature of an ego-consciousness, it is evident that this feeling is brought to the fore

far more frequently in the competitive situations of group play than is the case during the less socialized conditions of the controlled situations.[9]

From such experiences in the group gradually develop those social patterns of behavior, like gregariousness, coöperativeness, competitiveness, in which the self in relation to others is observed and in which we become more expressly aware of our relationship to others.

We shall attempt more fully in later chapters (Chapters 21–23) to show how our simpler motive patterns develop into the more complex motives which appear at the level of daily social living. Enough has been said here to suggest that however important the simplest human motives like hunger and sex may be, the play of human motives is very complex and highly charged with many attitudes relating to self-love, to power, and to other types of drives which are ingrained in us as members of the social group. So important are our regard for ourselves, our patterns of self-love and self-respect, and our need to control (and not be controlled by) our fellows, that we will *not* just eat "like animals" whatever is thrown at us, however hungry we may be. The story of frustrated love affairs and embittered marriages is often the story of "hurt feelings," feelings that we are not respected or are being shoved around, *not* a story of sex deprivation alone. The motives all get woven into a unified system; and *awareness of self in relation to others* is part of this system.

SUGGESTED READINGS

Cannon, W. B., *The Wisdom of the Body,* New York, Norton, 1939.
Gruetzkow, H. C., and Bowman, P. H., *Men and Hunger,* Elgin, Ill., Brethren Publishing House, 1946.
McDougall, W., *An Introduction to Social Psychology,* London, Methuen, 23rd ed., 1936.
Mead, M., *Sex and Temperament in Three Primitive Societies,* New York, Morrow, 1935.
Morgan, C. T., and Stellar, E., *Physiological Psychology,* New York, McGraw-Hill, 1950, 2nd ed., chaps. 18, 19.
Newcomb, T. M., *Social Psychology,* New York, Dryden, 1950, Part 2.
Young, P. T., *Motivation of Behavior,* New York, Wiley, 1936.

---

[9] F. L. Goodenough, The use of pronouns by young children: a note on the development of self-awareness, *J. gen. Psychol.,* 1938, 52, 333–346.

8   EMOTIONS

From one point of view emotions consist of stirred-up responses of certain parts of the body—a gasp, a pounding heart, dilated eyes, cold sweat. From another point of view, emotions are stirred-up states of consciousness, masses of turbulent feelings and impulses. Such viewpoints are good, and we need them both. But we need still another viewpoint, too. We need a view of the whole person, whose whole body (not just certain organs) and whose whole consciousness (not just specific feelings and impulses) are jointly involved in a unitary response; the emotion is not a local but a general response of the whole person.

Emotion involves in some way everything that is going on; it involves memory, thinking, imagination, and even the perception of your surroundings. In one of his short stories Ambrose Bierce describes the strange tricks which emotional stress can play upon a man's perception of the world. A southern planter stands on a railroad bridge high above the river below, about to be hanged by northern troops.

He closed his eyes in order to fix his last thoughts upon his wife and children. The water, touched by gold by the early sun, the brooding mists under the banks at some distance down the stream the fort, the soldiers, the piece of drift—all had distracted him. And now he became conscious of a new disturbance. Striking through the thought of his dear ones was a sound he could neither ignore nor understand, a sharp, distinct, metallic percussion like the stroke of a blacksmith's hammer upon the anvil; he wondered what it was, and whether immeasurably distant or near by—it seemed both. Its recurrence was regular, but as slow as the tolling of a death knell. He awaited each stroke with impatience and—he knew not why—apprehension. The intervals of silence grew progressively longer; the delays maddening. With greater infrequency the sounds increased in strength and sharpness. They hurt his ear like the thrust of a knife; he feared he would shriek. What he heard was the ticking of his watch.[1]

Such experiences—merely extreme or dramatic examples of the way emotion can pervade our whole being and warp our ways of thinking and perceiving—suggest that we might gain much from the concept of *tension*. The concept of tension served us as an introduction to the problem of motive. In the cases considered in earlier chapters, the motivated activity usually springs from tensions of some sort accumulating within the body; the tensions may, for example, spring from the vital organs or the striped muscle system. But in the case of emotion we usually refer to instances in which the tension arises from an outside stimulus, rather than from the inside (like hunger pangs); we may say in the case of emotion that outside pressure is applied to the living individual in such a way that a great deal of tension quickly accumulates. Instead of developing needs—need for food, or activity, or a gratifying sensory stimulus—slowly on our own terms, we may be quickly overwhelmed by some outside situation, some violent noise, some physical injury, some gross slight to our confident picture of ourselves which throws us completely off balance. We are frightened, upset, embarrassed, or enraged. All these responses we shall call emotions. Other terms have been used by other writers, and there is no need to quarrel over definitions. Simply for our own present purposes, the term will be used to indicate responses to these more or less overwhelming outside pressures acting upon us. The most common characteristic of all these responses is a rapid increase in the general level of tension, that is to say, in the amount of excitation in the body. This usually takes the form of increase in tension of the striped muscles, and likewise of the unstriped muscles of the arterial walls and of the digestive system. There may also be a marked increase in activity of some of the duct glands, as shown in sweating or in the flow of tears; among the ductless glands the adrenals are of special importance (cf. page 62).

If one undertook to classify the various types of emotion, one might begin with sheer excitement, that is, with the active but generalized

---

[1] A. Bierce, *An Occurrence at Owl Creek Bridge*, in H. R. Warfel, R. H. Gabriel, and S. Williams (eds.), *The American Mind*, New York, American Book, 1937, p. 1167.

display of energy. Eyes open wide; muscles tighten; heart pounds. Superimposed upon this general or undifferentiated excitement there may be a specific response like "exhilaration" or "rage." We may say that the very nature of sudden, intense stimulation is to produce much general excitement and also, as a rule, a more specific tension to which we may give some more specific name, such as "surprise" or "thrill" or "fright" or "irritation."

Perhaps the emotions of early infancy are mostly of the "general excitement" type without very much of the specific in them. We noted on page 41, in relation to the general process of growth, that there is development from the diffuse to the more and more specific and recognizable pattern of facial response. Motion pictures of the newborn who have been dropped from the attendant's hands, or kept beyond their normal feeding time, or pricked with a needle, or in some other way disturbed permit no very clear recognition of the nature of the stimulus. There is a sort of general turmoil going on to which no very specific name can be given. But the emotional expressions of older children can be spotted with fair accuracy (compare page 43). The maturation sequence (page 42) seems to be largely responsible for the specific emotions of fear, rage, grief, etc., which begin to be recognizable after a few months of growth have occurred. Yet there remains some general commotion, some nonspecific, diffuse excitement in *all* emotions; no emotional response is 100 percent specific and completely distinct from all other emotional response.

Emotion may be aroused by things favoring the individual or by things threatening him. In general, those activities which suddenly fulfill the individual's needs, like the lonely, anxious child's glimpse of his returning mother, or the sick child's first chance to get up and walk again, lead to excited smiles which tend to take the form of laughter—even frantic giggling—when the stimulus is more intense. I may break into a roar of mirth with some slight stimulus if "everything's going my way." A rival slipping on a banana peel may bring a heartfelt response. We may, then, see that laughter may be regarded as one of these emotional responses to a sudden overwhelming stimulus. Yet most of the emotional responses for which we have names are disturbing, rather than gratifying. Grief, rather than joy, would be emphasized in most lists of emotions. Many of the emotions have to do with gross threats to the individual: attacks, injuries, dangers, losses of treasured persons or possessions. Good studies of such responses have been plentiful in recent years, and a few will now be reported.

Fear

A number of different kinds of responses have been studied under the heading of fear.

Quite striking is the "startle pattern," seen when, for example, a revolver shot is fired close to the individual's head. The pattern involves the turning of the head, the twisting of the trunk, general cringing or shrinking, and acceleration of pulse and breathing. Other fear patterns appear in response to other kinds of stimuli. Indeed, whenever fear is

TABLE 2. Fear Symptoms Reported by Troops in Combat Divisions (Based on Surveys of Combat Veterans in Four Infantry Divisions, April, 1944)[2]

Symptoms	Percent Reporting Occurrence of the Symptoms			
	Division A (So. Pac., 2095 Men)	Division B (So. Pac., 1983 Men)	Division C (Cen. Pac., 1299 Men)	Division D (Cen. Pac., 643 Men)
1. Violent pounding of the heart	84	78	74	68
2. Sinking feeling in the stomach	69	66	60	57
3. Shaking or trembling all over	61	54	53	39
4. Feeling sick at stomach	55	50	46	39
5. Cold sweat	56	45	43	39
6. Feeling of weakness or feeling faint	49	46	36	34
7. Feeling of stiffness	45	44	43	31
8. Vomiting	27	21	18	8
9. Losing control of bowels	21	12	9	4
10. Urinating in pants	10	9	6	3

closely observed we are likely to find that we need special names for it, such as apprehension, or dread, or terror. When the stimulation is carried *beyond a certain point,* disorganization appears. The energy spills over throughout the living system; the central and autonomic nervous systems are both fully involved. We then see not only the

---

[2] S. A. Stouffer (ed.), *The American Soldier: Combat and Its Aftermath*, Princeton, Princeton University Press, 1949, vol. 2, p. 201; abstracted without modification.

elevation of blood pressure and the wild pounding of the heart, but a more general condition of profound upheaval. Normal, healthy young men subjected to terrifying combat conditions report the responses shown in Table 2. Many of these responses, such as items 6, 7, 8, can of course occur in many other conditions of upheaval; when emotion is intense it resembles in some respect the extreme responses due to other causes.

Emotional responses differ greatly from person to person. Fear is aroused more easily in one baby than in another, just as it is more easily aroused in one adult than in another. One undertakes to measure the sensitiveness of the individual to such disturbing stimuli by finding how much it takes to upset him. Reminding us that navigators speak of a ship as safely loaded up to a certain point called the "Plimsoll" mark, G. L. Freeman speaks of the Plimsoll mark of each individual, the point beyond which he may not safely be loaded with strain or violent stimulation. In selecting men for the North African campaign of 1942, it was necessary to get some individuals to serve in traffic control posts in which they would have to make quick and accurate decisions regarding the routing of tanks and trucks in the midst of shellfire and aerial bombardment, and while receiving constantly changing orders. They were put through a series of nerve-wracking tests. It was then possible to say something about the Plimsoll mark of the individual and to select only men who could "take it." Most of the men selected made good on the job. In Chapter 24 we shall glance at other methods developed in the British and U. S. armies for eliminating from overseas assignments men who were unable to keep their heads when handling tense and very difficult situations. One of the main things that such tests aim to do is to find out the crackup point, the Plimsoll mark at which disorganization appears. But if the man is safely above the Plimsoll mark, the investigator is also interested in finding out how smoothly and how effectively he can function.[3]

Rage

One of the most striking of emotional patterns in infancy is the response to interference. If one pinions the child's elbows at the

---

[3] G. L. Freeman, in a personal communication.

sides, or even if one gently holds the head with cotton or felt pads while testing the eye movements, one is likely to get squirming, thrashing, kicking, prolonged holding of the breath, even to the point of turning black in the face—a primitive rage response. Interfering with movement at one point is likely to arouse general restlessness, i.e., an increase of movement elsewhere. In the study at Ohio State University in which there was a brief interference with newborn infants' breathing this tendency to scattered responses in other parts of the body was just as marked as the tendency to move the head.[4] But this extensive study likewise revealed

TABLE 3. Age and Sex Differences in the Proportion of Outbursts Involving Retaliatory Behavior

Sex	Percentage of Total Number of Outbursts					
	Under 1 Yr.	1 Yr.– 1 Yr. 11 Mos.	2 Yrs.– 2 Yrs. 11 Mos.	3 Yrs.– 3 Yrs. 11 Mos.	4 Yrs. and Over	All Ages
Boys	0.0	9.4	10.4	25.7	30.0	18.0
Girls	0.8	2.8	11.5	25.3	26.3	12.2
Both sexes	0.7	6.3	10.6	25.6	28.0	15.9
Age and Sex Differences in the Proportion of Outbursts Involving Motor or Verbal Resistance						
Boys	27.3	71.2	40.4	39.2	60.0	46.4
Girls	12.3	42.9	20.8	56.3	60.9	40.5
Both sexes	13.9	55.6	36.6	41.8	60.5	44.2
Age and Sex Differences in the Proportion of Outbursts Involving Display of Undirected Energy						
Boys	100.0	78.0	73.1	65.2	45.0	67.8
Girls	86.9	78.7	83.3	29.6	29.0	63.2
Both sexes	88.9	78.4	75.1	59.9	36.3	66.1

quite marked individual differences from child to child. The unorganized responses, or display of "undirected energy," became less and less frequent and were replaced more and more by specific retaliatory behavior and verbal protest during the years of early childhood, as Table 3 shows.[5]

When the teacher of a class in psychology asked her students to re-

---

[4] K. C. Pratt, A. K. Nelson, and K. H. Sun, The behavior of the newborn infant, Ohio State Univ. Stud., *Contr. Psychol.*, 1930, No. 10.

[5] F. L. Goodenough, *Anger in Young Children,* Minneapolis, University of Minnesota Press, 1931.

cord all anger episodes in the course of a week, she obtained the data given in Table 4. Some students were often angry, or remained upset for

TABLE 4. Responses Made During Anger[6]

	Degrees[a]					
	V	IV	III	II	I	Total
Gross bodily responses directed at offending object						
Excited talking or angry exclamation	2	2	10	13	5	32
Angry, sarcastic, sulky retort	0	6	8	9	3	26
Restless behavior	2	2	7	7	2	20
Refusal to speak or look at offender	0	7	3	5	3	18
Violence to inanimate objects	1	2	2	4	1	10
Sudden exit from room	1	0	1	4	1	7
Grimace or glaring or staring at offender	0	0	0	5	0	5
Violence to offender (slap, shake)	0	1	0	2	0	3
Refusal of food	1	0	0	1	0	2
Pleasant reply	0	0	1	1	1	3
	7	20	32	51	16	126
Expressive movements						
Unpleasant facial expression	2	8	6	10	4	30
Biting of fingers or lips	0	3	6	2	2	13
Clenching teeth or hands	4	2	2	1	3	12
Body tense	3	4	0	2	1	10
Stamping foot	1	1	1	3	2	8
Tears in eyes	4	0	1	1	2	8
Eyes flashed, stared, popped	0	1	0	1	1	3
	14	19	16	20	15	84
Activities of sympathetic system and adrenal glands (mainly)						
Gasp, heavy or rapid breathing	1	2	7	11	7	28
Hot feeling	3	5	5	4	2	19
Flushing	0	1	6	5	1	13
Fast heartbeat	2	0	8	2	0	12
Swallowing, choked feeling	2	0	2	0	0	4
Nausea or "sinking" in stomach	1	2	1	0	0	4
Trembling, weak feeling	1	0	0	1	2	4
Cold hands, dry lips	0	2	0	0	0	2
Loss of desire to eat	0	0	2	0	0	2
Headache, dizziness	0	0	2	0	0	2
	10	12	33	23	12	90

[a] Self-rating scale I–V used. V was most extreme anger ever felt by subject. I was least ever experienced.

[6] G. S. Gates, An observational study of anger, *J. exp. Psychol.*, 1926, 9, 325–336.

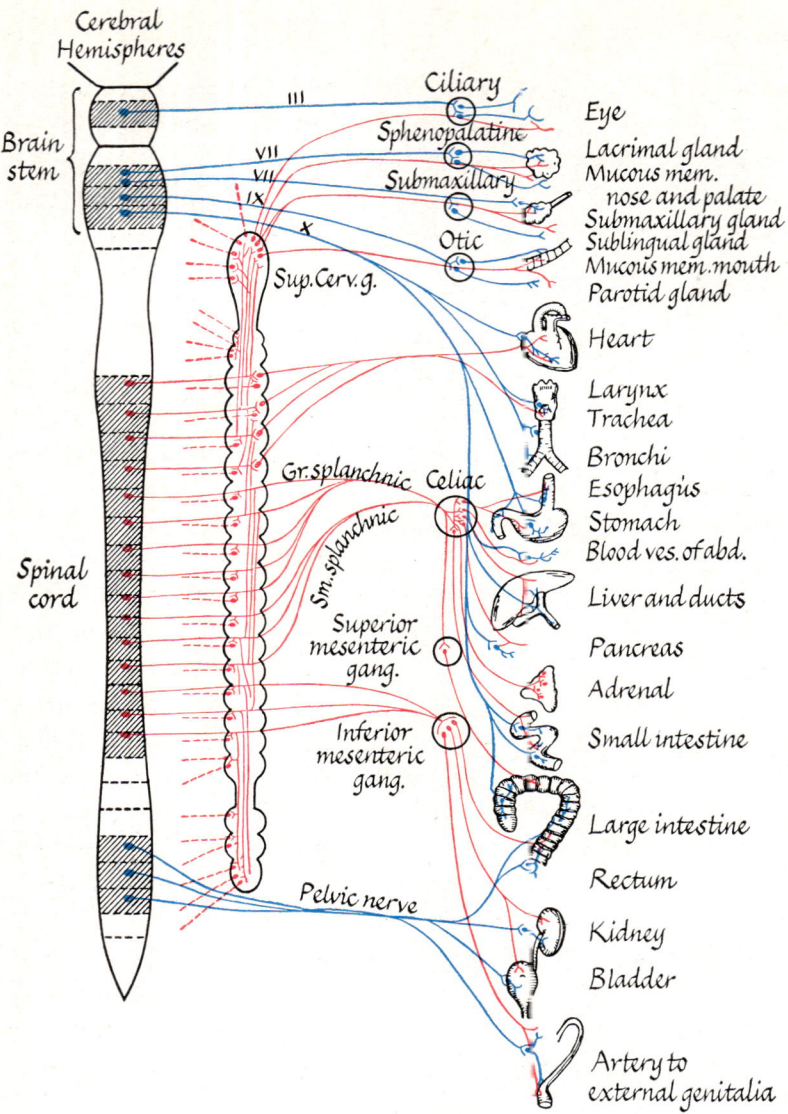

Figure 14. The Autonomic Nervous System

The efferent, or responding, branches of the autonomic nervous system shown in relation to the central nervous system. At the left is a conventionalized representation of the spinal cord leading up to the brain, the center of the central nervous system. At the right are diagrams of the vital organs controlled by the autonomic system. The three divisions of the autonomic system are (1) cranial, (2) sympathetic, (3) sacral. The cranial and sacral divisions are shown in blue; the sympathetic, in red. (Modified from Meyer and Gottlieb's *Experimental Pharmacology*, Urban and Schwarzenberg and J. B. Lippincott Co. By permission of the publishers.)

a full day, or even more, when badly upset. Others maintained an Olympian calm most of the time. There are, however, two problems here to be distinguished, as we shall see in more detail later: (1) sheer degree of susceptibility to rage; (2) capacity to keep going despite rage, i.e., capacity to keep one's annoyance under control. (Compare page 90.)

Emotion and the Autonomic Nervous System

Much research has been done on the physiology of emotional responses, especially on the physiology of rage. The excited state leads to vigorous activity of the sympathetic system (compare page 48).

In Figure 14 is shown the general relationship between the central nervous system (brain and spinal cord), on the one hand, and the system known as the autonomic nervous system, on the other hand. The autonomic nervous system consists of bunches of nerve cells and their nerve fibers, connected with the central nervous system but lying outside of the bony covering. There are three main strands or groups of fibers to be considered. Near the top and at the bottom of the figure one notices in *blue* two groups of fibers which play a large part in controlling the glands of internal secretion, the duct glands, and the unstriped musculature of vital organs, such as the gastrointestinal canal and the walls of the arteries. These top and bottom portions of the autonomic make up the *parasympathetic system*. This is concerned largely with the urgent needs of the organism while not in danger, such as nutrition, oxidation, elimination, growth, self-repair, and sex; broadly speaking, the vegetative activities. It plays, however, some part also in connection with struggling or emergency functions, as is evident in the violent spasms of the digestive system during fear, etc.

Between the cranial and the sacral system will be observed in *red* many small fibers of the *sympathetic* system, leading into those organs which are specially active in emergency responses of the body, including the arteries and some of the endocrine glands. It will be seen that the heartbeat, the increase in blood pressure, the liberation of adrenin, all of which are related to the maintenance of the body on a war footing, are controlled largely by this system of fibers.

The sympathetic and parasympathetic are the two great divisions of the autonomic nervous system. The autonomic is in general independent of direct voluntary control, although it is in continuous interaction with the central nervous system. A few people can learn by voluntary control to alter the pulse, the blood pressure, and the stomach contractions; and in the great majority of us who cannot exercise such voluntary control, there is nevertheless a constant give-and-take between our brain activities—our thinking, our deliberate decisions, our general attitude toward life—and the tone and function of the autonomic nervous system. Indeed, those *psychosomatic* conditions which were mentioned on page 56, such as the ulcerations and high blood pressures which stem from our overconcern with or worry about problems of life, are typical instances of ways in which the central nervous system plays its part in disturbing and causing hyperactivity of the autonomic system.

The study of these aspects of the physiology of emotions helps to explain why the different emotional patterns have so much in common. In all such responses there are massive changes in the general level of bodily tension shown in the striped muscles and in the unstriped muscles. Even in such different states as rage and intense pain, the response of the sympathetic system is very much alike. The sympathetic system acts diffusely, not in a different pattern for each of these emotional conditions.

Emotions, as we have seen, are not just a matter of a single organ; they involve a complex bodily pattern. One of the most frequent laboratory procedures is to study the responses of the respiratory and circulatory systems and to find how the excitement is betrayed, how it waxes and wanes, and how it varies from state to state and from person to person. One typically finds that, as the intensity of the response increases, the ratio of the time spent in breathing in to the time spent in breathing out—the inspiration-expiration ratio—increases from its typical normal 1:5 up to as much as 1:2 or even 1:1.

In such states of stress there are also electrical changes in the body. Currents are set up within the body and in addition there is a drop in the body's resistance to a weak outside current which the experimenter passes through it. Autonomic upheaval results in increasing perspiration, and perspiration facilitates good electrical conduction, so that a current passed through the body encounters during such states much less resistance than under normal conditions. The resistance which the body offers is measured by the method shown in Figure 15; this drop in resistance is called the *galvanic skin reflex*.

This reflex has been extensively studied in states of stress and of effort. The experimenter ordinarily uses a very low voltage—4 to 6 volts from dry cells—and the subject does not even feel the current. Yet as the current passes through, the varying resistance of the body causes a varying galvanic response. Such responses are very marked during startle, fear, rage, pain, and effort. Indeed, in many states involving stress, the galvanic skin reflex is associated more with "effort" than with what we would ordinarily call "emotion." Thus Darrow attached this kind of apparatus to his body, and as he drove about in Chicago traffic he noticed the movements of the galvanic needle indicating changes in his body resistance whenever he had to make a decision, even if it was just a question of shifting gears.

The galvanic skin reflex has been extensively used in the study of stress arising from disturbing personal situations. It has, for example, long been used in research with psychiatric patients. In a study by Wells, mental patients who had apparently lost contact with reality so completely that they were "inaccessible" (eyes closed, paying no attention to anything in their environment) nevertheless showed characteristic electrical changes in the body when words were mentioned which referred to earlier emotionally significant episodes in their lives. One goes around carrying within himself a readiness to electrical responses to those stimuli which "strike home."

The galvanic skin reflex is also often studied in the various *lie detector* procedures, frequently along with changes in respiration or blood pressure. Suppose that the individual actually knows certain details concerning a crime, and that words referring specifically to those details are presented, one at a time, interspersed in a list of other words. These "critical" words arouse sudden anxiety or fear. It is not a case of general fear or anxiety which anyone would show in a police court or under general suspicion. Rather, it is a question of knowing what to be anxious about, knowing what words are significant, which innocent persons do not. Thus when a purse had been stolen, a series of words indicating specifically the contents of that purse were mixed in with "innocent" words.[7] The question was not how much general fear the person would show; it was a question of response to those particular words. Among three women, only one responded specifically to words naming the

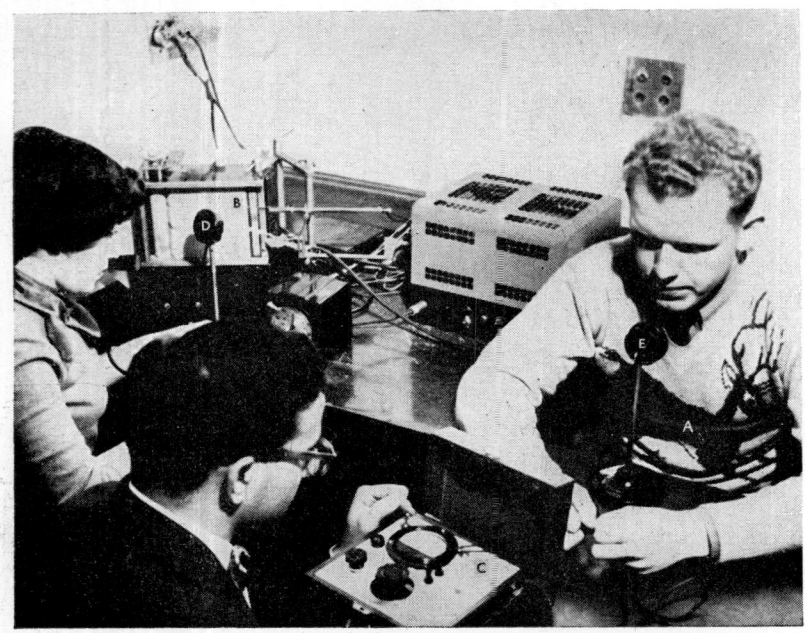

Figure 15. Bodily Changes Accompanying Emotion

The subject (at right) is asked to give his associations to a variety of words, some emotion-evoking, others neutral. As he reports them, changes in skin resistance to an electric current, fluctuations in breathing rate, and the time required to respond are measured.

The subject is wearing a pneumatic girth recorder (A), which records changes in breathing rate on a revolving drum (B). He is holding electrodes attached to a galvanometer (C), which registers changes in skin resistance. The experimenter speaks the stimulus words into a voice key (D) and the subject reports his associations via his own voice key (E). Both stimulus and response are recorded on the revolving drum (polygraph) in such a fashion as to make it possible to measure the time elapsing between them.

contents of the purse; and she promptly confessed. Even when a suspect is asked point-blank whether he committed a certain crime or not, there is often a marked difference in the physiological patterns of the guilty and the innocent. There are a good many studies indicating that while a

---

[7] C. G. Jung, The association method, *Amer. J. Psychol.*, 1910, *31*, 219–269.

guilty person can control his verbal expressions, it is very much harder for him to control the delicate inner responses which are reflected in his pulse, breathing, and electrical changes. Hence the tendency to make a good deal of these methods in police court procedure.[8]

Figure 15 brings out the expression of emotion. In this experiment, "emotionally loaded words" were found to produce responses characteristically different from those evoked by a series of "neutral" words.

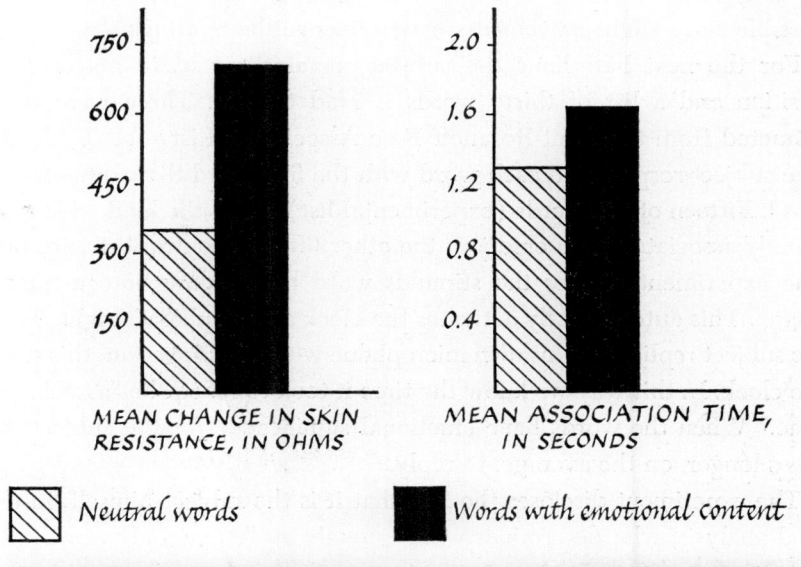

Figure 16. Bodily Changes Accompanying Emotion

The results of the experiment in Figure 15. The two graphs compare changes in skin resistance and association time accompanying the subject's response to each class of words. The mean changes in these two factors are greater for the emotion-evoking words than for the neutral words.

The subject, a male undergraduate student, was not aware of the purpose of the experiment. He had consented to be a subject at the request of one of the two experimenters who was a personal friend. Although he later confessed that the equipment had made him wonder "what was going to be done" to him, he asked no questions. He seemed slightly nervous.

---

[8] F. E. Inbau, *Lie Detection and Criminal Interrogation*, Baltimore, Williams and Wilkins, 2nd ed., 1948.

The subject is first seated in a chair close to the table on which the galvanometer rests. He is told to grasp the electrodes in his palms. Changes in his palmar skin resistance are then read from the galvanometer. This subject's only reaction to the electrodes came later in the experiment when he complained about the necessity of grasping them so tightly for so long a time. Next a pneumatic girth recorder is fastened around his chest. Changes in breathing are automatically recorded on the polygraph once the experiment starts. The subject sits as quietly as possible since slight movements may influence the readings.

For the next half hour the subject remains seated in his original position and a list of thirty words is read to him. These have been extracted from the Kent-Rosanoff Free Association List (see Table 6). The subject responds to each word with the first word that comes to his mind. Fifteen of the words (experimental list) are of the kind which are usually associated with emotion; the other fifteen (control list) are not. The experimenter gives the stimulus word by speaking into a microphone. This automatically activates the clock at the subject's right. Then the subject replies into his own microphone with an association; this stops the clock. In this way we know the time it took to react, the "association time." When the words have emotional significance for the subject, he takes longer, on the average, to reply.

The experiment discloses the fact that it is the subject himself, in the final analysis, who determines what is really an "emotional" word. And

TABLE 5. Summary of Results

	Mean (Average)			S.D.[a]		Median	
	Control	Exp.	P.[b]	Control	Exp.	Control	Exp.
Changes in skin resistance (ohms)	350	670	.05	490	390	210	600
Deflection of galvanometer	4.20	5.80	.10	2.3	2.6	4.0	5.9
Association time (seconds)	1.30	1.60	.05	0.35	0.48	1.40	1.60
Inspiration/expiration ratio (mm.)	0.28	0.32	.40	0.13	0.11	0.25	0.29

[a] S.D. is a measure of the amount of variation of individual observations from the mean. Cf. page 377.
[b] P is the likelihood that a difference of the magnitude given here would occur by chance alone.

although, as Figure 16 shows, the designation "emotional" does have some objective validity, since the experimental list produces a higher mean change in skin resistance and a longer mean reaction time than the control list, some words which were on the control list receive stronger responses than some words on the experimental list. Thus this

TABLE 6. Responses to Individual Words
Control Series

Word No.	Stimulus Word	Response Word	Skin R-Change	Deflection	Time	I/E
2.	Music	Nice	.1	3.0	.78	.25
3.	Deep	High	.4	5.0	1.17	.11
4.	Table	Chair	.1	3.5	.59	.11
7.	Mountain	High	.5	6.5	1.37	.16
10.	Cabbage	Salad	.1	3.0	1.37	.13
11.	House	Bad	1.9	10.4	.98	.25
14.	Lamp	Light	.3	5.0	1.76	.29
15.	Sheep	Wolf	.2	4.0	1.17	.29
17.	Bread	Wine	.2	5.0	1.56	.25
19.	Carpet	Sweeper	.3	2.5	1.37	.60
20.	White	Black	.2	5.0	1.17	.40
23.	River	Stream	.2	1.0	1.17	.50
25.	Fruit	Apple	.1	2.0	1.37	.25
27.	Whistle	Noise	.1	1.0	1.76	.25
28.	Cottage	House	.6	6.5	1.95	.29

Experimental Series

Word No.	Stimulus Word	Response Word	Skin R-Change	Deflection	Time	I/E
1.	Dark	Light	.2	3.0	.78	.18
5.	Sickness	Health	.7	7.5	1.56	.18
6.	Beautiful	Nice	.5	7.1	.98	.20
8.	Anger	Fear	1.0	9.5	1.95	.22
9.	Girl	Boy	.8	6.0	1.17	.40
12.	Dream	Good	.1	4.5	1.17	.50
13.	Trouble	House	1.9	5.0	1.95	.29
16.	Religion	Law	1.9	10.0	2.14	.50
18.	Afraid	Dark	1.0	6.5	1.95	.31
21.	Wish	Fulfilled	.6	4.0	1.37	.29
22.	Baby	Girl	.8	5.0	1.56	.22
24.	Bath	House	.6	1.0	1.56	.40
26.	Man	Woman	.4	4.0	1.56	.29
29.	Man	Woman	.3	3.0	1.76	.25
30.	Priest	Wife	1.3	10.5	2.74	.50

subject responded to "house" with the word "bad." Later he said that although at the time he had experienced nothing unusual about the word, he thought he might have said bad because he did have a good deal of trouble at *his* house. For him, then, the word house was emotionally loaded although it does not appear on the experimental list.

A particular source of difficulty for this subject was the words priest and religion. On both he took a noticeably longer time than usual to find a response and on both his skin resistance change was noticeably higher. His responses themselves were also somewhat unusual. Later he said he had felt a little uncomfortable at the time, but he had no idea why this might be so. He did however recall, on being questioned, that his mother now wanted him to teach in a Sunday school and that although he had attended once he was very reluctant to do so again. Table 5 summarizes the results of this experiment. Table 6 shows the subject's responses to the individual words.

Although the autonomic system produces rather diffuse upheavals, not permitting a sharp differentiation from one emotion to another, the patterns of *striped-muscle* response often tell a very different story. Earlier (page 41) we noted the gradual progression from the diffuse responses of early childhood to the much more precisely patterned responses of the adult; this is at least in part a question of maturation. Since the process of maturation offers clear-cut developmental patterns in the sphere of striped-muscle activity, we should expect the different emotions, of whatever type, to register differently in the striped muscles insofar as sufficient maturation has occurred. It is partly for this reason that facial expression can be differentiated in children a year old much better than among the newborn (page 44).

But there is a temptation here to put all the weight upon factors intrinsic to the individual and to forget the molding effect of the social environment. People living in a specific human group develop specific ways of smiling, scowling, sneering, etc., so that what finally emerges is not 100 percent a matter of maturation, but includes also the effects of learning; to some extent we smile or scowl or sneer in the way in which our own social group does. In Klineberg's study of facial expressions among the Chinese, we have evidence that the standardized expressions of rage take on a form somewhat different from the forms which prevail among ourselves. The Chinese gentleman may make use only of changed expression around the eyes, for it is forbidden to him to use the mouth as we do. That would be "bad form"; the mouth has been eliminated as a rage-expressing organ.

The Interpretation of Emotional Expression

Owing to the fact that the community directs attention to the expression of the emotions, it follows that to some extent all of us learn to notice and to interpret facial (and other) bodily expressions. How well can this be done? How well can we differentiate among the various emotions expressed by others? And how do we differ from one another in this capacity to understand the facial expressions of others? Are the differences among us solely differences in skill in making out what the faces of others indicate? If so, can each of us learn to "size up" the emotions of others well enough to make an effective adjustment to them? Let us try to answer these questions.

First, it is probable that we cannot innately tell such expressions apart. While there is good evidence that there is some maturation of the various specific facial responses, it does not follow from this that we have any innate ability to *interpret* these facial expressions. We probably begin with no knowledge, but very early learn to recognize different patterns in the faces of others, and later learn that someone else's facial expression goes with a kind of feeling which we ourselves have had and which we have learned to call by a specific name.

College students catch on, though with large individual differences, to the ways in which emotion is being registered; and we can sometimes teach them to improve their performance. In short, we learn to identify other people's expressions. But we can do so only insofar as the social group has a definite way of expressing emotions. And the differences between the customs of different social groups are one reason why the Chinese frequently fail to size up how we feel about things as they watch our faces, and why we fail in sizing up their faces and reach the conclusion that Orientals are "inscrutable," just as we ourselves may seem inscrutable to them.

We learn in the same way to size up the meaning of *posture* and *gesture;* we learn what to expect from taut muscles, from "drawing oneself up straight," from a free-swinging gait or a "mincing pace." We also learn to interpret the tone of the voice—the sigh, the happy, or sentimental, or grieved, or enraged voice—just as we learn to interpret the startled, or pleased, or amused face.

But when we spot the emotional tone of a living face, or even of a photograph, we are responding to more than the expression of the moment. Even when the face is completely relaxed, it bears the marks of many years of habitual emotional expression. If you contrast the face of a living person with that shown in a death mask, or even that of a waking person with that of a person under deep ether anesthesia, you will immediately become aware of the fact that the normal face is alive with the record of a lifetime's experiences, that the face is full of habitual expression, of habitual muscular contractions; the habitual rage, fear, disgust, pleasure, excitement, or sympathy of the face, as shown countless times in the past, has left its mark. Through the nerves which control the facial musculature, one keeps his habitual pattern going—or, we might almost say, his habitual emotional mask. Not that the term mask need mean anything misleading or evasive. Yet there is often a mask or screen between the outside observer and those subtle inner states which at the time are hidden by the habitual or stylized expression of the face. It is on this basis that one can read, with some degree of success, the habitual patterns, and can therefore size up personality to some degree from the face. The chronic deep prevailing outlook, whether of joy or grief, fear or rage, which serves as the fundamental tone of the individual's life is manifest to some degree even when there is superimposed upon it the dramatic expression of response to a particular incident.

But this is not the only way in which we express the chronic effects of such internal tensions. While most people have only limited knowledge of what goes on inside their bodies and only limited voluntary control of the physiological core of such disturbances, there is evidence that this physiological core, chronically maintained from day to day, has a great deal to do with health and disease. If there is constant stimulation or excitation of the body, yet no outer visible expression, we may reasonably suspect that the accumulated tension is finding some less obvious outlets. We usually find, in fact, that these dammed-up or unexpressed tensions are of profound importance.

Take for example the individuals studied by Carl Binger,[9] 24 young adults who had grown up with an extreme sense of dependence upon their parents, yet wanted to assert their own individuality. During adolescence they had craved the opportunity to stand on their own feet and get free of parental control; yet they were afraid to break free, really afraid of the loss of the dependency relation, afraid of the loss of love which this would entail. After a long series of struggles, probably mostly unconscious, to become free of this overdependence, they finally came to a crisis period in which there was a desperate effort to free themselves. The result was the precipitation of serious high blood pressure, requiring medical aid. When their life histories were studied, it was apparent in most cases that they had never really been aware of the fact that they were blocking the expression of their intense emotions day after day, year after year, and hence paving the way for a subsequent physiological breakdown.

Even more striking is the case, reported by Harold Wolff,[10] of a man whose day-by-day anxieties could be directly followed by studying the ulceration of the stomach wall. An accident had made his case available for study; as a child of nine he had rushed into the kitchen, smelled something good on the stove, dipped out a spoonful and swallowed it. It was a soup so hot and so thick that it burned through the esophagus and the surgeon found it impossible to open the passage again. The surgeon had therefore made an aperture lower down into the stomach wall, and since that time the patient had been dependent upon this opening, or fistula, into the stomach. This man, now in his twenties, was perfectly willing to be studied scientifically; in fact, he got a job at a New York hospital in which his day-by-day responses to stress could be studied. He allowed the doctors to utilize the opening into the stomach and to turn out part of the stomach wall so that it was directly visible. In this way the flow of blood in the mucous membranes of the stomach could be observed. From time to time little ulcerations, little bloody points, would appear on the surface as the man became worried. You could di-

---

[9] C. A. L. Binger, *et al.*, Personality in arterial hypertension, *Psychosom. Med. Monog.*, 1945, No. 8.

[10] H. G. Wolff, Disturbances of gastrointestinal function in relation to personality, *Ann. N. Y. Acad. Sc.*, 1943, 44, 567–568. See also S. Wolf and H. G. Wolff, *Human Gastric Function*, 1943.

rectly see how his emotional situation was causing an increase in acidity, an increase in the amount of movement, and an increase in the flow of blood—three things which indicate an abnormal condition. When stress became severe, actual ulceration was manifest. One day, for example, it was reported to him that the records of certain patients had been lost. It was this man's responsibility to keep these records, and when he heard of their loss, he became anxious. The little ulceration points on the stomach wall immediately appeared.

From evidence of this sort we may say with confidence that what we call emotions involve both brain events and visceral events. It may be convenient for certain purposes to pick out that spot in the body which represents a visible nucleus for emotional activity; emotional processes such as rage, or fear, may appear today in the stomach wall, tomorrow in the action of the sweat glands or the heart. But these are merely the most conspicuous points. Moreover, it is not the vital organs alone, but just about every bodily process that is involved when emotional activity is going on. This pervasiveness of the effects of emotional excitement is evident in many investigations of the processes of perceiving, learning, remembering, recognizing, thinking, imagining—in fact, in almost every activity in which we take note of our environment and adapt ourselves to it. Love is blind; often we cannot see blemishes in those for whom we care (or in ourselves). Or emotion may sensitize us to see what we fear. In Bartlett's experiments students looked at pictures of army and navy officers and found in these pictures a threatening attitude which actually arose from the students' own fears. There is really a very close interplay between emotional processes and those processes which we ordinarily regard as straightforward, cold, logical, matter-of-fact responses to the environment.

The Theory of the Emotions

Those interested in the physiology of emotions have not been content to study only the vital organs and the autonomic nervous system but have begun to ask what the brain itself is doing during the emotional responses, and have attempted, on this basis, to formulate a theory of the emotions. They have used the best modern surgical and electrical techniques to ascertain whether the brain as a whole or particular parts of it have characteristic functions in relation to emotional responses. Of great interest is a series of studies initiated by Cannon at Harvard which, after being followed through by Masserman and others, have now given us a rather surprising yet on the whole credible and useful picture of brain dynamics during emotion.

The question which Cannon[11] asked himself was whether there are particular parts of the brain which are centers for emotion, in the sense that an animal possessing an active brain center of this sort could show emotion, whereas one deprived of it could not. Just as one might remove

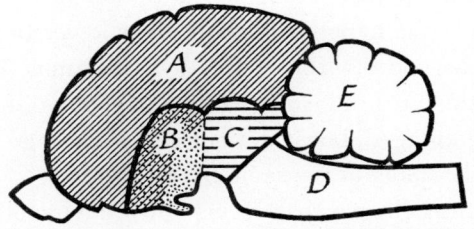

Figure 17. Section Through a Mammalian Brain

A, the cerebral hemispheres; B, the diencephalon, or between brain (which includes the thalamus); C, the mesencephalon, or midbrain; D, the medulla oblongata; E, the cerebellum. The dotted part in B is the center for the emotions. The crosshatched portion in A and B can be removed without interfering with emotional display. Once the emotional center is cut into, however, emotional reactions apparently disappear. (Modified from P. Bard, in C. Murchison, ed., *The Foundations of Experimental Psychology*, Clark University Press, Worcester, 1929.)

a man's sense of smell by destroying the mucous membranes upon which the sense of smell depends or deprive him of speech by cutting the nerves which lead to the lips, mouth, and tongue, so one might be able to ascertain where emotions are localized by finding the region which, when cut out, would prove its essential relation to emotional response. In this spirit a series of experiments were done by Cannon and his colleague Bard, which, as Figure 17 brings out, show that one may remove the forward portions of a dog's brain, slicing backward, without affecting emotional display until one encounters the region which is dotted in the diagram. If one injures the dotted region the emotional responses

---

[11] W. B. Cannon, *Bodily Changes in Pain, Hunger, Fear, and Rage*, New York, Appleton, 2nd ed., 1929; *The Wisdom of the Body*, New York, Norton, 2nd ed., 1939; P. Bard, in C. Murchison (ed.), *The Foundations of Experimental Psychology*, Worcester, Clark University Press, 1929.

are no longer present. This led to the idea of a definite *emotional center* at this dotted portion of the brain, the region of the hypothalamus. (The general layout of the brain is roughly similar in dogs, cats, and other higher mammals.) A dog deprived of the higher brain centers still bares its teeth and snarls if this "dotted area" remains, but a dog deprived of this area does not.

The more recent evidence from Masserman[12] shows, however, that the matter of localizing emotion in the hypothalamus is not so simple. The normal animal shows other brain responses in addition to the response in the hypothalamic region. To demonstrate that rage is more than just a local response in the hypothalamus or other lower brain center, Masserman placed electrodes within a cat's hypothalamus. Electrical stimulation of this dotted area did cause spitting erection of hair, and arching of the back, *as if* enraged, but it did not cause real rage; indeed, the cat went on eating its dinner at the same time.

In discussing the behavior that occurs when the hypothalamus is stimulated, Masserman remarks: ". . . The activity induced by hypothalamic stimulation is mechanical, diffuse, stereotyped, stimulus-bound, and seems to carry no greater emotional connotation than would the contraction of a skeletal muscle induced by the stimulation of an efferent nerve. . . . Pseudo-affective reactions differ significantly from those in motivationally determined emotional states."[13]

It has become evident from such studies that one may tinker with various parts of the body and produce local effects, but that these local effects in an injured animal are somewhat different from that highly focused and integrated behavior which we call rage, which seems to involve in man and in animals the interaction of the brain—both higher and lower centers—with autonomic processes.

If this is true regarding rage, it is true also regarding fear and the other emergency responses emphasized here. Indeed it is almost certainly true regarding experiences of exhilaration, excitement, thrill, surprise and joy—the positive or outreaching responses as well as the responses to threat and danger (compare page 89). It is likely, too, that

---

[12] J. Masserman, *Behavior and Neurosis*, Chicago, University of Chicago Press, 1943.
[13] *Ibid.*, pp. 35–36.

in those motives considered in Chapter 7 and in all those complex physiological processes considered in Chapter 6, and indeed everywhere else in the life of the organism, there is interaction between brain and other portions of the body in all those types of behavior which we call psychological. Relative isolation may characterize the self-repair of an injured cell or the slow growth of bone or muscle; it may at times be well worth while to neglect the rest of the body and emphasize a local region. The separation of the local region from the rest of the body, however, is never absolute; and in the case of those complex integrated behavior patterns with which psychology is concerned, the interrelations between central and autonomic nervous systems, and between these two systems and the muscular and glandular systems, always remain questions of primary importance.

The fact that emotion is a process involving the body as a whole, including brain and vital organs, must be stressed if a good working theory of the emotions is to be developed. One of the most influential of the theories is the one offered by the American psychologist William James and the Danish physiologist Carl Lange, and known as the James-Lange theory. This theory holds that when we perceive an emotion-rousing stimulus, a mass of physiological responses promptly occurs within us, such as the pounding of the heart and the drying of the throat; and that these physiological responses give rise to nerve impulses which reach the brain, giving us sensory impressions reflecting the nature of our inner physiological upheavals. According to the James-Lange theory, the emotion consists simply of these masses of sensory impressions which are initiated by the physiological upheaval. This would mean that the physiological upheaval *precedes* rather than *follows* the mental state or experience which we call an emotion. Instead of saying, "We see the bear, are afraid, and run," or "We lose our fortunes, are sorry, and weep," William James suggested that "we see the bear, run, and are afraid"; that we "lose our fortunes, weep, and are sorry." Of course it would have been better to say not just that we run, but that we run while our hearts are pounding, our breathing is rapid and violent, our throats dry, our eyes dilated, and so on. The point that James wanted to make was that the physiological upheaval which arises upon perception of the stimulus is the basis of the emotion; the emotion is simply the conscious reflection of this upheaval. It is the response of the brain as we feel our muscles tighten, our stomach sink, our heart pound, that defines an emotional experience. Try to imagine the emotion, said James, when you have subtracted from it all these feelings, these poundings, these quiverings, shakings, drynesses, sinkings of the stomach, and so on. What will be left? Nothing. This theory of James and Lange is called a *peripheral* theory, because it emphasizes the outlying regions of the body rather than the brain; *central* theories emphasize the brain.

Is the theory correct? The interest of the physiologists in the question is reflected in their attempt to test experimentally what happens when one removes this or that portion of the total system, just as was done in Cannon's studies of the hypothalamic region. Naturally it seemed appropriate to the physiologists to test the James-Lange theory by cutting, in an experimental animal, the nerve fibers which bring impulses from the vital organs to the brain, to see whether the emotion could continue despite the removal of these impulses from the viscera. Many years ago Sherrington[14] cut the fibers coming from a dog's vital organs to its brain and found that the dog continued to show what seemed to be rage behavior. We need not discuss whether this was the whole rage response or only part of it, for it was enough to show that emotion could not depend *solely* upon the viscera. Even more crucial evidence was sought by Cannon, who believed that the peripheral theory was on the wrong track. It occurred to him to prevent the changes in the vital organs from occurring, so that he might know for certain that there simply is no vital-organ change which might be reported in consciousness. He proceeded to cut the outgoing fibers to many of the vital organs and in this way obtained evidence that rage or ragelike behavior in a cat remained even when the visceral changes could not occur. Again this showed at least that emotion could not be *solely* a question of the viscera. This fits well with Cannon's own belief, already cited, that emotion depends upon hypothalamic activity as contrasted with peripheral activity. It must be granted that at least *part* of what we call emotion is still present even when these operations have been carried out. This certainly limits to some degree the applicability of the James-Lange formula.

---

[14] C. S. Sherrington, *The Integrative Action of the Nervous System*, New York, Scribner, 1906.

On the other hand, the experiments of Masserman, mentioned above, indicate that there is much more going on in emotion than can be located in the hypothalamus. At this writing it appears reasonable to conclude that the peripheral emphasis has something to contribute, that the emphasis upon the central nervous system has likewise something to contribute, and that it may be appropriate at present to stress the dynamic interaction of many phases of bodily activity. There would still be, from this point of view, a good portion of truth in the James-Lange emphasis upon the importance of muscular and vital-organ activities, and at the same time a good deal of legitimate emphasis upon active hypothalamic response and upon response in the higher centers of the brain.

It seems likely from Masserman's work that the spitting and fuming of the cat, the barking and snarling of the dog, may be only aspects or parts of the complete rage pattern. These isolated responses of the dog whose higher centers have been removed have sometimes been called "sham rage" and this would seem to be a good name for it; better still, however, might be the term "ragelike barking," etc., simply giving a name to what actually occurs.

One reason why it is important to get the theory as straight as we can at this time is the fact that human emotions, in everyday normal situations and in periods of catastrophe or breakdown, and likewise also in those chronic disturbing emotional states which can cripple the individual, seem to depend not solely on local brain change, but to a large degree on how the individual interprets the world around him, which certainly involves more than one spot in the brain. While it is valuable to know what goes on in primitive violent responses to interference, such as the infant's thrashing and kicking, or in the primitive response to fear, as in the startle pattern, the day-by-day realities of emotion involve a much more subtle perception of challenge or threat to the individual in which the quality and form of the emotional response vary with the perception of the situation.

Indeed, it is doubtful whether it is really useful for us to think of a primitive *unchanging core* of fear or rage, *plus* our perception of the situation and our deciding that it warrants our getting angry or frightened; the whole thing is more complex, more fluid, less rational, and at the same time much less primitive. Our emotions undergo education, like everything else, as we grow, and they become differentiated (see page 88) and undergo learning (see page 102) in a way which makes it essential to recognize, on the one hand, the delicate interaction of the primitive visceral machinery and, on the other, the complex brain machinery upon which learning processes depend. *Emotion is an integrated response of the organism as a whole that occurs whenever a crisis is met or a threat to the fulfillment of our wants is offered.*

Whatever aspects of the theory we emphasize, it is important to remember that basically emotion is a state of excitement, that it usually serves a biological function in energizing the individual, that it puts him vigorously into an adaptive—or, if excessive, a maladaptive—response to some life threat. We shall certainly have to discard the idea, earlier very prevalent, that the higher centers act simply as dampers, checking the activity of lower centers; that you get full-fledged emotions best when you inhibit or block off the lower centers from the controlling effect of those centers which are concerned with thinking. This view does not at all square with the facts. It turns out that the lower centers are typically acted upon by the higher centers in a positive way, not a negative way. The higher centers, as we perceive something disturbing to us, are very active, and they have their direct exciting effects upon the lower centers. The lower centers in turn serve likewise to stimulate the higher centers. The emotional response is an integrated total; as Arnold[15] says, it is an *excitatory* response; it depends typically upon many complex interactions between excited regions. The different emotions differ from one another in a manner depending on the whole pattern of response in brain, autonomic nervous system, muscles, and glands, and are therefore complex, variable, and often hard to identify.

Such a theory allows a large place for individuality in emotion and its expression. We have already seen that there are differences in brain dynamics from person to person, and likewise in the dynamics of autonomic, endocrine, and other visceral responses. To the constitutional factors a considerable place must be assigned; and these constitutional factors are being constantly worked upon by stimulating or inhibiting effects. The individual not only learns what to fear and what to get angry

---

[15] M. B. Arnold, An excitatory theory of the emotions, in M. Reymert (ed.), *Feeling and Emotions, the Moose-Heart Symposium*, New York, Macmillan, 1950.

at (page 89); the very quality of his fear and of his rage depends upon how intelligent he is, what distinctions he can make, what the society around him has to say about rage and fear as permissible or nonpermissible responses in certain situations, and all the things that have gone into his own experience in dealing with things which may first threaten him. Fear and rage which are blocked and not given overt expression may remain, as we saw, gnawing at one's vitals; but they are somewhat different things from rage and fear overtly expressed. Surprise, excitement, joy, are likewise different things in a society which eagerly encourages all such positive responses and in a Puritan society which soft-pedals them.

Mood and Temperament

As we look upon emotions as consisting in part of specific episodes of intense response and in part of chronic dispositions to response which are not at the time given full overt expression, we may have a clue to two personality traits which everyone knows to be connected somewhat with emotion: *mood* and *temperament*. We may look upon mood as the persisting emotional disposition of the individual—e.g., his disposition toward jollity or despair, toward irritation or panic, but kept within limits. There may be changes of mood, but there are also more or less stable differences in mood from person to person, stable enough to permit clear identification of a characteristic mood, week in and week out, year in and year out. When a mood is as stable as this, we speak of a person's having a certain *temperament*. We saw above (page 26) some evidence of a constitutional factor of temperament. This may very well be traceable in some degree to the chronic dispositions in infancy to laugh, to smile, to cry, as we noted earlier. Such constitutional factors, however, do not have absolutely controlling power over the subsequent development of temperament; and the happy or depressing effects of life experience can profoundly change the outlook or feeling tone. Mood can often be changed by music, or indeed in many cases simply by changing the color which prevails in the living quarters of the individual person. So it would be too intellectualistic to say that a cheerful or a despondent mood is merely a question of the sheer practical realities which the person faces in his life. There may be a completely irrational readiness to respond in one way rather than in another. Just as moods may be irrational, so temperament may, so to speak, be irrational. Perhaps we might say that where life circumstances are prevailingly very good or prevailingly very bad we may trace mood and temperament very largely to the actual life situation which people confront. If it gets good enough, almost everybody will be cheerful, and if it gets bad enough, almost everybody will be disturbed or depressed. But within a less extreme range of life situations, where things are neither wonderful nor terrible, there is a very large place for an individual temperamental factor. The successful man in good health may be morose; the man who has encountered bad health and bad luck may nevertheless be cheerful.

The Control of Emotion

In the society in which we live there is a craving for emotion and also a fear of emotion; a strong demand that life should be warm and reassuring, not cold and dry, and at the same time a skepticism about emotion, in the expectation that it may interfere with efficiency. We deprecate the performance of the musician who, we say, has "perfect technique but lacks emotion," while we grow very scornful of the judge or the scientist who, as we say, allows emotion to interfere with his thinking. Although many a modern educator says frankly that he hopes that "the whole student" can be educated and not just the student's intellectual operations, and that he hopes the student's emotions will become more mature and better integrated with his life, others speak as if emotion were a weed likely to interfere with the useful growth of a technically competent citizenry.

Perhaps there is a certain amount of confusion in these discussions, especially if it is true that, whether we like it or not, we just do not ever succeed in eliminating all emotion. Perhaps part of the problem is that there is not enough consideration of the situations in which this or that kind of emotion is useful, and of the huge factor of individual differences which may enable one person to respond emotionally in such a way that it adds to the effectiveness and happiness of his life, whereas another person at that degree of intensity damages his capacity to think straight. We might at least emphasize the fact that it is not emotion as such that is good or bad, but its relation to the life activity which is going on, its integration with that activity and perhaps above all the individual's awareness of the fact that the emotion is there and must be acknowledged and dealt with at a mature level. Most of what is really meant when people attack emotion is infantile emotion or explosive emotion which gets out of control. Emotion which is an aspect of intense and vital response both to the sudden good things and to the sudden threatening things of life would seem to be essential to making sound and effective adjustments. Perhaps, therefore, the thing to which we should pay chief attention is the question whether one is *aware of his own emotions, and of the fact that they do present a problem to be thought about.*

Emphasis has been placed on cases like those from Binger (page 103) in which people carry a load of emotional response of which they are not aware at the time. Such a load of emotionality, though not at the level of panic, may nevertheless be disruptive, may do things to a person. It may, for example, interfere profoundly with his adjustments to urgent tasks. What can be done about such a situation, without, of course, robbing him of his capacity for emotional response?

There are several things that can be done. (1) One method of reducing this chronic tension based on fear or rage is to teach the patient explicitly the arts of relaxation in the manner, for example, developed by Edmund Jacobson.[16] The patient is taught to recognize the tensions present here and there in his body; he is trained to note the tensions of hands or arms or trunk or esophagus or stomach, to notice what happens when tension increases or decreases and ultimately to get voluntary control over the muscles involved (compare Hudgins and Menzies, page 134). (2) Another approach is the gradual building up of a person's self-esteem, so that he will not constantly live in fear of failure. He builds up objectively, and by constant friendly reassurance based on realities, a basis for greater confidence in life, trusting that fear and irritation will gradually decline under such changed conditions. (3) Another method is to encourage the individual in the habit of relaxed and free discussion with others, including parents, teachers, classmates, family doctor, and, if they are available, the psychiatrist or counselor or clinical psychologist, regarding things which are at the background of his mind; the grad-

---

[16] Edmund Jacobson, *Progressive Relaxation*, Chicago, University of Chicago Press, 2nd ed., 1938.

ual development of this habit permits him to recall chronic stresses which he may never have faced frankly. This process, when developed in its most full-fledged and complex technical form by a specialist who is expert in studying these matters regarding which we have never been frank with ourselves, is called psychoanalysis. While lying quietly on a couch in the psychoanalyst's office, the person talks about anything that comes into his mind, frankly avows whatever he feels, allows all his old worries and anxieties, feelings of guilt and hostility to come into consciousness, and voices them. Out of a release process of this sort, in the analyst's presence, he comes to terms with emotions regarding which he has never been clear. As the origins of these emotions become evident, he hopes to be able to look them in the face and take hold of life confidently. There are several other psychiatric (and also educational and religious) methods of coping with sustained tensions of this sort (compare page 128).

If the question is asked which is the best method to use in dealing with these prolonged tensions arising from emotions which have no complete overt expression, the reply would have to be that there are big individual variations, depending upon the person and upon his problems; even the capacity to relax shows wide variations. Some people, moreover, become rigid, tight, and defensive early in life, and find it a terrific effort to acknowledge anything about themselves. Others are more or less explicitly aware of most of their problems, and can "spill" the difficulties without much inhibition. Here again there is some evidence of constitutional factors related to the ability to screen off certain impressions about oneself. But whether we recognize constitutional factors or not, at least by the time a person has become concerned over such a problem, his lifetime of mental habits is the one thing with which we have to cope first, and practical emphasis has to be placed upon the methods of reassuring him, giving him faith in himself, giving him confidence that he can solve his problems, helping him in the little techniques of remembering things that he may ordinarily not remember but which may still be unconsciously bothering him, and, above all, adding to the motivation that makes him want to carry through and master his problem.

Emotional reëducation is a very complex process. Sometimes an educational or esthetic or religious experience may cause a realignment of emotions in a way of which the professional psychoanalyst and the counselor may be rather envious, for it may take them very much longer. The chief thing, however, upon which stress must be placed here is the very rich and complex nature of the process of emotional response, and the necessity of knowing a great deal about the individual's personality and problems before selecting a method which might be specially helpful in his case. We shall return to these problems in the next chapter, in which the conflict between various impulses will be more directly considered, and from time to time later in the book, when more complex factors in personality formation will be considered.

In the meantime, by way of summary, it should be stressed that civilized man is equipped with all the complicated machinery which his primitive forebears needed in order to hit hard or run fast in times of stress, though he lives in a complex environment in which relatively little of this primitive explosive response is permitted. It may at first glance seem far-fetched to lay so much stress upon emotions of which we are unaware; but the more closely we look at it, the more directly we see that there is a piling up of emotional tensions under civilized conditions which inevitably means that there is a great deal in our response to a crisis which is more than just the moment's response; it draws upon a backlog of lifetime damming up of tension. Why did I get so sore over such a little thing? Why was I in a cold sweat just because I might be late? Why did that one little tune throw me off balance for the whole day? Why do I feel so good, so awfully good today? Just because the sky is blue? These little irrationalities of every day are irrationalities only if we take them out of their context. We are really sore or irritated or despondent or elated partly because of the momentary stimulus, very largely because of the background, the huge mass of physiological response that is waiting there. It may be that the little remark which made us so sore came from the person against whom there has been a piled-up resentment, or that we are so afraid of a major failure that some little thing like being marked late in coming to class takes on an importance all out of proportion to its significance.

In all these cases civilized man is a creature with an almost infinitely more complex and powerful emotional readiness for life than is evident if one attends only to the official, rational, and obvious relations between immediate stimuli and responses. We learn much from the physiological responses of animals when in rage or fear; but since animals do not as a rule block their emotions over long periods as does man, the major problems of emotion lead on from this simple point to the more complex problems of conflict and of the challenges, social conventions, pressures to social conformity, in which man's emotions have to play their part. Accordingly, what we can say here about emotion is only an introduction, and the theme will constantly recur in new contexts.

SUGGESTED READINGS

Cannon, W. B., *Bodily Changes in Pain, Hunger, Fear and Rage*, New York, Appleton, 2nd ed., 1929.

Darwin, C., *The Expression of Emotion in Man and Animals*, London, Murray, 1872.

Grinker, R. R., and Spiegel, J. P., *Men Under Stress*, Philadelphia, Blakiston, 1945.

Jacobson, E., *Progressive Relaxation*, Chicago, Univ. of Chicago Press, 2nd ed., 1938.

James, W., *Principles of Psychology*, New York, Holt, 1891, chap. 25.

Jersild, A. T., and Holmes, F. B., *Children's Fears*, New York, Teachers College, Columbia Univ., 1935.

Morgan, C. T., and Stellar, E., *Physiological Psychology*, McGraw-Hill, 2nd ed., 1950, chaps. 2, 16, 17.

Murchison, C. (ed.), *A Handbook of General Experimental Psychology*, Worcester, Clark Univ. Press, 1934, chap. 6.

Ruckmick, C. A., *The Psychology of Feeling and Emotion*, New York, McGraw-Hill, 1936.

Sheldon, W. H., and Stevens, S. S., *The Varieties of Temperament*, New York, Harper, 4th ed., 1942.

Woodworth, R. S., *Experimental Psychology*, New York, Holt, 1938, chaps. 11, 12.

9   CONFLICT

Paul loved his mother to his dying day, and he hated her for all he was worth. He started lovingly home with a huge bouquet of roses for her. On the way he decided the girl friend would like them, and he would get something else for his mother on her birthday the following week. All sorts of little things were brought home as pleasant little surprises for Mother; then as he presented them he would think of something awfully smart, something that showed some little foible of hers in a light not too pleasant, and it would just "slip out." There would be a sort of half smile on his face and she would burst into tears and go upstairs; and he would hate himself and wonder why he had done it.

He could not remember the time when he had not loved her: infancy, early childhood, all those years of difficult adjustment to a crowd of boys that looked upon him as a sissy. She had understood, protected, been wise, but she had been bossy at the same time. She planned in advance where he was to spend his week ends, what girl he should ask to the dance. The time came when he just couldn't take it. "Mother," he said, "I've got to be myself." She had stared, not comprehending. From that time on the little rift had broadened more and more, until almost everything that he did was tinged with love and hate, white and black.

It is typical of human conflict both to want and to reject the same thing, to love and to hate the same person. Whatever a person does to fulfill one of these motives opposes or blocks the other. There is no way out. The more satisfaction he gets from one aspect of a thing, the greater the frustration from the other aspect. Sometimes there are not just two but several motives, each one of which blocks the remaining ones.

Hector Berlioz shows how a conflict may pervade the whole personality:

> Two years ago, before my wife's health had become hopeless and when it was the cause of great expense to me, I dreamt that I was composing a symphony. On awakening next morning, I recollected nearly the whole of the first movement, which I can still remember was an allegro in 2 time, in the key of A minor.
>
> I had gone to my table to begin writing it down when I suddenly reflected: "If I write this part I shall let myself be carried on to write the rest. The natural tendency of my mind to expand the materials is sure to make it very long. I may perhaps spend three or four months exclusively upon it (I took seven to write *Romeo and Juliet*); meantime I shall do no feuilletons, or next to none, and my income will suffer. When the symphony is finished I shall be weak enough to allow my copyist to copy it out, and thus immediately incur a debt of one thousand or twelve hundred francs. Once the parts are copied I shall be harassed by the temptation to have the work performed; I shall give a concert, in which, as is sure to be the case in these days, the receipts will barely cover half the expenses; I shall lose what I have not got; I shall want the necessaries of life for my poor invalid, and shall have no money either for myself or for my son's keep on board ship!" These thoughts made me shudder! I threw down my pen, saying, "Bah! I shall have forgotten the symphony tomorrow." But the following night the obstinate symphony again presented itself, and I distinctly heard the allegro in A minor, and, what was more, saw it written down. I awoke in a state of feverish agitation, and hummed the theme. The form and character of it pleased me extremely; I was about to rise . . . but the reflections of the preceding night again restrained me. I hardened myself against temptation. I clung to the hope of forgetting. At last I fell asleep again, and when I awoke next day all recollection had vanished forever.[1]

Conflict had ended in the complete victory of one contestant over the other. This may seem the essence of personal misfortune; one loses something that he cherishes because it competes with something else. Yet still harder situations arise. You may be hung up between two alternatives, unable to decide, and at least for the time being lose both of your goals and be ridiculed or punished for your indecision at the same time.

Norman Maier[2] has made some studies of this same problem in animals. A hungry animal is trained to jump through a little window to get his food. The other window, however, is so fixed that it cannot move

---

[1] Hector Berlioz, *Memoirs of Hector Berlioz* (annotated, and the translation revised, by Ernest Newman), New York, Knopf, 1932, pp. 477–478.

[2] N. F. Maier, *Studies of Abnormal Behavior in the Rat*, New York, Harper, 1939.

when he touches it. He jumps from his station, not knowing which window is the right one. Half the time he gets through; the other half he bumps his nose and falls into a net beneath. Of course the animal could soon learn which is right. But Maier keeps changing the situation. Whatever was the right move to make on previous occasions may at any time be made wrong. The animal gets mixed up. There is simply no telling which is the right window. He is punished for making the very decision which he had earlier learned to make. A particular solution, like "the window on the right," gets to have a strong positive value for the animal, but because it has led at times to a bad result, it has also a strong negative value. After much experience with this insoluble problem, the animal finally stands stock-still, unable to decide. From such long tension with no possibility of solution, the animal frequently develops a nervous condition to which the name "experimental neurosis" is given. A man in such a situation is likely to feel, "Whatever I do is wrong."

A somewhat more complex type of blocking in a choice situation is one in which it is difficult for the animal to make out what the situation actually is—whether it is a good or a bad situation. Hungry animals are trained to respond positively to a circle; circle and food are presented together. But when an ellipse is shown, no food is given. Now the ellipse is gradually made more and more like a circle, until there is almost no difference between them. Is it or is it not a food signal? The problem is too much for the animal. If it is a dog, as it usually is in these experiments, he breaks down, barks, whines, fidgets about, tears at the harness, even "goes to pieces" in a severe nervous upset. In fact, he loses many of his earlier habits, and becomes a disorganized dog that it will take several months to calm down. Human beings are often caught in this way by signals which have more than one meaning; a smile may mean friendliness, but can we be really sure that the joke is not on us?

It is possible, then, to differentiate between two kinds of conflict: In the first, you have *two opposed ways* of responding to the *same situation*. In the second you cannot *differentiate between two situations*, although it is urgent for practical purposes that a differentiation be made.

Still a third type of conflict appears when one is moving forward along a familiar path pursuing some goal, and a new and fascinating opportunity comes along. Shall we give up the old and dart off in the direction of the new, or stick to the good old comfortable ways that we already know, taking no chances? Again this appears even at the animal level. The dog with his nose buried in his food dish hears the whistle of his master; he may look up, hesitate, resume eating, or follow the familiar summons. Probably the commonest of everyday sources of human conflict lies in this fact, that one is drawn at the same time to two or more different kinds of satisfying objects, and it is a question which is more satisfying. An evening to spend—shall it be a party at the roadhouse, or tickets for the theater? Or, in long-range terms, there is that offer of your family's support in getting into medical school, and also that very attractive idea of going into the business next June with Roy. He will be able to give you a start, and it will take years to get ready for medicine; but you did so much want to be a professional man. Here the conflict is a question primarily of two forces acting at the same time. But each one, in its turn, pushes you about like a leaf in a cyclone.

Perhaps the most painful conflicts of all are these, in which there are two or more strong pulls acting upon us, but in which the issue is what kind of person we want to be. There must be a decision between two kinds of "me"; one cannot be both. One must choose between "me" as that professional man with his prestige, and "me" as the fellow making that easy money. Often the conflict is not just between the two ways of life but primarily between the two pictures of oneself as he sees himself following each of these different ways of life.

Symbols

Before a choice is made, conflict may go on a long time in imagination. This may add to the strain. The person knows that the show tonight will be good, but that if he goes to it he will miss a good party. He thinks them over, tries to imagine what each will be like. He has to make a decision not between immediately present goals, but between symbols within his imagination—pictures in the mind's eye or words which he toys with to represent the alternatives. As he thinks it all over and one or the other possibility becomes more real, he begins to realize more and more keenly that he is losing the other. The grass is always "greener on the other side of the fence"; "blessings brighten as they take their flight"; "distance lends enchantment to the view." These proverbs and slogans bring out the fact that as we start to make a decision, we realize more keenly what we are losing in not taking the other alternative. The very fact of swinging toward one goal makes the other more attractive. As we bring one alternative nearer to us, we specially prize the one that goes farther away.

Wright[3] has some observations bearing upon this point. People walked into a cafeteria with their trays, eying the pies which were displayed in rows in front of them. They studied the pies in the front row, looked past them and reached for one of those in the row beyond, though the latter were exactly the same (equally clean, etc.) except that they were a little farther away. We have to be sure not to miss that extra good thing we would lose if we took what lies nearest to us. If, as we contemplate a choice to be made, each line of action, as soon as we reject it, becomes more attractive, we have a severe type of painful helplessness. Often the frustration of our wants when clear-cut and unavoidable is less distressing than a situation that offers some slight hope to us, but one which we repeatedly find to be beyond our reach. As Leah Levinger puts it: "When all possibility of choice is eliminated or avenues of escape blocked, the organism is able to find a tolerable existence within these borders. It is in the other cases of ambiguity and possibilities of escape that time after time prove to be illusory that it would be more probable that a deep type of disturbance would appear."

Frustration

In all these cases described so far, trouble is inescapable. Whether you follow one alternative and reject the other or get "hung up" between the two, there is a blockage of at least one course of motivated action. The general name for the blockage of motivated action is frustration; one may say that frustration is the usual result of conflict. There are several sorts of things which can occur under such frustration. One is aggression, the liberation of those struggling reactions, or attacks upon the environment, which are found even in the newborn (cf. page 91).

In most situations which are not known to be hopeless, the aggression

---

[3] H. F. Wright, The influence of barriers upon strength of motivation, *Duke Univ. Ser. Contr. Psychol. Theory*, 1937, *1*, No. 3.

frequently succeeds more or less in removing the sources of frustration. The first response is diffuse and chaotic, without much direction, and is often ineffective in removing the source of the frustration; but since this violent response is the initial reaction of most small people in infancy and early childhood, it is the one that is likely in the long run to develop into a well-organized habit based on experience in dealing with the environment. The "frustration-aggression hypothesis" states that frustration regularly leads to aggressive behavior, and that aggressive behavior is ultimately the result of frustration.[4] It is true that the exponents of this theory have in general admitted many exceptions, but as a general proposition it is well worth studying. Take for example Robert Sears' demonstration that when people have estimated the good qualities of their various friends, then have discovered that they themselves are failing on a test, and are again asked to evaluate these friends, they bring them down a peg. Their estimations of their friends are more "aggressive" after they themselves have been frustrated.

Or consider these stenographic records of comments by sleep-deprived subjects:[5]

3:30 A.M. Two observers arrived. Group of four S's in one room sitting and talking. "Can we eat?" (E: "No.") "Oh, gosh, are we subjected to that, too?" "You're up pretty late, aren't you, Doc?" "Don't you think you'll be missing your sleep?"

3:40 A.M. An E ostentatiously lit a cigarette. Group of five S's sitting together. "Where's this particular entertainment you offered us? How about some stories?" (E told dull joke; no laughter.) "We discussed cannibalism earlier in the evening." (E: "Would you eat human flesh?") "We may yet tonight." (Meaningful look at one of the E's; much snickering among S's.)

3:50 A.M. "What would happen if we would walk out?" "I suppose you'd blackmail us." "I bet it would wreck your experiment if we did. Let's leave."

5:15 A.M. "Are all psychologists mad?" "They're all queer. I've been watching 'em for a couple of hours." "Everything in this experiment was done 60 years ago—everything." "It's kid stuff."

5:30 A.M. (One S addressed an E as "Doctor.") "Don't call him Doctor; you must be a freshman." (Mumbling agreement from other S's.)

---

[4] J. Dollard, *et al., Frustration and Aggression,* New Haven, Yale University Press, 1939.

[5] Robert R. Sears, Carl I. Hovland, and Neal E. Miller, Minor studies of aggression: I. Measurement of aggressive behavior, *J. Psychol.,* 1940, 9, 275–295. Reprinted in part in T. Newcomb and E. Hartley, *Readings in Social Psychology,* New York, Holt, 1947.

The hypothesis is of special importance in those cases when a person seems to forget a frustration, seems to drop a matter when he finds he cannot have what he wants, or never admits even to himself that he has been frustrated. The frustration-aggression hypothesis would say that he merely *seems* to drop it, but that he is "stewing" inside, whether conscious of the fact or not. Some studies of anger show that a turmoil may be going on long after an insult is received (page 92), and other studies indicate that even when a difficulty is never consciously recognized, the individual remains in a state of strain (page 113). This may be shown, for example, in repeated dreams involving violence, or in little drawings or doodlings of knives and ropes which one does in idle moments.

It seems in general to be a fact that when frustration has been experienced, the tension does not just evaporate. The state of strain within the body has no way of merely "dying out," any more than gas or water in a tank can just naturally get out; there has to be some specific way of adapting to the strain. Tension which develops within the body has to be converted into some other type of energy manifestation; and if one can find something active to do, if he can find some substitute object of aggression, some hard work, some tough assignment to be licked, he may then be able to "vent his spleen" in that way. It seems today very naïve to believe that the insults a person has encountered, or the serious setbacks he has experienced, can really leave him untouched, doing nothing but smiling happily, ready to go forward and take it on the chin once again. It may appear on the surface that this is all that happens. But those who are really able to take it on the chin are as a rule either people who have discovered some way to look at the situation so as to get a larger perspective on it, and are consequently not much frustrated by what happens, or else people who have discovered some energetic activity upon which to expend their activities when frustrated, so that there is no need to take it out on the cat or the wife. Aggression is probably a primary response to most human frustrations, at least in our type of civilization.

But there are other ways of responding to frustration. One of these is apathy, a sort of gradual crumpling up, or withdrawal into inactivity, a slumping into a sort of "what can I do" or death-feint reaction, probably based on past experience to the effect that a given situation is really hopeless and that just knuckling under is the only thing one can do. When a group of workers in an Austrian village all lost their jobs because of the economic dislocation of their country, so that there was no work to be had in the village, a great many of them at first became frantic and tore about trying to discover some form of livelihood. Others went into a sort of "dazed resignation" in which they lost all zest in life, went mechanically through routines, too apathetic to make use of their new leisure for reading or recreation, but simply lived like vegetables. Most of those who had begun by being excited and agitated ultimately gave up and likewise became apathetic.[6]

There is always also a place for withdrawing into the activities of a more satisfactory world—something interesting to do, even a daydream. And there is also a place for falling back into *earlier and more childish habits* as exemplified in the experiment by Barker, Dembo, and Lewin.[7] In some cases children who had been allowed to play briefly with very attractive toys, then frustrated by being given less interesting ones, began to show babyish behavior. A child who had previously talked into a toy telephone began to use it merely as a rattle, etc.

There seem to be big individual differences in the way in which people are able to cope with their frustrations. One way of studying these individual differences is through a picture test devised by Rosenzweig[8] in which the individual has a way of letting off steam, or expressing aggression, in each of the pictured situations. "Go sit on a tack!" He may, however, say something very different. He may turn the aggression upon himself. Thus in Figure 18–1, instead of thinking of some tart remark at the expense of the driver, he may take the blame upon himself, disparage himself, ask, so to speak, to be excused for living. A characteristic remark of a self-disparaging sort is, "I was standing too near." There is also a third way of handling the situation: using a lighter touch, parrying the blow, making an impersonal situation out of the problem, with nobody to blame. If the other person is blamed, the reaction is called

---

[6] M. Lazarsfeld and H. Zeisl, "Die Arbeitslosen von Marienthal," *Psychol. Monographien*, No. 5, 1933.
[7] R. Barker, T. Dembo, and K. Lewin, Frustration and regression: an experiment with children, *Univ. Ia. Stud. Child Welf.*, 1937, *18*, No. 1.
[8] S. Rosenzweig, The Picture-Frustration Study, Adult Form, copyright, 1948.

Figure 18. The Rosenzweig Picture-Frustration Test

The subjects are instructed to write in the blank box above each picture the very first reply that comes to mind. These are the first four in a series of situations in this test. (From the Rosenzweig Picture-Frustration Study, Adult Form, copyright, 1948. Reproduced with permission.)

extrapunitive; when one throws the blame on oneself it is *intropunitive;* it is *impunitive* when a way is found to avoid blame.

The investigator counts the number of times that the subject uses each of these three procedures, and draws a tentative conclusion regarding personal predispositions. If he finds, for example, that extrapunitive responses occur in relation to nearly every picture, he concludes that he is dealing with a really hard-boiled customer, ready to strike out whenever trouble comes his way. The saint, the timid soul, the bootlicker, and the kowtower would all be inclined to make a multitude of intropunitive responses. The person who can really by-pass his frustrations gives many responses in the impunitive category.

The test may also be scored in another way, in terms of the three ways in which the subject handles the fact that he is frustrated. (1) *Object dominance* means that he emphasizes that the situation has got the better of him: "There's no help for it." (2) *Need persistence* means that he emphasizes that the need which has been blocked is still continuing: "I'll make it next time." (3) *Ego defense* means that he strives to protect his self-esteem, "to save face," and not acknowledge that he has been worsted: "Who cares?" The test is relatively new, but it seems to have considerable value in spotting at least those who are extreme in their habitual tendency to respond in one rather than either of the other of these three possible ways.

Coping with Conflict

But suppose there is conflict. What can be done about it? Are there any broad principles for the resolution of conflicts, once they have arisen?

Yes, and the first step lies in looking squarely at them, more squarely than we usually do. In general, modern practical experience in working with people in trouble has reinforced the good sense of the view that the trouble often begins with the individual's imperfect realization of the factors at work within him, and that the cure consists of helping him to get a larger view of the situation. It is almost never possible to take the conflict in hand directly and simply talk the person into giving up, without a struggle, one or the other of the things he wants to do. If either of his desires were as weak as all that, he would not have got into trouble.

If he is miserable because of an inner conflict which he himself does not understand, it is seldom possible to get rid of it simply by explaining it at the surface level, because his fear of facing it will persist during the conversation and he will manage to reject all explanations that will show him things he does not want to know about himself. It is not so much that he is fighting you as that he is fighting his own vague perception of things in himself that he cannot face squarely.

There are two things, however, that a friend or counselor can do. (1) He can create an atmosphere of friendliness in which the man in trouble will be less afraid to acknowledge what he wants, and especially what kind of person he really perceives himself to be. (2) He can show the relation between the man's immediate wants and the larger wants or plans he may have for his life; he may give perspective. Even if the conflict is fundamental, the man may grasp, as in the case of two conflicting positive goals, that each has long-range consequences, that he must acknowledge the fact and make a choice, that he must face the trouble and move forward.

It is possible of course to reply that these are not real solutions; they are palliatives. But they are reducers of tension; and as tension is reduced, perspective becomes in turn more clear. There are even some cases in which all the trouble can be removed by getting a broader perspective, particularly by analyzing the situation to see what you really want in each of the opposed goals. You may find, for example, that the two things you want are not really in opposition at all. Or you may find that one (or both) of the conflicting goals becomes much less important when considered in a broad perspective, so that one (or both) may be dropped without sorrow. We may regard all types of modern psychotherapy (treatment of psychological difficulties) as involving to a high degree the patient investigation of the subject's real goals—finding out what is really causing the trouble and how to pick out the major goals which one wants, and finding substitutes for the other goals that cannot be integrated with them, or finding an unsuspected new way of obtaining integration.

This process of resolving conflict by redefining the goals is discussed by Max Wertheimer[9] in terms of this example: As two boys played bad-

---

[9] M. Wertheimer, *Productive Thinking*, New York, Harper, 1945.

minton, one found that he could win with even his most careless stroke; the other found that no matter how frantic his efforts, he could never win a point. By and by, after much frustration because no real game eventuated for either one, it suddenly occurred to the better player to suggest a different way of going at the whole thing. "Instead of my trying to beat you, let's agree to see how many times we can get this bird flying back and forth before anybody misses. Let's fix it so that we can both keep this going a long time." In this way the satisfaction of batting the birds, getting the exercise, and competing each time against their previous record, instead of competing against each other, solved their problem jointly and coöperatively. The result was that they found the satisfactions that go with a vigorous outdoor game, but lacked that particular type of person-to-person competition which had earlier been assumed to be the only kind of fun offered by the game. It was a change in the assumptions about goals that solved the problem.

Often our conflicts arise from the same difficulty which at first bothered these boys: our assumption that in order to succeed, we must cause someone else to fail. This creates trouble. One wants "big killings" in an enterprise which may injure other people, an enterprise for which one really has little respect. A person wants to get high recognition for achievement in his professional training (all A's in college, for example), and at the same time not to make the beating of other individuals the primary goal, for his friends have their own goals also. A good deal of close thinking may be required. At one large university it has been possible to train professional people in that type of coöperative endeavor in which four or five men work on their research together, receiving a doctor's degree for their joint labors, instead of each man's striving to write the most brilliant research paper of the year.

Even in the most serious problems of personal maladjustment which come to modern therapy, one finds constant exemplification of the need to seek a new vantage point for viewing our goals. Often our goals are so formulated as to seem hopelessly in conflict. In the type of personal counseling known as "nondirective therapy,"[10] it is the regular procedure to try to find out in a friendly, permissive conversation what the client

---

[10] C. R. Rogers, *Counseling and Psychotherapy*, Boston, Houghton Mifflin, 1937; Donald Snygg and A. W. Combs, *Individual Behavior*, New York, Harper, 1948.

really wants in his life, and how he sees himself in relation to his goals. It turns out sooner or later that he has been maintaining an artificial picture of himself which he has strenuously defended, lest he become aware of other aspects of himself which seem to be less lovely. In the course of time, however, as he says more and more explicitly what he really wants from life, it becomes clear that he really does want to know himself and what he can effectively achieve; this desire may relax him and give him a new view of the ways of achieving his goals instead of self-defeat through trying to be all sorts of people at once. He may discover a kind of person within himself who is not really in conflict, but relatively single-minded.

In the more complex process of therapy known as psychoanalysis, one works slowly toward self-recognition in order to achieve self-realization (page 114). This means that one gives up various tinsel trappings, various "portraits of the artist as a young man," which are incompatible both with one another and with the central self that one basically wants to be. This does not in any sense deny that many people have set up for themselves goals which they cannot in fact hope to achieve. This is one instance in which full knowledge of self may not be a sufficient clue to the resolution of conflict. The point, however, is that the only way that conflict can be resolved is to repattern the picture of life and of oneself in such a way that the various unrealistic aspects can be pruned off, and the more realistic ones built into a harmonious whole. Or if there are truly incompatible aspects, one must decide what is important, and explicitly and firmly reject those that are in conflict with it, finding a way to redirect the energies that are invested in the activity which he is now giving up (page 128).

While the methods just defined aim at the resolution of conflict, there is another way in which people try to handle such situations, namely, by escaping from the conflict. Either a conflict situation is simply barred off, so that it no longer belongs in the world in which one lives, or one turns his back upon it and flees. This occurs quite commonly in various types of self-deception of the "ivory-tower" sort. It occurs, for example, in well-to-do people with kind hearts who give Christmas presents to the blind people at the corner and drop a quarter into the Salvation Army kettle, feeling in this way that they have done their full share to alleviate such poverty as exists in the world. In some degree, of course, all of us do this. Perhaps none of us could live if we fully faced the moral contradictions involved in our ignoring the suffering of a large part of the human family while we enjoy our comfortable standards of living. We even ignore many of the troubles of friends and relatives. A certain amount of running away passes for normal.

Nevertheless there are times when a common tendency like this may be developed to the point of bringing a person into gross disharmony with his immediate environment, and here we are likely to refer to such a person as an "escapist." He may carry this to the point of denying the main facts about himself, and we call him mentally ill. He is no longer just John Smith; he is the greatest inventor of all time. So he writes letters to the President about the damage done to the world by the dogs across the street that keep him awake at night. He may actually be a futile, confused person, afraid of himself, frustrated and in conflict because of his failures, but able through such an escape from reality to make himself important. Or, finding all doors closed to them and no great good things in life, people may settle for an easy solution in the form of believing themselves suffering heroes, and frantically denounce the Catholics, or the Jews, or the millionaires, or the Communists, or almost anybody.

In the matter of escape from unbearable conflict and the building up of a world of imagination or fantasy which frees us from part of the frustration, it is hard to know where to draw the line that separates "normal" people from those who are technically insane or "psychotic." From our everyday escapes to these last-mentioned ones is a gradual transition, not a sharp break. But it is a common feature of insanity or psychosis to escape from the real social world by creating a simpler world in which to live. Many of these people, beaten by life, construct for themselves a delusional system in which all the members of their families are out to defraud them, deprive them of their property, deny their friends access to the hospital. Even the people who come to visit may be people with masks who come as spies. The doctors and nurses are in league with the forces of evil, and almost every reference to the world's affairs is veiled in symbolic suggestion of the engines of torture which are actually going to be brought to bear upon the distraught patient.

It may at first sight seem a far cry from these horrible delusions to the quiet, placid delusions of many a psychotic patient who pictures the world's troubles as of no concern to him, while he lives as Napoleon or as God. Actually, however, even the most morbid and apparently terrifying delusions may be a device for freeing the individual of many of his own basically unacceptable ideas about himself. He may, for example, have hostile feelings toward other members of his family; but being unable, through feelings of guilt, to accept the fact that he has these hostilities within himself, he may manage in time to see the hostility as coming from them toward him, rather than from himself toward them (cf. page 424). This mechanism of "projection," as it is called by the psychoanalysts, is, after all, an escape from conflict, namely, the conflict which comes from two incompatible views of the self, in one of which the person is hostile, while in the other he is a noble spirit free from all hostility and malice. The latter view crowds out the former, and the hostility deep within him is assigned to or "projected upon" those whom he hates. Shifting the scene so that it is other people who are hostile, he finds escape from personal conflict which arises from the need to hate and the need to be noble at the same time.

The Will

When we can neither *resolve* conflict nor *escape* from it, we often feel ourselves to be making a free and spontaneous (or indeed sometimes an arbitrary) choice between the alternatives; and by a sheer act of will we put to rout one of the offending tendencies. As William James[11] put it, "We feel in deciding as if we ourselves by our own wilful act inclined the beam." The will is a conception relied upon to define our own participation as free agents in a conflict situation which would be hopeless as long as we remained the mere football of conflicting pressures. Using the analogy of the chemist's balance, we may say that although the weight in favor of one impulse may be greater than that in favor of another, we may throw *effort* into one of the scale pans,

---

[11] W. James, *The Principles of Psychology*, New York, Holt, 1890.

and in that way make a decision in favor of the weaker of the two impulses. Effort, then, is said to be an essential part of this process of voluntary decision. (See Figure 19.)

But it cannot be claimed that we understand this process very fully. A good many people believe that this sense of spontaneity (or arbitrariness) in making a choice is illusory. They remind us that we are by no means aware of all the forces at work within us, and suggest that unconscious forces (unknown impulses) are the things which enter into the scale pan. The sense of effort is real, but is a necessary result of the fact that there simply has to be a mobilization of more energy in order to overwhelm the brute force of the larger weight in the opposing pan.

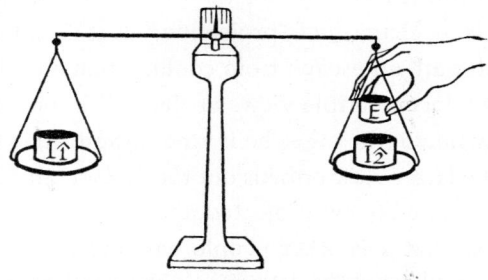

Figure 19. An Act of Will

When two impulses, I_1 and I_2, are equally strong, a little effort, E, determines which will win.

The effort is real, but the thing that motivates the effort is some unconscious motive or motives of the sort considered earlier (page 129). A good many people, having made a tremendous effort to do something out of a sheer sense of duty, have later decided that really there was some other motive which was prompting them all the time. Or that the sense of duty was really a complicated name for a way of winning the respect of parents or others whose respect they deeply needed. Again we repeat, we do not actually know very much about what goes into this process called the will; but it is reasonable to try to make the thing intelligible, and at least there is a good deal that becomes less mysterious when we note that many of the mainsprings of our conduct are not so very evident to us at the time we make a decision.

Along with this conception goes a view developed by William Mc-

Dougall,[12] to the effect that instead of spontaneous or arbitrary effort, it is really a certain struggle relating to self-respect that goes into the scale pan. He uses the phrase "self-regarding sentiment" to describe the pattern of attitudes toward ourselves which makes us reject the cheap and easy line of conduct. A certain standard of rightness or nobility, "a decent regard for the opinions of mankind," or the respect of others is the thing which adds itself to the weaker of the two forces, and thereby wins the day.

Still another way of defining the will is through the concept of manipulating symbols (page 120). While at first sight appearing to contradict the James and McDougall conceptions, this may actually be regarded as in some degree a confirmation of them. It occurred to Hudgins[13] to test the hypothesis that what we call the will is a habit that has been built up within our bodies—a habit of the sort which psychologists call a *conditioned response*. A conditioned response is a learned response in which one behaves in a situation as one originally behaved in another situation that occurred at the same time. If, for example, the child's bottle is brought to him at the same time that a tone is sounded, the child's typical response to the bottle begins to appear when the tone is sounded even before the bottle is brought within sight or reach. Hudgins' hypothesis was that the will is a simple conditioned response. He undertook to show that the will is simply a habit which has been built up within us by training. A simple way to prove such a point would be to take muscles which we cannot ordinarily control by our will and train ourselves by the simplest available method to respond with these muscles. Later on we shall find ourselves developing the ability to move these muscles, and we shall therefore find that what used to be involuntary has become voluntary, i.e., a matter of the will.

Let us see what can be done with this conception. Hudgins chose the muscles which contract the pupil of the eye, which ordinarily cannot be controlled by the will. The pupil can be observed through a special short-range telescope known as a pupillometer. The experimenter, sitting a few inches away behind a screen, can observe very accurately the di-

---

[12] W. McDougall, *Introduction to Social Psychology*, Boston, Luce, 1908.

[13] C. V. Hudgins, Conditioning and the voluntary control of the pupillary light reflex, *J. gen. Psychol.*, 1933, 8, 3–51.

lation or contraction of the subject's pupil. A bright light was flashed into the eye of the subject, and the contraction of the pupil was observed and measured. The experimenter then trained the subject to flash the light into his eye himself by means of a hookup in which the subject powerfully squeezed a hand dynamometer that was in circuit with the light bulb and with a bell. In this way the subject's own activity in contracting his hand muscles threw the light each time into his eye, and thus contracted the pupil. During several hundred of these self-stimulations, the subject said to himself each time the word "contract." In accordance with the general law of the conditioned response, we should expect the word "contract" to result in the contraction of the pupil, because it always occurred while light was contracting the pupil; and this is what happened. It was now possible simply for the subject to say the word "contract," and the pupillary contraction occurred. After this he needed only to whisper the word "contract," and finally he needed only to say the word inwardly to himself, i.e., to *think* the word. To think the word "contract" involved some remnants of the original activity, and thus provided inner clues which stood for the complex situation involving the light. In terms of a simple habit of the conditioned response type, one may say that in the end phase the inner responses represented by the word "contract" were sufficient to cause the pupillary contraction.

In a somewhat similar way Menzies[14] found it possible to produce a voluntary contraction of arterial muscles. First the subject placed his hand in ice water and the arteries contracted. Later he placed his hand in the ice water after whispering a word. Eventually his whispering of the word was sufficient to lead to the contraction of his arteries. Thus as one says words associated with the outer environment (in this case with the cold water) he sets going lines of appropriate behavior related to that outer environment.

Putting this conception together with those borrowed from James and McDougall, we find a good deal to suggest that the will is the name for a complex inner process which influences our behavior so that we are less easily bowled over by the sheer brute strength of impulses taken in their own right. We talk to ourselves, bring up alternative ways of

---

[14] R. Menzies, Conditioned vasomotor responses in human subjects, *J. Psychol.*, 1937, *4*, 75–120.

phrasing our situation, picture the consequences of our various modes of response, and try to size up how well we shall like each one. Instead of being at the mercy of our immediate physical surroundings, we are guided by what we have learned about the outcomes of various types of procedure, and symbolize these various possible outcomes in such a way that finally one course seems better than any other. Even so, considerable effort may be necessary in seeing the thing through. As already indicated, the impulses which are pitted against one another may all be pretty strong, and the quest of the goal may be just as difficult when it is far away as when it is near at hand; indeed it may be harder to start on a course of action that will take six or eight years of work than to shovel the early snowfall from today's sidewalk. Often the inner processes which play a controlling part in such a decision are centered, as we saw, in the need for self-respect. From this point of view a weak-willed individual would be a person with only a vague conception of himself and no self-regarding sentiment, or a person who had never developed the habit of responding to those forms of self-defense and self-enhancement which go with maintaining a good name for oneself. A person who, like Rip Van Winkle, always has good resolutions but never at a critical moment carries them through is a person with "no will."

Whether this is a real explanation of the will it is certainly much too early to say. We can, however, be fairly sure that the will is a complex process occurring under conditions of conflict; that it does regularly involve some sense of self, some need for integration, and the subordination of impulse to the pattern in which self-respect may be achieved. Even when the will takes the form of the will to do something which most of us renounce, such as the will to tyrannize over other human beings, it may still involve a conception of the self and a capacity to repudiate short-range pleasures for the sake of this ultimate fulfillment of the picture of the self. Popularly, the will is always something good, but a desperado and an exploiter also may have a "strong will."

There are at least three kinds of people who show no will, namely, (1) low-grade mental defectives, (2) those suffering from advanced deterioration of personality in certain psychotic conditions, and (3) those suffering from acute confusion due to a fever or drugs. In all these cases there is a faulty development of or a disintegration of the picture of oneself, and of the capacity for picturing to oneself different alternatives and making the choice between them. It is this feature of the process of the will which we should like to emphasize at this point. Some other aspects of the will will be encountered later in connection with the study of the growth of the self and of the conscience (Chapters 21 and 23).

SUGGESTED READINGS

Dollard, J., et al., *Frustration and Aggression*, New Haven, Yale Univ. Press, 1939.
Freud, S., *A General Introduction to Psychoanalysis*, transl. by Joan Riviere, New York, Liveright, rev. ed., 1935.
Guthrie, E. R., *The Psychology of Human Conflict*, New York, Harper, 1938.
Horney, K., *New Ways in Psychoanalysis*, New York, Norton, 1939.
Horney, K., *Our Inner Conflicts*, New York, Norton, 1945.
Hunt, J. McV. (ed.), *Personality and the Behavior Disorders*, 2 vols., New York, Ronald Press, 1944, chaps. 11, 14.
Lewin, K., *A Dynamic Theory of Personality*, New York, McGraw-Hill, 1935, chap. 3.
Luria, A. R., *The Nature of Human Conflicts*, transl. and ed. by W. H. Gantt, New York, Liveright, 1932.
Maier, N. R. F., *Frustration*, New York, McGraw-Hill, 1949.
Plant, J. S., *The Envelope*, New York, Commonwealth Fund, 1950.
Snygg, D., and Combs, A. W., *Individual Behavior*, New York, Harper, 1948.

10 SENSING AND PERCEIVING

Ordinarily we think of ourselves as keeping pretty closely in touch with the world which surrounds us. Actually, however, we take in only a small fraction of what is happening. Through our bodies pass constantly many radio waves of which we are unaware. Certain high and low tones which a dog or a bat can respond to, infrared and ultraviolet light, and dozens of other physical and chemical processes leave us untouched. We are equipped, however, with specialized organs, like eyes and ears, which sift out some of the welter of energies with which the world is filled, and enable us to respond specifically to some of its aspects. This elementary capacity to become aware of an aspect of the world we shall call *sensing*.

But even if our eyes, ears, etc., are well equipped to bring the world to us, there is just too much going on to permit us to respond to everything at once. We are being continuously bombarded by energy acting upon the many organs of sense. At the moment, as you read, your eyes are doing a job; but there are sounds to be listened to, or ignored as irrelevant; pressure from clothing, or book, or chair; sensations of strain from muscles; perhaps a little hunger, or fatigue, or excitement, or irritation, vaguely reflected in sensations from the interior of the body. We are not ordinarily aware of all these contributions from our senses. That which impinges upon our eyes and ears and skin, that which wells up from within the trunk or within the muscles, cannot be assimilated all at once; and even if it could be, it would be of little use to us if it came as a blur or medley of unorganized impressions. One of the reasons for the mass response of the little child (page 41) is an inability to select;

but both through growth and through learning more and more selection gradually becomes possible.

In responding to the world which our senses report to us, we make not an indiscriminate mass response to everything at once, but a more specific integrated response to certain features that have relevance for us. This process by which we select, from the enormous masses of impressions being fed into us by our senses, a few which have relevance to our conduct, and among these give emphasis and organization to one primary impression—allowing the rest to serve as background—we shall call *perceiving*. Perceiving is a way of coming to terms with the environment, playing up certain features, playing down other features.

In the first instance, of course, contact with the environment has to be made. We begin with the question of the mechanisms of the body, the sense organs, that make such contact. Whereas the most primitive forms of life have no such sense organs and make rather vague and inefficient contacts with light, warmth, acids, the effects of gravity, and so on, the process of evolution has resulted in sense organs with extreme sensitiveness to particular types of energies at work. A sensitive spot on the skin upon which light exerts a chemical effect gradually develops into an eye. The eye is an instrument containing cells which are extremely sensitive to the energies of the light waves. Similarly, the skin develops a vast number of specific spots which are very sensitive to pressure. A system of delicate mechanisms develops which are sensitive to the commotions in the air and register the effects in such a way that we hear sound. In every case of response to the environment, we are dealing with cells which are specially sensitive to a particular kind of energy; these cells, along with cells which support them, make up the sense organs.

Thresholds

One of the first things to do in studying the sense organs is to find just how much stimulation it takes to excite the sense organ in such a way that we become aware of some feature of the environment.

Individuals differ considerably in such sensitivity. Try, for example, holding a watch a few feet from the right ear, noticing the maximum dis-

SENSING AND PERCEIVING

thing to emphasize is the fact of making a more vigorous response to that which is relevant to our goals, so that other things tend to fall into the background. You can study this process by using a single figure like the Köhler cross (Figure 21). There are three different ways in which you can gaze at this cross: First, simply relax and note how many seconds you see the figure with the black as the cross and the white as the background; record the moment when a shift occurs, the white becoming the cross and the black the background, and so on for each subsequent shift; keep this up for three minutes. Second, bring in the factor of voluntary attention by giving emphasis or accent to the black, trying to hold the black cross in view as long as possible and keep the white as background. When the white becomes dominant, try at once to bring back the black, and keep it dominant as much of the time as you can for three minutes. Count seconds as before, making tallies to indicate how long each one remains. Third, make the white the foreground and the black the background, and count again for three minutes. Then, comparing the three methods, you can easily get an idea of the relative weight to be assigned to the voluntary factor. A certain amount of reversal or oscillation will occur no matter what you do about it, and the black will tend to win out over the white. At the same time, it is clear that a large role must be assigned to voluntary factors, perhaps the same sort of internal factors that we mentioned in the case of the Hudgins experiment (page 133). The term *sensing* having been used to refer to the raw fact of becoming aware of a stimulus, perhaps it is now clear why we use the term *perceiving* to refer to the *selective* and *integrative* activity by which we apprehend meaningful wholes.

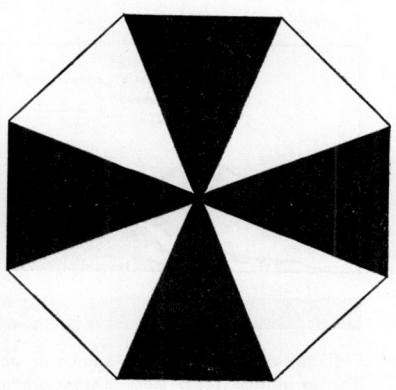

Figure 21. The Köhler Cross

(George W. Hartmann, Gestalt Psychology, copyright 1935 by The Ronald Press Company.)

Another thing you will notice in this experiment is that the four different arms of the cross do not behave independently. If the cross shifts, it shifts as a whole. You do not get one of the arms of the white figure and three of the arms of the black figure combining. Nor are you able mentally to cut the whole pattern up into pieces like a mosaic pattern, and reassign them at will. There are definite factors of organization within the total field which you see. This is one of the fundamental facts about all perception; it has to be organized. You may try as hard as you like to see the room in which you sit as if it were upside down. You may try very hard to regroup the stimuli so that the walls seem nearer to you than the book. You cannot really do very much to break down that

Figure 22. Cues to Distance

Clearness of detail (also known as aerial perspective) is an important cue to distance. The mountains seem more distant when partially obscured by a haze than when they stand out clearly.

ordered structure of the world which you have learned since babyhood to accept as real.

Actually, the organization is very largely the result of your lifetime experience in interpreting the impressions from your sense organs. It is easy for an experimenter (or even a conjurer) to deceive you by offering you stimuli which do not mean what they ordinarily mean in a different context. The Easterner in Colorado, accustomed to judging distances by haze, underestimates the distance of the mountains (Figure 22). Instead of showing a factor of disorganization in perceiving, this merely shows that throughout life you have learned to interpret certain cues as meaning certain sizes and distances, and you cannot by any arbitrary act disturb the basic habits thus learned.

You do indeed find that a shift in the organization of your perception occurs from moment to moment, in which you see new relationships which previously you had overlooked. These shifts, however, are not piecemeal, but are in line with your earlier experience, and with your present attitude and expectation. Your process of thinking, too, as we shall see more in detail at a later point (Chapter 17), consists of a series of more or less orderly steps in reorganization, that is, in passing from one organized view of a problem to another, not of a mere jumble of new connections.

But there are big differences between people in their habits of perceiving, and in any individual's habits of perceiving as he goes from one task to another. People differ very markedly, for example, in the energy of their attack upon a problem. In a difficult task which at first looks like sheer nonsense, as when we cannot make sense of a street scene or a difficult sentence, some of us wait for the clues to come to us. Others strike out for clues. Still others formulate some general abstract principle which might work in each case, and then actually perceive the problem in the light of the general view they have developed.

Four Aspects of Perceiving

We now have the problem of defining what factors inside the individual must be understood when we are coming to terms with the environment in the manner to which we have given the name perceiving. There seem to be four different aspects which always have to be considered.

1. The *sensitivity* of the organism to a particular kind of stimulation. This means studying the structure and function of the sense organ (and of the nerve cells which carry impulses from sense organs to brain).
2. The *qualities* (colors, tones, etc.) which this stimulation yields.
3. The influence of the amount and kind of *past experience* which one has had with this kind of sense experience.
4. The *set* within the individual, since perceiving is influenced by goals which he is pursuing (page 69). (It will be remembered that motivation is an important kind of set.)

1. As an illustration of the *sensitivity* factor as related to the structure of the sense organs, we may note the differences in perception of color which occur in color-blind, "color-weak," and normal color-seeing peo-

ple (see Figure 23); the kind of differences that appear in tone-deaf, partially tone-deaf, and normal-hearing persons; the absence of certain taste experiences in certain people—the inability to taste certain chemical compounds is a well-known hereditary trait which runs true in certain families.

2. Under the head of *qualities*, we may take account of the wide variety of colors, of tones, etc., that enter into experience, and of the ways in which these may combine or blend.

3. Under the head of *past experience*, we have to note how very differently a machine looks, or a symphony sounds, to those who have and those who have not become familiar with such material. One man sees or hears not much more than a blur; another immediately selects and integrates sense impressions into a meaningful whole. As you confront a foreign language or a new art form, or indeed even a first lecture on a new subject, you pass from a stage of jumble and confusion to a stage of being able to pick out things which make sense, and finally to put these together into a well-organized form. Experience, then, leads to the question of patterning. Not that patterning is always present to a high degree, and not that it is solely due to experience. Some patterning, as we shall find, is definitely a question of the way in which the sense organs and the brain are made. But a prominent feature of the patterning process comes from the kinds of personal experience previously gone through. There are large individual differences in what we perceive, resulting from our training and experience; we sometimes see the face of a stranger as "impassive" and he may see our face as "impassive" because each of us has had different training in interpreting the slight changes of expression (see page 101).

4. Examples of the role of *set* are the tendency of the starving person to perceive the outlines of food objects in the passing clouds, or the tendency of the frightened man to see thieves in the forest shadows, or your tendency when waiting in a doctor's (or dean's) office to hear your name spoken before it really is. If each of us has a pattern of motives different from the next person's, there will be individual differences in perception traceable to these motives (page 83).

The organization of perception, the way in which sense perceptions are integrated, is a process to which all four of these phases contribute.

Figure 23. Individual Differences in Color Perception

The parrot in 1 was colored by a person with normal color vision. Parrots 2 and 3 were colored by persons who could distinguish only two colors. The individual who colored Parrot 4 could distinguish red, green, and violet; but when yellow was next to green he saw it as red, and when it was next to red he saw it as green. The three color-weak individuals used more colors than they could distinguish, for they relied on differences in shading rather than actual color differences in their attempt to approximate normal color vision. (From McDowall's *Handbook of Physiology and Biochemistry*, John Murray, 1944; used by permission of the publishers and of Dr. H. Edridge-Green.)

The fact that our perceptions are organized, and not just a jumble, depends partly on the bodily organization of the sensory apparatus which supplies the raw sensory impressions, partly on the natural groupings into which our sense impressions fall (colors, tones, etc.), partly on the articulation of the various components through experience, and partly on the role of set in shaping the percept so that it is relevant to present activity. These processes can all be regarded as aspects of one basic and universally present factor: *the adjustment of the perceiving individual to the environment in relation to the particular problem or task in which he is engaged.*

Without at all using the same approach which we have employed, Leo Stein has come to much the same conclusion:

People commonly assume that they can see, and need only learn what they should look at. My experience contradicts this, and insists on the all-importance of learning to see. The what will take care of itself if the how has been acquired. . . . I shall now tell how I went about the business of learning to see. . . . The problem was to see, and then to learn what was particular about this way of seeing. There is no use speculating when one can experiment; so I began to experiment. I put on the table a plate of the kind common in Italy, an earthenware plate with a simple pattern in color, and this I looked at every day for minutes or for hours. I had in mind to see it as a picture, and waited for it to become one. In time it did. The change came suddenly when the plate as an inventorial object, one made up of parts that could be separately listed, a certain shape, certain colors applied to it, and so on, went over into a composition to which all these elements were merely contributory. The painted composition on the plate ceased to be on it but became a part of a larger composition which was the plate as a whole.[4]

Here it is evident that all four factors—the structure of sense organs, the qualities which they convey, past experience, and present motive—are playing a part in an individual's whole activity. Exactly the same is true in this more dramatic account by W. H. Hudson, whose experience reflects the presence of all four factors:

When the sun grew hot overhead and the way was over open savannah country I would see something moving on the ground at my side and always keeping abreast of me. A small snake, one or two feet long. No, not a small snake, but a sinuous mark in the pattern on a huge serpent's head, five or six yards long, always moving deliberately at my side. If a cloud came over the

---

[4] Leo Stein, *Appreciation: Painting, Poetry and Prose*, New York, Crown, 1947, p. 215.

sun, or a fresh breeze sprang up, gradually the outline of that awful head would fade and the well-defined pattern would resolve itself into the mottlings on the earth. But if the sun grew more and more hot and dazzling as the day progressed, then the tremendous ophidian head would become increasingly real to my sight, with glistening scales and symmetrical markings; and I would walk carefully not to stumble against or touch it; and when I cast my eyes behind me I could see no end to its great coils extending across the savannah. Even looking back from the summit of a high hill I could see it stretching leagues and leagues away through forests and rivers, across wide plains, valleys and mountains, to lose itself at last in the infinite blue distance.[5]

The Development of Perception

All this would suggest that we are not at the moment of birth able to perceive the world in the manner in which the adult perceives it. The baby's eyes may be open, and he may indeed be rolling them slowly toward the moving light. But this does not mean that he sees the light as you and I see it. He may respond to a loud sound by startle. This does not mean that he hears what you and I hear. There is, as a matter of fact, a good deal of evidence that his first perceptions are pretty well blurred; it takes him a long time to disentangle the various components of the world that is bearing down upon him. Even at a year of age, according to the studies of the Swiss psychologist Piaget,[6] the child has not as yet developed a world of sharply defined things. Rather, he lives in a world of blurred impressions. Ask the mother, for example, to bring her twelve-months-old child to the clinic, and let the child sit in her lap, relaxed, and have a good time with the examiner. The examiner holds his watch for the child to see, touch, and handle. He takes it and holds it up, and puts it beneath a pillow to the child's left. At a signal the mother allows the child to dive for the watch, which he successfully does, and plays with it for a moment. The experimenter takes it again and now, slowly, in front of the child's eyes, carries the watch over to the other side—that is, to the child's right—and puts it under a second pillow. Again he signals to the mother and the child is free to do as he pleases. What does he do? He dives for the watch under the pillow where he first found it. "The watch" is not an object which he was able to separate from its contexts; for although he had seen it move

---

[5] W. H. Hudson, *Green Mansions*, New York, Hartsdale House, 1920, p. 276.

[6] J. Piaget, Factors determining human behavior, in *Harvard Tercentenary Publ.*, 1937, pp. 32–48.

to a new point, it was for him a part of a context—under the pillow to the left. It was where it had previously been found. It was in that blurred total which lies to the left of his body that the watch was to be sought.

The French psychologist Roger Cousinet gives another example. The child calls pitifully for a balloon with which another child is playing. When the adult goes and gets him a balloon and hands it to him, he is utterly miserable, for the single object, the balloon all by itself, is not what he wanted. What he saw was the gross unanalyzed pattern of the child playing with the balloon, standing, patting, letting it rise and fall on its string. What has happened is that the little fellow has this strange, pretty object in his hands; but he has not that mass total which earlier he enjoyed observing and which he wanted. It was not possible, by separating the balloon from its context, to gratify his wishes.

In the same way Werner[7] has shown that up to three years of age or even older there is a great deal of blurred perception in which the emotional and impulsive aspects of things are hopelessly enmeshed in their outlines as things in space. Thus, for example, the tripod as it stands erect is perceived as "proud." The impression of vigor, energy, boldness that goes with this erect posture cannot be separated from the sheer fact that there is a complicated mechanism of wood standing at a particular point on the floor. The child experiences, in terms of all that has come to him in the past, each thing which he experiences. He is not able to sort out clearly the different items of color, shape, activity, and, above all, the feeling tone and action value which each object has. He experiences things in terms of what they mean to him as sources of pleasure and pain, and above all in terms of what they mean in relation to action. A hammer, for example, is not simply a metal and wooden object lying on a table. A hammer is a "thing to strike with." Indeed a good deal of this tendency to define things in terms of their use, to perceive them in terms of what you do with them, probably continues for years; even a six-year-old, asked to define a mommy, may say that "a mommy is to sew." And while part of this may arise from difficulties in describing things, Werner suggests that part of it lies in the way in which the child perceives.

---

[7] H. Werner, *Comparative Psychology of Mental Development*, Chicago, Follett, 1946.

It is probably true that there is in general a tendency for the child to develop from a global (blurred) to a more analytical type of perceiving, and then to a more integrative type of perceiving in which he combines into an organized structure, or well-defined pattern, the separate parts which he has been able to sort out from the original blur. Indeed, so many things in the world are new to the child that he is doing this a large part of the time.

Yet all of us, at *any* age, when confronting some new thing, have to go through these stages as we deal with unfamiliar things. When you take a field trip to the factory and see a mass of wheels, belts, shafts, levers, and hear various grating and rumbling sounds, you are almost like the lover of classical music who is making his first venture into the concert hall where ultra-modern music is rendered—you literally cannot "take it in." As you are conducted from bench to bench, as you see what each man does as he tends his machine, as you go to the powerhouse, as you see the blueprints for the new building, as you hear the plans for the development of the factory to take over new tasks, you get a sharper and sharper perception of one detail after another; and finally you have a large number of such components and their interrelations so clearly in mind that you may literally see what the factory is doing. You may visit some other factory at a later date, and as you walk down the assembly line you may literally see the automobile being put together—something you certainly never really saw in the first instance. In the same way, as you learn to pick out the sounds of the various musical instruments as they play a complex composition, and get the component elements more and more sharply defined, you become able to form organized totals and really *hear* the music. How far you can go in learning to perceive accurately and comprehensively will depend partly upon constitutional capacities (the man with a good ear and musical talent will progress further in less time in responding to new music than most of us can). Partly, however, it will depend upon how much you care, how strong the motivation is; the man not interested will never hear.

While all of us pass through these three levels of perception—the undifferentiated, the differentiated, and the integrated—there are big individual differences in what we do at each stage. We noted large differences in the *sensitiveness* of the sense organs (in visual acuity, capacity to differentiate tones, etc.). If for no other reason than this, there have to be individual differences in the variety and richness of the sense qualities which each of us experiences from music, painting, etc. Likewise, each person has his own kind of *past experience* in using his sense equipment, leading to more and better *analysis* (differentiation) on the part of one man or to more and better *integration*. Differentiation and integration depend also partly on the ability one has had to go forward to a maximal achievement ("high ceiling") in a given sphere, e.g., the musician proceeding to a much finer capacity for the integration of musical expressions than the ordinary person. Finally there are great individual differences in *motivation*—for example, the amount that one cares about the world of tone or color, making distinctions and new combinations, developing new ways of analyzing and of interpreting sense impressions to give richer satisfactions.

In a recent experimental study Douglas[8] presented to her subjects a series of 60 pictures, first badly out of focus, then more and more clearly focused, by means of a tachistoscope (a brief exposure apparatus). The following are typical reports from the subjects:

(Slide No. 6—A Landscape, André Kertesz, Paris)
Focal point
0.0. This exposure shows a rather dim flash of light toward the top, with a strip of unlit area in the middle and then a still dimmer and more diffused light toward the bottom of the picture.
1.0. The same impression as before, with the light at the top growing brighter and the light area at the bottom stretching out more toward the side, becoming a—almost a strip of light along the bottom of the picture.
2.0. In this exposure I was unable to see anything other than in the previous exposure.
3.0. In this, the top light has become diffused and has gone over toward the edge of the picture, so that the corners are now more eliminated —are more illuminated (*laughs*) than they were.
3.5. Here, one definitely gets the impression of the—of a sky, either at a sunset or sunrise, with clouds—with the sun shining through the clouds, thus getting a sort of diffused light of the sun through dark streaks which show considerable shading, horizontal strata of clouds

---

[8] A. G. Douglas, A tachistoscopic study of the order of emergence in the process of perception, *Psychol. Monogr.*, 1947, *61*, No. 287, 1–133.

with the sun behind them, possibly at the bottom being reflected from a bright object such as a body of water.

4.0. This exposure, I would be unable to add anything to the observations of the previous one.

4.5a. This definitely appears to be a landscape with a cloudy sky and the sun at about 3 o'clock angle, apparently. Vague impression of a road and fields, with the sun's rays being diffused on it in—in a dull sort of way through the cloudy sky. Apparently the light which I observed at the bottom and had previously thought a reflection may be a roadway or something of the sort in this landscape.

4.5b. At this point I think I'm looking at a seascape again, as before, rather than a landscape, with the water rather rough, but still the cloudy sky and the sun only partially shining through it in spots, light being diffused otherwise. There is a dark line in the water which looks as if it might be a pier, or breakwater, or something of that sort.

4.5c. Again this is a—would seem to be a marine seascape, though the pier has disappeared from this particular view, and one gets an impression of a point of land jutting out into the water which is rough, which is reflecting some sunlight, and the filtered sunlight is showing through the clouds in the sky. . . .

Well, I'll be damned! This is a landscape with a very diffused light from the sun illuminating the landscape. The sun is hidden behind the clouds and is filtering its light through them. There is a light body of clouds toward the center of the picture, with the clouds definitely darkening as the horizon is approached. As a result, the background of the horizon is quite dark, and it can only be dimly perceived. The entire layout of this landscape reminds me of two possibilities. I would say, first, that it more than likely is an area of farm in a rather broad valley. Terrain is slightly rolling, with the plant portions very carefully cultivated. One can see what might be the outlines of fields with differing crops occupying three major areas in the picture, the background slightly to right of center, and then, at about the same distance in the background, a small area to the left. On the other hand, the area to the left just mentioned as possibly being a farm seems to show some buildings which might conceivably, then, be a community. There is also the possibility of a community's appearing at the right edge of the flat area mentioned before, just to the right of center in the background. One can see three roads in this picture, each of them tree-lined, which makes them stand out very much. If it were not for those roads, one might suspect that this could be an army air installation—or an army or navy air installation, with the land carefully levelled for fields, and there are some buildings which might be hangars in the front ground. However, one would doubt that this would be an air installation with trees outlining the roads so carefully and clearly as they do here. In the lower left-hand corner,

SENSING AND PERCEIVING 153

we can see a clump of vegetation, which makes it quite clear that this picture is taken from a hill overlooking the lower level. There is some—also some strips of vegetation further on down the hill on something which, in general, looks like Scotch broom, though not in bloom.

(Slide No. 46—Through a Doorway, Roger Parry, Paris)

Focal point

0.0. Oh, my goodness. This is a piece about a foot wide, running in the vertical completely off the screen on both sides, both ends on the bottom, and it has grey streaks running vertically through it.

1.0. Same type thing, only it's more diversified—more scattered.

2.0. It's as though you had turned a picture of a rough tree on its side.

2.5. Of course, it could be a wind-blown landscape on its side, too, in that there are things running down which might be like trees bending over in the wind.

3.0. Get the feeling as though the left part of it might be something like an X-ray picture. The right part of it be—would be the undeveloped film or it could be the type thing you get when you're looking at a . . . prepared on a slide.

3.5. It looked like a X-ray of a fish.

4.0. This is the first time that a definite feeling of roughness or of blotched . . . has come out all through the picture. You get a feeling that there are little ridges and—parts that stand up. I can't quite— the word I want. But I still can't attach any name to it. I—I don't know what it is.

4.5a. It gives you the impression that it's a ship. You're looking over the side of the ship, and there's a man coming up the side. The only trouble with that is the part that should be the water isn't water, because it doesn't have the right feel. It feels more like sand than water. Consequently, I don't know what it is, but there's apparently —is a man coming up the side of it.

4.5b. I get the same thing, no matter how . . .

Wow, brother! What I thought was a man is a bottle, and the ground is right—a sailing vessel. . . . And what I considered as the boat is apparently the side of a wooden house. . . . Well, I got the feeling that you had some pine cones spread through the picture.

The following are the experimenter's comments on the results:

The pattern of this constructive process appears to have been duplicated with imposing fidelity in every slide progression. . . . The gradations of the sequence are not always equivalent in time nor in intensity, but they adhere to a uniform course approximating three phases of transformation:

1. A beginning sensory stage: Here is a purely descriptive level in which the

sensory data are acknowledged and defined by whatever means are available to the subject. The restricted nature of the data . . . is indicated by the limited variety of classifications into which the descriptions are fitted. . . .

2. Transitional stage: The evolution of perceptual experience out of sensory materials is manifestly a turbulent activity. The faintest and most primitive announcements of the onset of these throes are not at all well directed, but they are nonetheless expressive of the state of restlessness which erupts when the sensory stage is no longer sufficient to support the developmental progress. . . .

3. A final interpretative stage: This is largely an acceptance level, implying that the tentative possibilities of the preceding stage have somehow been discriminated among and that a choice has been reached which now can be named with satisfaction. That the choice carries factors in it which far exceed the original sensory stage in which it took root is further evidence of the constructive treatment to which it has been subjected in development.

Douglas does not use exactly the same language that was used earlier in this chapter. It is believed, however, that her analysis approximates the analysis given earlier in terms of *global*, *differentiated*, and *integrative* phases of perceiving.

SUGGESTED READINGS
General

Boring, E. G., *Sensation and Perception in the History of Experimental Psychology*, New York, Appleton-Century, 1942.

Ellis, W. D., *A Source Book of Gestalt Psychology*, New York, Humanities Press, 1950.

Murphy, G., *Historical Introduction to Modern Psychology*, New York, Harcourt, Brace, rev. ed., 1949, chap. 20.

Sherif, M., *An Outline of Social Psychology*, New York, Harper, 1948.

Woodworth, R. S., *Experimental Psychology*, New York, Holt, 1938, chaps. 17, 18, 27.

Woodworth, R. S., *Contemporary Schools of Psychology*, New York, Ronald, rev. ed., 1948, chap. 5.

Needs and Perception

Ansbacher, H., Perception of number as affected by the monetary value of the object, *Arch. Psychol.*, 1937, No. 215.

Braly, K. W., The influence of past experience in visual perception, *J. exp. Psychol.*, 1933, *16*, 613–643.

Bruner, J. S., and Goodman, C. C., Value and need as organizing factors in perception, *J. abnorm. Psychol.*, 1947, *42*, 33–44.

Bruner, J. S., and Krech, D. (eds.), *Perception and Personality*, Durham, Duke Univ. Press, rev. ed., 1950.

Bruner, J. S., and Postman, L., Symbolic value as a determinant of perceptual organization, *J. soc. Psychol.*, 1948, 27, 203–208.

Krech, D., and Crutchfield, S., *Theory and Problems of Social Psychology*, McGraw-Hill, 1948, chaps. 3, 4.

Levine, R., Chein, I., and Murphy, G., The relation of intensity of a need to the amount of perceptual distortion, *J. Psychol.*, 1942, 13, 283–293.

Proshansky, H., and Murphy, G., The effect of reward and punishment on perception, *J. Psychol.*, 1942, 13, 295–305.

Schafer, R., and Murphy, G., The role of autism in a visual figure-ground relationship, *J. exp. Psychol.*, 1943, 32, 335–343.

Sherif, M., A study of some social factors in perception, *Arch. Psychol.*, 1935, No. 187.

11 SEEING

When we look at the sky on a cloudy night, seeing only a few faint stars, and when we watch the traffic on a sunny day, we are, strictly speaking, using two completely different sets of sense organs. We have one set of delicate sense cells scattered through the retina of the eye which mediate our responses under conditions of adaptation to the *dark,* another which we use when adapted to the *light.*

The first type of sense organs, the *rods,* is scattered throughout all the retina except that little central pit, the fovea, from which we derive our sharpest and clearest impressions. For this reason, we never get really very sharp dark-adapted vision. You can easily check this by looking at a cluster of faint stars some night and noting that a star disappears if you look squarely at it, but reappears again when the eye is angled a little bit away from it. Moreover, night vision, when the most complete adaptation to the dark is realized, lacks all color, except insofar as a star of a definite hue casts its light upon the fovea. You remember how the colors in the landscape die out in the evening. The reds and oranges disappear first, and then the wave of disappearance moves over to include blue, so that all color is gone. This is a matter of the gradual substitution of dark adaptation for light adaptation, the rods taking over the process of vision.

During most of our waking hours we are using another type of sensory cells, the *cones,* which are also scattered through the retina, but are more highly concentrated in the very region in which the rods are lacking, namely, the fovea, the region of clearest vision. The cones are used under conditions of adaptation to light, and they mediate to us impressions

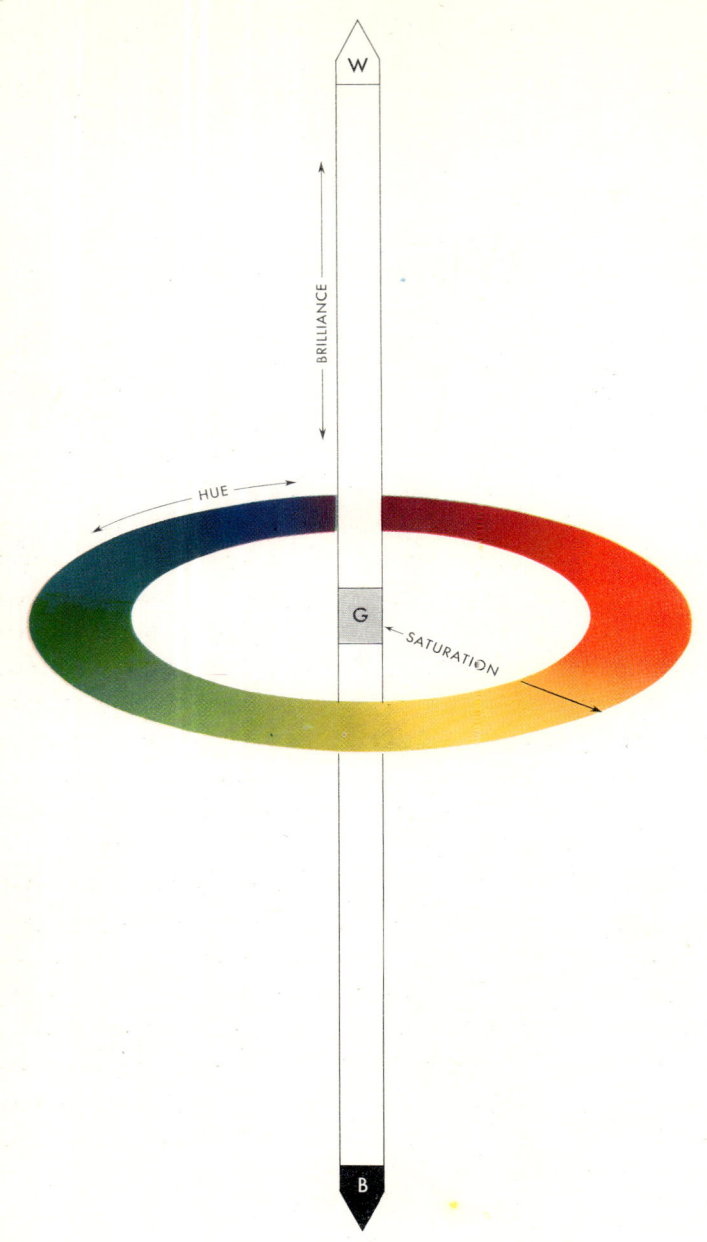

Figure 24. Double Color Cone

The interrelations of the various visual qualities of color arranged along a double cone. Only the vertical axis and the central cross section through the cone are shown.

Hues, the colors of the spectrum, are arranged in circular fashion. Colors opposite each other on the circle are complementary colors. Any given hue increases in *saturation,* or purity, from the center to the periphery of the circle. Changes in the relative *brilliance* are represented vertically, from black at the bottom to white at the top. Thus the darkest red would be near the bottom of this figure; the brightest red near the top.

of color. Almost all the discussion in this chapter will deal with light-adapted vision.

Visual Quality

In the preceding chapter we saw that in every act of perception we are concerned with (1) sensitivity, (2) quality, (3) past experience, and (4) set. In referring to rods and cones we have already touched upon sensitivity. Let us look at the matter of the elementary qualities given us in visual perception. These are usually grouped under three main heads: hue, brilliance, and saturation. *Hue* is color from the point of view of position in the series given us by the rainbow or spectrum. *Brilliance* is the degree of experienced intensity, independent of hue; the brilliance series extends from white to black. *Saturation* is the degree of purity of the hue, its degree of freedom from admixture with black, gray, or white. Tints and shades have lower saturation than pure colors. The colors of the spectrum are represented along the edge of the cone, an artist's representation of which is shown in Figure 24. The continuum from white to black appears on the vertical axis. Within the figure you can pass from the mid-point, a neutral gray, toward any hue (on the circumference); the saturation increases as you do so.

While it is convenient to regard hue, brilliance, and saturation as independent, you will nevertheless recall that as you get to very high or very low brilliance, the colors tend more and more to verge toward white and black. In other words, you get further and further away from pure hues like the purest rose reds or grass greens when the stimulus is raised to a level of very great intensity approaching white, or reduced to a very low intensity approaching black. For this reason it is customary to use the double color cone shown here, in which it is possible to represent by a point on the figure every visual stimulus in terms of the interrelations between hue, brilliance, and saturation. At the edge of the circle which separates the two cones, there is pure red; but if you go diagonally upward you will have to retreat, so to speak, toward the center, for you cannot get a very *brilliant* color that is also pure in hue. "Red hot" turns into "white hot" as the temperature goes up. We have to recognize more and more dilution of the red by the white.

Other elementary phenomena are those that have to do with the interrelations between different color experiences. There is the fact that any given hue can be mixed with some other hue which will so neutralize it that all hue is lost, leaving only a gray. Thus for every red there is an appropriate green, and for every blue an appropriate yellow, which will wash out the effect, and the pair will be reduced to gray. (This refers to pure spectral hues, not to the painter's pigments, which are far from pure.) Two hues which neutralize each other are called *complementaries*. Every hue has, in the same way, its *contrast* hue. If you display any patch of colored paper, for example, on a gray background and gaze at it steadily for twenty seconds or so, a margin or fringe of the contrast hue will appear around it. Thus on a gray background a yellow fringe will appear around a blue patch, a red fringe around a green patch, and so on. In general, the contrast hues are the same as the complementary hues; the same hue which will neutralize a given hue will also appear as its contrast hue. The relations of the hues in terms of complementaries and contrasts can be read from the color cone in Figure 24.

A third way in which colors may be grouped is in terms of their *after-images*. After you have stopped gazing at a brilliant orange-colored sun in the late afternoon you may continue to see it—a positive after-image—and then see a blue or purple disk before your eyes—a negative after-image. In the same way, after staring a long time at some blue lettering on a signboard, you may see yellow letters darting about. Red and green similarly change places after one of them has been stared at. The hues of the negative after-images are in general the complementaries of the hues which have given rise to them.

Colors fall to some extent, therefore, into natural pairs which cling together, so to speak, whether in the matter of mixture, or in the matter of contrast, or in the matter of after-images. Indeed, there are still further examples of this tendency to form pairs, as is shown by the experiment to test what colors we can see when we are not allowed to use the fovea. As you gaze at a point in front of you, the experimenter moves a colored stimulus out from the center into the region of indistinct vision until the hue is lost (the appropriate cones needed for color vision becoming fewer as we move out from the fovea). In this experiment red and green disappear at about the same point and, farther out, blue and yellow likewise disappear at about the same time. Red and green remain associated as they have in all the experiments described so far, and the same is true of blue and yellow. Another example of this tendency for the same colors to continue to appear as pairs is the fact that men who are color-blind or color-weak—that is, men who fail to perceive the various reds and greens which most of us see, or are rather inefficient in differentiating them from each other and from yellow—usually show failure in response to red and failure in response to green as if the two things were somehow connected by some basic property of the retina. They are not only at a disadvantage in traffic; their wives have to pick out their neckties. The following case was carefully studied:

1. Color names convey no meaning to S. He was able, however, to distinguish achromatic from chromatic colors though he could not match hues. He distinguished between chromatic colors with respect to their "strikingness."
2. Among the achromatic colors he distinguished black as the most intense and applied the terms "dark" and "bright" in reverse order from normal. "Black paper gave him a stronger sensation than white paper or even the direct view of a bright electric light which was for him 'unpleasantly glaring.'"
3. An ordered row of achromatic surface colors was not perceived as a series. Black and white were identified correctly. S does not use, nor know the meaning of the term gray.
4. S could compare achromatic film colors with respect to their brilliance though he could not identify them as achromatic colors.
5. S could not equate chromatic and achromatic colors with respect to brilliance.
6. Contours, when steadily fixated, blurred very rapidly and often disintegrated in spite of an initially large difference in brilliance. As contours blurred, color of the object began to approximate that of the ground. Other objects in the field, tridimensionality of objects, volitional attitude of S were all factors affecting changes of form, contour and blurring of objects.[1]

We now come to the problem of tracing these simple visual experiences to their physiological foundations. There is a series of physiological events which are run through in a given order whenever we *see*. These events are: (1) Light enters the pupil, is focused by the cornea and crystalline lens, and acts upon a substance in the retina; the chemical result is to excite the rods or cones. (2) The excitation of rods or cones arouses a series of nerve-cell changes. (3) The nerve cells, send-

---

[1] W. D. Turner and H. R. DeSilva, The perception of color and contour: an unusual case, *Amer. J. Psychol.*, 1934, *46*, 537–557.

ing their fibers through the optic nerve, connect with other nerve cells. (4) The relay finally reaches the visual brain center in the back of the head, the excitation of which gives rise to the experience of seeing. (See Figure 25.)

Failure of any of these points to function can cause partial or complete failure of vision. Defective cones, defective optic fibers, and defective or grossly injured visual centers can all impede or prevent visual experience. There are many other examples of the dependence of visual

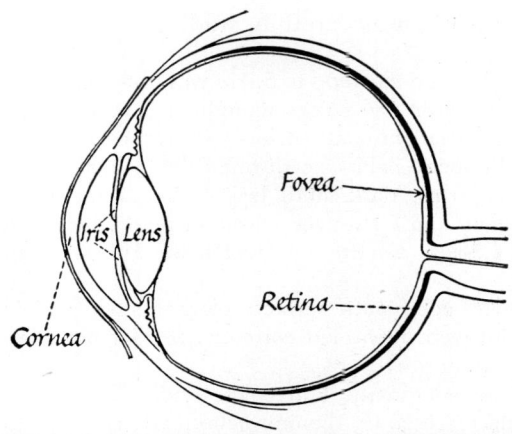

Figure 25. Cross Section Through the Human Eye

The lens, by changes in thickness, focuses the light rays on the retina, the light-sensitive tissue of the eye. The fovea is the region of clearest vision. The area where the nerve fibers from the retina join to enter the optic nerve, which branches off at the right, is the so-called "blind spot."

perception upon the physical structure of the visual apparatus. Our failure to make fine differentiations in indirect vision, that is, through the sides rather than the center of the retina, is partly due to the fact that the sense organs lie farther and farther apart as one moves out from the center of clear vision. Another example of the dependence of vision upon bodily processes is the fact that chemical factors may and frequently do interfere with clear seeing (it is easy to poison the optic nerve or visual centers with alcohol or narcotic drugs). Alcohol may cause visual hallucinations; rich visual hallucinations, both in waking and in dreaming, may be produced by hashish, mescal, and other drugs.

There is good evidence that no matter how well your eyes work, you do not see *until* the visual part of the brain responds. The capacity to give rise to visual experience is possessed by no other tissues in the body except the particular portion of the brain, in the rear, low down, that specializes in this particular process. Electrical stimulation of the visual brain center with an induction coil causes experiences of light; indeed, you can get them by falling on the back of your head. It has recently been demonstrated[2] that the subdivisions within the visual brain center are very highly specialized. The various elements of the retina are, so to speak, "projected" in corresponding form upon the visual area of the brain; points on the retina and points in the visual area of the brain are arranged on the same general plan. Thus while the organization of our perception depends upon experience, the sheer anatomical arrangement of the nervous system is orderly. The organization of perception is partly dependent on the orderly dynamics of brain function.

There are some other interesting examples of this principle. One is the fact that when a response occurs at one point, there is often a counter-response at another point. We might even regard color contrast as an example of the body's setting up in one region something that balances what goes on in another. The parts of the body are not isolated from one another, and the fact that you perceive a patch of light in one region may induce physiological effects in retina and brain such that you see another patch of complementary color in another region.

It takes time for a maximum effect to result from the stimulation of a retinal element; thereafter, when the stimulus is no longer at work, there is a period of waning or loss of effect. There is a good deal of *after-discharge* (continued activity without fresh stimulation) within both sensory and nervous elements, and during this after-discharge there are after-effects in consciousness. We may assume, in fact, that the red positive after-image of the red object which you continue to see after the stimulus has actually been removed is related to the phenomenon of after-discharge (both in sense organs and in nerve cells). Sometimes positive after-images are almost exactly like the original sense impres-

---

[2] S. L. Polyak, *The Retina*, Chicago, University of Chicago Press, 1941.

sions. Often an activity which we have carried out energetically for a long time seems still to be going on after we have tried to stop it. A person has been looking through the microscope, for instance, for hours; and when he gives his eyes a rest, the movements of the amoeba seem still to be there. This tendency of an activity to continue, even though the stimulus has ceased, is known as *perseveration;* it is almost certainly connected with the slow dying-down of brain activity. There are big individual differences in perseveration, and they seem to be connected with the fact that one person can turn to a new activity at the drop of a hat, whereas another can only slowly drag himself along. Even in very small children there are great individual differences in the ability to shift from one activity to another. (Cf. page 81.)

Past Experience

A very large role in the determination of our visual percepts is played by our past experience in dealing with the world of color, shape, distance, etc. A distant object may, for example, throw upon the retina a tiny diamond-shaped outline with four lines projecting from it, and that is all we have to go by, but we instantly perceive it as a square-topped table. All through the first year of life, each of us experiments with his visual impressions by trying them out, acting in one way or another. We learn such things as these:

1. Things which overlay others are nearer.
2. Things which are less sharply outlined are farther away.
3. Objects take up less and less of the visual field as they recede.
4. Therefore, of two things which fill equal proportions of the visual field, the nearer is the smaller (cf. Figure 26).
5. Things which cause more strain in focusing are nearer.

All these rules (and several others) are "monocular" cues; they hold for the single eye, whether the other eye is being used at the time or not. But in addition, when using the two eyes *together,* we learn certain things by experience from the way in which the two eyes are affected; i.e., we receive "binocular" cues as distinct from the "monocular" cues. Among these are (1) the fact that the more work we have to do to keep two eyes pointing at the object (strain of external eye muscles) the nearer the object; (2) the fact that the greater the difference in appearance between the impressions perceived by the two eyes, the nearer the object (effect of parallax). This second point is well brought out by the stereoscope, making use of cards so designed that the two eyes receive very different stimuli representing the same object, as from two different points considerably separated in space.

What you will be able to combine in such binocular studies will depend largely upon your actual past experience as to what *can* be com-

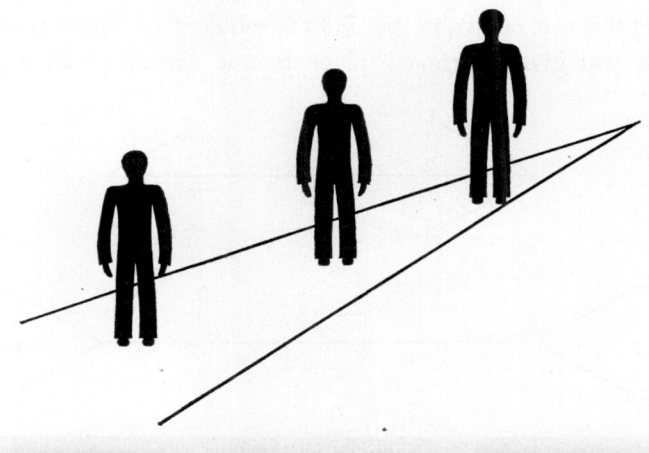

Figure 26. A Monocular Cue

If all of a group of objects project images of equal size on the retina, the object that is perceived as nearest will appear to be the smallest.

bined. The fact that you are limited by your experience is shown in studies of "retinal rivalry." Look through the stereoscope at a figure in which the right eye is exposed to a red field and the left eye to a green field. Your experience in dealing with the world has not provided you with much opportunity to see things as being completely red all over and completely green all over at the same time. You simply cannot "take it." Being a pretty well-organized individual, rather than two persons living in the same skin, what you do is to see one or the other, not both at once. Typically, you will see one for a number of seconds or even a half minute or so, and then the other will drive the first out. You will alternate, but not fuse or confuse. There are certain conditions in which your experience *will* allow you to accept a compromise between apparent contradictions (Hecht contrived a box which filters red light into one eye, green into the other; you get true color mixture), but in the ordinary confronting of the world of perception, you cannot. You must have it one way or the other. The patterning process here depends partly upon structure—two retinas serving one brain—but partly upon the experience you have had with the world.

There are some cases of figure-ground relationships (as with the Köhler cross, page 143) in which you go part of the way toward achieving this sort of rivalry, but not the whole way. These are instances in which you give a primary place to one aspect of an experience,

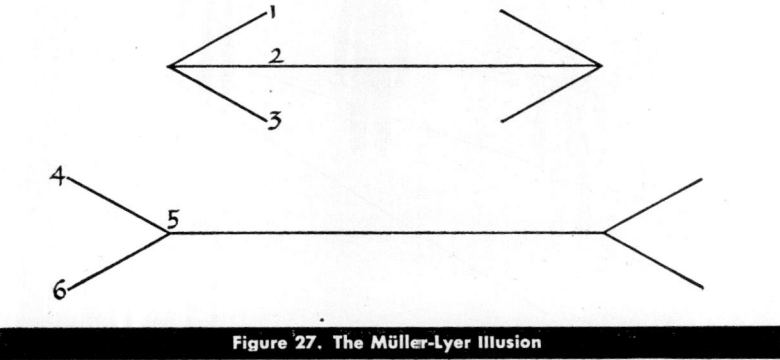

Figure 27. The Müller-Lyer Illusion

relegating the other aspect to a subordinate position. In the faces in Figures 31 and 32 you see at one time a given face and not the other. Indeed, a group of subjects trained to take note of one face never noticed that the other supplementary aspect constituted a face at all, and vice versa.

Other examples of the role of past experience in perception are supplied by interpretations which, while accurate in some situations, become misleading in others. Take, for example, the illusions shown in Figures 27 and 28. Typically we learn to judge distances in terms of lines. In the Müller-Lyer figure (Figure 27), for example, we make a comparison between the two horizontal lines and are surprised to find that they are of equal length. What we have actually done is to group the three lines 1, 2, 3 together at a point to the left of the 2, and 4, 5, 6 together at a point to the left of the 5, thus comparing a distance shorter than the horizontal line with a distance greater than the horizontal line. Our customary habit of letting the eye fixate a cluster or nest of lines has led us to judge the distances *between the centers of these clusters* rather than the *true length of the horizontals*. We are responding to familiar clues in a slightly inaccurate way. In the same way in the Poggendorf figure (Figure 28), with the parallel lines cutting a third line diagonally, the reason why the diagonal line comes out at what appears to be the wrong point is that we are actually comparing the two points that are indicated by the letters A and B. Illusions are habitual responses to familiar cues, in which we use a response that is ordinarily correct, but in the particular case leaves out an essential part of the situation. The conjurer who takes advantage of our usual habits of perceiving to make us see what "isn't there," follows the same principle; the small child has not learned to see as we usually do and is therefore usually not deceived by the conjurer. He simply does not see the point of a trick, because the illusion which the adult perceives is not experienced by him.

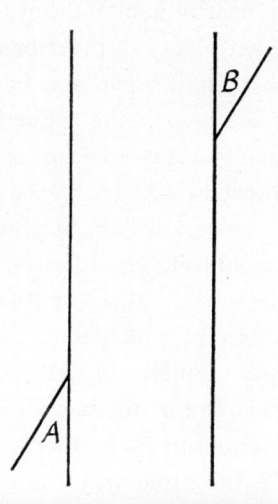

Figure 28. The Poggendorf Figure

Again, the part played by past experience is well brought out by the phenomena known as *constancies*. We judge each new impression not in terms of its intrinsic value alone, but in terms of the way in which we feel it should be interpreted on the basis of past experience. A piece of coal, for example, is always "black" for us no matter in what kind of light we place it. A piece of chalk is "white." Actually, however, the piece of coal reflects back to you a great deal more light than the piece of chalk; physically, it is nearer to white. The fact that you perceive it as black no matter in what light you put it, and the fact that you perceive the chalk as white no matter in what light you put it, result from your lifetime of experience in dealing with these "black" and "white" things, your habits of observation. This is called *brightness constancy*. In the same way the red scarf continues to seem red to you no matter how you carry it about from a dark to a bright corner of the room, and even if you put it under a yellow light. The redness is more or less fixed, whereas actually it would be a very light tint or a very deep shade, or indeed almost a brown, if you saw it in brilliant or subdued artificial illumination before you had any experience of how it "ought to look." This is *color constancy*. Similarly, a group of men in a ballroom are seen as of "normal size," although one nearby is many times as big as another at the end of the room, for we get plenty of practice at perceiving human figures as of normal size. The men of equal size in Figure 26 seem to differ greatly, because we cannot help being influenced by the context, with its cues suggesting varying distances from us. This is *size constancy*. The influence of the context in which objects are seen has also been recently demonstrated in connection with brightness constancy. Wallach found that white objects, objectively differing in brightness (reflecting different amounts of light to the retina), will be seen as equally bright under special circumstances, in which their backgrounds play an important role. They will appear equally bright provided the ratios of the amount of light they reflect to the amount of light reflected by their respective backgrounds are equal to each other.[3]

In the same way the outlines of an object, such as a tennis racket, actually impress upon your retina some very different contours from moment to moment, yet you see the object as a tennis racket—*object constancy*. Every object in the room around you is seen under a new guise from moment to moment as your head and eyes move, and the interrelations also keep changing constantly; yet for you the objects remain constant, because you are interpreting in terms of your experience—what you know objects to be. You see the bookcase as the bookcase, not putting together the various complex lights and shadows, lines and contours, as would be the task of the infant when first pressed with such changing and fleeting impressions. As an infant you had to learn to sort out impressions, weave them together and stabilize them, interpret them as objects no matter how much they changed. (See page 138.) The constancies—the constancies of size, shape, color, and object

---

[3] H. Wallach, Brightness constancy and the nature of achromatic colors, *J. exp. Psychol.*, 1948, 38, 310–324.

—are among the clearest exemplifications of the role of experience and familiarity with the world; they give it its organization. At the same time they demonstrate that it is possible to find order, security, and stability in the ever-changing panorama of sensory impressions.

Illusions are actually not freaks of nature, but simply instances in which the ordinary constancies that serve us well most of the time mislead us in special cases. Most of the time we make pretty good contact with the environment by relying on our senses in terms of our past experience; most of the things have the meaning which our experiences give them. But it is never possible to predict perfectly whether our familiar habits will be appropriate in relation to a new type of situation. It is therefore relatively easy to rig a situation so that everybody is misled. Indeed, 100 percent of the time it is easy to capitalize on normal people's perceptual habits so that people see a ball roll *up* hill.[4] It is possible to use the same lines to make people see very different objects at different times.[5]

There has been a great deal of research recently on the way in which a person in a plane perceives his relation to up and down—frequently he misjudges very badly—and experiments have sought to find out just how he determines what is "up." He judges, of course, by the context; but it is surprising, to say the least, to find that even when his own head is straight up and down with reference to the earth, the things around him can cause him to experience his own body as tilted. In a recent study Asch and Witkin write:

> In a number of cases the Ss were asked, at the conclusion of the standard procedures, to step into the tilted room, and to stand upright in it while facing the back wall. It often happened that the room was then perceived as completely upright by the S despite his full knowledge of the tilt and despite the effort required to stand upright on the tilted floor. Even more striking were the

---

[4] This is one of the demonstrations used by Adelbert Ames at Hanover, New Hampshire.

[5] Such experiments have led at times to the philosophical view that we simply build up an "external world" through habitual responses to sensory impressions; that the raw impressions from our senses lead us to cope with the world more or less well, if everything happens according to plan; but that we can *know* nothing at all about the intrinsic nature of the world lying beyond our senses, the world which we believe to be "out there" as we interpret the raw, changing, fleeting impressions from our senses. Problems of this sort, lying beyond experimental science as now constituted, cannot engage us here; but they are legitimate philosophical problems, and the philosophically-minded will recognize their interest and importance.

S's observations about his own position. Now the S reported that *his body appeared tilted*. The tilt, which was in a direction opposite to the objective tilt of the room, was most marked, and evoked deep astonishment. The evidence is clear that the S tended to perceive his body in the same manner as he perceived the other objects in space, and that the position of his own body was in this case determined by the main lines of the visual field.[6]

In spite of the uniformity in the results of such experiments as described, there is still a large factor of *individuality* in the way in which original dispositions and types of personal experience come to structure the perceived world. The love of symmetry, balance, regularity, and order, for example, is much stronger in some people than in others, and the capacity to organize visual perception in terms of such esthetic factors has led to the development of tests of "art judgment."

Here we are plainly dealing both with past experience and with present sets. The role of constitutional factors in such esthetic responses is unknown. A comparison of the art forms of different primitive societies suggests that social training can do a great deal to make people develop different ways of seeing and hearing, and that the preference for one or another artistic expression is derived partly from the fact that one person sees or hears differently from the way others see and hear. But even if we could imagine two people seeing or hearing in exactly the same way, we should probably have to admit that one of them might like a given picture better than a second picture, while another might like the second better than the first. There are, then, different ways of perceiving and also different ways of feeling toward what is perceived. Social training can certainly develop a love for certain kinds of simple rhythms and symmetries. Along with the love of order, some societies group the love of novelty or originality; others seem inclined to cling to the familiar and classical, to the point of disparaging novelty and originality. There is also the love of the massive, or powerful, as against the slight or the delicate. Compare the Egyptian with the Greek. There is, moreover, a large individual factor which, whatever its origins, appears very early. One child enjoys heavy, massive contours; another enjoys delicate lines.

---

[6] S. E. Asch and H. A. Witkin, Studies in space orientation. II. Perception of the upright with displaced visual fields and with body tilted, *J. exp. Psychol.*, 1948, 38, 455–477.

Set

In referring just now to the arts, we suggested the vital role of set (page 69), e.g., of expectations and of motives or drives, in shaping both our feelings about things and also the very way in which they are perceived in the first place. We see partly in terms of what we want to see. This was easily demonstrated in a laboratory study by Robert Levine,[7] who presented 80 different objects, one at a time, behind

Figure 29. Subject Viewing One of R. Levine's Figures

In R. Levine's experiment, black and white drawings of various objects were made to appear ambiguous by being presented behind a ground-glass screen. The subjects, who had been deprived of food for varying lengths of time, were required to identify the objects.

a ground-glass screen to subjects who had gone without food for various intervals of time (Figures 29 and 30). As the food deprivation increased up to six hours, the subjects tended more and more to interpret these indistinct forms as food objects (cf. also page 65). They were like

---

[7] R. Levine, I. Chein, and G. Murphy, The relation of the intensity of a need to the amount of perceptual distortion: a preliminary report, *J. Psychol.*, 1942, *13*, 283–293.

explorers and drivers of caravans who in times of hunger and thirst have visions of rich fields and cool springs. This tendency to perceive in a way determined by our needs is related to the fact that the wish is father to the thought. The general name that has been given to this tendency to perceive, remember, forget, think, and imagine under the influence of drives is *autism*.

In the same way, the words that represent our basic values, the things which we care about in life, are easily read when presented briefly on the screen. We may formulate what is happening here by saying that in

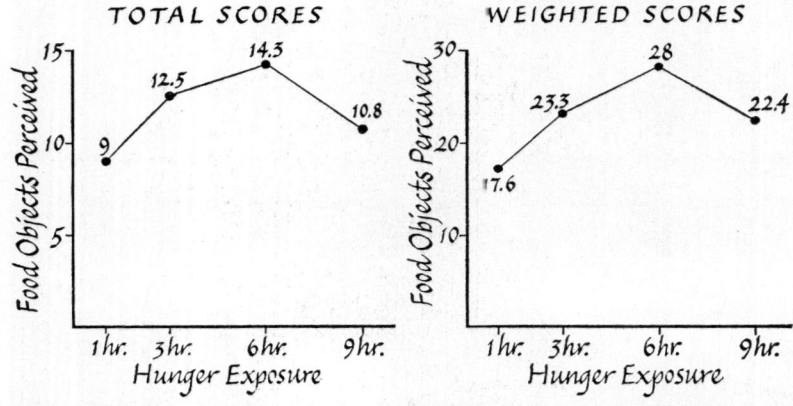

Figure 30. Average Scores in R. Levine's Experiment

The average number of ambiguous objects which Levine's subjects perceived as food objects increased with the number of hours since they last ate, up to six hours. When the scores were weighted in terms of "strong" and "weak" food responses, the relationships among the scores for the different time intervals were essentially the same. This experiment demonstrates that needs play a role in determining what we perceive. (From R. Levine, I. Chein, and G. Murphy, J. Psychol., 1942, 13, 291.)

an indistinct total one seizes upon or gives emphasis to that which satisfies a drive. If this is true, it should be possible to arrange that certain features shall become centers of perceptual response, figures against the background, simply by consistently associating them with the satisfaction of drives. In Roy Schafer's experiment[8] two circles were used. Drawing a wavy line through the middle of each, and supplying a dot for the eye, he cut each figure in two, so as to yield four different

---

[8] R. Schafer and G. Murphy, The role of autism in a visual figure-ground relationship, *J. exp. Psychol.*, 1943, 32, 335–343. As we go to press, we learn that repetition of this experiment does not confirm its results. Caution in its interpretation is therefore advisable.

faces in all (see Figure 31). He showed each of the four faces to his subjects, requiring them to learn the names which had been assigned to the faces. Sometimes he gave his subjects a small amount of money; sometimes he took money away. As the faces were shown, the subjects' task was simply to learn the names in association with the faces; they remained unaware of the purpose of the experiment, which dealt with

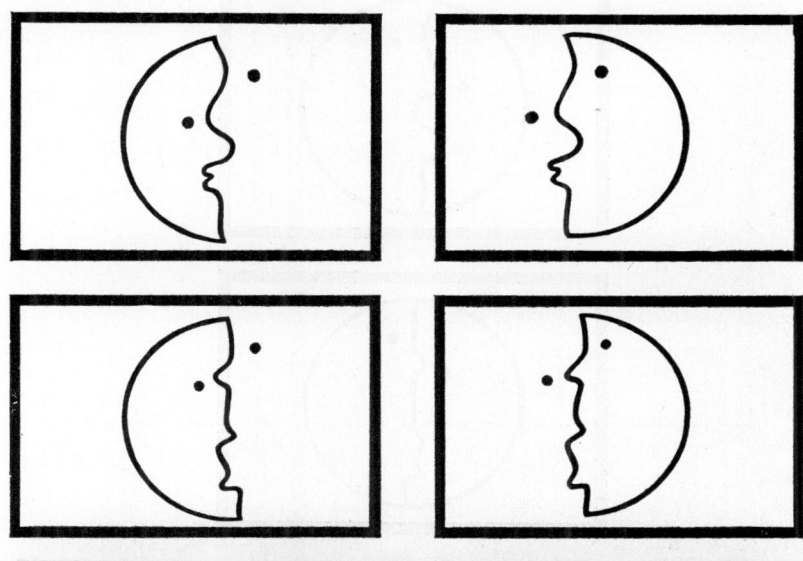

Figure 31. Four Stimuli in R. Schafer's Experiment

Each of the four "faces," made by drawing a wavy line down the middle of two circles and putting in a dot for an eye, was shown to a number of subjects during a series of trials. Some subjects were given a small amount of money whenever one set of faces was shown, but had to give up money when the other set was shown. For other subjects the "reward" and "punishment" procedure was reversed. The faces were then put together and the subjects were asked which faces they recognized. (This and Figure 32 from R. Schafer and G. Murphy, *J. exp. Psychol.*, 1943, 32, 338, 339.)

the *shaping of their habits of perceiving by the effect of rewards and punishments*. Later, when the complete circles were shown (Figure 32), each subject saw the face that had been associated with money; he could not see the face which he had been shown when money was taken away. (Faces which were "rewarded"—associated with money—by some subjects were "punished" by other subjects.) The subject developed, in other words, a *selectiveness* in perception in accordance with the rewards and punishments of past experience. Each subject saw the face that he had been "rewarded" to see, and was unable to make out the outline of the face with which punishment was associated. Even when the experimenter traced the outline of the "punished" face, it was rejected by the subjects as not being really a face at all. This last response, this sheer rejection of something unpalatable, is like the everyday denial of the

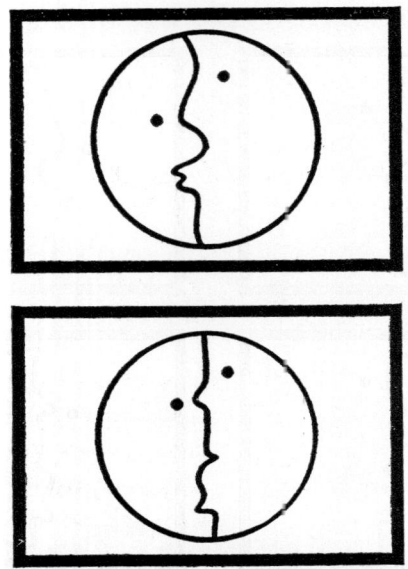

Figure 32. Two Stimuli in R. Schafer's Post-Training Series

When the "faces" in Figure 31 were put together, as shown here, the subjects were able to see *as faces* only those that had been "rewarded" in the training series. They were unable to recognize as faces those that had been associated with "punishment." The subjects had learned to perceive in a definite way during the training procedure.

existence of things which are just too much for us. When Murray Staal[9] made his subjects intensely miserable by having them wear a heavy gas mask, with discomfort from heat and from pressure on the face, they tended strongly to avoid seeing words related to air, heat, weight, etc., and instead saw neutral words not connected with their distress.

There is also at times an active set to discover reality, and to get away from the simple process of seeing what one needs. In Robert Levine's experiment (page 169), *after 6 hours* the subjects (who were now really

---

[9] M. Staal and L. Plotkin (in press).

hungry and would like to be going across the street to some real food instead of pretending to see food) were seeing *fewer* food objects in the cards (see Figure 30).

Indeed all these various tendencies show clearly that the effects of reward and punishment do not tell the whole story. There is more to say about the role of *set* when the subject is presented with a stimulus; we have not yet considered the important part played by *actively looking for clues to reality* (page 145). Bruner and Postman[10] have shown that there is a great deal of active *search for meanings*. In one of their experiments they frustrated their subjects' efforts to find a meaningful interpretation, by too short an exposure of indistinct words, and by bitter and sarcastic remarks as to how badly the subjects were doing. The result was not only to cause the subjects to read the indistinct words as having aggressive meanings (the frustration-aggression concept) but also to block their tendency to experiment with new ways of perceiving, so that they made no progress from session to session in interpreting the words, whereas the (unfrustrated) control group benefited from repeated opportunities for practice. The subjects *learn* to perceive when conditions are favorable for learning.

In another experiment Bruner and Postman told their subjects that words briefly presented would refer either to *colors* or to *foods*. Here the lack of a clear unitary set resulted in their taking considerably more time to read the words than when they were told simply that the words would refer to color. Perception, like action, is subject to conflict and to the delay which conflict brings.

Social Sharing of Visual Perception

Both the role of past experience and the role of set in guiding visual perception are brought out by our tendency to see things as other people around us see them. A classical study in this field is the work of Sherif. He made use of the fact that a point of light appearing in complete darkness appears to move. This is called the *autokinetic effect* (autokinetic means self-moving). It had been known to the astronomers that a man standing on a hilltop watching the stars in the

---

[10] J. Bruner and L. Postman, Perception under stress, *Psychol. Rev.*, 1948, 55, 314–323.

open spaces between clouds saw them move about in one direction or another, and that this was not due simply to the relative motion of the stars compared with that of the clouds. Indeed, if you bring the night sky into your laboratory in the form of a stationary light completely surrounded by utter blackness, the light will move about for you just as well. Sherif showed how delicately the apparent movements of the light respond to the social stimulation acting upon the individual. He began by testing the effects of simply telling the subject that the light, as soon as it appeared, would move to the right (or the left) and that he was to estimate the distance in inches. For the present writer, serving as subject, it moved typically eight or ten inches. In general, if other people tell us that the light will move, it moves for us.

This suggested to Sherif a systematic experiment on the way in which a person perceives when he is a member of a group, the other members of which report how they see things. In Sherif's experiment groups of three or four subjects would get together in the laboratory. When the light appeared, each subject called out how far it moved before it disappeared again, and each made a written record of his response. The experiment has been repeated by many investigators. Under these conditions almost no one fails completely to get the autokinetic effect. Each person quickly establishes his own general tendency—e.g., to see it move about three inches, or six, etc.—but of course varies somewhat from his own average in either direction from one judgment to the next. If the individual is alone with the experimenter, this average estimate remains pretty stable over the working period. But when a subject has worked alone for a hundred trials and is then brought into the group situation with others, he usually shows the pressure of his companions, in the sense that he finds his way *toward the group average,* a figure which represents the group as a whole. The result is what is called a funnel-shaped relationship, as plotted in the curves in Figure 33. During the course of three sessions of a hundred experiments each, there is a drift away from any extreme position, whether high or low, toward the middle. This throws interesting light upon the popular opinion that there is always "safety in numbers" and that the average man's view is probably the most accurate. Here, actually, there is always one individual who is more accurate than the average man, namely, the one who shows the *smallest* amount of reported movement! It is not the average man who is most free of errors. We are all responsive to group effects to some extent. The experiment throws light on the broad problem of the formation of group ways of perceiving, the standardized ways of looking at things which each one of us develops in everyday life in response to those about us, as when a child reared in a strongly Republican or Democratic community just "can't see it" in any other way.

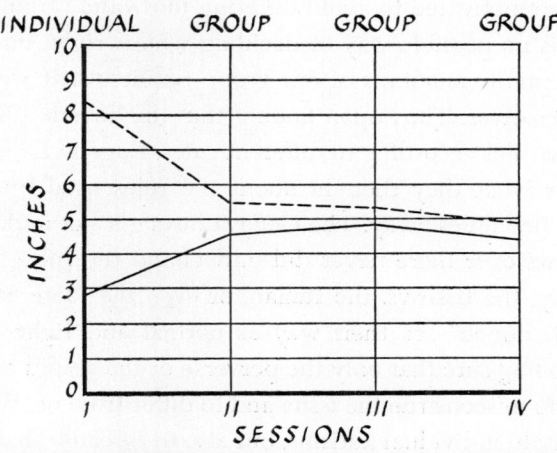

Figure 33. The Autokinetic Effect and Group Norms

A stationary point of light in a totally dark room appears to most observers to move. Making use of this phenomenon, known as the autokinetic effect, Sherif asked subjects to report the extent to which the light moved. The curves show the median judgments, in inches, made by two subjects, working first alone (individual) and then together (group). Over a series of group sessions the judgments converge, giving rise to a funnel-shaped curve and reflecting the influence of the group situation on individual judgments. (From M. Sherif, *The Psychology of Social Norms*, Harper & Brothers, 1936.)

What are the motives at work here? In Robert Levine's experiment (page 169), food deprivation was the thing that influenced the structuring of perception so that food was seen. Likewise in Schafer's experiment (page 171) there was a tangible reward. At first sight there seems to be no such direct reward in the Sherif experiment. But we need to look more closely to see what the motivation really is. From the comments of many who have taken part in such experiments, and from many other studies in which one person expresses his uneasiness when his judgments differ from those of others, it is clear that the primary motive is the need to find oneself a typical member of a group, a need not to be queer or exceptional or deviant. Many individuals feel out on a limb when they differ from their fellows. The group presses upon them to conform, and not to stray too far from the fold.

This is not necessarily an irrational response. There may at times be some real reasoning here; for we may conclude that what most people see is probably based on facts. But whether we reason about the matter or not, we are motivated to avoid differing too widely from others. And when there is no possible way of deciding who is right, our need to be normal, acceptable members of our group requires that we perceive as the group perceives. Thus upon finding that the boys in different Swiss cities play marbles according to different rules, Eugene Lerner asked the Geneva boys what they thought about the rules used by the boys at Neuchâtel a few miles away. The Geneva boys got hot under the collar: "Those fellows over there never did understand the rules, anyhow." In the same way, the Irish vs. the Italian, or even the "98th St. bunch" vs. the "99th St. bunch" see their way as normal and right. We get our dander up, being sure that only the perverse or the stupid could manage so basically to misconstrue the issue and to differ from us. We may refer, then, not only to individual autisms, but also to "socially shared autisms." When we have learned to see it as others see it, we may cling to this group effect. Sherif's subjects retained the group tendencies even when they were tested alone later. But there are big and rather stable individual differences in the response to such social pressure.[11]

In view of the universality of the "socially shared autisms" which make us see things as members of our own group perceive them, the question arises whether there is anything the individual can do to free himself from this type of partisanship, either in his own isolated experience, or as a member of a social group. Experiments dealing with this question are in progress in several American laboratories. The first answer appears to be that we can learn to correct our errors in perception just as we learn to correct our errors in action. The marksman firing at a target and making a certain constant error learns systematically to correct for this error. He learns, for example, to shoot in a direction which

---

[11] E. W. Bovard, Social norms and the individual, *J. abnorm. soc. Psychol.*, 1948, *43*, 62–69.

seems to him a little to the southwest in order that his northeast bias may be overcome. In the same way a person may learn to lean over backward and make judgments which to some degree reduce his autistic response. This is all to the good. But there is a much more radical approach, namely, to turn the eye of observation upon himself, and perceive more fully what he is doing when he allows an autistic response to gain headway. He may learn to see more clearly just how his wishes have been pushing him around. This demands effort and practice, and it usually requires working with someone else, or in a group which contains widely varying viewpoints, for we cannot lift ourselves out of the rut alone.

If each of us has characteristic ways of autistic perceiving and thinking with regard to everything from food to politics, does it follow necessarily that we are just a hodgepodge of disconnected, autistic habits? Not at all. We may, as a matter of fact, have a small, hard core of autisms referring to our primary needs, such as the need to see ourselves favorably; and all the more complex problems may arise from this simple core. In this way autisms prove to be not disconnected bits of mosaic, but expressions of one central, ever-repeated thesis. Each person has his own pattern of autisms; but, instead of being a medley of discordant elements, each has a more or less unified system of attitudes that serve his chief aims in life, including the aim of defending himself against unattractive pictures of himself, his family, his social group.

In reviewing the materials in this chapter on the process of seeing, we may bring together the four factors which we have stressed: sensory equipment, quality, experience, and set (including motivation). It would be a great mistake to conclude that each of these four factors works independently of the rest. Actually all four are at work all the time and are simply aspects of one unified whole. (1) Perception of the world utilizes the sensory mechanisms provided by the body; (2) it expresses the qualities of experience which are specific to these different sensory functions; (3) it integrates these qualities in a manner reflecting past experience—we see as we have learned to see; (4) it expresses present set—we look for, and often find, what we want. It might be urged by some that organization is a fifth factor separate from all the others; and indeed we have found much evidence that organization, or the capacity to give structure or integrated form to what we experience, is very basic. Actually, however, we shall not add organization as a fifth process, simply because organization is present all the way through. There is organization of the sensory equipment, organization of the qualitative material contributed by the senses, organization in the whole process of learning through experience, and organization in the system of motives which are operative at a given time and which work with the integrated material supplied by past stimulation.

It may be worth while, in attempting to show how the four factors are interrelated and how they demonstrate the principle of organization, to look at some experiments conducted at the end of World War I by Gelb and Goldstein, in which brain-injured men were studied with regard to visual perception. These were men who had suffered injuries to the visual centers in the brain, but who were not made completely blind. Over and over again Gelb and Goldstein found that the result of injury was not to remove some single part of the visual field and leave all the rest of the process of seeing unaffected; rather, they found that injury or impairment involved a *reorganization* of the whole process of seeing. In that type of brain injury which has resulted in a *micropsia*, a tendency of part of the visual field to show everything in reduced size, the man thus afflicted sees men and automobiles as you would see them looking down from the Washington Monument or a high mountain; he sees whatever lies in the microptic field as a miniature. Suppose now that a cross is so placed that part of it falls within this region of micropsia, the rest of it remaining within the sphere of normal vision. Does the man see the cross as reduced in part, but most of it remaining normal? No, he does nothing of the sort. It is not possible for a human brain to function in a piecemeal fashion such as this. The cross remains a cross. He sees the cross either as all large or as all small. This, moreover, is not just a question of having a great deal of experience with crosses. The effect is an illustration of the principle of organization and integration, as noted earlier in the case of the Köhler cross (page 143). Things fall into stable and orderly patterns rather than into unstable and disorderly ones.

Another example: When you are shown figures like those in Figure 34 for a brief exposure, you tend to reproduce them in the form appearing underneath, balanced, complete, and orderly—the tendency known as "closure." There are marked individual differences in the speed of closure,[12] as in other perceptive responses. Seldom will anyone reproduce a figure under these conditions in the asymmetrical or incomplete form in which it was actually shown. This is testimony to the orderly way in which the brain is built. But, in addition, past experience introduces order and system into material of the type presented; and order rather than disorder also arises from motivation, in the sense that you need order if you are to control the world. Gelb and Goldstein's brain-injured men were struggling after all to make contact, to "come to terms" with

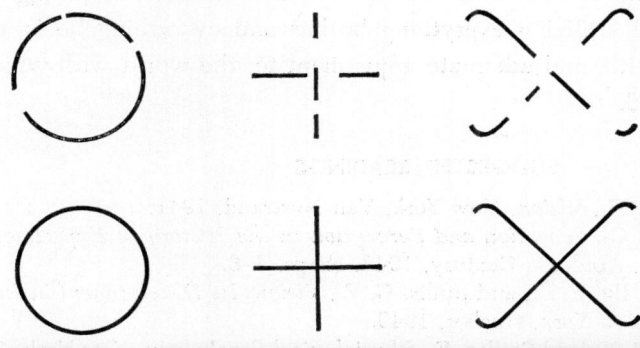

Figure 34. Examples of Closure

their environment; they were not machines indifferent to the forces acting upon them. It is not a question of having a "conscious desire" to see a cross; it is rather the fact that life is a serious business for both a normal and an injured man, and our job is to make as much sense out of the world as we can. The chances are that the motivation of the brain-injured man was even stronger than it would be in the case of a normal man—namely, the motivation to see not in a confused manner, but in terms of a plan which can be understood and followed. On the basis of much experience, each of us has found out something about the way in which things hang together in this world. Casting our eyes about, we estimate the size, distance, etc., of an object on the basis of past experience. In this sense the struggle of these brain-injured individuals to see things as they are is like the phenomenon of the "constancies"

---

[12] L. L. Thurstone, *A Factorial Analysis of Perception*, Chicago, University of Chicago Press, 1944.

(page 166), in which present impressions are taken *not* in their raw form but as we think they "ought to be" in order to represent things as they are. Perception tends, then, to round itself into stable, orderly, dependable forms, partly because, in the long run, brains have evolved as organs which are effective in introducing a certain amount of order into the chaos of the universe, and partly because individual experience and individual needs make as much order as can be made out of the individual environment. However useful it may be to break the individual up into parts and study each one separately, these cases seem to suggest the operation of the general law of life—the struggle of the individual, utilizing everything he has and everything he is, to make contact with, and adequate adjustment to, the world with which he is confronted.

SUGGESTED READINGS

Bartley, S. H., *Vision*, New York, Van Nostrand, 1941.

Boring, E. G., *Sensation and Perception in the History of Experimental Psychology*, Appleton-Century, 1942, chaps. 3–8.

Gesell, A., Ilg, F. L., and Bullis, G. E., *Vision: Its Development in Infant and Child*, New York, Hoeber, 1949.

Morgan, C. T., and Stellar, E., *Physiological Psychology*, New York, McGraw-Hill, 2nd ed., 1950, chaps. 7, 8, 9.

Woodworth, R. S., *Experimental Psychology*, New York, Holt, 1938, chaps. 12–16.

12 HEARING

Hearing is ultimately derived from the sense of touch. From the sense organs for touch there developed sense organs which were especially sensitive to the pulsations of the air: the first primitive ear. What evolution has done is to make these sense organs more efficient.

The fourfold classification of processes entering into perception may be used here again. We may differentiate (1) problems of sensory apparatus, (2) problems of quality, (3) problems of the effect of past experience, and (4) problems of set.

To understand the action of the sensory apparatus, let us begin with the kinds of commotion in the air which come to us, the different aspects of this commotion which act upon the body through its sense organs, and the various kinds of activity set going in the sense organs and the nerves to the brain. This will lay a foundation for understanding the elementary experiences in the world of hearing.

Sensory Equipment

The impact of a resounding body like a tuning fork upon the air, the blows which it gives the air, squeezes the molecules of the air together, as shown in Figure 35. A moment later, because the air is elastic, it begins to return to its original, more evenly distributed state. There is, then, a series of pushes and pulls in the air. When you speak, you actually push the air with your lips and tongue. Your breath hurls out a sound more or less explosively. There are regions of *condensation* and in between them there are regions of *rarefaction* of the air. A region of high condensation moves away from you at something over 1000 feet a second; trailing behind the region of condensation there is a region of rarefaction, then another region of condensation, and so on. While the speed of sound in air is approximately constant, the condensations may be more tightly packed together at one time than another; you may beat the air with a great many pulsations or only with a few in a second. But the rate at which the commotion is propagated away from you remains constant.

The frequency of pulsations, or *cycles,* the number of these phases of condensation and rarefaction per second, determines the pitch of the

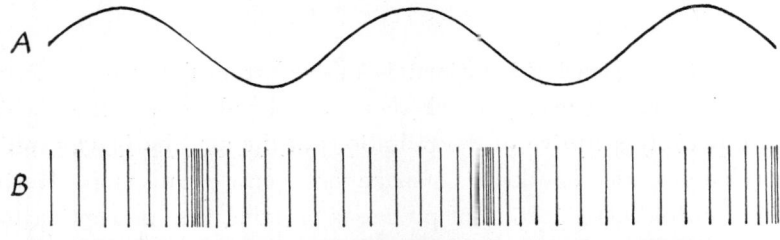

Figure 35. Wave of Compression

Air consists of widely separated, evenly distributed molecules. The blows of a vibrating object, such as a tuning fork, upon the air momentarily squeeze the molecules closely together (condensation). A moment later the air molecules return to the distributed state (rarefaction) and a neighboring set of molecules is squeezed together. The wavelike effect thus produced is represented above. The portions of the wave in which the lines are close together represent the areas of condensation; those where the lines are far apart are areas of rarefaction. Such waves, moving away from their source at a constant rate, give rise to the experience of sound when they come in contact with the ear.

tone. In middle C, for example, as given by the tuning fork, there are 256 of these cycles of condensation and rarefaction per second; and at an octave higher there are 512. The air vibrations cause the eardrum and the little bones of the middle ear (see Figure 36) to vibrate. This sets going vibrations in the fluid of the cochlea, in the inner ear; these vibrations stimulate the basilar membrane (Figure 37) which as it responds pulls upon the delicate hair cells, which in turn stimulate the nerve fibers that lead toward the brain.

It is evident that the basilar membrane has a great deal to do with the hearing of pitch, for its fibers vary in length much as do the strings of a harp. Just as a harp has short strings for high pitch, long strings for low pitch, so the basilar membrane, when uncoiled and spread out, would

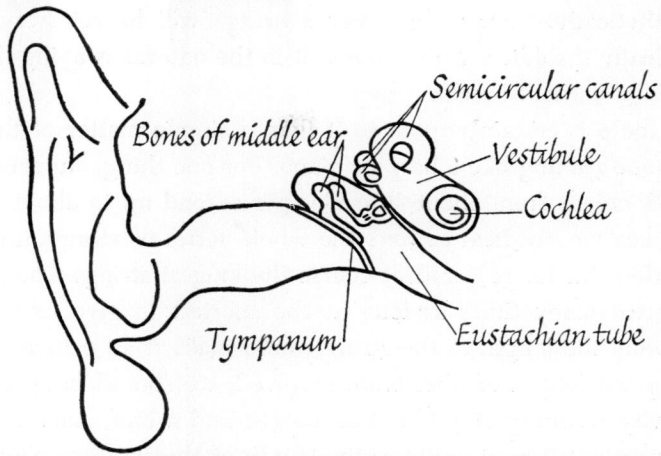

Figure 36. The Ear

Sound waves are directed against the eardrum (tympanum) by the external ear. The vibration of the eardrum sets in motion the bones of the middle ear. These transmit the vibration to the cochlear fluid, which stimulates the receptors (see Figure 37). The semicircular canals and the vestibule are important in maintaining equilibrium.

give a somewhat harplike arrangement. This membrane's basic mechanism of response appears to be *sympathetic vibration*. Thus when you press a piano key down quietly and then sing the appropriate note, the pulsations of your voice will set going an air column to which the particular string of the piano is sensitive. It then begins to respond

Figure 37. Organs of the Inner Ear

* Section through the organ of Corti, the receptor organ for hearing. The mechanical action of the bones of the middle ear serves to transmit vibrations to the cochlea. Wound about spirally in the cochlea in the inner ear is the basilar membrane. The vibrations of the fluid in the cochlea cause different parts of this membrane to vibrate. These vibrations stimulate the nerve endings in the hair cells. These are the impulses which finally go on to the brain and provide the basis of our auditory experiences.

sympathetically. In the same way a bridge will be set swaying sympathetically if soldiers march across it in the natural swaying rhythm of the bridge without breaking step.

But there is certainly more to it than a simple matter of the basilar membrane's acting like a harp or piano. For one thing, our sensitiveness to tones ranges from about 40 cycles per second up to about 20,000 or more (i.e., we can hear *as tone* the whole series of vibration rates that are within this range); and of course the longest strings would have to be a great many times as long as the shortest to give us this range. (Doubling the length of the string would make it an octave lower.) If nothing but length of fiber were involved, we should have a range of sensitivity reaching only about an octave and a half, since the longest strings are only about 2½ times the length of the shortest. Nevertheless, it must be remembered that the damping and tension of individual strings may alter their characteristic frequency while vibrating; you can alter the vibration rate of a rubber band by pulling upon it, and you can slow down a tuning fork by putting wax on it. It is believed by many that these factors of damping and tension may enable the basilar membrane to do what is required by the theory.

But it is a mistake to think of a single fiber as responding to a specific wave length. The issue is more complex; we might better think of belts or broad regions of response to a given pitch rather than of a single fiber working at a time. Yet the results of diseases of the inner ear, as well as experimental evidence, point to some degree of selective response to pitch from one end of the basilar membrane to the other, the shorter fibers responding to higher frequencies When the short fibers are injured, there is relatively more impairment of response to higher tones.

When once the sympathetic vibration has been set going, there is stimulation of the hair cells, which then excite the delicate nerve endings, different fibers thus serving different portions of the basilar membrane. The impulses are transmitted by several way stations to the temporal region of the brain, back of the temple. Injuries to the temporal region cause distortions or blockages in the reception of sound, just as the different portions of the visual cortex have specialized functions, each serving a portion of the retina (see page 161). There is apparently a fine subdivision of the auditory cortex, each subdivision receiving impulses from a portion of the basilar membrane. But whereas the retina is spread out so that it can serve the perception of space, the auditory apparatus gives the range of tone experiences from high to low, and does not in itself give perception of space (the localization of sounds will be treated a little later, beginning foot of this page).

Auditory Qualities

Pitch is one of three primary attributes of tone. The other two are *loudness*, which depends upon the sheer amount of energy in the sound wave, and *timbre,* or tone quality, the attribute that differentiates voices, piano tones, violin tones, etc., when equally loud and at the same pitch. Timbre results from the fact that, in addition to the fundamental tone, a vibrating body also gives off higher tones, so that the air wave is actually a composite wave. You hear the pitch as determined by the fundamental, but you also hear a tone quality which is determined by *the number and relative intensity of these overtones,* as Figure 38 shows.

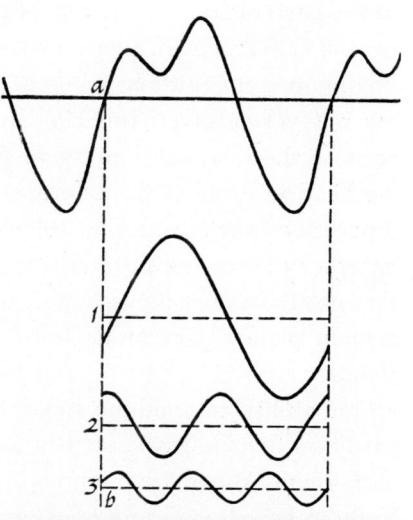

Figure 38. Timbre of a Violin

The composite curve shown in the upper wave records the vibration produced by a violin and gives rise to the experience of tone quality. Analysis shows this curve to be composed of the three vibration rates represented below it. When measured on lines parallel to *ab*, the altitude of the composite curve is the algebraic sum of the deviations of curves *1, 2,* and *3* from their lines of reference (the dotted horizontal lines). (From D. C. Miller, *The Science of Musical Sounds*, New York, The Macmillan Company. By courtesy of the Case Institute of Technology.)

Past Experience as Exemplified in the Localization of Sound

Just as we found in visual perception, so we find here in auditory perception, that the sensory equipment yields particular qualities which are modified and organized together on the basis of earlier experience. An obvious illustration of the effects of experience working in conjunction with the equipment and the qualities given us by the sense organs is our capacity to localize the source of a sound. In locating the sound, the relative intensity (energy) of the air vibrations at the two ears is of great importance; we have learned where to "place" a thing on the basis of such differences of intensity. Of some importance likewise are the differences in phase of the two waves; at one ear the air is in maximum condensation, while at the other ear at that moment the air has not yet received full condensation, etc. Turning the head helps because the relative intensity in the two ears changes, and because, as the head is turned, the differences in phase are altered. We learn by experience how to interpret the differences in phase just as we learn to interpret differences in intensity. If the head is so placed that the two ears get the same intensity and the same phase (as in the case of the median plane), we cannot tell from what point in the plane a sound comes.

Our ability to combine tones, and to hear them as music, depends partly on their intrinsic quality but partly on our experience in dealing with them. When two sounds are perceived simultaneously, we are likely to hear them as more or less independent of each other *unless* we have the attitude that they belong together, and *group them* together. If, for example, a distant railway whistle is emitting a tone at middle C, and a child across the street is chanting a nursery rhyme on the G above, we do not hear the two tones as a chord. They are unrelated. If, however, we respond jointly to a group of tones coming from the same instrument or as part of the same ensemble which is rendering music, we may hear the whole as a chord.

But sometimes it is a chord, sometimes a discord; can we find the principle that determines which it will be? Part, at least, of the answer lies in the relations between the rates of the different tones. The octave, in which the higher pitch has twice the frequency of the lower, enters into many familiar chords; a musical fifth, in which the vibration rates bear the relation 3:2, is acceptable; and the major third and minor third, with ratios 4:3 and 5:4 respectively, are also acceptable. As we get to ratios which are arithmetically less simple, like 15:8, we get discords. (Such facts as these led the ancient Pythagoreans to the view that numbers are the clue to all beauty.) These and other relations among vibration rates yielding various tones and chords are shown in Figure 39.

On the other hand, we can to some extent *learn* to find satisfaction in tonal relationships which were formerly unacceptable to us; the history of music is full of examples. Henry T. Moore[1] presented various chords to a group of college students to see whether there was a *change in preference* (as there has been in the history of music from the Greeks to the present). He sounded various chords, some of which involved very simple tonal relationships such as the octave and the musical fifth, and some of which were much more complex. After many sessions of

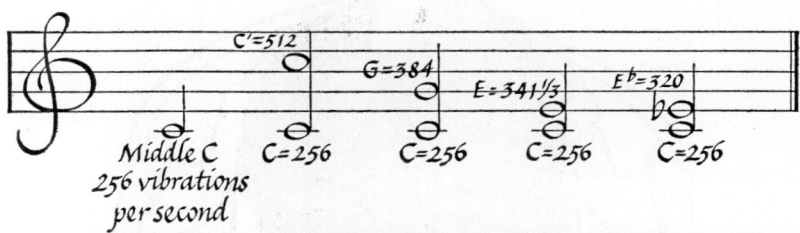

Figure 39. Chords and Vibration Rates

The vibration rate of C', the C above middle C, is twice that of middle C; the ratio is 2:1. The vibration ratio of the major fifth, G and C, is 3:2. The ratio of E and C, the major third, is 4:3; that of the minor third, E♭ and C, is 5:4.

experimental listening to such chords, he found that those chords which at first were satisfying in their simplicity became more and more boring, while those which at first could not really be heard as acceptable chords came to be heard as chords. Earlier we noted that *we learn to see;* Moore's study shows that *we learn to hear.*

This was the point that Mortimer Adler[2] made when he presented music in four different forms to large numbers of college students. Classical music was played sometimes in its *original* form, sometimes in rearranged *chaotic* form, sometimes in *sentimentalized,* and sometimes in *dull* form. The conclusion to which he was driven was that the students who preferred one or the other of the debased types of music proved to be people who had not really been able to *hear* it at all, that is, to make

---

[1] H. T. Moore, The genetic aspect of consonance and dissonance, *Psychol. Monogr.,* 1914, *17* (whole no. 73).

[2] M. J. Adler, Music appreciation: an experimental approach to its measurement, *Arch. Psychol.,* 1929, No. 110.

sense out of the musical selection itself. Those who *heard* the original form preferred it.

Students of the arts remind us that painting, sculpture, and architecture are "space arts," and music and poetry, which appeal to the ear, are "time arts." Just as we group and organize visual impressions in space, we organize auditory impressions in time. We learn to group events in terms of two's, three's, four's, or even sometimes five's, sixes, or larger numbers of units, as we learn in childhood to respond to poetry

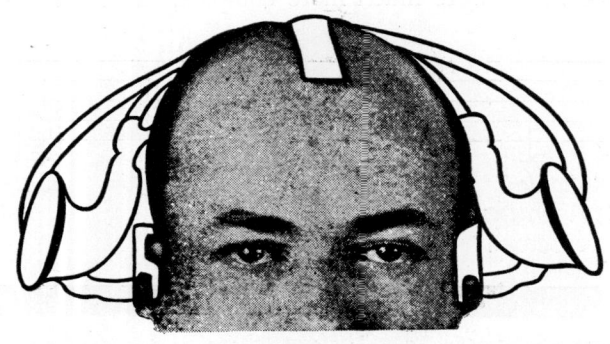

Figure 40. P. T. Young's Pseudophone

(Modified from P. T. Young, *J. exp. Psychol.*, 1928, 11, 400.)

or music, giving them rhythmical structure as we listen. When, for example, we hear waltz time, we group together the accented and the two unaccented beats as a single unit, or measure; we group together a sequence of such measures as a musical phrase. Just as we find it easy to take in five or six visual units at once, and just as the difficulty increases very rapidly as we try to bring this up to eight or nine units, so in hearing we can handle a group of four easily. ("Common time" is 4–4, and the commonest kind of line of poetry has five feet, as in "The próper stúdy óf mankínd ĭs mán.") We can, with effort, reproduce seven or eight (some people even more) digits or letters when read to us at the rate of one per second; but in the enjoyment of the arts we want fewer units. Indeed, you will hear 6:8 time not as six separate units, but as two groups of three.

Just as we learn to combine and integrate auditory impressions, so we integrate auditory with other sensory impressions; for example, we can understand a speaker more easily if we watch his face. Sometimes, however, the information from two different senses is contradictory. In general we rely so heavily on vision, especially in regard to matters of spatial localization, that direct competition between visual and auditory cues gives the visual ones the advantage. P. T. Young[3] has studied this effect with the *pseudophone* (Figure 40). When the pseudophone is used in ordinary fashion you hear what is on the right as if it were on the left, and vice versa; but when you *look* at an object which is evidently serving as the source of a sound, the pseudophone effect fails, for the eye dominates over the ear.

Set

Just as we see in some respects in terms of what we are set to see, so we tend to hear in terms of what we are set to hear. We pick out what is related to our needs, and give it emphasis. We hear our friends mentioned in the midst of the buzzing of group conversation— we hear their names when actually mentioned and indeed we may hear them even when no one has actually mentioned them, for we select and emphasize certain sounds which interest us. So also, in hearing the political speech or the sports news over the radio, we hear what is important for us, what fits into our needs, and miss or confuse a good deal of the rest.

An experimental device for bringing out the role of set in giving structure or organization to what is heard is the phonograph disk developed by Skinner under the name "verbal summator." This consists of vowel sounds which are heard by naïve subjects in terms of words that portray their own preoccupations. Thus normal subjects may hear in these meaningless vowel sounds references to food, dancing, moving pictures, or books in which they are interested. If they are tired, they are likely to hear references to fatigue. Disturbed patients hear in terms of their dis-

---

[3] P. T. Young, Auditory localization with acoustical transposition of the ears, *J. exp. Psychol.*, 1928, *11*, 399–429.

turbed expectations, as Shakow and Rosenzweig[4] bring out in a study of patients at Worcester State Hospital.

In the same way Herbert Spohn has devised an auditory situation in which two series of words are completely superimposed upon one phonograph disk; that is, after a disk has been made with a series of words, it is played through again and the experimenter utters certain new words which exactly fill the interval that was originally filled by the other words. The final disk thus contains a series of double verbal stimuli; for example, the word *defeat* and the word *employ* are presented simultaneously. Which word does the subject hear? Or, if neither one, what does he hear? The subjects display their preoccupations by the reports they give on what they hear. As they sit in a physically uncomfortable position with spine arched, shoulders squared, arms folded upon their chests, they hear in a blurred auditory presentation many words referring to strain, effort, annoyance, and a number of words relating to hostility or aggression (as they actually begin to experience hostility toward the experimenter). Some of these hostile words they hear are really there on the disk, but are not as frequently heard under relaxed conditions. Some of the significant words that they "hear," which tell how they feel, are not on the disk at all. It has been estimated that ordinary conversation goes along quite well if we hear 65 or 75 percent of the actual elements of speech which are uttered by our neighbor; so it is easy to grasp why a slight degree of indistinctness may permit quite a large degree of autistic organization. Not only past experience, but also present set, enters into this process of giving structure to what is heard, so that each person to some degree hears in terms of his needs and attitudes.

SUGGESTED READINGS

Boring, E. G., *Sensation and Perception in the History of Experimental Psychology*, New York, Appleton-Century, 1942, chaps. 9–11.

Morgan, C. T., and Stellar, E., *Physiological Psychology*, New York, McGraw-Hill, 2nd ed., 1950, chap. 10.

Stevens, S. S., and Davis, H., *Hearing: Its Psychology and Physiology*, New York, Wiley, 1938.

Wever, E. G., *Theory of Hearing*, New York, Wiley, 1949.

Woodworth, R. S., *Experimental Psychology*, New York, Holt, 1938, chap. 21.

[4] D. Shakow and S. Rosenzweig, The use of the tautophone ("verbal summator") as an auditory apperceptive test for the study of personality, *Character & Pers.*, 1939, 8, 225.

13 TASTING, SMELLING, AND THE GENERAL SENSES

Sight and hearing, the two great sources of our world of communication with one another and the medium through which a large part of our civilization is carried along, are in a way superimposed upon some simpler processes of sensing which are older in the race and represent more direct and primitive contact with our environment. Sight and hearing are often called "distance receptor processes," in the sense that the energies which come to us from things seen and heard must travel a distance, in contrast to those senses which represent our own direct contact with the environment. When we smell or taste or touch, the thing with which we have commerce actually touches our bodies. Smell and taste are often referred to as "chemical senses," because the particles which excite these senses actually interact chemically with our receptors. The sensory processes which make contact between our skins and the immediate world outside us in terms of touch, pain, warm, and cold, tell us not what is going on at a distance but what is going on in the immediate world to which the skin is exposed. And as we shall see, these relatively simple sensory processes—simple as compared with sight and hearing—have their own great importance in civilized living, and not merely as means of maintaining our physical existence.

Taste and Smell

The senses of taste and smell are very intimately associated and we shall consider the two together. A great deal that you refer to in terms of the taste of your food is actually a blend of taste, smell, and sensations of temperature, touch, etc., from the food in the mouth.

Actually there are only four tastes: sweet, sour, bitter, and salty; and these correspond to four chemical classes of stimuli. Chemical solutions act upon little "taste buds" in the tongue and mouth, and the taste receptors within these initiate the nerve impulses to the brain. The particles floating in the air which give rise to the sense of smell have to act chemically upon the mucous membranes of the nose. It is not possible at present to identify a few truly *elementary* smells, and to connect them with the chemistry of the floating particles.

In exploring the environment, smelling almost invariably comes before tasting. One might indeed challenge our statement that sight and hearing are the distance receptors, as contrasted with smell. Actually, however, the particles from the things we smell do not as a rule drift very far from the things themselves; and it was in the active sniffing of food, etc., that our animal ancestry developed the two interrelated processes largely as an adjunct to the selection and the devouring of that which proved good as food. In ourselves the enjoyment of a food begins as the door from the kitchen opens, or even as the housekeeper's words start us smiling, sniffing, and making ready for the repast.

And there is an enormous difference between the simple smell and taste satisfaction at a subhuman or savage level and the very rich, complex, exquisite balance of smell and taste qualities as the experienced cook has learned to combine them. Even with all this skill in preparation, the cook must be careful that the dish is served at the right temperature, and that nothing from the touch experiences of the mouth will interfere with the balance; let the dish be lukewarm instead of hot, or have a sticky or oily consistency, and everything is ruined. Experiences of "taste," then, are very complex, highly developed experiences into which civilized men for a very long time have poured their ingenuity; and they represent the huge difference between simple sensing at a primitive level and the rich cultural exploitation of our sensory equipment to give us our greatest satisfaction. About the same thing could be said regarding the enjoyment of smell in the world of gardening and in the world of perfumes. In the garden, a very rich and complex visual pattern is frequently combined, especially in the gardens of the East, with rich and complex experiences from the sense of smell; and often the odors of the garden are combined into fantastically complex and appealing effects by the perfumers' art.

Most infants show strong positive responses to sweet things and negative responses to bitter, sour, and salty things, and a little later they make definite and fairly uniform responses to many strong odors; but as they grow and learn, they show very marked individual differences. Thus a seven-year-old boy frequently made himself a drink of very salty water as a mid-afternoon snack. The taste for sour and bitter things may likewise develop early. Many soda fountain drinks are bitter. Other children are made sick to the point of nausea by these same things. Children appear to differ even more in their sensitiveness and response to smells; and adults, when experimented upon, differ greatly in their conception of what is pleasant and what is unpleasant. Two hundred subjects were asked to rank 10 different odors from 1 to 10, 1 representing the most pleasant, 10 the least pleasant of the series. Although a good many of the subjects experienced cinnamon as pleasant, there were some who ranked it as the *most unpleasant*.[1]

While restaurateurs and the writers of advertisements for the cuisine have perhaps reached the greatest heights in extolling the gratifications of "taste" in a complex sense, the poets have far outdone them when it comes to describing the elixir of satisfactions which may come from the world of flowers.

> *There are some powerful odours that can pass*
> *Out of the stoppered flagon; even glass*
> *To them is porous. Oft when some old box*
> *Brought from the East is opened and the locks*
> *And hinges creak and cry; or in a press*
> *In some deserted house, where the sharp stress*
> *Of odours old and dusty fills the brain;*
> *An ancient flask is brought to light again,*
> *And forth the ghosts of long-dead odours creep.*
> *There, softly trembling in the shadows, sleep*
> *A thousand thoughts, funereal chrysalides,*
> *Phantoms of old the folding darkness hides,*
> *Who make faint flutterings as their wings unfold,*
> *Rose-washed and azure-tinted, shot with gold.*[2]

---

[1] K. Gordon, The recollection of pleasant and unpleasant odors, *J. exp. Psychol.*, 1925, 8, 225–239.

[2] Charles Baudelaire, "The Flask," in *The Poems and Prose Poems of Charles Baudelaire*, New York, Brentano, 1919, p. 25.

The sensitivity which could make men write this way is partly, no doubt, a question of their constitutional make-up, but different cultural groups have exploited different sensory qualities in different ways. The reader will have no difficulty in recognizing the different modes of cultural exploitation of these gratifications of sense in different parts of the world at different periods.

We have considered the sensory apparatus and the elementary qualities supplied by smell and taste. Only a word needs to be added regarding the great role of past experience, for it is already evident from the associations formed between smell, taste and other senses, as shown in the quotation above. It is even more vividly brought out in the factor of experience which appears in the case of "acquired tastes," the way in which the tea taster learns to differentiate odors that accompany the (bitter) tea taste, the ability of the lover of wine or cordials to pick out qualities—such as "bouquets"—which most of us fail to recognize, and the capacity to take in the rest of a wide variety of qualities so as really to appreciate and enjoy what the more primitive "taste" overlooks. These are all evidences of the huge role of past experience. The role of set is very evident in the case of our expectations and desires as they relate to foods and in the case of our fears as they relate to medicines with a disagreeable taste. Let the eyes be closed, and the child may pass into almost a paroxysm of distress from the very same fluid in the mouth which he will fully enjoy if he thinks it is a syrup instead of a "medicine." The initiates at fraternity rites have long been subjected to these effects of fear and desire, paying unwitting tribute to the fact that the experience is to a very considerable extent guided by the demands and emotions of the moment.

Touch

The receptors for touch include various small "corpuscles" in the skin, near which or around which are found the delicate nerve fibers, transmitting their impulses to the brain. As you stimulate the blindfolded subject's skin with a bristle, you find that touch is experienced only at certain spots. Other receptors below the surface give us the sense of *pressure* which we sometimes experience even in the absence of skin contact as such. As in all perception, the characteristic kind of quality associated with these impressions is localized in a particular region of the brain; the touch impressions are transmitted to a region at the top of the head, near the middle. The disorder or obliteration of this region means inability to experience touch. Frequently gross brain injury may involve an inability to interpret, that is, to give *organization* to the various touch impressions. Thus one takes hold of a billiard ball in the dark, and thinks that it is an inkwell or a fountain pen.

Figure 41. Touch Substituting for Sight

Left, the head of Michelangelo's statue of Moses. Right, the head reproduced by a man who lost his eyesight in World War I and who based his work on impressions derived from careful tactual examination of the statue. This man was not a sculptor before he became blind. (From G. Révész, *Formenwelt des Tastsinnes*, Martinus Nijhoff, 1938.)

Everyday examples of the role of past experience in giving structure to touch appear in the complex experiences of texture in which we report upon the hardness or softness of something touched, or its dryness or wetness. In these instances we often use both surface and deep pressure experiences simultaneously, and also we take note of the sharpness or fuzziness of the edges. Frequently also, we use warm and cold impressions to eke out and complete the synthesis. The role of past experience, that is, interpreting by analogy with something encountered earlier, is very evident as you watch the experienced dealer in textiles or abrasives deftly pick out the exact cloth or emery paper which he needs but which is scarcely distinguishable from others of the kind by the uninitiated. An equally striking case is the development by the blind of special skill in interpreting through the fingertips, as shown in the Braille system. Over a period of months or years the blind reader goes on gaining skill and speed in his capacity to interpret these patterns of little raised points on the paper. But Figure 41, by a blind sculptor, shows the limitations of touch without sight.

Warm and Cold; Pain

The anatomy and physiology of the temperature receptors are still imperfectly understood.[3] But it is easy to show that the sense organs for the temperature senses are scattered through the skin, as are those for touch. As you map the skin with a suitably cooled or warmed stylus, you find, in addition to the spots which are sensitive to touch, other spots which give the experience of warm, and still others which give the experience of cold. (This does not, of course, mean just one receptor for each "spot.") A stimulus at high temperature will extend its energy through the region, so that pain is also aroused and you get a burning sensation. In the same way, cold may be sufficiently extensive and intensive to give you the experience of painful cold. Incidentally, this is an interesting exemplification of the difference between a physical and a psychological analysis. Cold, physically speaking, is simply the absence of heat; but psychologically speaking, the deviations from the neutral region of temperature experience (where neither cold nor warmth is experienced) may take the form of warm or cold, both of which are equally real, and each of which may be combined with pain experience. This is easily brought out in various experiments. If you use a stylus at high temperature and apply it carefully to a cold spot, and if the stimulation is intense enough to reach the threshold of the sense organs, the brain will get the usual impression that it always gets when an impulse from this spot follows its course to the appropriate brain center—you will experience cold. This is "paradoxical cold." In the same way, a very cold stimulus acting on a warm spot can give you an experience of

---

[3] See C. T. Morgan and E. Stellar, *Physiological Psychology*, New York, McGraw-Hill, rev. ed., 1950, chap. 11.

warmth. If once you get the receptors working, they send the accustomed impulses to their accustomed locus in the brain, and that particular locus when excited will give you the appropriate experience and not some other kind of experience ("specific energies of the brain").

When a warm stimulus reaches a sufficiently high temperature (and covers a sufficient area), it may simultaneously arouse cold and pain experiences. All three types of impulses come crowding into the brain at once. We have learned, of course, to interpret this compound of impressions in terms of temperatures higher than those which are just "warm." Again using the concept of the threshold, we note that the threshold for cold is a good deal higher when using a warm stylus than when using a cold one, but that ultimately the warm stylus will set the cold mechanism working, too, along with those for warmth and for pain. This is what ordinarily experiences of heat actually involve. It might be remembered that pain is not necessarily disagreeable. In everyday life (e.g., a hot shower), the warm, cold, and pain are all involved; you do not object (up to a certain point). Cold and pain are combined when face and hands are exposed to the wind on a winter day, and again, up to a point, you do not find this disagreeable. Experiences of warm and cold are greatly affected by habit and by attitude, so that a very cold object may, when touched, be experienced as burning hot, or hot objects experienced as cold, depending on the expectation of the moment.[4]

The receptors for pain appear to be the free nerve endings of the skin and the interior of the body. Thresholds are very low; from an evolutionary viewpoint, this is easy to understand. Anything going wrong, anything constituting a threat to the body, sets trouble signs working while stimulation is still at a low level. One little nerve fiber which is all agog, as in the case of a toothache, can overwhelm the whole organism with almost unbearable distress. There appears to be only one kind of pain experience where single nerve endings are involved; that is, the pain from a stubbed toe or a cut face would be the same if you could get down to the ultimate units of the experience. But a good deal of pressure

---

[4] Incidentally, warm and cold appear to contribute nothing to our awareness of the spatial world. In L. J. Stone's experiment (*Arch. Psychol.*, 1938), radiant heat given off from points arranged in various ways on the skin resulted in no perception of pattern at all. It is the touch experiences that combine with the visual, the auditory, and those from the muscles (page 199) to give us our world of space.

is frequently mixed in with the pain, and of course the number and distribution of the pain receptors vary with the region and the type of injury.

This elementary pain quality is usually unpleasant, but not always so. We have for centuries used the phrase "pleasure and pain" as if pain were equivalent to unpleasantness. Actually there is no one sensation which is always pleasant, and no one which is always unpleasant. There are even instances in which we enjoy inflicting pain upon ourselves or having others inflict it upon us. Some of these are instances of putting on a pose, serving as a suffering hero, etc.; but this does not prove that all of them are. Often we crave an intensity of experience as in "thrill," even if it yields pain. The very fact that a "red-hot" cup of coffee or a violent effort in climbing or skiing causes pain is part of the fun. But it is likely that pain at a very high level of intensity is always unpleasant. Most pain is certainly a danger signal, for pain is part of the organism's machinery providing a tendency to get the organism away from that which is damaging.

Kinesthesis

One of the most important of all our senses, the kinesthetic sense, is the sense that keeps us constantly adjusted to our own bodily position and activity. As the muscles contract, the sense organs wound around the muscle spindles and located in tendons or joints, initiate nervous impulses which come up through the spinal cord into the brain centers. Now any sort of effective response to the environment involves not only taking in aspects of the environment itself, but taking in at the same time what we are doing in relation to that environment, so that we neither overshoot nor undershoot the mark required by the situation. Kinesthesis is the name for the sensory processes which report to us on activity of muscle, tendon, and joint, enabling us at each instant to adapt the body to the moment-by-moment changes in the outer situation. Figure 20 (page 139) shows how we test the kinesthetic sense in lifting weights; as we lift, we estimate the weight.

Responses to kinesthesis are what contemporary scientists and engineers would call a feedback system (cybernetic system is the technical term). A feedback system is one in which any activity in progress sets going a device that holds it within check, keeps it within limits, prevents it from overstepping the bounds within which it can function. A thermostat, for example, is so set that if the temperature goes above a certain point the heat is thrown off, and if it goes below a certain point the heat is thrown on. The principle of homeostasis (page 15) is an exemplification of the general principle of the feedback system; the inner environment must be constant, and any activity which would interfere with its constancy is promptly held in check, so that constancy can be maintained. Kinesthesis exemplifies this same principle. When you reach for a book, you have to be able to stop your movement at the right point. You have to make just enough effort in throwing a ball from third to first base. In every little daily act like handling knife and fork, or tying a knot, or writing your name, you are delicately adjusting the expenditure of effort so as to do just enough of what is required and not too much. If you once have an opportunity to see a man with an injury to the kinesthetic system, such that the reports from his muscles as they contract do not reach his brain, you will see how grossly he overreacts or underreacts, in a jerky, chaotic fashion. You train your muscles; you learn in relation to each situation the amount of muscular contraction required of the muscles involved, and the way in which they are to be coördinated. You can watch the child year by year learning to skip rope or throw a baseball so that things are attuned to his effort. The kinesthetic sense is very sensitive. You are ordinarily able to report a swing of the extended arm through a single degree or two of a circle. You quickly adapt to new situations; when standing you correct for the rolling and pitching of a boat or the swaying and bumping of a fast bus on a second-class road. Somehow you maintain your balance.

The mechanisms involved in muscles, tendons, and joints are supported and helped out by other mechanisms in the inner ear shown in Figure 36 (page 183) and in the cerebellum. It will be noted that the vestibular apparatus is sensitive—"static sensitivity"—to movements of the fluid in such a way that all three dimensions are taken care of. Much aviation research has been done in recent years to ascertain how a man can maintain an awareness of up and down and of his relation to space in general though whirled about in a cage or on a tilting board. Here, as elsewhere, the different senses interact and fuse their reports; kinesthesis aided by sight does a very much better job than the kinesthetic and static without the use of sight.

While ordinarily we are not explicitly aware of the impulses coming from the muscles, tendons, and joints, we can practice observing until we are aware not only of kinesthetic sensations, but of their slight variation from moment to moment. Edmund Jacobson,[5] a physiologist at the University of Chicago, has experimented on the individual's awareness of these tightened muscles all over his body, and has shown that he may learn not only to detect but to *increase or decrease the resulting tension* (page 113). Jacobson's evidence that all of us are doing a great deal of contracting of our muscles while unaware of the fact fits in also with evidence from Wenger and others (page 103), who have successfully measured the amount of "residual" tension, that is, tension which remains even when we think we are relaxed. Wenger's data bring out strikingly the large individual differences in such residual tensions, and suggest that we vary from one another a good deal in the degree of tightness or prevailing tension level. This proves to be not just a question of maintaining ourselves in a constant state of strain, but actually in some sense a preparation or readiness for overt action. Many experiments have shown that when you are ready to do something, you are actually tightening the appropriate muscles. Thinking of doing something is to a considerable extent the beginning of doing it. If you are tense, it is largely because you are actually starting something—or a number of things. Indeed most conflict is starting several things at once, like Stephen Leacock's knight who went galloping off in all directions.

Organic Sensitivity

A wealth of impulses comes from the vital organs and from the inner machinery generally. In addition to warm, cold, pain, and touch, which are initiated from inside the body as well as from the skin, there are other impressions related to hunger, thirst, maternal and sex cravings, fatigue, and general well-being or distress, which are specific to this internal region and not found elsewhere. We never learn to take sharp cognizance of these experiences in such a way as to analyze them

---

[5] E. Jacobson, *Progressive Relaxation*, Chicago, University of Chicago Press, 2nd ed., 1938.

and give them names; in the gross statement, "I am hungry," there is nothing corresponding to the fine analysis and differentiation we have when we report on what we are seeing. We never make social capital for communication out of these experiences in their own right; even in the case of those of profound personal importance such as the maternal and sexual feelings, emphasis is placed rather upon the person loved or upon the context of our feeling. A French philosopher noted how different the world would be if one's gastric contractions rather than the contractions of one's vocal chords were used as the basis for interpersonal communication.

The organic and the kinesthetic processes work together, and indeed work in conjunction with the other senses, in giving us a general report on "how we are" or "how we feel." The very fact that we do relatively little sharp analysis of our sensations of these types makes it all the easier for us to slant our interpretations of what is going on inside the body; the role of motivation or drive in giving structure to our experiences becomes therefore very obvious. It is quite possible for a person who is in the blues or says he feels so "lousy" that he probably has the grippe, to take his temperature and discover that it is normal, and then suddenly decide to go for a hike or go to a movie in the blithest spirits. The hypochondriac is a person who interprets a medley of internal impressions as meaning illness rather than health. The more diffuse and unstructured, the less adequately named and finely differentiated these inner impressions are, the more they are subject to free or even arbitrary interpretations and naming. Often we can profoundly color the way in which we "feel" by our wishes; if there is a dance, the way we "feel" may be quite different from the way we "feel" if there is an exam about to be taken.

Nevertheless, these impressions from within the body are not altogether chaotic, or altogether changeable and fluid. They have a common core from day to day, and perhaps even from year to year. You feel "like yourself" most of the time, in the sense that your habitual and characteristic muscle tone with consequent kinesthetic response, and the habitual sensations from stomach, arterial walls, etc., are more or less recognizable from one phase of life to another. The rapid physiological changes of adolescence may occasionally make the boy or girl actually feel that he or she is no longer the same person as before; and in disease there may be such marked changes in these organic and kinesthetic components that the person is worried as to whether "he'll ever be himself" again. For the most part, we get through these periods of feeling strangely about ourselves with only superficial worry; but occasionally a hospital patient wakes up feeling that he is not the same person he has always been. He may say: "I am Joe Stone, but I am not really Joe Stone. This is some other guy." What is happening is that the familiar inner mass of sensory impressions, the "here I am" kind of experience, is gone. The sense of personal identity is to a considerable extent a sense of the good old familiar inner mass of sense impressions. Though they may be fluid and indistinct, they are nevertheless recognizable, and it is constancy and recognizability that count. Superimposed on this common core, of course, are the varying sensations of the hour.

The interaction between the different senses is so close that a further word needs to be said about the fact that every sense impression is colored to some degree not only by what is going on in the appropriate sense organ, but by what is going on in the *other* sense organs. Interest in this process is focused on the problem known as the "intersensory effects."[6] This relates to the sensory qualities in any given modality of sense experience which arises from what is going on in response to the stimulation of other sense organs. Thus a light at which we are looking seems brighter when a tuning fork is sounded. A tone sounds louder when a light is flashed. What is happening is that the various channels in the body provided by the nervous system transmit energy from one region to another, and actually intensify the effects in the brain at a point remote from the point at which the primary effect is felt. Whatever you are doing, in fact, is reinforced by other stimuli which are acting upon you.

Long ago the French physiologist Féré called attention to the fact that any stimulus whatever can intensify any activity whatever that happens to be going on at the time. Suppose you are writing a letter and someone turns on the radio. Perhaps you bear down harder; perhaps you write faster; perhaps you merely fidget more vigorously. But energy fed into the bodily system has to produce a result. As you walk along the street, a whistle blows, or a child starts to cry; you may walk at a brisker pace,

---

[6] G. M. Gilbert, Intersensory facilitation and inhibition, *J. gen. Psychol.*, 1941, 24, 381–407.

tread more heavily. For this reason the intensity of any response is in some degree determined by the entire energy level of the living system, and not simply by the energy which is coming in from a given receptor at a given time. (This may remind you of the distraction experiments, page 142.)

We may now summarize the material developed in these four chapters on the process of perceiving. First, there must always be excitation of a receptor or group of receptors, the thresholds of which are low enough to permit their response and the delivery of energies along the incoming nerve pathways until the brain is reached. Second, a specific quality, whether of color or tone or touch or pain, etc., has to be experienced; this seems to be an attribute depending upon the specific region excited, the *specific energy* of that part of the cortex. Third, there are interactions between this incoming energy and various other parts of the brain; and insofar as the brain has been modified by earlier experiences, we should expect to find that the impression is interpreted in the light of past experience. Whether it will be sharply separated from earlier experiences or lost in a blend, whether it will be given accent or emphasis as contrasted with being left in the background, will depend upon our previous experience in dealing with this type of sense impressions in various contexts of experience. Finally, what we are concerned to do, what we are trying to make out of the environment in the service of our needs, will play a very potent role in the structure or organization given to these impressions as they come to us; we will draw on one rather than another type of earlier experience to serve as context depending upon our present concern with the stimulus. A dinner bell may be just a quaint, interesting old trophy at a country hotel unless it is an hour past dinner time and we are ravenously hungry, in which case the sound of the bell is almost music in our ears.

The idea of perception which we develop in consequence of this emphasis is very different from that in which we regard perception as a sort of photographic registration of the environment upon ourselves. In some high-school textbooks of physics, for example, we might almost get the idea that in seeing and hearing we simply register the sights and sounds around us. The physics in the situation is important, but there is enormously more. Experience is important; motivation is important; the life history which has given shape to experience and to motive is important; and therefore individuality in perception, or variation from person to person, is everywhere evident. There is a very large place for human individuality not just in the matter of sensitiveness of the receptors, but in terms of degree of maturity, degree of experience, and past and present motives acting to give structure to the sense impressions.

This conception of individuality in perceiving is well brought out in the psychological test methods in which a person shows how quickly or how easily he can shift from one way of perceiving to another (page 143), or how effective he is in finding in a situation what is concealed there (page 295), or the speed and facility with which he carries out a perceptual learning process or a process of working from the simple to the complex so as to round out and stabilize what he perceives. There are, then, very rich and complex individual differences in perceiving which reflect the structural differences between persons, their differences in maturity, their differences in experience, and their preoccupation with the task at hand.[7]

SUGGESTED READINGS

Andrews, T. G. (ed.), *Methods of Psychology,* New York, Wiley, 1948, chaps. 9–11.

Boring, E. G., *Sensation and Perception in the History of Experimental Psychology,* New York, Appleton-Century, 1942, chaps. 12–13.

Jenkins, W. L., A critical examination of Nafe's theory of thermal sensitivity, *Amer. J. Psychol.,* 1938, *51,* 424–429.

Morgan, C. T., and Stellar, E., *Physiological Psychology,* New York, McGraw-Hill, 2nd ed., 1950, chap. 11.

Murchison, C. A. (ed.), *A Handbook of General Experimental Psychology,* Worcester, Clark Univ. Press, 1934, chap. 20.

Woodworth, R. S., *Experimental Psychology,* New York, Holt, 1938, chap. 13.

---

[7] Perception has been discussed on the assumption that the process begins with the action of physical energies upon the sense organs. There is, however, a considerable body of experimental work requiring the subject to name materials which are in opaque containers a great distance away. The results, which show correct responses far in excess of chance expectations, have led some psychologists, including the present author, to conclude that "extrasensory" perception—i.e., perception not involving physical action on the sense organs—does actually occur. These results are not at present widely accepted as material for psychology, but the necessity of full investigation seems clear cut. The interested reader is referred to J. G. Pratt, J. B. Rhine, B. M. Smith, C. E. Stuart, and J. A. Greenwood, *Extra-Sensory Perception After 60 Years,* New York, Holt, 1940; Gardner Murphy, "Parapsychology," in P. L. Harriman (ed.), *Encyclopedia of Psychology,* New York, Philosophical Library, 1946.

14 LEARNING

Everything we are and everything we do is a product of our original make-up molded through a long process of interaction with our environment. Some of our interactions with food, water, oxygen, and physical injury are matters of physics or chemistry, and not strictly subject matter for psychology; but almost all those interactions which represent our struggle to make contact with our environment and bend it to our needs, our efforts to get the greatest satisfaction from the world and avoid being hurt in the process, are psychological, and come under the head of the *process of learning*.

When psychologists discuss learning, they do not mean simply sitting at a desk and committing things to memory. The term learning covers every modification of behavior to meet environmental requirements, from picking up simple habits like nodding to mean "yes," through the acquisition of complex skills like skating, up to the most intricate development of personal philosophies of life. It is through learning that one molds the raw stuff of human nature into the concrete individuality which one possesses.

The cues to this learning process are largely in the problem of need, that is, in problems of general or local tension whether arising from inner wants or from pressures applied to us from outside (page 67). No matter how the tension or imbalance arises, the infant begins his learning by making *restless movements*. In the course of time, some of these bring him into contact with food, or water, or warm embrace, which offers a satisfying way out of his distress. In subsequent states of distress, his restless movements lead a little more quickly to the goal. As needs recur, he tends to do those things which relieved tension at an earlier time. Nearly all studies of learning indicate rapid progress at first in the elimination of false starts or errors, and then, as less and less remains to be done, smaller units of progress per unit of time spent. Finally the smooth-flowing operation of the newly acquired habit yields about the quickest and easiest adjustment that can be made whenever a potential satisfier lies within reach.

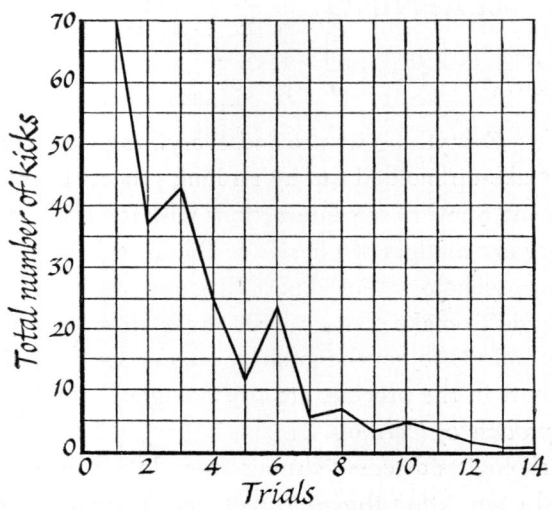

Figure 42. Elimination of Useless Movements

With more and more learning, fewer and fewer useless movements are made. The curve shows the number of times an infant kicked his legs in trying to grasp a rattle in fourteen successive trials. (From M. W. Curti, *Child Psychology*, Longmans, Green and Company.)

Figure 42 shows the elimination of one kind of useless movement. If instead of concentrating on only one kind of restless movement like kicking, we noticed also the thrashing and squirming, the contortions of the neck, the whole display of physical energy, we would see that all the processes which get the individual nowhere toward his goal tend to disappear as the learning process goes on. Kicking is only one example of "random activity." Random activity declines as the individual concentrates his energies more and more on the specific movements—in this case the appropriate movements of the arm—which finally receive prac-

Learning to write typifies the process by which many complex skills are acquired. The young child who is learning to write is clumsy and awkward. His movements are erratic and accompanied by a good deal of muscular tension, as is evident from the great pressure exerted on the pencil. In the older child, writing becomes smoother and more coördinated, but it is still accompanied by undue tension. The boy grasps the paper hard with his left hand and gives close attention to the form and quality of each line. At the adult level, coördination is smooth and unbroken. Writing as a task has become secondary to the content, and motor tension is at a minimum.

Figure 43. Learning to Write

tically all the energy which is used, as he carries out that particular act which has proved fruitful in adapting to the environment. General tension is reduced.

The small child learning to write must bear down hard on the paper, roll his eyes and perhaps his tongue across the page, twisting his neck and fidgeting, as energy goes into almost every part of his body. As he masters the art, less and less "wasted motion" occurs. Finally, in the adult, energy distribution and movements involved in writing have become very specific. (See Figure 43.) Mowrer tells how his small son asked to be picked up at first by extending both arms; later simply raising them slightly; later still, lifting one hand (as long as the adult world did what he wanted); finally, making a well-aimed gesture with one finger. One of the earliest careful records of child behavior shows how habit was established by hitting upon a specific act which brought the desired results; and how a child's voice and gestures came to be used, at eleven months, as an effective way of controlling the big world of people around her:

> For her own speech, the small set of spoken words she owned was of little use; indeed, as I have said, these were only exclamations. For talking to us she used a wonderfully vivid and delicate language of grunts, and cries, and movements. She would point to her father's hat, and beg till it was given her; then creep to him and offer the hat, looking urgently into his face, or perhaps would get to her feet at his side and try to put it on his head; when he put it on, up would go her little arms with pleading cries till he took her, and then she would point to the door and coax to be carried outdoors. She would offer a handkerchief with asking sounds when she wished to play peekaboo; or a whistle, to be blown; or a top, to be spun. When she was carried about the garden or taken driving, or when she crept exploring and investigating about the rooms, she would keep up a most dramatic running comment of interest, joy, inquiry, amusement, desire; and it was remarkable what shades of approval and disapproval, assent, denial, and request she could make perfectly clear.[1]

Sooner or later the responses which thus serve the need are fixated, and the behavior can be said to be learned. This does not mean, of course, that restlessness will not recur. But it does mean that when it recurs, one finds one's way more quickly to the source of satisfaction. The process of learning may be conceived in the first instance essentially in terms of the reduction of tensions; learning is an acquired tension-reduction process. This is at least an important part of the total process.

It is easy to demonstrate experimentally that this sort of thing occurs in the young adult, such as the college student, who is assigned a series of difficult learning problems of various sorts when he takes a course in

---

[1] M. W. Shinn, *The Biography of a Baby*, Boston, Houghton Mifflin, 1900, p. 237.

experimental psychology. Take for instance the mirror-drawing task (Figure 44). To draw correctly when everything is upside down, or backside to, is so bewildering a task, with the good old reliable eyes and muscles misleading us so badly at every turn, that it is almost hopeless, and such thinking as we do is likely to be ineffective; so we have essentially the same kind of blind trial-and-error activity that a child has in finding how to control buttons, or stockings, or kiddie cars, and to get the results he wants from the people around him. We must be able to keep in mind that we should substitute left for right, or up for down. But keeping it all in mind is quite a different matter from actually executing new movements which are appropriate. Figure 44C shows typical errors in the course of learning. These curves indicate what typically happens as trials continue.

Another experiment that is rather similar is the maze-learning experiment (learning the shortest way through a maze or labyrinth), in which there is a gradual reduction of errors until a smooth performance appears. The human adult learns this kind of complex motor task just about as animals do (though rats are a shade better at it, on the average, than students), and it is legitimate to speak of a "generalized form of the curve of learning"—at least for this kind of learning. The important facts are that (1) what is relevant to the satisfaction of a need is fixated; (2) the rest is eliminated; (3) progress, at least in this kind of learning, is gradual, not made all at once.

The Simplest Types of Learning

Our first approach has emphasized the reduction of random movement and false starts. But the process of learning involves much more. If you look at the various situations in which the process of learning occurs—you learn to sing, to ski, to debate, to get along with people—you find a wealth of scattered materials that have to be integrated if you want to understand the basic processes that are going on. It may be worth while to look first at some of the very simplest types of learning, to see just what happens, and then consider some of the more complex types in the light thrown upon them by the simpler ones.

We might begin with those instances in which a drive leads to diffuse behavior that can be satisfied by a wide variety of things. Children all

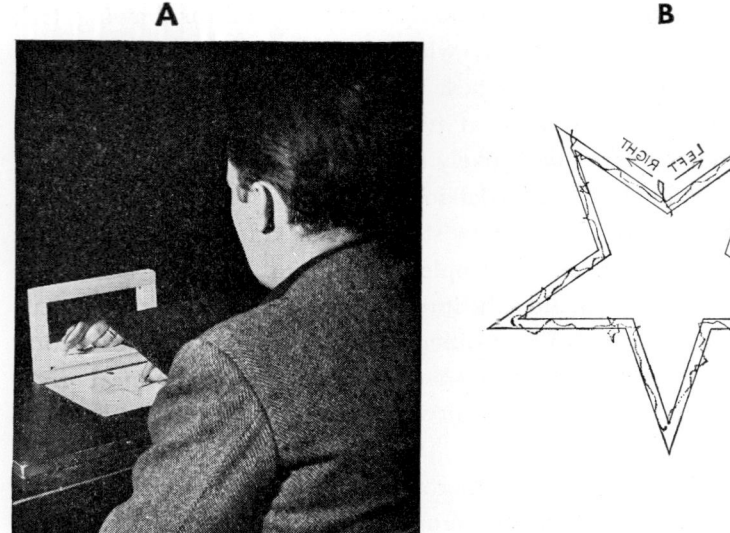

over the world are hungry; in some places they are given rice, in some places bananas, in some places strained carrots, in some seal blubber or candle grease. Their hunger is satisfied; their hunger tensions cease. Day after day, week after week, they come to *expect* this kind of food when hungry. After a while this becomes the normal way of satisfying hunger. If now they are offered a different kind of food—if, for example, the carrot-eating child is offered candle grease—it is spewed out. Candle grease is a perfectly good food for Eskimo children, who are used to it, but it does not fit the style or pattern laid down among ourselves. It is a strange, unacceptable, nonsatisfying food. This is not, however, because children are born with a need for a particular kind of food and an instinctive rejection of other kinds of food; you can actually watch the habituation taking place along different lines in different cultural groups. In instances of this sort, we are dealing not with the building up of some arbitrary motor response of the individual like teaching a child to grasp a bottle or teaching a seal to balance a ball on the tip of its nose; rather, we are dealing directly with actual satisfiers of needs, which have proved to be very good satisfiers on the basis of actual experience with them as the means by which satisfaction has been brought about. We satisfy the drive in one way rather than in another, and in time it becomes the

LEARNING

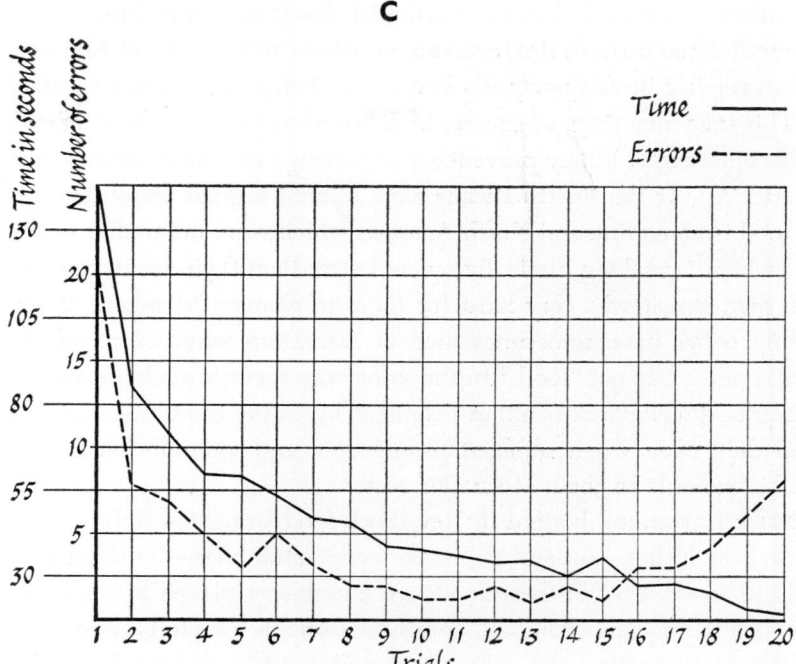

Figure 44. Mirror Drawing

A. The subject must trace the outline of a star as he sees it in the mirror. This means that not only the star but the hand and its motions are reversed. He must not cross the edges of the outline. Each complete tracing constitutes a trial and is timed.

B. A sample first trial. The difficulty of this task is shown by the number of times the edges are crossed; each such crossing is counted as an error.

C. These two curves, which consist of points that represent time and error in each of twenty trials, show that the task is learned gradually. In the later trials the subject's speed and accuracy are greatly improved. The slight rise in the number of errors reveals that toward the end he sacrificed accuracy for speed.

familiar, the right, and the normal way of satisfying that particular drive.

This process is sometimes called canalization, or channeling. The term was coined by the French psychiatrist, Pierre Janet. Just as, after a rain, the water on a hillside comes tumbling down in a million little brooks and rivulets which feed into larger brooks, and finally into rivers which pour into the sea, so the hunger impulses of the individual, which are at first diffuse—ready to turn to this or that or the other food—become canalized or channeled in one particular direction. When hunger arises, the individual turns to rice, or strained carrots, or bananas, or blubber, or whatever has been specifically learned as being the hunger satisfier.

This tendency may, of course, be labor-saving and efficient, or, when it becomes rigid, it may prevent a great many new satisfactions. During World War II the Puerto Ricans were offered a great many new types of food from continental North America which were unfamiliar to them, but which (speaking dietically) were better than their accustomed codfish diet. But it was very hard for them to change. Members of meat-eating tribes have sometimes died of starvation while surrounded by grain; grain was not "food." In the same way surveys made in American urban centers have shown that people go on eating the traditional American diet, even when superior protein-rich and vitamin-rich diets are made available to them at smaller cost.

Mary Lukomnik[2] bought in New York food stores ten different foods with which her student subjects were unfamiliar—"outlandish" or "goofy" foods. Five of these foods were regularly placed in small quantities on the subjects' tongues, and these came in time to be preferred to the "control" foods used only occasionally. When three subjects came to the experiment after a 24-hour fast, they showed this effect much more strikingly; they rapidly developed a preference for the foods given them frequently. P. T. Young[3] in the midst of a long series of food-preference studies finds familiarity a significant factor.

Most types of learning, however, involve, in addition to canalization, a certain amount of substitution of new stimuli which are not in themselves satisfiers of drives. Instead of directly satisfying your drive, you come to respond to a signal which is not in itself a satisfier of a drive, but which *stands for* or *represents* something which could satisfy the drive. The dinner bell, or the mention of pie, may make your mouth water. Animals as well as people learn in this way. Thus as his master's footsteps come across the floor at the regular feeding time, the dog pricks up his ears and begins to salivate. There is nothing about the footsteps or the dinner bell which in themselves satisfy hunger in the way

---

[2] M. Lukomnik, An Experiment to Test the Canalization Hypothesis, Master's Essay in Columbia University Library, 1940.

[3] P. T. Young, Studies of food preference, appetite and dietary habit. VI. Habit, palatability and diet as factors regulating the selection of food by the rat, *J. comp. Psychol.*, 1946, 39, 139–176.

the carrots or the rice can satisfy hunger. Response to the dinner bell and the sound of the footsteps is not canalization; these are not in themselves drive-satisfying things. But they are *signals* which, so to speak, get us ready for drive satisfaction.

A great deal of research has been done on this kind of learning, notably by the Russian physiologist Pavlov, who emphasized that if salivation occurs in response to food, it will also begin to occur in response to stimuli which precede or accompany food. He called these responses to signals, or to substitute stimuli standing for them, "conditioned responses." So important is this principle that some psychologists regard the process of conditioning, or the formation of conditioned responses, as the clue to all learning. Even the most complex ways of adapting ourselves to the environment might turn out upon analysis to be ways of responding to signals which prepare us specifically for a situation that will put an end to our tension. The stimulus which arouses the response prior to all learning is called the *unconditioned* stimulus (or the original stimulus); the one which owes its effectiveness to the fact that it has been presented with (or shortly before) the unconditioned stimulus is called the *conditioned stimulus.*

Even in the first two weeks of life the child establishes clear-cut conditioned responses to his food. He makes himself ready for the arrival of the mother, or he responds to the "get ready for feeding" signal as if the food were already at hand, as Marquis[4] demonstrated experimentally. Children a few months older, whose foreheads were touched when candy was placed in the mouth, soon opened the mouth as soon as the touch on the forehead was felt.[5] When such conditioned responses have been firmly established, they become rather stable, and we can count upon a ready and full response whenever the substitute stimulus, or "conditioned stimulus," is given. But when the conditioned stimulus is no longer attended or followed by the stimulus which brings satisfaction (e.g., when the signal for milk is not actually attended or followed by milk), the conditioned response begins to weaken or fail, and finally dies out. It is then said to be *extinguished.* It can be built up again, or *reinforced,* by again using the unconditioned stimulus along with the

---

[4] D. P. Marquis, Can conditioned responses be established in the newborn infant? *J. genet. Psychol.*, 1931, 39, 479–490.
[5] F. Mateer, *Child Behavior*, Boston, Houghton Mifflin, 1918.

conditioned stimulus; indeed, if it has been lost, it can usually be brought back by reinforcement more quickly than it was initiated in the first place. Often a conditioned response which has disappeared on an earlier occasion may reappear—*spontaneous recovery*—but as a rule such recovery is undependable. Moreover, the word "spontaneous" leaves the question open as to what is going on inside the body, or acting upon it, which brings into fresh expression a response that has dropped out of sight.

If a habit based upon a conditioned response is to be given any real life and endurance in human experience, if it is to be given any stable and important place in the system of habits which make up our daily round of activity—if it is, in short, to be built into our personalities—*it must be reinforced* from time to time. One cannot live forever on the basis of a habit once built up by conditioning, without further reinforcement. This is the same as saying that if a signal standing for some satisfaction situation ceases really to stand for that satisfaction, the signal loses its power.

A conspicuous feature of conditioning is the range of individual differences; often some subjects take more than twice as many trials to establish a conditioned response as others do. As we have seen, an important factor is *set* (page 69); but these individual differences appear to depend also on constitutional factors, such as sheer adequacy of the nervous system to form connections, and doubtless upon other physiological factors. Figure 45, from Campbell and Hilgard,[6] shows the typical wide variation from subject to subject in the number of trials needed to build up a conditioned eyelid response to light—how quickly some condition as compared to others. The original stimulus was a puff of air to the eye, followed by a light in 0.4 second. The criterion of successful achievement of conditioning was five consecutive movements of the lid in response to the "light" (before the puff).

Competition Between Responses

Frequently a pair or a group of conditioned responses, all well established, may interfere with one another, in the sense that the

---

[6] A. A. Campbell and E. R. Hilgard, Individual differences in ease of conditioning, *J. exp. Psychol.*, 1936, *19*, 561–571.

LEARNING

act of making one of the responses makes it impossible to carry out the other response at the same time. One cannot at the same time do two or more contrary things all of which have been learned. If you have learned to enjoy being "kidded" but to get tough when "insulted," and

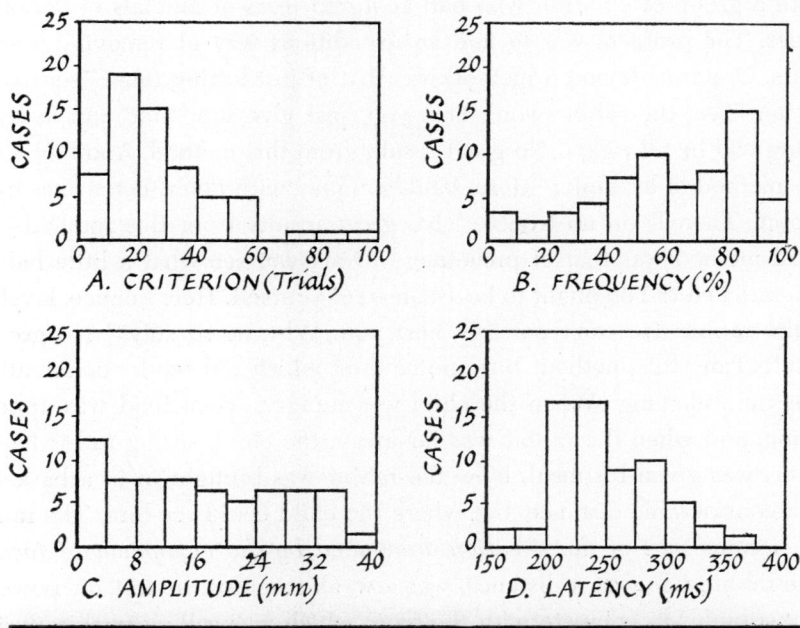

Figure 45. Individual Differences in the Ease of Conditioning

In this conditioning experiment, an attempt was made to condition the eyelid response of 63 subjects. A puff of air (the unconditioned stimulus) was followed in 0.4 second by a light (the conditioned stimulus). Individual differences in the ease of conditioning become apparent when we note, in A, that most of the subjects required less than 40 trials but that some were not conditioned after 70 or more trials. Individual differences are also revealed in B, the distribution of frequency of response (in percent); in C, amplitude of the responses (in millimeters); and in D, promptness of response (latency, in milliseconds). (From A. A. Campbell and E. R. Hilgard, J. exp. Psychol., 1936, 19, 565.)

you now encounter some rather acid remarks from a friend of yours, you are receiving both signals at once, but you cannot be amused and furious at the same time. One bright morning when feeling good you handle the situation well; at another time, perhaps when feeling sour, you blow up. But you do not show both of these responses at once. Attempts have been made to define what kinds of responses have the "right of way," to determine what kinds of responses are "dominant" over other responses in cases of competition between incompatible ways of behaving.

Such a conflict between conditioned responses was studied in an experiment by M. C. Jones[7] on the elimination of children's fears. She dealt with a group of children who had acquired fears of animals of various types. The problem was to find an expeditious way of removing these fears. One time-honored method was that of just letting them "get used to it": "See, the rabbit won't hurt you, just give him time and everything will be all right." No great results from this method. Another was the method of example: "Here, Paul, you play with Peter. Peter likes the rabbit. There'll be no trouble." No great results from this method. A third method was that of preaching: "Don't you see what a little baby you are, Peter? You ought to be ashamed of yourself. Here's a nice, lovely white rabbit. He can't possibly hurt you. Why be so silly?" No great results from this method. But one method which did work consistently was the following: When the child was hungry, when food was appetizing, and when the rabbit was far away, the child, sitting in his high chair, was given his meal. Now the rabbit was brought in in a basket, at a considerable distance, but where the child could see him. The rabbit became *part of the situation dominated by the enjoyment of food*. The rabbit, being at a distance, was a weak stimulus; he lost his power as a stimulus to compete with the food, which was calling forth a positive happy total response, and he became an aspect of this happy situation.

In Figure 46 two opposed responses, fear of the rabbit and enjoyment of the food, are indicated as possible when S_2, sight of the rabbit, occurs. If the food is appetizing, the child hungry, and the rabbit far away, a positive response to food can carry over to the rabbit. In other words, we succeed in eliminating the fear response. If fear gets stronger than joy, it may come back. Indeed, after the child had begun to get rid of his fear, the rabbit one day bit him, and the whole process had to be started over again.

Moreover, if we make the least mistake by having the child not hun-

---

[7] M. C. Jones, The elimination of children's fears, *J. exp. Psychol.*, 1924, *7*, 382–390; see also A laboratory study of fear: the case of Peter, *Ped. Sem.*, 1924, *31*, 308–315.

gry, or the food not appetizing, or the rabbit too close, then the fear response may dominate over the joy response, and the child actually come to *fear his food* and to fear the entire situation. In general, this principle by which, during conditions of competition between incompatible responses, one of them wins the right of way and annihilates the other, may be called the principle of dominance. Of course the question of

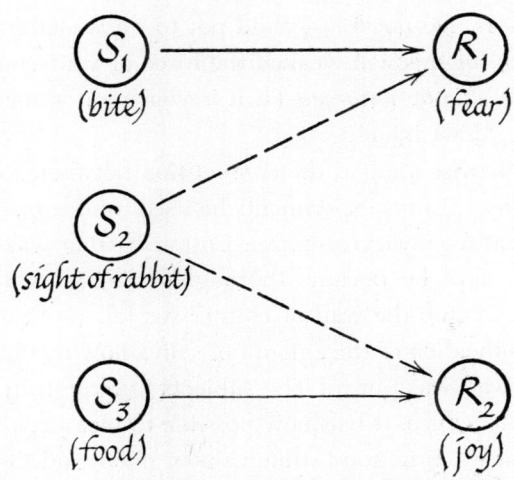

Figure 46. Competing Responses to the Same Stimulus

A child who had been bitten by a rabbit developed a fear of rabbits (S_1 and R_1). An effort was made to eliminate this fear response by a reconditioning procedure, in which the sight of the rabbit (S_2) was consistently made part of a situation in which the child was enjoying food. Thus another response to the sight of the rabbit—joy (R_2)—became possible, but it and the fear response (R_1) could not both appear at the same time. The fact that the child intensely enjoyed his food and that the rabbit was at a safe distance eventually permitted the joy response to become dominant.

what is dominant is a question of fact, not of theory. *The principle simply states that not compromise but victory of one response over the other is the rule.*

In using the principle of dominance in order to win the battle against a habit, it is of the utmost importance to "load the dice in our favor" by making sure that the desired response is stronger at a critical moment than the response we wish to eliminate. A very common mistake is to ask a friend to make a good resolution (in relation to a habit he wants to drop) just before an occasion when we know he will be very strongly tempted to break it. The result is likely to be a head-on collision between the "good resolution" and the habit just at the time when the habit is at its strongest. It is much better to let the habit training begin with a success by making the resolution strong at a time when the opposition to it is not likely to be able to compete successfully with it, keep the factors supporting the new habit strong enough to win, and gain strength by repeated successes. Do not tell a child not to do something which you know he will do, for this will weaken the force of your command. Wait till the command *can be enforced* (if it is worth enforcing); if it is not worth enforcing, don't issue it.

Razran[8] has likewise studied the competition between food responses and other responses. In his experiments he used mint drops and pretzels as stimuli to elicit a salivary response. Cotton batting was put into the subject's mouth until he became thoroughly familiar with the whole process. Once a minute the wad of cotton was taken out and weighed, thus giving an indication of the amount of saliva flowing during the minute, and a new wad was put in. The subjects became fully accustomed to this routine procedure. It was now possible to measure the amount of normal salivation when no food stimulus was given, and the individual's characteristic amount of increased salivation when the mint drop or pretzel was given. The experimenter then began to use other signals which regularly meant that the mint drop or pretzel was coming; colored papers, metronome ticks, nonsense syllables were presented in such regular fashion, along with the food, that the subjects developed a clear salivary response to each such conditioned stimulus. Now, however, interesting individual differences began to appear. In a group of subjects, a few showed consistent and regular increase in salivation whenever the metronome ticks or other signals were given; they were getting ready for the food. Other subjects never did condition. Still others, paradoxically, conditioned "in the wrong direction"; that is, they actually showed significantly less salivation when the signals were given than before. An experimental situation like that faced by Razran's subjects is shown in Figure 47.

---

[8] G. Razran, Attitudinal control of human conditioning, *J. Psychol.*, 1936, 2, 327–337.

Perhaps this result is really not such a paradox. We might remind ourselves that in everyday life we exhibit a bundle of conditioned responses which are likely to get in each other's way, so that some of them, though well learned, cannot function. Sometimes we are ready to go along with

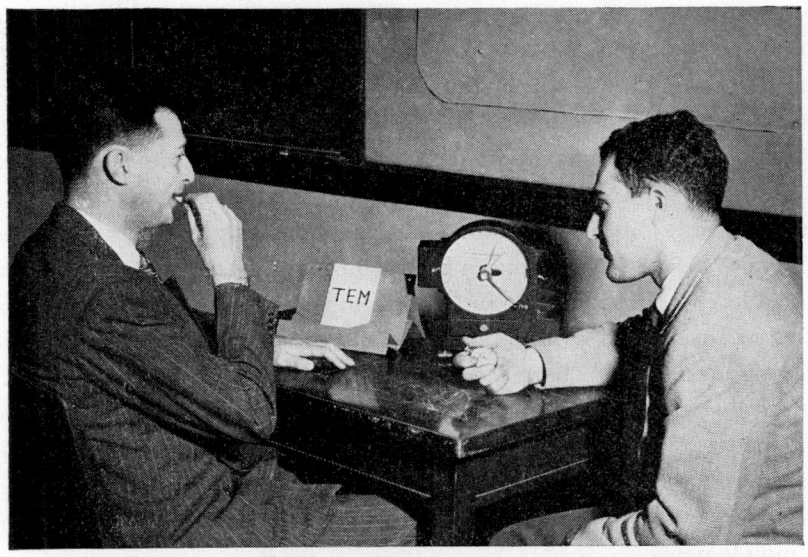

Figure 47. Salivary Conditioning in Human Subjects

An attempt to condition the salivary response to a nonsense syllable, TEM. In a preconditioning series only the nonsense syllable was presented to the subject at regular intervals. In the conditioning series shown here, the subject is placing a mint on his tongue (unconditioned stimulus), after being presented with the nonsense syllable (conditioned stimulus). The nonsense syllable and mint were presented a number of times in this order and following each other at a constant interval. The amount of salivation before and after the conditioning series was measured by weighing rolls of cotton that had been inserted in the subject's mouth. If the amount of salivation following presentation of the nonsense syllable is significantly greater after the conditioning series than before, we may conclude that conditioning has occurred.

other people's expectations, but sometimes we resist; and even a well-organized habit may fail to appear if other people are expecting us to go through our accustomed paces. This is probably because another conditioned response, a hesitant or challenging set of the body, had the right of way. Some of Razran's subjects may have resisted the response which the experimenter was trying to build up, so that conditioning did not occur. They may have had a sort of "so what?" attitude toward the experiment, not being interested in developing conditioned responses to mint and pretzels in this highly artificial situation in which perhaps the role of guinea pig meant little to them. The third group of subjects, who did condition but conditioned in the wrong direction, may have been more explicitly defiant. They may really have felt, "Why should I condition for you?" Hostility could actually mean, in relation to the signal, that there would be less salivation than usual. (There are several physiological possibilities as to how defiance could dry up the mouth.)

These interpretations are tentative; but Razran's experiments suggest, as do those of M. C. Jones, that when the usual stimuli for competing (incompatible) lines of conduct are simultaneously presented, the result is not fusion or compromise between the responses, but the obliteration of one response and the full appearance of the other. There are real cases of fusion and compromise *at a more complex level of response* (compare page 128); here the problem is what happens to *simple elementary conditioned responses* when they cannot all occur at once. The evidence suggests (though it is too meager to prove it conclusively) that the typical result is the triumph of one and the obliteration of the other responses, rather than chaos, compromise, or fusion among the competing elements.

The reader may now glance back at the opening paragraphs of this chapter and compare the issues raised there with the experiments offered by students of the conditioned response. Conditioning is certainly learning, but it seems very different from our first examples. In the typical learning situation of a very simple sort, you have a motivated individual more or less free to move and to act in a situation which is blind to him, who after a great deal of groping and fumbling manages to come upon the tension-reducing stimulus or goal object. As he encounters this general kind of situation on repeated occasions, he does less fumbling, eliminates more errors, and gets more quickly to his goal. The learning process involves a relation between his methods and his motives, his means and his ends. In relation to learning of this sort, the conditioned response formula and the canalization formula seem to leave out part of the problem, because in the case of both conditioning and canalization the organism stays put and *we bring the goal object to it*. We put chocolate drops in the child's mouth as we touch his forehead; we do not let him hunt for the chocolate. The conditioned response and all similar elementary clues may indeed be very helpful in showing how connections are formed between responses to goal objects and responses to other things in the environment; but somehow the struggling individual, groping blindly about the world, unsatisfied and seeking a way, is left out. This is by no means necessarily a disadvantage in the simpler formulas, for they may do their job quite well; but the fact is that only a part, not the whole, of the learning process, or the situation of the learning individual, is described when conditioning itself is described. The course of wisdom would seem to be to understand conditioning (and canalization) as well as we can, but also to grasp the larger context in which these processes occur.

Another part of the larger picture which has to be brought in is the fact that the individual is really always subject to a variety of drives (page 83). It is not a "useful abstraction," but a distortion of reality, to speak of him as if a single drive were the thing operative in the learning process. Moreover, there is a variety of things which the organism can do; even if we build an apparatus which severely restricts what he can do, he will bump, pull, scrape, turn, scratch himself, and he may do all sorts of things that are not foreseen by the experimenter. The whole question is what it is that we want to understand. If we want to understand the ideally simple behavior of an animal learning an ideally simple response to an ideally simple drive situation, it is not hard to set up laboratory experiments which will provide the information. They have, in fact, very definite advantages. But the case could be argued with reasonable plausibility that at the level of organisms which have nervous systems—and these are the ones we are chiefly interested in—the typical, the normal, the basic situation is one of interaction between many components, with struggle, confusion, and uncertainty, with multiplicity of drives as well as multiplicity of situations, all of which invite and at the same time threaten the individual. These are the things that characterize the core of the learning situation. At least it is more characteristic to have a free-roaming individual who is subject to many drives, and able in some degree to select from a variety of competing satisfactions, or of means of escape from dangers and threats, and able to continue in pursuit of his ends by virtue of his own activity.

Investigators who prefer to look upon learning in this way often use what we might call "problem" situations. We have already mentioned

Figure 48. A Stylus Maze

A stylus maze used with human subjects. The maze consists of a series of grooves to be traced with a metal stylus; the subject is prevented from seeing the pattern of the maze by a screen. He begins at the entry, which is nearest him, and traces his way to one of the two goals in this maze. The experimenter notes the number of errors (blind alleys entered) and the time required for each tracing.

the maze situation (page 209) in which the subject makes one movement after another and, as he eliminates through experience those which get him nowhere, ties together the various appropriate steps in the total response, so that now the series is rapidly run through without mistake. The maze experiment and a great many that are like it stand midway, as far as complexity is concerned, between the simple connection-forming situation which we have in conditioning and the challenging think-it-out kind of situation which we encounter when there is a chance to save time and effort by analyzing the situation and making short cuts. Figure 48 shows a stylus maze of a kind frequently used with human subjects. This intermediate kind of learning illustrates how maze learning allows some activity which goes beyond sheer fumbling or random behavior, as is well brought out in a study by Perrin.[9]

At the completion of the first trial [the subject] had a scheme of the path in mind that he represented [roughly as a rectangle]. He adopted in this trial, and followed consistently throughout the experiment, a working method which he described as that of "conscious trial and error." Each day he attempted to work over in the general direction he knew the path to extend, with the aid of such specific segments as he could retain. He would follow any given path to the end, the "hump." There he might or might not get a cue for the proper turn. . . . If he got it and it turned out to be the correct one, well and good; if not he would work around in a haphazard fashion, and eventually recover his bearings. He made no special attempt to reason out situations or to formulate plans or theories. He did consciously attempt to discriminate and memorize. He thinks he learned the maze, "as a rat learns it—assuming that it is conscious—by trial and error method and an associative memory control."

[This subject] adopted on the start a trial and error method, but with this, in the first trial, and throughout the ensuing trials she assumed a decidedly rational, thinking attitude toward her task. She conceived the idea of exploring one side at a time, but it did not prove to be a successful procedure. The results of [subsequent] trials were general orientation—the general spatial relations were learned first. . . . She was [alert] for familiar passages but she made more elaborate anticipatory judgments and plans—"The next time I reach this corner I am going to turn north and see what happens.". . . At the fourth trial she started out with the general working idea of eliminating useless movements. . . . She thinks about the maze as she learns, in verbal terms, sometimes spoken aloud, such as: "Never went up here so far before; yet, this is O.K., guess I'll try this path today.". . . By trial 16, she believed there were four different paths in the maze; just how much is common route she doesn't know. . . . By trial 28 she is firmly convinced that there is more than one path—stated that she used to come down a long path in the middle of the maze, for the last three or four trials she has been entering it from the right, at a place much lower down than usual—that is the path is perceptibly shorter than it formerly was. Therefore she concluded, there are two ways of getting into it, and therefore two paths in the right part of the maze. She hit upon the

---

[9] A. C. Perrin, An experimental and introspective study of the human learning process in the maze, *Psychol. Monogr.*, 1914, No. 70. The introspective reports refer to trials performed on the modified Hampton Court maze used by Watson and Carr with white rats.

idea of learning one of the paths in the maze and letting the others go. At (the 33rd trial) she has the situation under control—that is she can go through one of her paths without error. At the conclusion of the experiment she had not discovered the nature of the other paths; but technically the maze was learned.

This kind of trial and error, plus tying together the learned elements in the right order, looks at first sight very different indeed from simple conditioning. Yet it is true that these types of learning do all have a good deal in common, and it would be well to note what they have in common before proceeding to still more complex processes. They all show, for example, the phenomenon of reinforcement: satisfaction following an activity appears to make that activity more likely to occur again. There is likewise elimination of those responses which have failed to provide satisfaction. All kinds of learning show the effects of cumulative practice. They are all interfered with when contrary habits are set up. They all disappear when the goal object is removed, so that one goes through the motions without getting the final satisfaction. Let us tentatively conclude that there is a common core of things that appear in all learnings; or perhaps more accurately, that up to the present time, with our limited knowledge of what goes on in the individual, there are certain external signs of the learning process which we can always find if we look closely enough, together with much else that goes on inside about which we are still unaware. We may say that conditioning and canalization involve the general attributes which all learning involves, but that they are relatively simple types of learning and that other more complex types contain, in addition to these simple elements, other more complex aspects. As we go on we shall try to bring out various other complex phases of the learning process which we should not expect to find at the simple level considered so far.

The Acquisition of Skill

We must now take a closer analytical view of the ways in which skill is acquired in meeting some complex demand. A field of research in which a great deal of investigation of the learning process has been carried on is that of spoken and written language, the acquisition of symbols and the capacity to group them together in utterance so as to convey meaning or to give organized coherent response to groups of symbols such as words and numbers uttered or written by other people. Simply because we want to get at the very beginnings of the process of learning a particular skill, we usually use a language response in which the experimental subject has no skill; we use typewriting, telegraphy, or some other manipulation of language symbols as they are first acquired. Here we will take one of the classical studies, the studies made by Bryan and Harter[10] over fifty years ago of the acquisition of the "telegraphic language," and fully confirmed by more recent data.

One of the first things that stands out in the analysis of the process of learning telegraphy is the change in method as the subject proceeds. The task is at first blurred and vague; the subject does not even know how to make good dots and dashes, let alone how to string them together. He learns to make his dots and dashes (just as the beginner, working alone without aid, learns to typewrite by the "hunt-and-peck" method, responding to each separate letter). After a fair degree of skill has been achieved, he finds himself responding to a series of letters functioning as a group. He finds a whole word slipping out through the fingers, so to speak, as a single unit. When this has been achieved with the word, the phrase or even the whole sentence may slip out in the same way. We find that the individual is working at the "word habit" or "phrase habit" or even "sentence habit" stage. This type of progress may be described by saying that he is forming *higher units;* or we may speak of a hierarchy of habits, in which the letters are organized into words, the words into phrases, etc., so that the telegrapher is no longer even aware of the individual letters. The same tendency to pass from letter habits to word habits, word habits to phrase habits, is found also in learning to *receive* telegraphic messages.

If you plot on a learning curve, like that in Figure 49, the progress of the individual over a period of weeks, you find that there are spurts and also periods of relatively little or no learning. The explanation of the resulting flat spaces, or *plateaus,* is often to be found in lack of interest or effort, or in the fact that one has reached as high a performance as he can ever reach unless he improves his basic mode of attack on the task.

---

[10] W. L. Bryan and N. Harter, Studies in the physiology and psychology of the telegraphic language, *Psychol. Rev.,* 1897, *4,* 27–53; 1899, *6,* 346–375.

At the right-hand end of such curves, if sufficiently extended, there is also a flat line of quite another type, beyond which no further gain is made. This is ordinarily called the *physiological limit,* and it represents the maximal achievement of the individual. It must, of course, be agreed that in everyday life most of us reach a "good enough" level of achieve-

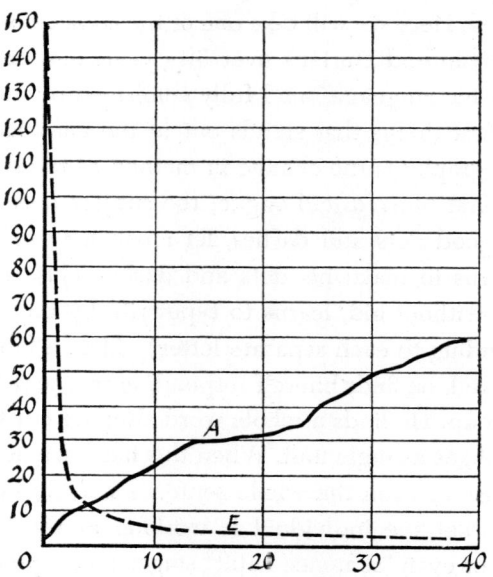

Figure 49. Practice Curve for Telegraphy

Curve A shows the number of letters per minute one man was able to receive during successive trials over a period of weeks. Curve E shows the number of seconds he required to receive five letters. Note the plateau, the flattening out of curve A, between about the fourteenth and the twenty-third week. (After Bryan and Harter, from J. Peterson, J. exp. Psychol., 1917, 2, 217.)

ment which we regard as our physiological limit, but which is really a prolonged plateau from which there is not sufficient motivation for us to lift ourselves. The fact still remains that ultimately a physiological limit is reached.

Despite the fluctuations and variations from person to person, there is a general form of the learning curve and it is of the sort shown in Figures 44C and 49. If you smooth out the irregularities in the curves, you find that the sorts of gain are those which can be explained on the assumption that as you near your limit, it takes more and more effort to make a certain gain. This will give you a curve of "diminishing returns" (mathematically, an exponential curve).

One might perfectly well regard the general curve for learning telegraphy or typing, or any other skill, as actually a composite of several curves in which learning to pick out and integrate the letters and other symbols which are perceived is a somewhat different thing from learning to make appropriate manual movements, and in which there are integrations into higher units from time to time. It has sometimes been argued, therefore, that what seems to be a good simple curve of learning is really the mass result of putting several processes into one curve. We must admit this. At the same time there is some value in noting that most of the curves of learning for different kinds of processes are essentially similar, and that frequently no great damage is done by putting together into one curve these different kinds of learning which go on simultaneously, so as to represent the whole trend of the individual in mastering his task.

At the same time it is fundamental not to overlook a basic distinction between learning when we are set to learn and the everyday process of blundering ahead with no great change from day to day because we are not *set* to learn. We may ignore the possibility that we might learn—or change—or we may actively refuse to learn (cf. also Razran, page 218). Often enough we are "well enough pleased"; and unless the itch to improve gets under our skins, no automatic gain from repetition occurs (in our handwriting, our manners, our viewpoints, or even the skills upon which our business or professional success depends). The sudden shift from *repeating* to really "catching on" is described by Thomas Wolfe in these words:

> He learned to read almost at once, printing the shapes of words immediately with his strong visual memory; but it was weeks later before he learned to write, or even to copy, words. Although he followed accurately all the other instruction of his teacher, he was walled in his ancient unknowing world when they made letters. The children made their sprawling alphabets below a line of models, but all he accomplished was a line of jagged wavering spear-points on his sheet, which he repeated endlessly, and rapturously, unable to see or understand the difference.
> "I have learned to write," he thought.

Then, one day, Max Isaacs looked suddenly, from his exercise, on Eugene's sheet, and saw the jagged line.

"That ain't writin'," said he.

And clubbing his pencil in his warted grimy hand, he scrawled a copy of the exercise across the page.

The line of life, that beautiful developing structure of language that he saw flowing from his comrade's pencil, cut the knot in him that all instruction failed to do, and instantly he seized the pencil, and wrote the words in letters fairer and finer than his friend's. And he turned with a cry in his throat, to the next page, and copied it without hesitation, and the next, the next. They looked at each other a moment with that clear wonder by which children accept miracles, and they never spoke of it again.

"That's writin', now," said Max. But they kept the mystery caged between them.

Eugene thought of this event later; always he could feel the opening gates in him, the plunge of the tide, the escape; . . .[11]

Transfer

The reader will of course note that actually the material to be typed from day to day or the telegraphic message to be transmitted differs somewhat from any which has been received before. Yet somehow the skill acquired is useful in the new cases. An accomplished singer can look at a score never before observed and can go forward into his task, taking into consideration the requirements of expression, the demands of his audience, the limitations of his accompanist, etc. He not only transfers to the new situation what he has learned at an earlier time, but integrates the various activities that are called for in order to sing to the satisfaction of his audience. Indeed, most everyday learning is not recapitulation of steps taken earlier; it involves appropriate transfer of skill to new situations. The man who plays golf well, the man who can think on his feet in making a speech, the man who is handy with tools or with the finesse of social etiquette is a person who is transferring earlier habits to new situations on the basis of analogy. Indeed, if one looks closely, one finds that all learning, whether simple or complex, involves transfer. In simple conditioning the child who has picked up a fear of a furry animal will also show fear of a fur muff or even of a handful of

---

[11] Thomas Wolfe, *Look Homeward, Angel,* New York, Grosset and Dunlap (by special arrangement with Charles Scribner's Sons, c. 1929), pp. 86, 87.

cotton batting. The child who has learned that a certain tone of voice goes with a storm that is brewing in his mother's attitude toward him is plaintive or disturbed when he hears that tone of voice even when new words are uttered, or when some other person's voice uses it.

All learning, as far as we know, is subject to transfer to new situations. One never learns a response which thereafter functions solely in a specific situation. If one acquires a taste for Bach, or for Italian folk songs, a Bach composition which one has never heard before, or a new Italian folk song will bring greater pleasure because of the preparation which has come from earlier experience. The amount of transfer is often considerable, and appreciation may lead on to an appreciation of Mozart, or of folk songs other than the Italian. In the same way, in the learning of means toward ends, as in all the ordinary experiments on the acquisition of skill (page 226), the habits acquired are useful to us even in dealing with material different from that used earlier. Indeed, if this were not so, it would hardly be worth while to acquire skills at all; the typist would, for example, be able to respond only to the specific copy previously learned, and our spoken language would consist simply of the mechanical reiteration of the same words and phrases in relation to stereotyped recurring situations. Indeed, in a sense, the essence of the whole process of learning lies in the flexibility with which the ingrained response may find its place and usefulness in relation to relatively new situations.

This issue as to the degree to which the response to the new is determined strictly by the elements previously learned, and the closely related question how it is that we can ever do something that we have never exactly learned to do before, have occasioned a great deal of discussion in educational circles. We went through a period fifty years ago in which it was presumed necessary to deal with certain formal powers of the mind—giving the student Latin to strengthen the memory, mathematics to make him accurate, economics or philosophy to enable him to think critically, etc. Then experiments by Thorndike and Woodworth, followed by many others confirming their results, indicated that identical elements appearing both in the old and in the new material are indispensable in making transfers from the old to the new. Consequently the new is not really new; the reason why the new attack is effective is because old elements recur. But emphasis began later to be placed upon the fact that there is always fresh *integration,* reorganization, or insight; it was emphasized that a complex fresh situation involves more than the sheer addition of previous elements, without ever a flash of any integrating tendency.

Perhaps these controversies have been necessary, but today it seems that some of the sharpness with which these distinctions were drawn is rather overdone. Growing and learning are processes of gradual, flexible, ever-changing redirection of the living individual, in which the recurrence of absolute identities is necessarily an abstraction. If a dog has learned to salivate at 256 cycles (page 213) and now he hears a tone at 400 cycles, there is transfer, but it is a little hard to put one's finger on the *identical elements* in the tones. Furthermore, as we have seen, there is constantly a leaping together of components previously acquired; the production of higher units involves really a fresh synthesis. The transfer process in everyday life is of this type. This statement applies to the learning not only of skills, of school subjects, of vocational capacities, but also of social habits and personality traits. Habits and traits are plastically redefined from moment to moment, sometimes with a rather small amount of reworking, sometimes with a great deal. If a small child has learned courtesy, or coöperativeness, you expect him to carry over the phrases, not the essential ideas; but as his understanding grows he carries over larger and larger clusters of ideas which are applied in new ways.

There is no sense in denying that transfer is certainly based, at least in part, on sheer similarity or overlap between what has been learned and what now confronts us. The similarity of the new to the old may be of a very simple or of a very complex sort. Razran[12] found, for example, that conditioned responses to patterns of lights might be elicited by patterns which had features in common with those that had been encountered earlier. He also measured the flow of saliva while his subjects ate pretzels, sandwiches, or candy, and as they were eating he flashed on a

---

[12] G. Razran, Studies in configural conditioning, V, Generalization and transposition, *J. genet. Psychol.,* 1940, 56, 3–11.

screen, one at a time, common English words like *dog, flower,* or *sign.*[13] Conditioned salivary responses were then established to these words. Later, he presented to his subjects words which had some features in common with the original words. A word which had some overlap with the original in terms of letters or sounds, like *glower* or *shower* in relation to the original *flower,* produced a considerable salivary response; and overlap or close relation in meaning, like *animal* or *terrier* in relation to *dog,* produced even more. When the new word is very similar in both form and meaning the response is very large; it is over half as much as it is to the original word. Table 8 is of interest in suggesting that we can

TABLE 8. Average of 20 One-Minute Measurements Obtained from Four Subjects

Conditioned Words	Generalization Words	Percent of Specific Generalization
Dog	Animal	22.2
Dog	Bark	56.8
Dog	Cat	38.1
Dog	Terrier	50.3
Dark	Light	40.1
Dark	Mark	36.1
Flower	Glower	35.1
Flower	Pansy	42.2
Flower	Petal	45.1
Flower	Shower	20.2
Sign	Signal	69.2
Sign	Signature	65.1

measure the degree of transfer appearing in given subjects in an involuntary response as a result of a wide variety of different elements and patterns which show overlap between the stimuli used in the first place and those used later. In the same way you solve any problems, impersonal or human, by responding not to a single element but to a pattern that is somewhat similar to a pattern with which you have had experience.

Along with the problem of transfer goes the problem of "negative transfer" or *interference*. The fact that we have learned to do a specific thing in one situation and that now the situation calls for something

---

[13] G. Razran, Semantic and phonetographic generalizations of salivary conditioning to verbal stimuli, *J. exp. Psychol.,* 1949, 39, 642–652.

quite different means that the new response will be hard to make because we are carrying over too much of the old into the new. If we learn, for example, to cancel all the *a*'s or *b*'s in the following,

cxwja	pftrn	hdpfl	rqbst
nfanb	gizfr	zogrn	mltqm
cbcgl	jbnts	zssa	ornfp
taxfr	wafqm	jntmn	zsrqn
jmbnt	tdban	ipond	tngyb

and now the problem is to cancel all the *p*'s and *q*'s, we carry over from the old situation into the new one various habits of response to the *a*'s and *b*'s which interfere with our effective attack upon the *p*'s and *q*'s. Transfer, in other words, is an important clue to interference.

An especially interesting form of interference is known as *retroactive inhibition*. This is the process that appears when something has been learned and another task somewhat similar to it is presented; learning the new makes the earlier material harder to reproduce. We shall come back to this problem in connection with memory (page 264), but it is of interest to see that the basic principles of learning, such as transfer, as they apply to simple conditioned responses, also apply in very complex memory tasks.

The reader will already have noted that a good deal has been said or implied about the process of *organization* as we learn. The role of organization is at times rather small, at times very great. It is perfectly appropriate to emphasize the sheer connection of stimuli in a simple type of conditioning in which dogs salivate in response to tuning forks. It is also important, however, to recognize that there may be interaction among different stimuli. One stimulus may inhibit the action of another (page 262). At times the number of factors to be taken account of in the learning process is very large indeed. We have already seen that the very layout of the sense organs and central nervous system provides us with the capacity to give organization to what is presented to us; while part of our tendency to perceive in terms of patterns depends upon experience, part of it is there from the beginning. Naturally students of learning are interested in the fact that the critical phase in the acquisition of a skill may involve the capacity to pass from a piecemeal to an integrated form of response (as in going from a letter habit to a word habit).

But more is meant here than the assembling of elements into composites which are practiced over and over again, as in the case of letters forming words, and words forming phrases. What is meant is that for the first time in his life the individual encounters several different stimuli which have never been related before and yet he responds in an integrated way to the whole pattern. In the classical and much quoted experiment of Köhler[14] in the Canary Islands, chimpanzees were shown to be capable of grasping complex relations never previously encountered. While chimpanzees, like all other animals, learn to some extent by "fumbling and success," "trial and error," they also learn in a way exemplified by the following observation: One animal had reached through the bars of her cage for a long time with her arm to try to reach a banana which was a few feet away from the cage. She had apparently about given up and turned away toward her blanket which lay in the corner of the cage. Suddenly, in the twinkling of an eye, she grasped the blanket, whisked it out through the bars, flapped it up and down, managing to hit the banana with it and then to rake the banana in with it. Such an instance is frequently called "insight," indicating the capacity to put into fresh relationships matters which were never previously brought into relationship with one another.

The question of interpreting just what is happening will vary from case to case, depending upon the amount of pattern perception the organism has, and the amount of experience it has had from which transfer might be expected. From the present viewpoint there is some primitive perception of form prior to training, which will give a certain amount of integration of elements, or insight; a great deal of further organization is added, however, by the life experience of the individual. In the case of this particular ape it would, for example, be of interest to know the history of her previous use of sticks and tools of all sorts, and to what degree the analogy of raking with a stick and raking with a blanket might have been built up by such experience. Some recent experiments somewhat similar to Köhler's early work have shown that

---

[14] W. Köhler, *The Mentality of Apes*, New York, Harcourt, Brace, 1924.

the animal's life history makes a huge difference in the type and degree of insight shown.[15] This still leaves us, however, with the important fact that such integrated perception does really occur and that frequently there is a sharp break between earlier integrations and newer ones. (Compare also page 297, where the problem of insight is treated in relation to the thought processes.)

The extent of transfer or of interference which will actually appear depends not only upon the maturity and competence of the individual, his capacity to discern and make the most of similarities, but also upon the degree to which transfer serves the achievement of his goal. If he carries over his responses from one situation to another, but immediately fails in the new situation to get the satisfaction which the earlier response brought, the process of transfer will begin to fail (page 213). Transfer may occur the first time, but if not reinforced it may peter out.

Pavlov's laboratory (page 213) investigated this process in the following way: Sound the tuning fork at middle C and give the dog his meat; continue until the salivation response to the tone is well established. Then sound the tuning fork at a higher pitch, but this time withhold the food. The *first* time that this is done there is considerable transfer; salivation occurs after a higher or lower tone as well as after the tone which was used in the original training. But the salivation which occurs the first time when you start to study transfer rapidly disappears in response to these other tones, if not reinforced. Whenever you sound the middle C, you give the food. But when you sound these other higher or lower tones, you withhold the food. A process of differentiation occurs. You can now find out how fine a discrimination can be made by bringing the upper tones slowly down in each new experiment until it is very close to the original tone; but while you reinforce the original tone you do not do so with this tone which is to be differentiated from it. You can find out how close the two tones have to be before failure of discrimination occurs (so that the dog salivates about the same whether he is hearing the original tone or the secondary tone).

In the same way language responses acquired by a great deal of vocalization, trial and error sounds which approximate in greater or

---

[15] H. G. Birch, The relation of previous experience to insightful problem-solving, *J. comp. Psychol.*, 1945, 38, 367–383.

lesser degree those that are made by grownups, serve their role as things to be said when a cat appears. It may be *ca*, or it may be *at*, or it may be *kit*, or *kitty*, or various other things; the important thing is that it be reinforced by bringing smiles or actual contact with the furry animal which is the consummation of the child's drive at the moment. Now along comes a squirrel or a chipmunk or a puppy, and it is greeted by the same verbal response which was made to the cat. We have here a typical instance of transfer. But now the process of differentiation can be studied. The child's response to the puppy as a "kitty" does not bring the familiar and expected results; there may be a little indication that he has made a mistake, that he is doing things in the "wrong" way. Or he may simply be completely misunderstood. In any event, language responses, like other overt responses, are carried over by transfer to new situations insofar as they actually work or serve drives; if they fail to do so, they are dropped out and relatively permanent habits of differentiation are established.

These simple characteristics must not obscure the fact that at the level of mature human learning the problem of transfer involves *active search* for common features (whether simple or complex features) that may make effective transfer possible. Being *set* to find similarities may often be fundamental. In his study of the ability to resist propaganda, W. W. Biddle[16] exposed students to propaganda relating to American interests in the Caribbean. Later he explained how the propaganda had worked. Later still he presented new propaganda, this time relating to American interests in the Pacific. In general, he found that those who detected and resisted the propaganda were those who explicitly recognized the similarity in the material dealing with the Caribbean and with the Pacific and *made their own transfer*. It was not the *amount* of overlap in the material but the *discovery* and utilization of it in the student's thinking that made the difference.

Efficiency in Learning

Humankind long since discovered a very effective way of preventing learning from getting under one's skin or doing much to

---

[16] W. W. Biddle, *Propaganda and Education*, Teach. Coll. Contr. Educ., No. 531, 1932.

change one, and it is still used in many schools and colleges in many parts of the world. It consists of having children, or young adults, chant over and over again the specific phrases or numbers that have been assigned by the teacher, or mechanically go over the phrases which are supposed to give them a key to American history or everyday good citizenship. In the motor sphere it consists of endless duplications of the same process in the naïve hope that practice makes perfect. The common word for it is drill. Even when one wants from one's learner nothing at all but the ability to parrot phrases or to march in goose step, the method is not very effective, because it works against the grain. We begin with this negative instance, so highly wasteful of human energy and ingenuity, so cramping to alert flexible adaptation to the complex problems of living, because it brings out so well all the things that real learning is not.

The first thing that effective learning involves is motivation. The child in the one-room school may or may not want to know the names and dates of all the Presidents. There are two possibilities of getting positive motivation. In an occasional case he may have some political interest. But in the vast number of cases, he simply wishes to avoid being kept after school (or feeling the birch rod). In these latter instances the motivation is "extrinsic." There is no desire to learn; there is only a desire not to be punished. A conditioned response can be established by these means. But, as we have seen, if not reinforced, the response is likely to extinguish. That is one of the reasons why the material driven into the child by drill is quickly lost and why 99 out of 100 people cannot tell you much about the elementary geographical and historical facts they learned in school.

Even more serious is the fact that there is often not even a simple and direct conditioning to tie up the facts in the lesson with the existing motivation. A fear of punishment does not actually glue the attention to the page; at best, it draws it away from the swimming pool and the other positive motivations of the moment. This negative method, relying upon punishment, may draw the child into a region in which something *may* catch his interest, but he is likely to waver or daydream. Only those moments in which there is actual attention to the task can be counted as moments of learning.

How different it all is if one has taken the time and trouble to find out the outlook and interest of the child, or the adolescent, or the college student, and fit the material into it! In the case of the college student one typically must work from large to small, from life outlook to specific detail. Instead of putting a pre-medical or pre-business student through a series of motions in the hope that years later he may find them useful, the modern plan is to take the necessary time and trouble to show the student what his professional life will actually consist of; to proceed then to show him how particular subject matters are related to his work; and to follow through to the specific content of each particular course, so that he may see how each topic is related to the course as a whole, just as the course is related to his professional preparation as a whole. Finally he gets to the point where he grasps that the psychology of learning or the psychology of thinking, quite aside from being of interest in itself, is a phase of the process of being an effective medical or business man, or being a civilized and mature human being, or both.

Individual students, however, differ greatly in their interests and in their rate and form of learning (page 220); and if a particular method does not work in a particular case, the thing for the individual to do, rather than throwing up his hands in despair or resorting to mere drill, is to follow through the necessary steps to see *why*, after all, he is studying a given chapter and what relation it has to his larger goals. If these larger goals or motives are related by one method or another directly or indirectly to a subject matter, it can be effectively learned; otherwise not. Figure 50 shows that sewing-machine operators could learn a task when it was made real to them that they *could* succeed.

Secondly, and in close relation to the problem of motivation, there is the problem of perspective, or the perception of the relation of one step to another. It is easy enough to pick up the separate turns in a maze, but even at the simplest animal level it is necessary then to connect the various turns with each other, so as to be able to run in a rapid orderly fashion through the maze as a whole. As the telegrapher takes in a word with his ears, he is already effectively preparing to take in the next word, and his hands have already been at work transmitting the message received a moment ago. There is overlapping in the sense that as you do anything you are already preparing for the next thing. This is simply part of the larger process of keeping one's perspective in time, and seeing the relation of each step to what follows

In the same way there is the question of a larger context, in grasping the meaning of historical, or scientific, or any other kind of material. One will do well in reading any textbook to spend a half hour or hour getting

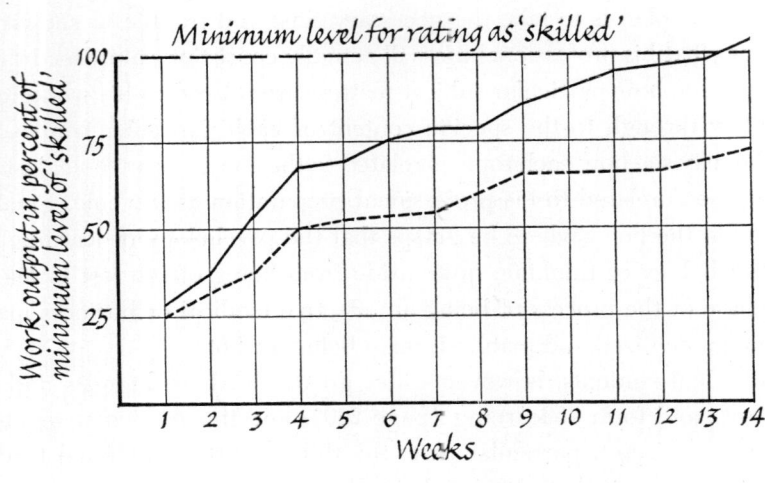

Figure 50. Effect of Motivation on Efficiency

Sewing-machine operators were told that a rating of "skilled" would be assigned when the weekly output reached a certain level. One group was told that they might achieve this rating—the goal became real to them. Another group was not given this encouragement; to them the goal remained unreal. The effect of these two motivating circumstances on efficiency is shown in these two curves. (From A. J. Marrow, in G. Watson (ed.), *Civilian Morale,* Henry Holt and Company, 1942.)

the plan of the subject matter as a whole, in order to see how each chapter fits in. How often the instructor, despite all his efforts, finds the beginning student halfway through a course without having even noted the chapter sequence or the general design of the course as a whole! From this principle follows one very specific principle to be noted again in the chapter on memory, namely, the fact that you will do well when memorizing anything to get the scheme of the thing as a whole and to go through it as a whole, time after time if need be, rather than breaking it into pieces and then trying to fit the pieces together.

A further general rule relates to the general economy of effort as it prevails in all human activities. Don't "kill yourself" trying to learn all the details of a thing at once, but work through it for a reasonable length

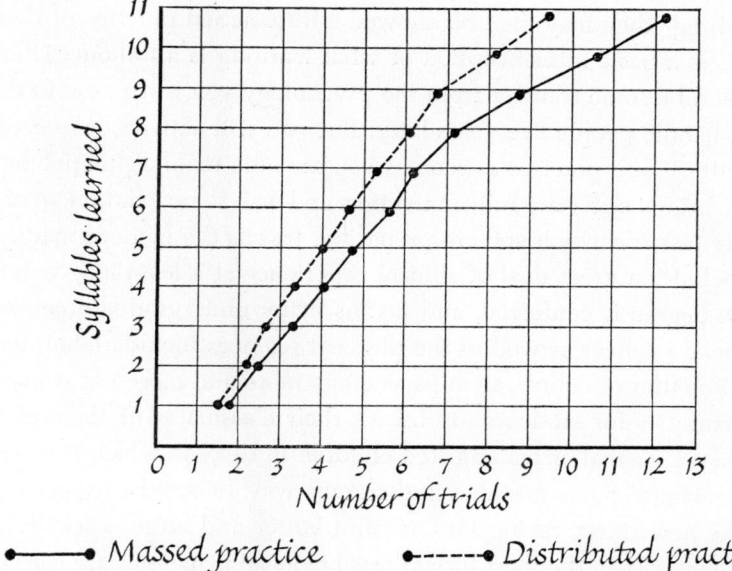

Figure 51. Effect of Distributed Practice

Two groups of subjects learned the same list of nonsense syllables. Distributed practice was used with one group; i.e., a rest period intervened between each trial. Massed practice was used with the other group; i.e., no rest intervals were given. As the curves show, the group using distributed practice learned more syllables more quickly than the group using massed practice. (From C. I. Hovland, J. exp. Psychol., 1939, 25, 625.)

of time, and then on some other occasion, after a rest, work through it as a whole again. This is the principle of "distributed practice," or "spaced repetition," as against massed practice. It applies to motor learning as well as to the memorizing of words, etc. The kind of spacing you need will depend partly on the material, partly on you. Work out your own best method. (See Figure 51.)

Finally, and in many ways most important of all, *put into practice what you learn*. What is learned is of course learned in a particular situation, often a situation in school or laboratory or classroom, or some other situation quite different from that in which the skill will actually be used later. Sometimes it is assumed that there is an almost miraculous capacity to transfer what has been learned in the college library or laboratory to some complex professional or social situation which occurs years later. We tell our students that when they have had years of "sound basic training" they may then be allowed a little actual practice of their skill. This is a basic misconception of what learning is all about. There may indeed be some transfer from the psychology you learn now to the way you handle people five years later. But you will actively learn very much better if you practice as soon as you are able to, and practice in a way that brings out your full motivation and has some relation to the actual life task for which you are preparing. Just as the modern medical school includes a great deal of clinical experience at a level long before the M.D. degree is conferred, and just as many undergraduate courses in the social sciences as well as the physical sciences include laboratory work as a matter of course, so in psychology more and more use is made of opportunities for students to observe their classmates or themselves or to observe normal or maladjusted children in cases in which they can "try their wings," make mistakes in their own way, benefit by experience, and make new starts, taking into account larger and larger varieties of relevant facts. Even the most formal psychological principles are learned better when you constantly apply them. This is true partly because the motivation is greater. Partly it is because what you learn can actually be transferred; you get actual practice in the very process of transferring. Partly it is because you have a chance to learn in the school of experience where the errors and misconceptions lie, and to prune them off and get a fresh start. In all these respects you can be sure that the thing you learn is really the thing you want to learn. At the same time a class project may enable you to gain experience working with other people who are likewise in need of learning the same things, so that learning to adapt yourself to other people, i.e., the social context in which the skill is used, goes hand and hand with learning the skill itself.

So far, we have been thinking of efficiency in learning such things as academic subject matter. We might extend the discussion to efficiency in learning the things that are useful in personal relationships. Why do we not effectively learn to get along with people—and with ourselves—and why do we fail in the simple process of eliminating habits that cause us distress?

In hunting for the answer, let us note that although frequently the responses which are fixated are those that reduce tension, learning does not invariably achieve this result. It might be very convenient if learning *always* involved the satisfaction of our major needs or the reduction of our major tensions. Actually, however, there are countless examples in daily life of the way in which a response may be fixated and continued with tenacity although it fights against our most important needs. Why has the response not been eliminated? Take for example the misery that comes to many people through the endless devices that they use to show off, to gain status, to utilize big words, to tell anecdotes about the celebrities they have met; and in the same category, the various bids for pity, fishing for compliments, etc., which punctuate their everyday conversation; in the course of time all this may become so boring to their listeners that the only result is well-earned scorn. They nevertheless go on with such habits. Why do they?

There are two possible answers. (1) The first is that their need is so intense that they are unaware of the fact that they are not getting the results they want; to some slight degree, each act of showing off, each episode of fishing for compliments, creates in them some slight satisfaction, in the sense that they seem to themselves to be gaining their ends. This would overpower their very vague perception of the blunders they are making. (2) A second possibility is that when sufficiently intense, the tension heightens the response (cf. page 87) and drives it deeper and deeper into us, making us so tense and rigid, so incapable of fresh exploration, that there is literally no other response available to us. In this connection there is an experiment of Hamilton's in which both men and animals were taught to escape from a difficult situation.[17] A small room offered an opportunity for escape through any of four doors. Under normal conditions subjects could quickly learn the right way out; but when the punishment was made severe, so that the tension to escape was terrific, the result was often a blind struggle at the same door over

---

[17] G. V. Hamilton, A study of trial and error reactions in mammals, *J. Animal Behav.*, 1911, *1*, 33–66.

and over again. Or after making a shift from one door to another, the individual went back to the very door which had just been tried and found to be locked. The experiment suggests that when tension reaches a given *level*, reactions are rigidly fixated and incapable of modification. One finds in the behavior of the frightened and confused juvenile delinquent, and in the morbid, repetitious, futile, and stereotyped behaviors of nervous sufferers, many instances which seem to point to the same dynamic principle.

Both of these factors are combined in many of the "bad habits" of normal people. We may actually make ourselves sick when caught in such a vicious circle of tension and futile response. Let us take as an example a rather common pattern of behavior in normal businessmen. Physicians who have had occasion to study these men when they crack up with ulcers or high blood pressure have pointed out that, as a result of business competition and a frantic desire to gain wealth, power, and prestige, these men have developed "maladaptive fixations." One of them develops, for example, a hearty rage with regard to some frustration to which he is subjected, and reacts with a mounting tension. He gets into a situation, however, where no blowing off of steam is really possible. He believes that his competitors are unfair, but he must maintain a poker face and not show how irritated he is. He may get caught in the toils of this circular rage response, and go on steaming and blustering at a higher pitch. On page 56 reference was made to cases of organic evidences of such prolonged tension.

It is usually suggested in such cases that a substitute method of expression be found: for example, learning against what or against whom an aggressive outlet may be found; or better yet, getting so deeply down into the causes of the individual frustrations that one can remove them and thus free himself from the annoyance. In the same way with regard to any of us, there are the two outlets: first, finding a way in which we can hit, and hit hard, without entailing fresh sources of distress, such as feelings of guilt for having reacted unfairly; and second, getting nearer to the core of the matter, finding out why these things frustrate us so much. If there are things that we "just have to have," then failure to get them will automatically involve this kind of damming up; when a broader perspective is found, whether we have to have this rather than something else can be seen in terms of a conception of relative values.

These cases of maladaptive fixation throw light also on a basic *inability to learn* which one often finds in perfectly normal people. They can learn with rapidity and efficiency all sorts of complex problems in history or mathematics; but for such a simple thing as learning to avoid giving offense, learning to avoid putting their foot in it, making themselves ridiculous, or even making themselves sick, they seem to have no capacity. It is hard to learn to look at things in a radically new way, partly because of the effort involved in getting away from the familiar paths of thought and action, and partly because there is so large a possibility that what we should find out about ourselves in the process would not look so good. This inability to learn, or "emotional stupidity" as it has sometimes been called, is in the long run a question of fear of exposure to situations with which we do not want to cope. A good many of the basic maladaptive fixations are due to this bristling up, or fighting back, of the individual against his situation—basically against recognizing that the situation exists. If he perceives the situation in such a way as to make it all rosy, and cannot bear to consider any alternative way of viewing it, he fails to carry out the trial-and-error activity or the fresh reorganization which would make possible the discovery of a real solution.

Often a child in the clinic who has "reading difficulties" is a child with a very bright older brother or sister with whom he simply does not want to compete, and any attempt to read at a level appropriate for his age would occasion too many direct comparisons. It is simpler to get out of the situation and not compete at all: "I just am not a good reader and that's all there is to it. Indeed if I can be a bad enough reader, I may get enough attention, pity, solicitude, to balance in some degree the inadequacy which I feel." In the same way the college student who makes a C− is not really competing with those who make A; there is not much likelihood that his work will be repeatedly and conspicuously compared with that at the top. He can simply take things in his stride from day to day and not be noticed. If he has sneaking suspicions that he *might* be able to make a straight A or even get an occasional A+ on a term paper, he may well be deterred from it by recognizing that what he would actually draw would be only a B−, or at best a B, and here he would be in danger of being compared with someone else who had actually made the A grade. Avoiding competition is a particularly common and effective way of avoiding the process of learning.

It therefore becomes evident in this whole survey of the different types of learning that it is motivation that guides us to the achievement of a goal, and that the means to the goal can never do the job if motivation toward the goal is lacking, or if these forms of response lead to rigid acts which rule out the possibility of flexible adaptation. In other words, even the last-mentioned cases relating to failure to learn show that needs are central to the entire problem of learning. One may consciously be highly motivated to learn, but at the same time put up a good fight against learning, and succeed in the latter struggle better than in the former.

The Theory of Learning

The theory of learning has proved to be both a stumbling block and a major stimulus to progress in experimental psychology. All serious psychologists are concerned with the theory of learning. Many of them do research in this area, and a considerable number have written systematic treatises in which there is an endeavor to bring into orderly form all the basic facts about the ways in which we learn. While it is not possible to do justice to all this material here, it will be worth while to indicate a few of the storm centers of psychological controversy, the types of data upon which theorists rely, and the general trends now prevalent regarding the interpretations of these data.

First, the *facts* upon which all theories must be based relate to *connections formed*. Some of the best connections are those between goals and the means which reach them, so that we learn the means to a given end. Connections are also sometimes formed between things which happen together, as for example between lightning and thunder, though there is no clear-cut *goal* involved. The importance of motivation is clear in most learning, but it is not clear that motivation provides *all* the clues there are.

Moreover, the fact is very evident that there is a relation between the complexity of an organism, particularly the complexity of its nervous system, and the complexity of the things that it can learn. This offers a direct temptation to compare different species of animals. At the same time there is a direct temptation to compare the learning processes of the immature human being with those of the mature one, and to try to define principles of learning which relate to the growth and maturity of the individual as the basis of what it can learn and the way in which it can learn. It is possible, for example, to regard simple connection forming (the lightning-thunder kind of association), or perhaps simple conditioning, as something universal in all members of the animal kingdom, but to say at the same time that certain types of learning, like integration or insight, depend upon achieving a certain level of development. In other words, it does not follow that some one simple formula for learning covers all the facts regardless of the individual that is doing the learning.

Nevertheless, any scientist wants to find a generalization which will embrace as many facts as possible, and we do find in psychology today a tendency to line up on one or the other side in a basic controversy about the nature of learning. We might phrase the matter in this way: There is a basic difference between those whose interpretation of learning is in terms of what the organism can be observed to do, and those whose interpretation is in terms of what is conceived to go on inside the organism as it learns. These two views can be called respectively the peripheral and the central views of the learning process.

Of course this does not mean that those with a peripheral emphasis deny the importance of the man's or animal's insides—for instance, the brain. It means, rather, that they insist that we can actually see the behavior and make some sort of order out of it; that the laws of learning and the curves of learning relate directly to observed facts; that we cannot see the brain processes which occur while learning is going on; and that we might as well not speculate about what we cannot observe. On the other hand, those with a central emphasis are inclined to believe that since all the really important things in learning *do* go on inside, particularly in the individual's set and point of view regarding his situation, the best thing to do is to develop experiments in such a way that they will make a critical decision between one central theory and another. They accept the peripheral facts, but they state that these facts will take a different form in animals with different kinds of brains; that they vary with the maturity, health, and previous activity of the brain; and that it is worth while to do one's theorizing in such a way that it will deal directly with these critical inside events. They look forward to the time when surgery, drugs, and other methods will give us a more direct view of what the brain is doing.

It goes almost without saying that those who emphasize the conditioned response type of learning or the acquisition of very simple skills will prefer the peripheral emphasis, and that those who emphasize new ways of viewing a situation will hence find an important place for factors of interpretation and insight (page 297). A good example of the difference between central and peripheral emphasis is found in the way of explaining the fact that there is a tendency to repeat an act if it reduces a tension—a fact about which there is general agreement. Earlier this was widely known under Thorndike's term, "the law of effect"; today it is common to refer to it as "the law of primary reinforcement." According to this principle, the tension reduction which follows from the interaction of an organism with a goal object—for example, the eating of food—reinforces the behavior that has just been completed and makes the animal more likely to do the thing that brought it into contact with the food. Now this is the last move made by the animal before it reached its goal, or by the child or man as he achieved what he had been struggling to achieve. One tends, ever afterward, to do the thing that brought the reward because of what Thorndike called the "stamping in" effect of the reward upon the organism But the peripheralist in espousing such a view has no use for a subjective term like the "pleasantness" experienced by the organism (and indeed the small child and animal cannot tell us about such "pleasantness"); so he is prone to emphasize the sheer proximity of the goal to the specific activity which brought the organism into contact with it. He states that the tension reduction follows immediately upon contact with the goal, and therefore that the acts which permit such tension reduction are stamped in. He sets up his laws of learning simply in terms of the time-space closeness between these events. The goal is said to have a tension-reducing effect, the effect being considered as far as possible in terms of the vital organs, as shown for example in the hunger contractions. We therefore have relations between drive, activity, and food, and we need not bother particularly with the central nervous system.

On the other hand, from the viewpoint of a central emphasis, we might as well face the fact that the man (and, as far as we know, the animal) is alertly concerned about the things he wants, and learning is a process which goes on as he energetically strives to get them. Learning is a matter of a relation between a goal object perceived and the satisfaction experienced when the act is completed. Or we may go further and say that the object which brings satisfaction *has become for us a different object* after we have had contact with it, and the object which brings distress likewise has a different meaning for us. Suppose that a flickering object appears at a distance, and a small child crawls toward it. He reaches out his hand. The object proves to be a dangling ribbon and he gets a good deal of fun manipulating it and putting it in his mouth. In another situation the flickering object is pursued and he reaches out his hand. This time the object is a candle flame, and he gets burned. He develops a tendency to approach and reach the ribbon, and to keep away from the flame. From the point of view of a central theory of learning, the objects have now become quite different objects from what they were before. One is not just a vaguely flickering thing; it is a *threat,* while the other is a *promise of enjoyment.* The objects have taken on a meaning in terms of potential satisfaction or frustration. Learning consists of changing the meanings of things for us. The signals to which we respond have taken on meanings, good or bad. From this point of view, learning is basically a change in the way in which we perceive things around us. Naturally it has been suggested by some psychologists, in studies of such processes, that learning is essentially a change at the level of perception, and that the changes in behavior follow from fresh ways of perceiving. Learning is basically a way of recognizing our environment in a new fashion, so that certain things take on a positive or a negative value for us.[18]

These issues have not been completely settled by any means. Controversies rage today in the psychological journals as new experimental

---

[18] See for example E. C. Tolman, Cognitive maps in rats and men, *Psychol. Rev.,* 1948, 55, and There is more than one kind of learning, *ibid.,* 1949, 56.

studies are published. The kinds of experiments already mentioned under the head of autism (page 170) could be used as ammunition for the central view, i.e., the view of learning in terms of perception. In support of the peripheralist view could be cited studies showing that you can train a rat to perform a series of acts such as pulling a chain and turning on a light, and all without considering the rat's point of view.

Yet integrations of the two theories are also possible. While probably most of the reorganizations of behavior that occur in learning may well occur at the level of perception, there may nevertheless be certain concatenations of activities of which we are unaware, certain simple weavings together of various components of our responses, through the unconscious agency of the nervous system. The basic and universal law of learning would be a law relating to the connection between things, whether the things are simple and their connections simple, or whether they are complex and their connections complex; and motivation or the tension state of the individual would be one of the things which facilitate this process of making connections. From this point of view it would be legitimate to regard learning as modification both of behavior and of the way of perceiving. From the present writer's point of view science is full of cases in which the same phenomena must be seen in two ways, and it is perfectly possible in the case of learning to regard the matter both as it looks to us from the inside and as it looks to the observer from the outside.

SUGGESTED READINGS

Hilgard, E. R., *Theories of Learning*, New York, Appleton, 1948.
Hilgard, E. R., and Marquis, D. G., *Conditioning and Learning*, New York, Appleton, 1940.
Köhler, W., *The Mentality of Apes*, New York, Harcourt, Brace, 1924.
McGeoch, J. A., *The Psychology of Human Learning*, New York, Longmans, Green, 1942.
Miller, N. E., and Dollard, J., *Social Learning and Imitation*, New Haven, Yale Univ. Press, 1941.
Murphy, G., *Personality*, New York, Harper, 1947, Part 2.
Tolman, E. C., *Purposive Behavior in Animals and Men*, New York, Appleton-Century, 1932.

15 REMEMBERING

So great is the role of individual personality in remembering that we might almost say: Show the same thing to any two people, and they will remember two different things. This is the heart of the "psychology of testimony," as known to any court of law. It can easily be brought out in a homemade experiment such as that illustrated in Figure 52. The subject is asked to stand before a desk with his eyes closed and the following instructions are read to him: "Directly in front of you is a desk with a number of objects upon it. When I give you the signal, open your eyes. Observe the objects on the desk. Then at a second signal from me [after five seconds] you will close your eyes." Immediately afterward the subject is taken from the room and asked to make a schematic representation of exactly what he saw on the desk, labeling the objects and including a description of color and material.

Everything that happens to the individual persists for a certain length of time. As we saw earlier, the impressions made on the sense organ or brain do not instantly fade out (page 169). There is a trace which fades gradually, just as the impression requires a certain amount of stimulation to work up to its peak. The reader will remember the after-images (see page 158) which betoken the continued effects, in the sense organ or brain, of something that gave rise to a perceptual response. Even when all after-images are gone, the man with whom we have been talking is still almost present, and after he has left us his voice seems to linger. These after-effects in the "mind's eye," or the lingering of the voice in the mind, are called "memory images." After you have been looking at the game or listening to the symphony, there may be a prolonged play of various after-effects within you, perhaps based upon the reverberation continuing in the nerve cells of the retina and in the nerve cells of the visual or auditory parts of the brain. Sometimes we call back the

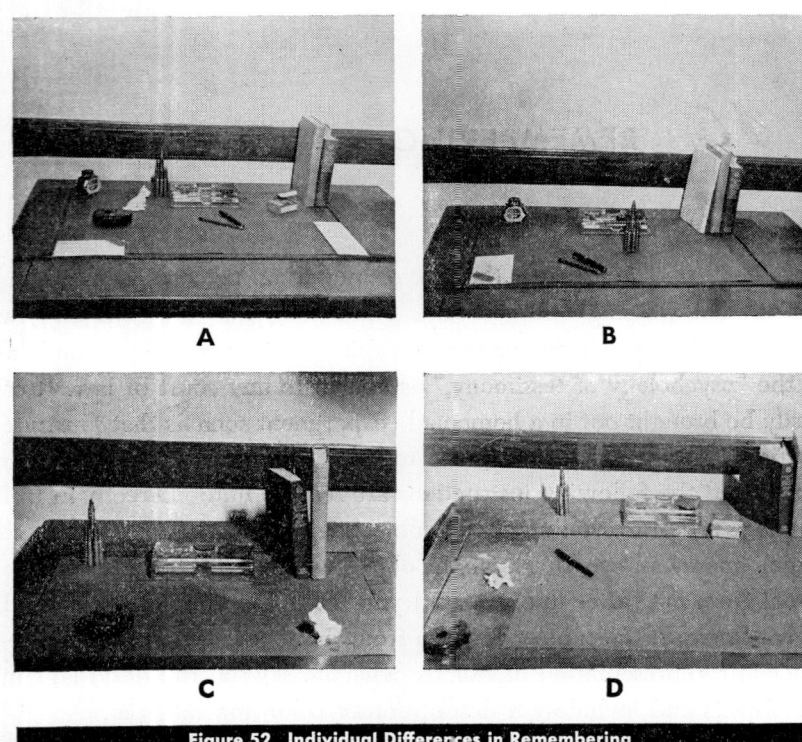

Figure 52. Individual Differences in Remembering

Three subjects looked at the desk top in A for five seconds. Then, from memory, they made schematic drawings of what they saw. In B, C, and D the objects are arranged in accordance with each subject's drawing. It is apparent that each individual remembered in his own characteristic way. Thus B forgot the dog, changed the position of the bullets, added a third book, but left out a number of other objects. C organized certain key objects in a more or less symmetrical fashion. D preserved the helter-skelter arrangement of the original, but left out objects or changed their position.

impressions of faces or voices after they have been completely absent for a while; these we would likewise call memory images. It is likely that the memory images depend upon a rearousal of the same brain regions which were originally active in the first perception.

At any rate, memory images are hard to differentiate from weak sensory impressions. An experiment by Perky[1] undertook to find out how people differentiate between percepts and images. The object was to see how far a person could be fooled into taking for a subjective image what is actually an objective fact. Perky conducted the subject into a well-lighted room, seated him before a screen, and asked him to project upon it the visual image of a leaf, a tomato, or a banana. Concealed in the room behind the screen were two well-drilled confederates of the experimenter, acting under instructions conveyed by him from the lighted room by hidden electric signals. As soon as the subject started to project his imaginary banana on the screen, the experimenter gave the signal, and the confederates threw a very faint picture of a banana on the back of the screen, very gradually increasing its intensity till the subject reported that he had a good image. The unsuspicious subject, intent on his effort to conjure up an image, mistook the picture for his own; and even though the banana was standing on end, whereas he had tried to see one lying on its side, he invented some plausible explanation of this discrepancy, and went away without discovering the deception. This result was obtained, not from one subject alone, but from 27 college and graduate students, men and women alike, with no real exceptions.[2] We may definitely say, on the basis of this and other experiments, that faint images are often indistinguishable from faint sensations.

Some images, however, are far from faint. Francis Galton[3] found that when asked to recall the breakfast table, some people saw with striking vividness the toast and the fruit and other objects in their appropriate places on the white tablecloth. Others, indeed, brought back impressions with such complete clarity and vividness that the experience was like the original scene, and they were willing to certify that it was just like a full-fledged reproduction of the original. Popularly it is often assumed that this capacity for actually seeing what is not there is a mark of insanity, but this is very far from the truth. Many normal people do

---

[1] C. W. Perky, An experimental study of imagination, *Amer. J. Psychol.*, 1910, 21, 422–452.

[2] The phrasing of this summary is borrowed from R. S. Woodworth and A. T. Poffenberger, *Experimental Psychology*, 1920 (mimeographed).

[3] F. Galton, *Inquiries into Human Faculty and Its Development*, New York, Macmillan, 1883.

have visual images at this level of intensity; one finds in almost everyday classroom situations two or three people whose habitual mental furniture consists of lifelike full-bodied mental pictures which they cannot distinguish, in clearness and intensity, from sense perceptions of the external world.

An eminent psychologist who had for a lifetime carefully studied his own images had this to say about them:

> My mind, then, is of the imaginal sort. . . . I have always had, and I have always used, a wide range and a great variety of imagery; and my furniture of images is, perhaps, in better than average condition, because—fearing that, as one gets older, one tends also to become more and more verbal in type—I have made a point of renewing it by practice periods. I am able now, for instance, as I was able when I entered the class-room nearly twenty years ago, to lecture from any one of three main cues I can read off what I have to say from a memory manuscript; or I can follow the lead of my voice; or I can trust to the guidance of kinaesthesis, the anticipatory feel of the movements of articulation. . . . When it is a matter of preparing a lecture on a definite plan, of dividing and subdividing under various headings, I draw up in the mind's eye a table of contents, written or printed, and refer to it as the hour proceeds. . . .
>
> When I am working for myself . . . I experience a complex interlacing of imagery which it is difficult to describe. . . . My natural tendency is to employ internal speech; and there are occasions when my voice rings out clearly to the mental ear and my throat feels stiff as if with much talking. . . .
>
> . . . I turn now to the topic of visual imagery, which is always at my disposal and which I can mold and direct at will. I rely, in my thinking, upon visual imagery in the sense that I like to get a problem into some sort of visual schema, from which I can think my way out and to which I can return. As I read an article, or the chapter of a book. I instinctively arrange the facts or arguments in some visual pattern, and I am as likely to think in terms of this pattern as I am to think in words. . . .
>
> The term "visual schema" is, of course, itself equivocal. . . . But I must warn the others to whom this sort of imagery is unknown, not to think of a geometrical figure printed black on white, or any thing a hundredth part as definite. I should be sorely puzzled to say what colors appear in my schemata, and I certainly could not draw on paper my pattern of a particular writer or a particular book. I get a suggestion of dull red, and I get a suggestion of angles rather than curves; I get, pretty clearly, the picture of movement along lines, and of neatness or confusion where the moving lines come together. . . .
>
> . . . my mind, in its ordinary operations, is a fairly complete picture gallery—not of finished paintings but of impressionist notes. Whenever I read or hear that somebody has done something modestly, or gravely, or proudly, or humbly, or courteously, I see a visual hint of the modesty or gravity or pride

or humility or courtesy. The stately heroine gives me a flash of a tall figure, the only clear part of which is a hand holding up a steely grey skirt; the humble suitor gives me a flash of a bent figure, the only clear part of which is the bowed back. . . .[4]

The same psychologist suggested that each student evaluate his own images by a method like this:

1. Think of a bunch of white rosebuds, lying among fern leaves in a florist's box.
    (a) Are the colours—the creamy white, the green, the shiny white—quite distinct and natural? . . .
    (d) Can you call up the scent of the rosebuds? . . .
    (e) Can you feel the softness of the rose petals?[5]

If you use a scale with values from 0 to 5 to measure the vividness of your images, you would give a score of 5 to cases in which the image is as vivid as the original sense presentation, and grade other images accordingly down to the zero point, at which no image can be called up at all. If you now average the intensities which you give yourself for each one of *many* such images in each of the modalities—visual, auditory, etc.—you can get a very rough impression of your predominant imagery. It is true that if we took a few more examples and chose them from areas where you had different types of experience, the figures would vary.

But this will serve as a rough introduction to our problem of individual differences. It will at least bring out this main fact: Some students will typically use the higher numbers like 4 and 5, and will be likely to assume that most people around them see things, hear things, etc., in the same vivid way in which they do. They will run up against the case of the individual who reports no visual imagery at all, who says that he never sees things in his mind's eye. They are likely thereupon to become a little skeptical and irritated and to wonder if he is not deceiving them or himself. On the other hand, among equally normal members of the group, there will be some who use only very low scores like 1 or 0, or indeed a few who use nothing but 0 all the way across, and who may deny the existence of imagery. These people are likely to be quite irritated

---

[4] E. B. Titchener, *Lectures on the Experimental Psychology of the Thought-Processes*, New York, Macmillan, 1909, pp. 7–13.

[5] E. B. Titchener, *Experimental Psychology*, New York, Macmillan, 4 vols., 1901; Vol. 1, *Qualitative Experiments*, Part I, Student's Manual.

with their friends who have used the 4's and 5's, feeling very sure that nobody really does have "pictures in the mind's eye," etc., except, perhaps, in a far-fetched poetic sense. The reality of the very great individual differences in imagery is a perennial source of interest and surprise to people who start with the assumption, "We are all pretty much alike." The important problem for psychology, of course, is to find in what respects we are pretty much alike, and in what respects we vary as greatly as we do in this case.

As to the reasons for these individual differences, we can only guess, as we so often do, that constitutional differences in the make-up of the brain, influenced by biochemical factors such as the endocrine substances in the blood stream, make part of the difference; and we can point out at least some important environmental influences in the fact that formal schooling can apparently reduce the vividness of imagery and that some people can expressly *cultivate* their imagery.

Perhaps partly because those who are interested in their images tend to cultivate them not only in one field but in all fields, there is a tendency for those rich in one kind of imagery to be rich in other kinds. It used to be held that if a person was a "visual type" he would be conspicuously lacking in auditory imagery, and vice versa. As far as we know, there is, on the contrary, a tendency for good imagery in one field to go with good imagery in others. A more significant contrast is between the people who remember and think in terms of *images* and those who remember and think primarily in terms of inner speech, i.e., *words* which are actually manipulated silently, inwardly, as symbols of things earlier experienced. Even if your imagery is good, you often remember things not by calling up images of them, but by naming them to yourself and to others; you use language to bring back early experiences. Try, for example, to recall the Lord's Prayer or the opening lines of "America" or "The Star-Spangled Banner," and after you have done so, compare your memory for words with the images which came along with the words.

Try now to remember the rules about efficient learning given in the preceding chapter (pages 235 ff.); cast about in your mind to see what it was that you really took hold of and succeeded in storing away. What will come back will almost inevitably take the form of a series of propositions phrased in terms of words, in which the actual print on the page, the material which you can actually visualize, plays only a small part in the total. At least, most people do most of their remembering (and a large part of their thinking; compare page 295) in terms of words. The use of words is picked up, as are other skilled acts in childhood, as one connects words with the things for which they stand. The two great devices for organizing, fixating, and symbolizing the world for yourself, so that you can recall it and adapt to it, are images and words; and in the long run words predominate.

There is, however, a very *different* way of utilizing images in recall which is quite uncommon in adults, but not infrequently found in children. It consists in actually reëxperiencing the original sense presentation, i.e., seeing or hearing all over again, in a way which is felt to be quite different from just calling up an image, and may be at a level of considerable vividness, as contrasted with the faint and poorly perceived impressions in the Perky experiment (see page 251). When a person's imagery is in this way essentially indistinguishable from his original sense impressions, it is called *eidetic* (from Greek *eidos*, a copy). A number of investigations, beginning in Germany and continuing in this country, have been made of eidetic images in children of school age. Objects are presented which a child may continue to see long after the stimulus has been removed.[6] For example, one child had seen in a picture a suitcase on which appeared a label with the word RICHMOND. When he recalled this picture, he clearly saw RICH; then later, RICH O; then again RICH. It was not a question of just *remembering* the word he had seen, for this was easy enough; nor was it a question of *imagining* it in the mind's eye, for many of us could call up fairly good mental pictures of an eight-letter word. Rather, it was a question of *seeing* it again; and when the O appeared from time to time, it appeared in the right place.

It is important to notice exactly what is involved here, and how different it is from our usual experience. Many of us recall a great deal after a brief glance, and we may persuade ourselves that we do this simply by photographing the impression on our minds and calling off the details from the inner picture. Actually the adult very seldom does this; he works by a radically different method. At least let us try to experiment

---

[6] H. Klüver, "The Eidetic Child," in C. Murchison (ed.), *A Handbook of Child Psychology*, Worcester, Clark University Press, 1933, pp. 643–668.

and let the reader form an impression of his own about how he actually works. Look at the letter square closely, and memorize it fully. Have you

        T   F   X

        N   P   Z

        O   J   Q

now got to the point where, if you shut your eyes, you can really see it? Now practice it for another minute, visualizing as well as you can. Now, *covering the letters,* start by recalling the letter at the lower right-hand corner, and from the image in the mind's eye read diagonally up to the upper left-hand corner. Is this difficult? Then did you really have the thing photographed on your mind, ready to be recalled? You could have done this easily if you had been reading from a photograph; compare your own efforts just now with what you actually do when you look at the letter square and read from lower right to upper left. What you did learn to do was to reproduce the letters *in the order in which you learned them,* that is, from left to right and a line at a time; this is something quite different. It is not characteristic of the ordinary adult to bring back a "photographic reproduction"; what he does is rather to pick out material and organize it in his own way or at least "string it together" in his own way. Likewise, as a person recalls a scene, he describes the chief features and relationships, not the original totality. Often he remembers not so much what he saw as what he said to himself as he saw it. Figure 53 shows the effect of our labeling of things on our remembrance of them. As one glances around a new house, he notices this feature or that, so that he can write home about it; he looks back and forth, pouncing upon one detail after another. Mother can practically always floor us by asking about something which we did not notice. It would be convenient if we *could* read off from our memory images; seldom does this work. With the eidetic individual, however, to produce the letter square or

REMEMBERING

photograph at which he has gazed is a relatively straightforward matter; he *can* read off from his memory image.

Eidetic imagery is certainly more common in early childhood than later, and formal schooling seems to work against it. One learns year by year to replace images with the words and numbers which make up formal schooling. Yet eidetic images are sometimes found in adults, and

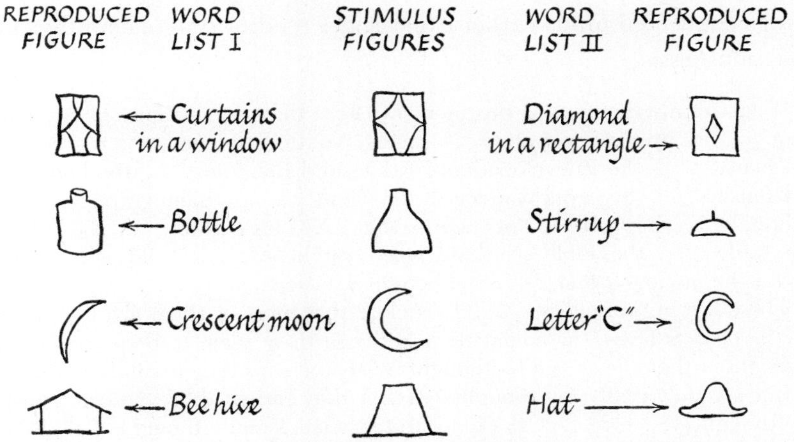

Figure 53. The Effects of Labeling

The reproduced figures are drawings of the stimulus figures done from memory by different individuals. The reproduced figures differ from the stimulus figures depending on the labels in the two word lists. For example, when the second stimulus figure was shown and labeled "bottle" a bottle was drawn; but when it was labeled "stirrup" a stirrup was drawn. (From L. Carmicheal, H. P. Hogan, and A. A. Walter, in *J. exp. Psychol.*, 1932, 15, 80.)

they may be an important part of the mental equipment of poet, painter, and composer. There is a good deal of evidence that Goethe and Blake were eidetic.

We might think of the eidetic as a rather curious class of person; actually he is merely at an extreme point on a scale on which all of us are distributed between one extreme and the other.

Association

When two things are experienced together, they tend to be remembered together, or experience with one of them recalls in one form or another the experience with the other. This is the general principle of association. The principle is the same whether a scene reminds you of another scene, or a word reminds you of another word; i.e., images and words function in the same way. Note how, in this reflective comment on the working of his own mind, Theodor Reik's associations arising from the perception of outer objects and then arising from restirrings of old memories are interwoven, all expressing the fact that things connected in his earlier experiences tend to drag each other into consciousness:

> What are my thoughts at this moment? I see the pussy willows on my bookcase . . . a prehistoric vase . . . spring, youth, old age . . . regrets . . . the books . . . the Encyclopedia of Ethics and Religion . . . the book I did not finish. . . . My eyes wander to the door. . . . A photograph of Arthur Schnitzler on the wall . . . my son Arthur . . . his future . . . the lamp on the table . . . the table . . . my wife bought it . . . I did not want to spend the money at first . . . she bought it nevertheless. . . .
>
> These are my thoughts. . . . It is clear that most of them are determined by the objects I see; the connections between them seem to be made only by the sight of the objects and by thoughts of the persons they remind me of. . . .
>
> But are they really my thoughts? Aren't they rather abbreviations, clues to my thoughts . . . ? . . . If I want to tell what I really thought, I shall have to fill the gaps between these clues. . . . Here is what I really thought. . . .
>
> I see the pussy willows on my bookcase . . . they are in a prehistoric vase that I brought with me when I came from Austria . . . the flowers remind me of my youth in Vienna . . . I am getting old . . . the next year I shall be sixty . . . I regret that I have not enjoyed my youth more . . . I try to console myself . . . I worked, I achieved something . . . I wrote many books . . . Twenty? Thirty? . . . the Encyclopedia . . . reminds me of the second volume of my Psychological Problems of Religion which is not finished . . . the door . . . leaving . . . dying . . . the photograph of Arthur Schnitzler . . my son was named after him . . . I once wished that Arthur would become a writer like Arthur Schnitzler, whom I loved . . . Schnitzler was once a physician . . . I hoped my son would study medicine . . . but he had to break off his studies. . . .[7]

Here is a rich web of associations. Yet all of them, as far as we can see, are the rearousals of old connections, established in Reik's experiences, and guided by the recency, the frequency, and especially the vividness of such connections, and, as we shall now examine more closely, the role of the *set* prevailing at the time.

[7] Theodor Reik, *Listening with the Third Ear*, New York, Farrar, Straus, 1949, pp. 28–30.

In order to be associated, things must in general be experienced together or at least one of them only shortly before the other. The lightning brings back the memory of the thunder (usually either the rumbling sound inwardly heard, or the word thunder, or both). The same laws of habit formation that seem to apply to acts of behavior, as recounted on pages 225–228, apply also to the connections between words and between images; apparently this is one of the cases in which nature does not pay any attention to the distinctions which we sometimes like to make between "subjective" and "objective" events. This would mean, then, that mental connections may obey the same basic laws that hold for the conditioned response (page 213), in which we are dealing with "objective" phenomena.

This leads to the question, Why cannot we establish conditioned responses where *sensory* rather than *motor* phenomena are involved? Why can there not be sensory conditionings? Appropriate experiments have been set up to answer this question and they have shown some of the circumstances under which such sensory conditionings occur. A useful study is that by Ellson.[8] In Ellson's experiments, tones were presented sixty times in conjunction with a light; most subjects came to "hear" (not just "imagine") tone when the light went on, even though the tone was no longer sounded. These tones could be called "hallucinations" if one likes. Indeed, we use the word hallucination typically for a sense impression in which there is no externally acting physical stimulus at the time. Sense impressions, however, as we have seen (cf. page 251), are qualitatively the same thing whether they happen to be faint sensations or just images; they are often indistinguishable to the person who has them. Let the philosophers have their very good problem as to what the ultimate nature of the real physical world is, and let us as psychologists accept the simple fact that the dynamic laws of psychology apply to experiences like tones and colors just as they do to acts like talking and swimming.

This principle of association is of major use to us in all sorts of ways in relation to remembering, thinking, and imagining; and we shall frequently come back to it. In the present connection, association simply

---

[8] D. G. Ellson, Critical conditions influencing sensory conditioning, *J. exp. Psychol.*, 1942, *31*, 333–338.

states the fact that the cue to all recall operates so as to bring up either the appropriate *image* or the appropriate *word*, or *act*, or *set;* indeed, as you can see in the man struggling to recall a name, more than one of them may be involved. The knitting of his brows, and the tension that you can see around his mouth and speech apparatus, together with the pictures that come up in his mind's eye as he tries to bring back the name, show that he has learned quite rightly to expect things to come back if certain cues precede them. Just as the actor gets his cue before he says his line, so the response comes back when appropriately signaled for. But the signal must be appropriate; it needs to be connected by earlier experience with actual production of the response. One may make all sorts of heroic efforts, acts of will, without being able to recall; but then, as Emerson said, it may come "sauntering into the mind as if it had never been called for," if, in fact, some little cue, some little word or gesture starts going the appropriate lines of association.

Often there are a number of cues all at once which may add to one another's effectiveness, and often the strengthening of one or many cues through much repetition may bring the cue to a dependable level. Typically you "overlearn" in the sense that you have set going in yourself all sorts of different cues any one of which would work. You may then get very tired so that only one or two of these cues are still available, and still you may seem to function as well as ever. But the trouble is that the large margin of safety which you think you have may be pared down so far that in the fatigue or excitement of the critical moment like the examination, or the recital, or the speech, the remaining cues cannot compete successfully with the disturbing cues which come from your examination of your eager audience.

Recall

Shepherd Franz[9] had the task of helping to synthesize the two parts into which a man's memory had fallen; in one mental state the man recalled events up to 1914, in the other, events since 1915. (He had been in a mine explosion and suffered various kinds of shock.) Franz was trying one day to get him to recall incidents in the African campaign in which he knew the man had taken part. He spread out be-

---

[9] S. I. Franz, *Persons One and Three,* New York, McGraw-Hill, 1933.

fore him a map of Africa, and the man saw the name of the little town of Voi. Suddenly his whole manner changed. "I had a monkey," he said. Then there came flooding back into his memory the tragic incident of the pet monkey killed by a leopard at Voi. The emotion, the keyed-up state, proved helpful in unlocking the vast storehouse of memories, and the African campaign was soon brought back.

This is an example of the process of *recall*. The term *recall* is ordinarily used when you are seeking some specific thing you have learned; you try to recall and you succeed or fail. Actually all the wrong names that come crowding into your mind as you try to remember a specific name are cases of recall, too; that is, there is failure of intended recall at the same time that there is recall of much that is not wanted at the time, just as you may bring back, when you are practicing a motor skill, many erroneous moves along with the right ones, you may be responding to cues which throw you off, lead you away from your goal. There are also in daily life countless times when you are not looking for anything in particular and are glad enough to accept what comes to mind; these are also cases of recall. If you hear an anecdote and say, "That recalls another story about ———," or if someone says to you, "Do you recall the old man who lived in the yellow house?" these are appropriate uses of the word recall. Usually, however, in experimental studies we are interested in the accuracy of recall, and for that reason we measure the percentage of items which are reproduced when they are wanted. In the method of paired associates, we give pairs of them, like these:

    angel spider
    test   vermilion
    ocean decade
    tree   queen

or like these:

    cat   21
    fog   49
    tricycle 11

and later present the first item of each pair, requiring the item which was paired with it.

Studies with this method show that recall is much more effective if you are very specific in the way you are set to form your original associations. Suppose the interval between *angel* and *spider* is 5 seconds, and that between *spider* and *test* is likewise 5 seconds; the former association is enormously stronger because as you read you are set to regard these two words as a pair. You recall much more effectively if you have set yourself to form particular associations; thus, if you are shown a series of colored cardboard cutouts and your attention is drawn to the *shapes*, you do a very bad job when later asked to recall the order of the *colors* seen.

The role of set is equally striking in the act of *recalling*, as is brought out in a type of test in which people are asked to designate the countries in which different cities are located, as compared with naming the cities located in these countries. Suppose your task, for example, is to name a city in each of the following countries: Italy, Poland, Greece, Spain, Japan, Scotland, Canada. This task is compared with naming the countries in which you would find each of these cities: Madrid, Warsaw, Naples, Corinth, Edinburgh, Vancouver, Yokohama. The trouble with the latter task is that the forward associations from the cities to their countries are not complicated by any competing associations, whereas the name of a specific country—for example, Italy—may perfectly well be associated with many different responses, such as Rome, Naples, Florence, Genoa, etc. In a sense each tendency will trip the others up. They are all involved in mutual interference. This overabundance of associations is an everyday part of our difficulties in quick recall. We may have too many facts at our fingertips to give a brisk answer. The novice may be able to answer more quickly than the advanced student in such a case, because he literally does not know too much; this is usually what we mean by a "glib" answer.

This is only one of a number of kinds of *interference* in the flow of association. Earlier we mentioned several types of interference and inhibition (page 231), any one of which may be operative in your present inability to recall something you need. One common difficulty is trying *too hard* and unintentionally arousing irrelevant, interfering associations; what you need may be relaxation. Of special interest in many life situations are cases where the interference lies basically in one's motivation. Take a case in which children in a vocational center were actually unable to function effectively because they deeply feared the material that was being used in the tests.[10] Rationally, you might say that they would do better through need to master the task, but human beings are seldom as rational as that.

Our major source of systematic study in recent years of the role of motivation in blocking recall is the systematic work of Sigmund Freud, especially his volume *The Psychopathology of Everyday Life*. He emphasizes that frequently we fail to recall things that we know perfectly well, and get ourselves into highly embarrassing situations, for a reason which really expresses a motive of ours, although we do not acknowledge this to be the case. We cannot remember the name of the close friend, or the telephone number of the business associate, or what the girl friend wore to the dance, or the wife's birthday. We plan a week-end trip which will take a good deal of money, and then after it is too late on Saturday noon to get to the bank we discover that we have not nearly cash enough; was there some possibility that there was somebody we might meet on that week end whom we very much did not want to meet? We are constantly forgetting appointments with people we "should so love to meet." Freud tells how a man hunted up and down to find a beautiful book which his wife had given him on their wedding anniversary. He failed utterly. Later on, after a long period of relative estrangement from his wife, he loved her again as intensely as before. It now occurred to him that he would like to have that book, and he went immediately to the bookcase, reached behind some other books, and brought it out. He had forgotten the book; there is no doubt of that fact. But in a sense something deep within him knew where the book was. To avoid arguments about whether his "unconscious mind" knew about it and what the unconscious mind is, let us just say very simply that part of him knew where the book was, but something blocked his recall of it. The thing that blocked his recall was, of course, his hostility to his wife. He did not want to recall things associated with her and, in particular, with the wedding anniversary. Failures of recall, says Freud, along with slips of the tongue, embarrassing remarks that are the opposite of what we mean to say, are good examples of the dynamic control of the process of association. Things can be recalled when they are really wanted. It is not a

---

[10] R. Sears, Motivational factors in aptitude testing, *Amer. J. Orthopsychiat.*, 1943, 13, 468–493.

question of whether we say or think they are wanted or not, but whether they are *really* wanted or not.

We might therefore add to the various *aids to recall*, in terms of concentrated attention, keeping in good condition, etc., the highly practical rule in relation to recalling promises, dates, appointments, obligations: Really want to recall. If you don't really want to recall, find out why you don't. One does not have to go 100 percent of the way with Freud, or give this motivation factor the weight he gives it, to get some practical benefit from always looking for answers to the question: What was really at work to make one name come back so easily, another with such great difficulty?

From such interferences as these it is only a short step to the interferences that are offered by our sheer preferences for some items over others as things to be remembered. "She's quite a handful, that woman" is the opening sentence in a story which Kenneth Clark[11] presented to a group of students; the story dealt with a powerfully built "muscular" woman whose prowess put to shame a man of ordinary build. Men and women forgot different kinds of things when they recalled this passage. In the same way a narrative about a "son who tried to outwit his father" was remembered differently by British and by Hindu students, the former playing up the moralistic and playing down the esthetic aspects of the tale, the latter doing the reverse.[12]

It has indeed been boldly suggested by some psychologists that *all* failure to recall is due to interferences, and none of it due simply to the passage of time. They cite as evidence the extremely interesting studies suggesting that we forget nothing during the hours of sleep (Figure 54). Perhaps when awake it is inevitable that one activity should constantly block another (see the discussion of interference, page 231).

And if powerful drives can *interfere* with recall, they can also signally *assist* recall. Life may be built largely upon the foundation of a few significant events which made their mark because of their relation to our wants and which we recall because of their continued relation to our

---

[11] K. B. Clark, Some factors influencing the remembering of prose materials, *Arch. Psychol.*, 1940, No. 253.

[12] F. C. Bartlett, *Remembering*, Cambridge, Cambridge University Press, 1932.

REMEMBERING

wants. Werner Wolff tells of a memory that was sustained by such a life need:

I can recall an early remembrance as though it had occurred yesterday, one moment that has affected my life many times since then and will, undoubtedly, continue to affect it. I can remember sitting in a room which was swarm-

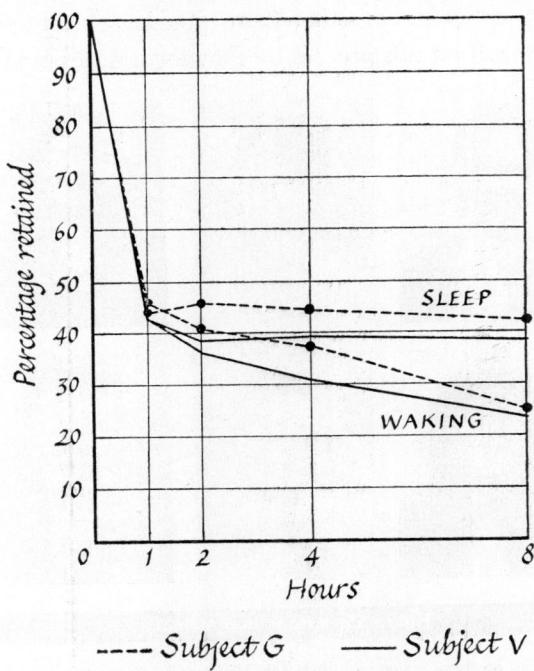

Figure 54. Retention After Sleep and Waking

Nonsense syllables were learned by two subjects before they went to sleep. The number of syllables retained at any given time drops with an increase in the number of waking hours. That practically no forgetting occurs during sleep was shown by tests given immediately after the subjects awoke.

ing with people. I was alone in spite of the fact that I was sitting between my parents. All eyes were focused on my father's younger sister. She had just finished giving a piano recital, and as the applause burst forth from all directions I happened to look at my father. His eyes were shining and he had an expression of great joy, an expression I find impossible to retell on paper. Mother turned to me smiling and said: "Daddy is so proud of auntie." From that day to this I fervently hoped that an action of mine would bring that look back. I can pick out incidents throughout my childhood in which that picture has intervened and caused me to take another path. It has forced me to try many things far above my abilities, and it has made my failures much more disheartening. I am completely sure that I will remember that incident unto my dying day and that it will affect my actions and decisions until then.[13]

Recognition

Recognition is the capacity to indicate which people, which pictures, or words, or other items you have experienced before. We may experiment on this process by showing a series of faces and then

Figure 55. Recognition Memory

Look at the faces of these boys and girls for 15 seconds. Then turn to page 433 and see how many faces you can recognize.

later showing another series, so as to see how many are recognized. (See Figure 55.) Recognition ordinarily involves a much more passive response than recall, and you usually feel less strain in the process. You may at times, however, make an effort to recognize, which turns out to be a question of initiating the appropriate *set* for the things you are seeking. This process of seeking to recognize something that you want in a presentation is something that we encountered before (pages 145–146); we considered one aspect of it when we were studying the active phases of perception, i.e., looking for something that you want. Indeed

---

[13] Werner Wolff, *The Personality of the Preschool Child*, New York, Grune & Stratton, 1946, pp. 14–15.

the process of recognizing depends upon the basic principles of perception that have already been considered. Your ability to recognize something depends first upon all the factors (page 145) that have enabled you to attend to the original stimulus, including its structure and its figure-ground relations; second, upon your past experience with the kind of material presented (you will be less likely to err in recognizing things if you have had long experience in perceiving them); third, upon the factor of set, especially upon the strength of your motivation to recognize. What you are set to recognize will play a large part in what you will discover. Students hearing a lecture on the New Deal and later given a test tended to recognize the material that harmonized with their own political viewpoint.[14]

The role of motivation appeared in the following experiment on the recognition of faces of racial groups:[15] Pictures were cut from the Howard University classbook, representing Negro students, and from the Columbia College classbook, representing white students. Later on, the Negro faces were mixed with other Negro faces which had not been seen previously, and the white faces were mixed with other white faces not previously seen; these two large groups of faces were then shown to several classes of white psychology students. The students were asked to pick out from each group the faces they had seen before. These students had also on an earlier occasion filled out an attitude schedule to indicate their general attitude toward Negroes (page 485). The score in *recognition* turned out to depend largely upon the *attitude* of the subjects toward Negroes. Those whose attitudes were friendly to Negroes proved to be skillful in picking out the Negro faces they had seen before from among the others. Those who were less friendly toward Negroes were not so skillful in telling the new faces from the old; they had apparently not found it worth while to respond to individual faces. Perhaps they were just against the group as a group, so that their ability to recognize individual faces was handicapped. They had failed, perhaps, in making differentiations among faces for the simple reason that they did not want to see individuality in faces.

---

[14] A. L. Edwards, Political frames of reference as a factor influencing recognition, *J. abnorm. soc. Psychol.*, 1941, *36*, 34–50.

[15] V. Seeleman, The influence of attitude upon the remembering of pictorial material, *Arch. Psychol.*, 1940, No. 258.

From what has been said here it would appear that recalling and recognizing are basically processes of association similar to those processes already encountered in studying the nature of learning. What has been learned can be brought back, whether it be a motor response or a glandular response, or an image, or a word. The better practiced a thing is, the more likely it is to be recognized in a new context.

But this does not tell us quite all that we ought to know about recognition. After all, how do we know that the face is the right face, that the word is the right word? Are there not failures of recognition? Do we not often find ourselves in a strange town, yet overcome with that curious feeling: "I have been here before"? Do we not in the midst of a conversation suddenly have the eerie feeling that the whole conversation has run the same course at some indefinable time in the past? However little we may understand these experiences ("paramnesia"), they at least point to the fact that failures of recognition do occur. M. Leeds,[16] among others, has shown that this kind of false recognition is likely to occur at certain times; in his own experience it occurred especially often when he was fatigued. The discovery that recognition is not infallible has led to the view that recognition is really just a matter of making a confident response in picking out things with which we had contact at an earlier time. We gradually build up habits of well-organized response, saying "no" to some things and "yes" to others. Perhaps it is this habit of well-ordered, confident behavior that is going on when the word "recognition" is used; when a man is recognizing something he has a confidence that is not present when he is blundering ahead and merely making guesses. But is not "confidence" partly a question of personality, not just a question of accuracy in spotting what we have encountered before? Yes, certainly. From this viewpoint the amount "recognized" would be much higher in a very confident person than the amount "correctly recognized." To tell the truth, personality *also* enters into every score we have in learning, or recalling, or indeed any psychological process.

SUGGESTED READINGS

Allport, G. W., and Postman, L., *The Psychology of Rumor*, New York, Holt, 1947.

---

[16] M. Leeds, The experience of déjà vu, *J. Amer. Socy. Psychical Research*, 1940.

Bartlett, F. C., *Remembering*, Cambridge, Univ. Press, 1932.
Ebbinghaus, H., *Memory* (trans. by H. A. Ruger and C. E. Bussenino), New York, Teachers College, Columbia Univ., 1913.
Franz, S. I., *Persons One and Three*, New York, McGraw-Hill, 1933.
Stern, W., *Psychology of Early Childhood* (trans. by A. Barwell), New York, Henry Holt, 1924, Part 5.
Stern, W., *General Psychology* (trans. by H. D. Spoerl), New York, Macmillan, 1938, Part 3.
Woodworth, R. S., *Experimental Psychology*, New York, Holt, 1938, chaps. 2–4.

16   IMAGINING AND DREAMING

Imagining

When you imagine, you rearrange the material you have experienced earlier. Sometimes the result is a jumble, based largely on the sheer recency, frequency, vividness of the associations you have formed, as when you dreamily doodle or make a nonsensical picture pieced together from things recently seen, or as when you listen to a boring lecture. Sometimes, however, the thing imagined is well organized and fully meaningful, under the predominant influence of some set which gives direction to your flow of ideas. We may illustrate these two extremes by the imaginative play of two children.

Eva, three years and four months old, had often heard the tale of little Red Riding-Hood, and one day she told it to us, but purposely changed it, and thoroughly enjoyed our astonishment. As characteristic of childish caprice we may mention that after a short time only the words wolf and Red Riding-Hood remain to remind us of the fairy tale, and, in the end, even these remnants disappear, and the whole tale is concerned with other things.

There was once a little girl called Red Riding-Hood and she had a red cap. And the grandmother, she was ill. And the wolf—well, now where is the wolf going? He went to the grandmother and then the grandmother was afraid. Then she dressed herself quick and went quick to Else. And the father of the grandmother—and the grandmother when she was well, then she went into the forest too with Red Riding-Hood and the wolf went into the garden with them too. And then they runned away fast. And the wolf has runned too and then they runned to the water-tower and then the wolf said: "I can run as quick." And the daddy was afraid too of the wolf. And Red Riding-Hood has cried too and the wolf bit her finger and made it bleed. And Red Riding-

Hood's kitty cried. And the wolf went to kitty but then kitty screamed; he runned quick in the wood and kitty didn't cry any more.[1]

Here each element is related to the child's experience, but organization through one controlling interest is lacking. In the second example (from an older child, and based on memories from a later period) one can see more order and unity:

Mrs. Comphret lived on the cellar stairs. She was short and plump and comfortable, and she was always smiling. Sometimes she sat out on the cellar door in the sun and smiled. When the days were warm the cellar doors were opened and my sister and I played on the cellar stairs with Mrs. Comphret. She did not talk much but was just comfortable and smiling and slow and quiet. We liked to feel her there. I never went to school or any where without stopping to talk to Mrs. Comphret, or if we were in a great hurry at least we whispered good-by.

This is the story of a child's imaginary companion, and the need for just such a person becomes clear when we are acquainted with the child's real mother.

The mother was, like Mrs. Comphret, a small woman, but there was no plump restfulness, no quiet smile. Instead she was alert, quick, dominating. The next thing to be done must be done at once. It did not matter where the development of an important game might be, it was time right now to go out, or to wash one's hands, or to put one's things away. . . . Her mother's voice was quick, charged with nervous energy, immensely disturbing. . . . She always intended to be very fond of her mother but before she quite accomplished it the voice would break in upon something very important and then she would be angry and very far away.

Mrs. Comphret was the personification of the things she had wanted in a mother and had not found. Gradually, as the relationship with her father had grown more satisfying, that need had grown less insistent. Mrs. Comphret, quiet, restful, slow, and smiling, died. . . .[2]

This typical product of childhood imagination shows how a need may help to shape a train of images which become more and more substantive. But in the adult, too, the inner world of needs, worries, preoccupation joins with the outer world of sensory stimulation to give rise to trains of imagination or fantasy.

---

[1] William Stern, *Psychology of Early Childhood* (translated from 3rd ed., revised and enlarged by Anna Barwell), New York, Holt, 1924.

[2] Frances G. Wickes, *The Inner World of Childhood*, New York, Appleton, 1929, pp. 162–164.

One morning I was reading in bed, with concentrated attention and much interest, my son resting beside me. The night before, the boy complained of a slight indisposition, which made me a little anxious, for during the war he had been ill with pleurisy, and I could not banish the fear of pulmonary tuberculosis. . . .

At a certain moment I become aware that I cannot understand a passage of my book. . . . I have the intuition that here is something worthy of observation. . . . As I become aware that I am making special efforts to understand the text, I realize the subject of my phantasy (the disease), and I recollect the boy coughed a few moments ago. (I did not become cognizant of this at the moment the coughing occurred.) I have no difficulty in retracing the concatenation: If there were any hoemorrhage I should have to run to the nearest doctor, who, however, is not a lung specialist. Neither has Dr. X., who lives close by, any special knowledge of tuberculosis. To whom should I go during the night? Perhaps I should do better to wait till morning. But in the meantime the boy might be dead. (Here the thinking ended.) I add that the ideas were represented visually, but obscurely, and accompanied by a certain amount of emotion. . . .

Finally, I may lay stress upon the circumstance that it is an outer stimulus—the coughing—reinforced by an emotionally emphasized recollection—my fears for the boy's health—which is the occasion of the phantasy.[3]

While memory may be regarded as a way of bringing back an earlier experience, imagining may be regarded as a way of presenting to ourselves something that has not yet existed, and perhaps never will. A thing imagined may therefore differ in any degree from a thing remembered, depending upon the degree to which we changed or reorganized the old materials. Imagination always depends upon material retained from the past, but it always involves the formation of a pattern which is new. Though none of the elements is new, the combination is new. You can perfectly well imagine a green elephant with pink stripes, because elephants, stripes, pink, and green are ingredients in your previous experience. Blind men do not remember the visual appearance of elephants unless they saw them or pictures of them before they lost their sight. André Gide tells how he struggled to convey to a blind girl what colors were like, using the analogy of music, and how utterly bewildered she became. Color-blind men cannot imagine colors in which they are wanting any more than you can imagine the tones of musical instruments other than those you have actually heard. When images are combined in

---

[3] J. Varendonck, *The Psychology of Day-Dreams*, New York, Macmillan, 1921, p. 367.

new ways, the same laws of association operate as are present in the case of memory.

Nevertheless, the study of imagination differs greatly from the study of memory in the matter of emphasis, because a few of the laws relating to memory take on very special importance when we are dealing with imagination. Take the matter of set. What will be remembered by a group of young adults about the *past* year's college activities will be much more alike than what will be *imagined* regarding what may happen *next* year, largely because the set given by each person's interests and drives plays such a big part. In fact, the role of set is a primary clue to the understanding of imagination. Imagination may seem to be utterly free and uncontrolled, but the appearance is deceptive. Earlier (page 258) we found that free association is not really free; the factor of control is always present. Even when imagination runs wild, there is a clue to it. "Though this be madness, yet there's method in it." Let us look for the "method," that is, the control or set that operates.

Often this is a question of drives, so that we may begin the study of imagination with an emphasis upon the role of drives. Arctic explorers subjected to prolonged hunger and cold tell us of the rich feasts and the verdant pastures of which they dream. In his journeys across far northern Canada, Rasmussen[4] has described the insistent recurrence of such fantasies. The blood stream which bathes our nervous system bears the effects of drugs, foods, and hormones; what we imagine depends partly upon health and physical state. William James spoke of the way in which alcohol may color the world, and the fact that even a cup of coffee may transfigure a man's philosophy.

During World War II intensive investigations were made of the process by which the visceral states guide the course of imagination. A group of conscientious objectors volunteered for a prolonged study of their thought and action during semi-starvation. Some of the reports by observers and by the men themselves make clear the control of their lives, thoughts, and imaginings by the deprived state of their bodies (compare page 65).

But it is not only the visceral drives which can operate to guide imagi-

---

[4] K. Rasmussen, *Across Arctic America*, New York, Putnam, 1927.

nation. In the same way, the activity drives play their part in the daydream of the skiing week end or the long hiking trip; and the sensory drives guide imagination, as we imagine a charming garden, or a program by a first-class orchestra. Typically, several drives work at once. The social drives (page 411), moreover, such as the drive for prestige and the drive for power, play a huge part in the "long long thoughts" of the ambitious boy who makes his great fantasies of future achievement. Thus one brings into the imaginative process everything that one has and everything that one is. Indeed, the artist and the scientist reveal themselves most fully through the devices by which their deeply ingrained values and interests steer the course of imagination.

How are we to study the process of imagination at close range? A simple method is the "chain association test." Typically, we present a single word and allow the subject to give a string or chain of words associated with it. The set which has been established in the subject is to allow each word which he utters to serve as his cue for the next word, and so on. One gets such a chain of words as the following: table—chair—furniture—house—roof—dome—peak—spire—chapel—religion—ceremony—prayer—God—good—salvation; or in a person more inclined to scientific rather than religious associations: table—chair—wood—tree—forest—forestry—botany—laboratory—microscope—refraction—light-waves—mathematics—Einstein.

It is true that in such a series certain elements that occur to the individual are usually skipped, in the sense that something goes on between words which never gets expressed. Thus, after giving the word ceremony, there is a pause. Did the subject, after saying "ceremony," recall a wedding but prefer not to say this word, or did he stop for a moment, mentally blocked, not knowing what to say and perhaps not even knowing that he was stopping? Just as a drive can keep the associations running, so it can provide a powerful aversion to the utterance of the word, and thus act as a form of interference (page 263). It is exactly these blockings or interferences which interest the psychoanalyst, as pointing to associations which a person may fear to recognize, things which for one reason or another he would rather keep out of sight. In experience with this method, it has often been found that associations related to guilt, shame, terror, etc., are frequently blocked out. In spite of all such difficulties the chain association method does show a good deal of what is "on one's chest"; it usually betrays the preoccupations of the individual.

It is for this reason that a somewhat similar method has proved valuable with children in the normal course of taking an intelligence test. The child is asked to say as many single words (i.e., not in the form of sentences) as he can. From our present viewpoint, the significance of this item will lie not in the light it might throw on the intellectual level of the child, but rather in the evidence it gives us regarding his preoccupations, interests, fantasies. The child may of course begin by naming objects around the room, or clusters of objects suggested by them; but he is likely very soon to get started on the hobbies or anxieties or problems with which he is concerned. Such a test is naturally one of a group of tests with which personality studies in childhood may be concerned (pages 458 ff.).

Motivation or predisposing drive is therefore our first guide to the study of fantasy. Fantasy is the general term for the spontaneous flow of imagination. Fantasy denotes those spontaneous expressions of drive which in their more highly developed form we call daydreams, or even the imaginative core of a work of art. One would speak of a poetic conceit, a fresh metaphor or simile, as a case of fantasy; it is simply the elaboration and connection of such fantasy material that give us a poem like the following:

> *That orbèd maiden, with white fire laden,*
> *Whom mortals call the moon,*
> *Glides glimmering o'er my fleece-like floor,*
> *By the midnight breezes strewn . . .*
> — Shelley, *The Cloud*

It is possible to get people to make up fantasies in a test situation by introducing a permissive and casual atmosphere; and we may even go a considerable distance toward standardizing a test of fantasy. One of the commonest procedures is to invite your subject to make up a story, giving him something to start with. A child may be asked to tell a story about a bear or an airplane, or to tell a story suggested by a picture. It is possible to find connections between such fantasies and everyday recurrent events in one's life. For that reason it is often useful to the clinical psychologist to get fantasy material from his subjects, whether children, adolescents, or adults. Indeed, they may be able in their stories to express things about their preoccupations, worries, aspirations, which they would hesitate to tell or would be unable to tell in person-to-person conversation, or things of which they themselves are not conscious. Material of this sort can be dealt with by the examiner either impressionistically or objectively. For example, he may emphasize what he believes the stories mean as expressions of the child's personality. At a simpler level, he may simply score the objective aspects of what is said, as to the relative frequency of nouns, proper names, references to the self, etc. In one experimental study it was possible by the latter method to show objectively that psychiatric patients told stories which were characteristic of their recurrent worries.[5]

Usually the examiner undertakes a more interpretative approach to the story material. Such uses of picture material are especially associated with H. A. Murray and the work of the Harvard Psychological Clinic. From Murray's viewpoint the story is expressive of the interaction of two things going on within the individual: (1) his needs; (2) the pressures or environmental stresses acting upon him. The interaction of a "need" and a "press" is called a "thema." The way in which a thema guides the process of perception is called "thematic apperception." The *Thematic Apperception Test*, as developed by Morgan and Murray, consists of a series of standardized pictures, regarding the responses to which we now know a good deal; the examiner is familiar with the kinds of things which the pictures draw out from normal and disturbed subjects of both sexes and at various levels of age and intelligence. The Thematic Apperception Test is used widely in clinical practice. It may bring out striking differences in predominant interests and worries, as shown in the following data from Sarason[6] for mentally handicapped girls. A girl is looking at a picture of a boy who sits at a table with a violin lying before him; she herself is rebellious against authority, and

---

[5] E. R. Balken and J. H. Masserman, The language of phantasy. III. The language of the phantasies of patients with conversion hysteria, anxiety state, and obsessive-compulsive neuroses, *J. Psychol.*, 1940, 10, 75–86.

[6] S. B. Sarason, Dreams and Thematic Apperception Test stories, *J. abnorm. soc. Psychol.*, 1944, 39, 486–492.

full of feelings of guilt: "The boy is supposed to take violin lessons—he doesn't care about it—he's sort of sleeping—he doesn't care to take violin lessons by the expression on his face—he didn't care to take lessons in the first place—he didn't listen to his elders—if he did he would take lessons."

The fact that the subject may make up a story in a manner which is much *freer* than that in which he would carry on a direct conversation about himself frequently permits the interviewer or examiner to go on from the test to a much more productive conversation with him than would otherwise be possible. The test may be useful in getting life histories or attitudes toward jobs, or help the individual to understand his own feelings toward his family, his girl friend, etc., or stir up within him an awareness of needs of which he had never been explicitly aware before. The test may therefore lead toward deeper self-understanding.

Imagination may at times flow directly into action; indeed, the reader will recall the idea (page 133) that any inner symbol which is *directly connected with action* will tend to start that action. Of course, the words or other symbols which are related to that action and the consequences may also be aroused, and may *deter* us, so that conflict (page 121) may arise. In the long run, though, imagining a thing is a good part of doing it. Education, therefore, consists largely in helping people to imagine vividly the doing of the things that will really fulfill their long-range or lifetime wants, and not just their whims; it is this vivid imagination that keeps us on the road. Indeed, all the way from the well-trained hypnotic subject who does whatever you say because he can imagine this vividly and cannot imagine anything different,[7] to the disciplined soldier whose muscles are directly geared to commands, imagination consists of a trigger system in action. When you are imagining an act, your muscles are actually beginning to tighten up as if carrying out the act, as Jacobson's electrical studies of the muscles so clearly show.[8] It is largely for that reason that waking imagination tells us so much about what a person really *is;* and, as we hope to show, the imagination that appears in the dream may in some ways present the same picture.

---

[7] M. B. Arnold, On the mechanism of suggestion and hypnosis, *J. abnorm. soc. Psychol.*, 1946, *41*, 107–128.

[8] E. Jacobson, *Progressive Relaxation*, Chicago, University of Chicago Press, 2nd ed., 1938.

Dreaming

As far as we know, dreaming is simply imagining while one is asleep; yet the process of sleeping changes the very structure, form, content, and personal significance of the process of imagining, and we are probably on safe ground in believing that we can learn even more from it than we can from waking imagination.

We might begin the study of dreaming by looking at its similarities to the processes of waking imagination, and then look later at some of the differences. Let us take the case of Robert Louis Stevenson, a man who could imagine all sorts of things real and fantastic, exciting and commonplace, prosy and poetic, and who could enrapture all sorts of people with his amazing inventions in story and verse. On the basis of years of experience in imagining, and in supporting himself with the products of his imagination, it was his judgment that dreams were often the best source of his story material. His waking interests, and the skill in story writing which he had developed in his waking life, were somehow carried over into the dream process; but at the same time he saw that dreaming actualized these capacities and brought them to a richer fulfillment than his best waking efforts could command. He phrased this whimsically by saying that many of his best plots and most extraordinary denouements came from the "little people," "the brownies," whom he set up as figurative personages to describe the deeply unconscious process which shaped his dreams. His stories developed as his dreams were recalled and rearranged. He gives us a series of instances in which the "little people" made up, he says, a better plot than he could have contrived consciously. In his sleep there was capacity to define a plot, to provide suspense, and to drive forward the material to the climax which the story required. He tells us of cases in which the final consummation, the final release from the tension of a climax situation, was developed through a perfect solution which he himself (consciously) would never have planned.

A good deal of this can certainly be ascribed to the influence of set, just as a similar process in waking imagination would be ascribed to set. A good deal also can be ascribed to the rich storehouse of his past experience, which similarly would be ascribed to past experience with a man wide awake at the time. In the two essentials, then, of set and past experience, we find the dream doing with consummate skill what the waking imagination would likewise undertake to do. We also find here in the dream a fact that we had occasion to note when mentioning the blockage which occurs in the chain association test, namely, the fact that processes of which we are unaware, or unconscious dynamic processes, may profoundly influence the course of association. Thus we seem to find that dreams have in common with waking imagination at least three things: (1) Their course is guided by the prevailing set, which may derive from any motive or combination of motives; (2) they rearrange the materials of previous experience; (3) what appears in consciousness is only part of a complex process of which the individual himself is often incompletely aware.

But what about the *differences* between dreams and waking imagination? There are at least two primary differences: (1) Dreams are often irrational, chaotic, crazy, to a degree not realized in daydreams or other waking fantasies. (2) Dreams take us much further away from the mere repetition of our daily round of experience, and frequently achieve great creative expressiveness.

The first of these qualities, the tendency toward the irrational and the incoherent, may be due to the condition of the brain as we sleep. It was suggested by William James that large parts of the brain are inactive, or out of commission, in the sleep state; and that for this reason the processes of association cannot take all the routes which they would ordinarily follow. Consider this analogy: Imagine a great flood through the Midwest, such as occurred in the summer of 1947, and work out an itinerary for a motor tour through the inundated region. You will have to choose here and there the routes that happen to be open, and you will find yourself in a series of detours. Perhaps the course of the thought in a dream may in the same way involve an endless series of detours. The thought will differ a good deal from the form it would ordinarily take. A good many of the bizarre or crazy dreams of everyday experience may well be due in some degree to this kind of disorder in the associative network. This does not mean that all the processes of association are blocked or that all associations are abnormal. Nevertheless, the associations are rather chaotic, and those that do appear do not seem to the dreamer to be queer, as they would seem if he were alertly aware of the whole perspective of the event. You become in the dream a simplified and at the same time less organized person; not enough of the facts of your experience are present through your consciousness to make you realize the absurdity of what occurs. You form your associations and accept them at their face value.

When the brain is reduced by the sleeping state to a simpler, more mechanical, less integrated kind of activity, it becomes easy for one thing

Figure 56. Effect of Physical Situation upon Dreaming

The effect of a heavy blanket pressing on a sleeping man's feet is reflected in the two dream images shown. In the one at the left, the man dreams he is a flying Mercury, entirely free except for the foot that is fixed to the pedestal. The freedom of the upper parts of his body probably reflects his deep physical relaxation as he goes to sleep. But as pressure from the blanket begins to control the dream he is running after a street car, his movements hampered by a heavy robe whose ends are flapping around his feet. (From L. H. Horton, J. abnorm. Psychol., 1919, 14, 168.)

to suggest another by sheer similarity. Horton[9] shows how a dream may portray the dreamer's physical situation (Figure 56).

D. B. Klein[10] found that dreams produced by hypnosis were likewise capable of exploiting simple physical similarities. He found that metal pressed against the forehead would give rise to dreams of cold weather;

---

[9] L. H. Horton, Levitation dreams: their physiology, *J. abn. Psychol.*, 1919, 14, 145–172.

[10] D. B. Klein, The experimental production of dreams during hypnosis, *Univ. Texas Publ.*, 1930.

and having found that the hum of a tuning fork would give rise to dreams of airplanes, he combined these two elements by pressing a cold metal object against the forehead at the same time as he sounded the tuning fork. His subject dreamed of standing in a snowstorm beside a hangar waiting for an airplane to come in. Dreams of falling seemed to arise frequently from movements of the feet. Klein found that he could produce dreams of falling feet first if he pressed on the foot of the bed, dreams of falling head first if he pressed on the head of the bed. When one subject told Klein that she was having repeated dreams of falling feet first—that is, in the course of the usual dreams of the night—he asked her if he could examine the bed and found that the springs were broken at the foot. As she turned in her sleep, her feet would thus be sure to fall a little. This material of Klein's is similar to the data secured earlier by Horton. We can say fairly safely that associations of a simple, normal sort are formed in the dream. If in this way fragments of normal association are separated from their context, chaos is pretty sure to arise.

As to the second respect in which dreams differ from daytime fantasy, namely, their tendency to get further away from our experience, the possibility occurs to us that perhaps the dream can say things that we ordinarily cannot say, or do not want to say, or cannot concentrate upon sufficiently to say. But if you are unable to say a thing bluntly, you can hint at it in symbolic form. One of the most obvious attributes of dreams is the fact that they symbolize. Often the dreamer's life situation, not just his physical situation, is portrayed. Christopher Isherwood, in his autobiographical novel *Prater Violet,* tells of an experience immediately preceding the full impact of Hitler's rise to power. Isherwood is at Brighton with an Austrian movie director whose family has been isolated in Vienna. He feels *guilty* for not having the courage and moral energy to condemn what is happening in Europe, guilty for being so unworried in the face of his friend's anxiety. He has also been called a "Momma's boy" by this same friend. During the train ride back to London he has a nightmare.

First of all I dreamed that I was in a courtroom. The State Prosecutor was a hard-faced, middle-aged, blond woman.
. . . Then I went into the British Embassy, where I was welcomed by a cheerful, fatuous, drawling young man. . . . He pointed out to me that the

walls of the entrance hall were covered with post-impressionist and cubist paintings. "The Ambassador likes them," he explained. "I mean to say, a bit of contrast, what?"[11]

The dream reflects, symbolically, the depth of Isherwood's sense of guilt and contrasts it, almost satirically, with his conscious attitude of unconcern.

Most people who have published and analyzed their own dreams agree that a great deal can be said in a few words or a few pictures. Classroom collections of dreams confirm this view. A student tells of a dream in which he is wandering along a road by a lake; on the other side of the road stands a row of buildings with high towers. He treads his way carefully until, to his horror, he discovers that one of the towers is beginning to shake and totter and is going to fall on him. He wakes up in terror, as the tower falls. He realizes as he awakens that he has long felt that his father is overpowering him, towering over him, making all sorts of terrific demands upon him, insisting on what course of life he should follow, threatening to withdraw financial and even moral support if he opposed his father's wish. What he has done in the dream, according to his own report, is to throw into picture form the sense of being overpowered. The symbol may at times be chosen purely because of its simplicity and eloquent directness, and at other times, of course, because it is less painful than the thing for which it stands. A person may use a sort of shorthand in which he represents to himself the things that terrify, without actually having to say, in all their horror and ugliness, the things which he would like to be able to say. In all probability the symbol will not be understood at first by the dreamer. But in this instance the dreamer realized: "The tower symbolizes my father." Even if a dreamer does not at the time grasp what a symbol means, it is possible that in reconstructing his experience he will come to the conclusion that it could have served such a purpose, though he was afraid to recognize it at the time.

This dream of the tower will serve as an introduction to Freud's theory of dreams. According to Freud, the dream is a device for realizing a wish, but it resorts to symbolism, in the sense that we are unwilling to

---

[11] Christopher Isherwood, *Prater Violet,* New York, Random House, 1945, pp. 54, 55.

IMAGINING AND DREAMING

say openly what our wishes are; instead, we use symbols to tell the story. In studying dreams, Freud came to the conclusion that there is often great resistance to recognizing the meaning of the symbol. It is for this reason that a special technique was developed by him and his followers, the psychoanalysts, to enable the individual to grasp what he has to say to himself in the dream.

The way in which Freud formulates the matter is to dispose first of the dreams which directly fulfill a wish, and require no symbol. A child has been skating and having a wonderful time, but is called in and told to go to bed. In the dream she goes on skating. The adult may occasionally have a direct wish-fulfilling dream, too. You have an appointment that you must keep at nine in the morning. You wake up at eight and you face the banging alarm clock with a good deal of disgust. You shut it off, turn over, go to sleep, and now you dream that you make the nine o'clock appointment. You thus keep the appointment on a make-believe basis, without actually giving up the extra sleep.

Except for these so-called "comfort dreams," however, most adult dreams, Freud believes, relate to deeper tensions regarding which we are not willing to accept the full reality. In a civilization such as our own, in which there are strong taboos and restrictions regarding sex, it is not surprising, says Freud, that there should be a great deal of double talk, a great deal of evasion and symbolic reference in the dream, in the sense that the demands of the individual which are socially reprehensible, and regarding which he feels guilty, cannot be directly portrayed. But they can be portrayed in a sufficiently disguised form to permit him to sleep on, without his grasping quite what he was doing. He thus works out a compromise between the two wishes: first, the wish which is symbolized by the dream; second, the wish to escape feelings of guilt which would be all too directly aroused if the whole story were told in an open fashion.

Even the nightmare is explained by Freud in terms of wish fulfillment. Perhaps a process of wish fulfillment has been started in symbolic form, but the disguise becomes rather thin so that the dreamer vaguely begins to grasp the whole force of the dream; there is, then, terror in relation to this breaking of the taboo. He who dreams such things is "guilty"; terror arises; the bear or monster which pursues may symbolize in one way or another the avenging forces in society. Indeed, if the dream does not appear to be wish fulfilling at all, Freud reminds us of the legitimate distinction that has to be made between the sheer physiological tension of the wish as it operates unconsciously, which he calls the *latent dream,* and the surface or symbolic representation, which he calls the *manifest dream.* It is perfectly true that if we grant this distinction we recognize all sorts of ways in which the surface manifestations may be very unpleasant, as in the nightmare, while actually a wish-fulfilling process has been going on at a deeper level.

There are two obvious difficulties about the Freudian dream theory, regarding which there has been an argument now for fifty years. First, as the dreamer recounts the dream to the psychoanalyst and tells him of all the things which come to mind in connection with the dream—the process of *free association* which follows the recounting of the manifest dream—he is likely to feel that he is letting a good many cats out of their bags, and he may come to indicate not only to the doctor but even to himself that probably he has been dreaming just as the Freudian theory required. Many patients who go through the process come to accept the Freudian theory, even if they did not do so at the beginning. If, however, it be remembered that both the account of the dream and the free associations which follow this account are necessarily guided by autistic factors, both in the doctor and in the patient, it is difficult to see how conclusive objective proof can be given of the real meaning of dreams. And it is of course true that psychoanalysts, and other psychiatrists of many different schools and viewpoints, get different kinds of dreams from their patients, offer different kinds of dream interpretations, and finally send their patients away with very different conceptions of what the dream was trying to say. We still have not got a scientific, objective, experimental dream psychology. We do have some good experiments— for example, Poetzl's demonstration that things presented to us, but *not noticed,* tend to crop up in the dream[12]—but we need far more.

The second difficulty relates to the belief that the interpretation of symbols can somehow reduce all meanings to one formula. If the process of imagining is a highly individualized one, it follows at the same time

---

[12] O. Poetzl, Experimentell erregte Traumbilder in ihren Beziehungen zum indirekten Sehen, *Z. ges. Neurol. Psychiat.,* 1917, 37, 278–349.

that the process of dreaming is likewise highly individualized. If we compare, for example, the dreams of Coleridge, Stevenson, and De Quincey—all tremendous dreamers, we may say—we can see in these examples the extraordinary differences in content, style, form, theme—in fact, everything that goes into the dream. Even if we could show that there is a certain nucleus of primitive, latent dream material in all three, the rich individuality of these three poetic souls would nevertheless appear in the dream material which they developed from such a nucleus. The Freudians may, of course, reply that they never deny such individuality; but in practice, as in theory, almost all their labor goes into the process of reducing themes to a common basis in unconscious wishes and in their symbolic manifestations. It is fundamentally true, and of major importance, as Freud has pointed out, that in the isolation of our sleep we may confront realities more candidly than when awake. But the realities that one confronts do not arise from any single impulse or any single fear; they are often a mirror of the individual's world. In a dream he acts out almost unlimited possibilities about himself and the world. He tells much about himself, to himself, in the process. But the experienced student of dreams, and of personality as a whole, may see implications which the dreamer himself has missed; and in the long years before we have a really scientific dream psychology there will be room for all kinds of serious, thoughtful dream interpretations, aimed not only at the discovery of the individual's impulsive life, or of his personality weaknesses, but also at the discovery of his resources, his imaginative powers, his immediate and ultimate goals.

SUGGESTED READINGS

Freud, S., *The Interpretation of Dreams* (trans. by A. A. Brill), London, Allen and Unwin, 1937.

Jaensch, E., *Eidetic Imagery* (trans. by O. Oeser), New York, Harcourt, Brace, 1930.

Murray, H. A., *T.A.T. Manual*, Cambridge, Harvard Univ. Press, 1949.

Stern, W., *Psychology of Early Childhood* (trans. by A. Barwell), New York, Holt, 1924, Part 6.

Stern, W., *General Psychology* (trans. by H. D. Spoerl), New York, Macmillan, 1938, chaps. 18–19.

Symonds, P. M., *Adolescent Phantasy*, New York, Columbia Univ. Press, 1949.

17 THINKING

You may stub your toe against a little idea or a big one. Thinking is a name for processes which range all the way from the smallest acts of discovery to the great boulders of science and invention. Basically, the processes always involve something new. Indeed, we have seen that even perception, and certainly learning and imagining, always involve adding something to what you already have, and in the process of adding, transforming it. And this is true of thinking, too.

We must begin, as in the case of these other processes, with the role of needs. A person does not think because he thinks, but because he has a need. We have already seen, even in imagining for its own sake (e.g., daydreaming), that there is a need at work. And in general those who have many hours of leisure, and no acute needs, enjoy basking in the sun, and perhaps are the least likely to come up with time-shattering discoveries. It is the artist, the scientist, the engineer, who have cultivated the need for new experience, new ideas, within themselves, who find the thoughts catapulting into their heads. The youthful composer or inventor may occasionally struggle with the way in which a musical or a mechanical idea can be brought to perfection; in a few years we find him bristling with such needs, popping like popcorn, unable to rest as a host of new problems, all pressing for solution, swarms in upon him.

These cases may answer in a practical way the question: "What is the difference between thinking and imagining?" In thinking there is a definite answer to a question and we strive to find it; in imagination there is no one answer, and a large field in which the mind may play.

No one would deny that computing an arithmetical answer is thinking; for there is an answer, and the problem is to find it. But the poet or the storyteller or the dreamer is not limited to one answer, and we speak of his activity as imagination. The line is not hard and fast, and we shall not quibble or deny that the distinction is relative, not absolute.

The needs are at first diffuse and scattered; they have to be focused, made explicit, their interrelations defined, their practical relation to means of solution worked out. All this points to the fact that over and above the role of needs in the creation of something new, there is the problem of *learning one's way to the goal,* the problem of acquiring a technique. One is not born thinking. As we shall see in this chapter, experimental work has driven home clearly the fact that we have to *learn to think,* just as we have to *learn to perceive.* For this reason we cannot agree with the popular idea that there is a basic distinction between perceiving, learning, and thinking. Perceiving and thinking are two closely related forms of learning to cope with the environment. The earthworm's learning to avoid an electric grid may not be called thinking, for it is a relatively simple process; but thinking extends over such a wide variety of activities that there is always an argument as to where we should begin to use the term. Do dogs, for example, think? If they do, is it possible that cats, mice, sparrows think? If we deny thinking to dogs and then start going up the animal series, shall we admit that monkeys think, or perhaps that chimpanzees think? In the same way, if we deny that newborn infants think, shall we introduce the term thinking suddenly when some particular kind of intellectual competence appears, or shall we recognize a series of gradations? The viewpoint of the present analysis is that the thinking processes that arise when we are pursuing goals are of a great many kinds, and of many different degrees of complexity, and that, whenever we can, it is worth while to tie these processes to what we already know about the learning processes. This would make it possible to say that in the more complex types of learning there occurs much which differs in degree from that which appears at a simpler level; but that even the processes which appear to be utterly distinct from sheer learning processes may be better understood if we study their origins.

The simplest kind of thinking is the forming of elementary associations. Betty, for example, at the age of a year and a half was regularly taken by an adult with a market basket to see the huge wild sheep at the zoo. She phrased this as "Go see Baa." Later, when anyone walked out of the house with the market basket, she called cheerily after him, "Go see Baa." That is to say, an association had been formed between a person's leaving the house with a market basket on the one hand and seeing sheep on the other hand. This might be called the most elementary kind of thinking, the direct forming of associations. There is of course transfer to a new situation, for an adult's leaving the house with a basket is not the identical situation in which Betty learned the response when she was herself part of the group which went to the zoo. But the new situation has enough in common with the old to permit transfer (page 228).

When once such an association has been formed (her phrase, "Go see Baa," can be called a conditioned verbal response to the situation if one likes), the next step is, as is true in all learning processes, an extension of transfer, or wider generalization. One carries over the response to a wide class of situations. Naturally one often carries it over too far. The child picking up a word applies it to all sorts of things where it does not fit (page 235). Just as we saw earlier, he must now learn to give up this "overextension of his line" and note where the generalization is socially acceptable. This involves pegging the objects with appropriate names, the kernel of the process of *abstracting*. The child learns that certain hairy four-legged creatures are "dogs"; but he constantly encounters new animals which are not exactly like any he has seen before, and the question is: Can they be called dogs? What things can be denoted by the words which have been picked up? Where are the limits to which their use may be extended? He tries the word *dog* on all sorts of other animals, some of which may be of about the same size and general appearance as those he has already encountered. You can see him at the zoo trying out the label on the wolves and the foxes. He tries out the term also on the raccoons and even the guinea pigs when he first naïvely encounters them. The question is simply: How far is the transfer permissible, e.g., how far does it actually work in bringing him warm and approving smiles?

THINKING 289

Concepts

It is remarkable how early the small child makes a transfer from one situation to another—grasps a common feature which the two share—and as he babbles and chatters to himself begins to use the same sound for all those things that have something in common—the beginning of *language*. One of the earlier systematic studies of an infant's day-by-day mental development reports the following (when the child was a little less than a year old):

The fourth sound, however, which developed through many variations (such as "M-gâ," "Gâ," or "Gng") to a clear "Gông," "A-gông," and even "Gone," was plainly an echo. It was used as loosely as it was pronounced: the baby murmured "Ng-gng!" pensively when some one left the room; when she dropped something; when she looked for something she could not find; when she had swallowed a mouthful of food; when she heard a door close. She wounded her father's feelings by commenting "M-gâ!" as her little hands wandered about the unoccupied top of his head. She remarked "Gông!" when she slipped back in trying to climb a step; when she failed to loosen a cord she wished to play with; when she saw a portière, such as she was used to hide behind; when she was refused a bottle she had begged for. It meant disappearance, absence, failure, denial, and any object associated with these.

In just this fashion, Preyer's boy used his first word of human speech, at about this age. "Atta!" the little fellow would murmur when some one left the room, or when the light went out—using a favorite old babble of his own, just as our baby did, to help him get hold of a grown-up word, "Adieu" or "Ta-ta," which carried the meaning he was after. The idea of *disappearance*—of the thing now seen, now gone—seems to take strong hold on babies very early; I have known several other cases.[1]

But it is not as easy as you might think. The child has not only to find *common features* to permit appropriate transfer and later to find *names* for them, but to fit his own names (that is, "baby talk" or "nonsense sounds" or both) into those upon which the grown-up world insists. In accepted adult language, he is learning to break up the world into a pattern like the pattern that other people recognize, and to accept *their* terms for the things they see. To you and me it is self-evident that north is "up," south is "down," and if a town is by a river, one end of it is "up," the other "down"; but the town looks flat to the child. Maxim Gorky tells of his own rather similar struggle to make sense out of the grown-

---

[1] M. W. Shinn, *The Biography of a Baby*, Boston, Houghton Mifflin, 1900, p. 228.

up world, when, one day, his grandmother came to visit him from a distant city:

I asked her where she came from, using the verb form which implies coming by foot.

"From up north, from Nizhny," she replied, "but I didn't walk it; I came down by boat. You don't walk on water, you little scamp."

This made no sense to me at all. Upstairs there lived a gaily-dressed Persian who wore a beard; and downstairs, in the cellar, there lived a withered, yellow Kalmuck who dealt in sheepskins. And I got up to one and down to the other by the way of the banisters; and if I had a fall, I just rolled down. But there was no place for water. So her "down" from "up north" on water could not be true; but it was a delightful muddle.[2]

In the same way the adult throughout life is up against the job of trying to work out the real clue to a number of different impressions, to get the real heart of an experience, so that he can be sure that the rule which applies to one case applies to all other cases within this group. In his chemistry or his history or his psychology, he starts to make generalizations by finding common features. If it is a red powder with a certain smell, a certain weight, a certain mode of reacting in the test

---

[2] Maxim Gorky, *Autobiography of Maxim Gorky* (translated by Isidor Schneider), New York, Citadel Press, 1949, pp. 3, 4.

tube, does it come within the category which he has learned to *label* with the name of a specific compound; or as he learns about Marx's economic interpretation of history or Veblen's theory of the leisure class, can the show-off behavior of certain individuals who display their wealth

Figure 57. The Vigotsky Test

The photograph on page 290 shows the parts used in a test devised by I. S. Vigotsky and now widely used to test the ability to think conceptually. The pieces are spread out roughly into a circle and the subject is told to arrange them in four groups on the basis of a principle that he is to discover. The performance is scored according to the number of hints given and the time taken in arriving at a solution.

The photograph above shows the pieces arranged correctly into the four groups. The correct criterion for grouping is similarity of size and height. A number of other groupings—shape, color, etc.—are possible, but these criteria are not correct. (Modified from E. Hanfman and J. Kasanin, *J. Psychol.*, 1937, 3, 523.)

come properly under the heading "economic behavior"? This process is called concept formation; a concept is a symbol which stands for a specific quality possessed in common by a number of stimuli.

It may be necessary to find not just one common factor running through a series of items, but two or more common factors. One of the best ways of investigating this capacity is a test developed by Vigotsky,[3]

---

[3] See E. Hanfmann and J. Kasanin, A method for the study of concept formation, *J. Psychol.*, 1937, 3, 521–540.

which has been used in clinical practice. You are given blocks which differ from one another in size, height, shape, and color, as shown in Figure 57. You are told to group them into four groups. The experimenter notes your behavior as you try grouping things in one way or another; he tells you only that you are right or wrong. Actually the things that count in the test are height and size; there are these four categories: large tall, large flat, small tall, small flat. The subject who groups according to color or shape, or makes any other error, is told that he is wrong. He must learn for himself to use the two criteria, height and size, in his grouping, and to make his form categories accordingly. It is evident that in such a process it is of paramount importance to be able to maintain a certain direction—that is, maintain a specific set, not to be distracted from the task—and that this set involves a readiness to take account of different attributes of the blocks at the same time. We have, therefore, a rather complex kind of thinking activity. We should expect that the capacity to deal with a problem of this sort would depend in considerable degree upon the kinds of set which various individuals utilize in their attack upon the problem. We find not only that the brain-injured and other handicapped people may be incapable of keeping such categories in mind, but that the perfectly normal person frequently loses the thread and lapses back into a simple method, looking for color or shape even after finding it to be irrelevant. The *concrete attitude* is often dominant over the attitude of looking for abstract categories, the *abstract* or *categorical* attitude.

In fact, Hanfmann[4] has shown that there appear to be at least two fundamental types of set in relation to this Vigotsky task, called a perceiving set and a conceiving set. The people who use the perceiving set look hard at the blocks and wait for the natural groupings to suggest themselves. The latter group, the conceiving type, try from the beginning some sort of rational basis for the groupings; they are seeking abstract principles.

This distinction in terms of perceiving versus conceiving has something in common with a distinction made by the psychiatrist Kurt Gold-

---

[4] E. Hanfmann, A study of personal patterns in an intellectual performance, *Character & Pers.*, 1941, 9, 315–325.

stein,[5] in comparing normal with brain-injured persons. He found that patients with injured or diseased brains may group things together, although incapable of genuine abstract thought. Suppose the task, for example, is to group together yarns of different colors. Your subject seems to understand the task; you have told him to put all the reds together, all the blues together, etc. At the end, however, it turns out that he has put all the reds of exactly the same shade together; the reds that are slightly lighter or slightly darker he has not used. In explaining his response he says that those others are "light red," and that these here are "dark red." He has been able to follow the direct cue from his eyes and to put things side by side *if they look exactly alike;* but to get the abstraction that all red ones are to be put together is too much for him.

A woman with brain disease was unable to copy a square, and it was obvious that the figure did not mean anything to her. However, she could copy the following model:

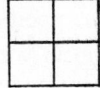

Asked what it was, she explained that it was a window. It could be demonstrated by many examples that if she recognized a model presented to her as a concrete object she could always copy it; if not, she failed. When she was unable to copy a model because it did not mean anything to her, she sometimes changed it so that it assumed for her the characteristics of a concrete object, and then she was able to copy it. Faced with a square:

she produced the following:

  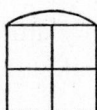

---

[5] K. Goldstein, *The Organism*, New York, American Book, 1935.

When asked what these figures meant, she answered, "The windows of a church." She drew not meaningless squares but three church windows in a position in which they might actually be found; apparently where we see an abstract geometrical figure she had seen a concrete object.[6]

This brings out the importance, in thinking, of maintaining not just a picture in one's head, but an abstract idea. In fact, this abstract idea is usually fundamental in giving the mental set which is essential for the solution of the problem. Such an abstract idea may be maintained by the use of a word—in the earlier instance, the word *red*. Something more than the sheer presence of the word, however, is involved, as is evident from the fact that a brain-injured patient, even when he keeps saying to himself the word *red*, cannot follow through and respond to the abstract principle. It would appear that the word is important as a way of crystallizing and maintaining a certain set, but the set is a more complex response. Similarly, in Hanfmann's experiment mentioned above (cf. page 292), it appears that we are dealing with something deeper than the presence or absence of a specific word operative in the activity of the subjects. Though her subjects were people with normal, not injured, brains, they nevertheless took basically different attitudes toward their problems, attitudes which probably were fairly deeply ingrained personality dispositions.

Although the role of set is important in so elementary a function as matching yarns, its importance becomes even more profound in relation to the types of thinking which we call problem solving, finding an escape from a difficulty or pursuing a goal despite the presence of obstacles. Set often provides the main theme of the task. Suppose we take, for instance, the experiments of Ruger which deal with mechanical puzzles. A large number of intelligent adults went to work on the task of extracting the various triangles, circles, and whatnot, from these complex puzzles; they gave a full report of how they began in each case, pointed out the kinds of attitudes that were present as they worked, and the kinds of things that helped them along or held them back. Typically, the subjects began with an exploratory attitude; there was a good deal of trial and error, poking about, blind pushing and pulling. There was also much trial and

---

[6] K. Goldstein, *Human Nature in the Light of Psychopathology*, Cambridge, Harvard University Press, 1947, pp. 39–42.

error by means of words inwardly spoken, and also trial and error in the manipulation of images, trying to imagine how the thing would look if a certain move were taken. The following example of trial-and-error activity, with narrowing down of the *area* of activity, appeared in working on a puzzle of the chain-and-ring type:

> I tried this [puzzle] at first idly, but then, as I progressed, I had a dim idea that I was doing something and gave careful attention. As I did this I saw that I had not merely made a difference, but had entirely freed the end of the chain which I had used as a loop and that therefore I could entirely free the chain from the stick. I saw this a little before I came to it, but not when I started the movement of the loop through the hole nor even when I passed the rest of the ring through the loop.[7]

There was much transfer from earlier experience with puzzles, and transfer from one puzzle to the next. The subjects phrased these problems in terms of their earlier experience.

But despite the great amount of trial and error and the obvious transfer from earlier experience, there was also much fresh perception of the situation. The reader who has had a go at mechanical puzzles knows how quickly he resorts to phrases like this: "The heart must come out before I can move the bar," "There are two bars that have to be slipped over here before I can do anything with this triangle," etc. Sometimes, with these subjects, the puzzle would suddenly take on a new appearance, as if its parts had recombined; instead of working piecemeal with one piece at a time, the subjects would find a whole new cast or organization of the material taking place. This reorganization is often called "insight." Such insights did not occur in all puzzles with all subjects, but they were rather common. Although they seemed to be "bolts from the blue" in some cases, usually they betrayed a relation to earlier experience with this type of task. The subjects showed, in fact, all shades and degrees of insight, from instant complete insight to a complete lack of it.

> "I knew how to do it as soon as I saw it. A visual image of the corresponding part of the Heart and Bow came on first sight."
> "I have no idea in the world how I did it. I remember moving the loop of the heart around the end of the bar, and the two pieces suddenly came apart."

---

[7] H. A. Ruger, The psychology of efficiency, *Arch. Psychol.*, 1910, No. 15, p. 23.

"I tried random fumbling for several minutes purposely to see if anything would turn up. . . . I was only inattentively aware of what I was doing and did not plan it out. Was shocked with surprise when the rider came off."

"I got it off in a way I had decided I couldn't. I saw a little way ahead that it would come off."

In the same person in the same task there might be both blind trial-and-error behavior and insightful behavior. In other experiments, such as those of Durkin,[8] it is clear that insight may appear in a very high or a very low degree. Methods of work may vary from almost pure "poking about" to almost pure insightful reorganization, with most people mixing the methods, oscillating, working from simple to more complex methods, or even at times falling back from the more complex to the simple. In the long run, experience permits larger integration and more insight appears.

In all such experiments we find a good deal of difference between the person who is making his first attack, and the person who has been making such attacks for a long time. Habits, including higher-unit habits (page 225), are formed. We might think of insight as a rather dramatic case of the sudden formation of a higher unit. The larger these units and the greater their number, and the more effective the associations between them, the more skill one has in a particular task. If this is true of the manipulation of keys on the typewriter, it is probably true of the manipulation of words in solving a verbal problem, or the manipulation of chess pieces in solving chess problems. In each case one learns to manipulate appropriate material by forming larger and larger units. Indeed, there have been several studies of the psychology of chess which show that it differs very little from the learning of simpler tasks. One learns how to look at and how to organize problems in terms of larger and larger units.

But the capacity for integration or insight at any given time and the capacity to make oneself more and more capable of achieving such insight are not to be determined solely in terms of amount of previous experience. General intellectual level has a good deal to do with the matter (pages 358 ff.); general health and alertness are important. As

---

[8] H. E. Durkin, Trial and error, gradual analysis and sudden reorganization; an experimental study of problem solving, *Arch. Psychol.*, 1937, No. 210.

Max Wertheimer used to say, a man with a bad cold (*Schnupfen*) may merely "associate"; the person who is completely himself, who is functioning with all his powers as a human being, is more likely to achieve a complex integration. Especially important is the motivation in relation to the task—the kind of alertness which comes from really wanting to achieve the integration, and not merely to dabble with detail in piecemeal fashion.

There is one rather frequently forgotten fact, however, about motivation. A person may be overmotivated and become so tense as to spoil the job; or he may allow his attitude to be focused not upon the task but upon himself. Ruger found that by far the most effective way of approaching his problems was what he called the "problem attitude," i.e., concern with the problem itself, forgetting the attitude of concern with himself and with the question of how well he was doing. In the same way, even in an abstract verbal problem, the attempt to make a good showing and to prove oneself right can interfere with cold logical reasoning.

The last few paragraphs have related to the role of *set* in the course of thinking. One kind of set—a set toward reality—may reduce errors; another—such as a set to find what one wants to find—may increase them. Nearly always, however, there is more than one set at work; a person may be trying to find a short cut and at the same time to consider every possible clue and leave no stone unturned, or to save trouble and at the same time to prove himself a genius. Often the set keeps changing; one loses the thread. It takes the child many years of growth and learning to develop the set of looking for essential relationships between the things he encounters, rather than just piling one upon another. As a six-year-old looks at a picture he *enumerates* the things he sees—"Then a man, and a lady and a chair and a door"—whereas the ten-year-old *interprets* what is going on. In the same way the child strings together items and lays them side by side. In his many studies of children's thinking, Piaget[9] shows that it is characteristic to *juxtapose* rather than really to integrate when one learns. But it is not only children that do this when the going gets hard. The adult likewise falls short of real integration.

---

[9] J. Piaget, *Judgment and Reasoning in the Child*, New York, Harcourt, Brace, 1928.

When T. M. Abel[10] presented students with orderly narratives, and later asked for recall, she got many replies involving sheer juxtaposition of ideas. Perhaps the reader may have encountered examination papers like this one:

> And the brain is there on top of the spinal cord and it is divided in parts front and back and the front is what we act with (motor) and maybe think also and the back is where sensations come in such as e.g., seeing and perceiving with the eyes which is why you see stars when you bump your head I mean on the back and there are nerve cells in all these parts and they are specialized.

The fact that adults as well as children do this kind of thinking is evidence that the capacity for adequate thinking is not just a question of growing up, but also a question of learning to look for relevant things and of learning to integrate them. To some degree, we really can learn to keep ourselves aimed at the task. Indeed, there is enough transfer from one task to another to warrant using the phrase "learning to think." We have found in this study of thinking all the basic earmarks which we earlier found to characterize the learning process: *set, practice, formation of higher units, transfer of learning to new situations*. Typically one has learned to think *in an area where one has had earlier experience;* it does not follow that there is a great deal of automatic transfer of thinking ability to areas in which one has not as yet had experience. The theologian may make absurd statements about science, or the physicist about social relationships.

Indeed, if we do justice to the great importance of *set* in thinking, we find ourselves forced to recognize that the set to find the true answer is one of many sets that can be important. The set to reach a conclusion in accordance with one's fundamental biases is one of the most important, and it is often nip and tuck as to whether the set to discover the facts will be as strong as the set to find what we want to find. If it is hard to establish the facts, and the whole situation is confused, the greater the role of bias (cf. autism, page 170); but even in as cold a task as reasoning with syllogisms, many investigations have shown how personal bias enters in. Take these propositions used by Janis and Frick:[11]

---

[10] T. M. Abel, Unsynthetic modes of thinking among adults: a discussion of Piaget's concepts, *Amer. J. Psychol.*, 1932, 44, 123–132.

[11] I. L. Janis and F. Frick, The relationship between attitudes toward conclusions and errors in judging logical validity of syllogisms, *J. exp. Psychol.*, 1943, 33, 73–77.

Instructions: This is a test in reasoning. You are to check each of the following arguments as "sound" or "unsound." A sound argument is one in which the conclusion follows logically from the premises. Do not concern yourself with the truth or falsity of the premises. (Note: "All" in logic means *each and every* case. "Some" means *at least one* and perhaps *all* cases.)

1. No Bolsheviks are idealists and all Bolsheviks are Russian. Therefore,
s   some Russians are not idealists.
u

2. The Eskimos are the only people who eat nothing but meat and it is
s   found that all Eskimos have good teeth. So we may conclude that no
u   people who eat only meat have bad teeth.

3. Many brightly colored snakes are poisonous. The copperhead snake is not
s   brightly colored. So the copperhead is not a poisonous snake.
u

4. Some Russians are idealists. All Bolsheviks are Russians. It follows, there-
s   fore, that some Bolsheviks are idealists.
u

5. All poets die young but many professors are old, so we may conclude that
s   not all professors are poets.
u

6. There is no doubt that some drugs are poisonous. All brands of beer con-
s   tain the drug alcohol. Therefore, some brands of beer are poisonous.
u

7. All poisonous things are bitter. Arsenic is not bitter. Therefore, arsenic is
s   not poisonous.
u

8. Some sailors are not able to swim. All Nantucketers can swim. Therefore,
s   no Nantucketers are sailors.
u

In response to these propositions, students tended to draw conclusions that were in accord with their personal views, though not warranted by the data given. Similarly, Lefford,[12] using material of the following sort:

The reality of any phenomenon is established by scientific investigation and treatment. The existence of God does not lend itself to scientific investigation and treatment. Therefore, the existence of God is not real,

found in a large student group a great piling up of errors when emotion entered as bias into the judgment, as compared with control material of an unemotional sort.

---

[12] A. Lefford, The influence of emotional subject matter on logical reasoning, *J. gen. Psychol.*, 1946, *34*, 127–151.

We said above that the theologian and the physicist may exhibit areas in which they have not learned to think competently. The same is true of us all. The psychologist has his own limitations due to his own special training in certain areas and his absence of training in others; no one altogether transcends the limitations and biases of his own special experience and training. But it is the ideal of the educator to train those types of universal soundness and rightness in thinking which can be recognized in every sphere of activity, and the psychologist should be the first to recognize the importance of this achievement whenever it is realized in actuality. But men whose thinking is equally sound in all areas are hard to find. The trouble is that it is so often assumed that studying particular books or subject matter will automatically engender such universality of competence. What we know from studies of thinking up to the present time suggests that we have to go at the matter the hard way, exposing the student constantly to more and more problems, giving him more and more experience, enabling him to discover more and more of his own weaknesses, and hoping that to some slight degree we can at least in certain cases give such an attitude of *wanting* to think straight, such a love of truth, that it may actually leaven the whole lump of attitude toward life, in terms of a quest for that which is sound and can be validated.

Individuality in Thinking

So far, we have been looking for generalizations about the thought processes. At the same time, there is a very large factor of personal idiosyncrasy in the way one thinks. Recent studies of the thinking of college students have shown a fascinating variety and individuality in the form, style, speed, proneness to cold vs. emotional types of thinking, the likelihood of getting blocked through fear of encountering results which one does not want to encounter, and all the personality factors that have already been considered in relation to imagining (page 276). In one study, for example, we are introduced to the *rigid* student, whose mind is effective provided that her basic *ways of thinking*, her casehardened methods, do not have to be altered.[13] Another type, the

---

[13] L. B. Murphy and H. Ladd, *Emotional Factors in Learning*, New York, Columbia University Press, 1944.

scattered student, can nibble freely over many spots in a large pasture, and think clearly here and there, but cannot follow an orderly or disciplined path of thinking through anything. A third type, the ivory-tower *escapist*, can learn almost anything that is abstract and difficult, provided that it does not touch upon the sore spots, the emotional, social, esthetic, ethical problems of daily living. In terms of the family's point of view about political questions, for example, she wants it understood that "their daughter is a fine scholarly woman of whom they can be proud"; and her picture of herself is such that any dabbling in the practical social consequences of a theory—e.g., in race relations or international relations, etc.—would be altogether too terrifying. The result is that she literally does not and *cannot think* in such areas.

More common perhaps than any of the others is the student who has exploited a particular field as something at which he is good, and thinks of other fields as fields in which he is "no good." The picture a student has formed of himself is so clear that he can easily make an attack upon any subject that comes within the category of things at which he is good; but try to introduce him to any other sort of topic, and his mind goes fuzzy. He may or may not have been poor at it in the beginning; the important thing is that he has become far worse through the conscious, or more likely unconscious, process of simply refusing to make contact with something which might possibly reveal his inadequacies. Or it may not be a question of absolute adequacy or inadequacy; in comparing himself with his big brother or someone else whom he idealizes, he may fear that he would show up unfavorably.

The case of Hortense shows some of the relations of personality to thinking:

Hortense is the sort of person who likes to impress others with the fact that she is extraordinary. Her whole behavior is calculated for effect. She would like to be something special and tries by suggestion to influence other people to accept this ideal. If others believe in her, her self-confidence is greatly increased, and she outdoes herself still more in the display of her fascinations.

Her show-off mechanism takes on various forms. She throws crumbs of information around as though she were very well informed on scientific matters and were very well educated in general, and conjures up far-distant, and, to her, fine-sounding, worlds, in order to attract others to her. At the same time she treats other people with condescension in order to emphasize her superiority.

She is able to maintain this attitude only at the beginning of a new situation, at the first meeting with people. The foundations are too frail, her actual feeling of self-confidence too much disturbed, for her to be able to preserve the attitude. Looked at more deeply, she is tormented by great fears and by a very wavering self-assurance, so that she is quite empty and is shivering inwardly. When strong emotions threaten to overpower her, she cannot maintain her pretentious attitude and does not feel so imposing and superior any more, but very small, helpless and dependent. She then feels constrained, overshadowed, delivered up to others who are stronger than she is. She offers defiant, rebellious resistance, shows her teeth, puts on again her air of originality, is, however, full of a fear which does not leave her in peace, but which, indeed, pursues her constantly. She does not intend to let herself be caught, others are not to see through her artifices or to dare to criticize her; she herself will provide the mask which fits her, and no one has anything to say about it. But finally she becomes exhausted and has to give in. This is the conflict and battle which takes place again and again, in which she is overcome, but which she always takes up again rebelliously. This is a battle for nothing less than her prestige and the wish to dictate to others how and in what way she is unique. A really creative substance is entirely lacking. She conceals ignorance behind vague, indefinite, relative statements, whose meaning is just as obscure to her as it is to others, but in so doing she would like to pose mysterious riddles and once more make herself interesting. By means of this vague, indefinite behavior she avoids committing herself and leaves a way clear for retreat.

She is quite intelligent and also has artistic interests, but because she has shut herself off from full participation in an objective or personal problem, she can progress only up to a certain superficial point which is quickly reached. She has decided possibilities for development which should be encouraged and strengthened. Her further development will depend very much on whether she succeeds in throwing off her mask. Even though there may be occasional outbursts of defiance and restrained indignation on her part toward her surroundings, she can probably overcome her difficulties, particularly with friendly encouragement and assistance.[14]

The cases noted so far seem to emphasize emotional and motivational factors primarily. There are, however, still other factors in thinking which appear to go quite deeply to the roots of individuality, and to relate in some degree to a basic style or mode of attack, such as we can see in the tiny infant who proceeds either globally or in piecemeal fashion (page 25), who is smooth and even in performance, or jerky and staccato. We shall return later to these matters of personality style (pages 496 ff.), but this is the place to say that individuality in thinking

---

[14] *Ibid.*, pp. 187–188.

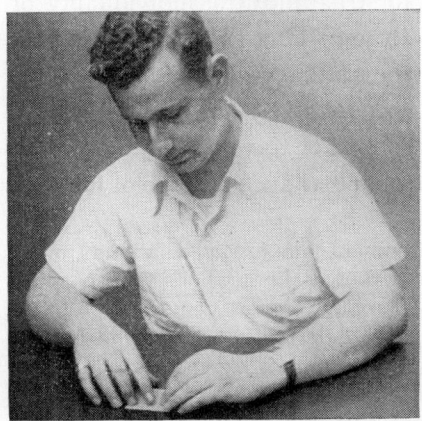

In these five photographs the subject is at first eagerly confronting the pieces of a difficult jigsaw puzzle. He pauses temporarily to figure things out, then he bends over the puzzle and is closely involved with a new approach. Finally he relaxes as he realizes that he is nearing the solution. These changes in posture and expression reveal fluctuations in attitude and changes in motivation.

Figure 58. Thought Processes and Goals

is as much a question of style of attack on tasks and goals as it is a question of the emotions which block thinking.

One more obvious point about the morbid tone which enters the discussion when we begin to talk about "impairment of one's thinking by emotion." There is often a positive as well as a negative aspect to this question of the relation of emotion to thought. Emotion may be the greatest stimulus, the greatest release, the greatest polarizer and canalizer of all energies, including those of thought. Much of the world's greatest thought arises from the passionate demand to prove a case or discover a solution. We come back, then, to the point already emphasized: the fact that thought processes are not dissociated from the world of our needs and impulses, but betray both the weaknesses and the strengths which are given by our struggles toward our goals. And much of this is often reflected even in the postures and expressions of the individual in the process of working through a problem. (See Figure 58.)

Finally, lest it be thought that the various aspects of thought can simply be enumerated and left like pieces in separate boxes—one piece relating to motive, one to personality style, one to past experience, one to present set, etc.—three students' short-answer reflections on the same problem will conclude this chapter. They show how the same material was effectively used by these individuals in radically different forms. Thinking was good in all cases, but the attack upon the question which was asked required enough thought to strike into the individuality of each person, and he came through with something that served his purpose well. Often less important than the accuracy of the answer is the portrayal of individuality which each account gives. The original lecture covered essentially the content of Chapter 2 of this book; the examination question was as follows: "Discuss the inheritance of sense of humor."

Student A. Both heredity and environment are involved. Infants often manifest jolly or phlegmatic temperaments. But if the mother's time is spent largely with the child, she may stimulate its jolly temperament.

Student B. Whatever the genes may do to determine strength and health, which I suppose is important, the thing that counts is exposure of the child to comics, movies, etc.; he picks it up by learning.

Student C. If by inheritance is meant that these personality traits are directly taken over from the parents, I disagree. The genes may *limit* what a child may become, but *positive* things come from the environment

SUGGESTED READINGS

Dunker, K., *On Problem Solving* (trans. by L. S. Lees), Washington, Amer. Psychol. Assn., 1945.

Durkin, H. E., Trial and error, gradual analysis and sudden reorganization; an experimental study of problem solving, *Arch. Psych.*, 1937, No. 210.

Goldstein, K., *Abstract and Concrete Behavior*, Psychological Monographs, 1941, No. 239.

Stern, W., *Psychology of Early Childhood* (trans. by A. Barwell), New York, Holt, 1924, Part 8.

Wertheimer, M., *Productive Thinking*, New York, Harper, 1945.

Woodworth, R. S., *Experimental Psychology*, New York, Holt, 1938, chaps. 29, 30.

18 CREATING

It is common in everyday life to assume that there are two kinds of mental activity: first, that which reconstructs the past; secondly, that which initiates the new. But the examples already given may help to show that the two modes of activity are inextricably intertwined. Indeed, there is something old and something new about everything we do. Creation, or initiation of the new, differs only in degree from activity which is primarily concerned with reproduction of the past. Whether in art, in science, or in daily life, each act is the carrying forward of a previous activity in relation to a present situation that is never the exact duplication of a situation already encountered.

We are all creators in a way, and under the stress of strong feeling or a big idea we may say something that rings out in real eloquence. George Thomson tells of an experience among the Irish peasantry which makes it clear that the ordinary person is not so very different from the poet:

One evening, strolling through this village, perched high up over the Atlantic, I came to the village well. There I met a friend of mine, an old peasant woman. She had just filled her buckets and stood looking out over the sea. Her husband was dead, and her seven sons had all been "gathered away," as she expressed it, to Springfield, Massachusetts. A few days before a letter had arrived from one of them, urging her to follow them, so that she could end her days in comfort, and promising to send the passage money if only she would agree. All this she told me in detail, and described her life—the trudge to the turf stack in the hills, the loss of her hens, the dark, smoky cabin; then she spoke of America as she imagined it to be—an Eldorado where you could pick up gold on the pavements, and the railway journey to Cork, the transatlantic crossing, and her longing that her bones might rest in Irish soil. As she spoke she grew excited, her language became more fluent, more highly colored, rhythmical, melodious, and her body swayed in a dreamy, cradle-like accompaniment. Then she picked up her buckets with a laugh, wished me good night, and went home.

This unpremeditated outburst from an illiterate woman with no artistic pretensions had all the characteristics of poetry. It was inspired.[1]

Sensitiveness

But it is our problem in this chapter to consider in greater detail and with sharper emphasis than heretofore that aspect of imagining and thinking which leads to the production of the new.

In Walter de la Mare's study[2] of the early memories of men of literary genius, one is reminded of the extraordinary individual differences in the sensitiveness of children to the different kinds of sights, sounds, smells, rhythms that make up the salient aspects of their own personal worlds. Each child is more sensitive or less sensitive than another to the pattern of the rain, the touch of the wind on the cheek, the song of the robin, the curious slate blue of the distant village roofs. In Walt Whitman's poem, "There Was a Child Went Forth," all the little strands of the poet's early Long Island experience are woven into the texture of his adult personality.

> *There was a child went forth every day;*
> *And the first object he look'd upon, that object he became;*
> *And that object became part of him for the day, or a certain*
>   *part of the day, or for many years, or stretching cycles*
>   *of years.*
>
> *The early lilacs became part of this child,*
> *And grass, and white and red morning-glories, and white*
>   *and red clover, and the song of the phoebe-bird,*
> *. . . all became part of him.*

Such sensitiveness to the environment, and love of its colors, tones, relationships of space and time, enter into the trend of mind from which creativeness springs.

Thomas Wolfe[3] is describing Eugene Gant at the age of six:

---

[1] George Thomson, *Marxism and Poetry*, New York, International Publishers, 1946, pp. 8–9.
[2] W. de la Mare, *Early One Morning*, New York, Macmillan, 1935.
[3] Thomas Wolfe, *Look Homeward, Angel*, New York, Grosset & Dunlap (by special arrangement with Charles Scribner's Sons), 1929.

Eugene was loose now in the limitless meadows of sensation; his sensory equipment was so complete that at the moment of perception of a single thing, the whole background of color, warmth, odor, sound, taste established itself, so that later, the breath of a hot dandelion brought back the grass-warm banks of Spring, a day, a place, the rustling of young leaves, or the page of a book, the thin exotic smell of tangerine, the wintry bite of great apples; or as with *Gulliver's Travels,* a bright windy day in March, the spurting moments of warmth, the drip and reek of the earth-thaw, the feel of the fire. . . . (p. 81)

. . . he felt the golden world in the thousand mixed mysterious odors and sensations. He loved the smell of cellars, cobwebs. . . . (p. 84)

. . . the smell of stored apples in the cellar . . . of pears ripening on a sunny shelf, and of ripe cherries stewing with sugar on hot stoves before preserving. . . . (p. 85)

And now, whetted intemperately by what he had felt, he began, at school, in that fecund romance, the geography, to breathe the mixed odors of the earth, sensing in every squat keg piled on a pier-head a treasure of golden rum, rich port, fat Burgundy; smelling the jungle growth of the tropics, the heavy odor of plantations, the salt-fish smell of harbors. . . . (p. 86)

In beginning with the fact of individual sensitiveness, we are trying to see how this sensitiveness becomes related to creativeness. Such individual differences are evident in the earliest response to the types of play material with which very tiny children can cope, and out of which they can make something that is satisfying to them. Children have always played with mud pies, snowballs, broken bits of stone or china which attract them, which they treasure or try to put together. And human society even at the simple level of the Eskimo makes toys for children such as little sleds or kayaks, noting the kinds of things which particularly delight them. The children make their own copies of the objects which the adults have made for their children in miniature form. In our own society nowadays we use not only the familar blocks out of which houses and towers can be made, and the traditional doll house and the human figures that go with it, but also materials that are manipulated especially easily by very small children, such as finger paints—a compound of flour, water, and coloring matter which the child can smear and push about as he likes. These finger paintings show strikingly the different individual sensitivities to color and to darkness and brightness, the early impulses to symmetry or to asymmetry, and the tendency toward subdued even tones or toward sharp contrasts (cf. pages 459–460).

Such love of color, line, surface, etc., appearing at an early level, may become the root from which later artistic activity springs. The same is true of expression in the sphere of literature; as we note the child's earliest toying with words we may see the beginnings of a literary imagination. In the realm of music, spontaneous hummings and chantings in three-year-olds are easily written down and made into acceptable songs.

In the case of those who become scientists, one often notes in childhood the delight in the orderly processes of nature and in wheels and pulleys, and the contrivances which produce mechanical effects. In the life history of Sir Isaac Newton one finds an early joy in the spatial and temporal relationships and in the mechanical laws governing the things expressed in them.

It is not only the world of the senses that gives joy to the creator; it may also be the world of *relationships,* such as the relationships with which mathematics and science deal. Aldous Huxley, in his story of Guido, might well have been referring to the childhood of such a man as Isaac Newton. "What I saw was Guido with a burnt stick in his hand, demonstrating on the smooth paving stones of the path, that the square on the hypotenuse of a right angled triangle is equal to the sum of the squares on the other two sides." Guido, who has had no contact with geometry or mathematics, explains the Pythagorean theorem in a completely original, though involved, manner. And after the explanation, he says, with an expression of delighted relief, "You see it seemed to me so beautiful, so easy." Like music, the sense of form in mathematics seems to fulfill a wide range of needs which in their entirety constitute Guido's personality.[4]

To be creative, therefore, appears to mean, among other things, that the individual is sensitive and selective to certain kinds of material, both by way of directing attention to them and by way of enjoying making new combinations with them. In this process the learning activities, of course, blend intimately with the most primitive processes of sensing. The canalization process, as we have seen, is going on. Reds or blacks may satisfy the child and help to play a larger and larger part in the early finger-painting construction; wheels and pulleys may play a rapidly

---

[4] A. Huxley, *Young Archimedes,* New York, Doran, 1924, p. 290.

increasing part in the earliest satisfactions in mechanical manipulation. There has to be some satisfaction in the beginning; but this satisfaction may become more and more specific and intense in relation to the material with which one has early experience. It is equally evident that conditioning is likewise occurring, as one gives names to things, and becomes thereby conditioned to the names. "I am making a train; I am building a boat." These are typically ways of providing continuity from one activity to another, of reminding oneself in a later play period of what one has done before, and projecting into the future the fulfillment of that upon which one is already bent. Many of the responses to toys, tools, etc., are likewise acquired by observing, grouping, forming higher units, exactly as in learning to telegraph or acquiring any other motor skill. Indeed, this same individuality of responsiveness and selectivity is clearly reflected in the creative products of young adult amateurs, even when the stimulating materials are arbitrarily limited. (See Figure 59.)

Creative Skills

Just as there are great individual differences in early sensitiveness, so there are great individual differences in the ability to learn what can be done with each kind of material provided. We are dealing not entirely with an abstract or general "ability to learn," but primarily with the knack or special gift of learning particular responses which result in particularly satisfying results—exceptional speed or manual skill or good form. The child who takes quick and effective advantage of an opportunity to learn specific skills is the one about whom we say "he is gifted" in painting, music, or science, or whatever it may be.

In making such comparisons, it is not sufficient to talk of the child's general "learning ability" as such. It is clear that, as the child matures, his ability in some fields of activity far outstrips his abilities in others. If we compare the early experiences of Mozart and of Goethe, we find Mozart constantly forming interesting or even exquisite new melodies, and Goethe delightful verses. In addition to their sensitiveness, and in addition to their ability to learn, there was a marked predisposition toward learning particular kinds of things; it was this aptitude in learning which marked the unfolding of their talent. In Charlotte Bühler's

Like everyone else, the artist is a unique personality and perceives in terms of this uniqueness; it is his perception that transforms fact into a work of art. This is well brought out by these four paintings representing the artists' impression of the same subject. The marked differences in texture, color, composition, and size express the individuality that has gone into each painting.

Figure 59. Individuality in Creativeness

studies of the life histories of many men and women of creative power,[5] one finds countless illustrations of this early differentiation of individuals in terms of their special proneness toward one or another kind of learning process.

Many children are sensitive to rich and varied smells and to the rich and varied sounds of words; but in addition to such sensitiveness it takes immense verbal *skill* to define as could Baudelaire the world of imagination to which the smells hold the clue (cf. page 193).

Often one can directly witness the unfolding of creative talent. As children are exposed to new opportunities to acquire skill with words or color or musical tone or scientific instruments, some can only repeat or give back the separate elements already given them, while others quickly leap forward to make the freshest and most interesting combinations. For reasons already considered (page 309), the new material that appears has order and is not chaotic; it is as a rule only the disturbed child in whom the material spurts up like an undisciplined geyser. Order is of the nature of the creative process, not only in a genius, but in the ordinary person. The degree, style, type of order, and the extent to which the material differs from material that the individual has already encountered, together with the degree of satisfaction which the individual and other human beings derive from the combination, are all among the things that must be considered important in evaluating the process of creation.

Skills which begin in this simple way rapidly elaborate themselves by the processes of learning already considered (page 228). As one learns to combine words, or tones, or colors, or the parts of a simple erector set, i.e., as one achieves more and more generalized skill with the material, one builds up higher units. Learning what colors go well with other colors, and how the light and shade combine to give a peculiar effect, one puts the principles of color combination together with the principles of light-shade construction and gets a broader conception of the feeling tones that can arise from complex patterns in which both kinds of principles are used. More and more principles are being integrated as one works toward a synthesis which is as broad as the material

---

[5] C. Bühler. *Der menschliche Lebenslauf*, Leipzig, Hirzel, 1933.

allows. In the same way the budding engineer learns to see the relations between fuels, heat, and work done, and the relations between wheels and the belts they move, and he puts the principles together so as to realize in action a new design which, while using the same fuel supply, will move the belt faster. From such an accumulation of higher units there comes the capacity to build a new structure or pattern.

Along with this process of working from the simple to the complex goes the emergence of *new needs;* for, as we saw earlier, the accumulation of materials that satisfy needs leads us to become bored or satiated, and we crave new combinations. Something new must again be created. Just what it shall be is largely a question of set, especially a question of mood. What is needed is not a new element, but a new structure, and one which contains the old but goes beyond it and is related to it in terms of set. Usually the set is in the direction of developing what is already implicit, or in the direction of offering contrast to what is already given. In this way the poet balances not one word against another word, but a phrase against a phrase, a line against a line, a stanza against a stanza; and having written his stanza, he knows that his poem is inadequate until another stanza is written to intensify the effect or produce a contrasting effect. In Milton's "L'Allegro" and "Il Penseroso" we see how one whole poem initiated a need for another; the poet had accented the gay and lyrical to such a degree in "L'Allegro" that he had to set up a sort of counterpoise in the more somber and serious mood of "Il Penseroso." These poems of Milton also show how great is the role of mood—or, more broadly, the role of set—in all creation.

The process by which the accumulation of satisfying materials leads to the need for more complex materials of the same general sort, under the influence of a prevailing mood, is shown in Coleridge's great poem "Kubla Khan." A student of English literature[6] traced Coleridge's travels and reading through a twenty-five-year period during which he accumulated that rich storehouse of materials which appears in the image of the "Damsel with a Dulcimer." Coleridge had built together in this poem a great many units gathered over the years; these accumulated materials were ready and waiting to leap into fresh integration. At times,

---

[6] J. L. Lowes, *The Road to Xanadu,* Boston, Houghton Mifflin, 1927.

however, the mood may be especially favorable to a massive integration of a whole encyclopedia of experience. In the case of the dream which brought him the poem "Kubla Khan," one may see the fulfillment of years of "incubation." What was needed to effect this fulfillment was a particular mood, a certain way of thinking and feeling which drew to itself by association all the phrases and all the images which had ever occurred in that mood, and the articulation of which could be achieved only in complete attention to that process, free of all distractions. In a morning dream Coleridge constructed a long, complete poem, of which the fragment known as "Kubla Khan" is all that remains. Upon awakening from the dream, he began immediately to record the poem from his memory of the dream. After completing eighty lines, he was unfortunately interrupted by a business visit. He tells us how, after he had transacted his business, it was utterly impossible to put together again all the shattered pieces of his dream creation, or to recapture the essential mood. The poem stands today as an amazing monument to the processes of accumulation and incubation, and to the importance of a favorable mood in achieving an integration. Even in the waking state, the interruption of one's mood is for most people the end of the creative process.

Just as we may learn what is most stimulating and constructive in aiding such an integrated creation, so from the works of poets and scientists we may learn what is likely to block the creative mood. In addition to sheer physical interruptions, there are many dynamic factors in the individual personality which make it impossible at a given time to go forward. As we saw in connection with psychoanalysis (page 129), the fear that a certain thought will emerge may paralyze us. Not only does one predisposition block another predisposition—for life is always selective—but in addition we may feel totally blocked in the sense that the whole direction required by the creation may be one we fear to take. If, for example, a person has been ridiculed as a child for his poems, the entire region represented by poems may be full of sore spots, and he may hardly be able to find the way. Or if the material of a particular poem deals with an early love affair about which he had to blush when the other boys laughed, the mature love poem may find itself blocked in the very process of being written. All this points to the necessity of making the most of favorable moments and especially of moments when one is free of this sense of outer constraint or inner annoyance.

The same holds true for scientific creation as well as for artistic creation. The scientist finds himself frequently blocked in the development of a mode of thought which would solve his problem, and it is only when he is finally relaxed and free of tension that the problem becomes clear. He may be blocked by having too many ideas at once and he may need a chance to relax and sort them out, letting some of them fade and others take clearer form. The individual may be blocked not only for the moment but for a lifetime by the false assumptions, the erroneous sets which have come from all his early training and outlook. He may also be blocked by the set which he shares with all the people of his time—the fact that the community as a whole has a wrong set toward the problem. Remembering also what was said earlier about self-consciousness and the "problem attitude" (page 297), we find that the scientist as well as the literary man may be blocked by the fear of seeming wrong, and may reach his highest creations when he is not thinking about himself at all, but is lost in the problem itself. Whether the idea which is being created is big or small, it needs a chance to be born in its own way, not forced at the very beginning into its parent's notions as to what sort of idea it ought to be.

When asked *how* he composed, these were Mozart's words:

What, you ask, is my method in writing and elaborating my large and lumbering things? I can in fact say nothing more about it than this: I do not myself know and can never find out. When I am in particularly good condition, perhaps riding in a carriage, or in a walk after a good meal, and in a sleepless night, then the thoughts come to me in a rush, and best of all. Whence and how—that I do not know and cannot learn. Those which please me I retain in my head, and hum them perhaps also to myself—at least so others have told me. If I stick to it, there soon come one after another useful crumbs for the pie, according to counterpoint, harmony of the different instruments, etc., etc. That now inflames my soul, namely, if I am not disturbed. Then it goes on growing, and I keep on expanding it and making it more distinct, and the thing, however long it be, becomes indeed almost finished in my head, so that I afterwards survey it at a glance, like a goodly picture or handsome man, and in my imagination do not hear it at all in succession, as it afterwards must be heard, but as a simultaneous whole. That is indeed a feast! All the finding and making only goes on in me as in a very vivid dream. But the rehearsal—all together, that is best of all. What now has thus come

CREATING 315

into being in this way, that I do not easily forget again, and it is perhaps the best gift which the Lord God has given me. When now I afterwards come to write it down, I take out of the sack of my brain what has been previously garnered in the aforesaid manner. Accordingly it gets pretty quickly onto paper; for, as has been said, it is properly speaking already finished; and will, moreover, also be seldom very different from what it was previously in the head. Accordingly I may be disturbed in writing, and even all sorts of things may go on around me, still I go on writing; even also chatting at the same time, namely, of hens and geese, or of Dolly and Joan, etc.[7]

And if this be true of music, compare with it the words of the mathematician Poincaré:

It is certain that the combinations which present themselves to the mind in a kind of sudden illumination after a somewhat prolonged period of unconscious work are generally useful and fruitful combinations, which appear to be the result of a preliminary sifting. . . . This, too, is most mysterious. How can we explain the fact that, of the thousand products of our unconscious activity, some are invited to cross the threshold, while others remain outside? Is it mere chance that gives them this privilege? Evidently not. . . .

All that we can hope from these inspirations, which are the fruits of unconscious work, is to obtain points of departure for (our) calculations. As for the calculations themselves, they must be made in the second period of conscious work which follows the inspiration. . . . They demand discipline, attention, will, and consequently consciousness. In the subliminal ego, on the contrary, there reigns what I would call liberty, if one could give this name to the mere absence of discipline and to disorder born of chance. Only, this very disorder permits of unexpected couplings.[8]

These sudden insights or moments of reorganization have occasioned much controversy, because they suggest two opposed theories of what the mind is and how it works. One conception is that the mind is ultimately a synthesis of pieces, each of which has its own internal characteristics. These must be put together in a particular way to achieve unity. The other conception emphasizes the overall unity of the organism and of the life process, and looks upon the pieces or parts as not completely independent but as reflecting the context in which they appear. From the former viewpoint it would seem rather mysterious that the parts "know how" to leap together into a new integration. From the latter viewpoint it is of the essence of thought, as of all life activity,

---

[7] Quoted from R. W. Gerard, The biological basis of imagination, *Sci. Mon.*, 1946, 62, 80.
[8] *Ibid.*

to function in a unified way, and the parts serve a function which is given by the very nature of the process that is going on. As we have already suggested, the first theory seems to be rather blind to the reality of much that is unified in life processes, and the second view seems to be rather blind to the amount of independent or autonomous activity that actually goes on. Certainly the second school of thought seems to have an advantage, at least in this respect: it has been impossible to show a piecemeal process of association in many of these cases of creativeness. The direct empirical study of the cases seems also to show that a very complex process of creation may literally occur all at once.

But there is more to be said. It has sometimes been urged that true creativeness must always be an inspiration, in the sense that the full answer to a problem must come all at once. It must be granted that in Rossman's collection of material on inventors[9] there is evidence that the long and weary accumulation of odds and ends of more or less relevant material may be suddenly and brilliantly consummated in a scheme which meets all the needs. At the same time, if we go through such material with a somewhat skeptical eye, we also find a good deal of evidence of many piecemeal activities, many moments of "little creativeness." Instead of suddenly rising to a new level at a single leap as if mounting a long flight of stairs, we sometimes find that each tread is only a few inches above the preceding one. Indeed, there are some cases that seem more like going up an inclined plane in which there is no sudden lift, only the "slow, dead heave" all the way.

Factors Favorable to Creativeness

It is worth while, then, to try to find out what it is that makes possible both the big creative moments and the little ones. What is the exact nature of those favorable states in which real progress comes? Certainly we can emphasize: (1) the fact of needs that lead to absorption in the problem; (2) freedom from distraction by self-consciousness or concern with irrelevant issues; (3) the appropriateness and stability of a particular mood which allows us to bring into focus everything that shares in that mood; (4) that peculiar state of mind in which we recog-

---

[9] J. J. Rossman, *The Psychology of the Inventor,* Washington, Inventors Publishing Co., 1931.

nize in the fringe of consciousness (or "out of the corner of our eye") something which is relevant to the problem. There is much more out in this margin than we can look at. We can throw the spotlight upon the immediate materials on hand, perhaps a half dozen or so of them, or groups of materials in the form of higher units, but we have to learn by an enormous amount of "working through" to get the feel of the materials away out at the edge of our mind which might be relevant to our problem. In the same way the conductor of an orchestra not only has to be attentive to the particular instruments which are leading in a given passage; he must be able to hear the individual variations in tempo and style which characterize the men in the remotest edge of his field of seeing and hearing. (5) In relation to this matter of alertness to all the materials out there "at the edge of the mind," we may go even further and stress the mass of material which has been accumulated in the past and of which we are not at all conscious at the time. This is what is meant by saying that the genius draws upon his unconscious (or subconscious). This is the theory of genius offered by Frederic Myers,[10] who did more than anyone else to show the process by which the accumulations stored up and ready for use, but not actually in consciousness at the time, can suddenly and definitely be drawn into a single integration. Myers suggested that we should think of all the vast realm which lies outside of consciousness as *subliminal,* that is, beneath the threshold, and that we think of the process of creativeness as an "uprush" of materials, almost as in the form of a geyser. When once conditions are optimal, a "subliminal uprush" characterizes the moment of peak creativeness.

It is worth while, however, to remember that these most dramatic cases are simply the upper end of a continuum, that there are all degrees of suddenness, of newness of material, and of dramatic quality. There is much everyday pedestrian "sweating it out," the thing to which Edison referred when he said that genius is one percent inspiration and ninety-nine percent perspiration. There are all types and degrees of creative activity.

This last fact makes it appropriate to emphasize that almost invariably there is a process of "hammering out," of reshaping, of filing and fitting,

---

[10] F. W. H. Myers, *Human Personality and Its Survival of Bodily Death,* New York, Longmans, Green, 1903, 2 vols.

which gives more finished form to the product. Even in the case of the inventors described by Rossman, some of whom have been at the business for a lifetime, a final invention which seems so perfect may lack some essential detail, some essential which will enable the product to do a successful job; or it may be perfectly sound yet cost too much to be commercially practical. There is, then, a need for a process of criticism, selection, and reorganization; and, indeed, little insights or supplementary insights or illuminations may come all along the way to support and implement the primary inspiration which has occurred earlier. Incidentally it must be remembered that inspirations often seem at first to be absolute, final, perfect, but may later be rejected or replaced by the creator himself; and at times these inspirations, however great they may seem to him, may be viewed by his successors as trivial and of little worth. In the long run it is the human community which decides how great, how new, and how important the results of a given illumination are.

So far as we know, this is the general nature of human creativeness, in which we all share. It is not limited to geniuses; or, if one likes, one may say that everybody has something of the genius—sometimes in a single field only, sometimes in more than one, depending both upon original gifts and upon both general and specific learning processes. The following quotation from the poet Housman will serve to illustrate these last points; in a way it will remind us that the poet should not stand on a pedestal, and it can remind us of things that we all sense in ourselves:

Having drunk a pint of beer at luncheon—beer is a sedative to the brain, and my afternoons are the least intellectual portion of my life—I would go out for a walk of two or three hours. As I went along, thinking of nothing in particular, only looking at things around me and following the progress of the seasons, there would flow into my mind, with sudden and unaccountable emotion, sometimes a line or two of verse, sometimes a whole stanza at once, accompanied, not preceded, by a vague notion of the poem which they were destined to form part of. Then there would usually be a lull of an hour or so, then perhaps the spring would bubble up again. I say bubble up, because, so far as I could make out, the source of the suggestions thus proffered to the brain was an abyss which I have already had occasion to mention, the pit of the stomach. When I got home I wrote them down, leaving gaps, and hoping that further inspiration might be forthcoming another day. Sometimes it was, if I took my walks in a receptive and expectant frame of mind; but sometimes the poem had to be taken in hand and completed by the brain, which was apt to be a matter of trouble and anxiety, involving trial and disappointment, and sometimes ending in failure. I happen to remember distinctly the genesis of the piece which stands last in my first volume. Two of the stanzas, I do not say which, came into my head, just as they are printed, while I was crossing the corner of Hempstead Heath between the Spaniard's Inn and the footpath to Temple Fortune. A third stanza came with a little coaxing after tea. One more was needed, but it did not come; I had to turn to and compose it myself, and that was a laborious business. I wrote it thirteen times, and it was more than a twelvemonth before I got it right.[11]

But an even fuller picture appears if we allow ourselves to see the *life history* of the developing creative gift, the steps by which one masters the art of creating. It happened that one of the group of gifted children who were studied years ago at Stanford University—Henry Cowell—later became a well-known musician. He told his story in a manner that highlights the way in which sensitiveness, learning, higher units, illumination integrate in a creative act.

It is doubtful whether any composer can have a well-working "soundmind" without going through a rigorous process of self-training to make it so. I will give as an example my own development; several other composers have told me they went through a similar progress.

As a child I was compelled to make my mind into a musical instrument because between the ages of eight and fourteen years I had no other, yet desired strongly to hear music frequently. I could not attend enough concerts to satisfy the craving for music, so I formed the habit, when I did attend them, of deliberately rehearsing the compositions I heard and liked, in order that I might play them over mentally whenever I chose. At first the rehearsal was very imperfect. I could only hear the melody and a mere snatch of the harmony, and had to make great effort to hear the right tone-quality. I would try, for instance, to hear a violin tone, but unless I worked hard to keep a grip on it, it would shade off into something indeterminate.

No sooner did I begin this self-training than I had at times curious experiences of having glorious sounds leap unexpectedly into my mind—original melodies and complete harmonies such as I could not conjure forth at will, and exalted qualities of tone such as I had never heard nor before imagined. I had at first not the slightest control over what was being played in my mind at these times; I could not bring the music about at will, nor could I capture the material sufficiently to write it down. Perhaps these experiences constituted what is known as an "inspiration."

I believe, had I let well enough alone and remained passive, that the state

---

[11] A. E. Housman, *The Name and Nature of Poetry*, New York, Cambridge University Press, 1933; the quotation is from pp. 48–50 of the 1944 ed.

of being subject to these occasional musical visitations would have remained, and that I would now be one of those who have to "wait for an inspiration." But I was intensely curious concerning the experiences and strove constantly to gain some sort of control over them, and finally found that by an almost super-human effort I could bring one of them about. I practiced doing this until I became able to produce them with ease. It was not until then that I began to develop some slight control over the musical materials. At first able to control only a note or two during a musical flow lasting perhaps half an hour, I became able, by constant attempt, to produce more and more readily whatever melodies and harmonies and tone-qualities I desired, without altering the nature of the flow of sounds. I practiced directing the flow into the channels of the sounds of a few instruments at a time, until I could conjure their sounds perfectly at will.

As soon as I could control which sounds I should hear, and turn on a flow of them at will, I was able, by virtue of studying notation, to write down the thought, after going over it until it was thoroughly memorized. I have never tried to put down an idea until I have rehearsed it mentally so many times that it is impossible to forget the second part while writing down the first.

I shall never forget the disappointment I experienced when I first wrote down a composition and played it. Could it be that this rather uninteresting collection of sounds was the same as the theme that sounded so glorious in my mind? I rehearsed it all carefully; yes, it was the same harmony and melody, but most of the indescribable flowing richness had been lost by the imperfect playing of it on the imperfect instrument which all instruments are. Since then I have become resigned to the fact that no player can play as perfectly as the composer's mind; that no other instrument is so rich and beautiful, and that only about ten percent of the musical idea can be realized even at the best performance.

I am able now to produce a flow of musical sounds at will, and to control just what they shall be. I am therefore able to work at any time, as the musical flow would continue indefinitely if I did not shut it off when I have not the time to work. The flow does not merely ramble on ambiguously, but centers about a germinal theme, which it proceeds to enlarge upon. I usually compose around a theme for several months before it develops into its final form as written. Because of devoting so much attention to finding the finest form beforehand, by trying the initial idea over mentally in every conceivable way, I rarely change a note after a composition is written.

Writing in form, I may add, is not a matter of pushing certain sounds into an unyielding mold; crudities of form tend to drop out unconsciously as further experience is gained. The experience of being in the throes of musical creation is distinctly an emotional one; there is a mere semblance of the intellectual in being able to steer and govern the meteors of sound that leap through the mind like volcanic fire, in a glory and fullness unimaginable except by those who have heard them.

The closest observation on my part has failed to reveal what the exact relationship is, if there be one, between my musical creations and the experiences which have preceded it, either immediately or remotely. I can only say that the musical ideas as they run through my mind seem to be an exact mirror of my emotions of the moment, or of moments which I recall through memory.[12]

But we do not need to take such testimony without corroboration. One experimenter[13] got some poets to write verses in her presence as she showed them a picture of Yosemite. We can see in the following the role of sensitiveness, skill, past accumulation, insight, trial and error, and "hammering out":

Poet J

The first thing that I think of is the rush of water at the base of the picture and the cool blue heights feeling distance. The importance of the picture at the top and bottom. When I examine it in detail the mist of the waterfalls seem most interesting and little evergreen trees suggest Christmas trees. The little clouds that float over the summit seem like desires that elude. Water has the suggestion of the timeless or eternal flowing on seeking something bigger than itself. I would say that the artist was outside of himself—that he had lost his personality in the vastness of nature.

5 min.: The figure of the man seems in keeping with the overpowering grandeur of nature. He is made so small that one discovers him only upon seeking him. The picture combines earth and unrest. It seems to bring the eternal quality of the hills and the changing of the water which reflects the mood of the sky. I call it a poem in colors. That is all I have. Well let's see. (pause)

1. The water swings to the timeless sea
2. And the peaks lift into eternity. (Would be glad if they cut off that radio)
3. While man is lost on the shores of time
4. Watching the changeless cool clouds climb (pause)
5. Above the trees that top the rocks. Perhaps not make sense.

        The water swings to the timeless sea
        And the peaks lift into eternity
        While man is lost on the shores of time
        Watching the changeless cool clouds climb
        Above the trees that top the rocks
6.   Forgetting the mandate of dull clocks.
        (Wish music would stop)

---

[12] H. Cowell, The process of musical creation, *Amer. J. Psychol.*, 1926, 37, 233–236.

[13] C. Patrick, Creative thought in poets, *Arch. Psychol.*, 1935, No. 178, pp. 53–54.

> The water swings to the timeless sea
> And the peaks lift into eternity
> While man is lost on the shores of time
> Watching the changeless cool clouds climb
> Above the trees that top the rocks
> Forgetting the mandate of dull clocks.
> "Rocks" rhyme with "clocks"

7. Here is the blue and green and earth
8. And man forgetting death and birth.

> The water swings to the timeless sea
> And the peaks lift into eternity
> While man is lost on the shores of time,
> Watching the changeless cool clouds climb
> Above the trees that top the rocks,
> Forgetting the mandate of dull clocks;
> Here is the blue and green of earth,
> And man forgetting death and birth.

11 minutes up to this point.

The Creator

We turn now from the creative process to the individual who creates. What kinds of people become especially creative? We shall begin with the Stanford University *Genetic Studies of Genius,* which comprise, among other things, an analysis of the early life histories of hundreds of outstanding creative personalities classified in terms of the area—literary, artistic, scientific, philosophical, military, political, etc.—in which they made their greatest contributions. Some of the main points that appear in this analysis are the following: (1) Looking at childhood achievements in and out of school, one is impressed by the high level of *general intelligence* of the group as a whole, and particularly of those groups in which competence in abstract thinking, such as scientific and philosophical thinking, appears. (2) Over and above these more general gifts there are *specific gifts* relating to particular subject matters: gifts for mathematics, music, poetry, and so on. General ability may be combined with more than one specific factor. For example, the high intelligence which makes a man a great jurist may enable him at the same time to become a great philosopher. And the specific gifts need not be narrow; a sculptor may likewise be a painter, as was the case with

Michelangelo. (3) The relative importance of *general* ability and of *specific* talents varies with the field of work, in the same sense that high intellectual competence is absolutely indispensable in some fields, but in some other fields is of relatively small importance as compared with special talent. To be of high general intelligence is important in any kind of scientific work, whereas in lyrical poetry sensitiveness of temperament and skill with words may far outweigh the intellectual factor.

As would be expected, one finds that early nurture and stimulation play a signal role in almost all cases. As one studies, for example, the nineteenth-century men of letters and science, one finds, over and over again, the special delight with which the parents or teachers greeted the development of the child's gifts. Just as gifted boys in Renaissance Italy or the Netherlands went to school to the great masters of painting, caught their spirit, and acquired their skills—often going even beyond their masters—so the great figures in British science and literature almost literally "went to school" to the masters whom they admired.

John Stuart Mill was brought up, so to speak, on one side of a table on the other side of which sat his austere and brilliant father, feeding him as much as he could take in terms of Greek vocabulary, Roman rhetoric and law, and later the historical background of English literature and politics.[14] At the age of thirteen, after a systematic workout in the realms of literature, history, and law, he was ready for long walks and talks with his father in which the primary subject matter was political economy. Later on came formal logic, and later still, psychology. The three fields in which he made his most distinctive contributions—namely, the fields of economics, logic, and psychology—were fields in which he was intensively trained. The boy was undoubtedly brilliant from the beginning; his father would not have been able to make such a mind out of poor material. There is likewise no doubt of a continuous pressure—as much pressure as the boy could take, and indeed, as we know from one of his emotional difficulties in later adolescence, sometimes *more* pressure than he could take.

In the same way, in the case of many a musical prodigy the father or mother has stood over the child, seen to it that every opportunity for hearing and playing an instrument was offered; all family interests and

---

[14] J. S. Mill, *Autobiography*, New York, Holt, 1873.

ambitions have been sacrificed to the maximal stimulation available for the growing child.

One may really doubt, however, whether these examples of the pressure put upon a gifted child differ very much from the day-by-day round of pressures applied in greater or lesser degree to many other children. They have shown some sort of gift or talent, something that occasions comment and hope, and so they are pushed by those who think they "ought to make something of it." The results depend not only on how much talent is there, but on how much pressure is applied, and how intelligently it is applied; upon the steps taken to enable the child to enjoy the development of his talent rather than feeling that he is overwhelmed with more pressure than he can accept, etc. The results probably depend more upon the child's incentive to develop the skills available to him than upon any other factor.

One may perhaps generalize, then, about us ordinary mortals by saying that (as in everything else) initial capacity achieves something specific only by virtue of specific learning processes. One can certainly say that more and better schooling both at school and at home, a greater variety of books and magazines, a wider variety of social contacts make a difference in the stimulation of creativeness It is not just a question of urging the child in relation to his particular talent; it is also partly a question of the broader resources which home and community offer, and of the amount of time and attention given by parents and teachers to the cultivation of individual gifts. According to Havelock Ellis' *Studies of British Genius*, even the matter of being first born or last born in a family seems to be of importance. Being a first-born son probably brought, in most cases, certain special privileges, such as special attention, or even special tutoring, travel, etc., not granted to later-born sons. But apparently the last-born child also had an advantage. In a large family he is often a sort of symbol to the parents of the end of a long period in which the rearing of small children was one of their primary tasks. Perhaps this made it possible for parents to concentrate upon their remaining youngest child, who would remind them always of the years when they had small children, and who could be given the benefit of all the family resources without fear that later-born children would find their needs unmet.

The Education of Creativeness

From these considerations regarding the importance of early opportunities and early experiences, there seem to be some rather definite rules which can be laid down which may be useful in giving the individual a chance to develop whatever creativeness he is capable of achieving. Not that we would set up as a fetish the idea that it is important for every child to try to be outstandingly creative, or that creativeness is the only way of fulfilling oneself or leading an effective or happy life. On the other hand, there is on the whole good evidence that creation can give a great deal of satisfaction, and that there is a great deal of potential creativeness which is being wasted through ineffective or even stupid methods. Society also needs creativeness not only from a few geniuses but from all members of the community. There seem, then, to be some practical things to be emphasized.

1. Certainly nothing can take the place of giving the small child his head, giving him freedom to respond to whatever he is sensitive to. Certainly no amount of drill or orderly regimentation in his life can ever make up for the mistake of depriving him of the opportunity to feed upon the colors, tones, words, rhythms, manipulations, and experimentations with the environment which delight his heart and give fulfillment to his need to do something significant with the world about him and his relation to it. A primary principle in helping a child to be creative is to let him have his way when he strongly needs a particular sort of gratification of sense, or word, or idea, that can be provided by parents, or neighborhood, or school, in the way of paints, crayons, stories, etc. Incidentally, when a child endlessly and repetitively stares at or manipulates a kind of material which does *not* give him deep satisfaction, it is likely that this is a substitute for something which has been denied him. What we are here emphasizing is the warm, primitive, spontaneous outgoing response to the things in the world which he craves and which give him satisfaction. A general impressionability in early childhood warrants offering the child opportunities for canalization of his early activity and sensory drives.

2. Along with this goes the opportunity for ego involvement, giving him the sense of adequacy and power in the manipulation of materials

which mean something to him. He is not just manipulating materials; he is *expressing himself* in the process. As the followers of John Dewey have put it, he is deriving satisfaction "from being a cause." It is he who makes the wheels go round, he who makes the colors come together in a startling and delightful new pattern.

3. With these two principles goes the great need for an opportunity to build up higher units, that is, to get deeply enough into the material to be able to combine not single elements, but masses with masses, and to get some sense of architecture. This means that the child will have an opportunity to develop a sense for form, so fundamental in getting the intrinsic "discipline" necessary in any artistic or scientific achievement.

4. If ego involvement is deep, this will mean that he will of course have many pangs of self-reproach when a pattern is not as good as he aimed at. In fact, the artist typically suffers such pangs; and of course he will suffer when he finds that his own drawing or invention is not up to the standard of big brother or his friend across the street. In a competitive society like ours, this may hurt him deeply. But we can shift the emphasis from competition to the *intrinsic* satisfactions of the work itself. We can reinforce the feeling that after all it is himself; he is different from anyone else, and the question of the value of the product as an expression of himself is largely independent of the amount of recognition which others give. We may help in some degree to free him from the competitive strain of our individualistic society, and give him the feeling that the creativeness is worth while in terms of what it means *to him*, and to those few or many who may be able to feel and sense what he is doing. If he can, in other words, *learn to be himself* in the process of creating, he can gradually free himself of the compulsion to outshine competitively every other person who works in the same medium.

5. When the fear arises in the minds of parents or teachers that the child may be becoming top-heavy, one-sided, narrow, an "eccentric genius" devoted only to his music, his mathematics, or his gift for social organization, they may understand more clearly how to handle the situation if they recognize that this narrow preoccupation is the result partly of competitive pressure rather than of the intrinsic nature of the task itself. While it may be true that certain eccentric geniuses will inevitably devote themselves narrowly to a single activity, we have already noted

the tendency of abilities to spread out or to spread over into related fields, and have noted that in most cases there is a high level of general intelligence, too, which makes it possible for the person to work effectively and to enjoy other related activities. The Stanford University studies, in fact, do not indicate that gifted children need to be narrow. The narrowness that may appear is more likely to come from a morbid preoccupation with status, the need to be something special, than from sheer talent or devotion to a special area as such. It is not enough to win the state championship in music, chess, dancing, etc.; one must enter a national competition, etc. This may be wholesome and genuinely stimulating to one child and very destructive to another. Emphasis was placed on the early expression of creative talent, but for its intrinsic value to the child, not for the sheer sake of outdoing others. What is suggested is that the child's creative satisfactions, whatever they may be, be given a free hand as long as they lead to genuine satisfaction in their own right. This will mean in most cases an area of special activity, but one which may perhaps change during the period of growth, with a good many side interests joining with the primary one.

In some cases, however, almost everything in life is poured into this one channel. Characteristic of almost all great creators is the fact that they somehow seem to *live* their work. So much of the self is involved in creation that it is no longer possible to draw a line between the artist and that which he produces. It is perhaps this quality of complete identification and involvement that is one of the keys to the nature of the creative process. Romain Rolland describes it well in his picture of Olivier at the piano.

> Olivier sat down at the piano with a sigh, and obedient to the imperious will of the friend who had sought him out, he began to play the beautiful *Adagio in B Minor* of Mozart. At first his fingers trembled so that he could hardly make them press down the keys: but he regained his courage little by little: and while he thought he was repeating Mozart's utterance, he unwittingly revealed his inmost heart. Music is an indiscreet confidant: it betrays the most secret thoughts of its lovers to those who love it. Through the godlike scheme of the *Adagio* of Mozart Christophe could perceive the invisible lines of the character, not of Mozart, but of his new friend sitting there by the piano: the serene melancholy, the timid tender smile of the boy, so nervous, so pure, so full of love, so ready to blush.[15]

---

[15] Romain Rolland, *Jean-Christophe*, New York, Pocket Books, Inc., 1949, p. 213.

Again Robert Schumann writes as the music came to reflect and convey everything that went on within him:

> But I can be very serious too, and sometimes for days together; but don't let that alarm you, for it is only when my mind is at work, and I am full of ideas about music and my compositions. I am affected by everything that goes on in the world, and think it all over in my own way, politics, literature, and people, and then I long to express my feelings and find an outlet for them in music. That is why my compositions are sometimes difficult to understand, because they are connected with distant interests. . . .[16]

6. Finally, the question must be honestly met as to whether this freedom to develop one overwhelming passion may not run counter in some degree to the need for social conformity. A word has already been said about the fact that there is no antithesis between freedom and discipline; discipline arises if material is pursued for its own intrinsic satisfaction. There is, however, a kind of discipline which relates to one's place in society, the need to adapt one's own activities to the requirements of others. This sort of discipline is likely to mean regularity in work hours and a certain orderly balance between work and play. The genius may "kill himself" for months, and then "be lazy." He may want to compose on the piano at 3:00 A.M. when others are asleep, or to write poetry when on a geology field trip and being given detailed instructions which must be remembered. The whole issue of discipline in this sense is a bit complicated, because (as in the case of all types of creativeness) work and play while in the process of creating have become the same thing, and the child or adult who really works while he plays in his creative task may be less quick than others to understand what is really meant by "working" in the sense of doing things he does not care to do. The problem of creativeness is not that the individual is neglecting his work, but that he is working along the lines of his own bent. As we noted, even his lopsidedness is usually not serious unless others drive him to increase it. There is need that he do some things he does not want to do, but not that he give most of his time to drudgery. Children of superior all-round ability can usually find interesting things to do with their time, and Holling-

---

[16] Robert Schumann, *Early Letters of Robert Schumann* (translated by May Herbert), London, George Bell, 1888, p. 270.

worth[17] showed that children of very exceptional intelligence could, working by themselves, avoid most of the waste and boredom that is involved when put through the mill with children of average endowment. The same general statement can probably be made regarding children with a special talent, as contrasted with those at a high intellectual level, namely, they can find much to do if the world does not block them.

But there is the problem, of course, of fitting into the administrative convenience of the school system or home routine which requires that other things besides this special interest of the child be given attention. The answer to such a question as this has to be in terms of a compromise. Rather than trying to legislate wisely about a compromise which will take a different form in every home and in every school, the plea of the psychologist will be phrased in terms of the largest amount of individual freedom which is compatible with the elementary needs of people about him; that is to say, the primary job of the psychologist is to emphasize that when growth of any kind is going on, it should be allowed to develop its own bent, with warm encouragement, and with every possible support, provided only that the healthy growth of others is not jeopardized in the process.

Sometimes the creative gift takes a *primary social* form: gift for social organization, leadership. These gifts like the others need to be given a kind of encouragement that is free from *forcing* on the one hand and from *blocking* on the other.

SUGGESTED READINGS

Galton, F., *English Men of Science*, New York, Appleton, 1875.
Genetic Studies of Genius, Stanford, Stanford Univ. Press, 3 vols., 1925–1930.
Hadamard, J., *The Psychology of Invention in the Mathematical Field*, Princeton, Princeton Univ. Press, 1945.
Hollingworth, L. S., *Children Above 180 I.Q., Stanford Binet*, Yonkers, World Book, 1942.
Patrick, C., Creative thought in artists, *J. Psychol.*, 1934, *4*, 35–73.
Rossman, J. J., *The Psychology of the Inventor*, Washington, Inventors Publishing Co., 1931.
Spearman, C., *Creative Mind*, New York, Appleton, 1931.
Stern, W., *Psychology of Early Childhood* (trans. by A. Barwell), New York, Holt, 1924, Part 7.

---

[17] L. S. Hollingworth, *Children Above 180 IQ, Stanford-Binet*, Yonkers, World Book, 1942.

19 INTELLIGENCE AND ITS MEASUREMENT

Among a group of children at play, we spot those who seem to be bright and those who seem to be dull in catching on to the rules of the game; and as we watch them at school we make a distinction also between bright and dull. Even about our dogs we say, "Wags is smart, Rover is dumb." We may say, as Aristotle did: "Reason, in the sense of intelligence, is not found equally in all animals, nor in all men." Distinctions in intelligence are recognized and used almost every hour of our lives. It is natural, in a scientific period, that we should try to be more precise as to what we mean by degrees of brightness and of dullness; in other words, it is natural to try to measure intelligence.

Within the same human stock, and indeed often enough within the same family, there are such big variations in intellectual power that one individual seems almost doomed to dependence upon another. We might make this concrete by giving a picture of two girls, neither of them a "freak," but simply representative of the extremes which we frequently encounter.

Josie . . . was a fast but careless power-machine operator. She was shy, but she overcame her feelings by acting in a rather rough and uncouth manner. She was eager to do well in her "profession," but she would work herself up into a nervous state and was unable to integrate and coordinate her behavior. Before being placed at Celeste's she had had some operating experience on pliofilm. At Celeste's she did well for the first two or three weeks when working on the larger salad-bowl covers. She made as much as $17 and $18 a week. Josie commented on her work as follows:

"The first day I only made 35 cents. I was nervous. I didn't know how to handle these things. You know they are round and if you haven't got a certain way to turn them they all go in and you have an awful time. He used to come and look at me. He used to have patience and come and show me. And the other girls help one."

She was then transferred to the making of smaller covers for milk and cream bottles. Here she had trouble, since more delicate manipulation was needed. Max (the owner of the Celeste Novelty Concern) had no more orders for the larger bowl covers, and he could not see why Josie was so slow and obstinate when working on the smaller articles, which were made on the same machine as the larger ones. He discharged her without giving her time to adjust to the new work, although he said she had been a first-rate worker on the salad-bowl covers. Since Josie was very anxious to have a job at once, and since she liked Celeste, her vocational counselor told her to return and see whether Max would take her as a floor girl until there should be more work on the operating machines. This she did, and was accepted, but she never made a good adjustment. She was full of complaints, such as, "You stand up all day and work twice as hard as I did on piece work and you don't make nothing, but it's true. I earn $5.00, and my mother spends more than that in one day. My mother needs a good rest, but when you haven't got no money you can't get a rest. You stand up all day and then you get in the train and you can't sit down and you get so tired. When I was on piece work, I don't know, I used to feel more ambitious. You may not think it's true, but when you're making out and getting money you don't feel so tired, but when you don't make nothing you feel so tired."

Under this strain Josie lasted about two weeks. . . . She went immediately to her placement counselor and said, "Operators are for their own selves; nobody bothers them. I think if you was there you would get disgusted too. I don't know, maybe I can't express myself right."[1]

This girl, when given intelligence tests, proved to be at the line which is technically drawn to differentiate the lowest normal from the highest feeble-minded. There is no sharp break or clear line of separation anywhere; it is a question of a technical distinction which may determine who needs institutional care, etc.

At the other extreme is Elizabeth:

Among Elizabeth's first toys was a set of cubical blocks with letters and numbers on four sides. One of the baby's favorite amusements was to hold up a block and point to one side after the other, for her entertainer to tell what was on the side of the block indicated. Gradually the game changed, and the baby held up the block, and pointed to the picture called for by the entertainer. At the age of 15 months she made no mistakes in finding the

---

[1] T. M. Abel and E. F. Kinder, *The Subnormal Adolescent Girl*, New York, Columbia University Press, 1942.

animals called for, and very soon afterwards she could find the letters in the same way.

One of her first books was *The Story of the Naughty Piggies*. The child seemed never to tire of hearing the story read, and by the time she was two and a half years old, when she sat in the lap of the reader, she could turn the page at just the right place in the story. About that time the two leaves in the center of the book loosened and dropped out The German grandma made a mistake in sewing them in, putting the second first. Elizabeth quickly discovered the mistake, and was very unhappy about it. She followed her grandmother about, asking her to fix it. The grandmother could not understand what the child meant, and finally appealed to the child's mother, who discovered what was wrong. Elizabeth was not yet three years old, and they could not believe that the child detected the difference between those two pages of the book. But after the grandmother ripped out the stitches and replaced the leaves in their proper sequence, the little girl showed unmistakable satisfaction and content.

At three and a half years of age, Elizabeth was spelling everything she saw printed and asking what the letters spelled, and she could recognize many words. At four years, she read the advertisements in the street cars, as well as everything in all the books she possessed. During all this time there was no attempt on the part of the parents to make their daughter precocious. They were pleased with her readiness to learn, but they did not look upon her as an unusual child.

In September, 1920, Elizabeth was enrolled in the first grade, in the public schools of Erie, Pennsylvania. She was then 3 years 8 months old. On her second day in school her teacher discovered that she could read anything that was placed before her. The principal put her in the second grade until she had time to investigate her case. She spent forty-two days in the second grade, during which time the principal observed her closely, and decided to place her in the fourth grade. Elizabeth had no trouble completing that grade in the remainder of the school year, the principal giving her some special help in spelling and arithmetic.

. . . Elizabeth is not a skillful writer, as far as penmanship goes, but she seldom makes a mistake in either spelling or punctuation, and the content of her letters and compositions is superior, even for the advanced grade in which she is now working. . . . Intellectually speaking, this child takes everything to which she is exposed, and she is not satisfied unless she understands the subject fully. Unfamiliar words or terms bring from her the question, "Just what does that mean?" She has a cheery disposition, and laughs often and heartily. She is contented in any environment, because her imagination makes it as she wishes it. . . . When she is reading or studying, she becomes so engrossed that it is hard to attract her attention to anything outside her book. . . . She is slow in her written work, and she is slow and rather awkward in some of her motor coordinations.

After less than a month in the fifth grade, in September, 1921 (age 7 years 8 months), Elizabeth was promoted to the sixth grade, where she is doing superior work. In the examinations at the end of the last semester she ranked about the middle of the class, due to the fact that she is still slow in her written work. But in comprehension she easily leads the class.

Thus far nothing has been done for this exceptional child except to move her along from grade to grade five times as rapidly as the average child can go.[2]

Now as we look at such a contrast we begin to ask: What goes into intelligence? That of course depends upon whether one is learning a complicated manual task, or how to handle oneself in a typical social situation, or how to dig out the facts from a history text. But perhaps there is something general that runs through all these things: a sort of general plasticity or readiness to adapt to situations, a capacity to tease out their meaning, to make sense of them, to take hold of them in such a way as to react more effectively to them. This would probably make intelligence the same as the ability to learn. It was in this sense that many of the pioneers in the area of intelligence testing fifty years ago attacked their problem. They confronted their individual child or adult subject with certain problems, the solution to which lay in ability to adapt to new situations, i.e., to learn.

Individual differences in ability to learn had indeed come to be emphasized as soon as Charles Darwin's theory of evolution began to sink into our habits of thinking. To the question: Where did humanity get its brains? the evolutionary answer is: Brains were an advantage in the struggle for existence. There has been a premium, throughout the whole history of life on this planet, upon the ability to adapt in relation to the difficulties of the environment and the competition provided by others. In the case of relatively defenseless animals like human beings, who can in no way stand up to tigers or elephants on the basis of speed or strength, there has been a constant emphasis upon intelligence.

Intelligence means, in the first instance, the ability to learn; and in general the *ability to learn* increases steadily with the *complexity* of the nervous system. Tests of animal intelligence bring out the things that can be learned with one kind of nervous system but that cannot be learned with a simpler one. Apes, for example, can learn to work for symbolic rewards, getting a poker chip for their labor, and cashing it later for food —which cats and rats cannot do—but apes in turn are behind three-year-

---

[2] L. S. Hollingworth, *Gifted Children*, New York, Macmillan, 1926, pp. 231–232.

old children in the matter of acquiring symbols to stand for purely abstract ideas, and combining these as the child does in his sentences. In studies of intellectual power, it is not the amount of time required to learn a simple task, but rather the level of complexity of the tasks the organism can solve, that makes the critical difference. In many tasks, for example, dogs learn more quickly than human beings. In the mazes of the sort shown in Figure 60 rats learn as well as or a little better than college students. The best test of all-round learning ability is not speed or

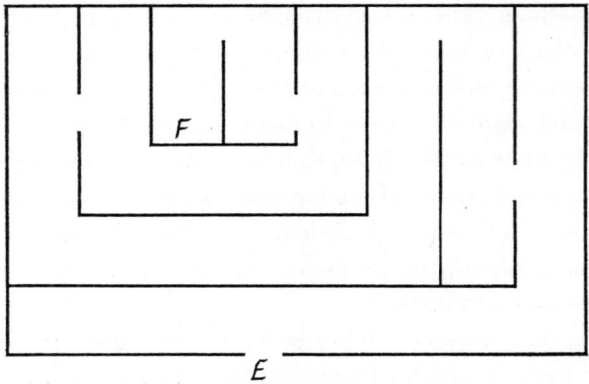

Figure 60. Maze for Animals and Human Beings

A simple maze like this one (which is unstandardized) can be used with both human and animal subjects. The entrance is at E and the goal at F. Learning is measured in terms of the number of trials required to eliminate errors (entries into blind alleys).

the number of errors made in some one task, but the level of complexity of the tasks that can be successfully tackled.

This gives some perspective to the question whether "ability to learn" is just *one* single thing. We begin to see that we are dealing not only with an all-round average general ability to meet difficulties, and solve them, but with abilities that vary somewhat with the task involved. None of us would seriously think that he could measure his friends' intelligence by assigning them one single difficult problem to do; he would need a variety of problems, and would look for some all-round capacity or group of capacities that entered into these varying tasks in greater or lesser degree. We may have to look upon intelligence as a composite of many different kinds of capacities to learn, depending upon the nature of the task undertaken.

Back of all this kind of thinking is the notion that living things differ in degree rather than in kind; we differ from one another in degree, just as mankind differs from its animal relatives in degree. This way of thinking makes it possible to conceive of our personal intellectual capacities as things which are not unique in the universe, but have their affinities with other processes that *adapt* living individuals to their environment.

This emphasis upon the increasing complexity of the brain and its relation to learning is pertinent also as one studies the child's increase in intelligence year by year. The human individual passes in childhood through stages of increasing complexity; at the same time the brain is increasing in size (it is nearly three times as large at 12 months as at the time of birth) and its inner structure is providing more and more complex functioning relations between newly developed nerve cells. The child can learn more and more difficult things as his brain becomes more complex. There is a popular misconception that a child at any given level learns more readily than the older child or the adult solely because he is more plastic. It is true that the child may sometimes be free from embarrassment and may be willing to make himself ridiculous as he makes a start at some new task from which the adult, knowing that he could not do it very well, may hold off. But in careful experiments it has been found over and over again that when you hold roughly constant the incentives that are at work, the adult human individual learns better than the child, and the older child better than the younger child.

Individual Testing

A hundred years ago, the French physician Séguin invented a simple device for studying the mentality of intellectually retarded children. He made use of form boards containing holes in which a child must place wooden blocks of the appropriate size and shape. In a general way, grossly defective children are likely to try to ram the pieces into any hole whether it fits or not; and one can gauge very roughly the child's mental capacity by his ability to grasp the spatial relations involved.

Late in the nineteenth century Francis Galton conceived the idea of measuring mental functions and experimented with some of the most ingenious pioneer devices; greatly influenced by him, the American psychologist J. McK. Cattell developed several types of mental tests. At the turn of the century, the great French psychologist Alfred Binet was contriving ways to gauge the intelligence level of children so that children of different age levels could be compared, and so that children of the same age could be compared in brightness with one another. In 1904 Binet was asked by the Minister of Public Instruction in France to devise tests which would differentiate intellectual capacity in children, so that those who were failing in school through an intrinsic mental defect could be separated from those who were merely lacking in interest and consequently making no effort.

It seemed to Binet that one of the great difficulties with the existing tests was that they assumed that the higher functions were simply a compound of a great many of the lower functions. It had often been thought before his time that if one could measure ability with form boards and other very simple tasks like naming colors or responding quickly to sounds or making distinctions between lines of different lengths, one could predict who would be able to solve logical or scientific problems. Binet went at the whole problem in a radically different way. It seemed to him that there was such a thing as intellectual level (page 335). A child might be a wizard at simple tasks and fail completely when encountering more complex ones. One might find a child who was not as quick as the average at the simple tasks, yet would nevertheless prove to be above the average at those which were more demanding. Binet therefore undertook to measure the more complex intellectual capacities. It seemed to him that at least three things would be involved in real intelligence: (1) the ability to follow directions; (2) the ability to make and maintain a given mental set, that is, to keep going along the lines laid down earlier in prosecution of the task; (3) auto-criticism, or the capacity to see where one is making a mistake, and to rectify it.

Binet's first experiment was done with thirty children of various ages, who were asked to do such simple things as to point to their noses or mouths, tell whether they were boys or girls, follow very simple directions given by the experimenter, hand the experimenter an object which he named such as a cup or key or string, and identify by appropriate names the objects shown in a picture. Binet knew, of course, that some children had better school opportunities than others, and that some learned more at home than others. But he was trying, even in these early tests, to select items which were fair for all children, in the broad sense that all children had been exposed to names for noses and ears, and to the habit of responding to simple requests from adults. He struggled—not completely successfully, as we shall see—to get at intrinsic intelligence not by "ruling out the environment," but by presenting tasks for which every child's environment would have prepared him if he had had wit enough to take full advantage of the opportunity.

Binet's first tests were very crude, and it was not at all certain that they were really "differentiating," in the sense that bright children would consistently do better on them than dull ones. He went on experimenting, adding new tests and working with more children, until in three years he had devised a *scale* of tests, *with tests appropriate for each age level from 3 to 12*. At the three-year-old level he found that most normal children could pass the item "points to nose, eyes, mouth," and the item "repeats sentences of six syllables," likewise "enumerates objects in a picture." The six-year-olds could mostly define right and left, as shown by indicating right hand and left ear, and could repeat sentences of sixteen syllables. They could define familiar objects in terms of use—"a knife is to cut"—they could tell how old they were and whether it was morning or afternoon. The seven-year-olds could tell what was missing in pictures of faces which lacked an eye, a nose, or a mouth. They could repeat five digits. They could describe pictures as scenes, not simply enumerate separate objects. They could count thirteen pennies.

The conception of a series of items of graded difficulty was of huge importance because it made possible the idea of comparing the child's age with the point on the intellectual scale which the child had reached. One might begin to think of the child as being bright or dull for his age in some sort of definite *quantitative* terms; thus one six-year-old is as bright as an average eight-year-old, or he is only as bright as an average four-year-old. Intelligence was a matter of comparison with those of the child's own age group and those of higher or lower ages.

It soon occurred to the German psychologist William Stern that this could be stated very simply in mathematical form by comparing two levels, the mental level and the chronological level. If the child was chronologically six years old, but could do what an eight-year-old ordinarily does, he would be one and one-third, or eight-sixths as bright as the average; indeed he could be given an *intelligence quotient* of 1.33. In the same way, if he were only two-thirds as far along as most children of his age, he would have an intelligence quotient of four-sixths, or .66. In other words, the intelligence quotient is the mental age divided by the chronological age, multiplied by 100 to get rid of the decimal point. Thus .66 becomes 66, etc.

Binet went on with testing for a further three-year period, and in 1911 published a still better scale based on a considerable number of further tests and profiting by his earlier mistakes. He had been experimenting to see at what age each test actually belonged, in terms of the fact that most normal children could pass it at the age expected. Thus he found that "defining familiar objects in terms of use" was suitable at the six-year level, at which it had earlier been placed, and that the test "describing pictures" was suitable for the seven-year level; but the item "showing the right hand and the left ear" he found too hard for most six-year-olds, so he moved it up from the six-year to the seven-year level. The task of defining what would be a good intelligence test was not one which could be thought out and studied theoretically; it had to meet the practical test.

Binet died in the year 1911, but the work of revising the Binet scale of tests went on. The major effort in this field was made by L. M. Terman at Stanford University, who in 1916 published the Stanford-Binet Scale. In 1937 this Stanford-Binet was itself revised, in a form very widely used. Many other revisions of the Binet have been published from time to time.

We have placed a good deal of emphasis upon the uncertain and groping character of Binet's progress in developing these tests, because nothing is more important than the recognition that we are dealing here with an empirical and practical problem. Even those who know children well cannot tell in advance just what a normal child will be able to do with a particular test situation, and what proportion of normal children will pass the test as the experimenter has defined it. Tests have value only insofar as they have been "standardized," that is, insofar as the procedure of giving and scoring the test has been thoroughly worked through and reduced to an order which anyone with suitable training can follow. This procedure includes, of course, the provision of suitable and representative norms of performance with which individual performance can be compared.

One of the things which had to be done with intelligence tests was to ascertain with certainty the order of their difficulty from the easiest to the hardest. Another thing that had to be done was to make sure that the results were not simply a momentary accident in any given case. If the test was a test of ability, we had to be sure that such tests when given over and over again, after a suitable period, would give scores which were fairly consistent from time to time, in the sense that those who were near the top at one time would remain near the top and those at the bottom would remain near the bottom (*retest reliability*). Above all, it was necessary to show that success on these prepared tests actually agreed pretty well with success in life tasks; in other words, the task must have *validity* in terms of its relations to recognized criteria by which we could judge it. If people who are found in life situations to be generally intelligent do not actually do well on the intelligence tests, so much the worse for the tests. The story of intelligence tests is a story of the struggle to meet these and other legitimate demands, and of the rather considerable success in meeting them. Binet very definitely did succeed in differentiating in a general way among those children whose school difficulties arose because they were actually limited in intelligence and those who were merely bored with school work. Not only did he make this differentiation, but he succeeded better than he knew in laying the general foundations for a method of intelligence testing, in the sense that adults who know children well and those who know adolescents or young adults well in a variety of situations do in general find that intelligence test scores agree pretty well with the average of their judgments.

This does not mean, of course, that the exact number derived for an intelligence quotient has any magic value. We shall see later that there are many instances of important factors which notably increase or decrease the intellectual level of the subject, and we shall likewise see a great many illustrations of very good performance in one task or life area side by side with very poor performance in other areas from the same person in the same period of life. The child's I.Q. gives his approximate present intellectual status as compared with others of his own chronological age; it does not infallibly tell where he came from or where he is going, nor can it tell about the variation of his abilities in response to different kinds of life tasks. After all, what Binet was up to was to contrive a general, all-round gauge of the capacity of the child to cope with tasks involving the ability to learn, especially to learn the most complex relationships to which he must adapt; and in this broad sense Binet was eminently successful.

But the test is not an automatic measuring instrument. It has a meaning to the person tested, and the examiner is concerned with the question of what it means to him and of his attitude toward it. Along with the matter of care in selecting the test goes care in the matter of administering it, being sure that you get the child's full coöperation, being sure that he is relaxed and at ease, is interested, is taking time to follow a leisurely and straightforward procedure which is his own spontaneous way of attacking the problem. A careful clinical psychologist makes use of all these precautions, refuses to test if the child is frightened or excited, or in poor health, puts no pressure on him, watches carefully all the way through to see how he is taking the situation, and writes qualitative interpretative remarks in addition to deriving the sheer quantitative I.Q. figure.

The adult often wants to know his own I.Q. From one viewpoint the problem is unanswerable with the Binet type of tests, because the I.Q. strictly refers to rate of mental growth; and if the adult has reached his intellectual growth limit (this is usually reached before 20) it does not make sense to compare his mental age with his chronological age. We can to some degree get around this difficulty by calling a certain chronological age the limit or maximum for purposes of calculation. Sometimes all adults are treated, for example, as at the sixteen-year-old chronological level, in the light of the evidence that at least a large proportion of us do not gain very much in raw intelligence (though we do gain in experience) beyond that point. This is a fairly good makeshift solution as far as the denominator of the fraction $\frac{MA}{CA}$ is concerned. But what shall we do about the numerator of the fraction? Suppose that a child during the growth period has been so brilliant as to have an I.Q. of 200. Now let us say that he has reached his chronological age of 16; shall we put down a mental age of 32? This is obviously preposterous. If, however, we have once set the chronological age of 16 as a limit, we cannot have men-

Figure 61. The Wechsler-Bellevue Block Design Test

One of the advanced block design problems in the Wechsler-Bellevue Intelligence Scale for Adults. The subject is scored for time and accuracy, and she shows tension as she encounters difficulty.

tal ages of any sort beyond the 16-year point except by arbitrarily assigning certain superior scores to categories like mental age 18, 20, etc. The whole idea of the intelligence quotient is poorly suited to the measurement of adult intelligence. We can get around this difficulty by assigning people to their percentage category—by saying, for example, that a given individual is in the "top 1 percent," or that another is at a point where only 25 percent of the whole group are brighter than he.

In recent years, the problem of testing adult I.Q.'s has been given a somewhat more useful meaning by the development of the Wechsler-

Bellevue test, a well-standardized individual test which is suitable for measuring adult intelligence. By this procedure it is possible to measure several different kinds of intellectual prowess in the adult and not only to give his percentage position with regard to each kind of intellectual prowess, but also to compute what is fairly usable as an intelligence quotient, in the sense that the figure is comparable to an I.Q. for a child. In Figure 61, one of the subtests of the Wechsler-Bellevue test is being administered to an adult subject.

Group Testing

The tests so far described are those in which one person is tested at a time. From the early years of testing the need was felt to devise intelligence tests which could be simultaneously applied to groups of individuals, and not simply to one individual at a time. To meet this need a great many group tests have been prepared. Some group tests are available for children, and some for adults. Notably in the United States Army in World Wars I and II group tests were administered to large numbers of recruits at a time. In World War I the Army Alpha test emphasized the following of directions, solution of arithmetical problems, ability to say whether certain words meant the same as other words; several other tests measured knowledge of (and skill with) words. During World War II the Army General Classification Test (AGCT) was used. This boiled the problem down to three primary functions on which the recruit could indicate "what he had": (1) vocabulary; (2) arithmetical reasoning; (3) a type of block counting in which piled-up blocks were shown, and the recruit had to figure out not how many blocks were in sight, but how many would have to be behind out of sight, to give the piles their observed height. The study of other intellectual activities was deliberately sacrificed in selecting only these three classes of tests. But a good deal actually goes into the ability to acquire vocabulary, likewise into arithmetical reasoning, and into the kind of imagination and thinking that are necessary to figure out how many blocks there must be. The practical follow-ups showed that in general the scores on these Army General Classification Tests agreed quite well with intelligence test scores based on sampling a wider variety of capacities.

What will make a good test of course depends upon the purpose for which it is developed. A test like the Army General Classification Test would not be suitable for choosing people for college entrance. Here we should need to emphasize much more heavily the question of reading comprehension, the general familiarity with the materials that go into a high-school education, and the ability to grapple with the kinds of problems that come up in college work. The test most representative of what is currently used here, perhaps, is the American Council on Education (ACE) test, which necessarily emphasizes skill, including that with words and with mathematical quantities.

At a still more demanding level is the Thorndike CAVD, a test involving items from areas of *comprehension, arithmetic, vocabulary,* and following *directions*. There are carefully graded series of items in each of these four fields, running from very easy to very difficult; the difficult ones are so hard that everybody reaches his "ceiling." That is to say, no one gets all the way to the top, solves all the items. For that reason this test can differentiate even among individuals who are very superior in any given function, whereas most tests only put the ablest people near the top and make no really suitable differentiation among them. But no single test does everything. If we want to assay all the intellectual capacities of the individual, we will combine different types of tests in order to get different angles on the problem. We may, for example, want to give an AGCT, ACE, and CAVD; and if we have time, we will continue to gain new information as other tests are added.

Performance Tests

So far we have been dealing with verbal tests, tests in which the instructions are given in words, and in which a good deal of the performance is in the form of words. From the beginning of intelligence testing, however, as we noted, performance tests, such as the form board tests, have likewise been used. In clinical practice we constantly encounter children with sense-organ defects who have difficulty in regard to verbal material. The partially sighted cannot, for example, read the verbal material; the hard of hearing may not hear the oral instructions well; and there are many children with other physical or mental handicaps who may be bright enough but who may not show it when a verbal test is used. There are likewise some children whose intellectual handicap is more severe in verbal than in other areas, and we may want to get a view of what they can do when they actually perform with their hands.

A good example of a widely used performance test is the Pintner-Paterson Performance Scale, which gives a general view of the performance ability of the child—not the same thing, of course, as intelligence in the verbal sense, but overlapping somewhat with it. There is a par-

Figure 62. The Healy Pictorial Completion Test No. 2

(Courtesy C. H. Stoelting Company, Chicago.)

ticularly good picture test known as the Healy Pictorial Completion Test No. 2, in which we can get an idea even of the very complex intellectual functions of a child without having to ply him with verbal questions (cf. Figure 62). In order to put blocks into the appropriate holes in the picture, the child has to do much more than just grasp the idea of fitting a shape into an appropriate hole. He has to grasp the kind of physical or social situation which exists for the children shown in the picture, and what makes sense in relation to it. The Healy Pictorial Completion Test No. 2 has been widely used in clinical practice, and often serves to throw light on the problems of a child in trouble (e.g., a delinquent) who may show a defective grasp of social situations.

The Distribution of Intelligence

In every one of the tests so far described, we find wide individual differences, from extremely poor to extremely good at each age level. This puts to us the question: "Do people tend to gravitate toward one or the other extreme on scales of this sort?" "Do they, in regard to the Binet test, or the Wechsler-Bellevue, or the Pintner-Paterson, etc., tend to come out near the top or near the bottom?" The answer is that more come out at the middle than at either the top or the bottom, and that actually they distribute themselves in the form of a bell-shaped distribution curve, known as the normal frequency curve (Figure 63). This type of distribution is usually found when complex human capacities, whether physical, social, or intellectual, are measured. When you measure people with regard to height, weight, speed of response, strength of particular muscle groups, or the kinds of social or personal qualities mentioned in Chapters 26–27, you find typically that there is piling up of them near the middle of the distribution, and a tapering off at the right as fewer and fewer people are able to make the higher scores, and a tapering off at the left as fewer and fewer people show grosser and grosser limitations.

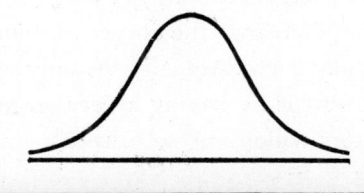

Figure 63. The Normal Frequency Curve

(Figures 63 and 64 from L. J. Cronbach, *Essentials of Psychological Testing*, Harper & Brothers, 1949.)

It is worth while to study more closely how frequency distributions of this sort arise. The fact that intelligence is normally distributed means that the number of cases within a given range—say a range of 10 points, like 90 to 100—will be greater when we are near the middle of the distribution than when we move out to the fringes, and that when once the form of the curve is defined we can tell in advance how many individuals will appear within any specific category. Normal curves arise from the fact that a great many different things enter into the determination of intelligence. You can look at this in either hereditarian or environmentalistic terms; and from either viewpoint you will see that intelligence is not a simple entity like a single specific gift which you either possess or lack. If only one thing were involved—if for example you were dealing with the effects of a single gene—those who received the gene would be *bright* and those who lacked it would be *dull* and there would be just two kinds of people. If there were two genes, there would be three kinds of people: those who get neither, those who get one, and those who get both. Since the individual has a 50–50 chance of getting each one, one-fourth of all individuals will get both; one-fourth will get neither; one-fourth will get the first but not the second; one-fourth will get the second but not the first. We can combine the last two, to comprise the two who get just one of the genes. If there are three genes, one person in eight will get all three, one in eight will get none; three will get two but not the other, three will get one but not the other two. As the number of genes increases, the curve will tend more and more toward a normal frequency curve. Actually the only way that you can get a smooth curve of this sort is by having a very large number of independent contributing factors which are, so to speak, drawn from a very large lottery or grab bag.

The same logic will apply if you look at the matter environmentalistically. If there were just good environments and bad environments and none between, there would be just two levels of intelligence. If there were, say, three kinds of environments—bad, average, and good—we would again get three sharply defined levels of intelligence. The environmental factors, as we have already seen, actually vary smoothly through a wide range.

Now when you are dealing with the interaction of heredity and environment, each of which involves many components, it is inevitable that you will have a smooth distribution curve, since each person gets a very large number of contributing factors, of much too complex a sort to be described with our present knowledge, but differentiating him from those who happen to be luckier or less lucky in the number of more or less independent favorable factors that combine. We are all to be placed somewhere on a continuum when any such attribute is involved, with most of us inclining toward the middle and relatively few trailing off at the upper or lower level.

When intelligence tests or any other kind of tests of complex functions are administered in the classroom you will typically expect to get approximately bell-shaped curves. This presupposes, of course, that the number in the class is rather large, and it ignores the fact that those who have gotten into college probably have had a somewhat more fortunate break than those who have not gotten into college, by virtue of either genetic or environmental factors, or both. This often means that the bell-shaped curve will be not quite symmetrical—in statistical language it will be *skewed*—owing to the fact that those normally at the left-hand end of the curve are not in college. Nevertheless, for most purposes, you can count on finding most distribution curves normal enough to serve ordinary purposes.

Genetic and Environmental Background

It is now time to draw together various lines of evidence and look more directly at the question of nature and nurture in relation to intellectual level. It will be recalled that a brief introduction to the problem was presented in Chapters 3 and 4. Let us look more closely at modern studies from which we can learn about hereditary and environmental factors. We may hold constant the influence of nature by working with identical twins, and study the types of variation in performance that appear when these twins are subjected to *different* environments, as compared with identical twins who grow up in the *same environment* and are subjected to more or less the same general pressures from parents and from siblings (brothers and sisters). From several studies we know that such identical twins are treated alike to a degree more marked than that which characterizes the treatment of ordinary brothers and sisters, and even the treatment of nonidentical twins of the same sex. We can, so to speak, put these twins, reared together, side by side with identical twins separated from each other in the first few weeks of life.

At the University of Chicago H. H. Newman has been interested for many years in this problem; he and his collaborators (cf. page 19) have succeeded in bringing together data on over twenty pairs of identical twins separated in early infancy. They were given medical, educational, and psychological tests, and were carefully observed and described by people familiar with child development. It was found that their *physical* resemblance was about as striking as that of twins who had grown up in the same home. We cannot, therefore, heavily stress the role of difference in physical upbringing; even the different food and regimen given the twins did not weaken very much the similarity which appeared in their physical development. When it comes to *intellectual* traits, the evidence is much more puzzling and complex. In a good many cases the twins separated in early infancy and growing up in different homes continued to resemble each other intellectually as if they had been reared in the same home. There were several cases in which twins A and B were as much alike as the same individual is like himself (in the sense of taking a test over again a year or so later). There were some cases, however, in which the pairs had become very dissimilar indeed; differences of 25 or 30 points or more in intelligence quotient sometimes appeared. The average degree to which those identical twins differed from each other in intelligence was significantly greater than we find in identical twins reared together. We may say, then, that the disparity in the environment seems to be getting in its work, but in a way which varies from pair to pair. It has not made the twins as dissimilar to each other as are the non-twin members of the same family.

Finally, going beyond physical and mental resemblance to the question of *social and personal qualities,* and using the observations of those who talked with these individuals and such crude personality tests as were available, these experimenters found that the resemblance was less close than in the case of intellectual performance. Particularly in the case of twins reared in grossly dissimilar environments (e.g., one growing up on a farm, the other in a busy urban environment), traits noted by observers and appearing on personality tests suggest that here the environment was able to produce rather marked differences. Using such methods as we have, then, we may say that when heredity is held constant, there is a wider variability traceable to the environment in social than in intellectual attributes, and a wider variability in intellectual than in physical attributes.

While twins offer the best types of evidence for the particular problem we have first emphasized, namely, the problem of holding nature constant and studying the effects of environment, there are other methods which can be applied on a large scale, and which are therefore worth using, even though heredity is not held constant in so strict a sense. Under this head come the investigations of foster children, whose intelligence level may be compared with that of their foster parents and of other children reared in the same home, and may sometimes likewise be compared with that of their "own" or "true" parents. It is possible, by bringing children into the home very early as foster children, or as legally adopted children, to expose them to the general environment which is also acting upon the own or true children of that particular pair of parents. If everything were attributable to environments alone, we should expect that such foster children would, in general, show the same average intelligence and the same variability as those found among the own children.

There has been much controversy as to how to interpret the quantitative information on these foster children, but we might as well give the reader some gross facts about the research and then see if we cannot find something important to emphasize which is independent of controversy over detail. From two major investigations—one by Barbara Burks[3] and the other by Frank Freeman and his collaborators[4]—it is clear that the I.Q. is definitely increased by virtue of growing up in a relatively favored home, as compared with growing up in one less fortunate. In some ways Burks' investigation was more carefully controlled, and it may be more heavily stressed here; for Burks took great care to rule out the artifacts which might have arisen if bright parents adopted the children who seemed very bright or who came from bright "own" parents. Such "selective placement" would have produced an artificial closeness of intellectual level between foster parents and foster children. If we wish to study the effect of the home as such, we must rule out selective placement or at least know how to allow for it. After making strenuous efforts along these lines, Burks succeeded rather well in finding a quantitative statement to indicate the degree to which a favored home might be able to elevate the intelligence quotient of a child placed early in that home.

This requires that there be some measurement not only of intellectual level but of the adequacy of the home as an environment tending to stimulate the child intellectually. The best thing we can do is to use a "scale of socio-economic status," allowing a certain amount of "credit" for each aspect of the home environment, like number of rooms, running

---

[3] B. S. Burks, The relative influence of nature and nurture upon mental development: a comparative study of foster-parent foster-child resemblance and true-parent true-child resemblance, *Yearb. nat. Soc. Stud. Educ.*, 1928, 27, 219–316.

[4] F. N. Freeman, K. J. Holzinger, and B. C. Mitchell, The influence of environment on the intelligence, school achievement, and conduct of foster children, *ibid.*, 1928, 27, 103–218.

water, telephone, magazines, etc., and assuming that socio-economic factors stimulate intellectual development. We can now arrange all the foster homes in terms of a distribution, so that we move from left to right, from the least stimulating to the most stimulating of these homes, so far as we can judge this from socio-economic factors.

Proceeding in this way, Burks compared the intellectual level of children in various homes with the actual socio-economic status of those homes, so as to indicate to what degree the homes might have been responsible for the higher intellectual levels. Actually the correlations between socio-economic status and intellectual level of the child were not very high; and by a mathematical method too complex to be described, Burks estimated that most of the variability in intelligence quotients among these children was due not to the home but to the stuff or stock of which the individual children were made.

The outcome is very curious and interesting. By Burks' methods of computation it is possible to show by about how many points of intelligence quotient the child had benefited by being transplanted early to a favorable home environment. If we note the fact that about a sixth of the whole range of socio-economic status is marked off by a single *sigma* (a statistical concept which will be considered on pages 377 ff.), we can ask what will happen if a child born into an *average* environment is placed very early in a home one sigma above the mean. The computations show that such transplanting of a child at birth (or in the early weeks) would tend ultimately to elevate his I.Q. from 6 to 9 points. If he were placed in a still better environment he would benefit still more. This, from Burks' frankly hereditarian viewpoint, is of great interest to us. Freeman and his collaborators do not state their data in so precise a form, and it is sometimes thought that their findings warrant a more environmentalistic emphasis. Let us take the Burks data as they stand; they show that a considerable effect on intelligence quotient can be wrought by a definitely favorable environment.

On the other hand, we must also bear witness to the fact that the results show definite limits. If we note on Figure 64 what one sigma means, and if we remember that not very many children can count on getting a home very much better than the kind of favored home (one sigma above the mean) that Burks was describing (and the majority not as good a one), we are bound to admit that under present conditions variations in the stock are going to make a huge difference. Indeed, even if everyone could magically be placed in such a superior environment, all the data of both Burks and Freeman show that wide individual differences would still remain.

One of the best follow-ups of this type of investigation was done by

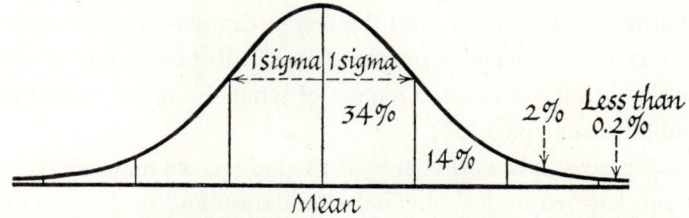

Figure 64. The Normal Frequency Curve

When a distribution of individual differences, such as height or intelligence, which are determined by many factors takes the form of a normal frequency curve, certain fixed relationships are evident from the general characteristics of the curve, regardless of the actual nature of the differences. One such relationship is the sigma, which is the measure of the variations of individual scores around the mean. In distributions in which the scores are all close to the mean, the sigma will be small; but if the scores spread out below and above the mean, the sigma will be large. The mathematical derivation of the sigma is discussed on pages 377 ff.

While the actual numerical value of the sigma varies from one normal curve to another (for a normal distribution of height it will be expressed in inches, for intelligence in I.Q. points), a normal frequency curve can always be divided into about 6 sigma distances laid off on the horizontal axis. The distance to the mean is about 3 sigmas; this distance includes 50 percent of all the cases in the distribution. One sigma above or below the mean includes 34 percent of all the cases; a sigma 2 sigma distances above or below the mean includes 14 percent of all the cases because the curve descends sharply at these points. At a point 2 sigmas above the mean and 5 sigmas from the left end of the distribution 98 percent of all the cases are included; only 2 percent are above this point.

Leahy, who compared the intelligence of children adopted in early infancy with the intelligence of the adopting parents (compare page 34). In Leahy's investigation the resemblance between the adopted children and their adopting parents was on the whole slight. (In terms of the correlation coefficient, page 380, we have $r = .2$.) This means that even after years of exposure to the intellectual level of the homes, the children's intellectual level cannot be attributed in any very great extent to the influence of these homes. Of course, if there had been in the group some outstandingly stimulating homes, and a few children especially responsive to what such homes offered, the figure might have been somewhat different. All we can say is that the investigation supports Burks in pointing to the fact that children do not automatically take over the intellectual level of the home.

In more recent years there has likewise been interest in various other ways of emphasizing the stuff of which the individual is made. Certainly the effects of birth injury point to the importance of having and using all that nature has given one, and the recent dramatic results achieved with various types of specially prepared food substances which nourish the brain also bring out another aspect of what the environment may do in individual cases (page 27).

Turning now to the other side of the ledger, we may ask ourselves just what can happen under maximal stimulation and under maximal deprivation; that is, we may ask what the environment may achieve when its effect is very much better or very much worse than what we are accustomed to. This places the emphasis upon the widest possible variations, to see whether, as we should expect, I.Q. variations become greater when environmental variations are greater. Under this heading we include cases in which the child has had to cope with some factor that interferes with his intellectual development. There are several kinds of evidence about this factor of *stimulation* or *restriction* in freedom to grow and in freedom to think. One aspect of the problem is the fact that while the intelligence quotient of a normal child in a normal home usually varies only 6 or 8 or 10 points, the I.Q. being roughly constant, it is a commonplace in institutions for defective children—where life is usually very monotonous, attendants are few, care is extremely limited—to see the I.Q. shrinking and contracting year by year. A child with an intelligence quotient of 65 in his own home would ordinarily hold his own year by year; but such a child in an institution is likely to drop to 60, 55, and 50 after a few years. Although he has gone on growing chronologically, he has grown very little in mental age. Such a child brought into a more stimulating setup frequently begins to go ahead again in mental age.

Another aspect of the problem of stimulation and blocking of mental growth is the matter of emotional stress which actually interferes with attention and thinking. While not in any sense wishing to suggest that the case to be described now is typical, it is at least of some real interest and has the advantage of being known personally to the writer, so that he can have no doubt regarding the facts.

Henry appeared at a nursery school in Westchester County, New York, in a rather unhappy and distracted state. He had almost no contact with the other children, except occasionally to pounce upon one of them without provocation. He played in the sandbox by himself a large part of the time, being interested neither in the other children's activities nor in the adults. One of the nursery-school teachers, eager to draw him out and make good contact with him, would come and sing to him for long periods, and this he greatly enjoyed. In fact, music was the only way of making contact with Henry. Study of his life history showed a mother who could not be bothered spending time with him, and who farmed him out to a nurse; she in turn could not be bothered with small children who were likely to get into trouble, so she kept him in a stroller. Handling him was an impersonal routine matter; the feeding, toileting, going-out and coming-in routine yielded very little warm give-and-take either with adults or with children. When he came to the nursery school, he had already undergone some sort of "turning in upon himself." His activity was not oriented toward the outer world, as it usually is with two- and three-year-old children.

His intelligence appeared to be quite limited. He was taken to a professional clinical psychologist, an experienced person who had administered thousands of tests, and who knew the rules of the game. She reported an intelligence quotient of 65, and recommended that the child be sent to an institution. The staff of the nursery school were unwilling to accept this suggestion and arranged for psychiatric visits. The child was gradually drawn out; points of contact were made with him. He found warm friends and interesting things to do. He was placed with new associates. His intelligence quotient began to go up. It went to 80. It went to 95. It went to 110. When last tested it was 150, and the child has made a good general adjustment, at the age of fourteen, after ten years of very attentive care.

Again let it be emphasized that this is not offered as "typical." The child's I.Q. had undoubtedly been pushed down for a long time by exceptionally bad environmental handling, and at the time of testing and at other times he was probably incapable of giving "everything he had" to a task. Perhaps it would not be altogether fanciful to remind ourselves that a spring which has been held down for a long time, but not too long, may make a great push upward when released. Also, one may say, if one likes, that there is even a little "artificial forcing" here. Some may doubt whether this 150 will be maintained. But after all, we are not trying to make a mathematical point. We do not know the whole inner story of what happened to Henry or what might have happened under different conditions.

We are, however, prepared to say that the idea of the I.Q. as something like an unchangeable birthmark has had a very vicious effect in the case of a great many children who are emotionally in a jam, and need to be brought out and given encouragement. It is not implied that this kind of handling would be needed or would be useful with all children. Again it must be emphasized over and over again, to avoid all fear of misunderstanding, that there are definite and often tragic constitutional limits. Children cannot be pushed beyond a certain point. What that certain point is depends upon the child, the home, the teacher, the total situation; this is no time for the fatalistic rejection of evidence in which constructive therapeutic achievements are often possible.

Likewise, there are data of social significance relating not to individual clinical cases but to handicapped social groups. The reader will recall an example given earlier: Bruce's data on white and Negro children in Halifax County, Virginia (page 33). There the intelligence quotients clustered around 80. In that particular case we have no way of knowing what could have been done if the environment had improved; the I.Q.'s would probably go up in any such case, but how much? Seldom in the story of underprivileged human groups have we been able to answer this kind of question.

At times, however, a flood of light on the general problem is thrown by cases in which some of the individuals are transplanted to a better environment. Particularly useful is the study by Klineberg relating to rural Negro children referred to earlier (see page 29). This suggests that in the case of grossly handicapped groups environmental opportunities must be given an important role in the analysis of their achievements. At the same time it must be heavily underscored that in

Klineberg's data (and in Bruce's data and in all others') individual factors, apparently traceable to variations in the stock, are of great importance. There are high intelligence quotients even in Bruce's grossly handicapped group. Even such a profound limitation of opportunity cannot erase individuality.[5]

When it comes to drawing conclusions from the sorts of data given here, we run into a great deal of prejudice and a great deal of vaguely defined resistance. From high-school students to professors of psychology, the issue of heredity and environment in relation to intelligence is one that is very difficult to handle without an emotional warping of our thought. Mostly, we want things to go on as they are, at least as they affect most of us; and therefore arguments relating to heredity and environment are almost sure to run into a snag. If, for example, we begin to think about the long-range importance of the human stock, and of the wide individual variations in competence which characterize our American population as a whole, some people are likely to become emotional and say that we are talking about "stock breeding," that the people who are interested in heredity want to arrange forced marriages between the supposedly bright and to limit the reproduction of the others, or that they have Fascist ideas about the superiority of some individuals over others, etc. The quiet straightforward investigation of variations in the stock as they appear in every class, in every race, in every human group, is a factual question and it is immature to allow emotional factors to disturb it. Nothing much is actually being done now by the community regarding heredity; indeed, very little money is being put into the study of the role of human stock variability in producing changes in the American population over the years. We simply do not know whether the brighter stocks are adequately reproducing themselves or not; the whole issue is caught up with our lack of knowledge about the precise way in which nature and nurture interact. We have studied these issues only in certain limited situations. The plea which the scientist must make is for much more and better research and thought about the long-range process of improving both the stock and the environment. And it is tragic, when

---

[5] Another careful study (J. Peterson and C. H. Lanier, Studies in the comparative abilities of white and Negroes, *Ment. Meas. Monogr.*, 1929, No. 5) shows that the differences between white and Negro children vary with the test used, and are mostly small and not statistically significant.

both kinds of improvement are so important, to become involved in a controversy as to which should be investigated. Both need to be investigated, and thought about, and, when good findings are available, to be considered democratically in terms of long-range public policy.

Regarding various environmental measures for improving intelligence, again there is likely to be much emotion if we undertake anything on a large scale. If we suggest, for example, that greater equalization of wealth, and therefore of educational opportunity, would probably be the most practicable way in which to raise the general intellectual level in a democracy, we are likely to be told rather emotionally that people find their natural level, and that ours is a utopian socialistic proposal which has no relation to human nature. Again what we need is better factual information and a more reasoned democratic analysis of the problem.

Fortunately we do not have to wait for all these happy consummations in order to help individual children who are suffering from social handicaps. There are ways of setting up a nursery school, an elementary school, or an orphanage in such fashion as to elevate I.Q.'s. Every psychological clinic in the country and a good many private clinical psychologists and psychiatrists are influencing intelligence test scores through stimulation or psychotherapy of one sort or another. The methods include the following: (1) giving the child confidence in himself; (2) enabling him to find greater satisfaction in life, and thus eliminating some of his hostility to his environment; (3) overcoming his ability to accept his own wishes and longings, and the attendant sense of guilt which may rack his conscience; and, perhaps above all, (4) exposing children steadily, year by year, to a range of interests and ideas which had previously been denied them. As we saw at the end of the chapter on creating, there is a wide area of new activities in which each child can be allowed to find fulfillment; and it is certainly among such children that the more dramatic intellectual as well as emotional and social improvements are to be observed.

Finally, it will be worth while to consider, in the light of these scattered findings, the present general meaning of nature-nurture research. It will not do us much good to state the effects of nature and nurture in terms of some broad abstraction, no matter how good, and let it go at that. In the case of foster-child studies, a great deal will depend upon the kind of stock represented by the children available for adoption, and upon what can be done for a particular child by a specific foster home that is available to him. Much will depend upon the school situation, too; for it may be the concrete school situation, or the personality of a particular teacher, that gives stimulation. A home or a school which may seem good to us may be lifeless and boring to a specific child. In the same way, an influence in life will have a meaning that depends in part upon the make-up of the individual who encounters it. All the data seem to indicate that the nature-nurture problem is a highly individual one, that a particular kind of genetic make-up can derive a great deal of benefit from a particular kind of educational or psychiatric handling. The same psychiatric and educational handling might not help some other child at all.

In the same way, there are a great many different kinds of educational and psychiatric help, the choice among which will depend upon the child's needs at the time. A Montessori school may help one, a progressive nursery school another, private tutoring a third, a new foster home a fourth, a wise and discerning psychiatrist a fifth. Each of these may be helpful in regard to certain individual children and not so helpful with regard to others. The problem involves A's meeting B; in it almost everything depends upon the particular attributes of the individual, A, that go to meet the particular releasing qualities present in the environment, B. This way of looking at the matter is of course not likely to give the neat generalization that may be wanted; we should like to be able to say what percentage of all variation in intelligence quotients in the United States is traceable to variation in heredity, and what to variation in environment. Without denying the value of a research investigation which aims at achieving such a generalized quantitative statement, the emphasis most appropriate in regard to most problems of development is in terms of understanding the reasons for the wide individual variations. We want to understand why we may expect the individual child to benefit a little, or a very great deal, in relation to a particular type of environmental situation. This means that we have to understand both the composition of the child's mind as a whole and the personality make-up which he might be able to release and to expand if placed in a new environment. In exactly the same way, the botanist or the horticulturist will want to know, with regard to a particular strain of perennials or bulbs, what particular types of acid or alkaline soil, what particular types of sunlight or moisture, will be available in a particular greenhouse or field, and he will want to *individualize the treatment* as far as he can. Indeed, if he is raising orchids or other flowers which require very special individual attention, he will show a medical man's interest in the whole flower in relation to all of its interactions with its environment. Perhaps a child is worth as much as an orchid, and the problem of education will ultimately be seen in individual terms.

The Theory of Intelligence

Is intelligence something general, in the sense that if you know how much intelligence a man has you know just how much intelligence he has in business matters, in politics, in community affairs, in his reading of the newspaper, in his handling of his children's problems? Obviously the variation in the effectiveness of his thinking as he moves from one field of activity to another is partly a matter of his interest, but there seems to be something more to the problem than that. We find that the children who are brightest in arithmetic may, despite serious interest and hard work, not be very good in social studies, and we find at the college level many an individual who though seriously motivated discovers that he has a true "blind spot" for science or for languages. We shall therefore have to rule out the idea that intelligence is simply a fund of intellectual competence which one has at one's disposal and that the fund is the same no matter in what area of life one sees fit to spend it.

But on the other hand we cannot possibly assume that *everything* depends upon the particular area. Can a man who is bright in business matters be at the level of a mental defective as he struggles to comprehend the newspaper? Do we ordinarily find that the woman whom we know to be bright at the sorority house turns out to be consistently stupid in other situations? Actually, when we take the trouble to test the matter, we find that on the whole there is a certain positive relationship between brightness in one field and brightness in another. We may summarize the situation by saying that there is something which might be called general intelligence, something which is a common factor running through all the different tasks; but that in addition to this general factor there are special abilities, abilities to deal with particular kinds of problems. We can symbolize the situation in the following equation, where G is general intelligence, S_1, S_2, S_3 are special abilities, and A is total ability:

$$G + S_1 + S_2 + S_3 = A$$

So far, we have stated the theory of general and specific factors as formulated fifty years ago by the British psychologist Charles Spearman. The extensive research of recent years enables us to state the case more accurately. It is clear that in between the general factor and the factors that are very specific to particular situations (like ability to catch errors while reading proof) there are capacities which are less general than the former and less specific than the latter. These are today called group factors. They relate to such capacities as the ability to understand words, the ability to handle numbers, the ability to imagine spatial relations.[6] The identification and measurement of these factors is called *factor analysis*.

Some investigators are sure that the different factors are as well defined in the small child as in the adult.[7] Others[8] think that as the child develops, his abilities become more and more specialized. They report that no matter what tests are given the child of four or five, the result is about the same level of competence; while as he grows older, his mind becomes more and more differentiated in the sense that there is less and less prediction from his ability *in one field* to his ability *in other fields*. This process of differentiation year by year is probably the result partly of factors of maturation and partly of the way in which the curriculum is organized, giving the child an opportunity to make a good impression in English or mathematics if he likes the teacher and is strongly motivated, while providing his mind with less exercise in some other area.

At any rate, we know from extensive data that at the level of the young adult the general factor is accompanied by a very large number of important factors which are less general. This, however, does not mean

---

[6] L. L. Thurstone, Primary mental abilities, *Psychometr. Monogr.*, 1938, No. 1.
[7] L. L. Thurstone, Psychological implications of factor analysis, *Amer. Psychologist*, 1948, *3*, 402–408.
[8] H. E. Garrett, A development theory of intelligence, *Amer. Psychologist*, 1946, *1*, 373–378.

that to all intents and purposes we can disregard the intelligence quotient, as we obtain it from a Stanford-Binet or a Wechsler-Bellevue, and that we should deal only with specific powers. That would be a misconstruction of the evidence. Actually what we do with the Stanford-Binet, or the Wechsler-Bellevue, is to combine scores which are of various origins and interact in the functioning of the adult's mind.

Even though on finer analysis the mind turns out to comprise different factors, it is often well worth while to know actually what the individual can do with typical *generalized tasks* in which he uses everything he can use. We find, for example, even though the mind is differentiated, that a good general intelligence test will predict rather well the grades that can be made in the freshman and sophomore years, in view of the fact that the student takes a broad, diversified curriculum. There is nothing surprising about the fact that an all-round test will predict rather well an all-round college achievement. As the individual moves onward, however, to more and more specialized work during his junior and senior years in college, the specific factors count more and more, and the more general factors less and less. We therefore find that intelligence tests predict the work of the last two years in college very much *less* successfully than the work of the first two years. This is as it should be; it means that a general test will not predict very well in the areas of specialization to which the individual is giving his attention. Emotional factors and factors of special interest of course increase the difference in achievement that appears between one field and another. Whatever the explanation, the mind has become molded into a fairly stable pattern by the time one has reached the late teens.

Since this is true, it unfortunately necessitates still further reservations about the meaning of nature-nurture studies. It is hard enough to know what to attribute to heredity and what to environment if we are talking about intelligence as a single homogeneous attribute like height. Granted that many genes and many environmental factors influence height, at least an inch is an inch and we can add inches together. But if intelligence is a complex expression of many interacting types of abilities which have become more or less differentiated in the individual who is tested, it becomes more and more difficult to try to specify to just what degree his intellectual level is a function of variations in stock or variations in environmental opportunity. Ultimately we shall need a good nature-nurture analysis not just of general intelligence but of each of the specific budding abilities which we watch year by year in a child. Until that time comes, we might do well to regard each unfolding capacity as the expression of a genetic disposition that is being warmed and nurtured in a particular direction. Since this is the picture regarding physical attributes, including those studied by medical science, we may presume that it is probably true also of psychological and social attributes. There is a very real and important place for the study of "general intelligence," along with the study of these specific developing potentialities; it is like the place of "general health," so important in medicine, but distinct from the specific health assets of the individual.

One can do a great deal of damage to an individual by assuming that if he would only *try* he could climb to every height; this is brought out in the case of Elsa.

. . . Elsa, a young girl of fourteen, was brought to a psychiatric hospital because she had become more and more unco-operative at home and had finally become mute, rigid, and indifferent to her surroundings. After a few months in the hospital she slowly began to take an interest in the people around her. Elsa was particularly fond of sewing and embroidering, but lapsed into her former depression at the least suggestion of doing academic work or reading a book. Records revealed that at the age of seven, when she was in the second grade, her I.Q. was 73. The intelligence level of her two sisters and brother was considerably higher, no one having an I.Q. below 110. Elsa's school record was poor, and she had repeated a grade in school on two occasions. Apparently neither her parents nor her school realized the nature of her limitations, and they tried to drive her to keep up with normal standards of intellectual achievement. This girl had the misfortune, for her, to come from a home where there was an aspiration level beyond her capacity and where there was no understanding of any line of conduct other than that of doing well in school.[9]

On the other hand, if anyone is still tempted to think of an I.Q. as one simple unalterable aspect of the individual's make-up, like a birthmark, it may be worth while to quote two other case studies in which heredity, home environment, health, are all featured by the psychologist, and the

---

[9] T. M. Abel and E. F. Kinder, *The Subnormal Adolescent Girl*, New York, Columbia University Press, 1942.

relations of intelligence to the individual's emotional life and whole personality are brought out.[10]

Caroline

One of the cases showing most consistently rapid mental development is Caroline. Caroline's parents are well educated; the father is in a professional occupation that requires advanced scientific training. She has a brother about three years her senior. The family's income has been ample, steady, and increasing throughout Caroline's life. They recently built a new home in a good suburban district.

The mother shows much interest in the theory and practice of child training. However, Caroline's brother was something of a behavior problem, and had been taken to a clinic for guidance before Caroline was born. His presence at the Institute during Caroline's tests was always a trial and a great disturbance. The mother seemed often to be far more concerned with Peter than with Caroline.

Caroline had few illnesses during her early years, but developed asthma at about four and one-half years. Since this age she has been very thin, has had repeated and severe asthma, has been kept in bed for long periods or else on a restricted schedule with long hours in bed.

At about 5 months of age she cried very much during the tests, especially the physical tests and measurements, and this behavior continued until after she was 2½ years old. She manifested strong drives to do things her own way, and to help herself without assistance (as in dressing). She had strong preferences for certain toys in the mental tests, protested at their removal, and she rejected new toys at first. Peter's presence was a disturbing factor at several tests. Her mother sent her alone to be tested at all but one test from 8 through 14 months of age. Caroline was never taken anywhere as a baby and never saw anyone but her own family. At 2 years she was "a regular chatterbox," followed her mother around the house talking and imitating her. She became very neat and orderly, always picking up things and putting them away.

As she grew older, Caroline's independence and drive to do things for herself developed into a *very strong* drive to excel, often in competition with Peter. She uses long words and elaborate sentences, strives to do well in all problems set for her, and delights in her successes. She often has a rather strained, tense look on her face. During her enforced rest periods, it is reported, she reads a great deal. Her classmates tend to dislike her, for she is overbearing and critical. Various indications point to the possibility that her intense strivings are compensation for feelings of insecurity and jealousy of her brother and that these compensations take a turn that makes her less liked by other children.

Several factors in Caroline's life appear to be operating to stimulate her

---

[10] N. Bayley, Factors influencing the growth of intelligence in young children, *Yearb. natl. Soc. Stud. Educ.*, 1940, Part II, 49–79.

to high intellectual development. There is a probability of good inherited ability; and emotional drives have made her put forth great effort in this direction. In addition, the nature of her health has been such that she has long quiet hours for reading and acquiring "book learning." There is little wonder here that Caroline's mental-test scores have greatly improved. What is more, her poor early scores coincide with a period during which the testing situation was very disturbing to her.

Lawrence

In Lawrence . . . we find very rapid mental development, generally, during his first two years, followed by a gradual regression toward the mean through eight years of age. Lawrence is the third and youngest child of parents whose ancestry is "Old American," cultured and distinguished. The father, a commercial artist, completed a six-year university course, the mother a five-year one. The family income is moderate, and was greatly reduced during the depression. They own their own home, which is a good, modern house in a very good neighborhood.

Lawrence is growing up in an environment where education and culture are taken for granted, in an artistically beautiful, very comfortably lived-in home. The father has various artistic abilities, like playing the violin, at which he is gifted. There is, in the home, an atmosphere of encouraging the children to go ahead on their own initiative, and a genuine appreciation of the artistic results of these activities. The sister is interested in music, the older brother in writing. Lawrence is adept at such things as making his own play costumes, in making toy villages and forts, in flower arrangements, in improvised dances, and in painting.

Lawrence was a small, wiry, excitable infant, though he was not overactive physically. During his first three years he was cared for by an elderly German woman who idolized him, read to him, and taught him German nursery rhymes. He did not seem to miss her when she left, and in spite of her attachment he is emotionally independent and self-sufficient.

Lawrence was excitable and rather easily upset by the measuring procedures. There was a period at 21 and 24 months and another around 4 years when his pronounced shyness prevented him from entering into the mental-test games until he had become more accustomed to the strange place. But once his reserve was overcome, he made very intelligent responses to the tests. He has not been interested in gaining adults' approval, and hence does not usually put forth much effort to succeed unless the task appeals to him. His concentrated effort goes to things he is interested in doing and these are not often the verbal mental tests. He usually enters eagerly into the performance tests and tests of manual skill, but has little enthusiasm for the Binet tests.

His mother says he is "temperamental." When he was 2 years old, she reported that he liked music very much and always listened when his father played evenings, remaining awake to listen. He appears to be sensitive, emotionally rather volatile, somewhat shy and introverted at times, with a good sense of humor and a lively imagination. His teachers report him as outstanding in his school work, talented, with an adult sense of humor, and very popular with other children. He is also very well liked by adults. His mother reports that, though he gets along well with children, he has little interest in their usual group play. He accepts them if they wish to join in his own projects in which he is intensely interested, and which are usually attractive to other children. These games are imaginative, "intellectualized," rather than active or energetic.

To sum up, Lawrence is physically small and immature; he has a history of infected tonsils and several severe illnesses, especially during his third year. On the credit side he has excellent heredity and a high cultural background, with a home atmosphere that encourages his creative interests. One *might* postulate that his poor start in infancy was due to physical immaturity, that some of the favorable factors fostered rapid mental growth until his poor health slowed it down after two years, and that, since then, his test scores do not reflect his actual abilities because these particular tests are not the right kind to measure them. Although such things are not measured in our tests, his exceptional artistic ability has been noted repeatedly by his teachers and others.

SUGGESTED READINGS

Gesell, A., Castner, B. M., Thompson, H., and Amatruda, C. S., *Biographies of Child Development*, New York, Hoeber, 1939.

Greene, E. B., *Measurements of Human Behavior*, New York, Odyssey Press, 1941.

Hollingworth, L. S., *Gifted Children*, New York, Macmillan, 1926.

Spearman, C. E., *The Nature of Intelligence*, London, Macmillan, 1927.

Terman, L. M., and Merrill, M., *Measuring Intelligence*, Boston, Houghton Mifflin, 1937.

Thurstone, L. L., *The Nature of Intelligence*, New York, Harcourt, Brace, 1924.

Wechsler, D., *The Measurement of Adult Intelligence*, Baltimore, Williams and Wilkins, 1941.

Wechsler, D., Non-intellective factors in general intelligence, *J. abnorm. soc. Psych.*, 1943, 38, 101–103.

20 THE PATTERN OF ABILITIES

Although the term "psychological test" still means to most people an intelligence test, one of the great areas of psychological activity in recent decades has been the development of tests of dozens of other kinds of personal abilities besides intelligence, e.g., tests measuring mechanical ability, musical ability, manual skill, quickness and accuracy in perceiving, etc. We have already seen, in fact, that the intelligence test itself measures not only *general* but also *special* skills (page 360), and that there are a great many special abilities which are not tapped by the materials used in a test of general intelligence. It is of the utmost importance to think of the individual human being's abilities as a *pattern of many different abilities*, not just as an abstract score in "general intelligence." Regarding some of the tests we have data showing typical scores during the years of early development, so that we can say something about the consistency of the scores during the growth period and how much can be accomplished through training these functions; in other cases we have no such data. In some cases we know to what degree these special kinds of aptitude correlate with intelligence test scores and to what degree they are independent of them. In many cases these tests of special abilities have been subjected to factor analysis or have been specially contrived as tests of factors which have already been identified. Often a test of some special capacity may be of very great practical utility even when these other types of information about it are not available.

A great many types of abilities which are important in relation to success in a given vocation or in a specific job can be tested one at a time.

This is very advantageous because a person might have *one* of the required aptitudes, but not all of them, and he might consequently do better to find a job which requires *his own* special pattern of ability. Job analyses may be carried through which show the amount and the level of difficulty of each kind of activity that goes into the successful performance of each specialized job. The vocational guide and the industrial psychologist have to know how to administer the appropriate tests, to score them, to interpret them, and to see them in relation to one another and to the life history and interests of the applicant for a particular line of training or industrial job. We cannot embark here on a systematic study of vocational or industrial psychology, but we must insist on the importance of distinguishing between tests of intelligence and tests of special abilities.

But the abilities which we test in a person today do not in themselves tell us how far he can go if he gets further practice and experience. We must differentiate between his fundamental aptitude and the achievement he brings to us today. The term aptitude as used here means simply the readiness of the individual, as we find him, to profit by further training. Suppose, for example, as he comes to us now at 20 years of age he is strong, quick, of moderate general intelligence, and with a high degree of interest in learning a semi-skilled industrial job rather quickly. We find in testing him that he has such-and-such aptitudes as shown in speed of response, accuracy of eye-hand coördination, and so on. Actually, however, he has never worked at this job and will be worth little the first day at the plant. Another man shows a lower level of success on aptitude tests but has achieved a rather high level of functioning as a result of special training. An achievement test will bring out how well the two will actually carry out the operation, and an aptitude test will give us a general view of how much to expect of each one after he has had the requisite training.

Whether you will administer an aptitude or an achievement test will depend entirely upon what you are doing. If you have the time and facilities to train a group of applicants, or if you are giving vocational advice rather early in the game to an adolescent who has some years of training ahead of him, you may want to emphasize aptitude and make some guess as to the limits which he will ultimately reach. If, on the other hand, you have to place the applicant here and now and it is too wasteful to let him blunder through with an ineffective performance during the first few weeks, or if you have a very large number of applicants for a rather short job and you must get the most done in the least time, you will probably want to rely most upon an achievement test. A very important exception was the wartime selection of men for new tasks, e.g., in the air forces. Here it was possible to predict fairly well, from a comprehensive battery of tests involving speed and accuracy of adjustment, who would be successful in training (Figure 70).[1] That is, *aptitude* for aviation had to be determined, rather than the applicant's achievements in previous life tasks (like driving cars or trucks).

Aptitudes begin to show themselves early. In some cases the effect of giving all children equal practice is to make them more and more *unlike;* i.e., increasing practice brings out more clearly the constitutional disparities among individuals. This appears generally to be true of motor skills. In many other cases, such as artistic capacities, early encouragement and training appear to do much more than simply "bring out" such abilities; they seem to do a great deal to develop imagination when less encouragement might stifle it. But as we suggested in Chapter 3, what is acquired, so to speak, from the environment is not something in *opposition* to what is given, but depends in a positive way upon what is given. It is the material actually given that undergoes the training.

We also find from such studies that children grow more rapidly in one function, more slowly in another. A child may be speeding ahead in one function, maintaining his position in the top quartile (quartile is the technical term for one-fourth of the distribution) in verbal comprehension, but perhaps be in the third quartile in mathematics, or vice versa. At every age level we want to be able to tell not only how well a child does in terms of some one capacity, *but how the different capacities are interrelated.*

It is of special importance to be able to assess the individual's abilities in his middle and later teens, when so many tens of thousands want guid-

---

[1] J. P. Guilford, Some lessons from aviation psychology, *Amer. Psychologist,* 1948, *3,* 3–11.

ance as to vocations. We may make concrete the conception of ascertaining the individual *pattern of abilities* by citing in full the case of Michael T.[2]

Michael T. was concerned about his vocational future. He did not think that he even had a start in the right direction. He was now 20 years old and urgently felt the need to plan a more satisfactory career. He talked about his problem with a friend who was attending college. This friend had been in a similar quandary only a short time ago. He had spoken to his psychology instructor, who had recommended a vocational counseling agency. Now the friend suggested that Michael go there. Because he was so anxious to receive help in his problem, Michael jumped at the suggestion.

Michael went to the vocational counseling agency the very next day. He was met by a receptionist to whom he told his desire to "take some tests" and be helped vocationally. The receptionist gave him a registration blank to fill out while he waited for a preliminary interview by the intake counselor. On the blank Michael was to note factual data such as his name, address, age, by whom he was referred, the occupations of his parents, his education, the jobs he held and whether he liked them or not. He also was to write what he wanted to discuss and what he wanted to become in the future. The information on the blank provided some background information, served as an introduction, and permitted the counselor to conduct the interview without having to interrupt it to obtain the specific facts.

The intake counselor received the filled-in registration blank and studied it before talking with Michael. (Among the functions of an intake counselor is the determination of whether or not the person can be helped by vocational counseling and which particular counselor may be best suited for him.) Michael had noted among other things that he was a high school graduate and in a job that he did not like. He also had written that he wanted to be an engineer and wished to discuss how or if he could "make it." He impressed the intake counselor as pleasant and bright but very tense and anxious. The intake counselor accepted his application and assigned him to a counselor experienced in handling young men with problems similar to Michael's.

About a week later, Michael was called for his first appointment with his counselor. (The time lag before the appointment varies with the number of people accepted for service.) The counselor had the registration blank and the notes from the intake counselor available before the interview. He also had a résumé of Michael's high school record which had been sent for by the intake person. In the first interview, Michael discussed the nature of his problem.

He said that he was anxious to know if he could study engineering. This was something he had had in mind for many years but his father did not think it wise. His father thought Michael would be much better off in business

---

[2] This case was supplied by Dr. Benjamin Balinsky, who prepared it in a form suitable for our purpose.

THE PATTERN OF ABILITIES

and had spoken to one of his business friends, who helped Michael obtain a job in a large firm. Michael said he was told by one of the executives that there was a future for him in the business if he worked hard and demonstrated that he could learn all that was necessary. He was promised eventual consideration for an executive position. Michael was then put to work in the stock room to learn from the bottom up.

Michael said that he did his work conscientiously and was praised for doing it well. However, two years had gone by and he was still in the shipping room. He said that he really did not feel he was making sufficient progress. He had spoken to his superior about transfer to a position where he could learn the technical aspects of the work but was told he was needed in the shipping department. Michael felt that he would like to leave the job and study engineering before he became too old to start.

However, he was quite anxious about his father's reaction. He had not spoken with him yet, but had spoken with his mother and older brother. They were both sympathetic and encouraging. Michael felt that they would back him in his decision, but he wanted to be sure that it was the right thing before he spoke with his father. He preferred to study engineering by day rather than take evening courses. He felt it would take too long in the evening and that he could not stand the extra burden of work while studying. So he needed his father's support. He said his father was financially able to support this plan and if extra aid was required his brother would contribute.

Michael said that he had done good work in mathematics and physics in the technical high school he attended. His school grades, according to the record, were exceptional. Michael was being modest. He also had liked chemistry and used to do hobby work in this at home. Michael asked if there were any tests that could predict his success in engineering school. Although there are no foolproof, perfectly accurate tests, there are some that have been found to predict rather well the level of engineering school success. When the tests taken are considered together and along with school grades and interests, their usefulness is increased.

An appointment for tests was arranged for Michael. The counselor recommended certain tests for him: measures of general *intelligence, spatial* and *manipulative aptitudes*, as well as an *interest* test. The general intelligence test would provide an indication as to how well Michael might do in college when compared with other students. The Otis Self-Administering Test of Mental Ability, Higher Examination, Form B, was selected as a measure of general intelligence.

This test measures general academic ability, not engineering specifically. It measures mainly how well one comprehends and reasons with words. It also contains arithmetical problems. These are some typical questions:

> The opposite of love is (?)
> 1 like, 2 anger, 3 hate, 4 strange, 5 lover
> If 2 pencils cost 5 cents, how many pencils can be bought for 50 cents?

A man does not always have (?)
   1 bones, 2 heart, 3 teeth, 4 nerves, 5 lungs
If the following words were arranged to make the best sentence, the first word of the sentence would begin with what letter? Print the letter as a capital.
   tests   pupils   mental   thousands   have   of   taken

Spatial aptitude tests measure functions more directly related to those required in engineering itself. In the simple tests one wants to know how well and how quickly the individual can grasp the way in which parts of different sizes and shapes will fit together. Not much in the way of *figuring out* possible relationships is necessary; rather the ability to *perceive* shapes and sizes so as

Figure 65. The Minnesota Spatial Relations Test

to fit them into their proper positions is what is needed. This ability is useful in some aspects of engineering but even more so in mechanical jobs. The more complex spatial ability tests require an understanding of physical and mechanical principles, and the ability to visualize how parts would fit together when they are not actually present. This often involves rotating the parts mentally and working from scale models or blueprints.

Three spatial tests were administered to Michael, each measuring certain aspects of spatial ability. Together their results would be more meaningful than one of them alone. The Minnesota Spatial Relations Test, the Revised Minnesota Paper Form Board, and the Bennett Mechanical Comprehension Test were the three selected.

The Minnesota Spatial Relations Test was administered with two boards. Each board has cutouts of different shapes and sizes. Most shapes have three sizes. There are 58 pieces available, and each piece fits into one cutout correctly. The examinee is to place the correct piece in the appropriate cutout. He does this as quickly as possible, first for one board, then for the other. The score is the time taken to fill in the two boards. (See Figure 65.)

The Revised Minnesota Paper Form Board consists of 64 geometric figures. Parts of the figures are given, with five whole figures in which the parts have been fitted together. The examinee is to choose the one of the five which is correct. This requires visualization of the patterns.

The Bennett Mechanical Comprehension Test, Form AA, has 60 items pic-

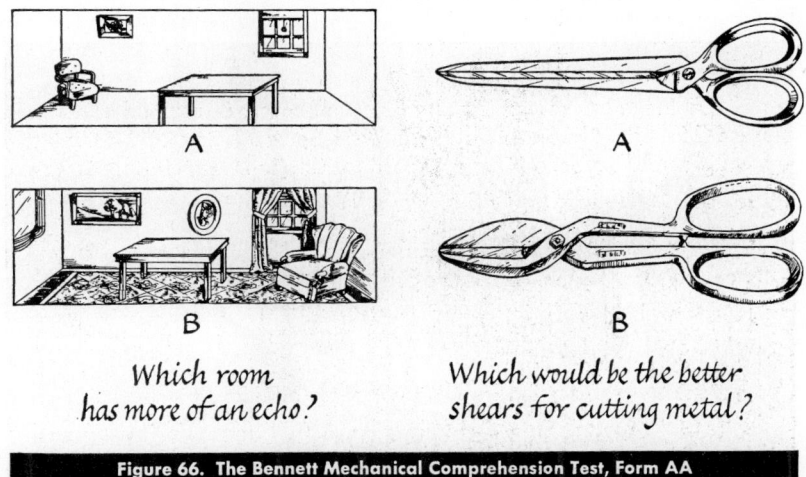

Figure 66. The Bennett Mechanical Comprehension Test, Form AA

(By courtesy of The Psychological Corporation.)

torially represented and arranged in order of difficulty. They involve comprehension of mechanical principles found in ordinary situations. The items shown in Figure 66 are illustrative.

Manipulative tests were also given to Michael. These measure rather specific psychomotor functions, like dexterity with small objects and large objects. This kind of aptitude is not as important for success in engineering as is spatial ability. However, the engineer usually shows good facility and speed in handling objects.

Michael was given the Finger Dexterity Test (Figure 67) and the Placing and Turning parts of the Minnesota Rate of Manipulation Test (Figure 68). The Finger Dexterity Test uses a plate in which there is a shallow tray for brass pins, and 100 holes in which the brass pins can be placed. Three pins are to be picked up and placed in each hole three at a time until the 100 holes have been filled. The score is the time it takes to do this. The Placing and Turning tests use a rectangular-shaped board with sixty round holes. Sixty disks or cylinders are used to fill the holes. In the Placing test, the examinee is to put the cylinders back into the holes in a standard manner as quickly as he can. Speed is essential. This is done four times and the score is the sum of the time on each of the four trials. In the Turning test the cylinders are in the board; each one is to be removed with one hand, turned over and with the other hand returned to the hole from which it was removed. The procedure is standardized. Four trials are given and the score is the sum of the time on each trial.

The counselor also wanted an interest test given to Michael to obtain some objective evidence about interests that could be related with the aptitude test results and the interview data. The test would be helpful in showing in what

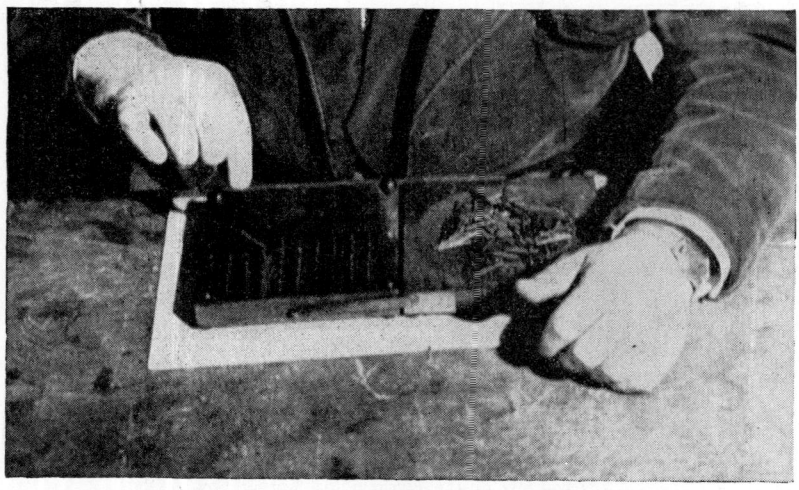

Figure 67. The Finger Dexterity Test

areas of work Michael was most interested. Interest tests generally consist of statements concerning hobbies, social and recreational activities, and vocational activities. They have been standardized by giving the test to people established in different vocations. The patterns of their likes and dislikes among the hobbies and other activities become the basis for comparison; an examinee's interests are compared with the interests which are actually characteristic of successful people in different vocational groups.

The Kuder Preference Record is a widely used interest test that has proven itself to have satisfactory validity. It consists of 168 groups or blocks of three statements each. The examinee is to indicate which of the three statements in a block he likes best, and which least. As he does so, he is building up patterns of statements that characterize people in certain occupations more than they characterize those in others. Scores in nine vocational areas are obtainable: mechanical, computational, scientific, persuasive, artistic, literary, musical,

THE PATTERN OF ABILITIES 373

social science, and clerical. An illustration of some of the blocks of statements is provided below:

      P. Visit an art gallery
      Q. Browse in a library
      R. Visit a museum

      S. Collect autographs
      T. Collect coins
      U. Collect butterflies

Michael's scores were as follows; note that "percentile" tells what percent of the group he *surpasses*, and "norm group" means the group with which he is being compared (the group on which the published norms are based):

Test	Percentile	Norm Group
Otis Self-Administering	42	Liberal Arts College students
Minnesota Spatial Relations	98	16–25 general population
Revised Minnesota Paper Form Board	94	1st year male engineering students
Bennett Mechanical Comprehension	95	Engineering school freshmen
Finger Dexterity	92	16–25 general population
Placing	68	" " "
Turning	83	" " "
Kuder Preference Record		
Mechanical	93	General adult
Computational	63	" "
Scientific	92	" "
Persuasive	45	" "
Artistic	38	" "
Literary	49	" "
Musical	28	" "
Social Science	62	" "
Clerical	41	" "

A report on the test results was given to Michael's counselor. The report indicated that Michael had made consistently high scores on the spatial tests, indicating that he probably had good aptitude for engineering. He had rated only at the 42nd percentile on the Otis Test; but this is in comparison with Liberal Arts students, and the latter generally do better on tests like the Otis than do engineering students, since it contains mainly language items. Michael's Otis score is not inconsistent with aptitude for engineering. The percentile score, although not too high, is not so low as to indicate great difficulty with such subjects as history or English.

Michael's score was in each instance above the average on the manipulative tests, and in some instances was excellent. Apparently his finger dexterity and manual aptitude are high enough to predict little difficulty in speed of assembling and handling objects.

The Kuder Preference Record shows highest interest in the mechanical and scientific areas. These two areas are closely related to engineering. He also showed fairly high interest in the computational area, which should serve him in good stead. The persuasive area, which is often significant for business, is relatively low.

Michael's counselor wrote him to return for another interview after the test report was received. During this interview the counselor asked Michael if he had done any thinking about his vocational plan and he replied that he had broached the subject to his father with the encouragement of his mother and brother. His father was not as negative as Michael had believed, and said if the counselor thought it advisable he would go along.

Figure 68. The Minnesota Rate of Manipulation Test

The counselor asked Michael how he thought he had done on the tests. Michael said he did not find them too difficult but was not sure how well he had done. The results were given in an indirect manner in terms of the chances for success of people who obtained scores like Michael's. In this instance the test scores were quite favorable. Michael thought that he would be able to make the grade and decided to go into engineering. He discussed various engineering schools and selected three to which he was to apply for admission.

Michael visited the counselor each time he was in town. He was doing very well. He graduated with high grades and was selected by a company representative for a position in a large electrical firm.

Some Statistical Terms and Ideas

If we want to see Michael's abilities in their broadest interrelations, and compare him with himself as he is a year later, or

THE PATTERN OF ABILITIES 375

with his classroom friends or engineering associates, we shall need to introduce the reader to the concepts which underlie all studies of the interrelation of test scores—concepts that have been developed in the world of statistics.

There are three ways of measuring the "central tendency" or point at which a distribution appears to be centered: (1) the average or mean, which is simply the sum of all the scores divided by the number of cases; (2) the median, or the midmost case; and (3) the mode, or the point at which the largest number of individual cases concentrate. In some distributions these three measures of central tendency may have quite different values. In a normal frequency distribution the mean, median, and mode all fall at the same point. When distributions are skewed, or when there are two or more modes, it is not feasible to use, without modification, some of the elementary methods we are going to describe next; for these methods are designed primarily for use with normal frequency distributions. (See page 345.)

Often we want to compare the scores on one test with the scores on another test. We may know that in general those who did well on one did well on the other, but there may be exceptions. The question of the size of the exceptions and their frequency is often of very great importance. We can say that two kinds of ability are "related," yet not be saying anything of value, because the whole question is how closely they are related. We might find that only now and then does a person superior in one test fall at the middle or below the middle in another; or we might find that the exceptions, though not overwhelming, are quite frequent. We need an exact scale to measure the correlation, or degree of agreement between sets of measures.

Two very commonly used correlation methods are Spearman's *rank-difference* method and Pearson's *product-moment* method. In the former we are simply interested in each individual's rank in each function. For example, his rank in spelling and in reading comprehension may be about the same. For the most part, those who are near the top in one are rather near the top in the other. We rank the individuals in each of the two tests, find the difference between each person's rank in one test and his rank in the other, square these differences and add the squares, as in the following example:

Individual	Rank in A	Rank in B	D (Difference)	D^2 (Difference Squared)
A	1	4	3	9
B	2	3	1	1
C	3	1	2	4
D	4	2	2	4
E	5	6	1	1
F	6	5	1	1
G	7	10	3	9
H	8	7	1	1
I	9	9	0	0
J	10	8	2	4

The formula for this is:

$$\rho = 1 - \frac{6\Sigma(D^2)}{n(n^2-1)} = 1 - \frac{204}{10(100-1)} = .79$$

where $\Sigma(D^2)$ is the sum of the squares of the differences, and n is the number of cases.

This ρ (rho, the Greek letter for r), the symbol for the rank-difference correlation, may be converted by means of a special formula to r, the symbol for the product-moment correlation. In this case, ρ (.79) corresponds to an r of about .81. In general, a correlation derived by the rank-difference method (ρ) is roughly comparable to a correlation derived by the product-moment method (r) to be described below.

In the *product-moment* method, we have a place for more exact information as to the scores made by each individual; we compare individuals not in terms of their rank, but in terms of the actual scores made. Here the basic problem that we must keep in mind is whether the person who is above the mean on one test is also above the mean on the other test; if he is, the fact will tend to increase any measure which shows a relationship between the two. On the other hand, if he is above the mean on one, and below the mean on the other, this will tend to pull down the correlation. Secondly, we want to know *how far* above or *how far* below the mean he is on each test; tests are frequently referred to as *variables* in this context. Actually it works out quite simply; we can multiply the amount by which he surpasses (or falls below) the mean in one function by the amount by which he surpasses (or falls below) the mean in the other one. If, for example, he is very far above the mean in both, multiplying one by the other will have a huge effect in pushing the correlation up. If he were very far above the mean in one and very far below the mean in the other, this would quite rightly pull the correlation far down. Our task, then, is to go right down through the array of cases and multiply these deviations (x) from the mean in one test by the corresponding deviations (y) from the mean in the other, remembering that multiplying a plus by a plus gives a plus, that multiplying a minus by a minus also gives a plus, and that multiplying a plus by a minus gives a minus. We assume each individual to have made the scores (X and Y) shown on page 380. It is evident at a glance that the positive xy products are in this case preponderant. Actually we should ordinarily not bother with the product-moment method if we only had 10 cases, but should reserve it for problems where we had at least 30 cases. Here, however, we are concerned only with the *method*.

We have still left out of account one thing. If we have measured in terms of very large units rather than small ones, we may get some huge figure like 50,000, which will not mean anything because it cannot be compared with anything concrete. We need to know what kinds of units we are working with, and how far individuals in our given group actually vary from one another in terms of these units. We take account of this by introducing into the formula an expression which shows how widely the different cases vary from one another—whether they are bunched close together or scattered far apart. The expression ordinarily used is the *sigma,* or *standard deviation.* As we saw earlier (page 351), a sigma is in practice usually about one-sixth of the full range.

Its mathematical definition must now be explained. We start with the fact that each case deviates from the mean and that this deviation can be measured. Square all these deviations, add the sum of the squares, then divide by the number of cases (this will give the mean of the squares). Now take the square root of this last figure. The resulting figure is the sigma: *the square root of the mean of the squares of the deviations.* It is this figure which we use to measure the variation of individuals around the mean. In the formula below you will see that a place is reserved for the sigma of the first variable and the sigma of the second variable. We need also to know *how many cases* were used in working out the correlations, since if it took 100 cases to yield a given

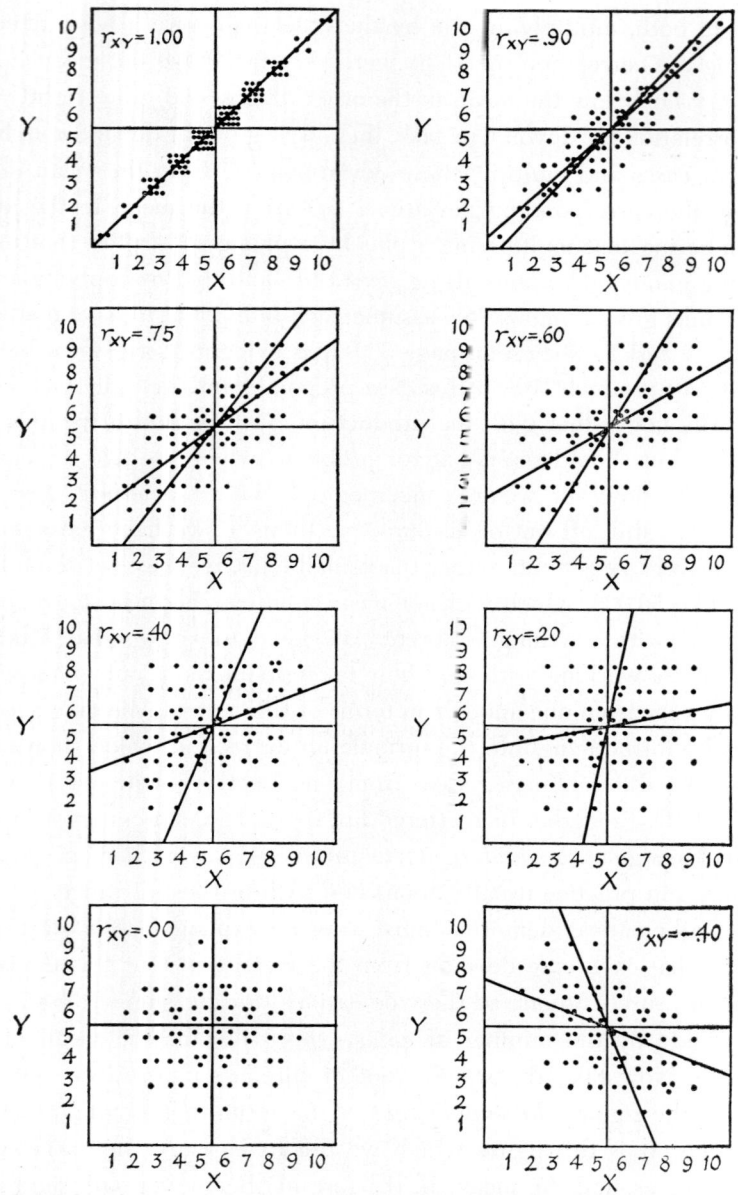

Figure 69. Data Yielding Positive, Zero, and Negative Correlations

total, the correlation would be much smaller than if we could get the same result with 10 cases. All this is taken care of by the denominator of the fraction, which shows that we multiply the number of cases by the sigma of scores (σ_x) on one test and by the sigma of scores (σ_y) on the the other. Actually, all that is involved in the product-moment formula is the conception that *we take the algebraic sum of the xy products and divide it by the number of cases multiplied by the sigmas of the two variables.* The formula works out mathematically so that perfect agreement in the scores gives a result of 1.00 (a perfect *positive* correlation) and complete absence of relationship gives a score of zero. If one variable is always down and the other is up by the same degree, we will get a correlation of -1.00 (a perfect *negative* correlation). Figure 69 gives an idea of the values of r (the product-moment correlation) obtained with various sorts of data.

It is customary to indicate, following the r, about how accurate the determination is, stated in terms of a "probable error." The probable error tells within what range the figures would fluctuate if we did further studies of the same problem. A phrase like $r = .50$, P.E. $= .05$, means that the product-moment correlation was .50 and that if we made such determinations from comparable groups over and over again this result would lie between .55 and .45 fifty percent of the time. It might stray further away sometimes, but very seldom more than 3 probable errors, so we are fairly safe in saying that the true figure is more than .35 and less than .65.

We are now ready for the formula,

$$r = \frac{\Sigma xy}{n\sigma_x \sigma_y}$$

where Σxy is the algebraic sum of the products of the two deviations

◀ These *scatter diagrams* yield sample correlations of various sizes. They are made by plotting each case on X and Y axes, each axis representing one of the two distributions of the scores being correlated. Thus an individual with high scores in both distributions would be represented by a single point in the upper right-hand corner of these squares; two low scores would be represented by a point in the lower left-hand corner, etc. If two distributions of scores are highly correlated positively or negatively ($r_{xy} = \pm.75$ or above), the points fall almost in one straight line. If two such distributions are not correlated at all ($r_{xy} = .00$), a given score on one test may fall anywhere along the scale on the other test and the scatter distribution will be nearly round. The other scatter distributions shown here are between these two extremes. (From L. J. Cronbach, *Essentials of Psychological Testing*, Harper & Brothers, 1949.)

x and y, n is the number of cases, and σ_x and σ_y are the sigmas of X and Y, respectively. Let us assume these scores:

Individual	Score X	Dev. x	Dev. x^2	xy	Dev. y^2	Dev. y	Score Y
A	85	+30	900	300	100	+10	65
B	75	+20	400	300	225	+15	70
C	70	+15	225	375	625	+25	80
D	65	+10	100	200	400	+20	75
E	60	+ 5	25	0	0	0	55
F	55	0	0	0	25	+ 5	60
G	50	− 5	25	+225	2025	−45	10
H	45	−10	100	+ 50	25	− 5	50
I	35	−20	400	+300	225	−15	40
J	10	−45	2025	+450	100	−10	45
Mean = 55			4200	2200	3750		Mean = 55

$$\sigma_x = \sqrt{420} = 20.4 \qquad \sigma_y = \sqrt{375} = 19.2$$

$$r = \frac{2200}{10 \times 20.4 \times 19.2} = .56$$

The higher the correlation, the more likelihood we have of putting our fingers on the actual dynamic factors that are responsible for it. In psychological test scores we frequently find scores that are correlated with one another to the tune of about .15 or about .2 which with a very large population may be many times their probable errors, yet which do not really help us very much to understand what is going on in the individual. For the most part, we are interested in the relation of psychological functions which are correlated .6 or .7 or better; as we study them, we may find why it is they go together.

There are two situations that will frequently recur in which we shall want to be able to use the correlation coefficient. (1) The first is in comparing scores on a given test with scores on the same test when it is given later, or with scores on some other test which is supposed to serve exactly the same purpose. This procedure is known as the determination of the "reliability" of a test. If we are basically testing ability and not chance factors which are here today and gone tomorrow, we should expect that test scores over a period would have some stability. The greater the stability, the higher the correlation between the test scores of today and those obtained later. Ordinarily, since we are aiming at reliability when

THE PATTERN OF ABILITIES 381

we devise a test, we feel that unless the retest reliability of a test is .8 or better, we cannot afford to pay much attention to it; usually we hope for .9 or better. If, moreover, there are two alternative forms of the same test and if we can really rely on one to do the same job as the other, we should expect people taking both tests to yield scores which should correlate with each other .8 or better. (2) Sometimes it is not possible to give a retest or to use an alternative form to get a reliability determination. But in a test having a considerable number of items, we may compare some of the items with the remaining items—for example, the odd-numbered items like the first, third, fifth, and seventh, with the even-numbered items like the second, fourth, sixth, eighth—and if there is really some one job which all the items in the test are helping to accomplish, people who make high scores on the sum of the odd-numbered items ought also to make high scores on the sum of the even-numbered items. The "odd-even" reliability of a test is simply this comparison of the total score made on the odd-numbered items with the total score made on the even-numbered items, and a mathematical correction we shall not go into here.

Now as to the use of correlation methods in comparing different tests of ability. In addition to the common factor which enters into all items in an intelligence test (some of the items are of course loaded with the common factors described above; cf. page 359), the verbal comprehension items are loaded with a verbal factor, the numerical items with a numerical factor, etc. Verbal comprehension items will be correlated with numerical items insofar as there is a general factor running through both; but the verbal and numerical factors will stand out distinctly. It is of very great practical importance to be able to say how well the verbal scores correlate with the numerical ones, partly because we want to see how big this general factor is which is shared by them both, partly because it is important to be able to compare each of these two factors with specific college attainments, such as work done in literature, science, etc. Over and over again it has been shown that the ability to do particular subject-matter requirements in college depends not just upon general intelligence, but upon the verbal, numerical, and other abilities which define the chief tasks to be performed in these courses. Consequently a very important use of the correlation coefficient is the prediction, from specific test scores, of competence in particular fields as compared with competence in other fields.

One other important use of correlation procedures remains to be emphasized. It is not enough that a test have a high reliability, or that we know that in general the scores will be stable over a period. It is important also to know that the test actually measures the thing it is supposed to test. If, for example, we have a test of reading comprehension, and if through some mistake the paragraphs to be read are in no sense typical of those which the individual actually reads and is required to read, the test may be very interesting and have high reliability in its own right, but may have no genuine *validity* as a test of reading comprehension. We might easily think up tests of numerical ability which would be based to a great degree on sheer ability to remember numbers and would not really bring out the factor of skill in the *manipulation* of numbers. When we have called a test by a name, it is up to us to demonstrate that it warrants that name, in the sense that it actually measures the function which has been named. This is known as determining the validity of a test. In order to determine the validity of a test, it is necessary to obtain scores from a considerable population who have taken the test and also to obtain validation scores indicating how well the individuals do in the actual performance measured by that test. If, for example, the medical schools and law schools wish to experiment (as they are already doing on a small scale) with medical aptitude and law aptitude tests, they will need to know not only what sorts of grades in medical and law school the students are likely to make on the basis of their test performance today, but how successful they will be in medical and legal *practice*. In this case the validity of the test could be defined as the degree of agreement between the scores of today and actual success in the field.

It must be admitted that frequently the obtaining of absolutely satisfactory criteria of validation is difficult. In the Air Force during World War II, for example, it was possible to predict fairly accurately from the tests how well the candidates would make out in flight schools as pilots, navigators, and bombardiers; their scores on tests devised by psychologists had considerable predictive power in telling what their learning ability in these three tasks would be (Figure 70). It was *not* feasible, however, to follow the men through actual combat experience, and get quantitative figures to indicate the predictive power of the tests for effectiveness in combat situations. Often we have to be content, then, with validity in relation to some criterion which is not necessarily the one that is most important to have. The ideal to which the psychologist aspires is to develop reliable tests that will predict, ever more accurately, future

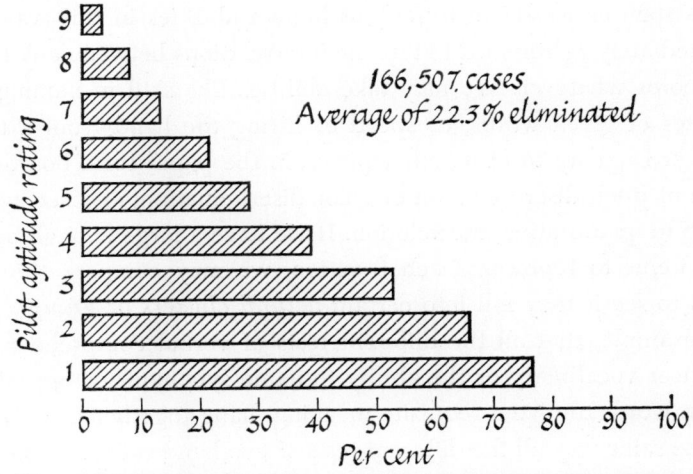

Figure 70. Validation of Test Results

The aptitude test scores of 166,507 candidates for A.A.F. flight training are broken down into nine classifications, from the lowest, 1, to the highest, 9. The percentage of those in each test-score classification who "washed out" during training is represented by the length of the bar. An average of about 22 percent were eliminated. (From A.A.F. Aviation Psychology Program, Report No. 2. By permission of the Office of the Surgeon General.)

performance in some chosen function. But we never expect perfect prediction. We are always working with the theory of probability—what we call in everyday speech the "laws of chance" or "the law of averages." A positive correlation which is of just the same magnitude as its own probable error will tend to jump about as we test fresh cases; indeed, in one out of every four subsequent experiments it will fall below zero, so that we do not have a positive correlation at all. Such a correlation is not considered statistically *significant*. Significance relates to the safety with which we can rely on the correlation. If the difference between two means is so great that such a difference would occur by chance only once in a hundred times, it is said to be "significant at the 1 percent level"; but if it would occur by chance in five out of a hundred times it is only "significant at the 5 percent level." In current usage an author sometimes says simply that a difference is significant; he usually means to refer to a 1 percent level of significance, or a still more rigorous one.

As soon as we begin to look at human abilities in this way, we can immediately go forward to test the interrelations between any two types of scores whatever. We may take abilities like skill in naming the opposites of given words, or speed of lifting the hand from a telegraph key, or capacity to fit together pieces in the paper form board, or even tests of pitch discrimination or color discrimination, and see any two of them in quantitative interrelation. If we have a large enough number of test items to represent each function, we may compare the different tests to see if they fall into certain *natural clusters or groups*. We find, for example, that all the different tests of verbal comprehension, such as sheer vocabulary or the ability to name synonyms or opposites or to fill in words to give a requisite meaning, hang together to some degree. In the same way all the different tests of eye-hand coördination, whether they involve reaching, grasping, or delicate manipulations to follow a moving object with the fingers, hang together to some degree. This supports the idea that the mind is made up of a certain number of fundamental factors. We might speak of a verbal comprehension factor whenever the understanding of words is involved; we might speak of a numerical factor whenever skill with numbers is concerned, and similarly of a spatial factor in which the ability to grasp and use spatial relationships appears.

With an understanding of the elementary mathematics of correlation, we may begin to see the rational basis for factor analysis. It is by correlation that you can prove that different processes do hang together and point to a basic psychological factor, like 'numerical ability."

Almost every kind of psychological process has been looked at in this way in recent years. Take for example the process of perceiving, in which at first glance we all seem to be very much alike. L. L. Thurstone has conducted a *factorial analysis of perception* (page 179) in which he has been able to show that in responding to visual material presented on a screen or printed on a page, some people have certain broad tendencies to perceive in terms of wholes, and are particularly quick and competent in filling in missing parts, in seeing relationships, and so on. The factor analysis of perception shows half a dozen very important basic mental modes of attack on such perceptual tasks. Each subject has his own strengths in certain areas, weaknesses in others. If you had made a wide enough sampling of a person's different ways of perceiving things, you could by analyzing his strengths and weaknesses, predict fairly well how competent, effective, quick, accurate he would be in taking note of new material which would be shown him. In fact, just this sort of thing is needed in industry and in Army, Navy, and Air Force research. In the latter you must be sure that a pilot can size up very quickly a new terrain, a new cloud formation, a new type of enemy plane seen in the distance; and you want to be able, from existing test material, to predict about how well he will function when the combination of all these various perceptual abilities is put to a sudden test. In the same way, much research has been done on motor coördination: the quickness, effectiveness, accuracy, and follow-through of movements made with hands and feet when quick signals are given.

So far, we have dealt with problems involving effective adaptation to a practical task, meeting reality in a direct way either through words, or through other symbols, or through bodily response. Factor methods can also be applied to the *emotional and feeling* life, to *esthetic* sensitivity, to the personal and social attributes of each individual. There are, for example, some fairly useful tests of response to music and of response to poetry and to pictures.

Just as all intellectual and motor aspects of the individual are somewhat plastic and subject to change—and the more so, the younger the individual—so we should be able to dispose of the idea that these factors represent fixed attributes or birthmarks of the person. They are very definitely limited by genetic constitution, as we know from the fact that although we can push or force a subject by intensive training to do a little better on any of these things, he nevertheless reaches a definite ceiling or limit (compare page 226). At the same time we do not, as a rule, know what the limits are *until* we have actually tried the thing out on a large scale over a considerable time. It is for this reason that in the practical situation—whether in education, in vocational guidance, or in industry—we must carry out our aptitude and achievement tests in a systematic and rigorous way and not speak of any given achievement as a *final* expression of what could be achieved unless the person has definitely been shown to have reached his real limit, with maximal motivation, and to have been at that point for some time. It is not surprising, then, that people who have the responsibility for guiding other people's lives are likely to want to get all the information they can as to both aptitude and achievement.

This way of thinking in terms of factors gives one the impression that the mind is a complex fabric of many constituents, many shades and tints, woven together in all sorts of ways; that the texture is not very tight, that it is likely to be pulled awry by various forces. New colors may appear in a new light which has never been suspected before. Wear and tear may alter the fabric; but it is also possible that strength may be more evident after such a challenge. Even this idea of a fabric is, of course, not dynamic enough, because the texture of the living body is not like the warp and woof of a fabric. The thing is growing, changing, adapting to new situations in a much more complex fashion.

It is well worth while to cut cross sections through the mind and to get numerical results indicating general intelligence, capacities, and achievements, whether in factor form or in terms of specific tests requisite for specific tasks. It is always worth while, though, to put a question mark at the end, and to note that we do not know what areas of flexibility may still remain in the individual, and what types of special incentive, interest, or stimulation may give dramatic expansion of powers which are at present only dimly glimpsed.

How confidently can we counsel people who ask for advice about their abilities? We certainly have the practical responsibility of informing a person who is only a shade above average in intelligence that he should not aspire to be a lawyer or a physician. We can certainly tell a person who is deficient in dealing with musical material that he should not try to be a band leader. We can certainly tell the conspicuously clumsy individual that precise manual manipulations such as those required of a dental technician are probably beyond him. We must be realistic in defining the limits. But at the same time we must remember that even very high endowment in any of these areas may not necessarily spell success, since a good deal depends on personal, social, or other qualifications for which the test may be inadequate. We can help the person, by a wide variety of test data, to see himself a little more clearly than he did before, and vocational and industrial guidance is therefore decidedly worth while. To pretend, however, that it provides exact numerical readings which will fit the man perfectly to the job is beyond any aspiration that can be reasonably entertained.

One other aspect of the practical problem of using abilities is, of course, the assessment of the personality as a whole. This we shall have to postpone until we have had a wider view of how personality is shaped in the community. After such a study of personality development has been undertaken, we shall return again briefly to the question of the guidance of the individual (page 437). The first step will be to consider the way in which the individual becomes *aware of himself,* and the significance of this fact for the development of his personality. This is the problem of the next three chapters.

SUGGESTED READINGS

Cronbach, L. J., *Essentials of Psychological Testing,* New York, Harper, 1949.
Spearman, C. E., *Human Ability,* London, Macmillan, 1950.
Super, D. E., *Appraising Vocational Fitness by Means of Psychological Tests,* New York, Harper, 1949.
Thorndike, R. L., *Personnel Selection,* New York, Wiley, 1949.
Thurstone, L. L., *Factorial Studies of Intelligence,* Chicago, Univ. of Chicago Press, 1941.
Walker, H., *Elementary Statistical Methods,* New York, Holt, 1943.

21 THE SELF

From all the evidence we now have, it appears that the newborn individual has no sharp or clear perception of anything whatever. The world is a huge blur, or as William James said, a "blooming, buzzing, confusion." For this reason we should not expect to have the child know that he is there, to have any recognition of his bodily outlines, to be able to pick out his voice from the medley of other sounds that assail his ears. There simply is no me or you, no here or there. We should not expect the child to know that there is an inside and an outside of his body, for he does not even know that he has a body. Indeed, it takes a long time for him to sort the world out and begin to recognize different objects, and to find the boundaries between his own body and the world so that he can sort it out and recognize it.

At nine months an infant was in the habit of exploring the world by moving her arms about over the counterpane. Whatever she touched was grasped and brought to her mouth. One day the two hands were both out exploring, and each one happened to discover the other; each hand brought the other hand to the mouth, as if it had been an outside object. There was for her no distinction between an outside object which she grasped, and a part of her own body. The same child had the habit of brandishing her thumb as her father entered the door. This activity punctuated periods in which she would lie sucking her thumb. There was a characteristic whimper of dismay if anyone pulled her thumb from her mouth. One day her father came in through the door as she was sucking her thumb. Out came the thumb and it was brandished in the characteristic salutation; but then immediately came the whimpering that occurred whenever someone pulled the thumb from her mouth. Though it was she herself who had done so, her attitude seemed to be: "Who has taken away my thumb?"[1]

Moreover, the experiments of Piaget on the recognition of objects, mentioned above (page 148), suggest that even at a year or so of age the child has still not spotted or identified objects as such, that is, objects as sharply detached from their environment. We may put all such data into perspective by saying that, as far as we know, the infant shows the same vague, slow, uncertain delimitation of the *self* that he shows regarding every other *object* in the world. One learns only gradually, for example, to recognize the visual outline of oneself, and to recognize one's voice, and to connect the two together.

The self is an object which is discovered, interpreted, put in its context, and adapted to, just as everything else is discovered, interpreted, put in its context, and adapted to. In time, one picks out the hands, the feet, the voice, and later on the picture of oneself in the mirror. One synthesizes these at first into a loose pattern, and then later into a more compact portrait. This is similar to the process by which, in the whole development of perception, one always goes through gradual differentiation of parts, followed by integration into a unified whole (page 150).

It is not surprising, then, that some parts of the total serve as "anchorage points" or are more important or real than other parts. The individual may seize upon the right hand or the nose or the voice as the thing about himself which is important. We remember how poor Cyrano de Bergerac had to live his life in terms of a morbid preoccupation with his nose, just as the more fortunate young Caruso built his life around a passionate preoccupation with the sound of his voice. Some people actually say: "I am more in my voice than I am in my face." Horowitz[2] studied two individuals who anchored their perception of themselves in this way: one in the nose, the other in the right hand; he found that over half of a group of college residents had some tendency to localize the self more at one point than another.

Most people, however, do not resort to such extreme or sophisticated ways of formulating the problem of what makes up the most important

---

[1] M. W. Shinn, *The Biography of a Baby*, Boston, Houghton Mifflin, 1900.
[2] E. L. Horowitz, Spatial localization of the self, *J. soc. Psychol.*, 1935, 6, 379–387.

parts of the self. As a rule they simply accept the good old totality of body, voice, name, as the self. Yet they may be much more disturbed if something is said to the disadvantage of the hands than if it were said to the disadvantage of the hair, or vice versa, depending upon what their friends and parents said about their hands or hair, and upon what has become most intimate and precious in their total conception of themselves.

But the self is the aggregate to which all these parts belong. What differs from one person to another is the degree of importance or of closeness of association of the self which each of these features possesses. For some, such as the handsome young Romeo, hair is essential; for others, it is so inessential that it can be shaven off in the summer, or even kept permanently shaved in the old-style German fashion. The Chinese gentleman thought of the self as magnificently represented in the long tapering fingernails which proved his superiority to any kind of manual work. The stevedore may actually be proud of the calluses on his hands which prove him to be hard and tough.

Since it takes the child so long to discover his own body and to form a picture of himself, it is hardly surprising that he shows a great deal of difficulty in telling where *he himself* stops and where other things begin. The writer saw a boy of a year and a half cringe in fear when *another person* approached a fire. This kind of "primitive sympathy," long before there is a rational understanding of other people's needs, has often been observed. Stern reports:

A child of two saw a picture that excited her sympathy: an eagle pouncing upon a chamois kid. Suddenly she put her little hand on the picture as if she wanted to form some defence between attacker and attacked; the same child a few months later saw, in a picture, a lamb caught in a thicket, and she tried to pull away the clinging thorny branch.[3]

In his memoirs Sherwood Anderson recounts an incident in his early childhood which shows clearly the absence of a boundary between the child and the outer world:

There was a small pot-bellied stove, red hot. . . . A great piece of iron turned yellow by the heat lay on the coals. It was for heating the water in a

---

[3] William Stern, *Psychology of Early Childhood* (translated from the 3rd ed., revised and enlarged by Anna Barwell), New York, Holt, 1924.

tub in which leather was put to be softened. My father grasped the hot iron in a pair of tongs and threw it into the tub. A great cloud of steam flew up. . . .

I had burned my hand on our kitchen stove. For some reason the heated iron, thrown into the tub of water, had made a great impression on my child's mind. I wondered if putting the iron into the stove to be heated had hurt it as

Figure 71. An Example of Empathy

A dramatic illustration of empathy. The man at the right, intent on watching the jumper, has unconsciously raised his own right foot as if he himself were trying to clear the bar. (From J. Tiffin, F. B. Knight, and C. C. Josey, *The Psychology of Normal People*, D. C. Heath and Company, 1940.)

touching the hot stove in our kitchen had hurt me. It had seemed to hurt. It had seemed to scream with pain.[4]

But we all continue to put ourselves in the place of others, sometimes even in the naïve way of doing what they do (Figure 71). This is called *empathy*.

The self, as we saw, is at first a physical thing to be discovered; but this matter of spatial localization, and the whole question of the physical attributes of the self, tend to become gradually less important as the

---

[4] Sherwood Anderson, *Sherwood Anderson's Memoirs*, New York, Harcourt, Brace, 1942, pp. 17, 18.

child grows up, and as he emphasizes more and more a variety of other things which may bring him a *reputation* or which may be *necessary for success*. This is especially true in the middle-class world in which sheer physique may tend to become less important than various types of ability and skill. Greater and greater importance attaches to such attributes of the self as intellectual gifts, social skills, talent for business, music, and the things which make us acceptable and important. Along with family background, it is these skills and achievements which differentiate us from others and serve as the basis of our being recognized and "placed" by others. While for the very small child the sense of self depends largely upon his body, e.g., how big and strong he is, he discovers in the early school years how many other things there are that enable him to get ahead, win prestige, and achieve what he wants. While sheer size and strength in a tough five-year-old boy may have enabled him to dominate the playground, these attributes yield, to some extent, to skill, agility, and quick thinking (in general, the things that go into sports), so that there may be a premium upon attributes which were inconspicuous earlier. The working-class child may still have to batter his way through his difficulties with his fists to a large degree, but the middle-class child is competing more and more in skilled activities in which strength, while important on the football field, is secondary to the use of head and tongue. Competence in school work becomes important, even when the children regard it as belonging to a sissy and speak of "red-appling the teacher." They develop a furtive regard for brains expressed in this or in any other way. There is deep concern for ability, whether it is openly expressed in admiration for high grades, or whether other types of brain work, such as the school paper, happen to win admiration. The important thing is that physical traits, while remaining important, have been gradually pushed aside to some degree in favor of things the child can do with what he has; the emphasis is upon skills and achievements.

It may be felt that we are overdoing the changes in the self-picture from year to year, and the point may be made that it is not the way we regard ourselves but our *bodies themselves* that are of primary importance. We might emphasize, for example, the "good looks" which a girl must have at any period. Even here, however, studies have shown that sheer *physique* as such becomes gradually subordinated to the charm, the grace, the skill, the social finesse and attractiveness which know how to make the most out of the raw physical attributes.[5] One learns how to look well, to talk well, to make oneself acceptable; much that is called beauty is as much a matter of skill as is the case with the masculine preoccupations mentioned earlier.

Being "good at" this and "poor at" that, whether it be music, or football, or dentistry, or selling vacuum cleaners—along with family connections and various other outside helps—is what provides a reputation in the neighborhood and in the larger community. What has happened, then, is that the picture of the self has gradually ceased to be primarily a physical thing, and has become more and more a group of traits which are loosely hung together and which go with your name and with your general perception of yourself. Each one of us is the person who did this, or knows how to do that, or whose social talents give him such and such a reputation. The self has become a system of traits—of socially important traits.

Eugene Horowitz reminds us that in his parting injunction to his son Laertes, Polonius says, "To thine own self be true." Polonius is here speaking about being true not to a portion of the body, but to the conception of the self as a system of laudable traits, as a totality of attributes which are recognized by others and by the person himself as worth while. "To thine own self be true" means to go on living in accordance with the concept of the self which has been built up during one's lifetime. "Do not indulge in impulsive acts which would defeat your concept of yourself as a worthy and admirable person."

It takes a long time to build up such a self. During the years before adolescence (for most children in our civilization this means the years in elementary school) the child slowly forms a concept of himself in terms of what he *can do* and in terms of what he habitually *does*, rather than primarily in terms of sheer physical appearance. But the rapid physical changes of adolescence may upset the process. Big changes are going on inside the individual; his body begins to look different and feel different, and his contemporaries begin to look different and respond to him in new ways. Maybe the girl who was a skinny little tomboy finds

---

[5] F. A. C. Perrin, Physical attractiveness and repulsiveness, *J. exper. Psychol.*, 1921, *4*, 203–217.

herself suddenly attractive to boys; maybe the boy who was good fun as a "tough little guy" suddenly becomes gawky, incoördinated, unsure of himself, at the very time that he finds himself unable to understand the sudden new warmth and appreciation that he may have for girl friends who used to be "just pals."

Truman Capote tells how the sensitive boy, Joel Knox, feeling himself changing, looked at a childhood snapshot:

> What a dumbbell! He would gladly be rid of him, this old Joel, but not quite yet; he somehow needed him still. For long periods each day he studied his face in a hand mirror: a disappointing exercise, on the whole, for nothing he saw concretely affirmed his suspicions of emerging manhood, though about his face there were certain changes: baby fat had given way to a true shape, the softness of his eyes had hardened: it was a face with a look of innocence but none of its charm, an alarming face, really too shrewd for a child, too beautiful for a boy. It would be difficult to say how old he was. All that displeased him was the brown straightness of his hair.[6]

A new self has to be discovered. Again as in our studies of trial-and-error perception (page 295) we find the individual trying to make sense out of what he sees, and trying also to make something that is *satisfying* to look at. He experiments with new life, with new ways, finds what others think of him, finds what he can do, what his self is. Often a picture of the self is crystallized in these years, for better or for worse.

Paul, who is highly intelligent, physically somewhat unprepossessing and below average in stature and strength, is talking to a psychological counselor.

S. I—uh—have the opinion that I'm inferior. That's the—that's the opinion I have.

C. You just know darn well that you don't measure up, is that it?

S. That's right. (*Pause.*)

C. Want to tell me some more about that?

S. Well, I'll tell you. I've been interested in anthropology to some extent, and especially criminal anthropology. (*Pause.*) Well, I'm continually—uh—I continually compare physiques of people, and I feel that mine is inferior, and I don't stop—I don't—I also believe that the behavior of an individual is an approximation of his physique, you might say That's what my belief is. I've read too much of Hooton (*laugh*). Did you ever hear of him? (*C. nods.*) I expected you did. [Footnote omitted.]

C. And—uh—as you look about on other physical types, you just feel that yours is inferior, the lowest of the low.

S. No, not exactly, I wouldn't say that.

---

[6] T. Capote, *Other Voices, Other Rooms*, New York, Signet Books, 1949, p. 127.

C. But you're far down in the scale? . . .
S. Well, for instance, I was small, and I envied people who were large. I was—well, I took beatings by boys and I couldn't strike back. I guess that had something to do with it. And I resented being always licked. I guess that has something to do with it.
C. You've had plenty of experiences in being the underdog.
S. Oh, yes. I've repeatedly taken setbacks. (*Pause.*)
C. Tell me about some of those.

The interview continues with Paul telling a number of specific experiences which have caused him to feel personally and socially inadequate, and stating how strongly he has wished he were "master of the situation."

C. Yet you feel that actually you can't be anywhere near the top.
S. No. It isn't my ability. Of course, there's no reason why I should think that I should be at the top, but I think there is some reason for not being where I am. I think I shouldn't be where I am right now.

Fortunately the record shows that as Paul's negative feelings about himself are frankly faced, he can begin to recognize some of his assets, and can define for himself a less anxious, more realistic goal.[7]

That there is a transition stage in which the loss of an earlier self leads to a sense of being without selfhood is dramatically revealed in the following material:

That JK should be the topic of so extensive a study results from his having passed through a peculiarly dramatic crisis in the development of self-determination and self-respect. In sharp contrast to his carefree, contented childhood he was troubled (at 18½ years) by severe self-consciousness, painful uncertainty as to his standing in the opinion of others and an irresistible submissiveness designed to win everybody's favor. He felt he had no personality of his own and therefore lacked any stable object on which to focus self-respect.

The longing for a new, stabilized self is clearly projected by Joseph Kidd in the story he makes up about one of the pictures in the Thematic Apperception Test (page 469):

"Gradually he began to realize that the greatest difficulty between himself and success lay primarily in his appearance. So over a period of time, having saved a small amount of money, he one day appeared in a small town in good clothes. . . . Very soon after, with the appearance of a well-to-do man of profession, he gradually became the center of attention and was smart enough to hold it and earn the esteem of the people. By his own imagination he built up a past life comparable to what people would expect; by gradual self-sug-

---

[7] C. Rogers, *Counseling and Psychotherapy*, Boston, Houghton Mifflin, 1942, pp. 144–147.

gestion won himself over to this position; and in a short time had established himself successfully in an enterprise in the city and lived the rest of his life in extreme comfort and security, showing that it is not what you *have been* but what you *are*."

Here we are given the pattern of success, from which we can infer the pattern of frustrations that would lead to failure. To make a good appearance, to have good clothes, to become a center of attention, to enjoy a high esteem-income, these are the conditions upon which success and happiness are founded and upon which depends the power to transform and ennoble oneself by autosuggestion. When Kidd was denied these gratuities of his early childhood, he passed into the fatal cycle of resentment and its suppression. When he was granted them again by his recent girl-friends he began to break out of the cycle, let aggression and cynicism come to the surface, and release his energies for more constructive enterprises.[8]

What can happen to an individual whose image of himself is *in conflict* is vividly told by Romain Rolland in *Jean-Christophe*.

The composer, Jean-Christophe, the hero of the novel, has risen to a position of favor with the local Grand Duke. He is called frequently to perform at the palace. He becomes the friend and teacher of the princess. For Christophe, the duke, the small German town, his status at the palace, all are interwoven into a way of life he has known since childhood. His affections, his hopes for the future, his tastes, the very substance of his life are bound up with Germanic feeling.

But gradually Christophe's sensibilities begin to revolt against "the false idealism of Wagner," the "massive sentimentality of the Flying Dutchman," along with the increasing Prussianism of his people. His revolt grows more open. He publishes a violent article in a Socialist newspaper denouncing German art and culture. One day shortly thereafter he is called to the palace. It has never occurred to him that the article will affect his position at court. But the duke pounces on him, upbraids him, orders him to leave the palace. Christophe is staggered. What he has written is just as surely a part of himself as his relationship to the palace and the tradition it represents. He is caught in a severe conflict.

He choked. He was almost weeping with shame and rage. His legs were trembling. He jerked his elbow and upset an ornament. He lost count of what exactly happened. He longed to thrust his fist into the Grand Duke's face; but he was crushed under a weight of conflicting feelings: shame, fury, a remnant

---

[8] Robert W. White, The personality of Joseph Kidd. III. Three years of ego-reconstruction, *Character & Pers.*, 1943, 2, 339–360.

of shyness, of German loyalty, traditions of respect, habits of humility in the Prince's presence. He tried to speak; he could not. He tried to move; he could not. He could not see or hear. He suffered them to push him along and left the room. . . .

He went up to his room, shut himself in and lay down. . . . Oh if he could only see no more, feel no more, no longer have to bear with his wretched body, no longer have to struggle against ignoble life. . . . About two o'clock, in an access of madness he got up from his bed, sweating and half naked. He wanted to go and kill the duke. He was devoured by hate and shame.[9]

It is easy to see that when Christophe's attachments and values are threatened it is also he himself who is threatened. He desires self-annihilation because he can accept neither picture of himself—neither the young rebel nor the artist of a culture for which he has only distaste.

The Self and Social Perspective

Awareness of *self* is closely related to awareness of the fact that *others* are also *selves*. The little child has at first no way of knowing what other people think and feel; he tends at first to assume that they think and feel as he does. While every child's experience differs from that of every other child in some ways, all children have to *learn* that their own is a "private" world to which others have no direct access. Walter de la Mare writes about Edmund Gosse as follows:

It was as though . . . his soul had suffered an avalanche when Edmund Gosse in his sixth year detected that omniscient moralist, his father, not in an untruth, but in merely having failed to detect a little escapade of his own. . . .

First he confesses that he was ashamed at having deceived his parents. "Of all the thoughts which rushed upon my savage and undeveloped little brain at this crisis, the most curious was that I had found a companion and confidant in myself. There was a secret in the world and it belonged to me and to a somebody who lived in the same body with me. There were two of us and we could talk with one another. It is difficult to define impressions so rudimentary, but it is certain that it was in this dual form that the sense of my individuality now suddenly descended on me and it is equally certain that it was a great solace to me to find a sympathizer in my breast."[10]

In connection with the study of perception, attention was given (page 170) to the fact that we unconsciously bring into our way of perceiving the vested interests or special personal needs which warp each situation in accordance with our demands upon life. Year after year the child

---

[9] R. Rolland, *Jean-Christophe*, New York, Pocket Books, Inc., 1949, pp. 103–105.
[10] W. de la Mare, *Early One Morning*, New York, Macmillan, 1935, pp. 198–199.

weans himself to some degree from the deep self-centered autistic ways of viewing the world which characterize him so very powerfully in the first years of life. For this reason attention must be given to a series of studies by the Swiss psychologist Jean Piaget, who has brought together at Geneva a series of lines of evidence showing how the child gradually becomes aware of himself, and how, in this process, he manages to free himself from some of the primitive autisms and biases which were there from the beginning. The modern study of the self has benefited greatly from Piaget's demonstration that as the child becomes more and more sharply aware of himself, he can "make allowances" for his own bias, can come to see where his own distortion of reality enters in, and can therefore to some degree achieve greater objectivity. From this it follows that awareness of self—the explicit recognition of it and the ability to make allowances by seeing it in perspective—is of major importance in the acquisition of mature ways of thinking.

Piaget has emphasized (page 389) that the little child's earliest experiences are without benefit of any distinction between what is happening "out there" and what happens "inside." There is at first no possibility of recognizing that a given experience is "just my experience," or that it is independent of "your experience," since there is no "I" or "you" or "outer world." For the infant, consequently, things are just what they seem to be. The child cannot make the distinction which we make when we say, "Of course it looks this way to *me,* but then I may be wrong," or "That's just *your* point of view; there are other points of view." The little child is incapable of this sort of recognition—that there are different points of view—simply because he is not even aware that he exists as something marked off from the rest of the world. The term used by Piaget to describe this inability to recognize the self, and consequently to recognize the limitations and the limited perspective given by one's own viewpoint, is *egocentrism;* the consequent tendency to assume that the way things *appear* to us, so they must be, is called *realism.*

Egocentrism does not mean of course that the child is conceited or proud of himself. It means simply that because he is not aware of himself, he can make no allowances for his own perspective. Though the child's egocentrism gradually declines, we find, even in the kindergarten or the first grade, a tendency to take at face value whatever *appears* to be so. A good deal that his parents do seems arbitrary. He cannot grasp the possibility of any viewpoint other than his own. Even the adult may at times say, "Anybody who sees it any other way is just prejudiced."

The child's first judgments of people are in these terms. Suppose that there is an especially exciting radio program at 9.00 p.m.; the four-year-old wants to stay up late like his big brother and hear it. When parents say "No," they are just being "mean." Cake and ice cream and other dissipations are good, but a time comes when a few more pieces of cake may mean from the parents' viewpoint the likelihood of getting sick. From the child's point of view this is just "Blah-blah"; it is the here and now of how things look that is the reality, and it is a mean old mommy who says you can't do what you want to do.

It is easy to experiment with realism, and to show how strong it is even in children seven or eight years of age. In one of Piaget's experiments a huge relief map of the Alps is prepared in such a way that the Geneva child recognizes the familiar mountain contours. On the various trails that lead up the mountainsides are placed little dolls which symbolize mountain climbers. Around the walls of the room are large photographs taken on the various trails, indicating how the Alps appear from each one of a number of different vantage points. Now as the doll is moved around from one point on the relief map to another, the child is asked to tell how the mountains look to the doll. The child does not understand the question as the adult would understand it. You and I would say: "From this point you would be able to see such and such; and this photograph over here shows about how it would look to people over there." Piaget tells us, however, that even for the child around seven years of age, the mountains simply have to look the way they look right now to him, as he stands beside the relief map. "What would the mountains look like to the doll?" The child's answer is: "They would look like this," pointing to the photograph which shows not how they would look to the climber but how they look to the child from the vantage point he now holds. He cannot grasp that the mountains will look differently from different angles, in accordance with the different vantage points of the climber. Realism still prevails; there is no possibility that they could look differently to anyone else.

From this fact of realism, Piaget reports, follows the little child's inability to differentiate between things that he imagines and things that actually happen. If you see it, that makes it real. The difference between appearance and reality has not become clear. The small child's nightmare, or even his daytime fantasy, may leave him frightened, so that for hours thereafter he may continue in horror, unable to grasp that the danger is unreal.

Another aspect of realism is brought out in those cases in which imagining something bad is the same thing as its actually happening; the distinction between imagination and reality is blurred, and to think of something makes it objectively real or at least likely to become real. This confusion of what is inside and what is outside, and the tendency to project our inner thoughts upon the outer world so that it mirrors our thoughts, are called "participation." A number of Piaget's research associates from various countries were asked to describe their own childhood experiences in participation. Many of these were similar to experiences which American students find are commonplace in their own life histories or which they can see in their own younger brothers and sisters. A good many, for example, told how as children they had been afraid to think of an accident such as a puncture of a bicycle tire, because sheer thinking of such a thing would make it happen. As your friend starts off in his car on the narrow mountain road, don't *think* of the possibility of his driving off the road. When in daily conversation someone mentions the likelihood of an accident, how often we say, "Don't think of it!" Knocking on wood appears to be a remnant of an old superstition that mentioning things makes them happen unless you avert the danger by a magical act (perhaps propitiation of a tree spirit?).

Closely related to realism and participation is the process of attributing to people, animals, and objects around us the same kind of feeling and thought that we have in our own experience. The fact that the self is still not well formed in early childhood makes it impossible for the child to grasp the different viewpoints and say, "I am conscious, but the tree is not conscious." And if he wants something and begins to talk about it, it is natural that when dogs and cats want something they begin to talk about it. Children accept stories of talking animals, and may become confused or angry when grownups solemnly assure them that animals never talk. They frequently attribute to their dogs and cats human feelings and ideas. They even have a tendency to attribute to puppets or the stone faces that one sees on the mountainside some kind of awareness of their surroundings, and the same wishes and fears that they themselves experience. A tree is sorry and dejected when the sun goes down. It droops until, with the returning sun in the morning, it picks up and asserts itself joyfully again. It is easy, therefore, for a child to enjoy stories in which animals and the forces of nature are portrayed in a personal form.

This tendency to attribute life and mind to everything is called *animism*. Animism is characteristic of many preliterate (primitive) societies which likewise make the sun into a person, look upon the running stream as benevolent and the forest fire as a demon. The men and women of our own cultural heritage found delight in Aesop's fable of the wind and the sun who both strove to make the traveler take off his coat; this is a prototype of the universal struggle of personal forces in the universe.

Piaget believes that the child outgrows his animism only slowly, a step at a time. For the tiny child everything is alive. For a child in the early school grades, things are alive if they move; for example, the stone that rolls downhill is alive, but when it lies still it is no longer alive. For the older child nearing adolescence (and for adolescents and adults), things are alive only if they move of their own initiative. Unless the student has studied biology, he may find that this rough practical conception of what it means to be alive is the one he uses himself.

There is much uncertainty as to whether these animistic tendencies occur in children universally. In one of the islands of the South Seas it was found that children never attributed life, purpose, or mind to inanimate objects around them, whereas in some American Indian tribes we find about the same picture as we did in the Geneva children studied by Piaget. Perhaps the truth is that an animistic tendency due to egocentrism is present in some form in early childhood in all societies, but is then either nursed along by fairy stories, animistic fables, etc., or held back, depending upon the cultural emphasis of the group.

Another aspect of egocentrism, as defined by Piaget, appears in the child's interpretation of his dreams. Again, if you have a sharp and clear idea of yourself, you know that a dream is something that "is part of you." Just as a small child feels that thinking about a thing is in some ways actually the same as encountering it, so dreaming about it is a real physical encounter with it. To the tiny child who describes his dream in the morning, the dream has come along the street, climbed into the window, and lain down beside him on the bed. The termination of the dream was the dream's departure out the window. Year by year the process of dreaming is better and better understood by the child; the dream is less and less a thing, more and more a process inside himself, until finally the child of ten or twelve describes the dream no longer as something external but as something which he himself produced. Insofar as we realize that we are doing things—that we are seeing, selecting from the world, placing an emphasis upon this and ignoring that—we are moving away from the earlier conception of our experience as telling the full and complete story of what is going on out there in the world. We are outgrowing our egocentrism. The growth of a sharp and clear picture of the self makes it possible to get perspective, and therefore to wean ourselves from egocentric tendencies.

Piaget has likewise studied the development of children's ideas of right and wrong, their process of *moral judgment,* through the various levels of growth.[11] He has thus been able to show that the kind of morality which makes possible social understanding and give-and-take depends upon some sort of perspective about the self. Learning how to play marbles with the boys, and cat's cradle with the girls, Piaget noted four stages in response to right and wrong. The little ones begin to play marbles in terms of simply shooting from the line, and watching the big boys to see how it is done. One must knock one's opponent's marble out of the square, and one's own marble must not go out while one is doing so. After the game, each of the little children, when asked who has won, says something like this: "I won, and John won, and you won, and we all won." He is enjoying the activity, but not making judgments in terms of success or failure, or fair and unfair. A little later, typically at around four or five years of age, he has learned the rules of the game, and he now seizes upon these rules and very rigidly adheres to them. It is now fair or right to put your foot here and to shoot your marble there; it is

---

[11] J. Piaget, *The Moral Judgment of the Child,* New York, Harcourt, Brace, 1932.

bad or unfair if you do not do this. It is fair if you follow the rules which the big boys told you; it is unfair if you do anything different. Everything is objectively right or objectively wrong; the moral rules are just as objective as the marbles themselves. There is no other way to play marbles. Fairness and unfairness are therefore exactly like physical laws, such as the fact that a marble will drop if you let go of it. This stage, which treats of right and wrong as external physical realities, is called *moral realism*. If a child is told that some children have different rules, he does not understand. When, for example, a Geneva child is told that children over in Neuchâtel, thirty miles away, play according to a different rule, this simply means to him that these Neuchâtel children don't play the *real* game of marbles. "Those guys over there never did play right, anyhow." (Cf. page 176.)

By seven or eight years of age, the child has gradually come to recognize that the rules are made by people, and that they are relative to human needs. Instead of being fixed and absolute and above all human wishes and needs, they are arrangements made by human beings. He is changing his whole conception of what is fair and what is unfair. You can put your foot across the line provided the other players can do so also. You can even shoot with a different kind of a marble, or you can have more than one shot, provided that everybody else can do the same. Morals are now gauged no longer in terms of moral realism, but in terms of *reciprocity*, that is, taking turns; and all is fair providing that it applies to everyone.

Still another stage appears later as adolescence approaches. Even reciprocity is not the highest ethical development, because your eyesight may not be as good as someone else's eyesight, or you may have a bad leg, or something else may be not quite on a par for all. Just as the lame child may be allowed to take his turn at bat in the American sand-lot ball game, despite the fact that someone else will have to run the bases for him, so in the marble game at Geneva things can be worked out to give the individual a little special help here or there when needed. Piaget summarizes this by saying that "reciprocity is tempered by considerations of equity." Equity means the recognition of the special circumstances, the special needs which characterize a given individual. The child, then, has gone even beyond the capacity to understand that other people have rights; he grasps that the need and outlook of another person may be different from his own. He recognizes the special problem, the special life situation, of each person.

In the same way, one can study children's ideas of right and wrong as they go through the process of learning to understand their parents' ideas of what is to be praised and what is to be punished. Piaget tells each child a story about a little girl who comes home from school, swings open a door, and unwittingly knocks over a tray of dishes and breaks them. He asks: "If you were the child's mother, what would you do?" The little ones all say: "Punish her." "How much would you punish her?" The small child replies to this: "How many dishes did she break?" Wrongdoing is an objective thing that can be measured in terms of the damage done. Whether she meant to do it or not is not part of the problem. This is again a case of moral realism; the rightness and wrongness are in the act itself, and the intentions or subjective considerations have nothing to do with it. The child of six or seven, however, has gone beyond this purely physical and external situation and has begun to understand points of view. He asks: "Did she mean to break the dishes?" Or "Was she specially careless?" He is working toward the recognition that the same external act may arise from different kinds of internal attitudes. Moral judgment becomes more and more personal and social, less arbitrary.

Every one of these investigations by Piaget serves to reinforce the fact that social points of view are not acquired all at once, but come slowly as a result of increasing experience, especially experience in dealing with the different outlooks and personal needs of other individuals. Society is ready to make clear to the child that there are other viewpoints than his own. The reason why this cannot be taught the child all at once lies in the fact of his own intense personal needs and personal preoccupations, and his sheer unawareness of the fact that his viewpoint is just his viewpoint. He may be aware of the physical attributes of his own person but not of what he is doing to his observations, not aware of the fact that he himself is a major factor which is coloring or giving shape to what he sees. It is only as he shares with other people in looking at the world and comparing notes, learning to correct for the factors which are purely personal, that he becomes capable of a broader social outlook. This is a major factor in his own socialization.

The child's parents play a primary role in giving him his earlier sense of being a person—of being in some ways like other people, in some ways different from them, in some ways emotionally dependent on others, in some ways independent of them. In and through it all, they help the child understand what a *person* is, and how one grows into being a complete person. The child is born without an identity; he achieves one through his contact with the world around him, chiefly through his contact with his parents. Their strength, their assurance, become his own. Sherwood Anderson tells of a dramatic moment in this identification process. He talks of his father, a dreamer, a teller of stories, and an object of mild scorn in the small midwestern community in which the Anderson family lived. And always the young Sherwood Anderson, the small boy, is somewhat ashamed of this man. Always he dreams of a father who is quiet and dignified, a man behind whose back the town will not snicker. Then one night the boy's father finds him alone, reading near the kitchen stove. The father takes the boy silently by the hand and in the darkness they walk to a pond outside of the town.

He was a man with big shoulders, a powerful swimmer. In the darkness I could feel the movement of his muscles. We swam to the far edge of the pond and then back to where we had left our clothes. The rain continued and the wind blew. Sometimes my father swam on his back and when he did he took my hand in his large powerful one and moved it over so that it rested always on his shoulder. Sometimes there would be a flash of lightning and I could see his face quite clearly.

It was as it was earlier, in the kitchen, a face filled with sadness. There would be the momentary glimpse of his face and then again the darkness, the wind and the rain. In me there was a feeling I had never known before. It was a feeling of closeness. It was something strange. It was as though there were only we two in the world. It was as though I had been jerked suddenly out of myself, out of my world of the schoolboy, out of a world in which I was ashamed of my father.

He had become blood of my blood; he the strong swimmer and I the boy clinging to him in the darkness. We swam in silence and in silence we dressed in our wet clothes, and went home.

There was a lamp lighted in the kitchen and when we came in, the water dripping from us, there was my mother. She smiled at us. I remember that she called us "boys."

"What have you boys been up to?" she asked, but my father did not answer. As he had begun the evening's experience with me in silence, so he ended it. He turned and looked at me. Then he went, I thought, with a strange new dignity out of the room.

I climbed the stairs to my own room, undressed in the darkness and got into bed. I couldn't sleep and did not want to sleep. For the first time I knew that I was the son of my father. He was a story teller as I was to be. It may be that I even laughed a little softly there in the darkness. If I did I laughed knowing that I would never again be wanting another father.[12]

We all need people not only to lean on, but to give us this greater sense of our own identity. We identify with others when they command attention, loyalty, allegiance.

The child's own awareness of self, then, comes not just from physical growth, but also to a large degree from the varying viewpoints which he encounters among other people, and from the fact that in order to live with people he must learn as best he can what their outlooks are. Awareness of self is in large measure a social product, not something that sheer physical or chronological growth absolutely guarantees. In fact, one frequently finds among underprivileged children, children who have had no chance to see through the eyes of others, that there is a delay in getting a social viewpoint, or a permanent inability to do so. Among many delinquent groups and among children in the Displaced Persons camps of recent years, one finds many who have so long been kicked about, and forced to depend entirely upon their own resources, that they are literally conscienceless and unaware of and uninterested in the needs or outlooks of other persons. It is through social experience that the child learns not only habits of coöperation but habits of taking into account the outlook of other persons.

At the same time, it is also important to stress that our increasing understanding of our own motives helps also in understanding the motives of others. We must to a very considerable degree understand other people's aims and feelings by having had such aims and feelings ourselves. Later we may hope to go beyond the first primitive process of "judging others by ourselves"; but at first we must to some degree judge others in this way when we are beginning to get an idea of what makes people

---

[12] Sherwood Anderson, *Sherwood Anderson's Memoirs,* New York, Harcourt, Brace, 1942, p. 49.

tick. All this amounts to saying that just as experience with other people's outlooks helps us to grasp that we ourselves have an outlook too, and are not the sole and absolute arbiter of all reality, so also experience in taking account of our own wants and interests helps us to take into account the wants and interests of others. It is worth while to say once more, for emphasis, that this whole process of developing awareness of others' needs and viewpoints depends partly upon the kinds of parents one has and the kinds of early contact one has with them and with other members of the family. The little child learns much of what he knows about human feelings and viewpoints by virtue of the closeness of his contact with his father's and mother's feelings and outlooks; he "projects himself into" their outlook. It is they who give him his first great experience of the process of seeing through other people's eyes—which leads us into the deeper dynamic problems of the next chapter.

SUGGESTED READINGS

Hilgard, E. R., Human motives and the concept of the self, *Amer. Psychologist*, 1949, 4, 374–382.
James, W., *Principles of Psychology*, New York, Holt, 1890, chap. 10.
Lecky, P., *Self-Consistency*, New York, Island Press, 1945.
Murphy, G., *Personality*, New York, Harper, 1947, Part 4.
Piaget, J., *The Child's Conception of the World*, New York, Harcourt, Brace, 1929.
Piaget, J., *The Moral Judgment of the Child*, London, Paul, 1932.
Sherif, M., and Cantril, H., *The Psychology of Ego Involvements*, New York, Wiley, 1947.
Snygg, D., and Combs, A. W., *Individual Behavior*, New York, Harper, 1949.

22 ASSERTION OF THE SELF

Just as the self is mapped out and its parts put together so that we perceive "the same old person" we knew before, so we build up characteristic ways of making much of the self, ways of playing up the attributes which make the self remarkable, or laudable, or lovable. The two-year-old in our culture says: "See what I can do," or "I am a good boy"; later: "I can spit further than you," or "I have a bigger car than you," or "I have more degrees than you." One makes the most of the self, one enhances it, asserts it. One likewise defends it, rejects slurs or unfavorable comparisons.

We might make a beginning in understanding the process of enhancing the self by noting that the infant derives an elementary satisfaction from his own physical well-being. Even in the opening months of life there is gratification in his own existence; as he rolls over, or pushes up, or plays with his toes, the infant enjoys the perception and the activity of his own body. He comes to love his body. It is the only self that he knows. Self-love may gradually grow from this seed into a ruling passion. It may be worth while here at the beginning to introduce the concept of *self-love* as developed by the Greek myth of Narcissus. The universal human experience of falling in love with oneself appears in this story of Narcissus' love for his own reflection in the water:

> While he drinks he is smitten by the sight of the beautiful form he sees. He loves an unsubstantial hope and thinks that to be substance which is only shadow. He looks in speechless wonder at himself and hangs there motionless with the same expression, like a statue carved from Parian marble. Prone on the ground, he gazes at his eyes, twin stars, and his locks, worthy of Bacchus,

worthy of Apollo; on his smooth cheeks, his ivory neck, the glorious beauty of his face, the blush mingled with snowy white; all things, in short, he admires for which he is himself admired. Unwittingly he desires himself; he praises, and is himself what he praises; and which he seeks, is sought; equally he kindles love and burns with love.[1]

It is likely that these old stories of the Greeks and most other mythologies tell of experiences which are shared to some degree by all human beings, especially in their early years. This perception by Narcissus of his own image is, of course, an infinitely more complex and more complete response to oneself than the baby is capable of. As we saw, the picture of the self develops only slowly. But the story suggests a thought which Sigmund Freud has developed on the basis of long years of close study of childhood emotions, namely, that as soon as there is any perception at all of one's individual selfhood, one loves it. As was said in Chapter 7, there is at first a general diffuse fund of outgoing positive response to the environment; and since the environment and the self are not clearly separated, why should not this outgoing positive response be devoted to one's own warm and active responses, i.e., to one's body, as well as to anything else? The child takes delight in the gratification of his own needs, as in the gentle touches and strokings of his own physical person by his mother, in the rhythmical babblings of his own voice, and in the inner rhythms of the muscles of limbs and of vital organs (pages 79 ff). He is at the same time taking delight in the mother's soft breasts, her gentle voice, her friendly and comforting and supporting ways; indeed, at first he may make no very sharp distinctions between her and himself (page 389). There may be a parallel development of self-awareness and awareness of others which for a while is one indivisible process (page 397). *Hence self-love and the love of others reinforce each other.*

Yet a differentiation must sooner or later set in. Insofar as the mother opposes the child's wishes, refusing to nurse him, or insisting that it is bedtime when he does not want to go to bed, there may be a reinforcement of this sense of difference. One's self, after all, is something that always goes hand in hand with the movement toward one's own gratification, and sometimes others will not play the game in so consistent a fashion. The child begins then to build up more and more a pattern of

---

[1] Ovid, *Metamorphoses* (translated by F. J. Miller), London, Heinemann, 1916.

making the most of the self. There are of course many other people besides his mother and father who sometimes gratify him, sometimes frustrate him, but no one can be counted upon every time; he is, so to speak, the only person who always votes on the right side.

COMPLIMENTS OF A FRIEND[2]

. . . . .
I know my own best friend is me.
We share our joys and our aversions,
We're thicker than the Medes and Persians,
We blend like voices in a chorus,
The same things please, the same things bore us.
If I am broke, then me needs money,
I make a joke, me finds it funny.
I think of beer, me shares the craving,
If I have whiskers, me needs shaving. . . .
For every sin that I produce,
Kind me can find some soft excuse,
And when I blow a final gasket,
Who but me will share my casket?
Beside us, Pythias and Damon
Were just two unacquainted laymen.
Sneer not, for if you answer true,
Don't you feel that way about you?

— Ogden Nash

What are the specific goals, the attainment of which will assert or make the most of the self? Four such goals are of great importance.

1. The first is the development of those *physical attributes,* such as strength and skill, which bring the things we want.

2. Another goal is the accumulation of *possessions.* In a society where property distinctions are so important, a child may treasure a Christmas present, or a dime that he gets for running an errand; later on, stamps or athletic trophies; still later, stocks and bonds. A person may act like a "dog in the manger" regarding the claims of others. Possessions become almost a part of an "extended self" or "larger self" which makes one's

---

[2] Copyright 1949 by Ogden Nash. Reprinted by permission of Little, Brown & Co. The poem first appeared in **The New Yorker.**

domain bigger and more worthy than that of the mere physical personage as such.

3. A third goal becomes evident when we notice that possessions may in some cases be important only as a means to *prestige or status*. A person may use possessions (relative to those of others) as ways of bringing himself the self-love which we call prestige, just as strength or good looks may likewise be used in competition for status. One may be unable to use one's possessions, yet show them off in what Veblen[3] describes as "conspicuous consumption." We are bewildered or amused at the Kwakiutl Indian chiefs who destroyed huge amounts of wealth to show off and shame the other chiefs who could not do the same; but we often spend to show that we can spend, not so much for what we get as for the sake of showing that we are not cheap skates, pikers. And many other things may be shown off, like a string of honors, or titles, or conquests, or votes in a popularity contest. So there is an important distinction to be made between sheer *possessions* and *status*, which may either be derived from possessions, or be independent of and at times more important than possessions.

4. Just as fundamental as the struggle for status is the struggle for *power*. One is gratified in successfully asserting his power against that of others.

Thus, in a competitive society like our own, the individual strives simultaneously for these four good things—for physical adequacy, for possessions, for status, and for power. In some human societies one may have status without having power or without having possessions. The holy man, for example, may be revered by all, yet actually be abjectly poor and count for nothing in the political system. In some societies, possessions bring little power and no prestige; the wealthy man cannot control the powerful warlords or politicians, and most people shrug their shoulders at wealth as of trivial consequence. In our own society, however, these values or "good things" are closely interwoven, and the individual struggles to get ahead simultaneously on all these four fronts; he is simultaneously striving to protect and to make the most of his physical personage and also to achieve possessions and status and power over others.

---

[3] T. Veblen, *The Theory of the Leisure Class*, New York, Macmillan, 1899.

These values, moreover, may be pursued in their own right, or in terms of competition between oneself and others. Among the Arapesh of New Guinea, not only is there no competition for material goods, there is also no competition for status or power.[4] It is sufficient for the individual child that he is accepted in the group. Under normal circumstances all children are accepted and made much of—not only by their parents, but by the whole community—and there is no need to be accepted *more* than anyone else is accepted. Indeed, there is no meaning in striving for a degree of acceptance which others cannot share. This seems strange to us; we regard competition for status as a universal aspect of human nature. Students of American history and of contemporary American life, as compared with life in other countries, emphasize especially the *status* goal as we pursue it competitively; it is common to describe American life in terms of *status competition*.

The Means Used for Assertion of the Self

What are the *means* available for reaching these goals that relate to self-enhancement, especially the goal of status? There are several which we all use.

1. You may assert the self by putting yourself into situations in which you are likely to win. In the "aspiration level" experiment,[5] the subjects who are working on a task are told how well they have done, and are asked: "How well will you do next time?" Some persons set a goal so low that they are sure to succeed, thus buying very cheaply the sense of victory.

2. You may assert the self also by playing for big stakes. In the "aspiration level" experiment, you may predict that you will make a phenomenal score. If you fall short of so remarkable a score, nobody will blame you, and in the meantime you can picture yourself as a person of huge potentialities.

3. You may assert the self by associating yourself with important people. Surely if you make the good fraternity or exclusive business or pro-

---

[4] M. Mead (ed.), *Cooperation and Competition Among Primitive Peoples*, New York, McGraw-Hill, 1937.

[5] F. Hoppe, *Psychol. Forsch.*, 1930–1940, 40, 1–62; R. Gould, An experimental analysis of "level of aspiration," *Genet. Psychol. Monogr.*, 1939, 21, 3–115.

fessional or academic group, you will be thought of as worthy of the honors which the members receive. Better tag along with the somebodies than be King of the Nobodies. (In a reversal of emphasis, some would rather be "first in a little Iberian village than second in Rome"; they cannot stand comparison with those above them.)

This matter of associating with people who strengthen us may be carried to the point where we lean upon them and are lost without them.

For Phillip Carey, in Somerset Maugham's novel, *Of Human Bondage,* King's School is a lonely place. A cripple, shy and sensitive, he finds it extremely difficult to make friends. When he does find someone he can like, in the boy called Rose, the intensity of his need for human companionship makes him want to exclude the rest of the school from the relationship. Phillip grows to fear the possibility that Rose may abandon him, and because of this fear he finds that at the very moment he wants Rose most, he dislikes him most. In a fit of rage one day, at the impotence of his position, Phillip insults Rose.

Rose shrugged his shoulders and left him. Phillip was very white, as he always became when he was moved, and his heart beat violently. When Rose went away he felt suddenly sick with misery. He did not know why he had answered in that fashion. He would have given anything to be friends with Rose. He hated to have quarrelled with him, and now that he saw he had given him pain he was very sorry. But at the moment he had not been master of himself. It seemed that some devil had seized him, forcing him to say bitter things against his will, even though at the time he wanted to shake hands with Rose and meet him more than half-way. The desire to wound had been too strong for him. He had wanted to revenge himself for the pain and humiliation he had endured. It was pride: it was folly, too, for he knew that Rose would not care at all, while he would suffer bitterly. The thought came to him that he would go to Rose, and say:
"I say, I'm sorry I was such a beast. I couldn't help it. Let's make it up."
But he knew he would never be able to do it. He was afraid that Rose would sneer at him. He was angry with himself, and when Sharp came in a little while afterwards he seized upon the first opportunity to quarrel with him.[6]

The need for self-assertion was so strong that Phillip leaned upon Rose when he could—but self-assertion there had to be even at so terrible a price. Fortunately, for most children there is a father or a big brother or an uncle; a mother, a big sister, or an aunt; an older friend, to whom the

---

[6] Somerset Maugham, *Of Human Bondage,* Garden City, Sun Dial Press, 1945, pp. 80, 81.

child can be close and with whom he can jointly face life's battles, so that to some degree he actually merges with them in such a manner as to use them to help form a picture of himself. One of the great teachers of philosophy at a woman's college had a stammer; several of her most devoted students began to stammer, not through insecurity, but because they

Figure 72. Identification

Playing "grown-ups" as these children are doing is not only fun, but a concrete means of identifying with adults. It affords a child a way of asserting himself by becoming, in imaginative play, like the adults he admires.

were trying to be like her. One always "pays a price" when one "takes over" someone else's self; but, as in this case, the strength one gains often makes it a good bargain.

4. You may assert the self by carrying this third method, associating with the strong, so far that you *identify* yourself with the strong or admirable people you know. We see the two-year-old boy put on his father's hat, seize his father's cane, talk as he thinks his father talks, and exercise authority. (See Figure 72.) Later, we see him emulating the policeman, fireman, soldier. The little fellow can be a big fellow by a sort of make-believe in which actually there is no sharp distinction be-

ASSERTION OF THE SELF

tween what he fantasies and what he senses himself to be (page 398). Since, as Piaget says, there is at the beginning no sharp distinction between the attributes of the self and the attributes of the world outside, the child can gradually inflate the self-portrait by making the most of the similarities he has to other persons. If there are models (like a friendly father) upon which he can closely form the outlines of his character, so much the easier; even if the father is rather remote and awesome, he can still identify with him in those aspects in which he can assimilate his power. The more meek and helpless the child, the more desperately he needs a strong person with whom to identify.

Most children identify with one person after another, experimenting to see who makes them feel safest and strongest. They identify with animals, too. The very little child gains strength by being a big bear or a roaring lion. Older children also love to identify themselves with fierce strong animals, but less directly; current names of boys' clubs and baseball teams include the bears, the hawks, the wildcats. And the grown-up world of sports has not only the Pirates and the Indians, but also the Tigers and the Cubs. One little boy, struggling against his own tendency to be babyish and clumsy and his tendency to run away, has found the world of animals a great help in reminding him what he was and what he wanted to be:

When Harry had been at the school for eight months his group planned to arrange a zoo with their stuffed animals. Each boy dressed his animals according to his own taste. When Harry arranged his animals he began with his stuffed elephant. He attached a sign to its cage which labeled it the biggest of all animals and the king of all elephants. Next came a cage for his favorite animal, the teddy bear, which he dressed in his own clothes. This was labeled "Clumsy, a bear only seven years old who is still clumsy at times." "Clumsy" was followed by "Hoppy," a lazy rabbit which killed only carrots. Last came his dog, "Lollipop, because he loves lollipops and eats them all the time." Together, they were Harry's way of stating clearly that he had at first to derive protection from the idea of being the animal king because only then would the defenseless and inadequate "Clumsy" be safe in leading the carefree existence of a lazy rabbit and accept the gratification which was represented by the lollipop.

A few months later, at Easter time, he felt he had to tell his Easter bunny how to behave. He admonished him: "Act like a real little boy and don't crawl around or climb on roofs. If you do that people will think you're a monkey and treat you like a monkey, and you don't want that to happen." The lazy and carefree Hoppy was slowly being replaced by a responsible citizen who recognized not only his obligation to reform but also his need to help others in abiding by acceptable standards of behavior.[7]

5. You may assert the self by looking at some aspects of yourself which are especially worthy, making them into the figure in the figure-ground pattern (compare page 143). The farmer who has done only little with his land can say: "I never was a hand to borrow money"—a real fact, but not a statement of all the facts. The student who is far behind in his work can always say: "I am not the kind that is always talking in class." Again a fact, but perhaps not quite all the facts in the picture.

6. You may very conveniently *recall* or *recognize* all that is favorable to the self, by virtue of the same dynamic processes that were considered in Chapter 15 (pages 260 ff.). Recall has been studied in a number of experiments. Zeigarnik[8] gave her subjects a group of tasks to perform, and let them finish half the tasks, but interrupted them in the middle of each of the others. Her subjects later *remembered* many more of the *unfinished* ones, in the ratio of nearly 2 to 1. Perhaps this is because a finished task has already ceased to be part of *my* concern, whereas an unfinished task is still something that belongs to me, something I might do well if I had a chance to finish. Follow-up experiments have interrupted some tasks when the subject understood that he had been doing badly. He was led to interpret completion as success.[9] Under these circumstances a person tended to remember more of the tasks in which he was doing well.

7. You can get other people to sing your praises, surround yourself with yes-men. If they say you are good, you must be good.

These are a few of the many ways of building up the self. We need not sit and dream of our amazing qualities or reconstruct the memory of what we did, so as to make it stupendous. We can, in each moment, make the most of our big muscles, or friendly smile, or possessions; and in the all-important competition for status we can put ourselves in a posi-

---

[7] B. Bettelheim, Harry—A study in rehabilitation, *J. abnorm. soc. Psychol.*, 1949, 44, 231–265.

[8] B. Zeigarnik, *Psychol. Forsch.*, 1927, 9, 1–86.

[9] S. Rosenzweig and S. Sarason, An experimental study of the triadic hypothesis: reaction to frustration, ego-defense, and hypnotizability, *Character & Pers.*, 1942, 11, 1–19.

tion where we look good to ourselves and can get others to agree with us.

It may seem to the reader that there is a certain amount of self-deception in many or all of these seven means of asserting the self. Fortunately, there are three additional ways of building up a good strong "satisfactory" self with whom we can live without conflict, which do not entail the need for self-deception. We shall conclude this chapter with a mention of these three methods.

8. Without being moralistic, we may note that the people who assert the self with the greatest inner satisfaction, free from bluffing and poses, are usually the people who try to get a balanced picture of all their assets and liabilities seen in perspective, and decide to accept all of reality and to secure help from friends or counselor in rounding out the picture. We have already said a few words about how this can be done (page 129).

9. People seem to enjoy themselves most when they derive satisfaction directly from the activities of life instead of pursuing each activity for the prestige or power they get from it. There is such a thing as pursuing music or literature or mechanical hobbies or recreation for the direct value they have in themselves, rather than to know more than others, or outshine them, or raise one's status. Friends may be people one likes, and likes to be with, whether or not they are the people whom one "wants to be seen with" as a symbol of belonging to the best set.

10. Finally, people need to love and be loved; and unless they are afraid of being considered weak in a hard-boiled world, they can vigorously develop a sense of the worth-whileness of themselves by accepting and giving love. Romain Rolland[10] illustrates this well in describing Olivier, one of two children of a middle-class French family. Olivier is delicate and fair. Throughout the early part of his life he suffers a succession of illnesses that leave him in a permanently weakened condition. As a result he is petted by his family. He becomes melancholy and introverted, a boy who "is afraid of death and very poorly equipped for life." He is backward. He prefers to avoid the society of other children. Their games, their robust play, fill him with dread. He cries easily. Morbidly sensitive, he begins to withdraw into a private world. He tells himself

---

[10] Romain Rolland, *Jean-Christophe*, New York, Pocket Books, Inc., 1949, pp. 173–174.

stories. He slavishly keeps a diary. He has a "burning, almost feminine, longing to love and be loved."

The possibilities already exist for the development of an adult who makes excessive demands for affection, who becomes frightened in the presence of strong emotion, who may erect hostile defenses against the world that threatens him, and who in general may be unable to adjust himself to society.

And yet in the fragile child we can already see signs that this is not to be the case. Although he is always to remain shy and retiring, he is able to express his feelings toward the rest of the world without fear or hostility. For the delicacy and sickliness are nurtured in a world in which the child is genuinely loved and respected. He receives the affection and care of his older sister Antoinette. He is loved by his mother, who is talented musically and imparts her feeling for music to the children. Olivier's father, the town banker, is generous, jocular, and easygoing. He loves his family and allows the children freedom that never becomes tinged with disregard. The family is influential, but above all it is surrounded by an atmosphere of warmth and friendliness that comes not only from itself, but from the tightly knit social structure of the small French town as well. So in Olivier, the constitutional weakness that might have produced an individual useless to himself and the world about him, interacts with the social and family environment to one day produce a highly talented pianist and an effective human being.

Sometimes neither love alone, nor self-understanding alone, can quite accomplish what an insecure or lonely child (or adult) needs, setting him free to believe in himself and giving him courage to be himself. Bettelheim and Sylvester describe the way in which a lonely boy who felt isolated from all other human beings struggled to make contact with them, and how through a *combination of love and understanding* they drew him out, so that he became free to participate in social give-and-take, first with a few intimates, then with groups of his age-mates.

A ten-year-old boy of superior intelligence had lived in various institutions since his birth. His adjustment demanded psychiatric attention only when self-destructive tendencies of long standing culminated in a suicidal attempt. His life had been characterized by scarcity and tenuousness of personal ties. During the process of rehabilitation, it became obvious that his self-destructive act was an effort to break through his isolation. This he revealed in a situation which was characteristic for him in the beginning of treatment. An explosion of rage had followed his awkward and ineffectual attempt to get close to other children by provoking their aggression. It was then that he said, "I went up on the Empire State Building and jumped off. After that everybody was my friend."

Although he had always lived in proximity to others, he neither knew how to react to adults nor how to get along with children. For him, adults were those who were bigger than he, individuals who by virtue of greater strength and size enforced rules, inflicted punishment and prevented children from "bothering them."

One counselor devoted herself particularly to him. Though he was for a long time unable to reciprocate the offered relationship, he immediately utilized the additional comfort which the contacts with the counselor offered. Toward the end of the first month, he expressed his first appreciation of her devotion when he snuggled against her. It took another month before he was able to ask any personal questions of her.

This breaking through of his isolation was apparently meaningful to him and he feared its return because his ability to maintain contact was still very tenuous. The arrival of a new boy in the dormitory became an immediate threat to him. However, he found means of reassuring himself; he asked his counselor to come over to his bed and asked to kiss her good night for the first time. . . . Walking close to her he said, "I am going to hang on to your arm for the rest of my life."

. . . He began to arrange tea parties in which he himself prepared and served all the food. He showed great concern that everybody should have enough to eat. These parties were at first limited to his favorite counselor, the person who for a long time had satisfied all his desires. Then he stopped grabbing food from the plates of the other children and gradually included them in his parties.

Since there had never been any pressure on his table manners, the spontaneous changes in this area are significant indications of his inner changes. His greed, his noisy smacking and sucking, gave way to the eating habits of a normal child. Thumb sucking was relinquished for the socially more acceptable chewing of gum. Personality changes paralleled this process of arriving at mastery of primitive needs through their unconditional gratification. While initially his time was spent mostly in daydreaming, he gradually began to participate in active sports, learned to swim and play baseball and showed pleasure in these achievements.

. . . He became able to face the "bad" past and also developed trust in a benign and manageable future, while he took his present existence for granted. Two successive dreams which he spontaneously related to his counselor illustrate this.

In the first dream, he was king of the universe, Superman. He had a million dollars and ruled everyone. In the second dream, he went to visit the orphanage. He was in the pool (where the older children had thrown him into the water and never given him a chance to learn to swim). He showed them how well he was able to swim and dive. All the children sat around the pool and admired him and liked him very much.

The first dream shows how he attempted to compensate for his lack of personal status in the orphanage by ideas of omnipotence. In the second dream, his recently acquired real achievements, swimming and diving, give him prestige among those with whom he used to have none. Thus the new strength permitted him a more assuring perspective on past and future. While the past had been bad, a similar situation would not again find him helpless.[11]

SUGGESTED READINGS

Adler, A., *A Study of Organ Inferiority and Its Psychical Compensation* (trans. by S. E. Jellife), Nervous and Mental Disease Publishing Co., 1917.

Davis, A., American status systems and the socialization of the child, *Amer. soc. Rev.*, 1941, 6, 345–356.

Freud, A., *The Ego and the Mechanisms of Defense* (trans. by C. Baines), New York, International Universities Press, 1946.

Greenberg, P. J., Competition in children: an experimental study, *Amer. J. Psychol.*, 1932, 44, 221–248.

Hunt, J. McV. (ed.), *Personality and the Behavior Disorders*, New York, Ronald, 2 vols., 1944, chap. 10.

Leuba, C. J., An experimental study of rivalry in young children, *J. comp. Psychol.*, 1933, 16, 367–378.

Murphy, G., *Personality*, New York, Harper, 1947, chap. 22.

Plant, J. S., *The Envelope*, London, Hildreth, 1950, chaps. 1–4, 16, 17.

---

[11] B. Bettelheim and E. Sylvester, A therapeutic milieu, *Amer. J. Orthopsychiat.*, 1948, 18, 191–206.

23 DEFENSE OF THE SELF

We have been describing the asserting of the self. At the same time there are constant *threats* to our picture of ourself, and we resort to all sorts of devices for *defending* it. We can reconstruct the damaged picture of the self not only by putting the good things into the figure but by energetically keeping the bad things out; we take pains to see that the less lovely and more vulnerable aspects are kept out of sight. We can strip the self-image of every weakness so that the enemy's barbs convey no threat. Or we can weaken the enemy by making him ridiculous or beneath contempt; we may see him as too puny to be bothered with. If he tries to insult us, we can parry the blow by belittling the relevance of his remarks. If he scores a direct hit, catching us in a lie, we can prove that he is a still bigger liar, or that ours was a white lie and his a black one. We may indeed act against our weaknesses by becoming strong, or "making believe" strong, in those very areas in which we are weak. We may develop blustering and self-assertive tactics regarding the very opinions about which we are inwardly most uncertain.

So as a supplement to what has been said about assertion of the self, let us examine, one at a time, the devices by which each of us defends the self.[1]

---

[1] The definitions of defense mechanisms given here are the writer's own. An effort has been made to state them so that their relation to general psychology, especially the psychology of perception and of learning, will be evident. For the technical psychoanalytic definitions, see W. Healy, A. F. Bronner, and A. M. Bowers, *The Structure and Meaning of Psychoanalysis*, New York, Knopf, 1929, especially pp. 198–254.

Psychoanalysis is based in considerable degree upon the theory of the *libido*, or instinctual craving, which is conceived to be essentially sexual, so that many activities which do not *seem* to be sexual are treated as sexual. Great emphasis is placed on the

1. First let us emphasize those processes of distortion of the picture of the self by which we manage to conceal from ourselves our less laudable motives, so that we make ourselves appear good, intelligent, reasonable, laudable—the process known as *rationalization*. In Shakespeare's *Much Ado About Nothing,* Benedick has made himself something of a hero by asserting his superiority to the shafts of Cupid. He is one who will never marry. When in the middle of the play he falls in love with Beatrice, he finds very good reasons why he should marry. "The world must be peopled." Everything is different now. The old arguments mean nothing. Theodore Roosevelt said that "under no circumstances" would he be a candidate for a third term; when he decided to run again, he commented that a man who had rejected a second cup of coffee certainly had a right to change his mind. King Leopold II, one of the great empire builders of the nineteenth century, undertook a colossal slave-driving enterprise in Central Africa in which many natives were crushed in getting rubber and ivory from the Congo basin. Very solemnly the king and his counselors drew up an elaborate explanation in terms of the advantages accruing to the natives in receiving the benefits of civilization and Christianity. Now we need not assume that the king and all his counselors were simply wicked men. In point of fact, economic advantage was probably the heart of the adventure, but prestige, power, and many other factors also entered the picture; and it is entirely possible that certain opportunities to help here and there to fight against tropical disease and to raise the level of native well-being may have played a minor part in the thinking of the king or of some of his advisers on the project. All that is necessary to make the enterprise laudable is to see that these minor factors are thrown into a central role, make them a figure in the figure-ground pattern of one's thinking, so that these are items that one notices and that other people notice. One can therefore refer to these items as primary objectives; they are primary in the sense that they are the things which attract attention, although not primary in the sense of the total weight they carry. The process which the Freudians call *rationalization* is this process which Benedick, Theodore Roosevelt, and

---

instinctive response of the infant to the parent of the opposite sex. Since the writer cannot give a brief summary of Freud's complicated theory it seems to him better simply to accept gratefully whatever he can from Freud, but to give definitions which express his own outlook.

King Leopold all showed. As Ernest Jones puts it, they found a good and acceptable reason for what they were doing or wanted to do. Whether this reason is the real or the chief reason is another question. But rational grounds for one's acts have been found, and in our rational civilization an "acceptable reason" for doing whatever we do is fundamental. Thinking may even at times consist in large measure of finding good reasons for things to which we are already fully committed.

So far we have not strayed from the ordinary realm of autistic reconstruction of perception, for the man who rationalizes is autistically controlling the figure-ground pattern (page 143). There may at times be cases, however, when we cannot, by any amount of distortion, make the present situation laudable or even bearable. We may then carry out a process known as (2) *turning away,* simply blinding ourselves to a situation; or another process known as (3) *undoing,* i.e., carrying out acts which "erase" the past and make it clear to us that the reprehensible acts of an earlier day never did occur at all. Lady Macbeth, with her endless washing of her hands, shows, among other mechanisms, the struggle to undo the murder which she has committed. The process is not always carried so far; sometimes, instead of a struggle to wipe out an unbearable memory, there is an effective stoppage of memory and the whole event is washed clean from the mind. As Friedrich Nietzsche remarked, "My memory says that I did it, my pride that I could not have done it, and in the end my memory yields."

4. If we carry out this process of undoing more radically and effectively, we may force the whole business completely out of consciousness. This process of forcing from consciousness is sometimes called *suppression.* (5) When the process of struggling against painful events is carried out unconsciously, so that we are not even aware of the process, it is called *repression.* McGranahan[2] successfully demonstrated by experiment that one can in this way unconsciously block out an unwelcome memory. He presented 100 nouns to his subjects, requiring them to reply with adjectives; if they gave adjectives referring to *color,* they were given a strong electric shock. His data suggest that some of his subjects not only avoided *naming* adjectives, but even failed to *think* of them.

[2] D. McGranahan, A critical and experimental study of repression, *J. abnorm. soc. Psychol.,* 1940, 35, 212–225.

At times we may be able to repress effectively the fact that we have done something or that we felt a certain impulse, and yet something may appear in consciousness to take its place. We have kept the meaning of the act out of consciousness, but not all ideas and feelings related to the act. Sometimes a sexual idea is repressed, but a book, a ring, an item of clothing connected with the idea comes into consciousness, the reason not being recognized at the time.

6. Sometimes when we cannot bear to recognize the reality of our impulses, and the guilt belonging to them, the impulse may be assigned to someone else. This is called *projection*. Thus we attribute to others the desire to do things that unconsciously we desire to do ourselves. Sears' data[3] suggest that a group of fraternity men tended to attribute to other men the stinginess and obstinacy which they themselves possessed to an unusual degree.

This process seems to be involved in many cases of *delusions of persecution*. Many a patient suffering from mental disorder believes that family and friends are plotting against him. He may attribute to them the hostile feelings which he himself actually has. In a study in Switzerland, Josef Lang[4] made an investigation of eleven patients, all of whom had developed delusions of persecution with reference to their families. They believed that members of their families were trying to poison them, defraud them of property, etc. Lang thought that perhaps the reason for this suspicion was the fact that the patient himself had deep hostilities to some or all of the members of his family. It would therefore be natural to expect that if he himself suffered from feelings of guilt because of his hostilities, he would get rid of these unbearable feelings by developing the belief, "It is not I who am hostile to them; it is they who are hostile to me." We might test this hypothesis, Lang suggested, in the following way: If the patient himself is the one who really harbors hatred, he will unconsciously choose as his persecutor the member of the family who is most like himself. He will *project* upon the person most like himself the guilt which he is unable to acknowledge. When association tests of the sort described on page 274 were given to all these eleven patients

---

[3] R. Sears, Experimental studies of projection, I. Attribution of traits, *J. soc. Psychol.*, 1936, 7, 151–163.

[4] J. B. Lang, *Jahrb. f. Psychoanal. u. Psychopath.*, 1913, 5, 705–755.

and to all the members of their families, it turned out in every case that the person against whom the delusion of persecution was entertained was the member of the family who was most similar to the patient himself. So far as a single experiment could ascertain, Lang's hypothesis seemed to be verified.

7. Somewhat analogous to this process of projection is the process of *introjection,* by which one attributes to oneself those traits which are actually the traits of someone else. The small child, as he identifies himself with his father, actually feels that he is in a sense as strong, as big, as wise as his father. The qualities of the father are brought within him. The process of introjection appears also at the adult level. The "small fry" or "little men" in a political movement may identify themselves with the "big shots" and feel within their own bosoms the heroic qualities which appear to be those of the leader. This was exactly the way the members of the S.S. in Germany felt toward their *Führer.*

8. Another method of protection against our less laudable attributes is to fight against them by developing the opposite qualities; this process is called *reaction formation.* A common illustration is reacting against one's childish dirtiness by being neat, correct, punctilious, and orderly; or reacting against one's more violent and cruel impulses by being "sugar and spice and everything nice." Lasswell[5] tells of a man who as a child had blinded a cat with a knife. Completely forgetting (repressing) the experience, he had spent his adult years in all sorts of philanthropies for the blind. One goes out of one's way not only to cover up, but to do *more than seems necessary* to cover up that which occasioned the original sense of guilt. It has been noticed by many a novelist that the very humble, meek, neat, correct people may turn out to be really the toughest, coarsest, and most violent when their masks are pulled off, just as Uriah Heep in Dickens' *David Copperfield,* a "very humble person," becomes as savage as a beast when once his shams are seen through.

9. If all these mechanisms fail, there is still a way to get out of the painful situation when the self is directly or indirectly sensed to be inadequate or laden with guilt. This way is to fall back to an earlier level of adjustment; this is *regression.* He who has failed in making love can

---

[5] H. Lasswell, *Psychopathology and Politics,* Chicago, University of Chicago Press, 1930.

go back to his earlier associates. He who has failed as an adult may go back to the childhood level of response. After all, this brings safety. During World War I, William McDougall[6] described four striking cases of soldiers who, terribly broken with war neurosis at the front, had gone back to childish ways, even to the ways of infancy, so that they talked baby talk, crept or walked on hands and knees, even showed a typical infantile facial expression. They had gotten away from the world of danger and threat by regression.

Much interest has been attached in recent years to the fact that under hypnosis people can sometimes be induced to relive the experiences of early years; they are "hypnotically regressed." They are told, for example, that they are celebrating their twelfth birthday and asked what they have been doing during the morning; later they are hypnotically carried back to the eleventh birthday, the tenth birthday, etc. When they are given mental tests and personality tests of various sorts the results often take a form which is about what would be expected of persons at these earlier levels. A typical example is the following definitions of the word "lecture" by a man in his twenties when "hypnotically regressed" to various earlier levels:[7]

Year	Month	
4	0	Don't know
5	0	Don't know
5	9	Raise cain. . . . Get a talking to
6	0	A talking to . . . when mom gives you the dickens
8	0	Scold. . . . Mummy usually fusses
11	0	Fuss; scold . . .
12	0	Fuss; scold . . .
14	0	To talk . . . given by school teacher
17	0	An instructive talk

The varying degrees of immaturity appear to be expressed in regressive behavior in a manner clearer than we should expect to result from bluffing or a conscious desire to show characteristic behavior at each of these early levels; control tests showed that the subject could not consciously put on an act characteristic of these age levels.

---

[6] W. McDougall, *An Outline of Abnormal Psychology*, New York, Scribner, 1926.
[7] H. Spiegel, J. Shor, and S. Fishman, An hypnotic ablation technique for the study of personality development, *Psychosom. Med.*, 1945, 7, 273–278.

Super-ego

In the early work of Freud, it was considered sufficient to explain these "mechanisms of defense" or processes carried out by the "ego"—the individual's orderly conscious activities as contrasted with the blind instinctive drives which dominated his unconscious mental activities. But as his work went on, Freud became convinced that the task of the ego was complicated by another factor arising from the process of *identification with parents* which we have already discussed (page 414). He became impressed with the fact that the child identifies with the parents as lawmakers or *disciplinary agents;* as he identifies with the parents he takes over their reproving or punishing attitudes toward himself, so that he comes to sit in moral judgment on his own activities. In other words, having described the ego as the system of activities consciously or unconsciously concerned with making contact with reality, Freud used the term super-ego to define the process by which in early childhood *we identify ourselves strongly with our parents as authority figures.* We see the four-year-old playing with pets or dolls, scolding and holding up to moral excoriation the puppy or the doll which is "guilty" of the very misdemeanors which he himself has actually committed. And in the same way we sometimes hear him talking to himself and turning a fusillade of moral terminology loose upon his own head: "You're a very, very, bad boy, and you can never, never go there again."

What seems to have happened is this: Very early he puts himself in the place of his parents with their great authority and power, and begins to see things, *as far as he can* (there are limits; cf. page 398), from their viewpoint. From this vantage point he can, through identification, make himself one with them, and thus condemn his own guilty act. He has carried the identification so far that an offense against the property code or the sex code is not just something that parents disapprove; he now disapproves of it *in his own right*. This process of self-reproof, of course, underlies the formation of a *conscience*.

The young boy, Harry, whom we mentioned on page 415, shows clearly some of the steps involved in learning to control himself through conscience rather than relying solely on external control from other people:

When Harry began to feel that he should cut down on his truancy, he asked that the doors of the dormitory building be locked. Submitting to external control seemed easier at that point than internal restraints. His request was denied and it was pointed out that it was never locked doors but only a person's decision which prevented him from leaving a building. Since in spite of his efforts the school provided no physical restraint, he had to create it for himself. Harry had strongly identified himself with a stuffed dog which he had brought with him to the school. During the initial phase of violent self-destruction, he treated it badly, spanked it, threw it around, flung it at people, and hung it by its neck. Now he tied it to the post of his bed "so that it wouldn't run away." A short time later, he received a teddy bear from the school. Each evening, he tied his arm to the teddy and fastened the teddy to the bed to prevent himself from running away.

A child had left the institution and Harry feared that someday he too might have to leave. In order to fortify himself against the tendency to truant which was revived by his fear he invented the following story:

"Once upon a time there was a little mule who ran away all the time. Finally he became the property of a little boy named Harry. The mule had been beat up a lot and was glad to have found a good home. Harry's father said he could keep the mule if the mule wouldn't run away. But one night the mule ran away and Harry ran after it to find it. He didn't come back and his father went out for them and finally found them sitting at the foot of a cliff with the mule in Harry's lap. [He added here as an aside, 'It was a very little mule, and they were both fast asleep.'] Things went all right for a while, and then the mule ran away again and Harry followed it again. This time it was a very cold night and the searching party looked and looked for them, but couldn't find them, and finally they told the police and the police looked for them, and then they found them at the foot of the cliff and the mule and Harry were dead. [At the end of the story he suddenly explained, 'You know, Harry, that's really me.']"

. . . In cases of staff sickness or for other similar reasons, a substitute counselor may be placed in charge of a group for limited periods of time. Approximately nine months after Harry's enrollment a young man was assigned to the group which included Harry. With newcomers, Harry was characteristically on his worst behavior. The substitute, who was very good with the boys and therefore well received by the group, lost his patience at one point and gave Harry a token spanking.

Some of the boys reported the incident to the director, who placed another counselor in charge of the group. This showed Harry, as well as the other children, that immediate action had been taken. The director then discussed the event with the group. He reminded them that when a child entered the school he, the director, made several promises, one of which was that the child would never be spanked. Therefore, because he thoroughly disapproved of physical punishment and wanted to live up to his promise, he had asked the substitute counselor to terminate his services to the school. He added that, while such action on his part was in line with the school's policies and his own promises, it was nevertheless not quite fair to the substitute. Harry's behavior had been so exasperating as to require more than average patience, and it was understandable that the substitute counselor lost his temper. Harry in particular could understand how a person might lose his temper since he himself did so continually. On the other hand, Harry's misbehavior warranted no retaliation in kind.

This made a great impression on Harry and he began to cry violently. Several times during the evening he went to see the director, making promises and violent threats in an attempt to get the counselor reinstated. It was explained to him that, although his feelings were understandable, there was nothing to be done. He was told that it was only natural that he blame himself for the counselor's difficulty, since it was his and not the counselor's fault which had brought about the situation.

In this incident Harry's behavior demonstrated for the first time that his conscience was developing. His guilt-feeling was based not on any direct act of violence, but on the fact that he had been instrumental in creating an act of injustice. From this moment on he never again acted quite irresponsibly.[8]

How much of all this is a conscious process, how much an unconscious one in the small child, we cannot say. But there is some evidence that in some children conscience soon becomes terrific, and overwhelms the individual with a terrible sense of guilt. There is also evidence that other children simply develop a realistic acceptance of the fact that other people approve certain lines of conduct and disapprove others, and adjust themselves to the standard of approval and disapproval *without* developing much conscience about it. From the Freudian point of view it would not be the super-ego at all if it were merely a question of judging in a practical way that "honesty is the best policy" and that we had better maintain a good reputation with our fellows. From a Freudian point of view it is only when there is a deep unconscious identification with the parents as authority figures, and the sense of right and wrong has been deeply ingrained within us and has tight control over us, that we may properly speak of super-ego formation. "I don't know why, but I know what is right and what is wrong"—this is pure super-ego. The practical value of all this will of course vary from person to person. Some noble and heroic acts have resulted from this kind of absolute and unreasoning moral judgment, but many a fanatic war and many an intolerant persecutor or bigot have also had this kind of absolute certainty about right and wrong—and about his being in the right.

---

[8] B. Bettelheim, Harry—A study in rehabilitation, *J. abnorm. soc. Psychol.*, 1949, 44, 231–265.

Individual Differences in the Use of Psychoanalytic Mechanisms

Regarding these and other devices related to the self, we must ask the question: But do *all* of us do *all* of these things, and if so, what determines which of the many devices we will utilize at a given time? In reply it seems likely that some people are more prone to use one, some more prone to use another of these various possibilities. One investigation by Saul Rosenzweig suggests that there is a definite relationship between certain personality tendencies and the tendency to utilize certain kinds of Freudian dynamics.

Rosenzweig believed that there might be a relation between (1) the tendency to repress and (2) the ability to be hypnotized and (3) the tendency to blame no one when frustrated ("impunitiveness," cf. page 126). In collaboration with Sarason, he offered the hypothesis that "hypnotizability as a personality trait is to be found in positive association with repression as a preferred mechanism of defense and with impunitiveness as a characteristic type of immediate reaction to frustration."[9] Their measure of repression was the tendency to remember jigsaw puzzles successfully solved rather than failed; they measured the depth to which the subject could be hypnotized (and with other subjects used suggestion without sleeping hypnosis); and they measured impunitiveness with the picture test mentioned above (page 124). The three groups of scores actually proved to be positively interrelated in the way required by the hypothesis. This is a good beginning. But the assumption that there are individual differences in proneness to one kind of defense mechanism rather than another is important enough to warrant a great deal of research. As a matter of fact, most dramatists and novelists constantly use this assumption; they give us their rationalizers, their repressers, their projectors, their undoers, assuming that each individual has characteristic forms of self-defense.

Extroversion and Introversion

We may also utilize the psychology of Carl Jung[10] in relation to this conception of individual proneness to one or another

---

[9] S. Rosenzweig and S. Sarason, An experimental study of the triadic hypothesis: reaction to frustration, ego-defense, and hypnotizability, *Character & Pers.*, 1942, *11*, 1–19.

[10] C. G. Jung, *Psychological Types*, New York, Harcourt, Brace, 1923.

type of self-enhancement or self-defense. This will not mean that we accept all of Jung's ideas any more than we accept all the ideas of anyone else; rather, we shall find a way in which we may reconcile his ideas with such evidence as we have.

Jung believes that each person is constitutionally predisposed to find his richest satisfactions *either* in the social world outside of him, *or* in his own inner life; he is *extroverted* or *introverted*. Believing in the value of this distinction between people who are directed to the outer world and people who are preoccupied with their own subjective world, we must nevertheless note that there is a great deal of evidence that these tendencies may change during an individual's life. Social experience modifies these tendencies to make one more extroverted, or more introverted. During the whole childhood period confidence and happiness in social relationships can be increased or decreased, and the child made more at home or less at home in the social world about him. There is the evidence of Lois Jack[11] that in certain situations shy and withdrawn children can definitely be helped by being trained into more confident types of adjustment; and there is a great deal of clinical evidence that children who in the early years are warm and outgoing are driven, through humiliation or social rejection, into an inner world where alone they can feel secure. A person can be battered down by a rough or frustrating environment, or one that is full of ridicule and humiliation, and be driven into those inner recesses in which he feels relatively free from the risks he runs in human society. When college students are given a series of "extroversion-introversion" questions such as the following:

Do you enjoy being alone?	Yes No
Do you enjoy speaking in public?	Yes No
Do you like to organize social gatherings?	Yes No
Are you always glad to meet prominent people?	Yes No

it becomes very evident that the responses indicate factors which are derived in considerable degree from the students' own personal experience. Extroversion seems to be related primarily to the fact that one has been accepted; and introversion, as it emerges from such tests, seems to express the response to fears which have arisen in socially frustrating situations, especially those in which one has been rejected or humiliated.

---

[11] L. M. Jack, An experimental study of ascendant behavior in preschool children, *Univ. Ia. Stud. Child Welf.*, 1934, 9, No. 3.

Fortunately we find in teaching and in counseling experience (as well as in such quantitative studies as those mentioned previously) evidence that there may be considerable change in either the extrovert or the introvert direction during the college years; one may be drawn out or driven back into one's shell.

From this point of view it would be reasonable to suggest that introversion as it appears in the light of our questionnaire methods is actually a defense mechanism, a mechanism of defending the self, not very different from those defined by Freud. In fact, introversion is not so very far from the Freudian mechanism of "turning away" mentioned above. Extroversion might in some cases be simply the happy discovery that one can cope with other people and be accepted by them.

Our generalization refers only to introversion-extroversion as they appear in questionnaire studies. The problem is really bigger; the tendency to respond more warmly to the outer or the inner world has many other facets. Many other factors, such as a rich and satisfying imagination, or the tendency to enjoy the reading of poetry, fiction, and other types of creative expression, may and often do involve a sort of turning inward *without* any morbidity. Nor is there any reason to deny that even if all children were lovingly accepted by their families and by everybody else, there would still be individual differences in the relative satisfactions which each would derive from (1) the faces, voices, social activities of other people, and (2) the inner world of imagination and thought. If we extended our questionnaires to deal with the whole vast domains of outwardly directed living and inwardly directed living, we would find much covered by these terms that is independent of the matter of escape from social rejection, and not related specifically to the processes of enhancement and defense of the self.

It must, however, be reluctantly admitted that in a competitive society like ours, these questionnaires serve a very real purpose in bringing out the successful and unsuccessful forms of response to social competition, social acceptance, and opportunities for membership in social groups; and the kind of extroversion and introversion that is related to social acceptance and rejection respectively is of basic everyday importance to the student's own personality adjustment. Using such an instrument, we must of course be on our guard to note the difference between what ap-

Figure 73. Recognition Memory

Which of these faces appeared on page 266?

pears at the surface of social response and what is going on underneath. An *apparent* extrovert may really be a shy, insecure person who is trying to be gay or confident; he may even be excited and boisterous. He may try to defend the self which has been injured or threatened by social rejection and to enhance it by pushing it into the limelight, pretending that it merits applause. An extrovert may be temporarily fed up with the crowd but go back to it the next month. Some mentally disturbed patients show a tendency to throw themselves, ranting or laughing, into perpetual motion, in a way which psychiatrists have sometimes called a "flight into reality," as contrasted with the "flight from reality" which appears in depressed, withdrawn patients. Even with these complications, however, and with these distinctions between surface and deep-level response, the concepts of introversion and extroversion still seem to be valuable; and inasmuch as they denote ways of avoiding hurt feelings or making the most of social acceptance, they seem to be concerned with assertion and defense of the self.

Compensation for Inferiority

Another series of suggestions regarding the ways of coping with personal inadequacy and social rejection should be mentioned in this connection, namely, the suggestions offered by Alfred Adler, the Viennese psychiatrist who broke away from Freud and set up his own school. It was Adler's belief that all individuals are born into a world in which they feel themselves weak, puny, ignorant, insignificant —in short, inferior. They look around and see the big, strong adults who march back and forth across the floor; who shout, sing, and whistle; who go and get the things they want; who tell the baby what he must do, pick him up, put him down, sometimes responding to his squeals and sometimes ignoring him; to whom he is beholden for all his satisfactions and protection. If he has a physical defect which makes him feel all the more inadequate, so much the worse for him. Or if the child is intellectually inferior to big brother, or less pretty than big sister, this may add to the trouble. But the sheer fact of being ignorant and helpless when a person begins life gives him the need to make the most of such means as he has for asserting himself. He develops a lusty yell, a vigorous technique of grabbing or controlling, all sorts of ways of preying on the feelings and especially the sympathies of the grownups around him, all sorts of direct and indirect ways of getting the better of big brother and big sister, or, indeed, of anyone who stands in his way.

Believing therefore that the child makes the most of such capacities as he can play up as an infant—as a relatively helpless person in a world of bigger people—Adler stressed the role of what he called compensation for inferiority, that is, the playing up of every kind of skill and strength that will enable the individual to overcome his limitations. It is not a question of one child's having "inferiority feelings" and another child's not having them. Absolutely every child feels himself at first inferior compared with others, if for no other reason than the fact that others are bigger and can do things which he cannot do; he therefore compensates for all he is worth. He asserts himself, shows off, bluffs, fishes for compliments, etc. His method of compensation, which depends on his surroundings, especially his family, differs from other children's methods; soon it is an important trait of his personality.

But some people, as the result of a catastrophe, may lose the method of compensation which has been developed. For example, if a child has learned to dominate his parents by a particular kind of coaxing, wheedling, or bluffing technique, and if one of the parents dies and the other remarries a much stronger personality, the child's early technique will fail, and he may come face to face with the fact that his devices for compensation are taken away; he may feel desperately inferior and build up all sorts of pitiful, complicated tricks to try to regain control of the situation. These "secondary inferiority feelings," which come after the first main compensations have fallen through, may cause havoc to his general adjustment. He may swagger, play sick, become a bully, or lose himself in fantasies of conquest. These cases are dramatic, but emphasis must be placed on the fact that for Adler everybody is inferior at first, and everybody compensates. But the situation is much more painful for some people than for others.

A typical record of a man suffering rather severely from inferiority feelings is the following:

C. You recognized before that when you were acting superior, you really were acting inferior. Do you want to carry that a little further?[12]
S. Well, I felt so nervous I didn't know what to say and everybody else was talking so smoothly. I sat in the corner while everybody else was being interested and consequently I just looked ridiculous because I didn't know what to say. So I adopted an air of superiority and acted like I wasn't inter-

---

[12] S. is exploring here his attitudes and experiences in a social situation to which he had referred in a previous interview.

ested. (Pause.) But I found out that that doesn't work. People don't like you unless you go out of your way to show that you like them.

C. I believe that's a good rule of personality.

S. . . . I have a couple of rules for friends now and I had to learn them the hard way. First go out of your way to do what they want you to do. That's what I didn't do until a month and a half ago. But I found it makes a tremendous difference. Then you have got to find out what a person likes to be called and call them that. . . . You don't have to be a good talker. People like you better and they say you sure are interesting if you just sit and look interested in what they say. . . .

C. Well, you have been doing a good bit of thinking about personality, haven't you?

S. There are a great deal of things I could say. People would be greatly surprised at me. When I go home I'm not going to be the same and I know my family will notice it. I used to be domineering. That was to cover up an inferiority complex. I had the air that I didn't care what anybody thought, but that doesn't get you any place. I just used to brush past things. I would brush past other people's qualities and "pooh-pooh" their ideas. (Pause.)

C. You feel you have experienced certain changes in your own personality.

S. I realize I'm changed and some of my friends have commented on it too. . . .[13]

It is typical of such inferiority feelings that a person tries one way, then another, of relieving the strain, trying especially to win approval and support from others, and making himself more and more dependent upon them.

James Joyce tells of young Stephen Dedalus as he learns to feel shame. Standing among a group of schoolmates he is quizzed by the grinning leader.

"Do you kiss your mother before you go to bed?" he is asked.

"I do," replies Stephen.

"Oh, I say, here's a fellow says he kisses his mother every night before he goes to bed."

The other fellows stopped their game and turned round, laughing. Stephen blushed under their eyes and said:

"I do not."

"Oh, I say," replies the leader, "here's a fellow says he doesn't kiss his mother before he goes to bed."

They all laughed again. Stephen tried to laugh with them. He felt his whole body hot and compressed in a moment. What was the right answer to the

---

[13] William U. Snyder, *Casebook of Non-Directive Counseling*, Boston, Houghton Mifflin, 1947, pp. 43 ff.

question? He had given two and still Wells laughed. But Wells must know the right answer for he was in the third of grammar. He tried to think of Wells' mother but he did not dare to raise his eyes to Wells' face. He did not like Wells' face. It was Wells who had shouldered him into the square ditch the day before because he would not swop his little snuffbox for Wells' seasoned hacking chestnut. . . . And how cold and slimy the water had been. . . . He still tried to think what was the right answer. Was it right to kiss his mother or wrong to kiss his mother? What did that mean, to kiss? You put your face up like that to say good night and then his mother put her face down. That was to kiss. . . . Why did people do that with their faces?[14]

From the present point of view the "compensations" of Adler may be regarded simply as *devices for asserting and defending the self*. Specifically, many of them sound much like the reaction formations of Freud (page 425), in which weakness has been turned into strength, inadequacy into adequacy. One puts one's best foot forward and plays the game hardest in those areas in which one's skill is limited.

On the whole, then, it would not be so difficult to draw these types of psychiatric inquiries (those of Freud, Jung, Adler) into the one broad scheme which we have been endeavoring to develop, namely, a scheme emphasizing self-assertion and self-defense. In all human societies the self must be asserted and defended. But in a competitive society like our own, emphasis must be placed upon the role of social acceptance and social rejection in guiding the struggle of the individual to develop the picture of the self as he wishes to view it.

Education and Therapy as Roads to Self-Knowledge

The dynamic activities just sketched in relation to self-defense may be regarded as devices usually involving even more self-deception than is involved in self-assertion—making the self invulnerable, free of weaknesses, and free of guilt. We may therefore ask whether there is not more to say about the process by which the individual learns, with greater objectivity, to see himself as others see him, or even to see himself as he actually is. There has been some research on this point suggesting that comparing one's self-evaluation with the evaluations given by others may, to a slight degree, reduce one's "defensiveness."

We may take a glance at some things which help. First, frank discus-

---

[14] James Joyce, *Portrait of the Artist as a Young Man*, in *The Portable James Joyce*, New York, Viking, 1947, pp. 253, 254.

sion with parents, teachers, and counselors may help. A person may wish to go deeper and get help from a psychiatrist or a clinical psychologist. Many individuals, when they learn to see through their own shams, and gain some degree of maturity, feel a great relief from the fact that the effort at self-deception is removed (cf. page 129).

It has been stressed continuously by therapists—e.g., by those who practice Carl Rogers' *nondirective therapy*—that the first hours of conference interview between therapist and client must be devoted largely to enabling the client to become aware of the things which he has seen only "out of the corner of his eye," or has not seen at all. In Rogers' technique this process is not conceived to require the hundreds of hours which are required by psychoanalysis. The client states his problem to the therapist, and the therapist occasionally repeats a phrase or recasts a sentence in such a way as to indicate that he has understood, that he is glad to give emphasis to that which has already been emphasized by the client, and that he would like to have the client go ahead. As the records indicate, this permissive atmosphere which allows the client to talk about his preoccupations may, at least in some cases, enable him to perceive his problems more accurately, and to live with less sense of guilt and frustration regarding aspects of himself which previously he refused to recognize.

The method of psychoanalysis is much longer and much more complex. But it also has a very large place for the process of coming to view the self more objectively, and of becoming more orderly and purposeful in the way in which one asserts and defends the self. One learns to accept and to become less defensive regarding oneself, more ready to view realities and to abandon the tricks of self-deception. The same is true of Adler's psychotherapy and of the new trends in psychoanalysis represented by Horney[15] and Fromm.[16]

Of rapidly growing importance is group psychotherapy, in which people share their problems, develop a sense of unity with others, and learn to face realities about themselves in an atmosphere in which *everyone* lays his cards on the table. This conception has pervaded educational thinking extensively, and has fused with the conception stemming from

---

[15] K. Horney, *New Ways in Psychoanalysis*, New York, Norton, 1938.
[16] E. Fromm, *Man for Himself*, New York, Rinehart, 1947.

John Dewey and progressive education, that we are healthiest when we are social creatures, and that our psychological illnesses are largely the illnesses of artificial separation from our fellows.

SUGGESTED READINGS

Adler, A., *Individual Psychology* (trans. by P. Radin), New York, Harcourt, Brace, 1932.
Appel, K. E., Psychiatric Therapy, in Hunt, J. McV. (ed.), *Personality and the Behavior Disorders*, New York, Ronald, 1944, Vol. 2, chap. 34.
Freud, A., *The Ego and the Mechanisms of Defense* (trans. by C. Baines), New York, International Universities Press, 1946.
Freud, S., *A General Introduction to Psychoanalysis* (trans. by J. Riviere), New York, Liveright, 1935.
Horney, K., *The Neurotic Personality of Our Time*, New York, Norton, 1937.
Jung, C. G., *Psychological Types* (trans. by H. C. Baynes), New York, Harcourt, Brace, 1923.
Sears, R. R., An Experimental Analysis of Psychoanalytic Phenomena, in Hunt, J. McV. (ed.), *Personality and the Behavior Disorders*, New York, Ronald, 1944, Vol. 1, chap. 9.

24 PERSONALITY MEASUREMENT

Now that we have embarked upon the ocean of personality investigation, and have seen some of the concepts which are used to assist us in understanding the individual's ways of adapting to his environment, it is worth while to ask about specific means of *testing* an individual's personality attributes and of *comparing individuals* with one another by means of such tests. In the case of intelligence and aptitude, it was found possible to compare people with one another; perhaps the same thing can be done when attitudes toward the self, conscience, extroversion, inferiority feelings, etc., are involved.

We may for convenience distinguish three broad classes of tests. The first comprises *methods of verbal report*, including questionnaires, check lists, and rating scales—devices in which the individual says something about himself or about someone whom he knows well. The second comprises *behavior methods,* in which we put the individual through his paces in situations similar to those in which we wish to understand and predict his behavior; we sample his personality in the behavior field just as we sample his intellectual behavior in an intelligence test. Third are the *projective methods;* as we shall see in Chapter 25, these aim to give us a more systematic and complete picture of the individual's many attributes and the ways in which they are organized together within his personality.

Verbal Report Methods

You would expect to find out more about an individual's personality through any one of the following methods: (1) reading whatever has been written about his life, either by others or by himself —the *life-history* method; (2) talking with him—the *interview* method; (3) comparing him with others by means of written answers to questions—the *questionnaire* method; (4) estimating and recording the degree to which he possesses certain traits, like honesty or generosity or obstinacy, and comparing him with others in respect to each trait—the *rating* method.

Life-History Methods

From the time of the earliest Greek character analysts (the best known of whom is of course Plutarch) to the literary biographers of today, there have been many intriguing and suggestive literary techniques for getting the meaning out of the life history, so that in addition to a sheer chronological record of the events in a person's life, one can get some conception of the unfolding of his personality.

Recent attempts have been made to develop a way to *standardize* the methods of getting the life history, in the sense that one makes sure to ask for the same general kinds of information about everyone, so that the data for one person can be compared, in appropriate respects, with those for other people. A literary biographer might be interested in the early childhood of one person, in the adolescence of a second, and in the middle years of a third, so that he might easily forget to ask about the early childhood of the second and third individuals or, finding that there is not much material on it, he might simply leave it out when his record is drawn up. The later student of this record may never know whether the material was available and was neglected, or whether it was unavailable. In any event the three life histories are not comparable. The aim of the modern student is to do as well as he can in getting the same sorts of information, and all of it as complete as possible, for all the people in his study.

The life history must include a systematic study of the person as he is today. An example of a good outline is this one from Hartley:

Outline for the Study of Individual as a Social Unit

Each person has an individuality which is unique, which represents an organization of characteristics which is probably precisely duplicated in no other person in the world. There are, of course, many elements in personality which are common to a wide number of people, but we are here interested in the patterning of elements which represents the individuality of the individual.

Please consider each section below carefully. Read the questions, then please discuss yourself in the light of those questions. Don't try merely to answer each specific query, elaborate upon the theme involved. Cover the different points raised, but don't limit yourself, don't restrict your discussion to the questions as stated. Present all relevant material in detail. In case of doubt about material to include, remember that it is better to put in *more* than *less*.

1. What are your skills? What are you good at and what are you poor at? Consider school, outside of school, home, leisure time activities, hobbies, vocationally useful aptitudes. What do you enjoy doing? What do you find unpleasant? Describe fully, giving details contributing to enjoyment, to lack of enjoyment. What would you like to be able to do better to secure more enjoyment?

2. What is your general approach to your associates? How spontaneous are you in your relations with them? To what extent do you hold back? Consider boys and girls separately. Under what circumstances are you most free? With what sort of people? Least free? Who are your intimates? What factors entered into your selection of each of them? How did you become acquainted, how did the friendship develop? What do you like about each? What do you dislike about them? List six people you can't stand having anything to do with. Describe each of them. What is there about each that you dislike? List six people whom you know who seem to be all right but with whom you wouldn't care to become intimate. Describe each. What is it you like about each? Why do you feel you would not like to know them better? Discuss each one separately, at length, and probe into the "Why's" of your statements.

3. What is your general reaction to those slightly younger than yourself? Considerably older? Do you consider yourself an adult or an adolescent? How does this self-evaluation affect your relations to others? Are you accepted at the level you consider yourself? Who does, who doesn't? What circumstances make you feel young? When do you feel old?

4. Where do you feel "at home"? With whom? What groups do you feel a member of? Identified with? Where, with whom do you feel you do not belong? What difficulties are introduced by these feelings of belongingness and not belonging? Discuss in detail, citing examples and describing instances.

5. When, under what circumstances are you most confident of yourself? Least confident? What specific fears bother you? How much do they disturb you (be specific)? In what ways do they interfere?

6. Describe situations in which you have inner conflicts, are drawn in two or more opposing directions. What are the bases of these conflicts? Which aspects generally win? Under what circumstances may the other aspects dominate?

7. When are you happiest? If you had a magic wishing wand and could wish for absolutely anything, what might you ask for? Discuss at length. What will Heaven be like? What will you be like in Heaven? Who else will be there?

Who won't be there? (If you do not believe in life after death, say so and develop this theme through fantasy.) What sort of thing makes you unhappy?

8. When do you feel tense, anxious, upset? Discuss how these feelings develop, describing the circumstances in typical cases, and how they recede. What factors create tension? Describe at least three situations, the most recent you can recall, in which you felt distinctly uncomfortable. Discuss the phases which contributed to your discomfort.

9. (Summary) For you, what seems to be the fundamental organization of life, into what major categories is living organized from *your* point of view? From your point of view, how are activities classified? How do you classify things? How do you classify people? Discuss in detail, citing examples.[1]

The Interview

An interview may vary all the way from a casual unplanned conversation to a systematic technique for obtaining information. Often the teacher's and the counselor's first interviews with an individual may be informal but gradually undergo crystallization as the people get to understand each other; or the interview may follow a uniform plan, but with flexibility in the way of talking and in the order in which questions are presented. A semi-standardized method was used in the Kinsey Report; in it a rather uniform way of getting information on many points was followed. Finally, for some purposes, the whole interview may be a completely standardized procedure in which the interviewer covers the same points with each person in the same way. While at one time there was a tendency toward extreme standardization, it has been generally agreed in the light of modern experience that more and better information is derived from a more flexible method.

In situations where highly personal questions are asked, the interviewer has to adapt to his respondent to some degree. Students of public opinion have done much work with the "open-ended interview," in which the respondent, instead of being forced into a *yes* or *no* reply, is asked such a question as, "How well is your farm doing this season?" or "How do you like the President's stand on the Taft-Hartley Act?" The data from such replies cannot be directly scored and tabulated as yeses and noes can, but they can be *coded*, e.g., arranged on a scale from maximal agreement or disagreement with the President's stand, etc.

---

[1] E. L. Hartley, *Problems in Prejudice*, New York, King's Crown Press, 1946, pp. 53–55.

The Questionnaire

When we need to standardize an interview, we can usually get the data equally well from a questionnaire, or list of prepared questions, such as the following:

> How old are you?
> How far did you go in school?
> Who is your employer?
> Do you have a telephone?
> Did you vote in the last presidential election?

Or questions dealing directly with individual personality such as:

> Do you often feel lonely?
> Do you feel resentful toward your father?
> Do you usually "kick yourself" if you make a minor mistake?
> Do you enjoy parties where everybody is "high"?
> Do you feel inferior to the other people in your family?

Since our interest in dealing practically with people has largely been an interest in helping them to adjust, or in choosing for certain specific tasks the people who are best adjusted, these lists of attributes have been inclined to emphasize maladjustments; indeed, many of them are called tests of *neurotic tendency*. One method of scoring is to count up the number of answers which indicate maladjustment; another method is to allow the subject to indicate his *degree* of response to each item so that the more serious difficulties can be given extra weight.

The method of *validation* of such procedures is to give a large number of questions to an experimental group which contains many people who are well adjusted and many who are badly adjusted, as shown for example by psychiatrists' reports, and then to pick out for further use the questions that are *differentiating*, in the sense that a much larger proportion of the maladjusted answer them in a given way than is the case with the well adjusted.

It must never be forgotten that the usefulness of such methods depends largely upon an empirical demonstration that these are the sorts of questions that people can and do answer honestly. For example, in the case of tests of adjustment, practical usefulness depends on whether those who, on other grounds, are considered maladjusted really do give answers reporting maladjustment. If this is fairly consistently true, it becomes possible to use such a method to "screen" people in a large group, with the idea that those with many signs of maladjustment—"neurotic" signs—may be given the special help they need. But so great is the human tendency to deceive others or oneself that it sometimes turns out that the most disturbed people report almost complete absence of all neurotic signs. In some tests it appears that to show a *great many* such signs, or to show *almost none at all,* is equally portentous of trouble.

One of the best-known examples of an objective method derived from the analysis of personality traits and the resulting attempt to get *yes* or *no* answers throwing light upon these traits is the Minnesota Multiphasic Personality Inventory.[2] Instead of calling for a printed record sheet, the questions (when administered as an individual test) are presented on cards which the subject reads and sorts into piles in terms of *yes, no,* and *doubtful*. To take a hypothetical example, if the item "I like mechanics magazines" calls for an affirmative answer, he puts the card in the *yes* pile. If it does not, he puts it in the *no* pile. If he is not sure, he puts it in the *don't know* pile. He proceeds in this way through 550 items. Actually, as he piles up the cards, a score is being piled up with regard to each one of many different dispositions of personality. The individual achieves, then, a certain gross total with respect to each of these traits or "dimensions" of personality. These many phases of personality are being tested all at once.

The validation of such a method is done with the procedure already indicated. The questions were originally chosen because the answers of people known to have certain traits were different from those known not to have those traits. Further validation is secured from time to time in current research by finding out to what degree one can actually predict the extent to which each trait will be manifested by specific individuals in *new* situations.

It is, however, a great mistake to assume that a personality questionnaire need be directed to a person's weaknesses. His strengths may like-

---

[2] S. R. Hathaway and J. C. McKinley, Booklet for the Minnesota Multiphasic Personality Inventory, 1943.

wise be considered, and some of the more interesting of these questionnaires deal with people's *interests* and *values*—the things they live for. A good example is the Allport-Vernon Study of Values, which gives the individual a chance to express his responses to six basic values defined by Spranger: the theoretical, the economic, the esthetic, the social, the political, and the religious. The first seven questions on the Allport-Vernon scale are as follows:

1. The main object of scientific research should be the discovery of pure truth rather than its practical applications. (a) Yes; (b) No.

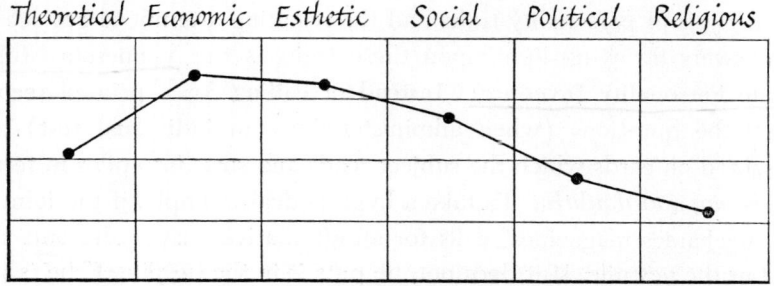

Figure 74. Allport-Vernon Scale Profile of an Engineering Student

This profile was arrived at by plotting the subject's score for each of the six values of the test—the higher the score the stronger the value. This freshman engineering student values the economic and esthetic most highly; religious values are weakest.

2. Do you think that it is justifiable for the greatest artists, such as Beethoven, Wagner, Byron, etc., to be selfish and negligent of the feelings of others? (a) Yes; (b) No.
3. Because of the aggressive and self-assertive nature of man the abolition of war is an illusory ideal. (a) Yes; (b) No.
4. If you were a university professor and had the necessary ability, would you prefer to teach: (a) poetry; (b) chemistry and physics?
5. Under circumstances similar to those of Qu. 4, would you prefer: (a) economics, (b) law?
6. Which of these character traits do you consider the more desirable: (a) high ideals and reverence; (b) unselfishness and sympathy?
7. In a paper such as the New York Sunday Times, are you more interested in the section on picture galleries and exhibitions than in the real estate sections and the account of the stock market? (a) Yes; (b) No.[3]

[3] Copyright, 1931, by Gordon W. Allport and Philip E. Vernon. Published by Houghton Mifflin.

PERSONALITY MEASUREMENT

A freshman engineering student responded to question 1 by marking (b) No; for him, the practical, especially the *economically* practical, always appealed over the theoretical. On question 2 he likewise said *no*, for he had no use for "egotists" and believed in "being decent to people." He was not enough of an idealist to say *no* to 3. On 4 he chose (b), because science always meant more to him than poetry. And so on through the long test (the whole test contains dozens of items and takes nearly a

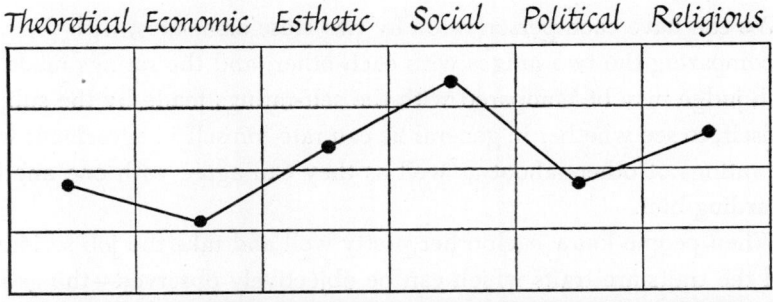

Figure 75. Allport-Vernon Scale Profile of a Liberal Arts Student

Compare this profile with that in Figure 74. This liberal arts senior valued the social area above all the others, the esthetic less highly, and the economic the least.

class hour for most students). His relative expression of value in the six areas is shown in Figure 74. A woman senior in a liberal arts college responded *yes* to question 1, for she wanted to *understand* the world; she was so concerned with the need for unselfishness in the world that she replied *no* to question 2; her idealism led to a *no* response to 3; her esthetic bent favored (a) over (b) in question 4; her love of justice led her to prefer (b) to (a) in 5. Question 6 caused a considerable struggle, but was finally decided in terms of (b) since sympathy was her own highest standard. On question 7 she decided she would put pictures ahead of business any time. Her profile on the whole test is shown in Figure 75.

Ratings

In comparing people with one another in any psychological trait, we may regard them as spread out along a scale from one extreme to the other, as for example from very high on originality to very low on originality. We often use a three-point or five-point scale such as these:

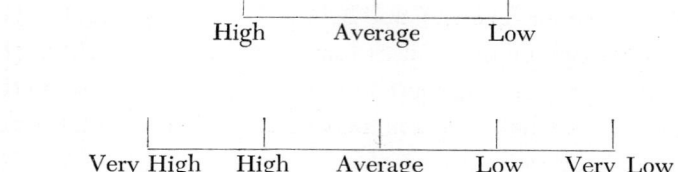

or

We can have each person rated by two close associates, with the idea of comparing the two judges with each other; and the ratings made by each judge may be compared with the self-ratings made by the subject himself, to see whether in general he can rate himself in agreement with the ratings of others about as well as they can agree with one another regarding him.

When people know each other pretty well and take the job seriously, and the traits are traits which can be objectively observed—things like "punctuality," "timidity," "stinginess," "sense of humor"—we can expect to find that the ratings of independent observers agree well, and have value in practical personnel work in industry or in education. When we go beyond the area of the immediately observable, and get into traits which are hard to observe or easy to disagree about, like "sense of fair play," we must define our terms and train our judges in using the terms. Perhaps even then we shall remain doubtful whether the ratings refer to objective facts; in other words, we are not very sure about their validities.

Sometimes it is possible to get away from self-estimates and the estimates of others regarding *traits,* and to rate people on specific *activities* actually observed. Thus in studying sympathetic behavior in small children, a group of observers rated sixteen different kinds of specific things that children had been observed to do when they saw other children in trouble (such as asking the teacher to help), so that the resulting sympathy *scale* (measuring the total amount of sympathetic behavior shown) was based directly on the observations.[4]

Yet it is always proper, in the case of ratings on questionnaires, to

---

[4] L. B. Murphy, *Social Behavior and Child Personality,* New York, Columbia University Press, 1937.

group a number of items together when they are known to be interrelated, and to measure the broad tendency or trait that runs through them all. We are therefore still measuring the traits of the person; but instead of asking for general impressions, we infer the trait from many concrete observations. It must not be assumed that a mere collection of odds and ends of behavior is important in itself; in such methods we are attempting to get a broad view of the *characteristic kinds of response that hang together and are typical of the person.* It means very little to us if he has a single nervous habit, like blushing occasionally or biting his nails. It means a great deal, however, if we find a number of interrelated behaviors all of which point to self-consciousness, shyness, nervousness, or the like. Practically always, then, from such methods we derive groups or *clusters of interrelated* items which are conceived to measure *specific traits.* If you found, for example, blushing, averting the eyes, high tension, quivering, stammering, hilarious giggling, alternation between reticence and excited shouting, you might possibly conclude that the person is socially shy or insecure, and that some of these attributes are direct, others indirect, expressions of this insecurity. You would therefore be using ratings (or questionnaires) to get a reliable general picture of such traits. You might even go beyond a specific trait like nervousness, or insecurity, or self-sufficiency, or extroversion, and reach a still broader general trait like "adequacy of adjustment."

One obvious difficulty with both questionnaires and ratings is the problem of bias, particularly the bias of the individual with respect to himself; and there is no easy way out of this difficulty. All we can do is to compare different sources of information with one another, and to make the best judgment we can as to where the truth probably lies. For questionnaires we try to provide cross-checks to see if different items scattered through the test give consistent information. If possible, we get corroboration from others who know the respondent well. For rating scales we ordinarily seek information from at least three independent observers, and we hesitate to accept the results unless the intercorrelations are of the order of .7 or better. (The average of the judgments of the three observers probably correlates with reality better than one judgment correlates with another.)

Aside from the question of the authenticity of the data produced by these verbal methods, there are other difficulties which are involved in them. Traits are not like a number of unrelated possessions that an individual carries around—like a quarter in his hip pocket, a match in his vest pocket, socks with red clocks, notebooks and letters in his coat pocket. On the contrary, traits *depend upon one another.* People who have certain traits must inevitably have other traits that are, so to speak, ways in which the first traits are expressed. For example, a man feels insecure, or inferior; even such different traits as bullying, blustering, blushing, may all arise from this insecurity. A person may have half a dozen different ways of expressing some basic trait. From day to day, and from situation to situation, he rings the changes on these half-dozen possibilities. The very fact that he shows one of these forms of response prevents him from showing one of the others at the same time; so if you went into it mechanically without knowing what you were doing, you might conclude that there was actually a *negative* relation between two traits, like blushing and blustering, which actually in many people are related not negatively but positively. We have to be on our guard when we have our measurement stick in hand lest we forget the intimate interrelations between traits which appear under different circumstances.

Yet, even if we take due account of the interrelations of traits, we find that much depends upon what is figure in the total figure-ground pattern. It may be possible to understand the traits pretty well, and even the way in which they hang together, and still not know what is *important* in the individual personality. For these reasons, methods have been developed in which there is an attempt to pick out the kind of attribute that is the core, or center, or root (radix) of the person, and in relation to which the others must be seen. Such traits are said to be *salient*. One easy way of bringing out salient attributes is by a *guess-who* test. We may ask the members of a group (such as a school room):

Who is always showing off?
Who is a real friend to everyone in the group?
Who goes around with a chip on his shoulder?

Despite all the limitations of verbal methods which have been noted, these methods are still widely used and are valuable when used with good clinical judgment. The data are easily secured in large quantity, are inexpensive to analyze, and can be repeated from one group to another so that valid comparisons can be made; finally, they can frequently help the individual to understand himself in comparison with the other individuals who have taken the test. They may therefore be decidedly useful to a person who wishes to gain in self-understanding.

Behavior Tests

We can sometimes frame an experimental situation which may bring out *individual differences in behavior* so that people become directly comparable with one another. Particularly well known and successful are the tests prepared by Hartshorne and May[5] in the Character Education Inquiry. Several hundred boys and girls from the fifth to eighth grades inclusive not only were asked a good many questions about their ideals and attitudes in the matter of honesty, generosity, self-control, and persistence, but were actually put into situations where they had a chance to be honest, generous, self-controlled, or persistent.

In one of the honesty tests, for example, the children had an opportunity to improve their scores by cheating on arithmetic tests, but a means was found by which the cheating could be easily detected. In party games when they had to pin the tail on the donkey, they could peek, and methods were devised to find out when they did so. Their actual generosity was gauged by the degree to which they were willing to give up their ordinary satisfactions, come early to school, and make up material for sick children in the hospital; or the extent to which they would exert themselves for the good of the group rather than solely for their own good as individuals. In all such tests it was possible to show changes between the fifth and the eighth grade that were related to the growing-up process and to the environment in which the child was growing up. The curves reproduced in Figure 76, for example, show the rapid increase in honesty in a group of children with backgrounds where honesty was emphasized by parents and teachers, and the decline in honesty in a group of children from a slum area where no premium was placed upon it.

It is worth while, however, to utter one word of caution regarding the

---

[5] The first of this series is H. Hartshorne and M. A. May, *Studies in Deceit,* New York, Macmillan, 1928.

advantage of these behavior tests over self-ratings and ratings by others. A behavior test may be a very good one, and yet it may cut a narrow slice, so to speak, through the person; it may sample such a small segment of what the total personality is, that its real predictive power may be much less than we would expect. Even an excellent item may fail to give us a broad conception of how the person is likely to function. A single test of *children's readiness to help other children in difficulty*

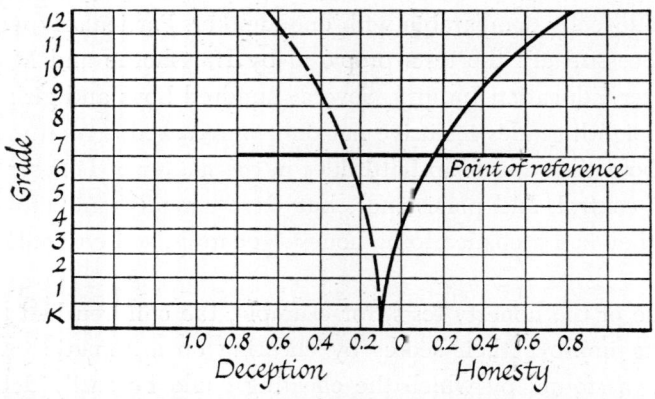

Figure 76. The Growth of Honesty

The growth of honesty in two groups of children, one group (solid line) from a favorable economic background, the other (dashed line) from a poor economic background. Composite honesty scores on a group of tests are scaled on the horizontal axis. With increasing age the group with the favorable background moves in the direction of honesty, the other group in the direction of deception. (Hartshorne, May, and Shuttleworth, *Studies in the Organization of Character*, copyright, 1930, by The Macmillan Company.)

(Figure 77) which brings out striking individual differences may fail to reproduce accurately the broad pattern of helpful and sympathetic behavior shown over a period of weeks. Personality is too complex to permit a trait to reveal itself fully in any one situation.

As to the origin of these broad dispositions we have, as usual, both constitutional and environmental factors to consider. Sometimes a constitutional low threshold for a particular reaction, e.g., for fear, may be clearly playing an important role in slanting an individual toward a particular type of trait, such as insecurity. In general, however, we know more about early experience than we do about heredity, and our emphasis is upon *conditioned responses arising in early experiences*, e.g., the feeling of insecurity and the manner in which these fear reactions have become *generalized*.

It is often a good thing to be able to give both verbal and behavior tests, and even to combine them in the same investigation. An effective combination of the two methods was used during World War II by the

Figure 77. Patterns of Helpfulness in a Behavior Test

In A, the little girl is in the play pen, but the toys she wants are outside. In B, a little boy is too shy to offer any help. In C, she gives "the baby" all the toys. In D, another little boy offers her a doll but guards the auto he himself wants. (From L. B. Murphy, Social Behavior and Child Personality, Columbia University Press, 1937.)

British armed forces and thereafter in the United States by the Office of Strategic Services, which set up some experimental projects for selecting men for difficult and dangerous overseas military assignments. It was not enough to talk to these men and observe them casually in familiar situations. It was necessary to set up a really comprehensive and severe procedure for "screening" them, so that serious mistakes would not be likely to occur. These men, some of them generals, some of them privates, some college students, some businessmen, all appearing in Army all-purpose uniforms and unidentified, lived together for three days in the company of the staff and went through a series of extremely difficult and often grueling experiences in which their personal stamina and imagination were tested. The ability to keep cool, assert leadership, get something done, avoid gross errors, could be tested in a practical way.

In the "stress interview test" the individual was given just twelve minutes to develop a "cover story" to explain why he was going through secret papers at 9:00 P.M. in a government office, and was mercilessly grilled by the staff in the process of showing up his inconsistencies and breaking down his story. In the "brook test" the candidate had to show his capacity to work with others by taking part in the construction of a way of getting across a brook.[6]

You are on a mission in the field, and having come to this brook you are faced with the task of transporting this delicate range-finder, skillfully camouflaged as a log, to the far bank, and of bringing that box of percussion caps, camouflaged as a rock, to this side. In carrying out this assignment, you may make use of any materials you find around here. When the job is done, all of you, as well as any materials you have used, are to be back on this side.

It was possible to observe the clear thinking, the speed, the self-control which were necessary to get the task done according to the plan.

In another test each individual had to put up a wooden structure, using assistants who unknown to him had been trained to misunderstand, mess up directions, etc.

At this the two assistants, who had been working in the barn, were asked to come out and help the candidate. They complied, but waited for him to take the initiative. These two members of the junior staff traditionally assumed the pseudonyms of Kippy and Buster. Whoever played the part of Kippy acted in a passive, sluggish manner. He did nothing at all unless specifically ordered to, but stood around, often getting in the way, either idling with his hands in his pockets or concerned with some insignificant project of his own, such as a minute examination of the small-scale model. Buster, on the other hand, played a different role. He was aggressive, forward in offering impractical suggestions, ready to express dissatisfaction, and quick to criticize what he suspected were the candidate's weakest points.

The two assistants were not permitted, by their secret instructions, to dis-

---

[6] OSS Assessment Staff, *Assessment of Men*, New York, Rinehart, 1948.

obey orders, and they were supposed to carry out whatever directions were given to them explicitly. Within the bounds of this ruling, though, it was their function to present the candidate with as many obstructions and annoyances as possible in ten minutes. As it turned out, they succeeded in frustrating the candidates so thoroughly that the construction was never, in the history of S [one of the screening centers], completed in the allotted time.

The results of this long series of exacting and grueling tests were apparently very successful; as far as the record goes, the men selected by these methods did even better in actual stress tasks overseas than men selected without the benefit of such screening. It may properly be objected that all such behavior tests are rather narrow; they tell what the individual does in a specific situation, but not what he would do in very different situations. This is the same old problem of transfer that we have encountered (page 228). Moreover, when we ask how "valid" these tests are, we come up against cases like the following. One of the men selected for an overseas assignment, operating behind the German lines in France, had been captured and tortured to make him produce military information. He had given none. When found by the Americans he had developed amnesia (impairment of memory) and of course had to be considered a military casualty. One might say that technically the man was a failure for the screening process because ultimately he did not hold together nervously; but he fully achieved the military expectations.

Despite the success achieved by such methods in wartime, we do not feel warranted in putting on so much pressure under peacetime conditions; hence most of our methods with adults have developed at a more leisurely tempo over the years. Almost everywhere we find some attention given to practical behavior tests in the industrial situation. If it is reasonable to expect an applicant for a skilled job to show what he can do with a lathe or in backing a truck around a corner, why is it not reasonable also to bring out something of his personality by putting him through practical behavior tests? With the possibility of such behavior methods before us, it may be surprising to learn that actually these tests have not proved the most useful personality tests. They have their great value. But in general it is very difficult to set up a duplicate of some future situation that has to be met; and even if we succeed, we do not really have a very broad basis for judgments. The OSS testing program had the men under observation for three days and got a great deal of information. It must be remembered that single items are usually of low reliability (see page 380), and it is rare in the industrial or educational situations that we want to know simply what will be done in some rather narrowly specified situation which lends itself to behavior testing in the short time available. More and more, what we want is a broader view of personality as a whole, hoping that in the broad view we may get that kind of overall conception of the person from which specific predictions can always be made as the occasion requires. As suggested above, the tendency is to *combine* the verbal and behavior methods—several of each if time permits. What educators, industrialists, professional men want are people regarding whose *broad dispositions* something valid can be said on the basis of a test that is not too time-consuming (supplemented of course by other information). To meet this purpose, a new way of looking at personality testing has been developed. This new way of thinking has actually developed side by side with, and has been much influenced by, the study of psychiatry and of child psychology, so that these various converging ways of thinking have given us a new kind of personality test, the *projective* tests, to be considered in the next chapter.

SUGGESTED READINGS

Allport, G. W., *Personality,* New York, Holt, 1937, Part 4.
Dollard, J., *Criteria for the Life History,* New Haven, Yale Univ. Press, 1935.
Hunt, J. McV. (ed.), *Personality and the Behavior Disorders,* New York, Ronald, 2 vols., 1944, chaps. 4–6.
Jarvis, L. L., and Ellingson, M., *A Handbook on the Anecdotal Behavior Journal,* Chicago, Univ. of Chicago Press, 1940.
Landis, C., and Ross, W. H., An empirical evaluation of three personality adjustment inventories, *J. educ. Psychol.*, 1935, *26*, 321–330.
Vernon, P. E., Some characteristics of the good judge of personality, *J. soc. Psychol.*, 1933, *4*, 42–57.
Zubin, J., *Quantitative Techniques and Methods in Abnormal Psychology,* New York, Columbia Univ. Bookstore, 1950.

25 PROJECTIVE METHODS

Personality tests which systematically undertake to get at the personality as a whole, rather than at specific traits or specific behavior, are usually called projective tests, because the individual in carrying out a task projects himself into the activity and thus reveals the kind of person he is. The aim, so to speak, is to see the individual all at once; to see the traits and their interrelations; to see the salience and figure-ground organization; to get both at surface indications and at deeper dynamics. As L. K. Frank[1] has phrased it, projective tests reveal the way in which the individual apprehends, understands, takes hold of a task; they reveal his inner or "private world." The "private world" of one individual is unique and different from that of any other individual. At the same time, projective tests aim to reveal the way in which the emotional dispositions of the individual, and his manner of striving with life problems, integrate with his perception, and serve to mold and guide this perception. The basic problem is to see how you perceive because of the fact that you are yourself. (See Figure 78.)

Projection then means much more than it does in Freud's terminology (page 424). It means that the dynamics of perceiving, the dynamics of feeling, and the dynamics of acting, all in their interrelations, should be revealed as we administer such a test. Instead of interesting ourselves in how well or how fast an individual carries out a task assigned—as would be the case with intelligence tests and most other tests—we are interested in the revelation of his personality through the style and form of his work;

---

[1] L. K. Frank, Projective methods for the study of personality, *J. Psychol.*, 1939, 8, 389–413.

through the grace or awkwardness, the steady or jerky quality of his response; through the interests, values, feeling tones which emerge; perhaps above all through the unconscious way in which he mirrors his own attitude toward his body, toward his reputation, toward the people around him. This seems to be a large order; but actually it is the aspira-

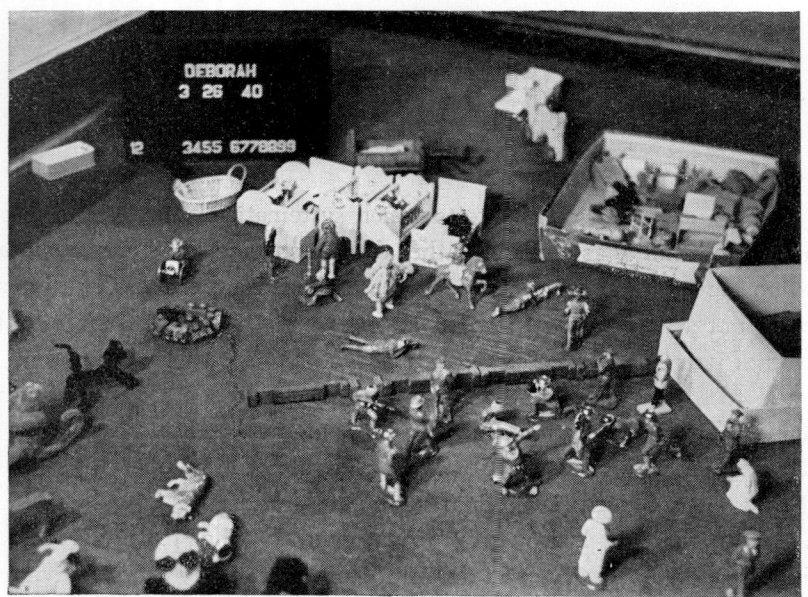

Figure 78. A Child's World Projected in Miniature Toys

This child's play reflects both her hopes and her fears. Understanding that war was coming, she arranged her toys so as to set up a barrier between home activities and the soldiers, but they gradually encroach upon the home area.

tion of every serious projective test to accomplish exactly this. As we shall see, the tests succeed in varying degree, depending upon the complexity of the problems with which they cope and the number of competent people who have taken part in the development of the method.

Projective Tests with Children

Projective tests with children will be described first. Typically, we take the material with which children like to play, and develop a method of using it, without at any time imposing upon the child something uncongenial to him. Children have always played with mud pies, clay, and other plastic materials, and such materials have recently been developed into a feasible laboratory form, of which *finger paints* are a good example. Finger paints are simply flour, water, and coloring matter, prepared in jars and spread out over a large piece of

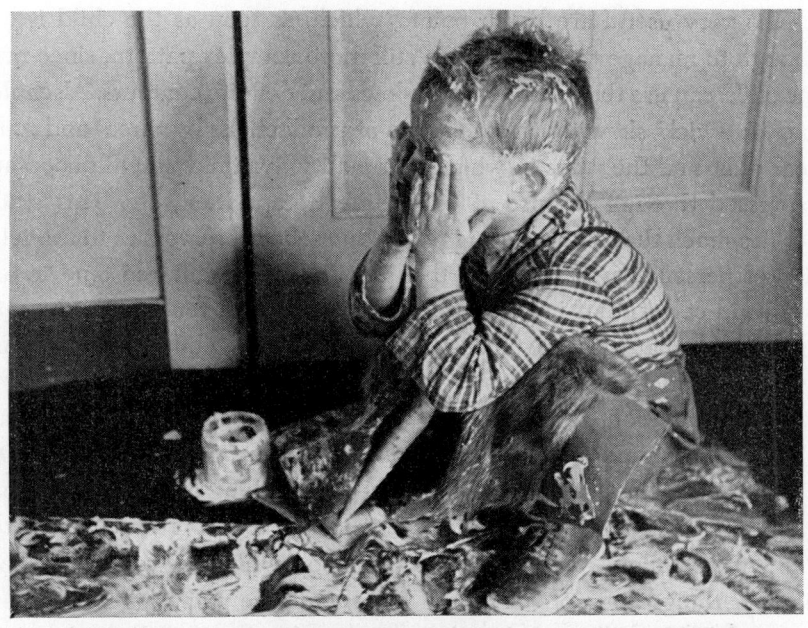

Figure 79. Sensory Toys as Projective Materials

In their play with a jar of cold cream children reveal much about their general approach to life. This little boy said, "I am changing myself into something fancy-like"— behavior in sharp contrast to that of the child who hardly dares touch the cold cream.

paper, so that the child can poke and smear as he likes; they are therefore practical and inexpensive, and very widely used. Children working with finger paints reveal in some measure the sense of expansion or retreat, the delight in vivid color, or in some cases the fear of it, and the smooth or jerky tempo which express the child's confidence or insecurity in relation to the materials or the situation. One gets an excellent opportunity to observe the slap-happy swish-splash manner of the child who loves all rich sensory material, and his freedom from fear or reproach or reproval; one can likewise see the frightened and insecure response of the child who has been ridiculed for being messy and reproved for making trouble for his mother at wash-up time. Such "sensory toys" as cold cream, dough, clay, have similar value; Figure 79 shows to what degree the primitive love of touch qualities and the fun of manipulation may combine with the dramatic fantasy delights of the small child.

Also very useful are brush paints, which, as soon as the child is old enough to manage them, give us a still more complex pattern, since now the child can use the brush to create lines and definite contours. Alschuler and Hattwick[2] show the great variety of productions by three- and four-year-olds, and the ways in which personality dynamics in childhood are expressed through the use of color, line, composition, etc. This study verifies much that had been suggested by earlier observers as to the relation of personality to painting: that gay and lively children tend to use the vivid colors, that insecure and somber children tend to the browns and blacks, that the more changeable and versatile children tend to use a wide variety of color, etc.

Two illustrations are given here of the brush paintings of four-year-old boys in the Sarah Lawrence College Nursery School (Figure 80). The top painting was done by an impulsive outgoing child with no sense of order; the lower one, by a child who has to get everything in *order* and to follow *rules* before he can cope with the world. See how he lines things up in orderly form. In general, the paintings by different types of children are samples of their ways of expressing themselves and there is nothing very mysterious about the fact that when groups of such paintings are shown to audiences, with brief descriptions of the children, most people can quickly tell which child produced which picture.

Much of what can be done with paintings can also be done with drawings. Drawings of a man have been used as measures of intelligence,[3] and such drawings may also serve as an index of a child's *conception of a human being*. Among his free drawings we may see his understanding of male and female, adult and immature, and his attitude

---

[2] R. H. Alschuler and L. W. Hattwick, *Painting and Personality*, Chicago, University of Chicago Press, 2 vols., 1947.
[3] F. L. Goodenough, A new approach to the measurement of the intelligence of young children, *J. genet. Psychol.*, 1926, 33, 185-211.

Figure 80. Brush Paintings by Two Boys

Brush paintings, through which children may express their individuality, are frequently as different as the children themselves.

toward his own person. The productions of gay, shy, graceful, or awkward children are characteristically different; some of the child's deeper feelings about his own body may be portrayed in the way he renders the body in the picture. The way in which for some children the masculine is idealized, the feminine debased, or the way in which adults are made severe and remote and children made warm and natural, may tell us much about how the individual child feels about the people around him. One child draws a strong authority figure, a sort of Lone Ranger or Superman type; another draws a man as something ridiculous, apelike, trivial, something to be hooted at and debunked. We wonder if just possibly the child could have unconsciously been referring us to his father or to some country cousin, or whether the world of the comic strips or of buffoonery in general has for some reason dinned itself especially deeply into his mind. We begin to wonder if we could not use the free or the figure-drawing situation as a way of teasing out some of our deeper feelings about what it means to be a man, to be a woman. Suppose the figure of the man is heroic, firm, confident, while the woman who is drawn next is ridiculous, fussy, a lorgnette-dowager type, or something in the manner of the traditional caricature of the New England schoolmarm, inflated into a position of authority which adds a basic hatred to the ridicule appropriately applied to her. Some clinicians raise a question regarding how male and female figures are represented on the page. Does one look down upon the other? Are they looking at each other? Are they back to back? Does one respond positively to the other? Figure 81 came from a boy whose immediate problems are that he is a runaway and a car stealer. He rationalizes about this drawing of his, saying that the boy is running for a bus to go to work; it seems likely, though, that there is so much *need to run* (from the cops and also from his own difficulties) that it just pushed itself into his first picture.[4] Some picture interpretations involve more complex considerations. Thus one may look for clues to drawings in *psychoanalysis*, with its extensive emphasis upon many symbols, the meaning of which is not consciously grasped by the subject himself; e.g., the fear or guilt associated with certain parts of the body may be unconsciously indicated.

---

[4] K. Machover, *Personality Projection in the Drawing of the Human Figure*, Springfield, Thomas, 1949.

Also very useful are the miniature life toys—the dolls, furniture, animals—in which we may see the gay, vivid creative constructions of children whose imaginative life has been encouraged and who are deeply at home in social relationships. We see the orderly, well-planned structure of the juvenile architect. But we also see frequent examples of rigid, tight constructions of children who know that to be orderly is the only way to avoid mommy's disapproval, and who dare do nothing to warrant a harsh look. There is here also a deeper dimension, a *symbolic interpretation of the world as the child sees it* (cf. pages 398 ff.).

Figure 81. Drawing by a Runaway Boy

(From Karen Machover's *Personality Projection in the Drawing of the Human Figure.* Courtesy of Charles C. Thomas, Publisher, Springfield, Illinois.)

Attitudes toward property and toward making trouble for adults are particularly evident at the nursery-school age. In L. J. Stone's experiments with balloons, for example, when the child is gently urged not only to play with the balloons but to step on them and smash them if he likes, we find the extreme range from those who jump and smash with the greatest of ease to those who throughout the experimental period will touch them only gently, fearing that any injury to property would be very naughty. A little child does not of course think these things out fully; he is simply revealing ingrained patterns which have been built up at home and in the play group, and which appear in the test situation so far as it is similar to the situations he has encountered.

Personality may also be understood by the way in which the individual distorts the material presented to him. Just as he may give you his picture of a man or a woman, or may show in his paintings or his play with miniature life toys a sort of sketch of what the world looks like to him, so his retelling of a story which he hears may reveal his basic ways of understanding and his basic feelings. Consequently storytelling has also been developed as a projective method; in it the child listens to the story and then tells it back so that it can be recorded.

Sometimes these and various other projective methods may all be administered to the same children. We may then compare the different methods, to see to what degree the characteristics attributed to the child on the basis of one test appear also in relation to other tests. We usually find that the data from the different tests agree to a considerable extent. But each method is unique, and independent of the rest; none is a perfect duplicate of the others. No test is a perfect duplicate, either, of any one particular life situation. Nothing in life is a completely valid index of anything else; therefore it would be impossible for any test to predict exactly what would happen in some other situation. The modern interest consequently is not so much in trying to get once and for all an answer to the question, how good is such and such a test? as in finding in what situations, with what individuals, a test is useful; what its practical values and limitations are in educational and clinical experience. From this point of view it is important to find out how close the relation is between various types of test response and various responses to other tests and to "life situations," and to know how to choose and combine a variety of different methods, so that we can cross-check and get wide and clear evidence regarding each attribute that is important in the child, and gain the rich perspective that comes from seeing the child in a great many different situations.

Projective Tests with Adults

While projective techniques have been extensively used with children, there is also a large place for them today in work with adults.

The most widely used of these methods consists of a series of inkblots prepared by the Swiss psychiatrist, Hermann Rorschach.[5] Having observed that the individual's way of perceiving is a revelation of the kind of person he is, Rorschach found that inkblots are an especially good kind of material to bring out wide individual differences in habits of perceiving. After much experimentation, he developed a series of ten

---

[5] H. Rorschach, *Psychodiagnostics* (Eng. trans., New York, Grune and Stratton, 1941).

inkblots, some in black and white, some also utilizing color, to be presented in a given order. The subject is asked to tell what he sees in each of these cards. Over a number of years Rorschach gathered the responses of hundreds of normal and hundreds of mentally disturbed individuals to these cards, and developed ways of scoring the responses so that they could be compared, person for person.

A simple type of inkblots is shown in Figure 82. Clinicians, however, are generally agreed that it is inappropriate at present to reproduce the original Rorschach inkblots, since the more widely known the actual blots are, the more they are spoiled for clinical use. You will therefore understand if somewhat similar blots are used for the present purpose. What do you see in them?

The responses are scored in three columns. The first column takes note of whether the individual responds to the whole blot, or to its large details, or to its small details, or to the white spaces within the blot. If he gives a response which shows that he is seeing the card as a whole, a W is entered in the first column. A large detail like "hand" is recorded with a capital D; a small detail with a small d. (We are overlooking several finer distinctions that can be made.) If he responds to the white spaces within the main outline, thus reversing figure and ground, an S is entered in the column. Each response, then, will be either W, D, d, or S.

In the second column we score all the responses that are the same with respect to certain attributes. We ask ourselves whether it was the *form* of the thing seen, or its *color*, which determined the response, or whether it was some combination of the two, etc. If, for example, the reaction to the first blot is "spider," it is clear that it was form which led to this way of seeing it, and we enter it as F. If, however, the emphasis is upon the color of the blot, as when the object is called "blood" or "fire," we enter the response as C. If the response is determined primarily by form and secondarily by color we enter the response as FC, form-color; if the color is more important than the form, we enter it as color-form, or CF. We must also make a place for the subject's response to *shading*, e.g., in perceiving rough or smooth surfaces and texture effects, or in the sense of a vista that comes from seeing the light shading and the dark shading as being at different distances from the observer. Another very important kind of response can be made; the subject may interpret the people (or

Figure 82. Inkblots as Projective Materials

The ambiguity of inkblots such as these three permits different people to see different things in them. By analyzing what is seen, the skilled interpreter can learn a great deal about the personality of the perceiver.

animals or objects) in the cards as *carrying out movement*. If the movement is one that he himself or other human beings can make, e.g., if he sees running, or dancing, or leaping figures, such responses are scored *M*. Flapping the wings or lashing the tail, characteristic of animals but not of human beings, is scored in a different fashion. Still other methods of scoring are used for the movement of inanimate things, such as flames or water.

While the second column has to do with the dynamics of perceiving in terms of *form, color, shading,* and *movement,* the third column takes note of sheer content—simply what is seen, not the manner of its perception. If the person sees animal forms, we score them *A*, and animal details *Ad*; he may see human forms, *H*, or human details, *Hd*, or elements from his knowledge of botany, geology, anatomy, or other areas of special interest.

In scoring any Rorschach test, all three columns must be fully considered, the first having to do with location, the second with determinants, the third with content. We now proceed to count up the total number of wholes, details, small details, spaces, in the first column; in the same way the number of forms, the number of colors, etc., in the second column; the number of animals, animal details, etc., in the third column. It is clear, then, that the Rorschach test is in the first instance a quantitative test; this is not true of finger painting or miniature life toys. It involves counting up how many of each kind of response there are in the total number of responses given by the subject. Typically, an adult subject will take from fifteen or twenty up to forty or fifty minutes in responding, and is likely to give somewhere between 10 and 60 responses.

We are interested in the relative frequency of the different kinds of responses. If column 2, for example, has a great many human movements and few responses utilizing color, or if column 1 has a great many whole and column 2 only a few human movements, we can make up ratios like ratio of M to C, or of W to M, upon which a particular interpretation can be based in the light of extensive clinical experience. We know, for example, that heavy emphasis upon color at the expense of human movement tends to mean an outward turning or emotional impulsiveness in relation to the environment, whereas a preponderance of movement over color usually means a rich inner imaginative life and a relative disregard of the emotional appeals of the social environment. The terms *extratensive* and *introversive* are used to describe these two tendencies respectively; they are similar to, but not identical with, Jung's extroversion and introversion (pages 430 ff.).

We now have to take two steps: first, show the fundamental logic that underlies the construction of the test, and second, show the degree of its practical utility. As regards the theory, this is not actually very complex, nor is it very far from the basic theory to which clinical students of human personality have been led by other routes. The theory is clear-cut, well proportioned, and reasonable. If you yourself settled down to the task of deciding what kinds of people would be likely to give what kinds of responses, it is likely that you would reason out rather well a large proportion of the realities which are actually there in the test. You would expect that people with an overwhelming demand in daily life to get things as a whole, people unwilling to look at them in detail, would respond to the Rorschach by giving more wholes than details, and so on. You would be pretty sure to come to the conclusion that consistent and constant emphasis upon sharp clear form is more of an intellectualized response than is the response to color, and that the response to color at the expense of form is likely to mean emotionality. As far as content is concerned, you would expect people who are quite different from the usual run of people to give a great many "original" responses, responses which are usually given by very few persons. You would expect banal and unimaginative people to give strings of animal details like hoofs or claws, etc., and not go far from this level into the region of the highly imaginative or creative. For the most part the principles thought out by Rorschach are based on more experience and deeper perception than the best of us ordinarily achieve. And for the most part they have been rather well validated. It is for this reason that we can obtain in a relatively short time a fairly good general diagnostic picture of the individual.

The second step involves the kinds of evidence there are regarding the actual success of the test. Sometimes the Rorschach test has been asked to meet the very severe requirement of predicting what kind of person a man or a woman will prove to be in life situations when there is no evidence whatever but the responses to the inkblots. The classical case here, the "posthumous case" (Rorschach died just before this case was published), concerns a very anxious "compulsive" man who felt a deep need to be *right* and was unable to face his own emotions, and whom Rorschach, just before his own death, described rather fully on the basis of inkblot responses alone.

This finding does *not* mean that everyone can achieve this kind of success in every case. In fact it is doubtful whether there is much meaning in asking, "How good is the Rorschach?" The real question is how good it is, with certain people doing the interpretation and working with particular kinds of human material. We can say in general that when working with clinical cases (most maladjusted people), experienced Rorschach workers can sufficiently surpass what can be achieved by other quick methods to warrant their being put on the staffs of clinics and hospitals and being widely used in private practice. Unfortunately a more exact statement of how good the test is cannot be made at this time.

There is another way of using the Rorschach which demands just as much of it, and this is its use as a *group* test. What can you do with a Rorschach to predict how well a group of freshman students will do with their college work and how well they will adjust to campus life? The work of Munroe[6] at Sarah Lawrence College indicates that by the use of the sheer *number* of trouble signs one can predict college adjustment to some degree from the Rorschach alone, when administered the week of entering college, and that except for intellectually very brilliant girls, the Rorschach is even better than an intelligence test in predicting the kind of academic work they will do at this particular college. It is not at present possible to generalize beyond the specific college concerned in this investigation.

A third sort of demand which may be made of the Rorschach test is for the expert to make a completely blind diagnosis of a cultural group to whom the test has been administered; that is, to tell, when supplied only with the responses to the test, what kind of human group, living

---

[6] R. L. Munroe, Prediction of the adjustment and academic performance of college students by a modification of the Rorschach method, *Appl. Psychol. Monogr.*, 1945, No. 7.

under what kind of cultural conditions, must have seen the blots in this particular way and made these particular responses. An exemplification of what can be done in this case is the work of Emil Oberholzer, on the basis of materials supplied him by Cora DuBois[7] from the people of the island of Alor in the East Indies. Oberholzer's description, based on such things as the predominance of *CF* over *FC*, emphasized the chaotic impulsive personality pattern which prevailed, and in this and many other respects was curiously close to the real situation as described by the ethnologist.

It would be absurd at this time to make extravagant claims about the Rorschach as revealing "the whole personality." No single Rorschach interpretation or even a series of them tells the whole story of the person's assets, liabilities, and deeper attitudes. It is, however, well worth while to gather material of this sort, and in everyday psychiatric practice as well as in many educational situations the test has proved to be well worth the time it requires. Although it takes only a few weeks to learn the elementary rules about scoring in the three columns, it takes years of training and clinical experience to learn how to see the interrelations between all the responses to all the cards, and make a mature interpretation.

The training comes, in fact, largely in learning to see responses in their interrelations. Thus the principles of Gestalt psychology relating to structure (page 143) are exemplified to a very high degree in the Rorschach test. Though commonplaceness of mind, for example, may be suggested by an excessive number of animals and animal details, such responses take on a very different meaning in the context of a performance containing many clear, sharply perceived forms, yet having a place also for a considerable number of human movement responses. The individual giving these animal responses may be a person with a well-trained and integrative mind who has studied animals as a naturalist and is preoccupied with them. Every response must be perceived in relation to the entire pattern of the subject's responses. Moreover, everything that the subject says and the way in which he says it, his tempo, his mode of attack, his indications of interest, give the experienced examiner a

---

[7] C. DuBois, *The People of Alor,* Minneapolis, University of Minnesota Press, 1944.

sense of the personality of the individual. While it is true that highly useful results can often be obtained by inspecting the scores alone, as already suggested (page 467), still the Rorschach test, individually administered in connection with psychiatric practice, is on a completely different level. It is frankly concerned with clinical synthesis or intuition of a sort which does not yet meet all our customary scientific requirements, yet remains a powerful tool in mature hands.

Picture Tests

The best projective tests give shorthand views of personality in action. One of the serious defects of the Rorschach is that it does not tell us concretely very much about the *content* of the individual's mind, the things with which he is preoccupied or the directions in which his fancy tends to move. The content of the mind as revealed in the third column is, as we saw, one aspect of Rorschach work, but it is a relatively small aspect, and one upon which it is important to get much fuller information. In view of our great need to know more about the characteristic thoughts and fantasies of the individual, it has been convenient to use photographs, drawings, and paintings which portray human beings in a variety of situations, and ask the respondent to "make up a story" to explain what he sees and to predict what would be likely to happen in such a situation. (See Figure 83.)

Best known of all such devices are the cards made up by Morgan and Murray, already considered in Chapter 16 (pages 276 ff.). The test method used by them assumes that the individual has certain recurring *needs,* and also that the environment *presses* upon him in particular ways that will be manifest in the way in which he interprets the picture shown. The assumed needs include the following: the need for aggression, for acquisition, for achievement, for dominance, for deference, for recognition, for order, for play, for sex, for autonomy, for seclusion. When the individual is under the influence of one or more of these needs and the environment presses upon him in such a way as to limit or give direction to his possible satisfaction of these needs, the story he makes up as he looks at a picture will characteristically express this need-press situation. This is the Thematic Apperception Test, or TAT.

In a sense, responses to the TAT do give an objective picture of the recurrent preoccupations of the subject. Fantasy material as revealed in the TAT agrees to a considerable extent with other fantasy material such as daydreams and dreams during the night (pages 281 ff.). The "validation" of the TAT lies, however, in its relation to general clinical descriptions, and in its capacity to predict, after a relatively short test time,

Figure 83. Picture Test

Pictures like this one can be used for the same purposes as those in the Thematic Apperception Test, individual subjects being asked to tell a story about each of a series of such pictures. Their interpretations will differ widely. Such stories often express personal needs and feelings that cannot be discovered by more direct approaches.

the types of personality imbalance which will appear in a period of psychiatric observation in a clinic or hospital.

Picture tests of various other sorts have been used in a more delimited way to gauge and assess specific dynamic tendencies. In the Picture-Frustration Test of Rosenzweig (Figure 18, page 124), the aim is to assess the relative strengths of the tendencies to respond to frustrations in one way or another. When frustrated a person may either attack the

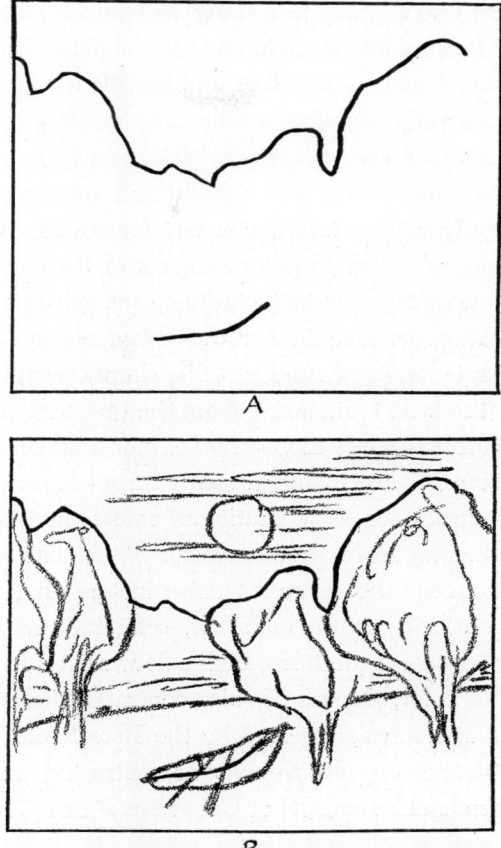

Figure 84. "Complete the Drawing" Test

A lover of woodland scenes and canoes, when presented with the outline in A, drew B—"A canoe lying idle near a riverbank waiting for the owner to go paddling." (Outline from E. F. Hellersberg, in *Amer. J. Orthopsychiat.*, 1945, 15, 690.)

source of his distress or turn his aggression inward upon himself or sidestep the situation and attack no one. These responses are called respectively *extrapunitive, intropunitive,* and *impunitive.* In the twenty-four pictures in the test there is abundant opportunity to pile up a considerable score along one or another of these three lines; and as we have already noted (page 430), we find important functional relations between these ways of handling responses to frustration and various other dimensions of personality.

Another interesting picture test starts with *incomplete* pictures and asks the subject to complete them in any way he likes.[8] This is something like the Thematic Apperception Test, but it calls for a *motor* response, not simply a description of what is seen. The results are interpreted in terms of *needs* and *fantasies* (cf. pages 469 ff., and Figure 84).

Something was said above about children's painting. Progress has been made recently with painting as a test for adults. Waehner[9] asked each of 55 women students to paint subjects of their own choice, and then a series of assigned subjects, including a self-portrait without a mirror. Each woman proceeded in her own way, chose her own brush, paints, size of paper, angle of easel, etc. She simply went to work, throwing herself into the task. Quite aside from the question of *what* is being painted, it is possible to study the *method* of painting. Under the heading of "factors of control" are included small form elements, presence of many curves or curved forms, separation of colors one from another, use of pale and dark color scale, preference for black. The antithesis of all this is what Waehner calls the extratensive factors (page 466), such as neglect of margin, large form elements, scattered, wide distribution, sharp edges, smearing, vague form, high color variety. In many of these —the selection of color, the use of color contrasts, the smeared or neat edges—we note attributes suggested by the Rorschach. There may be, for example, a strong response to *color* as contrasted with the concern for *form* (in Rorschach's terms, C or CF versus F or FC) and a contrast between whole and detail emphasis (W versus D). There is, however, a good deal here that is not found in the Rorschach; for example, the fact that one is creating something new means that one has a very wide choice among colors. Very similar to drawing and painting, in some cases, is the use of clay and of blocks to represent the world as one sees it—or, even more deeply, as one feels it.

Handwriting

The oldest of all projective methods is graphology, or handwriting analysis. Unfortunately, despite its long history and the

---

[8] E. F. Hellersberg, The Horn-Hellersberg test and adjustment to reality, *Amer. J. Orthopsychiat.*, 1945, *15*, 690–710.

[9] T. S. Waehner, Interpretation of spontaneous drawings and paintings, *Genet. Psychol. Monogr.*, 1946, *33*, 3–70.

many intriguing methods which have been developed, there is much conflict among graphologists regarding basic principles, and until recently there has been relatively little systematic scientific work showing what actually can be done. Even when particular groups and problems are well defined, it is still possible to argue as to how much or how little may be concluded from handwriting. Very little published information has been available until recently to indicate to what extent one can actually identify people with various personality tendencies by handwriting alone. In general, the best graphologists agree that there is grave danger in attaching too much attention to separate items considered piecemeal, such as the width of margin, the length of the t-bar, the angle of slant, and that it is important to study the handwriting pattern as a whole and then consider each specific detail in relation to the dynamic structure. Hence validation must be in terms of total interpretation, not in terms of the validity of the many different items considered separately. Enough has been done to indicate that successful matching of personality descriptions against handwriting patterns as a whole can be carried out to a degree not attributable to chance, and that professional graphologists vary greatly in success, although doing much better than novices. In Powers' large study at Dartmouth,[10] professional graphologists all did better than could be expected by chance guessing, but some did *very* much better than others. But graphologists have not as yet supplied us with a method which can be objectively used in successful prediction, as for example has been done with the Rorschach (page 467).

The Interpretation of Projective Methods

There are literally dozens of interesting projective methods on the scene today, each offering something worth while, but requiring the support of a great deal of careful research work before we can be sure where its usefulness lies. This means that the mature clinician will hesitate to draw confident conclusions from a single test.

Can several different projective tests be used to supplement one another? Yes, decidedly. We would expect that since all such tests seek evidence regarding personality as a whole, the projective methods would

---

[10] See G. W. Allport and P. E. Vernon, *Studies in Expressive Movement*, New York, Macmillan, 1933.

agree in a general way with one another, yet would not agree perfectly. Though we shall expect to find them saying more or less the same sort of thing about each person, different aspects of personality may sometimes be revealed by different methods.

With these ideas in mind, it occurred to three investigators[11] to pool their resources in administering projective tests to a large number of college students for whom a large amount of life-history and personality material, in and out of the academic situation, was available. From each one Rorschach responses, handwriting samples, and free paintings were obtained. The Rorschach expert, the handwriting expert, and the painting expert made independent analyses of the data resulting from their own personality methods.

The degree of their success was measured by the following method. The students were sorted at random into groups of four. Within each group of four, the task of each investigator was to match the projective responses with the character sketch. It was Munroe's job, for example, to tell which of the Rorschach records came from each of the four girls whose life sketches had been supplied her She had one chance in four of getting a given one right. In the long run a sheer guess will give one correct judgment in four.[12] Actually about 80 percent of the Rorschach identifications were correct, and the scores from the graphology and the free painting were nearly as good. Each of the methods taken separately agreed pretty well with the facts and pretty well with each of the other two methods. At some points the three methods agreed in some respects, although they did not agree with the life history. Each of the methods failed at specific points, yet in general they supplemented one another. Just as one can get a better view of a landscape by looking at it from different hilltops, so the view of a person one gets by combining several methods is better than that given by a single method. Indeed, for the mature clinician who wants to secure a broad view of an individual's personality so as to be really helpful to him the thing to do is to use these methods to supplement the life history. He can thus, for example, begin

---

[11] R. L. Munroe, T. S. Lewinson, and T. S. Wæhner, A comparison of three projective methods, *Character & Pers.*, 1944, *13*, 1–21.

[12] Of course, if she got three right, the fourth would have to be right, etc.; but if she got three wrong, the fourth would have to be wrong. In the long run the statistical chance of guessing right is one in four.

to ask questions about the person's difficulties and the direction in which he needs to be helped to grow.

The case of Pauline Butterworth shows how projective methods integrate with the life history and with observation of everyday behavior. Pauline is the darling of a very proper mother who wants her daughter to be a little lady, an "English story-book princess." At seven Pauline, immaculate and daintily dressed, walks with a mincing pace, speaks Boston English with textbook propriety. At lunch time she picks up her lettuce delicately and smiles as the other "sevens" discuss "bad manners" and give vivid demonstrations of the differences between "bad manners" and "very bad manners." On her Rorschach test she is very hesitant. "I would not have any idea about this one. . . . This is not a splash exactly. It is more of a blotch. . . ." She thaws out enough to call Card 5 a butterfly, sees a child, lapses back into inability to see anything definite, and sees a garden and flowers in the last card. The Rorschach analyst notes that Pauline is an "unchildlike child," writes that she is docile, coöperative, seeking praise and recognition, and believes that her development is being retarded by her desire to win approval through compliance. With the miniature life toys she is careful to make a realistic matter-of-fact arrangement, then carries the various members of the family through a day's routine in proper stereotyped fashion. But when night falls, the wild animals are in the woods, "jumping around." She goes back again to a routine day with the people; and again when the people are asleep "the animals jump around again in the woods." Even in this very proper little girl the need to bounce and jump crops out; she uses the animals as embodiments of a kind of life that is not permitted to proper little girls. It is evident that her quietness is a way of "being good." In the interview, when asked, "What do you like to play?" she says: "Quiet things. Not noisy games. But if a game teacher comes and likes to play noisy games then I like it, so I play for the whole playground time and I think it is only five minutes because it is so much fun."[13]

The case history alone tells us, so to speak, the things the individual has actually done. There may, however, be potentialities within him that have never as yet been realized but which may be suggested by the

---

[13] G. Murphy, L. B. Murphy, and T. M. Newcomb, *Experimental Social Psychology*, New York, Harper, rev. ed., 1937, pp. 289–297.

projective tests. Projective tests, then, if maturely used, may enable us to see the areas within which the personality may effectively develop.

There is a great temptation to set up a sharp contrast between verbal tests and projective tests; but since we do a good deal of our "projecting" in words, this is unwarranted. In fact, several good projective tests are wholly verbal. A particularly good example of what can be done with a well-planned verbal test is Alex Sheriff's "intuition questionnaire."[14] A group of women students in clinical psychology were asked to make up sentences to explain *why* a given hypothetical person showed each of the kinds of behavior indicated in the following items:

1. B. is always wanting to do something she has never done before.
2. X. feels upset if she hears that people are criticizing her or blaming her.
3. Z. often acts contrary to custom, or to the wishes of her parents.
4. R. said to her brother, "I hope you never marry."
5. J. sometimes puts almost too much time and effort into neatness.
6. W. never seems to stop and let herself think.
7. P. is easily influenced by her friends; lets herself be led.
8. E. is a girl who enjoys a good hot argument.
9. T., a twenty-year-old girl, turned down an invitation to a party in order to study for an examination to be held in a week.
10. This girl said, "I give myself utterly to the happiness of someone I love."

On the assumption that each individual, in explaining these behaviors, says something about *herself*, clinical psychologists were given the following directions for scoring the "intuition questionnaire":

Read each item carefully and score for presence of strain in the areas of self, family, and social. In any item, strain may be indicated for one, two, or three of these areas; score for each area indicated. Do not score one area more than once in any item.

Self: Content of response states or implies tension, strain, conflict, or insecurity in regard to the self of the subject of the item, or in regard to the life of the subject; for example, in re size, sex, physical makeup, abilities, disposition, past or present misdemeanors (guilt), "boring existence," "unsatisfying life," worry, anxiety, etc. *Example:* For item 1, the response: "B. has failed at everything she has tried so far, and looks for something at which she can succeed." . . .

---

[14] A. Sherriff, The "Intuition Questionnaire": a new projective test, *J. abnorm. soc. Psychol.*, 1948, *43*, 326–337.

Family: Where response indicates in regard to parents or sibs tension, hostility, ambivalence, strain, dependence which brings on concomitant insecurity, suppression by parents, friction between parents or sibs: it should be scored as "tension family." *Example:* For item 1, the response: "B's family have always held her down." . . .

Social: Tension, or lack of confidence in social techniques, social relationships, social approval, number of friends, mobility, probable success in marriage, friction with outside individuals or group, fear of "robbers," "rape," etc., are scored "tension social." *Example:* For item 1, the response: "B. has never had a date with a boy, and keeps thinking of the good times she would like to have." . . .

The students also wrote *autobiographies,* and evidences of tension in the areas of *self, family,* and *social life* were rated on these scales:

Rating Scales of Tension Areas: Self, Family, Social, and Combined Area

Self: [Adjustment to size, sex, physical makeup, abilities, disposition, past or present misdemeanors (guilt), "boring existence and unsatisfying life," worry, anxiety, etc.]
  1. *Extreme in tension in regard to self;* extreme lack of confidence, excessive in self-depreciation and unfavorable comparison—or compensatory and marked braggadocio. Perhaps intense guilt feelings, or feelings of inadequacy.
  2. *Marked unacceptance* of one or two items of makeup, but not as extreme as 1. (If to point of dominating whole personality, classify under 1.) May have many mild points of discomfort.
  3. *Lacks confidence in some particulars,* but for the most part is unselfconscious—or unaware—of assets or liabilities. Occasional tension or conflict about self, but not enough to be considered as characteristic.
  4. *Without much tension;* this person recognizes handicaps but accepts them realistically; or unaware, and not bothered. Little evidence for compensatory behavior to be found.
  5. *Full confidence;* accepts limitations and assets easily.

There was good agreement between raters of the questionnaire material, and also between raters of the autobiographies ("criterion"), as Table 9 shows. There was also rather good agreement between the two sets of ratings (questionnaire and autobiography), as Table 10 shows.

Such a study indicates the present effort to measure what the life history has to say, and to show how, and to what extent, projective methods can reveal the same themes, with a simple uniform method. But each method gives something that no other method can give; the heart of the

TABLE 9. Findings on Reliability (Correlations)

Questionnaire	Self	Family	Social	Combined Area
Rater A vs. Rater B	.90	.96	.73	.89
Rater A vs. Rater C	.73	.87	.60	.73
Rater A vs. Rater A	.93	.93	.73	.80
Test-retest (9 mos.) (Rater A vs. Rater A)	.76	.76	.76	.75
Criterion				
Rater A vs. Rater B	.64	.71	.49	.77

TABLE 10. Validity of the Questionnaire for Tensions

Tension	Correlation
Self	.76
Family	.57
Social	.71
Combined area	.71

Five minutes after the first questionnaires had been collected, the subjects were given fresh copies and were told that they were now to attempt in every way to disguise themselves in their responses to the items. In addition, they were asked to make their disguises plausible, so that the person who did the scoring would not be aware of their intent to distort the picture of themselves. This latter condition was imposed because it was felt that some subjects might otherwise leave items unanswered.

The correlations between the scores on the first and second responses to the questionnaire were: *Tension Self* = .62, *Tension Family* = .88, and *Tension Social* = .68.

problem of personality study is the integration of data from many sources.

SUGGESTED READINGS

Alshuler, R. H., and Hattwick, L. W., *Painting and Personality*, Chicago, Univ. of Chicago Press, 2 vols., 1947.

Klopfer, B., and Kelley, D. M., *The Rorschach Technique*, Yonkers, World Book, 1942.

Lerner, E., and Murphy, L. B. (eds.), Methods for the study of personality in young children, *Monogr. Soc. Res. Child Developm.*, 1941, 6, No. 4.

Machover, K., *Personality Projection in the Drawing of the Human Figure*, Springfield, Thomas, 1949.

Rapaport, D., *Diagnostic Psychological Testing*, Chicago, Year Book, 2 vols., 1945.
Tompkins, S., *The T.A.T.*, New York, Grune and Stratton, 1947.
White, R. W., Interpretation of Imaginative Productions, in Hunt, J. McV. (ed.), *Personality and the Behavior Disorders*, New York, Ronald, 2 vols., 1944, chap. 6.

26 SOCIAL ATTITUDES AND THEIR TESTING

When you see a salesman waiting in the outer room, his muscles taut from head to foot, his fingers strumming, his jaw locked tight, his eyes snapping, you know both that the deal is important and that straight-shooting methods are going to be used. When you see a student sprawling listlessly on the couch a half-hour before an exam, you know something about the way the examination looks to him. In other words, bodily posture tells you something about attitude. Almost any part of the body has something to say. When you meet a stranger with whom you want to strike it off well, you look closely to see what is written in his eyes and mouth, indicating his readiness for a smile or perhaps only for cold formality. Attitude in the first instance is the way in which the body is set or made ready for an oncoming situation. The psychology of attitude begins with the psychology of set, the readiness to move in one direction or another. And since personality is likewise in large measure a matter of readiness to move in one way rather than another, we need to explore the relations between attitude and personality. (See Figure 85.)

We noted earlier, however (page 68), that set or readiness to respond is not solely dependent upon muscular arrangements, but may consist of deeper inner readiness involving the autonomic system, and indeed the brain. In a good many cases one can alter the brain situation itself in such a way as to alter the set toward a task. We might glance back for a moment at the studies of perception and recall, in which the concept of set was used (pages 169 ff.), noting that set determines what a situation

SOCIAL ATTITUDES AND THEIR TESTING 481

Figure 85. Posture and Attitude

This man's posture as well as his facial expression reflects dejection, disappointment, apathy. Such attitudes, perhaps of long standing in this case, have found bodily expression which makes them clearly recognizable.

means for us. In the same way the processes of judgment and feeling move in one direction or another depending upon the readiness of inner mechanisms or action tendencies (page 298). At the drop of a hat you may approve or disapprove the suggestion made by your friend or your competitor; set is so strong that you forget to think it out. Your attitude (or set) is one of approval in one case, disapproval in the other. This is evidence that attitude is simply *one kind of set,* namely, set toward people or toward social situations. You would probably not speak of attitudes toward a nonsense syllable which make it easier or harder to learn it; here the word "set" would be sufficient. But if a man's set toward people or social situations—e.g., toward Russians or Communism—influences what he reads, hears, and remembers concerning world affairs, we would speak of *attitude.*

The psychology of attitudes is an area in which a great deal of research has been done in recent years, with emphasis upon attitudes toward other persons in home and community, and toward social groups and social issues such as race relations, labor relations, international relations. Typically we administer in an attitude test a set of questions like the following, asking our subjects to indicate agreement or disagreement or uncertainty:

After each question, indicate your attitude by drawing a circle around YES or DOUBTFUL or NO.

1. Should eighteen-year-olds have the vote?
   YES   DOUBTFUL   NO

2. Should Alaska be admitted to the Union as a State?
   YES   DOUBTFUL   NO

3. Do you favor a Constitutional amendment regulating child labor?
   YES   DOUBTFUL   NO

4. Do you consider the United Nations a help toward world peace?
   YES   DOUBTFUL   NO

Or we may use a five-point scale with attitudes ranging from "strongly approve" to "strongly disapprove":

1. We should make another attempt to get the Soviet Union to agree to the UN plan for atomic energy control.
   Strongly approve   Approve   Undecided   Disapprove   Strongly disapprove

2. Medical and dental care should be provided for all by means of federal taxation.
   Strongly approve   Approve   Undecided   Disapprove   Strongly disapprove

The following are typical items from a schedule of attitudes of whites toward Negroes:

Should white and Negro children have identical educational opportunities?
Is it desirable to have separate colleges for Negroes and whites?
Should all jobs be open to whites and Negroes without discrimination?
Are there any circumstances in which lynching can be justified?

In the following scale the questions all relate to the distribution of wealth:

Does the heavy taxation of the rich destroy our traditional American freedom?
Should the wealthy pay steeply graded income taxes?
Should every worker be guaranteed a minimum wage below which his income cannot sink?
Is extreme poverty always sufficient justification for a workers' strike?

When a series of questions all relate to the same general issue, like the United Nations, or the place of women in the professions, or the status of the Negro, we develop them into a *scale*—an interrelated set of items, without too much duplication and with an attempt to cover all the main points that are socially vital in relation to the issue.

These methods follow in general the plan described earlier for the investigation of personality by means of questionnaires and ratings. The dimension of personality with which we are working here is general attitude toward a particular group of people or a particular social institution; consequently the questions should hang together to some degree, and we would not expect a person's answer to one question to be utterly unrelated to his answers to the others. Attitude schedules of this sort, therefore, reveal high *reliability* in the sense that any batch of items from such a scale predicts fairly well the responses to another batch of items from the same scale. Of course reactions cannot be *perfectly* predicted item for item; but if a person is in general strongly favorable to the Negro as shown in items 1, 3, 5, and 7, you can be pretty sure that on items 2, 4, 6, and 8, a similar high degree of favorableness will be shown. The kind of reliability referred to is a matter of internal consistency. The commonest method of studying such reliability is simply to correlate the sum of the answers to the odd-numbered items and the sum of the answers to the even-numbered items.

Another way of stating this fact, that the items hang together, is to say that attitudes are *generalized*. An example which shows in a rather surprising way how broadly one's social attitudes may be generalized appears in the *social distance test* devised by Bogardus. This is a method of telling how close you feel yourself to be socially to a group of people, or how far from them you feel yourself to be. Take a group of nationalities and arrange them alphabetically along the left column of the page: Armenians, Belgians, Canadians, Danes, Finns, and so on. At the top of the page, put a series of steps indicating the degree of closeness of these individuals to yourself. To admit them to close kinship by marriage is obviously to accept them in a closer relationship than merely to admit them as member of your club, which again is closer than admitting them to membership in your community. This in turn is closer than admitting them to citizenship in your country. When you have twenty or more nationality groups thus indicated, you find that the *total degree* of acceptance shown toward *any ten* of them gives an almost perfect prediction as to the *total degree* of acceptance which will be felt toward the *remaining* ten nationality groups. This means that if you drew out of a hat the names of ten nationality groups—let us say Armenians, Finns, Greeks, Hungarians, Portuguese, and so on—and then had to predict the total degree of closeness or remoteness which would be shown toward Filipinos, Lithuanians, Norwegians, Turks, and so on, you would find a correlation of .95 or .96. Hence, attitude is *not* simply an isolated item of response; it represents typically a broad disposition which has transferred or generalized in the same sense in which other conditioned responses generalize. The disposition in this case is the disposition toward acceptance of "out-groups" or groups other than one's own.[1]

Social attitudes are in general pretty stable when you administer an attitude test a second time, say a month after the first test. Most people do not remember what they said before, and their reactions to individual items may change one way or another; but unless a powerful new factor comes in suddenly to produce a change, the general disposition as shown in the total score now and a month later indicates high stability. Attitude, then, is both *generalized* and *stable* at the adult level.

---

[1] E. L. Hartley, *Problems in Prejudice*, New York, King's Crown Press, 1946.

In turn, attitudes toward current controversial issues such as race relations or labor relations or political liberalism tend to be interlocked to some degree; those who favor basic change in some social institutions tend in the long run to favor change in others.[2] In view of this factor, it is proper to speak of a *generalized* tendency toward radicalism or toward conservatism if we define this term as degree of readiness or unreadiness to favor a thoroughgoing change in the social order. This does not mean that everyone is strongly radical or strongly conservative; it means that in general the position which people take on one set of issues is in some measure representative of their attitudes on other issues. But this general factor must be very generously supplemented by *specific* factors, varying from one social issue to another (cf. page 359). To be really effective in predicting social and political attitudes, one needs to know both the *general* disposition (e.g., slightly radical or very conservative, etc.) and the pattern of *specific* attitudes on economic, radical, etc., issues.

There is no need, of course, to rely solely upon purely verbal methods for the study of attitudes. There are picture methods such as those shown here (Figure 86), which agree pretty well with purely verbal methods. Attitudes of white boys toward Negroes were tested all the way from the kindergarten to the eighth grade by a series of picture tests.[3] In the rank test the child chose from a set of mixed white and colored faces the ones he liked best; prejudice was measured by the tendency to put all the Negro choices at the end. In the "show me" test the child was asked to point to faces in response to the question, "Show me all those you'd like to take home to lunch, etc." The child free of prejudice would be governed by variation from face to face, not *solely* by skin color. In the social situations test, a series of pictures (two are shown in Figure 86) is presented and the boy is asked to indicate wherever he would like to "join in and do what they are doing." In every case an all-white picture is compared with one which contains one or more Negro boys. Prejudice is measured by the number of cases in which the activity is accepted if

---

[2] G. Murphy and R. Likert, *Public Opinion and the Individual*, New York, Harper, 1938.

[3] E. L. Horowitz, The development of attitude toward the Negro, *Arch. Psychol.*, 1935, No. 194.

486   AN INTRODUCTION TO PSYCHOLOGY

Figure 86. The Social Situations Test

on an all-white basis, otherwise not. These three methods of Horowitz show steadily rising prejudice scores during the nine-year age span covered; and the three methods, which in the little children are largely independent, gradually become intercorrelated so that higher prejudice in one of the three goes with higher prejudice in the other two.

There are, of course, other possibilities in projective testing, such as making up pictures which may be interpreted by the subject to show how a Canadian, a Finn, a Greek would behave in such and such a situation. The TAT and other methods similar to it have already been successfully used as attitude material.

It is usually possible to predict actual behavior fairly well from attitude tests. One finds good Republicans, good Communists, good Christian Scientists, good Roman Catholics responding verbally in accordance with the life plan which they have laid down for themselves. But much depends upon knowing what kinds of attitudes one is dealing with. In cases where the attitude situation taps the personality in an aspect which daily life does *not* tap, there is no reason why one should expect a close relationship. Expressed attitudes toward punctuality in a midwestern college showed no relation to actual promptness in showing up at class. And in a study on the west coast of the United States, restaurant and hotel keepers who had been in the habit of accepting Chinese with the same courtesy as was afforded to whites, answered a series of mailed questionnaires by saying that they would be unwilling to accept Chinese patrons. What you will actually do on a business deal today is quite different from committing yourself in the mail to a policy which might lead to consequences that you are not altogether ready to face. It is like anything else human; we will get either consistent or inconsistent results depending upon the direction in which motivation and pressures impel. If we set the situation up carefully in such a way as to secure real interest and coöperation from our subjects, we will find that most people are willing to answer and can and do answer pretty well regarding themselves.

Attitude and Personality

All the material described thus far attempts to separate the attitudes, so to speak, from the personality itself, so that each can be more closely observed. This attempt might remind one of those modern surgical operations on the heart in which the surgeon lifts the heart away from the body for a few minutes—an operation that in some respects actually involves abnormal functioning of the heart, because ordinarily it is too deeply embedded and too deeply interwoven with life to be accessible to surgical instruments without endangering life. Using this figure of speech, we might say that attitude tests of the sort we have described so far do separate attitude from personality. There are, however, some outstanding recent attempts to study attitudes in their intimate relation to many other dynamic aspects of everyday living. Notable, for example, are the studies done at Berkeley, California, in relation to the problem of hostilities of certain white Americans toward other social groups, as shown in life histories, interviews, verbal and projective tests.[4]

These investigations show that hostility toward out-groups goes along rather consistently with certain traits of personality. In a large proportion of the very prejudiced individuals it appears from the TAT and from the case history that the subject has unloaded on to (projected upon) the members of other social groups the "undesirable characteristics" (related to aggression, sex, etc.) which he cannot bear to accept in himself. This is the basis of the scapegoat conception of prejudice, the conception that we assign to others the blameworthy traits which we cannot acknowledge within ourselves ("projection"; cf. page 424). While far from completely *explaining* prejudice, this has relevance in many individual cases.

Many other traits seem to be related to prejudice. Take the trait of rigidity, which means inability to adapt to a situation. Growing up in a rather self-contained, narrow world of values and attitudes, a person accepts the prevailing outlook. He sees the world as his own group sees it—"ethnocentrism." Consequently he hates the people that are hated by his immediate group. He has learned basically to rely upon the authorities and standards which regulate, among other things, the prejudices of the group. One has to have the "standard" prejudices to be a "normal" member of the group.

Can we get at this basic rigidity of personality and find a way to test it? Among the tests of rigidity is the following:[5] Maps of American cities are shown to the subject and he is asked to show how to get from point

---
[4] E. Frenkel-Brunswik and R. N. Sanford, Some personality factors in anti-Semitism, *J. Psychol.*, 1945, 20, 271–291.

[5] M. Rokeach, Generalized mental rigidity as a factor in ethnocentrism, *J. abnorm. soc. Psychol.*, 1948, 43, 259–278.

A to point B. He sees in relation to Map No. 1 (Figure 87) that the diagonal avenue does him no good. Having worked with a series of such simple maps, he is presented with a map like No. 2 (Figure 88). Here, of course, it does make a difference whether he uses the diagonal avenue or not. We find the rigid subject typically clinging to the plan which has

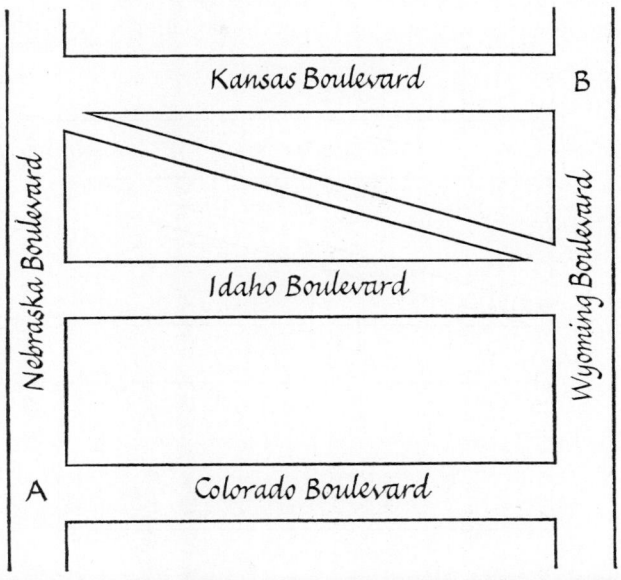

Figure 87. Rigidity and Ethnocentrism: Map 1

One of a series of maps used in the study of rigidity. In each case the task was to get from point A to B, but the diagonal avenue was useless. Subjects who worked with a series of such maps soon developed a set way of solving this problem. (Figures 87, 88, and 89 from M. Rokeach, in *J. abnorm. soc. Psychol.*, 1948, 43, 269.)

once been used and has brought success; he does not go in for "wild harebrained innovations." But the people who are relatively free from prejudice quickly solve problems of this sort, taking advantage of new opportunities such as the diagonal avenues which are now lined up appropriately to help them toward their goal. They appear to be people who feel no such emotional need to cling to a method which has been approved; they can look at a new problem on its merits. The differences in rigidity between the high-ethnocentric and the low-ethnocentric are equally clear in an arithmetical reasoning test by Rokeach (Fig. 89).

Personality factors are also easily elicited by the interview, questionnaire, and life-history methods, as in this "self-analysis of an avowed Fascist":

Ques. Are you easily irritated when people argue with you?
Yes. The one thing I cannot stand in any form is opposition.
Ques. Do you usually get upset when things go wrong?
Yes. When things go wrong I take it as a humiliating defeat.

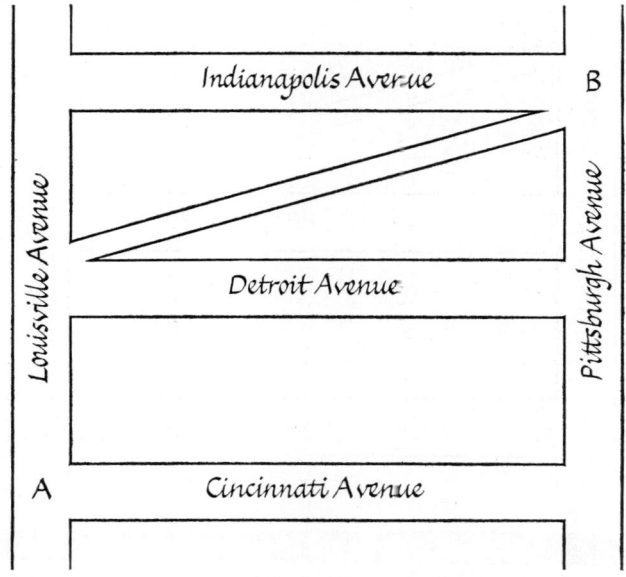

Figure 88. Rigidity and Ethnocentrism: Map 2

Subjects who had worked with a series of maps like that in Figure 87 were presented with this map. Here the diagonal provides a shortcut from A to B. Subjects who continued to follow the old route were classified as giving a rigid solution.

Ques. Is it hard for you to admit it when you know you are in the wrong?
Yes. It's difficult for me to retreat one step.
Ques. Do you feel uneasy (usually) when you are around people you do not know?
Yes. I don't trust them.
Ques. Are you considered mediocre in many of the things you do?
Yes, but this isn't news to me. I know I'm just fair in a lot of things I do. I think this is a poor question.
Ques. Have you often felt that some people were working against you?
Yes, but I suppose that is a natural feeling for suspicious people.

Ques. Are certain people so unreasonable that you hate them?
Yes. Anyone who opposes me I hate.[6]

This study is in harmony with the personality studies offered by the Berkeley investigators to show that personality is ultimately related to social attitudes.

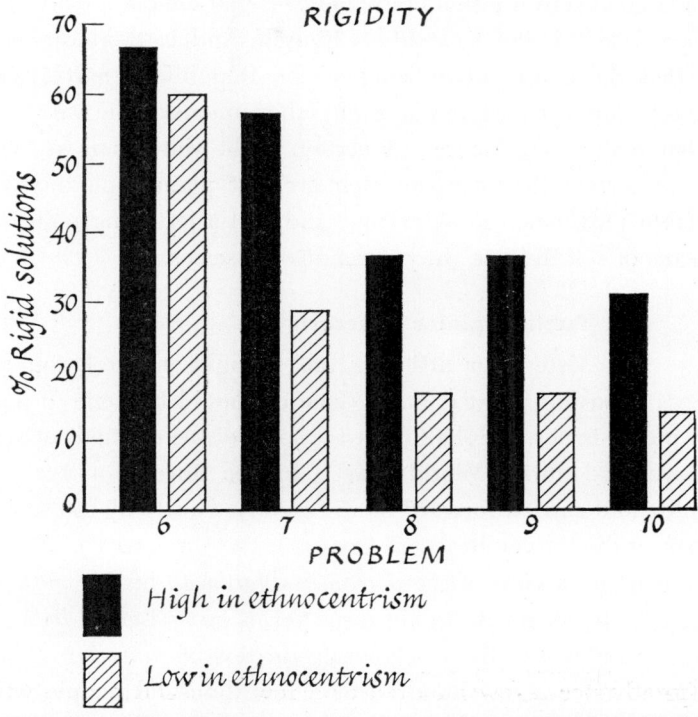

Figure 89. Rigidity and Ethnocentrism: Results

The height of the bars represents the percentage of rigid solutions of arithmetical problems solvable by rigid and nonrigid methods. Solid bars represent rigidity in subjects high in ethnocentrism; shaded bars, rigidity in those low in ethnocentrism. (Results for the map-experiments are highly similar.)

Of course we should expect social attitude to be related also to *self-interest;* e.g., social attitudes express the outlook and needs of one's own economic group. Often the individual influenced by economic self-interest honestly believes that the reason for his behavior lies in some-

---

[6] E. Rosen, George X: the self-analysis of an avowed Fascist, *J. abnorm. soc. Psychol.*, 1949, *44*, 528–540; quotation from p. 536.

thing quite different, such as sheer justice or reasonableness. If autistic response can enter into such matters as face-saving and relieving oneself of guilt, it can certainly enter into one's outlook as regards one's economic or social status. A certain very successful corporation lawyer in New York, whose intelligence, health, and energy all combined to give him a good start, quite literally believes that *anybody who wants to can succeed to the same extent as himself,* and is therefore entirely certain that the conservative wing of the Republican party, with its hesitation to support welfare plans and labor unions, is the only political party that makes any "sense." A certain night watchman at Western Electric is certain that wealthy men are just plain exploiters, that a strong labor movement is imperative, and that a left-wing policy is the only means of self-defense the community possesses.

Public Opinion Research

Often our attitudes are brought into relation to our judgments regarding what is being done or should be done in political or other public issues. We shall illustrate some of the methods of attitude study developed during World War II by the Bureau of Agricultural Economics, and carried forward more recently, mostly by the same psychologists, at the Survey Research Center at the University of Michigan. The aim is to get a view of the *person in relation to his life outlook* before one tries to formulate in yes-or-no terms just what he *believes,* or what his attitudes are. By an elaborate process of *sampling,* there are chosen in advance a few hundred or a few thousand people who are *representative* of a very large population; i.e., their proportion as to age, sex, education, income, etc., is the same as in the large population. The interviewer carries on a leisurely conversation, typically averaging three-quarters of an hour, in which he avoids the temptation to pin his respondent down to a yes or no; he asks what his general feeling is regarding some trend or policy. This is called the "open-ended interview" method. Since data of this sort cannot be scored in simple quantitative terms, they have to be *coded;* that is, a trained headquarters staff has to classify the responses—e.g., in terms of the kind of bias and life outlook —and show the relation of the responses to the age, sex, economic level, etc., of the respondents. But the coding yields a great deal more. It is also possible to code for various personality attributes, for degrees of friendliness or hostility toward the interviewer, for general morale, happiness, optimism, or self-sufficiency. In other words we can get personality data, attitude data, and public opinion data all at once. Such methods are quite sensitive in showing changes from month to month, whether in relation to one's general life problems or in relation to economic ups and downs, or in relation to the special force of the publicity or propaganda aimed one way or another at the public by the government, the press, etc. There is still some value in the short-cut methods which merely ask people *yes* or *no* and count up percentages, as in Gallup polling; but these methods, even when they are technically adequate in every other respect, tell us very little about the people from whom the responses come.

Since public opinion is sensitive to many factors, it must be studied *continuously;* one cannot rest on one's oars as some public opinion pollers did in September, 1948, after predicting what the result in November would be. Another fundamental matter requiring constant vigilance is adequacy of the *sample* that is used to predict the tendencies of large numbers of people. If we interview one person in a hundred, or a thousand, or a hundred thousand, we must be sure that we are not choosing for our interviews the people who are liable to answer our question in one way rather than another; they won't be representative of the whole population. In an election forecast, the people who are actually interviewed must be a fair sample of the much larger group which will go to the polls. And when, instead of merely reporting that 53.4 percent of the public favors one candidate or another, we are interested in seeing *from what kind of people what kind of attitudes are coming,* it is even more important to know whether we have a fair sample of each group.

A typical sampling method involves mapping out a city in terms of blocks and houses and directing the interviewers to call at the northwest house in the indicated blocks, and interview the people in the second-floor apartment to the west. The interviewers have to take people who have been chosen in advance on some carefully thought-out random basis which makes sure for example that the houses to the northwest in that particular city are not better or worse houses than the others. When we use such methods of random sampling, we are essentially groping in the dark with both hands, picking up masses of randomly distributed material, but we get enough cases to give a fair and representative picture. Here we can use the standard statistical methods and the theory of probability, and also double check upon our results by taking samples over and over again to see if they differ very much from each other, in exactly the same way that we establish that the dealing of cards or the throwing of dice is fair by analyzing it in terms of the theory of probability and showing that no one person has too many aces or throws too many sixes over a period of days or weeks.

From this point of view, the best modern sampling methods are quite good; and it is not surprising, therefore, that their predictive power is quite high. There is a popular prejudice to the effect that a sample should be very large. Actually, once you have chosen a few thousand (or for some purposes just a few hundred) people by a very systematic and careful sampling method, it makes little difference whether you add a few thousand or a few tens of thousands more. The important thing is that the samples you do select shall be rigorously fair and rigorously representative of all the factors—age, sex, education, ethnic group, and so on—that are likely to influence opinions.

Psychologists have worked long enough with such methods to be sure that opinion sampling, particularly when the open-ended interview is used, has implications not only for sociology and politics, but for the psychology of personality. One finds out constantly more and more about what individual Americans are actually like with respect to the changing pressures and threats in their economic and political existence, and in terms of the changing general climate of opinion in relation to the world situation. Opinion study has therefore become an important psychological method.

SUGGESTED READINGS

Krech, D., and Crutchfield, S., *Theory and Problems of Social Psychology*, New York, McGraw-Hill, 1948, Chaps. 5–9.

Likert, R., A technique for the measurement of attitudes, *Arch. Psychol.*, 1932, No. 140.

Murphy, G., and Likert, R., *Public Opinion and the Individual*, New York, Harper, 1938.

Murphy, G., Murphy, L. B., and Newcomb, T. M., *Experimental Social Psychology*, New York, Harper, 1937, Chap. 13.

Newcomb, T. M., and Hartley, E. L., *Readings in Social Psychology*, New York, Holt, 1947, Chaps. 12, 14.
Sherif, M., and Cantril, H., The psychology of attitudes, *Psychol. Rev.*, 1945, 52, No. 6, and 1946, 53, No. 1.
Thurstone, L. L., and Chave, E. J., *The Measurement of Attitude*, Chicago, Univ. of Chicago Press, 1929.

27 PERSONALITY PATTERNS

No term is more frequently used regarding personality than the word *trait*. It means a characteristic, a trend, a way of response, an attribute, an aspect. It means each of the various components or segments of the individual considered in a greater or lesser degree of separation from other traits. The habitual recourse to rationalization (page 425) or reaction formation (page 422) is a trait; qualities like courage, honesty, etc., studied by ratings or by tests (page 451) are traits. It will be our task in this chapter to look at some of the ways in which traits are found to hang together, to be articulated into a whole in the individual personality. We have really been working our way for a long time toward this idea of the *interrelation of traits*. In the matter of personality tests, for example, we found it possible in certain relatively simple problems (pages 447 ff.) to study traits more or less independently. Then as we came to behavior tests and especially projective tests, we found that we were beginning to deal with whole *patterns* in which the single trait arises from a system of interacting tendencies.

We may begin with the study of certain *organic* attributes of the individual such as those described in Chapters 3–6. Many of these are more or less persistent through life. Speed, strength, endurance; visual and auditory acuity; perhaps specific thresholds for rage, fear, or joy—these are examples of deep-seated and enduring dispositions which may be called organic traits, derived from specific aspects of the physical machinery of which we are constituted. A second group of traits consists of conditioned responses which have become generalized to a greater or lesser extent. They are the broad dispositions to react with rage, delight, and so on, in response to various classes or types of stimulation, and are in many cases the root material of the social attitudes just considered in Chapter 26. They are also among the root dispositions observed in projective tests. In the same way canalizations, it will be remembered, are subject to generalization, and we may visualize the individual as consisting in part of a group of generalized conditionings and canalizations. In the case of Pauline Butterworth (page 475), for example, we see how a conditioned response (based on need of approval) spreads until it cut a broad path through the personality and appeared in many different areas of expression.

But whether we emphasize constitutional or learned characteristics, we find ourselves confronted with a large number of persistent, deepseated traits which are essential ingredients in personality; and we must show how these are put together, study the forms of *interrelation* between personality traits.

1. One such interrelationship is a direct dynamic relation in which one trait *gives rise to* another. A gives rise to B whenever it appears:

$$A \to B$$

In Alfred Adler's description of compensation, for example (page 434), inferiority is A and compensatory behavior is B. (Chapters 22–23 explained many of the specific ways in which this occurs.)

2. Sometimes, however, there are two or more different ways of compensating (e.g., arguing or playing sick; cf. page 435). The second diagram shows the alternatives or possibilities when trait A may produce either B or C (or still other reactions):

$$A \begin{smallmatrix} \nearrow B \\ \searrow C \end{smallmatrix}$$

Closely related to this are the cases in which the basic direction being taken by the person may show itself at the surface in terms of contrasting types of behavior. In the investigations by Allport and Vernon,[1] a man was observed at times to walk very rapidly and at times to walk very slowly. Instead of concluding that his walking was simply inconsistent,

---

[1] G. W. Allport and P. E. Vernon, *Studies in Expressive Movement*, New York, Macmillan, 1933.

or that there was no rhyme or reason for it, Allport and Vernon studied his basic values in living. It was clear that as a business executive he had set for himself the major standard of being efficient. In order to be efficient he always saved time, walking briskly when there was nothing to do but get back to his desk. But when he was working out a plan, he would get up and stroll back and forth as he thought it out. Fast and slow walking were completely consistent when you knew his aims. In the same way the patterns of a man's being very tough and hard-boiled in the business world, very gentle and tender with his little son, may actually both spring from his feeling that he is a tower of strength upon whom others depend. He cannot allow his business to be jeopardized by weakness any more than he can allow himself a loss of temper when his child needs affection. The need to be *strong* is central to everything else. We may symbolize the relation of deep traits to superficial (often seemingly inconsistent) traits that result from them in this way:

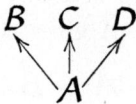

3. There is a broad category of behavior in which A leads to B and B leads back to A:

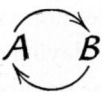

We may establish a seesaw relationship. We may, perhaps, compensate for our inferiorities by being noisy and then feel inferior because we have done so, then be noisy again, etc. There are many striking illustrations of this mechanism in which the circle, once having been established, keeps itself going. We get ashamed of what we have done and then are ashamed of our shame. You kick yourself for having kicked yourself. Or you grow afraid of your fear, or angry at your rage. *Whatever one does, one reacts to it by the very same quality of feeling which has just been generated.* These are the vicious circles into which the psychiatrist can often cut.

4. Then, of course, there are the cases of more complex interdepend-

PERSONALITY PATTERNS 499

ence in which three traits chase each other around in a triangular relationship:

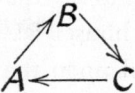

And there are cases in which each one of a system of attributes feeds into and reinforces or inhibits each one of the others. We may truly say, then,

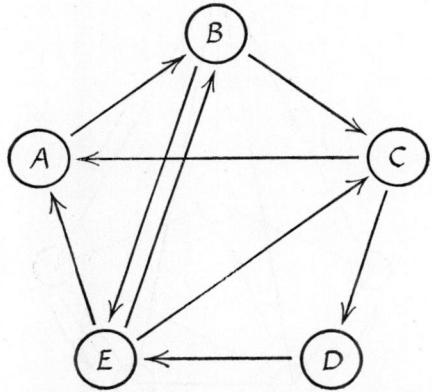

Figure 90. Diagram: An Interdependent, Dynamic System

Another way in which personality attributes may be related to each other. Each is linked directly to at least two others and indirectly to all the others. All of them together may thus be seen as dependent upon each other, as constituting a dynamic interacting system.

that we have an interacting, interdepending, dynamic system. A dynamic system is an example of the psychology of *Gestalt* or form,[2] in which everything is *interdependent*, not a piecemeal agglomeration. This conception of interdependence is illustrated in Figure 90.

5. The fifth type of interrelationship involves the search for a center or core of the system of traits. The reader who has grasped the implications of the material on the self and on the ways of enhancing or defending the self, is likely to be dissatisfied with all the accounts that proceed as if the traits were simply responses to inner or outer stimulation but had no real center. Actually, the view was developed earlier that for

---

[2] W. Köhler, *Gestalt Psychology*, New York, Boni, rev. ed., 1947.

most people in our society (and in many other societies) there is typically an *anchorage point,* a center which proves to be *one's view of oneself.* It might be possible, then, to say that from the vantage point of his outlook, his way of regarding himself as a whole, a person looks down from the apex of this pyramid upon the various interacting attributes which have already been sketched (Figure 91).

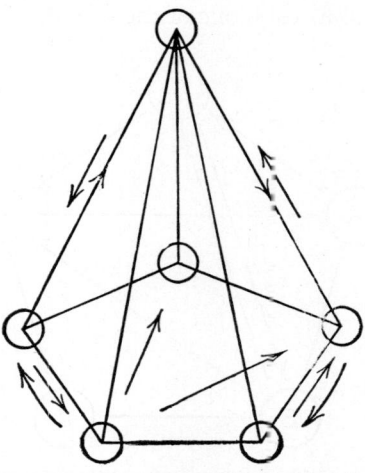

Figure 91. Diagram: Self-View as Anchorage Point

The apex of the pyramid may be regarded as representing the central anchorage point in a system of traits, the person's view of himself. It has a dominating position here, above the system of interacting attributes, because it may be conceived of as pervading and organizing all the attributes.

The individual does not, of course, see all of himself clearly. Much of the process of perception is foggy and confused. But he does have some broad, general conception of the sort of person he is, and he sees his traits in *some* sort of perspective. It is the very fact that he realizes altogether *too* clearly the implications of a trait like laziness or loss of self-control that leads him to try to fix up the picture for the sake of the self-esteem which he is so eagerly trying to maintain. He is constantly throwing his weight around, reinforcing one aspect or weakening another aspect of the total self-portrait. This is carried out, as we have seen, partly by the ordinary perceptual dynamics of figure-ground shift, and partly, at a less conscious level, by similar shifts of the sort the psychoanalysts have described (pages 421 ff.); in other words, the mechanisms already considered in the earlier chapters on the self are the same mechanisms that appear here in such a way as to help us to observe the interrelations of traits. If the person views himself in a certain way, it is because he has certain traits, interrelated in specific ways; there is a real, dynamic pattern within him which leads to his characteristic self-image. But of course *we* may be able to see many aspects of his personality structure (interrelations between his traits) of which he is unaware, and there are many which *no one* sees.

"Sizing People Up"

This study of the interrelations between traits makes a big practical difference when we are interested in "sizing people up" or in predicting what they will do in new social situations. We have to judge each aspect of behavior in the light of its context, and that means that we have to see how things hang together. A face that is always smiling may have very different meanings, depending on whether the smile is due to sheer exuberance of spirits (fed largely by a constitutional predisposition and good health), or is the nervous expression of an insecure person that arises directly from insecurity, or is a deliberate device for making friends and influencing people. Some traits, likewise, are here today and gone tomorrow, whereas others "stick." If a habit, for example, is a conditioned response of the simple sort described on page 213, it will *extinguish* when not reinforced, and you will be rid of it. If it is a direct expression of constitutional factors, or is a mechanism of defense (cf. Chapter 23), you will not be so lucky. The real test of a way of thinking about personality traits is the degree to which they enable us to understand others and ourselves, and predict what each of us will do. The acid test of such a conception is afforded by the methods in which we determine from a group of observations what a person will do in concrete situations, e.g., in stress situations (cf. page 454). We are able to recognize personality structure (interrelated traits) in one situation, and in the process of doing so we are capable, to some degree, of predicting what will happen if that same structure appears in another situation. In some cases we do this very explicitly by saying that the combination of weakness and strength, or the combination of consistency and confusion, which appears in a person in one situation would be bound to lead to vacillation and turmoil in him in a second situation. To some degree we make this judgment overtly and explicitly.

At the same time a great deal is done by "feeling ourselves into" the person, by getting the feel of what it would be like to have the various attributes as they appear in the first situation. We all do this to some extent. This depends on the *capacity for active identification,* getting the feel of the system of traits and of the self-outlook of the individual, imagining *how we would look to ourselves if we had the interrelated system of attributes which the other person has.* The doctor or teacher or counselor in the same way makes his integrations of personal attributes, feels himself into the situation by a process of active identification. *Sizing up traits, then, is always partly a question of spotting specific characteristics, partly a question of acquiring through long experience a capacity to respond to groups of traits as efficiently as one responds to single traits, and partly a capacity to make response to the other person's view of his own pattern of traits.*

Of course there is a great deal of autism both in the perception of others and in the perception of oneself. But one can get to a point at which he can actually demonstrate the reality of personality structuring by making predictions based on structure which are better than predictions based on perceiving individual characteristics in isolation. This is what the trained psychiatrist or clinical psychologist usually does, and in large part it is the rational basis for the successful appraisal of personality (as described in Chapters 24 and 25).

The Continuity of Traits and Their Interrelations

Suppose, then, that we have a picture of the individual with his own peculiar pattern of traits articulated, hanging together in the one organized way that we recognize as himself. Has he *always* had this pattern of hanging-together traits? Will he *always* have it? The answer to both questions is probably *no.* He learns and unlearns. He grows and in later years may begin to fail. If this is true, can we say when we study him today that we understand his whole personality? Have we not left out something very important—the continual change, the time dimension? We see him at a point on the path of life, but we cannot ever see clearly where the path lies. Most of our studies of personality involve "cross sections" through the person at a moment in time, or, at the most, over a time span of a few weeks or months. We see the individual at college or industry, or settled down in life, and we think we know what sort of person he is. But the question is: How did the forces that made him what he is today actually operate, and how will they continue to operate to make him different next year? What are the stable things and what are the changing things about him? In what respects can we assume that he will remain what he is? This problem is especially pressing as he changes rapidly during the early years; and if we want to be really helpful in the family, in the school, in the vocational center, in the clinic, or in community relationships, we shall have to study him over and over again at different levels of his development. We can do this to some extent by asking him to tell us his life story, and by getting similar life stories about him from those who have known him well. Better still, we can supplement these stories with direct observations and tests made over a period of years. Some examples of a history of this sort were given above (pages 473 ff.), where a group of observers pieced together a meaningful record of a person's growth, many phases of his life being interwoven to make him what the observers saw. Studies of this sort are called longitudinal, as contrasted with cross-sectional.

Naturally we should like to be able to begin our studies in earliest childhood. Sometimes we can fill in the picture by bringing together documentary materials like diaries, letters, drawings, school compositions. Better still are the cases in which we are able to determine during the individuals' infancy which ones we will study over a period of years, and carry out systematic observational and testing programs, over and over again. This method is illustrated by the work of the Fels Foundation at Antioch College in Yellow Springs, Ohio, where hundreds of children have been observed and tested for many years.

We begin to see the possibility of formulating clear working hypotheses, during a person's infancy, as to what is making him grow in one direction rather than another, and then actually testing these hypotheses by watching him year by year. We do not wish to be limited to observations relative to single attributes. We should not be much interested in knowing whether the ideas and attitudes at the six-year-old level reappear in the same form at the twelve-year level; rather, we are interested in how the hanging-together of attributes, the total pattern or configuration, manages to keep itself going despite marked changes in the growth and situational factors. Sometimes even the attributes which seem most striking, such as the sense of security and adequacy of the "tough little guy" of ten, are somehow lost in the shuffle as the body changes and the social situation changes, and four years later we find a worried insecure lad, unable to compete in winning the girls attention and resorting to rather pitiful show-off devices to try to reëstablish himself.[3]

There are some things that undoubtedly run consistently through from year to year; but along with them there may be great variations in the things that are evident at the surface (we have given examples; see pages 394 and 395). This underscores the question: What is really stable and enduring from year to year? We could characterize at least four sorts of functions that are pretty stable. (1) There are the organic dispositions which depend upon very early interactions of genes and environmental factors, like the low thresholds and other constitutional traits already considered (page 26). (2) There are the early conditionings and canalizations which have been built into the center of the personality, comprising the core of the systems of symbols, particularly the verbal habits. (3) There are the deep-seated habits of perceiving (page 146), which early become established and structured together. (4) There are the images of the self which, while variable and sensitive to changing external pressures, do have to expand from a fairly stable and definite core, and are held within limits by the conditionings, canalizations, and perceptual habits established in the early years. We can see in the adult, better than in the adolescent or child, the maintenance of these four types of continuing attributes, for neither the body nor its social situation is changing so quickly. From year to year much of the core of personality is maintained.

But you will also find reason to challenge the assumption that traits which appear now in one situation must infallibly appear in all situations. Whenever the environment changes, new pressures are applied to the individual. The attributes of personality cannot be defined solely in

---

[3] Our own summary of a case read at Berkeley, California, in the California Adolescent Growth Study.

terms of what is going on inside the person; they need to be studied in terms of the interplay of what is inside the organism and what is acting upon it from without. *There are probably no traits of personality that are just "bound to appear" regardless of the situation in which the person is placed.* What each environment or situation does is to permit one attribute or group of attributes to come out, while making it more difficult for other attributes to come out. This is, of course, educationally most important; because what we draw out from the person can be to some degree controlled by considering what is inside of him, and what the drawing power of future situations may be. It is exactly on the basis of such experience that the psychiatrist, or the group leader, or the teacher, builds up a situation that will, as he says, *bring out what is potential* within the individual child or adolescent.

The possibility of such molding, changing, drawing-out of potentials warns us against any conception of rigid and fixed continuity through life. We may be puzzled about this because many of the writers of literary biographies may want us to believe that a certain keynote or "leitmotif" is established early in life and that the individual clings to it forever. Lytton Strachey, in his vivid picture of Queen Victoria, tells us how the little girl, when first informed that she was to be the queen and empress, sat demurely for a moment deep in thought, and then said, "I will be good." Strachey tells us that this little slogan ran through all the complex national and international tasks and undertakings of the queen; that she was living true to a way of feeling which had been instilled in her earliest years. It is often quite tempting to pick out a single strand of this sort. Actually it would be safer to say that a central strand or slogan of life is formulated with relative distinctness by one child, and with no clarity at all by another; and that even when it is very distinct, its effect upon the subsequent life must depend upon the actual circumstances encountered. Victoria's determination, "I will be good," combined later with other loyalties, such as loyalty to her husband and to the policies of the Prime Minister, to produce an imperial policy which could never have been produced by sheer "goodness" alone.

But while Strachey has gone too far in tracing the queen's ways to a single guiding motive, his study of her shows what every systematic biography shows, namely, that there is some continuity not only of traits, but of the structure, the *system* of traits. Not only were her affections always strong, but they were always held in check and given direction by a sense of duty and responsibility that went with a typical nineteenth-century royal child's imperial conscience (super-ego); not only was she determined to *be right* and to *have dignity,* but everything in the empire with which she felt herself to be identified must "be right" and "have dignity." These were moral values which were made stronger with the years; and if she deceived herself as to what was right in India and the Middle East, her self-deception was not essentially different from that of the rest of us whose perceptual habits, and especially self-perceptions, are loaded with the stuff that makes things look as we need to have them look. There is continuity, then, in personality structure as a whole, not just because the elements survive from year to year, but because the *ways of living,* which are the individual's effort to come to terms with the world and himself, are persistent.

Do they *always* persist? No. Two things can happen. (1) A man may suffer catastrophe; he may lose his legs in an accident or his fortune in a bad investment, and the physical basis of his life may collapse. He can no longer continue his old ways; he must begin all over to learn some new ones, using old materials and habits as well as he can. Often he fails to find a new solid basis for life, and either builds a pitiful third-rate caricature of a life, or goes through the old motions, pretending that neither he nor the world has changed. So hard is the rebuilding that under a blow or catastrophe most people cling to the ways they know. (2) But it may also happen that good fortune throws into an individual's path a ticket to a much better way of living, in the form of a friend, or a lover, who gives life a new meaning; or a doctor or teacher who knocks away the canes or crutches of his self-imposed lameness and shows him how to walk, jump, and run. Here again, it usually takes a shock to do the trick, or a series of shocks. We cling to the old ways, experiencing the old ways of seeing ourselves as long as we can. But if the need is forced upon us to see the world in a new perspective, we may give up the comfortable continuity of a lifetime of bad habits. Now we may seem to our associates to be a "new person." For although we retain the continuities that arise from our organic make-up and many of our conditionings and canalizations, the figure-ground organization of our world perspective and of our perspective on ourselves can be permanently changed.

Personality Types

There are so many different things in the world to react to that we cannot possibly deal with each one of them individually. If we are describing a home, we have to be able to say how many chairs there are, and deal with chairs in such a way that we can be sure that everybody invited to a party can sit down, without bothering to consider who will be most ideally comfortable in which particular chair. In the same way we group most of the things in our experience into broad classes so that a whole class of things can be handled at once. Naturally we try to do the same with people. We want to say that there are friendly types and sour types; that there are extrovert and introvert types; that there are domineering and submissive types. What we are doing in each such classification is to ignore subtle individual differences and throw people into large categories which can then be contrasted.

The whole question is whether there really *are* any personality types of this sort. If, for example, there were a very smooth and even gradation all the way from the friendliest to the sourest, or from the most domineering to the most submissive, and if it should turn out that most people are somewhere *in between,* the temptation to classify people in contrasting types would actually mangle the job of describing them faithfully.

In our whole language and way of thinking we have a tradition so deeply favoring the use of types that it may be worth while to look closely at it for a moment. Ancient Greek and Roman medical men based their types upon the supposed fundamental fluids of the body: the blood, the phlegm, the bile, and the black bile. And we still speak of people as *sanguine* (from *sanguis,* meaning blood); as *phlegmatic* (from *phlegma,* meaning clammy humor); as *choleric* (from *chol,* meaning bile); and as *melancholic* (from *melan,* meaning black, and *chol*). These are expressions which continue in daily speech as if modern men still believed that these four body fluids laid down some basic law of life.

We have also from the Greeks the habit of making up little character sketches, like the sketches by Theophrastus, who tells us typically what the flatterer or the lover is like. Theophrastus does not link these types of behavior to bodily components, but he implies in a certain sense that, if you look about you, there are certain people who are flatterers and who are *all alike*. There would be, then, in our society the flatterer and the nonflatterer. Actually, if you noticed the small and large flatteries which constitute so great a part of the technique of social ingratiation, white lying, and adapting to "necessity," you would probably find that flattery is an attribute mingled in generous or stingy proportions with all sorts of other attributes in *every* person. So far the idea of personality *types,* or sharp, clear classes or groups of people, to be put into separate pigeonholes, does not seem to fit the facts very well.

It must be granted that we often get great satisfaction from building up a picture of clear-cut, well-defined cleavages between people. It is more fun if we can group our friends into types than if we have to place each person carefully on a distribution curve from one point to another (page 345). In the same way the literary artist who tells us about Leonardo da Vinci, or Beethoven, or Einstein, is much happier if he can put his finger on some distinguishing work by which he can show that Leonardo is a pure example of the artistic type, Beethoven the essence of the creative musician, and Einstein the true scientist. Similarly, in a large department store or industrial plant where there are a great many applicants for jobs, we may undertake to choose real "sales types"—people who are really typical of an effective sales force—or people who represent genuine "leadership types" to serve as executives. This is easier than to embark upon the very time-consuming task of measuring and assessing everybody's attributes in great detail.

And it must be admitted that if all that is desired is to lop off a certain part of the population and treat it as if it were distinct from the rest, the type method will serve the purpose. Thus, if the police force or the army wants people above a certain height, it can perfectly properly set its limit at 5 feet 2 and reject the rest. In this sense there is a physical type which is acceptable for the police force or the army, because by the very nature of the standard the individual either completely succeeds or completely fails to get in. If a certain "type of mind" is desired, meaning people who make a certain score, the police or army can reject those whose intelligence quotients fall below a certain arbitrary standard. This is a sort of typing by default, and it may have its purpose.

But in more basic and scientific terms there is grave reason for doubting whether people do fall into types at all, except in a few respects that are important enough to be considered below (page 510). What people *do* fall into, as a rule, is the normal bell-shaped curve already considered (page 345). If you indicate, for example, on the x axis the speed of response as shown in the speed of canceling letters, you get a normal curve. And if you administer rating scales or questionnaire forms delving into such traits as ascendance-submission or introversion-extroversion, again you get normal curves.

It may be said, in relation to such an argument, that the projective tests which attempt to reveal the personality as a whole do reveal some sort of real cleavages between types. We may be told, for example, that there is an extratensive type of people who are emotionally outgoing, and an introversive type who have a tendency to fall back upon their own inner resources (cf. page 466). But again quantitative data show that we are dealing with *questions of degree* in both respects, and that there are *all degrees* of emotional outgoing, *all degrees* of retirement into an inner world. It is the balance between the two—in fact, the structural interrelations of all the attributes—with which a projective test is chiefly concerned.

The same seems to hold true in relation to the *ideal types* of Spranger (page 446). The results of the Allport-Vernon test of Spranger's values show that we differ from one another in the *degree* of intensity of *each* value, not on an all-or-nothing basis. People do not fall into types. Some will say that there is definitely such a thing as a religious type or a theoretical type. But the administration of this test has in general produced smooth and normal distributions, not definitely demarcated types. The *degree* of the theoretical value, for example, varies from large to small through all gradations, and the theoretical value may coexist with other strong values.

In recent years there have been several interesting attempts to establish a basic *physical* typing of human beings and to show the relation of *personality types* to these basic *physical types*. The best of these methods of typing individuals according to their anatomical and physiological attributes are those developed by Sheldon and his collaborators.[4] Sheldon's emphasis is on the fact that there are three layers of tissue which make up the body during embryonic and later growth, and that any one of these layers may be developed to a greater or lesser degree. The inner layer from which develop the vital organs is the endoderm; the middle layer, giving rise to bone, sinew, and muscle, the mesoderm; the outer layer, from which the nervous system and skin are derived, the ectoderm. Each individual's anatomical development shows a certain balance among the three; perhaps an overdevelopment of one and an underdevelopment of the other two. The body build which springs from marked endoderm development is called endomorphy; similarly, the body build arising from a highly developed mesoderm factor is mesomorphy; and that from marked ectoderm activity, ectomorphy. It is possible, by photographing the individual and making careful measurements of the photographs, to indicate quantitatively the proportions among the three. The photographs in Figure 92 show first an example of an average physique, 3½–3½–3½. The second individual is 7–4–1; the 7 refers to maximal development of endoderm, and 1 refers to minimal development of one of the other two. The third individual is 2½–7–1; and the fourth is 1½–2½—6½. More commonly there are less extreme developments. A person who is slightly on the endomorphic side would be classified as 5–3–3, and so on. All of us, then, represent a combination, so to speak, of the three components; and in general—although not absolutely—the more we have of one, the less we are likely to have of the other two. An absolutely average person would, of course, be 4–4–4.

Such a scheme is offered by Sheldon as throwing light on basic personality constituents. It is asserted, on the basis of clinical interviews and ratings, that men high in endomorphy are typically dependent upon the primitive, earthy satisfactions of eating and digesting; they are socially warm, they are likely to be impulsive, easygoing, *bons vivants*. Men high

---

[4] W. H. Sheldon, with the collaboration of S. S. Stevens and W. B. Tucker, *The Varieties of Human Physique*, New York, Harper, 1940; W. H. Sheldon, with the collaboration of S. S. Stevens, *The Varieties of Temperament*, New York, Harper, 1942.

PERSONALITY PATTERNS 511

in mesomorphy are tough, hardy, athletic, noisy, and enjoy dominating persons and things around them. Men high in ectomorphy, in turn, are inclined to be thoughtful, withdrawn, sensitive, imaginative.

These are, of course, ideal types or abstractions, since pure cases of 7–1–1, etc., are very rare; but the *degree* to which each one of us possesses each of these three bodily components is regarded by Sheldon as

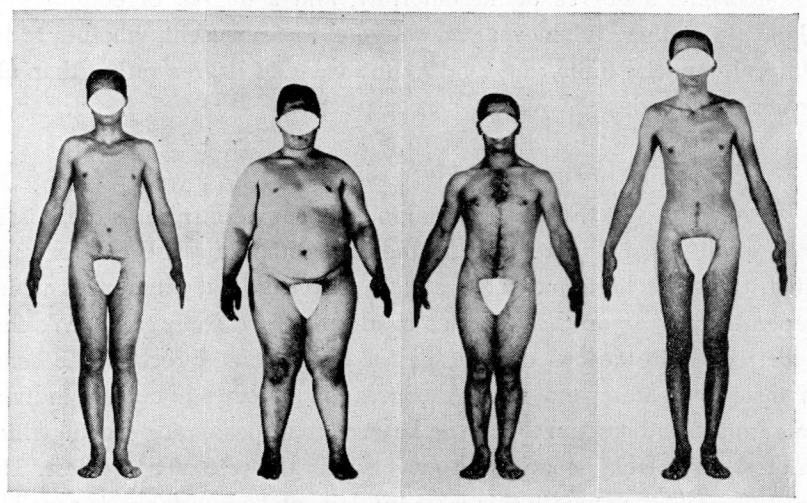

Figure 92. Physical Types

The individuals, from left to right, are of average physique, predominantly endomorphic, mesomorphic, and ectomorphic, respectively. Their somatotypes are respectively $3\frac{1}{2}$–$3\frac{1}{2}$–$3\frac{1}{2}$, 7–4–1, $2\frac{1}{2}$–7–1, and $1\frac{1}{2}$–$2\frac{1}{2}$–$6\frac{1}{2}$. (Courtesy the Constitution Laboratory, College of Physicians and Surgeons, Columbia University.)

correlated with the degree to which the corresponding personality characteristics are developed. Even though most psychologists remain skeptical, it must be granted that there appear to be, at the very least, some real relations between actual life-history data and the extreme degrees of anatomical development shown by this method. How close the relations are, however, has not been confirmed by independent research; and we may point to almost all the rest of the material in this textbook as showing that even if Sheldon's case is sound, all sorts of environmental factors may pull, warp, twist, redirect, and mold biological constitution. If, moreover, it should ultimately be shown that the personality relations suggested by Sheldon are very direct and important, and that they are stable throughout life, it still would remain true that each individual belongs on a *continuum* rather than being a full-fledged expression of a simple type; so that even this dramatic modern exemplification of a typing method does not really yield types in the everyday sense of the term. Rather, it reveals points upon a scale. Each of us consists of a *degree* of endomorphy, a *degree* of mesomorphy, and a *degree* of ectomorphy, blended together. Whenever you get good measurement, whether of biological or social traits, you tend to find cases of *degree* rather than all-or-none categories.

Yet There Is a Place for Types

In the case of two kinds of human attributes there is, in spite of all this, a definite need for the recognition of real breaks or gaps. First, there are here and there certain *constitutional* differences which depend simply upon the presence or absence of certain genes. We find with regard to various defects, as for example a defect in the sense of taste, a definite and sharp demarcation of certain human individuals from all others, purely on the basis of their possessing a gene which the rest of us lack, or lacking a gene which the rest of us possess. The most obvious case where this is of fundamental importance is sex. The other cases are numerically few and their social importance is small.

Second, there is an important kind of differentiation among people on the basis of the *social groups* to which they belong. Take first the case of social classes based on their economic status. In sociological studies like those in Middletown or "Yankee City," most people do fall into well-defined social classes. Most of them are middle-class or working-class people; there is not just one smooth curve which tells all about degree of social status. In large communities it is also possible to subdivide these classes further, e.g., to make a distinction between the "lower-middle" class and the "upper-middle" class in terms of clear-cut differentiation in people's buying habits, their habits in talking, reading, thinking, etc. Society, in other words, is stratified; and in spite of the fact that some people do make a higher level or sink to a lower one, they grow up and bring up their children pretty largely within the framework of their social class. You, for example, would definitely find it very hard to accept yourself as a member of the working class and give up all the little class identifications that you have built up. Insofar as these attributes are actually stamped into us so that we have the ways of thinking and feeling, the outlook and modes of self-evaluation which characterize people at a particular class level, there are, in spite of all difficulties, real types among us.

Moreover, where a racial group is sharply separated from some other group, it may also develop, for these social reasons, a real cleavage from the rest in terms of a basic way of thinking and feeling. We may say also that religious groups in the United States permit in some instances a genuine typing. To have a Catholic viewpoint, a Jewish viewpoint, an evangelical Protestant viewpoint may at times actually separate people in terms of sharp cleavages. Insofar as one thinks of oneself as a member of a given social class or religious group, the self-image necessarily differs from the self-image of those belonging to other groups.

We should expect, therefore, that there would be a real break—*discontinuity*—between social classes and between religious groups in terms of a whole set of feelings and attitudes.[5] In some recent studies[6] of the performance of boys from the lowest economic levels in Chicago on intelligence tests it became evident that they thought themselves sissies whenever they tried to do what the teacher or examiner wanted. It was almost a self-mutilation to find oneself doing too well. When the tasks were changed so that the boy could fit the task to the cloth of his own self-image, much more successful attacks on the tasks were made.

Moreover, this same sort of basic cleavage is often forced upon people in terms of their acceptability or nonacceptability to others in social situations. Life often forces us into one or the other of two contrasting categories and makes "types" out of us whether we want it or not. Even though people may differ in fact through a series of imperceptible gradations, you either do or don't make the fraternity; you either do or don't win your school letter; you either do or don't achieve success in the new business venture into which your capital is poured. The "sink-or-

---

[5] R. S. Lynd and H. M. Lynd, *Middletown in Transition*, New York, Harcourt, Brace, 1937.
[6] E. A. Haggard, A. Davis, and R. J. Havighurst, Some factors which influence performance of children on intelligence tests, *Amer. Psychologist*, 1948, 3, 265–266.

swim," make-or-break process is pretty characteristic of American life. People are forced into the ranks of the confident or of the hesitant. In many social groups the cleavage is clear and complete. A group of normally attractive women may at twenty show a normal distribution in most social attitudes; but after the pairing off has been going on a few years, those who remain unchosen would not be human if they had not developed a real insecurity. The unmarried woman may quite genuinely show characteristics which belong to a *type* created by her situation where marriage is expected but not guaranteed and the man is the asker.

Attitudes toward the self are often the result of clear-cut external conditions in which we succeed or fail in our own eyes and must therefore assume the form of *either-or, yes-or-no*. Thus on a test at the University of Minnesota[7] during the depression years, it was found that although attitudes on economic and political issues were mostly distributed according to the bell-shaped curve, *whenever the issue related to the self there was a relatively sharp cleavage, a tendency toward the bimodal.* In the same way propaganda studies[8] show that the effect of applying powerful pressure to people is frequently not simply to move them in the direction the propagandist intends, but either to catapult them along in the expected direction or to drive them into staunch opposition. Some move in the expected direction, others in the opposite direction. The result, therefore, of applying hammer blows like this is to break the material in two, to make people go with you or against you, depending upon their sense of identification with you or their awareness of the fact that you are invading their territory and demanding of them that they yield—in which case they get their dander up and move in the opposite direction. Whenever the self comes in you are likely to get forced decisions. The self is too central, too fundamental, too important to be jockeyed with in terms of little gestures here and there. You are either for me or against me and I take my stand accordingly.

It is partly for this reason that in therapy and in education changes in the picture of the self are frequently sudden rather than gradual. Indeed

---

[7] E. A. Rundquist and R. F. Sletto, *Personality in the Depression*, Minneapolis, University of Minnesota Press, 1936.

[8] W. H. Wilke, An experimental comparison of the speech, the radio, and the printed page as propaganda devices, *Arch. Psychol.*, 1934, No. 169.

the process of therapy is likely to be either a brilliant success or a complete "bust," depending upon whether we do or do not touch the possibilities of a reconstruction of the self-image. The material quoted above (page 435) from Snyder serves to reinforce this point.

You would expect, on this basis, that when there are incompatible pictures of the self, with resulting conflict and suffering, there will usually be a *knock-'em-down drag-'em-out* victory for one or the other. If there is not, we find the kind of material presented by Carl Binger and his associates (page 103). In the young men and women who have built up a picture of themselves as "good people," accepting their parents' guidance and affection, there gradually develops a sense of futility and helplessness because they cannot break away from parental domination. They despise themselves for their helplessness, their dependence upon their parents. They become more and more incapable of accepting the self-image as dependent, and yet they cannot completely renounce such an image and look upon themselves as dominant people, free altogether of parental control and affection. They do not dare to make the break. They carry around with themselves two self-pictures, one of which they cannot completely realize and the other of which makes them feel afraid and ashamed. Nor can they pretend that either picture tells the whole story. They manage over the years to keep themselves ignorant to a large degree of what is going on, until finally the necessity for taking a stand, the necessity for breaking completely with the parents, throws into sharp relief the hopeless nature of the opposition between the two images. Most of us, most of the time, avoid such conflict by setting up one or the other goal and self-picture, pushing ahead or "retreating in good order."

And just as there is discontinuity between selves, so there is discontinuity in personality type insofar as there are different *ways of enhancing the self* at a given time. We saw earlier, in considering the psychoanalytic mechanisms, that one may repress, regress, project, identify, indulge in reaction formation, etc. Many psychoanalysts believe that people tend to make habitual use of certain psychoanalytic mechanisms to the relative exclusion of others, one person being predominantly a rationalizer, another predominantly a projector, etc. (cf. page 430). We found that there are apparently personality types related to the *way in which one learns*. Apparently more is involved than one specific habit;

for the student shows these ways of working with different subject matters, and on successive occasions. Moreover, there appears to be a really deep-seated cleft among the students who have these different ways of working, as judged by teachers who know these students well. This would, in fact, be what we should expect if images of the self develop through finding that one is "good at math," "poor at languages," etc., and if in addition to the initial differences in individual ability there has been an exaggeration of the sense of competence in one area and the sense of helplessness in another, until people have actually developed lopsided pictures of themselves.

On the whole, then, despite all the difficulties we have raised, there *are* some real situations in which people can apparently be successfully typed. It is important not to prejudge the issue, we must always demand proof. We should, in other words, always treat people as distributed through a continuum *unless* we have positive evidence that we are dealing with sharp divisions and categories. We may use the categories if we know that they exist.

Finally, a general warning needs to be urged regarding personality types. The types are limited in their utility to the situations in which they have actually been observed. If you find in a particular social situation that every individual is either very outgoing or very withdrawn, you may be tempted to apply a general theory of introversion and extroversion. Perhaps, however, some people have been in that social situation before and "know the ropes"; perhaps others are new to it. Perhaps you find you can make yourself understood by half the members of a social gathering; the others stare stonily at you. It is possible that if you knew the backgrounds, the life situations, in which all your various people move and have their existence, you would actually find that the typing is very real and fundamental, for people with one social background often fail to grasp an issue as it is presented to those with another social background. And yet, when you set up a new situation in respect to which all your people have essentially the same experience, the types may vanish into thin air. Types are relative, in other words, to the concrete modes of reaction to the environment on which you have direct evidence, and it is unwise to assume that the types which are actually observed in one situation have any true predictive power for basically different situations.

This will mean, for example, that in situations in which people are aware of their membership in well-defined classes—as when the workers put on their Sunday best to attend the boss's funeral and sit in the same church with the boss's friends—there is likely to be a real cleavage in response along the lines of the attitudes which go with such membership. But in other situations, where there is nothing to remind us of such group membership—as when all of us stretch in the seventh inning of a ball game—we are not divided into well-defined types. For the most part, types arise from the fact that *situations themselves* throw us into activity categories; outside of such categories we keep ourselves on a normal curve in many activities rather than grouping ourselves into types.

SUGGESTED READINGS

Allport, G. W., *Personality*, New York, Holt, 1937, Part 3.

Jung, C. G., *Psychological Types*, New York, Harcourt, Brace, 1923.

Kretschmer, E., *Physique and Character*, New York, Harcourt, Brace, 1926.

MacKinnon, D. W., The Structure of Personality, in Hunt, J. McV. (ed.), *Personality and the Behavior Disorders*, New York, Ronald, 2 vols., 1944, chap. 1.

Murphy, G., *Personality*, New York, Harper, 1947, chaps. 26, 27.

Sheldon, W. H., with the collaboration of S. S. Stevens, *The Varieties of Temperament*, New York, Harper, 1942.

28 CULTURE AND THE INDIVIDUAL

I. Ethnological Evidence

As L. K. Frank has remarked, if a fish started to study its environment, the last thing it would notice would be the water. It is so immersed in it that it sees the moving things about it, rather than the all-encompassing fluid. The last thing of which human beings have really become aware, in their long history of studying themselves, has been the intimate way in which they express the social world of which they are a part.

Of course we have considered in every phase the interaction of the individual with the environment. But we have really taken the environment very much for granted. We have assumed, for example, our growing up with fathers and mothers, brothers and sisters, neighbors; a language which chops the world up into pieces designated by words; moral and legal sanctions; inventions which make the spread of words almost instantaneous; attitudes toward the past and the future. This social world of ours differs profoundly from other social worlds which are just as real and fundamental to many other groups of the human family as our own is to us. In some human societies the father is not part of the family group. The child has little to do with him; the mother's brother is the adult male to whom the child is responsible. Or the child may live in an "extended" family group with fifty relatives under one roof; all are part of his world. In some societies there is no sense of affinity with those nearby; many of them are enemies. In other societies everyone in the village is a friend. Personality is molded profoundly by the very nature of the social organization of which the family and the individual are expressions.

If, then, we wish to understand what we ourselves are, we shall have to cease taking our social environment for granted, and begin to compare social environments of various types and of many levels of complexity, seeing just as clearly as we can what the social surroundings do to the molding of action, feeling, and thought in the growing individual, and the way in which the relationships among persons constitute the supporting and stimulating pressures which make us so different from people who grow up in other social worlds. You know a man from Missouri, perhaps, by his tempo and the fact that you have to "show" him; a man from Virginia or from the Back Bay in Boston by his sense of tradition and fitness. If you take the boat across the two hundred yards from Matapedia in French Canada to Campbelltown, New Brunswick, you find yourself transported in ten minutes from one whole way of thinking and feeling about life to another—the French to the British. Every posture, expression, attitude reflects the rich background of an entire civilization.

It is going to be our task in this chapter to look at the relations between the individual and his culture—culture is the broad term indicating the whole social outlook, form of organization, and way of life—in the simple kinds of human societies which have no written language. In the following chapter a similar comparison of the relations of the individual and society will be made at a more complex level, in societies in which there is written language. Students of society distinguish between "preliterate" and "literate" societies. It is the preliterate ones, those without written language, that are our first concern.

Fifty years ago the great pioneer of American ethnology, Franz Boas, gave us a description of the Indians of Vancouver Island which has become almost legendary in its value in opening our eyes to the nature of culture; for he presented a picture of a community that in some respects is like our own, but in one sense is so extreme as to be a caricature of it. This is the culture of the Kwakiutl Indians, a fine, strong, vivid, self-reliant group, with efficient agriculture and fishing, and maintaining a rather high standard of living. Among the Kwakiutl chieftains life was a perpetual struggle for *prestige*, prestige as represented by wealth, and wealth tossed about in a frantic and unremitting effort to assert one chieftain's superiority to others. One chieftain amassed, over a period of months, vast quantities of blankets, copper kettles, and similar expressions of material wealth. He then invited another of the chieftains to a tremendous "potlatch," a feast and ceremony in which he destroyed his own blankets and kettles on a fantastic scale. The other chief was thereby challenged to make a similar display of destruction and to surpass the first. If he could not destroy blankets and kettles in an even greater quantity, he was put to shame. Thus, everything seemed to be coördinated to inflate the ego of the individual chieftain. In the same way, if he suffered dire misfortune—if, for example, his son died—his feeling was that unseen powers and the law of life itself had insulted him, and it was perfectly proper for him to slay the son of another chieftain. Here the ego sticks out like a big toe. Life is a problem of making the most of opportunities for display and for ego inflation.

If we turn for comparison to the Zuñi Indians of the Southwest pueblos, we encounter a quiet, strong, effective, slow-moving, level-headed group of agriculturalists, with an extraordinary equality of possessions and of status. Every man has enough; he tills the soil steadily and competently; no one seeks to be a leader. Positions of authority and responsibility are avoided if possible. The children are brought up to take no advantage of their superior wit or strength in competition with others. "Everybody should be alike." (In a similar group in the Southwest Pacific, the pidgin English phrase has been coined to describe this relationship: "All man he walk alongside.") Among the Zuñi, competition is muted, just as among the Kwakiutl it is exaggerated, in both the way and tempo of life, and above all in looking at oneself.

Nor is this type of contrast between competition and coöperation limited to the unique situation of the Indians of North America. If we compare the mountain Arapesh of New Guinea with the Manus, a seafaring people of the Admiralty Islands, we find an amazing antithesis. Margaret Mead[1] reports that the mountain Arapesh are a quiet, coöperative, gentle group. There is no struggle for possessions, for power, or for prestige. Every child grows up with a sense of belonging to the group as a whole; he is made much of, affectionately handled, and emotionally accepted

---

[1] M. Mead, *Cooperation and Competition Among Primitive Peoples*, New York, McGraw-Hill, 1937.

tutional living—economic, political, family, educational, religious, etc.—are closely interdependent. The same sort of interdependence that we saw in the personality structure (page 499) is found also with reference to the aspects of social structure studied by the ethnologists. We might

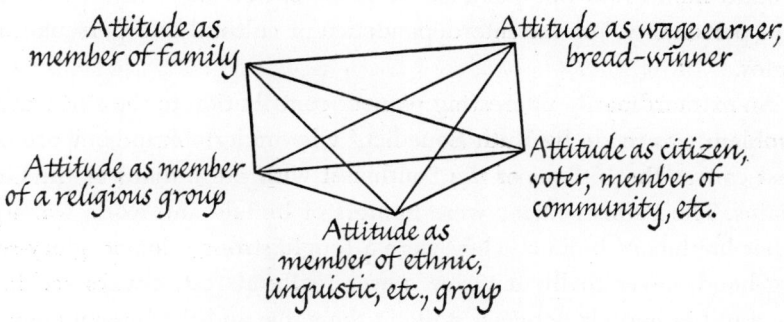

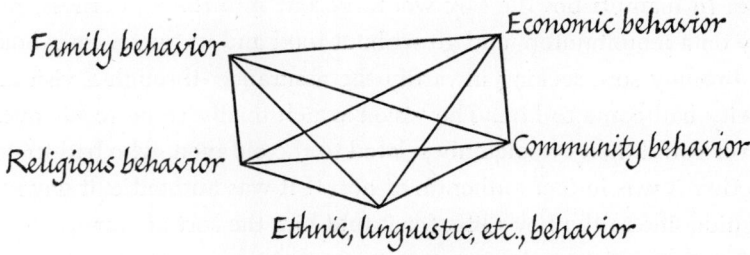

Figure 93. The Individual and Society

formulate in Figure 93 some of the possible modes of mutual influence which exist between institutional patterns. If it is remembered that, after all, the patterns exist *in the behavior of individuals* we shall hardly be surprised to find again that personality is a system of interdependent traits, each reflecting the life of the group as a whole. How could it be otherwise?

This way of thinking will avoid the difficulty of regarding economic institutions as something external to the individual and somehow driving a wedge into him. We shall be able to think, rather, of the individual as a sort of bearer or vehicle of all the ways of thinking, feeling, and behaving which characterize the group; we may think of the individual child, as he grows up, as taking over the interrelated system of attitudes, feelings, and forms of conduct which are expressed by the community around him. From this point of view one speaks nowadays of "culture and personality," or the interdependence of cultural and personal attributes.

An extraordinarily interesting pioneer contribution to the study of this problem was made by Ruth Benedict,[4] who undertook to compare on a vast canvas the Indians of the Southwest with the Indians of the Great Plains. The Plains Indians were hunters of buffalo and made war upon other hunters of buffalo. They were a tough, strong, violent, glory-seeking band, never really at peace, never really at rest, always seeking— even in the periods between stalking the game and the human enemy— the intense, the magnificent, the personally overwhelming types of experience. Their religion, for example, involved a highly individualistic struggle of the young boy for a form of *supernatural power and guidance*. In many tribes the boy would go out into the wilderness, preferably on a mountaintop, and go without food and water for long hours in the broiling sun, seeking inwardly the assurance, through a vision, that a deity had come to him. The vision which finally came to his overtaut nerves could then be solemnly related to the old men, who had to decide whether it was in fact authentic or not. If it was authentic, it gave a sort of guide line to the boy's life, for it told him the sort of warrior or medicine man or chieftain he was to be.

It was characteristic of these men of the Plains to seek always for *individual glory*, rather than for wealth or tangible signs of success. Thus at night when you stole *ten* horses, you might get one little feather to wear in your headdress. But if you went out on a bright moonlight night, approached the sentinel in the enemy's camp, slapped him in the face before killing him, and then stole a *single* horse, you received a *big* feather (grand coup). It was not how many horses, it was not material

---

[4] R. Benedict, *Patterns of Culture*, Boston, Houghton Mifflin, 1934.

wealth, it was the amount of danger that measured the extent of your glory. When huge bonfires were built in the evening and the braves sat around them, each one, as he tossed his pine knot into the fire, told a taller story than that of his predecessor. It was a "boasting contest" which simply duplicated and carried forward the extraordinary self-importance that had been spun in the tasks of the days preceding the meeting.

If, sometime, you drive over U. S. 66 through Sun Dance, Wyoming, this name, apparently so romantic, may perhaps remind you of the Plains Indian's ordeal of the "skewers." The brave was hoisted aloft with skewers driven through the muscles of the breast; and as the muscles were torn and he did not flinch, he gave final proof of the heroism which even hours of dancing in the broiling sun had not established among his equally tough and violent onlookers. As Benedict says, this was the sort of life that Friedrich Nietzsche had in mind when (in *The Birth of Tragedy*) he contrasted the cult of Dionysus, the wine god, with the cult of Apollo, the god of grace and beauty. To be *Dionysian* meant, for Nietzsche, to be *violent, savage, uncontrolled, orgiastic.* The Indians of the Great Plains, says Benedict, were *Dionysian.*

When one looks at the Southwest, everything changes. Here a steady, dignified, solemn, poised, graceful civilization, with beautiful pottery and silversmith work, maintains the charming and gentle traditions of communal life and religion. Life is public sharing, not private self-enhancement. Thus, no one would dare place a prayer stick in the ground alone, lest he be accused of black magic, for religion is a matter of the *group.* All must work in their religious exercises. Benedict regards these people as the embodiment of Nietzsche's other principle, the *Apollonian.* The Indians of the Southwest live according to the grace and beauty of Apollo rather than accepting the impulsiveness and violence of Dionysus.

These different ways of living get "into the blood"—are impressed upon the nervous system—very, very early. One sees aggressive attitudes, friendly attitudes, anti-social attitudes, taking on the social pattern in the behavior of very small children. So deeply ingrained are the attitudes that they are transmitted to the young for some time even after the *existence* pattern of life has changed; the Sioux boys of today, fifty years after the collapse of the Sioux hunting system, still play games that center in the life of the braves.[5]

A word, ethos, has been coined to describe the *feeling tone* of a civilization as a whole; the thing that makes the Great Plains orgiastic and the Southwest beauty-loving is *ethos*. Ethos is a comprehensive term that covers the spirit of a people—the rugged individualism of early America, the "methodical" approach of the German, the "reserve" of the British. But where a more complex society is full of internal contradictions and wide personal variations, it is held that preliterate societies are homogeneous, that people share the same spirit. This is one important feature in the characteristic personality pattern of the members of a cultural group; it is sometimes called the basic character structure. Other features which they share would be their religious and political ideas, their ways of working and playing, etc. But a strong case could be made that the ethos, as the fundamental feeling tone of life, colors all the ways of the group, and therefore of the individual as related to the group.

Now if this is so, i.e., if there is such a thing as a personality pattern that characterizes the members of a cultural group, it may be worth while to see if we can put to use the various *projective methods* and other personality research devices which we found to be so useful in our own society. Perhaps we can in this way discover the basic character structure of a social group. Accordingly, within the past few years, there has been a great deal of concentrated and successful investigation of the personality dynamics of preliterate peoples by means of such tests. An example is the study by the Henrys,[6] who showed that the doll play of the Pilagá Indian children of the Gran Chaco in South America could tell a psychologist, sitting in a New York office and knowing nothing much about the Pilagá civilization, the things that were essential to permit a good description of the nature of Pilagá social life.

In the same way, the Rorschach responses sent by Cora DuBois from the island of Alor in the East Indies to a New York psychiatrist, made evident to him the way of life of the people of Alor (page 468). From their responses it was clear that these people were suspicious, with-

---

[5] E. H. Erikson, Observations on Sioux education, *J. Psychol.*, 1937, 7, 101–156.
[6] J. Henry and Z. Henry, Doll play of Pilagá Indian children, *Res. Monogr. Amer. Orthopsychiat. Ass.*, 1944, No. 40.

drawn, anti-social, that they had no such warm and strong social support as would give them an effective, happy form of livelihood. Nor on the other hand were they capable of that tight, strong, military discipline, or despotic unification, which would have made them at least members of one co-working band; rather, they were disorganized, undisciplined, full of hatred, suspicion, and uncertainty. All this was clear from the form of attack on the Rorschach cards, just as it was clear from the autobiographies collected from some members of the group and by other projective methods. The ethnologist's account of the culture, which had not been reported to the Rorschach analyst in any form, corroborated the interpretations.

In most of these studies we see the adult world and the world of the half-grown child far more clearly than we can see the world of the infant; so it is hard to discover just how personality development in a culture *begins*. There is, however, some material bearing on the nature of earliest childhood among preliterate peoples which gives a picture of personality dynamics in the light of which the adult character structure can better be understood. An outstanding example is the study of the people of Bali by Bateson and Mead.[7] In their study of the children of a mountain village in Bali, they describe a number of the practices followed by the mothers which may perhaps throw some light upon personality development. After the usual maternal care and caressing in the first months, the mother rather suddenly turns to a different approach. She begins to *tease* her baby quite violently by refusing to pay any attention to his demands for affection, and "rubs salt into the wound" by borrowing a baby from another mother and caressing this other baby in plain sight of her own. Her own child, frantically jealous, screaming in a temper tantrum, gets no relief. The mother simply smiles as she goes on with the process of teasing. The child learns, after a couple of years of this, that his wails get him nowhere, that he does not get the response he wants, that he must learn to *withdraw* and find some sort of fulfillment within himself, rather than in the intense, warm relationship with his mother. He derives various satisfactions from the rhythmic movement of his body being carried in a sling over his mother's shoulder; he

---

[7] G. Bateson and M. Mead, *Balinese Character*, New York, New York Academy of Sciences, 1942.

gets the gentle, regular rhythms of her activity as she works. He learns also to imagine and daydream. He is given toys which represent not only the human body, but also its various parts; he is allowed to make the most of body consciousness. He maps out, then, one part of life as pretty safe for his own fantasies and for his own quiet indulgence in the adequate world that he develops within himself, by *withdrawing* from the intensity of social give-and-take.

Figure 94. Personality Development in Culture

The objects in the gutter fascinate this child and she goes after them. But culture, in the guise of the unmistakably restraining hand of the mother, says, "No, those things are dirty. You must not play with them." Through the agency of such forcible signs cultural sanctions are taught to children in our society at an early age.

Moreover, as the toddler starts to explore this interesting world, finding the little path between two buildings, the mother suddenly screams at him a horror-word—*arai*—which may mean that he is about to step on a scorpion. It means "Look out" raised to the *n*th power. By such means she scares him into staying on the straight and narrow path. Perhaps he learns more than just the rule of keeping out of trouble; perhaps he learns that life is a hazard in which one clings to all that is safe; perhaps, as Bateson would say, he learns *how to learn*, namely, he knows that the way to learn is to do meekly what he is told. This is by no means dissimilar to the experience of many children in our own culture, as Figure 94 dramatically illustrates.

There are, however, certain occasions in life when the early intensity of his demands upon life is given a chance to be warmed up again and put into full expression. There are grand ceremonial occasions of dancing and pageantry, and the great play which represents the violent struggle between the dragon and the witch, in which all the participants without reserve throw themselves into an exquisite intensity of feeling which would be comparable, in some ways, to our responses to a prize fight or perhaps to the last quarter of a close football game. There is, then, for the Balinese child a double organization of the world—a withdrawn, quiet, serene, gracious world, and a world of violent intensity. These two worlds mirror and perpetuate the early cleavage of the world between an inner, safe world and an outer, violent kind of world. Personality reflects early experience.

Social Roles

Of importance equal to the idea of ethos is another concept used by students of society. This is the concept that each individual is cast for a certain *role* in life, this role being determined by the institutional tasks which have to be done. We have already suggested that personality is partly comprised of a group of attitudes relative to the individual's life tasks. The idea, however, needs to be more fully developed. We shall have to consider not only the roles related to making a living, but also the many other roles which the individual will play as daughter or son, brother or sister, as parent, husband, or wife, as citizen, as member of a club or political party or religious or other organization. The individual typically fulfills many roles at once. *The roles which he has to fulfill mark themselves upon his personality.* He becomes in time the kind of person who sees things in terms of the tasks which he has learned to perform, and the performance of which gives him *status* in the community.

To make all of this concrete, we may look at the Iatmul people of New

Guinea.[8] The Iatmul are a strong, upstanding, martial, head-hunting people of New Guinea whose adult males found fulfillment in predatory activity against neighboring tribes. In periods when no war was afoot, they stood about in the men's ceremonial house for a large part of each day, boasting, swaggering, attacking and belittling one another with every variety of verbal onslaught. They were, so to speak, cast in the *predatory role* to such an extent that they had to go on with it even when there was no war to be fought with hands and weapons. The women, on the contrary, were a quiet, peaceful, well-adjusted group whose roles in life called simply for effective homemaking

But the plot begins to thicken. The men, victors in a war, have completed one of their military processions. Now a time comes when the women dress up in the finest regalia they can put on, and swagger even more magnificently than the men. What is the meaning of this? There are other occasions on which the women put on the dirtiest possible garb; they grovel in the dust, and allow the little boys to walk over them. What is this all about? Is this just the "queer" behavior of savage people? Actually, if one looks, one finds that there is always a reason, a complex and meaningful reason. It appears that the normal everyday martial role and swaggering behavior of the men has produced in the women a little more quiet domesticity than they really need or want; it has, moreover, made it possible for them to catch the spirit of display, and has prompted them to make the most of their "day in the sun" when they likewise can show off in the grand style. The women's procession results from the monotony and the strain of always being subordinate. But even this is not the whole story. The women know in their hearts that this martial show-off behavior is really not in accordance with their basic roles. They have overdone the role a bit. Perhaps there is a place to make obeisance to the little boys who will be military heroes in their time.

One gets the feeling that acting out *one* role is perhaps an inducement to playing *another* role which is a sort of reaction to it. In the same way, the over-hard businessman or the over-thrifty farmer may be glad on occasion to enact the casual, friendly role that brings out another aspect of himself which his ordinary role has blocked. The pompous man "lets

---

[8] G. Bateson, *Naven*, Cambridge, Cambridge University Press, 1936.

down" and becomes a "good fellow"; the society woman can go to her reunion and be "one of the girls." Each one of us may at any time find that he has been *overdriving one role*—as "grind," as "playboy," as "dutiful son," as "life of the party," as "smart woman." Each role in itself would give some satisfaction; yet each of us feels the need to choose from the roles available to us some other role or roles which will bring out some *other* aspects of our make-up.

There are, then, actually many roles to be lived. Sometimes one may be able to combine them all at a single time and in an appropriate way. A dignified, elderly, responsible leader of an ecclesiastical organization may, for example, be fulfilling the roles of benevolent father, patron and protector, paragon of all that is dignified and dependable in life as he sees it. He may feel no need for those vagaries, those chameleon-like shifts which characterize a person whose primary role gives him no such concentrated satisfactions, or offers them in such a lopsided way that a different kind of role must be developed in order to offer some variety. So, while some people find social roles capable of being harmoniously enacted all at once, it is characteristic of many other people to find that they can hardly bear the lopsidedness of life unless they shift about from role to role.

Roles, like every other type of social activity, have to be learned. Recent studies by Hartley, Rosenbaum, and Schwartz[9] show that small children in New York take years to understand what the different roles are that their fathers play in society, and to develop the idea that one may be a father, a postman, and a Roman Catholic all at once. A small Jewish child finds it difficult to grasp that one can be a Jew and an American at the same time. Each person functions differently in different groups, and it takes a long time to grasp that membership in a group may accompany membership in another group which calls for different behavior.

Since it takes so long to learn the roles which must be enacted by each person, it is hardly surprising that the child does a great deal of *experimenting with roles*. In his play we find him, so to speak, putting on one suit of clothes after another, one role after another, playing one part after another in his little drama; now he's a daddy, now a postman, now

---

[9] E. Hartley, M. Rosenbaum, and S. Schwartz, Children's use of ethnic frames of reference, *J. Psychol.*, 1948, 26, 367–386.

a fireman, now a pitcher, now a doggy, now a daddy again. We find the kindergartner and the first-grader playing the role of teacher's pet and tough guy, of mama's big boy and *enfant terrible* with different audiences —schoolmates, parents, grandparents. And in his own private world where he is sole observer, he experiments with these roles, and indirectly may try to find a way of putting them together. This reminds us of William James' celebrated discussion of all the different kinds of selves he would like to be: "Not that I would not, if I could, be both handsome and fat and well dressed, and a great athlete and make a million a year, be a wit, a *bon vivant*, and a lady-killer, as well as a philosopher; a philanthropist, statesman, warrior, and African explorer, as well as a 'tone-poet' and saint."[10]

We emerge, then, with the idea that the *integration of the self-picture* which we saw several times earlier is actually accomplished largely by *socially defined roles*, the definition and the integration of which are largely determined by the way in which society defines jobs to be done. These roles play a large part in defining the kind of picture of ourself that we can draw; for every society defines roles in its own way—there is a fireman in our society, but not in another society. Moreover, an important role like that of teacher has great prestige in one society, very little in another. The child catches on and enhances the self in his roles while playing. The way in which roles can be combined is culturally determined; a fireman in a city can hardly be a shopkeeper, but in a village he can do both, and be a minister and a carpenter as well. By endless experimentation, always looking to see if we appear in a good light and have fun enough to be interested in the game, we "try on" the different selves and find which features of one role "look well" with features of another. Most of this, of course, is done half-consciously. But the society around us, by supplying examples of the roles to be played, supplies us with ideas as to what we would like to become, first tentatively; then we are more and more assured, until we have decided to become a doctor, a businessman, a nurse, a librarian, etc. The study of culture and of social roles proves this to be a major clue to understanding the picture of the self.

---

[10] W. James, *Principles of Psychology*, New York, Holt, 1890, vol. 1, p. 309.

SUGGESTED READINGS

Bateson, G., Cultural Determinants of Personality, in Hunt, J. McV. (ed.), *Personality and the Behavior Disorders*, New York, Ronald, 2 vols., 1944, chap. 23.
Benedict, R., *Patterns of Culture*, Boston, Houghton Mifflin, 1934.
Kardiner, A., and Linton, R., *The Individual and His Society*, New York, Columbia Univ. Press, 1939.
Kluckhohn, C., and Murray, H. A. (eds.), *Personality in Nature, Society and Culture*, New York, Knopf, 1949, chap. 1.
Lasswell, H. D., Person, personality, group, culture, *Psychiatry*, 1939, 2, 533–561.
Linton, R., *The Study of Man*, New York, Appleton-Century, 1936.
Mead, M., *Coming of Age in Samoa*, New York, Morrow, 1928.
Murphy, G., *Personality*, New York, Harper, 1947, Part 6.

29   CULTURE AND THE INDIVIDUAL

II. Our Own Tradition

Sometimes we think of "savage tribes," preliterate peoples, as helplessly molded by their environment, whereas civilized men are free to choose their ways of life. All of us, however, are molded, from the cradle to the grave, by the ways, habits, customs, the whole culture around us. We shall introduce the molding of modern Europeans and Americans by their social surroundings in the form of a study which can be rendered in picture form: Efron's study of the *gestures* of four European groups and what became of those gestures under American conditions.[1]

Figure 95. Effect of Culture on Gesture: "Traditional" Jew

Thumb-digging movement—digging out an idea. (Figures 95–98 from D. Efron, *Gesture and Environment*, Kings Crown Press, 1941.)

---

[1] D. Efron, *Gesture and Environment*, New York, King's Crown Press, 1941.

Just as one learns from one's cultural group the specific acts of the hands or the tongue, so one learns from the cultural group the way in which to hold the whole body. One acquires a posture, stance, or gesture. As against the notion, for instance, that we are born with a tendency to express emotion through specific gestures, or indeed that whole races of

Figure 96. Effect of Culture on Gesture: "Traditional" Italian

Wide gestural radius; movement from the shoulder.

men differ innately in such expression, David Efron made a study of the way in which social groups differ in such expression as a result of environment. He made a comparison, by means of motion pictures, of four large groups of human beings: (1) a group of "traditional" Italians —Italians coming mostly from villages in southern Italy but living in New York City in a section where their daily round of activities largely involved others of their own cultural background; (2) a group of "assimilated" Italians—second-generation members who had foregone their earlier cultural habits and lived simply as Americans; (3) a group of "traditional" Jews, mostly from the semi-Ghetto existence of central and western Europe, living primarily within their own group; (4) a second-generation group of young Jews who were Americanized in their ways and their outlook. Efron's photographs show the striking differences between the ways in which the traditional Italians and the traditional Jews show their excitement, their joy, their fear, and their rage. Almost every fiber of the musculature of these individuals is thrown into dramatically

Figure 97. Effect of Culture on Gesture: 'Assimilated' Jew

No gesture over a period of about five minutes at a debate.

contrasting expressions which we all recognize and find in exaggerated form in the films or on the stage (Figures 95 96, 98). On the other hand, the two assimilated groups are devoid of these characteristic expressions from their Italian or Jewish traditions, are indistinguishable from one another and from other Americans. Figure 97, representing an assimilated Jew, is characteristic. As one young Italian said to the writer, "The hardest thing to learn about talking English is to hold the hands at the sides." The molding of the body has gone far beyond the question of learning to make a specific indication with lip or hand. The entire outgoing or withdrawing expressive pattern has changed.

What is the basis for the differences between these people? Take the fact that these traditional Italians lived in small villages where there was plenty of space, that most of them came from families that had been resident in the village for hundreds of years. Nobody, therefore, had any problem of being accepted in the group. Everybody knew who everybody else was. Every family was part of the village. Free sweeping gestures

Figure 98. Effect of Culture on Gesture: "Traditional" Italian

Symbolic gestures signifying "good," "sweet," "pretty."

seem to go with a free confident attitude. The traditional Jews, on the other hand, came from a Ghetto existence in which there was very little space and in which the outer world pushed in relentlessly upon them. The typical gestures are those of self-defense and withdrawal. As to the assimilation process, life in New York City, with all its confusion, nevertheless allows relative freedom to individuals and relative opportunity to take a stand and make a gesture as one likes; the mass of the residents gesticulate little; the traditional differences rapidly disappear in the new molding process which all individuals share.

This is just an introduction to the conception that each one of us reflects the ways of his group. But so far we have looked only at *specific behavior;* how about the *personality as a whole* as an expression of modern ways of living?

The Psychological Results of Our History

A book of this sort, if prepared for and used by Chinese students or students in India or Israel or Brazil today, might appropriately compare the development of personality in preliterate societies with the development of personality in their own more complex cultural heritage. It is reasonable to use, as far as we can, the ideas which proved fruitful in our study of simpler societies in the preceding chapter, but to keep our eyes open to the very great variety of forces which have flowed together to make the kind of society to which we belong, and to try to see how such a society molds our own individual characters. It is not our aim to teach history as such, but to remind ourselves of a few basic historical landmarks, a few basic trends, with which we are all familiar, and to see their psychological implications, i.e., to see how personality is molded by culture.

We may begin by emphasizing the important role played in our own personalities today by four huge contributing factors: (1) the civilization of the Greeks as it took shape in the literature, philosophy, and science of the great period of about 2500 years ago; (2) the civilization of the Hebrews as expressed, for example, in the Old Testament, and maintained and transmuted by the Christian tradition which grew out of it; (3) the Roman system of law and government; and (4) the western and central European traditions of the Celtic and German-speaking peoples, and the other preliterate folk who were in varying degree molded and assimilated at a later time into the Roman Empire and into the nation-states which are its present-day descendants. These people may all seem remote from us; but if we compare ourselves with the people of India, Burma, China, the East Indies, we begin to realize how much we have in common with the men and women of two or three thousand years ago who are culturally (if not always biologically) our ancestors.

Let us look at the Greeks. A strong, "swashbuckling" band of brigands, as Gilbert Murray[2] calls them, besieging a rich town on the east coast of the Aegean Sea and making their way home again, is portrayed for us in the great epic poems of Homer. These people, mingling thereafter with the thoughtful, artistic native people of the Greek peninsula and of the maritime islands of the Mediterranean, gave rise within a few generations to the imaginative, scientific, and immensely creative Greeks of the Age of Pericles, whose literature, whose basic artistic forms of expression, whose scientific and philosophical ways of interpreting the world

---

[2] G. Murray, *Five Stages in Greek Religion,* New York, Columbia University Press, 1925.

are still very much with us. Every capital and column you see on a large building is Greek; most of the scientific terms you use are Greek; the way you feel about poetry and about art is probably largely Greek.

The strong family loyalties, the moral intensities, and the passionate devotion to a unitary deity which characterize the ancient Hebrews, especially during the age of the great prophets, come to us for the most part through the vehicle of Christianity, in which these moral and religious emphases still mark out an area of life as real as the world of philosophy and science—indeed, for many people, even more real. If you discuss belief in God with a friend, your thinking is probably largely Hebrew, for the conception of a unitary personal God is unknown in most civilizations.

Both Greek and Jewish elements were, of course, assimilated by the civilization of western Europe, notably by the Roman Catholic Church; and after the Protestant Reformation, they have been found essential ingredients in every Christian mode of thought—or indeed, paradoxically, in every agnostic mode of thought that stems from the western tradition. Both the belief and the disbelief of today run in channels long since marked out by the believers and the doubters among the Greeks and the Hebrews. The skeptical science of today, with its faith in the unity and order of the world, was well known even in Socrates' time.

But it was not only the Mediterranean peoples, it was also the peoples of western and northern Europe that poured the life blood of their own thoughts and feelings into the making of modern western society. Certainly the Germans of Caesar's day and the Germans whom we discover in the literature of the tenth century of the Christian era already had the methodical, stalwart, orderly, law-abiding character, along with the touches of romanticism, which we find in the Germans of a later period. And certainly the intense romanticism and mysticism of many of the Celtic groups was carried over, in the tradition of King Arthur and his knights, and in other folk tales, into the immensely rich early French and English romantic literature which has played so large a part in the poetic and general esthetic feeling of the French- and English-speaking peoples. In all these ways the personalities of modern American men and women are shaped by the cultural tradition to which they belong.

But now we must come to the *economic* emphasis about which we wrote in the preceding chapter. The medieval system was founded largely upon the system of the *manor house,* the self-sufficient home and surrounding farm area within which all human beings were interdependent. The manor was a self-sufficient economic unit that bartered with other units, and was protected through the power of the great lord who, as knight or captain, provided relative safety against intrusion or attack from other manorial units nearby, or from the princelings from a more distant region. Ultimately the whole unit was founded upon two things: first, military force, incarnate in the knights in armor, a hard, relentless, self-sufficient man of arms; and secondly, the economic independence which went with atrociously bad roads and the futility and danger of travel. It was these men-at-arms who had saved Europe from chaos when the Roman Empire battled unsuccessfully against the invading barbarians; it was they who had stopped the march of the Moslems; it was they who had stood out against the terrible raids of the Vikings from the north; it was they who maintained local order and safety everywhere. "What does it mean to be a man?" People's answer was the picture of the knight. Even the squire, the yeoman, the bond servant or thrall, accepted this standard of masculine nobility. The fighting man was usually too tough for the arts, so he let the men of the monastery—and the women of noble lineage—carry forward the civilized tradition; but in time he learned from them, and listened to the romantic songs and stories which the womenfolk loved and encouraged.

It was this period of the self-sufficient man-at-arms which first gave us the great literature of chivalry—an age, speaking literally, of the man on horseback (*cheval* = horse). Not only were King Arthur and his Round Table representative of the spirit of the period; this spirit had so profoundly taken possession of men's minds that even while the manorial system decayed, the great works of English and French drama and fiction portrayed it magnificently. It was in this era that the great characters of Shakespeare were conceived. Men were ready at any time to draw their swords in defense of honor. Men capable of passionate heroism and of passionate love, without raising questions regarding how it will affect business, are the expression of a society in which readiness for rugged single-handed fighting like that of the knight is the bulwark of self-defense. In France and elsewhere in western Europe the same held true. The reader of *The Three Musketeers* will remember the kind of life which those young warriors led, and will find many of the same values. The great mass of people could not become warriors; they stayed in the class in which they were born. Perhaps most people accepted their "status in life" without a murmur. To some degree, at least, they saw through the eyes of their masters.

With the invention of gunpowder (and cannon, and other new weapons) and the consequent futility of this armed man on his armed horse (there was no safety even in his stone castle), and with the improvement in means of communication by land and sea, economic self-sufficiency was broken down, and the *market*—that is, a system of intercommunication and of distribution of goods for a money price—came into existence.

The breakdown of the ordered pattern and the development of a market with relatively free exchange, not only from county to county but from nation to nation, ushered in the commercial revolution, that great transition which began to emphasize a new kind of values: shrewdness, thrift, careful planning, an eye to long-range realities. Such an outlook is really more characteristic of the commercial outlook of the Manus people, whom we have already considered, than of the immediate ancestors of the merchants themselves. "What it means to be a man" is defined no longer in terms of courage and toughness, but in terms of astuteness and an eye to the main chance.

One finds in the same way that while religion had been largely a matter of *group* experience, now the religious viewpoints that are intensely *individualistic* become congenial. There had been many efforts to protest against the Roman Catholic outlook, many forms of Protestantism, before the era of Luther and Calvin. It was, however, with the rise of the commercial class and its individualistic view of life that the individualistic conception of religion found its most congenial harborage in Calvinism. Men were already growing lonely because of the fact that large family units were breaking up, people seeking their fortunes everywhere, some rising, some falling, and few knowing the people about them. They became even more lonely because of the fact that God inscrutably rewarded some and condemned others, and no church, no wife, no child, could influence His will. (This outlook gradually softened, but individualism remained.)

The shock of conflict between chivalry and the commercial point of view appears clearly in the contrasting viewpoints that every student of English literature encounters in the mid-seventeenth century. Think, for example, of the stately and restrained rhythms of John Milton—essentially expressing the newer, more restrained and rationalistic approach—in contrast to the romantic lyrics of Lovelace and Herrick which represent pure chivalry: "I could not love thee, dear, so much, loved I not honor more." Rationalism, practicality, self-control, all that it takes to get ahead in this world, become more and more central in the new business outlook. Together with this, of course, comes a less naïve belief in the traditional authorities, more critical challenging, a wider belief that man, by using *reason,* can find his way to the ultimate answers. This is a partial explanation of why rationalism and skepticism, as in the agnostics of the eighteenth century, became so prominent. The power of the authorities over men's thinking is declining; the mechanical conceptions of the world, developing in astronomy (though offered by Sir Isaac Newton in a profoundly religious spirit), gradually substitute a *mechanical* universe for the *purposive* universe of the personal Deity envisaged by Hebrew, Greek, and Christian thinkers. The authority of the Bible and the authority of the Church manifestly declined decade by decade, and morals ceased to be an absolute code expressive of the Deity, and became a series of human conventions agreed upon and followed because of social necessity.

Upon the heels of the commercial revolution followed the Industrial Revolution, the development of power-driven machines, usually placed in factories, in which the labor of those who tend machines produces in vast quantities better products than were ever produced by a small handicraft unit at home during the centuries preceding the transition. Harry Elmer Barnes remarked that the Industrial Revolution of the last century and a half has so profoundly changed our life that while George Washington would have been perfectly at home in the world of Aristotle, he would feel completely lost in the world of today. The Industrial Revolution has, of course, intensified the emphasis on individualism, practicality, science, skepticism, reasonableness which had been developed earlier by the commercial revolution. But it has introduced some ideas of its own. It has gradually prepared us to think less of *individual competition,* which was the heart of commercialism, and to awaken to vast, impersonal forces like modern corporations, which efficiently produce goods for an impersonal mass of consumers and make money for an impersonal mass of owners of securities. Many an economist today emphasizes the difference between competing with the man across the street and sharing in the vast enterprises of an oil company which in some distant land competes with another gigantic corporation.

The world has become even less personal than it was during the commercial revolution. Many organizations are so big that employers do not know their employees. The employees hardly know one another; the life of the shop and bench is impersonal. A man's friends may drive from another part of the city to work at a bench next to his own, but he does not see them except at work. Life, moreover, has become *mechanized* in the sense that he does a small operation in production like turning a particular nut on a car while the continuous flow of the production line moves past. Much of what we do is not really worthy of a full-sized human being. At the same time, people have gotten into the habit of moving about in quest of jobs to such a degree that, at the age of starting a family, less than half of all urban Americans live in the community in which they grew up, and the big cities are full of lonely people. The feeling of being *alone,* and of being a helpless creature battered about by machines, has added to the experience of emptiness that comes from doing trifling tasks that do not call for everything we have to give. Erich Fromm[3] believes that this loneliness, through loss of the stable *position* in society that existed in the medieval period, is a prime cause of our modern need for slogans and crowds, our need to be sure we are all right, our need to be doing what others are doing. This sense of *belonging* supports us and gives meaning to an otherwise meaningless loneliness, and a ceaseless going-through of motions. These are the words Gordon Allport uses to describe modern man:

He wakens to grab the morning's milk left at the door by an agent of a vast Dairy and Distributing system whose corporate manoeuvers, so vital to

[3] E. Fromm, *Escape from Freedom,* New York, Norton, 1941.

his health, never consciously concern him. After paying hasty respects to his landlady, he dashes into the transportation system whose mechanical and civic mysteries he does not comprehend. At the factory he becomes a cog for the day in a set of systems far beyond his ken. To him (as to everybody else) the company he works for is an abstraction; he plays an unwitting part in the "creation of surpluses" (whatever they are), and though he doesn't know it his furious activity at his machine is regulated by the "law of supply and demand," and by "the availability of raw materials" and by "prevailing interest rates." Unknown to himself he is headed next week for the "surplus labor market." A union official collects his dues; just why he doesn't know. At noontime that corporate monstrosity, Horn and Hardart, swallows him up, much as he swallows one of its automatic pies. After more activity in the afternoon, he seeks out a standardized day-dream produced in Hollywood, to rest his tense, but *not* efficient mind. At the end of his day he sinks into a tavern, and unknowingly victimized by the advertising cycle, orders in rapid succession Four Roses, Three Feathers, Golden Wedding and Seagram's which "men who plan beyond tomorrow" like to drink.

Sam has been active all day, immensely active, playing a part in dozens of impersonal cycles of behavior. He has brushed scores of "corporate personalities," but has entered into intimate relations with no single human being. The people he has met are idler-gears like himself meshed into systems of transmission, far too distracted to examine any one of the cycles in which they are engaged. Throughout the day Sam is on the go, implicated in this task and that,—but does he, in a psychological sense, *participate* in what he is doing? Although constantly *task-involved*, is he ever really *ego-involved*?[4]

In American literature we find evidence of various social changes which have affected American personality. When Benjamin Franklin, in *Poor Richard's Almanac,* advises: "Early to bed and early to rise makes a man healthy, wealthy, and wise," he is thinking of the farmer and the small handicraftsman who get ahead by virtue of personal effort. Shortly after 1800 we find in the writings of Washington Irving a beautiful picture of the developing leisure class, essentially like the leisure class of Britain, as an expression of the economic changes which have come with the commercial revolution. For a while an effective counter-movement against leisure-class conservatism was led by Thomas Jefferson and particularly by Andrew Jackson, who sang the praises of the farmer's life, and succeeded in building a strong political weapon out of the farmer group with its small holdings scattered up and down the Atlantic seaboard and west of the Appalachians. Here, for a while, as the French

---

[4] G. W. Allport, The psychology of participation. *Psychol. Rev.,* 1945, 53, 117–132; quotation from p. 121.

observer de Tocqueville showed in his great book, *Democracy in America* (1830), there was in everyday life a direct expression of the fact that men were essentially equal in their pioneer struggle for units of land on which they could maintain their homes and rear their children. Political democracy, social democracy, the feeling that one man was as good as another, the basic homespun pious virtues of thrift, self-control, courage, adaptability to every new test, hardihood in the face of inequities and dangers—all of these are rather clear illustrations of what we have called the *economic determination of character structure*. This was the main new factor in American character; the aristocracy was too small a group to alter the essential picture. But for a long time a struggle went on between these equalitarian forces and the newer forces of concentrated economic power (shipping, banks, etc., mostly on the Atlantic coast) which came particularly with the Industrial Revolution.

Mark Twain is a good example of a literary figure who played off against each other two pictures of American life—the equalitarian *Huckleberry Finn* and the industrialists of *The Gilded Age*, later lampooned in the silk-hatted cigar-smoking men of the political caricatures. The world of Dan Boone and Tom Lincoln is played off against the society world, and Horatio Alger builds a bridge between the two by describing the poor boy who struggles up to become a manipulator of power and property. American character, then, which was predominantly homespun and equalitarian in 1800, very definitely became more and more sharply stratified in terms of *classes*, as is evident in the political struggle between farmers on the one hand and business leaders on the other, which reached a crisis in the time of William Jennings Bryan and the Populists at the end of the nineteenth century.

Fortunately for our purposes, a brief yet clear picture of the development of American classes is given in the study by Robert and Helen Lynd entitled *Middletown*.[5] This is a study of a midwestern city, about which a good deal of information was obtained in a long systematic sociological survey. The Lynds aimed to compare the town in 1890 with the town in 1924, and went back for a follow-up in 1935. First they combed the diaries, letters, newspapers of 1890, and the memories of the

---

[5] *Middletown* and *Middletown in Transition*, New York, Harcourt Brace, 1929 and 1937.

older inhabitants, to sketch out what life was like in 1890, then brought the story forward.

In 1890 there was still a simple village life, with many of the "frontier" qualities still found in many parts of the United States at the time, in the sense that people lived in the consciousness that there was land to be had in the West for almost nothing; even among the settled townsmen there was the feeling of equality and freedom colored by the fact that one could move—to homestead land, for example—if one liked. It was a *one-class* town, that little town of 1890; one-class not in the sense that everyone owned the same amount of property, but in the sense that everybody was, as we say, *as good as* everybody else. The banker could sit in his shirtsleeves on his porch on a summer evening, see a worker go by, call out to him to come up and have a cigar and chat a while. The town was full of community activities, group singing, lyceums and forums, where people of all sorts mingled; and there was an articulate protest against "the trusts," the big business combines of the cities.

With the development of the town in the '90's, largely because of a gas boom and the importation of capital from the East, a rapid industrial expansion occurred. Before long the town had developed a *two-class* system, a business class and a working class. In 1923–1924, when the town was systematically studied, the business class numbered about one-fourth of the total, the workers three-fourths. Very few people had any doubt at all where they stood. Practically the whole town consisted either of persons who got their living by using their hands on tasks set for them by owners and executives, or people who manipulated symbols—that is, who made plans in terms of words and numbers, who dealt with concepts, ideas, expectations, rather than day-by-day material objects. *Personality patterns had already very clearly begun to express the cleavage.* When business-class and working-class mothers were asked what kinds of traits they were trying to develop in their children, the former had a place for independence and creativeness, whereas the latter clung mostly to the homespun virtues of thrift and obedience. According to the housewives' testimony, the *parents* of these two groups had more or less the same values and ideals—values, as a matter of fact, close to those of the Calvinist frontiersmen who had made up so large a part of the American stock heretofore; but by 1924 the cleavage was clear-cut.

It is therefore not guesswork to point out that different standards, ideals, and norms are developing according to class. These standards are not as strongly defined as those of European classes; the European classes have been there for a longer time. The American classes, at least in the Middletown setting, have something of the feeling of *uncertainty* and *confusion* that relates to recent changes. Many of the businessmen and their wives have come from backgrounds lower in the prestige scale, and many of the workers were farmers or small handicraftsmen in one-class towns before they got their present clear-cut working-class status. Of course not all of the people in Middletown in 1923 were the children of those who lived there in 1890; in fact, the majority of them were not. But the general picture given by the Lynds suggests that even among the descendants of the early Middletowners who were originally members of one big family, this split along class lines has occurred. Uncertainty, confusion, doubt, have gone with the recent changes, the business people not knowing how next year will work out, the workers sometimes hoping that their children will do better than they themselves have done, though at the same time dogged by the fear that the present job will vanish next month.

Running through the whole picture is what might be called *status anxiety*. Instead of simply being brought up as the son of a skilled glass blower, who will in time become as good a glass blower as his father, the boy or young man does not know what he can count on, where he will be a few years later, as machines take over much of the glass-blowers' work and layoffs in most of the factories are unpredictable and uncontrollable. But he tries to get ahead. The struggle to "keep up with the Joneses" dominates not only middle-class thinking, but all those many elements in the working class which look up to and to some degree try to copy and emulate the business-class world of ideas and behavior.

So far the picture is of Middletown in 1924. The depression knocked the life of the town to pieces and rebuilt it in a new form. One powerful business family bought up many failing businesses, acquired control over the banks and department stores, put a great deal of money into the local college, hospital, Y.M.C.A., and so on, and became a sort of dominant class all in its own right. The "X family," numbering in all about 75 people, is now the aristocracy of the city. The business class, no longer independent, strives to follow the standard set by the X family, suffers a good deal of insecurity as to what further misfortunes may do to them, yet still sharply maintains its ascendancy over the working class. With the New Deal legislation favoring labor organization, there developed in the middle '30's somewhat greater class consciousness, a somewhat more definite sense that labor could stick together. The movement was not everywhere successful, however; many elements in labor were unwilling to accept status as laborers and hoped that they, or their children, might in time improve their status. So even today the American class system is somewhat less sharply defined and well crystallized than that of western European industrial countries. It is nevertheless definite enough to give most people a clear picture of their own status[6] and of the class structure of their community, and status anxiety is at least as great as before.

As a result of such studies, social scientists have been emphasizing the conception of general or common features in American life which set it off in contrast to others, and utilizing the anthropologists' way of showing basic personality patterns characteristic of culture groups (see page 526). Table 11 brings out one anthropologist's conception of the way in which American women, as contrasted with women in two preliterate societies, are psychologically affected by our anxiety-producing culture.

Since this picture is relatively clear-cut, many have argued that there can be no escape from the increasing sense of frustration which must characterize American living until the time comes when equalitarianism and democracy can give everyone a sense of full participation and of equal status in the social scene. This need not mean, however, that right now there is nothing constructive to be done. There is at least one important opportunity, here and now, in the social order as it exists, namely, that children may grow up with more satisfaction in the daily round of their own activities; that parents and teachers may come to emphasize more and more the fulfillment of each child's individuality rather than competition with others, and give less and less attention to the question of grades, gold stars, prizes, special recognition which

---

[6] W. L. Warner (ed.), *Yankee City Series, 1941–47*, New Haven, Yale University Press, 6 vols., 1941–1948.

makes one child feel superior to another, and then later feel inferior. Indeed, a good many Americans think that an attack on the threat to personal security can be carried out on both fronts at once, working to develop more democracy and security in the community and at the same time giving children satisfactions which are not rooted in ego enhancement and status dynamics.

In this connection it is worth remembering that the old order often continues to persist along with the new, and that a great many of the feelings, ideas, attitudes of the one-class frontier days, and of one-class towns nearly everywhere in the United States, continue to appear even in the midst of a well-defined class system. In the New England town where the blue bloods live on "Hilltop," the great middle group in Ardville "south of the tracks," and the French Canadian mill hands on the "other side of the tracks," there very frequently come times when a community festival, or a county fair, throws the town almost back into its one-class way of feeling. And many Americans who outwardly acknowledge the reality of the class lines which separate the higher-ups from the lower-downs, refuse to kowtow even when they lose business; they still say, with Robert Burns, "A man's a man for a' that." How long these "traditional Americans" will last it is not our aim to predict; but these contradictions exist today between the (relatively) old democracy and the (relatively) new class system. American character today is a hodgepodge, with some people mostly expressing the older, others mostly the newer feelings. But in integration of attitudes, the development of *consistent* attitudes is easier for the middle and upper classes, for they can actually claim *status,* whereas the workers, though traditionally equalitarian in spirit, would like to rise in the system, and tend to imitate the ways and ideas of those who are so often called the "better class of people" in the community.

This has been written as if the pressures which have been described were more or less equal for all individual Americans, and as if the stuff of which we are made were more or less alike. We have pointed out in many connections that no one lives in exactly the same world as anyone else. Pressures and incentives differ; and no two human beings, not even identical twins, are made in exactly the same way. The argument would therefore affect different individuals in different ways. We all

TABLE 11. Comparison of the "Feminine Personality" of Two Age Levels and Three Cultures[7]

Personality Area	American Adolescent Girl, Common-Man Level	American Housewife, Common-Man Level	Samoan Adolescent Girl	Navaho Adolescent Girl
Mental functioning	Anxieties and drive for conformity reduce mental efficiency and imaginal creativity. But achievement drive counterbalances this reduction, in area of academic performance.	Reduced imagination and personal resources: ideas routine and concepts repetitive. Suppression of resources available for attacking emotional problems.	Is able to do all the numerous household tasks considered her responsibility by adolescence, in a relaxed, taken-for-granted way. No drive for achievement.	Practical, matter-of-fact. Not impressed with abstract goals or intellectual achievement for its own sake.
Impulse expression and control	Suppresses overt impulse expression. Conflict between inner and social demands.	Impulse suppression: fears spontaneity and impulsivity—wants to keep these under control. Resistance to mentioning sex.	Easy acceptance and expression of impulses, especially the sexual.	Conscious outer control in relation to social demands. But expresses instinctual urges freely, particularly the sexual.
Anxiety level and sources	High or pervasive anxiety, due to feeling that world is hostile, to feelings of affectional deprivation, to conflict between inner and social demands. "Adolescent withdrawal."	Feels the environment is against her and fears that she will not succeed in her struggle with it. Lacks feeling of control over own fate. Apprehensive about the new and unknown.	No evidence of anxiety. Extended kin system provides emotional support of an impersonal type. Adolescence not a period of crisis or stress; no conflicts or remote ambitions.	Lack of guilt feelings over infractions of the rules. Affectional deprivation not a problem—extended kin to give affection. Some adolescent withdrawal.

Picture of outer world	World seen as hostile, unfriendly, unloving.	World seen as usually unrewarding and frequently punishing for moral infractions. Viewed, further, as conventional, repetitive, and filled with petty detail.	World considered non-complex, orderly, non-threatening.	Very aware of the world about her and reacts to it on a practical matter-of-fact level. No generalized hostility toward older people.
Interpersonal relations	Finds it difficult to relate emotionally to peers. Manipulates them for own, anxiety-relieving purposes.	Sees other persons and relationship to them in terms of stereotypes. Interpersonal relations usually seen as troubled and strained.	Close emotional ties not usual; tendency to tone of impersonality in closest relationships. No evidence of this because of any inner strains; rather the social norm.	People seen as individuals, not categorized. Respect for individual differences. Interactions between persons depend upon individual choice rather than social "rules."
Motivations and adjustments	Need for more affection or approval; major motivation is to obtain these. Major means of gaining motivations and making emotional adjustments is through social conformity.	Feels that it is her duty to conform to the demands of the world about her and that the suppression of personal desires required to do this is necessary.	"To live as a girl with many lovers as long as possible and then to marry in one's own village near one's own relatives and to have many children" all in good time.	Not impressed with abstract goals or with intellectual achievement for its own sake.

[7] E. Milner, Effects of sex role and social status on the early adolescent personality, *Genet. Psychol. Monogr.*, 1949, *40*, 231–325; table from pp. 306–307.

know some perfectly placid, quiet, casual, friendly people who accept their place in life and make no bones about it, who do not interest themselves in being a "big wheel." We think of other people who are simply overwhelmed by the struggle for status at every phase in their development. The individual's *energy level* is certainly one factor here; but early experiences of frustration, or of "demanding" parents who apply the thumbscrews whenever one fails to do better than the boy across the street, play a huge role, too. Even when we turn our attention to a form of prestige struggle which knocks a large number of people out of the running—as for example the large group of business executives who annually succumb to gastric ulcers, to high blood pressure, and to coronary disease of the heart—we can still point out that many remain immune, either because physiologically they are especially sturdy in the organs that are so often afflicted, or because in a deep sense their psychological make-up is more secure and less vulnerable.

In this connection there is much value in Ruth Benedict's suggestion[8] that while every society applies certain kinds of pressures to its members, some people can take these particular kinds of pressures more easily than can others. If at birth, for example, people are distributed according to a normal curve with regard to their threshold for rage, or their sensitivity to frustration, an individual growing up in a highly belligerent society may make his adaptation to that society quite easily, whereas one belonging over at the left of the scale will not become really competitive and bellicose except under the greatest of pressures. The person born into a gentle society like that of the Arapesh will make a quick adaptation if his own temperament is gentle. Tough and violent characters among the Arapesh are simply "queer" people; they can make their adaptation to society only with very great difficulty. We might draw the conclusion, then, that all of us have the problem of adapting our original temperaments to those of the community, as expressed in its ethos (page 526). In any society, however, the middle range can make the adaptation without great difficulty, until the society has moved too far from what is congenial to human nature. Perhaps the intensely military or the intensely status-minded societies represent illustrations of social trends

---

[8] R. Benedict, Anthropology and the abnormal, *J. gen. Psychol.*, 1934, *10*, 59–82.

which finally get so far off center that the bulk of the human material can no longer make a decent adaptation.

We come, then, to the view that the individual, in responding to the social pattern, does a great deal more than simply *receive* the impress and *adapt* to the mold. He encounters one difficulty or another in making the adaptation. And if he is capable of asserting himself against its trends and getting others to follow him, he may be able in time to give a new push to the social trend of the period. Just as a revolution may start when most people are hungry, so a revolution in science, or in the arts, or in literature may begin when the existing forms of thought and expression seem shallow, hollow, and unsatisfying to a person who really has something to say. Granted that the rebellious temperament of the revolutionary may owe something to his own personal experience as a child rebelling against a father, his primary impulse toward social change may come from the fact that his needs are very different from those accented by the people of his group and period. He is capable of giving voice to something in himself which is not well represented in the culture, and he is therefore capable of serving as a guide to others who are in the same personal predicament. Hunger revolutions or scientific and literary revolutions, then, would ultimately all arise from a certain incompatibility between individual and social emphasis. This way of looking at the matter may perhaps serve to bridge the gap between those who have emphasized the "great-man theory of history," like Thomas Carlyle (who said that history consists of the lives of great men), and the adherents of the cultural determinism theory, which speaks of the intrinsic mass trends which a culture as a whole must supposedly follow, and allows no important place for the individual. Benedict's view gives the individual a real place, but what he would do with it would depend on him and on his society at the time.

What we have just said implies that personal frustration is in a sense a point from which new trends are initiated. Yet there is also another very important possibility, namely, that when all of us feel a certain need for more wealth, for greater knowledge, for freer political institutions, some one of us may have more *insight into ways of solving the problem* than the rest. *Not* because he is especially *frustrated*, but because he is *ingenious*, the inventor of an idea, or of a new art form, or of a mode of scientific thought, may offer a solution which ultimately all can in some degree understand and follow. Social change would arise, then, as much from *creativeness* as from *frustration*. In fact, frequently the combination of the two is what starts a series of new cultural processes going. Necessity is the mother of invention, but its father is the quest for a new idea.

SUGGESTED READINGS

Efron, D., *Gesture and Environment,* New York, Kings Crown Press, 1941.
Fromm, E., *Escape from Freedom,* New York, Rinehart, 1941.
Lynd, R. S., *Knowledge for What?* Princeton, Princeton Univ. Press, 1939.
Lynd, R. S., and Lynd, H., *Middletown* (1929), *Middletown in Transition* (1937), New York, Harcourt, Brace.
Mumford, L., *The Culture of Cities,* New York, Harcourt, Brace, 1938.
Tawney, R. H., *Religion and the Rise of Capitalism,* New York, Harcourt, Brace, 1926.
Warner, W. L., and Lunt, P. S., *The Social Life of a Modern Community,* New Haven, Yale Univ. Press, 1941.
West, James, *Plainville, U.S.A.,* New York, Columbia Univ. Press, 1945.

30 ONESELF AND OTHERS

"Know thyself," said Socrates; and the contemporary counselor, vocational guide, psychiatrist, educator say the same. Contemporary literature has made much of the portrayal, in novel, drama, and poem, of the inner world of one's own fantasy through which one tries to grasp what one is. At the same time the objective scientist has attempted by his tests and measurements to find a method of recording individuality which will give each person a way of comparing himself with others. He makes use of tests of ability, of interest, of value, of adjustment. Through the projective tests he releases and makes visible the deeper trends of feeling and attitude in all their rich interrelations. In group discussions the individual finds himself, understands his relation to the group more fully; and as the recorded interview is read back, the client or group member sees more clearly what he said, and what sort of person he seemed to the others to be. He not only learns to place himself on a distribution curve; he learns to see through others' eyes. He learns to think of himself as a unique synthesis of those attributes which his profile has brought out; he also learns by sharing each attribute with others. Reading of the joys and frustrations of others, he finds a mirror of himself. Reading the biographies and autobiographies of older people, he glimpses what he may become.

By all these means he passes beyond the sheer effort to portray a momentary static outline of himself. He begins to make a design for living. He begins to realize where his limitations probably lie, what types of freedom of choice are real in terms of his inner capacities, and what is the range of social situations and life settings among which he may choose. He begins to grasp that education is for him not just a question of sharing knowledge which others have shared; that his own interests and attitudes mean that even in a uniform curriculum his experience will be different from that of others. He begins to realize that because his personality is not the duplicate of anyone else's personality he will bring to each task not only a unique pattern of abilities but a unique pattern of tastes and attitudes. In consequence he will more quickly and easily learn certain subjects and acquire certain skills, and only slowly or with great difficulty acquire the knowledge and skills which come easily to other people. He may be able to realize through the study of autism and projection how little he has grasped of what he has been, and he may be on his guard lest a similar distortion begin to close the walls in upon him as he settles down all too early to a rigid and local professional outlook.

He begins to grasp that flexibility and rigidity are not given once and for all, that there is such a thing as becoming a different person as one becomes educated; he may become more and more flexible, in the sense of becoming more and more open and receptive to ideas, to points of view. Far from being a mere chameleon, ready to change color in each new environment, he finds that the very fact that he has real values and beliefs of his own, about which he feels secure and nondefensive, offers him the opportunity to consider with sympathy and true openness the equally legitimate beliefs and convictions of others. Above all, perhaps, he may have outlived the conception that inventiveness, creativeness, the capacity to do something original and distinctive, is given to just a few. He may have grasped the fact that creativeness, the readiness for plastic, flexible, ever-changing reconstructions of life, new ideas, new skills, new art forms, is in considerable measure open to everyone who wants it.

The principles which have been developed can now be summarized in a series of suggestions regarding the attainment of self-understanding.

First, in the matter of heredity, we may develop the habit of thinking of our genetic make-up as predisposing in one direction rather than another, but leaving room for a good deal of plasticity (pages 18 ff.). Our genes definitely set limits for intellectual and temperamental as well as physical qualifications; but no one knows except by empirical test where those limits lie, and the flexibility before achieving adulthood is so considerable that it is well worth while to explore to see where those limits lie, trying our hand at everything interesting to see what we can do, and how deep the satisfactions are.

Secondly, as regards the ingrained habits formed in the earlier years largely as a result of conditioning, we may remind ourselves that in themselves they have relatively little force, and tend to be extinguished except insofar as they are made rigid by continued self-conditioning through verbal symbols, or other inner circuits (pages 133 ff.), particularly those involving the image of the self (pages 421 ff.), which may make it seem dangerous to us, or just too great an effort, to undertake a change. Examples were given earlier of self-initiated changes, and extinction of conditionings which no longer serve a purpose. The principle of dominance seems also to be helpful; "fight Satan with fire," drive out one habit not by "sheer will power" but by another habit such as considering consequences in terms of self-respect.

Third, in relation to those canalizations which have become deeply embedded in us, and do not seem to be subject to extinction of the sort which applies to the conditioned responses, the way to turn them to good account is to permit *transfer to a related field* in which conflict or other difficulty can be avoided (page 228).

Fourth, while we may consider our ingrained habits of perceiving (autistic and otherwise) as tending to make us blind to other viewpoints, it is worth while to remember that they are essential building stones in personality and cannot be kicked out. If they are to be removed, a careful engineering job is called for. Those habits of perceiving enable us to find anchorage points, safety, and confidence in our habitual view of our environment. Hence any process of reëducation is long and arduous, and emphasis needs to be placed primarily on the discovery of *new values* which are satisfying in themselves, which will almost automatically give new frames of reference, new anchorage points for reperceiving the world.

When these perceptual patterns relate to the *perception of oneself*, the job may be either long and complex, or very simple and direct, depending upon the way in which a new self-image serves our basic goals. It is not worth while to make staunch resolutions about outgrowing our self-deception, and try to defeat our ordinary habits of self-observation by sheer force. Rather, the thing to do is to find new satisfactions in new ways of looking upon ourself. No process of self-deception need be involved in this effort; there is no need to deny anything that is there to be seen, or to follow any process of ostrich-like evasion. We may discover new areas of value and interest, gradually wrap them up within ourself, incorporate them within the inmost core of our individuality. That is exactly what we saw happening in the cases described earlier (pages 394 ff.).

But we have not found that all the process of perception, and in particular of self-perception, is at the level of direct conscious observation where it is easy to see all that is happening. Like the iceberg, it lies largely beneath the surface. It is for this reason that the skilled efforts of special counselors and educators, psychiatrists, or of seasoned teachers, ministers, family doctors may enable the individual to get beneath the surface, gradually face and deal realistically with the factors which are slanting his view of himself and his relation to the world. Every normal person needs some help of this sort. There is no sense in kicking himself because a certain amount of self-deception has been going on. Taking it realistically and casually, a person may, for his own good, seek aid in broadening the picture of the self in its relation to the environment.

Finally, the chapters which have just preceded may enable the individual to realize the relativity of his personality to the situation in which he is placed. No fatalistic conception of the self, as a package all wrapped up ready to be delivered, need be involved. Rather, the problem is to define our situation in life, find out to what degree our present personality is a specific response to that specific situation—the tasks, the pressures, the incentives, the rewards which the world offers us; and to think realistically what kind of world, what kind of situation we would like to have for our own. The choice of a life partner, the choice of a profession, the choice of a place to live, the choice of our hobbies, leisure-time activities, philosophy of life—all these are far from being simply questions of applying inner voluntary controls to our existing make-up; the decision regarding these matters will inevitably bring to bear upon us new forces which will transform us.

Mapping One's Own Education

In this task of making a design for life, education in the broad sense plays an enormous role. Not education in the sense of ability to retain specific items required to pass a specific examination, but education in the sense of extending the range and depth of knowledge, the number and subtlety and power of our personal skills, the degree of our understanding and appreciation of other people, the breadth of the vistas of our outlook. Education includes the principles by which effective living outside of the classroom is regulated; it includes the capacity to understand others and to participate socially in the development of group and community life.

Education which has as broad a goal as this has had to develop ways of observing individuals as they grow and learn; it has had to develop ways of measuring and assessing their growth and learning in each of these respects. The whole modern movement toward measurement in education can be used to support these more creative aspects of the task of the teacher. Progressive education means getting all the information we can about the individual, and considering his unique attributes as well as his interdependence with others. It entails getting all the evidence regarding his intellectual powers, his interests, his values, his viewpoints. It involves to a large degree the development of personal contacts between teachers and students through counseling or closer pupil-teacher relationships in the classroom. It involves a long-range picture of the growing individual, so that instead of just a series of marks on a cumulative record sheet covering a period of years, we can actually see him working through each school year, each vacation, starting in a little changed, a little modified by experience in each new setting. More and more we expect to see the whole developing individual, and attempt to guide not just a person who can make an A in math, but a person who has very specific intellectual, social, personal interests which have slowly grown and changed; a person who cares about this kind of music, that kind of literature, these particular sports, those particular campus activities. We try to find out whether the interest in math is related to a determination to succeed at engineering; to what degree math simply comes easy, like "falling off a log"; what the interest and competence in mathematics mean in relation to the personality as a whole. The aim is to view the whole person, all that he or she is in the college situation, in terms of the capacity to learn particular kinds of material, the readiness to grow in a particular direction. This is of course not quantitative science; it is a question of interpretation and evaluation. But it tries to *use* quantitative science in every possible way. Guidance of the individual follows directly in the same way from a counseling and teaching job based upon this degree of intimate understanding of the growing student. The answers to problems of the curriculum, of extracurricular activities, and of vocation arise from the broad view which the counselor and the student develop together regarding the latter's personality, how life looks to him, in what areas he is capable of growing.

On the basis of this kind of view of ourselves, developed partly by our teachers and counselors, partly by our own self, there develops a framework within which leisure and community life, marriage and family can become expressions of the whole pattern of what we are, in the process which Goldstein[1] has called self-actualization. The understanding of others will come in the same way partly by viewing them in the same broad terms, partly by discovering the specific points in which we share their outlook, and the specific points in which we differ. We begin in time to realize that we are in a certain sense locked within a particular frame of reference, and we can only momentarily, and in limited ways, expect to escape from it. Such a conception gradually enables us to grasp that others are also locked within their frames of reference. But these are, so to speak, semi-transparent; therefore each of us who is psychologically skilled can to some extent look into and through the special limiting conditions which determine the viewpoint of others. At the same time a certain greater tolerance comes from the recognition that we can never completely and absolutely enter into the little boxes which contain them, look out through their eyes, and see life wholly in their terms.

We might follow up the figure of speech by saying that just as we are all in our own boxes, so our boxes are ranged together, so to speak, inside of larger boxes which are determined by community, by religious or economic or other group viewpoints. We share our frames of reference with

---

[1] K. Goldstein, *The Organism,* New York, American Book, 1935.

others, so we see in terms of the group-determined outlook much more clearly than we do in terms of the outlook of other groups differentiated from us. As we have noted, the roles we play are the primary factors in

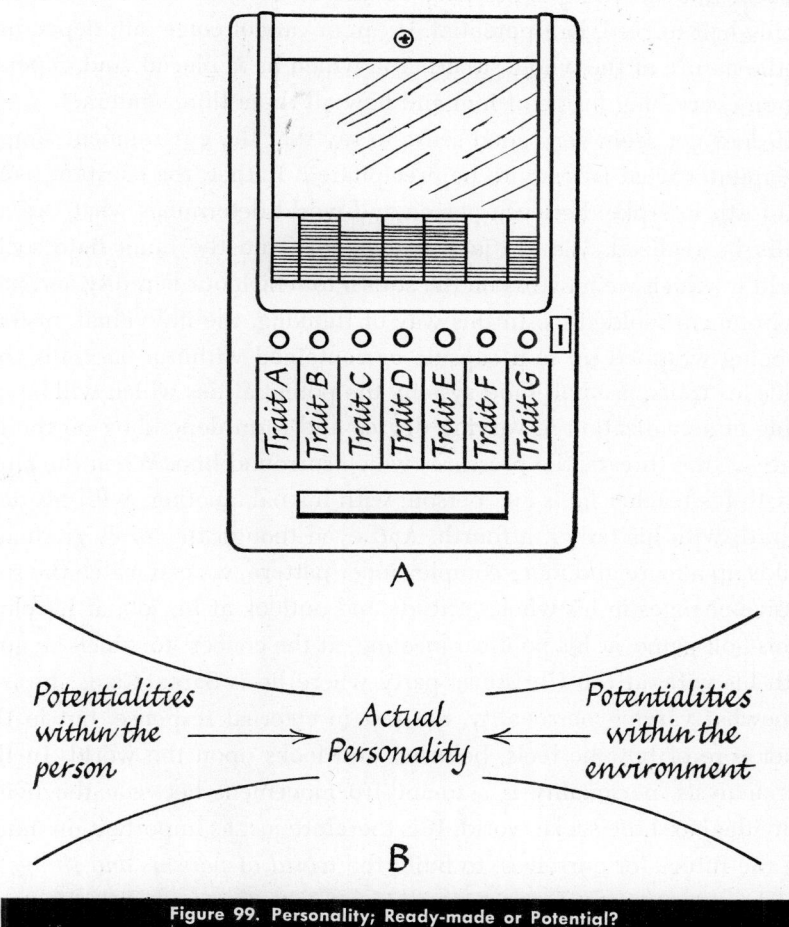

Figure 99. Personality; Ready-made or Potential?

determining these differential outlooks. These roles, as always, are determined partly by past social factors which we have shared, and partly by the immediate situations which press upon us.

This way of thinking may be summarized by sketching a difference in point of view between one of the traditional viewpoints of psychology and the scheme of thought which has been proposed here. In Figure

99A, a situation is pushing the individual, somewhat like pushing down a plunger on a gum or candy machine, eliciting one trait or another that is lurking inside the individual—it all depends on which plunger is pushed. But according to the view developed here, what is inside of him is only half formed, half potential. It can or cannot come out, depending on the nature of the whole situation in which he is placed, and depending on everything inside of him and how all these things interact.

It does not seem very good sense to say that the environment simply precipitates what is ready to be precipitated. Rather, the constant back-and-forth interplay between person and world determines what can actually be realized. We are just as dependent on the immediate social world in which we move as on the stuff into which our heredity and past environment molded us. In this way of thinking, the individual, instead of being wrapped up in a capsule or contained within a chrysalis that holds his traits, is a half-fluid system, the potentialities which will be capable of actualization in varying degree and form depending on the incentives, the threats, the pressures which surround him. When the child is with his teacher he is one person; with his pal, another; with his dog, a third; with his father, a fourth. And even though the adult gradually builds up a more and more complex inner pattern, we can watch the successive changes in his whole attitude and outlook at his job, at his club, at his golf game, at his political meeting, at the concert to which he goes with his wife, at the Christmas party where he is Santa Claus; he is a somewhat varying personality, not just in external response, but in the inner core of how he feels, believes, and looks upon the world. In the last analysis, personality is a to-and-fro movement between the living individual and the social world. It is therefore just as important, in molding the future for ourselves, to build the *world of persons and things* in which we want to move as to experiment with the inner habit systems which will make up so large a core of our future personality. But it is not a question of one or the other. With an honest effort at self-understanding, we can begin to decide, while life is before us, both what we really want to be "inside" and what kind of world we want to live in.

Understanding Others

In understanding *other* people—in sizing up our friend, our employer, our neighbor, our professional colleague, our teacher—all these principles likewise apply. Through using them, we may perhaps achieve a little more patience and perspective. These people are not what they are "just to be ornery," or because they are "just naturally nice people." There are reasons. Reasons lie partly in the potentialities for healthiness or abnormality, for warmth or coolness, for rigidity or flexibility, that are in the genetic composition; but much emphasis must also be placed upon reinforced conditionings, early canalizations, pictures of the self, conceptions of the environment, and the actual and imagined pressures which life offers them. Maybe people are what they are in very large measure because they see life in a certain way. Maybe if we saw life in the same way we would act according to the same pattern that characterizes them. From such a study of people come the practical rules about "sizing up" traits to which some attention was given earlier (page 501). Perhaps in a broader sense we may say that the chief value in studying people lies in developing a sort of attitude of accepting them for whatever they are, a willingness to look dispassionately at all that is there, joined with a very real readiness to explore the possibilities of change if there is a way in which we can help them. Rather than fatalism, what emerges from such a way of looking at people is the conception regarding the areas of flexibility, the areas within which change is to be expected.

A scientific psychology may help us to understand a person's motives better, may show him where is he defeating his own purposes, may free him from those inner contradictions and frustrations from which so much hostility and conflict arise. Science cannot decide which values in life are the best; but it definitely can show that many values involve suffering to the individual and to others, and are ultimately sources of mental ill health, and that other values are in accordance with deep human needs. Some satisfactions are short-lived or shallow, or embrace a relatively small portion of the personality. Others may be more enduring, capable of being built upon, and deeply pervading the personality as a whole. At the same time, science can show that there is a very great potential in us for understanding other people and for enjoying them and liking them rather than hating them, and that this potential can often be set free so that people enjoy life more deeply. If, by discussion with others who share our general outlook, we can discover the more enduring and the deeper types of satisfactions, there is no law or scientific principle by which with our present knowledge we can say that some other code is better. The problem is ultimately a question of getting the greatest possible knowledge about human beings in general and about oneself in particular, and applying it in the wisest way we can.

We must of course face honestly the disturbing fact that our own self-fulfillment may at times block the self-fulfillment of another person; we may need a scholarship to stay in college but in competing for it we may keep someone else out. Parents may have to make the hard choice whether to give their time largely to the great needs of a mentally defective child or to the needs of its normal brothers or sisters.

Fortunately, however, we find more and more ways to avoid competitive situations, more and more ways to stimulate fellow feeling. It used to be assumed, for example, that children of nursery-school age "just naturally fight"; but if we supply enough play equipment so that there need be no struggle for the inadequate supply of tricycles, sand-box tools, etc., and if we add equipment that *fosters group activities,* because a group can have a lot of fun together in using it, the ratio of coöperation to fighting will gradually shift. The whole development of social science thinking encourages the view that we are all mutually interdependent, and that in a society as complex and closely interwoven as our own it is likely in the long run that the deep fulfillment of each individual will tend to increase, rather than to defeat, the self-fulfillment of others.

GLOSSARY AND INDEX

Definitions are freely adapted from the following sources: *A Student's Dictionary of Psychological Terms*, 4th ed., by Horace B. English; *Webster's New International Dictionary*, 2nd ed.; *The American Illustrated Medical Dictionary*, 19th ed., by W. A. Newman Dorland; *A Briefer General Psychology*, and *Personality*, both by Gardner Murphy; and the present text.

Abel, T. M., 298, 330–331
Ability, 322–323, 359
  pattern of, 365–367; tests, 368–374
  statistical concepts, *see* Tests
Abstract attitude, *see* Categorical attitude
Abstracting, 288
  See also Concept formation
Acceptance, degree of, 484
Acculturation—*(1) Transmission of culture from one social group to another and its assimilation into the latter's culture. (2) The process by which an individual reared in one culture adapts himself to another:* 535–537
Acquired tastes, 194
Activity drives—*Craving for activity as such:* 79–82, 84–85, 274
Adaptation level, 140
Adjustment, 12–15, 147
Adler, Alfred, 434–435, 437, 497
Adler, Mortimer, 187–188
Adolescence, 57–62, 393–394, 401
Adopted children, 349, 351–352
Adrenal glands—*Endocrine glands lying near and above the kidneys:* 62–63, 87
Adrenin, 63

Adult attitudes, 61–62
Adult intelligence tests, 340–342
Afferent neurons—*Neurons that carry impulses toward the central nervous system:* 47
After-discharge, 161
After-image—*Sensation persisting after the original stimulus has ceased. In vision, after-images are positive if they are like the original sensation; negative, if their color differs from that of the original sensation:* 158, 161, 249
Aggressiveness—*Tendency to attack or injure, or to push one's own interests or ideas forward, or to carry out one's plans despite opposition:* 80, 121–123
Air Force, U. S., 382–383
Alcohol, 160
Alger, Horatio, 545
Allport, G. W., 497–498, 543–544
Allport-Vernon Study of Values, 446–447, 509
Alor Island, 468, 526–527
Alschuler, R. H., 460
American Council on Education test (ACE), 343
Ames, Adelbert, 167 n.

Anchorage point—*Point or center around which a specific process is organized, e.g., the self-view as the anchorage point of personality:* 389, 500
Anderson, Sherwood, 390–391, 405–406
Androgens, 58
Anger, *see* Rage
Animals, and human environment, 31–32
 conflict experiments, 118–119
 development experiments, 40–41
 emotion experiments, 105–106, 109
 intelligence tests, 333–334
 learning experiments, 233–234
 temperament studies, 23–25
Animism—*The belief or assumption that all objects, animate and inanimate, are conscious in about the same way that human beings are conscious:* 401
Anthropology, cultural, 28
Anxiety, and hyperthyroidism, 55–56
 and ulceration, 103–104
 status, 547
Apathy—*Withdrawal into inactivity:* 123–124
Apollonian—*Like Apollo; hence serene, gracious, beautiful:* 525
Aptitudes—*Readiness of an individual to profit by further training:* 365–367
Arapesh tribe, 412, 520–521, 552
Army Alpha test, 342
Army General Classification Test (AGCT), 342–343
Art judgment tests, 168
Arthur, King, 539, 540
Asch, S. E., 167–168
Aspiration level—*The level which one strives to attain:* 412
Assimilation, *see* Acculturation
Association, 262, 268, 273, 279–280, 412–413
 elementary, 288
 free, 273, 284
 principle of—*The tendency of two things that are experienced together to be remembered together:* 257–260
Association time, 98
Attention—*A narrowing of the range of objects to which the organism is responding:* 140–145

Attitudes—*Readiness to act in one way rather than another:* adult, 61–62
 concrete and abstract, 292–294
 problem, 297, 314
 protest, 72
 testing, 480–487; and personality, 487–492, 529; public opinion research, 492–494
 toward Negroes, 267, 483, 485–486
Attributes, and heredity, 23–25
 physical, 410
 transmission of, 10–12
 See also Traits
Auditory cortex, 184–185
Auditory impressions, 188
Authority figures, 427
Autism—*Movement of perceptual and thought processes in the direction of need satisfaction:* 170, 176–177, 248, 398, 423, 492, 502, 556
Autobiographies, 477
Auto-criticism, 336
Autokinetic effect—*Apparent movement of an actually stationary object:* 173–176
Autonomic nervous system—*The system that supplies the vital organs and smooth musculature with their efferent innervation:* 48
 and emotion, 93–101
Average, *see* Mean
Avery, G. T., 40
Awareness of self, 85
Axon—*The part of a neuron which conducts impulses away from the cell body:* 46

Balance, endocrine, 53, 59
Bali, 527–529
Balinsky, Benjamin, 368–374
Bard, P., 105
Barker, R., 124
Barnes, H. E., 542
Bartlett, F. C., 104
Basal metabolism, 53
Basilar membrane—*An organ in the inner ear upon which the perception of pitch very largely depends:* 182–184
Bateson, G., 527, 529
Baudelaire, Charles, 193, 311
Beethoven, Ludwig van, 508
Behavior, 2, 3, 68, 70, 106–107
 contrasting, 497–498

Behavior tests, 451–456
  combined with verbal tests, 453–456
  individual differences, 451–452
Benedict, Ruth, 524–525, 552, 553
Bennett Mechanical Comprehension Test, 371
Bergerac, Cyrano de, 389
Berkeley, Calif., 488, 491
Berlioz, Hector, 118
Bernard, Claude, 13
Bettelheim, B., 415–416, 418–420, 428–429
Bias, 298–300, 398
Biddle, W. W., 235
Bierce, Ambrose, 86–87
Binet, Alfred, 336–340
Binger, Carl, 103, 113, 515
Binocular cues, 162–163
Biographical method, 3, 4
Biological method, 3
Biological variations, 10–11
Birth injury, 352
Bladder tensions, 72
Blake, William, 257
Blocking—*Interference with memory, thought, activity, etc., usually as the result of emotional tension or conflict:* 119, 121, 263–264, 274, 279, 313–314, 329, 352
Blood pressure, 63, 103
Boas, Franz, 519
Body build, 28, 510–512
Body cells, 11–12, 16
Body functions, 35
Body needs, see Motives
Bogardus, E. S., 484
Bowel tensions, 72
Braille system, 196
Brain—*The portion of the central nervous system enclosed within the skull:* and dreaming, 279–280
  and emotional responses, 104–109
  and hearing, 184–185
  and learning, 245–246
  and seeing, 160–162, 164, 178–180
  and temperature receptors, 196–197
  and touch, 195
  complexity, 335
Brightness constancy, 165
Brilliance—*The degree of experienced intensity of a color, regardless of its hue:* 157
Bruce, Myrtle, 32–33, 354, 355
Bruner, J., 173
Brush painting, 460
Bryan, W. J., 545

Bryan, W. L., 225
Bühler, Charlotte, 310–311
Burks, Barbara, 19, 349–351, 352
Burns, Robert, 549
Business class, 546–548
Butterworth, Pauline, 475, 497

California Adolescent Growth Study, 59–61
Calvinism, 541
Campbell, A. A., 214
Canalization—*Progressive shifts in differential response to the various means of satisfying a drive:* 211–212, 220–221, 309, 325, 497, 504, 557
Canary Islands, 233
Cannon, W. B., 105, 108
Capote, Truman, 394
Carlyle, Thomas, 553
Caruso, Enrico, 389
Categorical attitude—*The readiness or capacity to respond to abstract attributes of objects:* 292, 294
Cattell, J. McK., 336
CAVD (Thorndike) test, 343
Cells, 51
  body and germ, 11–12, 16
  nerve, 45–48, 70, 335
Celtic civilization, 539
Central learning theory—*An interpretation of learning in terms of what is conceived to go on within the organism as it learns:* 245
Central nervous system—*The part of the nervous system that is protected by the skull and spinal column; it consists of the brain and spinal cord:* 48, 93, 109
Central tendency, 375
Cerebellum, 199
Chain association test, 274, 279
Channeling, see Canalization
Character Education Inquiry, 451–452
Chemical organization of life, 13, 51
Chemical senses, 191
Chicago, University of, 347
Chivalry, age of, 540–542
Chords, 186–187
Christianity, 538, 539
Chromosomes—*Minute bodies in the nucleus of a cell that play a determinative part in heredity:* 16
Clark, Kenneth, 264
Class—*A group of persons with such distinguishing characters as to af-*

Class—(*Continued*)
fect *social intercourse; especially differences in economic status:* 545
Class system, 545–549
Clinical method, 3, 5
Closure—*A basic principle whereby the tension initiated by an uncompleted situation is resolved by a tendency to complete the situation. For example, a briefly seen profile of a face without a nose tends to be reproduced with a nose:* 179
Cochlea, 182
Coding, 492–493
Coghill, G. E., 41, 49
Cold, experience of, 196–197
Coleridge, S. T., 285, 312–313
Color—*Hue or chroma within the spectrum, as contrasted with brightness and saturation:* 157–159, 173
Color constancy, 166
Comanche Indians, 522
Combat, fear responses, 89, 90
Comfort dreams, 283
Commercial revolution, 541–542
Compensation—*The process by which an individual seeks to balance a sense of inadequacy with a real or fancied superiority in some other aspect of his personality* (Adler):
inferiority, 434–437, 497
Competition—*A contest between rivals:* 326
individual, 543
status, 411–412
Complementary colors—*Spectral hues which when mixed give gray:* 158
Complexity, level of, 334–335
Concept—*A symbol which stands for a specific quality possessed in common by a number of stimuli:* thinking, 289–300
Concept formation, 291
Concrete attitude—*Inability or lack of set to respond to abstract attributes of objects:* 292, 294
Condensation regions, 181–182, 186
Conditioned response—*A response elicited by a stimulus which, although ordinarily biologically inadequate, has been presented along with a biologically adequate stimulus and hence has become an effective substitute for the latter:* 133–134, 213–214, 236, 246, 259, 496–497, 557

Conditioned response—(*Continued*)
competition between, 214–224
sensory, 259
Conditioned stimulus—*A stimulus that is biologically inadequate to elicit a response but which, as the result of conditioning, has become an effective substitute for the biologically adequate stimulus:* 213–214
Cones, 156–157, 159
Confidence, 268
Conflict—*Opposition between acts or tendencies:* 117–120, 396–397
and will, 131–136
escaping, 129–131
frustration, *see* Frustration
resolving, 126–129
symbols, 120–121, 133
Connector neurons, 47
Conscience, 427–429
Consciousness—*Awareness; one's immediate experience, as contrasted with inferences regarding the experience of others:* 86
Conspicuous consumption, 411
Constancies—*A group of perceptual phenomena which involve the tendency to interpret stimuli in terms of past experience and the context in which they are perceived so that perceptual objects (their size, color, shape, etc.) appear the same though perceived under different conditions:* 165–167, 179–180
See also Homeostasis
Continuity, 25–26
Contrast hue, 158
Coöperation—*Collective action for the common benefit:* 80
Coördination, muscular, 45, 49, 72
Corpuscles, 194
Correlation coefficient, 351, 380–382
Correlation methods, test scores, *see* Tests, statistical concepts
Cortex, cerebral, 48, 203
Cousinet, Roger, 149
Cowell, Henry, 319–321
Creativeness—*The capacity to produce through thought and imagination; capacity for original work:* 306-307, 554, 556
and creator, 322–324
education of, 325–329
favorable factors, 316–322
sensitiveness, 307–310

Creativeness—(Continued)
skills, 310–316
Cretinism—*A condition due to thyroid insufficiency in early childhood and marked by great retardation in mental and physical growth:* 54
Cross-sectional studies—*Procedure used in studying the normal course of development, wherein the average of measurements of a large number of persons at successive stages of growth is taken as standard. It is contrasted with the longitudinal method, wherein the successive stages of the development of one person are investigated:* 503
Cues, 162–163, 260
Cultural anthropology, 28
Cultural determinism, 553
Culture—*The complex whole that includes knowledge, belief, art, morals, law, custom, and any other capabilities and habits acquired by man as a member of society:* literate society, gestures, 534–537; psychological results of history, 537–554
  preliterate society, 518–529; personality development, 527–529; social roles, 529–532
Curiosity—*(1) Tendency to investigate any novelty that is perceived. (2) Tendency to seek information about anything:* 81
Curve, learning, 225–227
  See also Normal frequency curve
Cybernetic system, 198
Cycles per second, 182–184, 230
Cyrano de Bergerac, 389

Darrow, C. W., 95
Dartmouth College, 473
Darwin, Charles, 333
Defectives, mental, 135
Defense mechanisms—*Adjustments that enable a person to avoid facing a painful fact or an unpleasant situation:* 421 n., 422–426, 501
De la Mare, Walter, 307, 397
Delusion—*A belief so obviously contrary to the evidence as to be held only by a disordered mind:* 130–131
  of persecution, 424–425
Dembo, T., 124
Dennis, W., 35, 36

De Quincey, Thomas, 285
DeSilva, H. R., 159
Determinism, cultural, 553
Development, awareness of self, 388–407
  embryonic, 18, 41
  emotional and social, 34–36
  individuality in, 38–45
Dewey, John, 326, 439
Dickens, Charles, 425
Differentiating tests, 444
Differentiation—*(1) In development, the process whereby progressive changes occur in the characteristics of an organism. (2) In conditioning, the process whereby a response is conditioned to a specific conditioned stimulus:* 40–41, 151, 234–235, 359
Dionne quintuplets, 22–23
Dionysian—*Pertaining to Dionysus; hence wild, violent, orgiastic:* 525
Discipline, 328, 427
Discontinuity, group, 513
Disease, 28, 201–202
Distance receptor processes, 191
Distraction, 141–142, 203
Distributed practice—*Spaced repetition of an activity during learning:* 239
Dominance—*Differential effectiveness in favor of one stimulus, drive, or neural pattern:* principle of, 215–217
Douglas, A. G., 151–154
Drawings, projective, 460–461
Dreaming—*The occurrence of more or less coherent imagery sequences during sleep:* 74, 278–285, 401–402
Drill, 236
Drive—*Basic tendency to activity; the action tendency initiated by shifts in physiological balance (restlessness) is accompanied by sensitivity to particular types of stimuli so that eventually a consummatory response occurs:* 65–66, 132, 406
  activity, 79–82, 84–85
  and imagining, 273–274
  maternal, 74–76
  physiology of, 66–74; elimination habits, 72; hunger, 66–69, 209–213; oxygen want, 70–72; rest and sleep, 72–74; thirst, 69–70
  self-love and power, 83–85
  sensory, 82–83

Drive—(*Continued*)
  sex, 76–79
Drowsiness, 72
Drugs, 160–161
DuBois, Cora, 468, 526–527
Ductless glands, *see* Endocrine system
Durkin, H. E., 296

Ear, 182–185, 199
Eccentric genius, 326–327
Economic change, 521–522
Ectomorphy, 510–512
Education, 559–562
Effect, law of—*The law that one learns to make the responses that are accompanied or followed by satisfaction, and to eliminate those that are not accompanied or followed by satisfaction (Thorndike):* 246
Efferent neurons—*Neurons that carry impulses away from the central nervous system:* 47
Effort, 131–132, 142
Efron, David, 534–537
Ego—(1) *The individual's orderly conscious activities as contrasted with the blind instinctive drives which dominate his unconscious mental activities (Freud).* (2) *Group of activities concerned with the assertion and defense of the self:* 427
  See also Self
Ego defense, 126
Ego involvement—*Involvement of the ego (in a task, value, etc.):* 325–326, 544
Egocentrism—*Term used by Piaget to mean the individual's (especially the child's) absorption in his own activities, and his inability to see things from a social point of view:* 398, 401–402
Eidetic imagery—*Imagery that is peculiarly vivid, as if the individual actually perceived an object:* 255–257
Einstein, Albert, 508
Electricity, body, 13, 94–97
Elements, identical, 229–230
Elimination habits, 72
Ellis, Havelock, 324
Ellson, D. G., 259
Embryonic development, 18, 41
Emerson, R. W., 260
Emotional center, 105–106
Emotional instability, 63

Emotional stupidity, 243
Emotions—*Disturbed condition, with responses characteristically involving innervation of the autonomic nervous system:* and autonomic nervous system, 93–101
  and mental growth, 352–354
  and thinking, 299, 304
  constitutional factors, 110
  control of, 112–116
  defined, 86–89
  expressions of, 43–44, 88, 100–101, 146; interpretation, 101–104
  fear, 89–90, 109, 110–111
  galvanic skin reflex, 95–100
  mood and temperament, 111–112
  rage, 90–93, 106, 110–111
  theory of, 104–111
Empathy—*Direct apprehension of the state of mind of another person without, as in sympathy, feeling as he does. In sympathy, shared attitude is the chief matter:* 391
Endocrine glands—*Ductless glands whose hormonal secretions pass directly into the surrounding tissues:* 52
Endocrine system—*The endocrine glands and their interrelations:* 51–53
  and maternal drive, 74–76
  and sexual development, 57–63, 77
  interdependence of organs, 63–64
  thyroid functions, 53–57
Endomorphy, 510–512
Energy, specific, *see* Specific energy
  undirected, 91
Energy level, 552
Environment—*Group of factors potentially capable of influencing an organism:* 2, 9–10, 81
  adjustment to, 12–15, 147
  and heredity, 16–23, 32, 34–37, 347–348
  and intelligence, 34, 347–358
  and learning, 205
  and sex development, 62
  and stock variations, 32–33
  effect, on emotional and social development, 34–36; on intelligence and temperament, 28–32
  food and health factors, 27–28, 352
Equilibrium—*A state of balance between opposing forces or actions, etc.:* 14–15
Equity, 403–404

GLOSSARY AND INDEX 571

Escape, 129–130
Escapist, 301
Estrogens, 58
Ethnic group—*A group differentiated on the basis of common traits, customs, institutions, etc.:* 522
Ethnocentrism—*Tribalism or nationalistic standardization of ethics and laws:* 488–489
Ethos—*The feeling tone characterizing the outlook on life:* 526, 552
Evolution, 3
 and individuality, 8–12
Excitement, 87–88, 106, 109
Existence pattern, 525–526
Exophthalmos, 55
Experience, past, *see* Past experience
Experimental method, 3, 4, 7
Experimental neurosis, 119
Expressions, facial, 43–44, 88, 100–102, 146
Extinguished response—(*Experimental*) *disappearance of a conditioned response to a stimulus when the latter is repeated a number of times without reinforcement:* 213–214
Extrapunitive reaction, 126, 471
Extrasensory perception, 204 n.
Extroversion—*The tendency of an individual to direct his energies outward and to be absorbed in the things and activities of the world (especially other persons) about him:* 430–434
Eyelid response, 214
Eyes, *see* Seeing

Facial patterns, 43–44, 88, 100–102, 146
Factor analysis, 359, 384–386
Factors, constitutional, 110
 general and specific, 358–359, 485
 of advantage, 140–141
Fantasy—*Wish-fulfilling imaginative process:* 275–277, 470, 472
Fear, 89–90, 109, 110–111
 and conditioned responses, 216–217
Feedback system, 198–199
Fels Foundation, 503
Feminine personality, 550–551
Feral children—*Children reared from birth by wild animals:* 30–31
Féré, C., 202
Figure-ground relationships—*The "figure" is any part of the whole which stands out from the "ground" or*

Figure-ground relationships—(*Cont.*) *background. Figure and ground are mutually dependent members of the whole:* 143, 164, 267, 422–423, 500
Finger Dexterity test, 371
Finger painting, 308, 309, 459–460
Fixations, maladaptive, 242–243
Flexibility, 556–557, 563
Follow-through, 25–26
Food, and conditioned responses, 216–220
 and environment, 27–28, 352
 canalization, 210–212
 deprivation and set, 169–170, 172–173, 175
 lack of, as motive, 65–69
Forgetting, 2, 263–266
Foster children, 348–351, 356–357
Fovea—*A small point or region of the retina near the midpoint where vision is clearest:* 156, 158
Frank, L. K., 457, 518
Franklin, Benjamin, 544
Franz, Shepherd, 260–261
Free association—(1) *The free-flowing associations in the analytic situation.* (2) *A method whereby a subject responds to a stimulus, usually verbal, with any word, usually as quickly as possible:* 273, 284
Freeman, Frank, 349–351
Freeman, G. L., 90, 142
Frequency distribution, intelligence, 345–347, 350–351, 375, 508, 509
Freud, Sigmund, 263, 264, 282–285, 409, 421 n., 427, 429, 432, 457
Frick, F., 298–299
Fromm, Erich, 543
Frustration—*Barrier to the attainment of a goal:* 121–126, 396, 430, 470–471, 553–554
Frustration-aggression concept, 122–123, 173

Gallup poll, 493
Galton, Francis, 251, 335–336
Galvanic skin reflex—*Sudden decrease in skin resistance occurring during upsets of the psychophysiological balance of the organism, as in emotion:* 95–100
Gelb, A., 178–179
Gene—*Factor in the germ plasm that determines that in a certain normal*

Gene—(Continued)
  environment the organism will develop a certain specific trait: 16, 36, 512, 556–557
  and intelligence, 345–346, 360–361
  and temperament, 23–26
General intelligence, 322, 358–361
Genius, 317, 318, 322, 328
  eccentric, 326–327
Germ cells—Specialized cells, the sperm of the male, and the egg or ovum of the female, whose union in the fertilized egg gives rise to a new individual composed of body cells and germ cells: 11–12, 16
German civilization, 539
Gesell, Arnold, 19–20, 22, 35
Gestalt psychology, 468, 499
Gesture, 101
  and culture, 534–537
Gide, André, 272
Gifted child, 324–329
Gifts, specific, 322
Glands, see Endocrine system
Glutamic acid, 27–28
Goals, 127–129, 141, 220–221, 237, 244, 287
  assertion of self, 410–412
Goethe, J. W. von, 257, 310
Goldstein, Kurt, 178–179, 292–293, 560
Gonad—Generic name for the sex gland in animals of either sex. It produces the sperm cells or the ova, and certain specific sex hormones: 57, 62, 63
Goodenough, Florence, 44, 84–85
Gorky, Maxim, 289–290
Graphology—Method of depicting the characteristics of a person from his handwriting: 472–473
Gregariousness—Tendency of animals to live in groups. By extension, the human tendency to take satisfaction in the company of others: 85
Greek civilization, 538–539
Group average, 174–176
Group factors, 359
Group psychotherapy, 438–439
Group testing, 342–343, 467
Growth pattern, 3, 40, 53
Guidance, individual, 560
Guilt, sense of, 281–282, 283

Habits—Acts regularly or customarily repeated: 217–218, 225, 230, 259, 296, 501, 557

Hair cells, 182, 184
Halifax County, Va., 33, 354
Hall, Calvin, 23
Hallucination—An extremely vivid image in any sensory field. Usually the term is used only when the subject accepts the image as a present fact of the environment: 259
  visual, 160–161
Hamilton, G. V., 241–242
Hammering-out process, 317–318, 321
Handwriting analysis, 472–473, 474
Hanfmann, E., 292, 294
Harter, N., 225
Hartley, E. L., 441–443, 531
Hartshorne, H., 451
Harvard Psychological Clinic, 276
Hattwick, L. W., 460
Healy Pictorial Completion Test No. 2, 344
Hearing, auditory qualities, 185
  past experience and localization of sound, 185–189
  sensory equipment, 181–185
  set, 189–190
Hebrew civilization, 539
Hecht, S., 164
Helpfulness, 452
Helson, H., 140
Henry, Jules, 526
Heredity—Transmission of traits through family lines. Factors called genes within the parents' germ cells determine that the offspring, if permitted an environment normal for the species, will develop particular traits similar to those of the stock. Such traits are said to be due to heredity: and environment, 13–23, 32, 34–37, 347–358
  genes and temperament, 23–26, 556–557
Herrick, Robert, 542
Higher centers, 48
Higher units, 225, 296, 311–312, 326
Hilgard, E. R., 214
Hollingworth, L. S., 328–329, 331–333
Homeostasis—Tendency to uniformity or stability in the normal body states of an organism: 15, 51, 67, 69, 199
Homosexuality, 77
Honesty tests, 451
Hooker, Davenport, 41
Horowitz, E. L., 389, 393, 486
Horton, L. H., 280, 281

Hostilities, 131
    See also Aggression
Housman, A. E., 318–319
Hudgins, C. V., 133–134
Hudson, W. H., 147–148
Hue, 157, 158
Hunger motive, 66–69, 209–213
Huxley, Aldous, 309
Hyperactivity, 67–68, 94
Hyperthyroidism—*Excessive activity of the thyroid gland:* 55–56, 63
Hypnosis, 280–281, 426, 430
Hypochondria, 201
Hypothalamus, 106

Iatmul tribe, 529–530
Identical elements, 229–230
Identical twins, 16, 18–20, 347–348
Identification—*Tendency to view oneself as one with another person and to act accordingly:* 414, 427
Identity, sense of, 405–406
Illusions—*Perceptions which fail to give the true characteristics of a perceived object:* 167
Images, eidetic, 255–257
    memory, 249–257
    visual, 252–255
Imagining—*Manipulation of images:* 270–277, 300
    and set, 273
    and thinking, 286–287
    drives, 273–275
    fantasy, 275–277
        See also Dreaming
Impressions, 140–141, 166–167, 188
Impunitive reaction, 126, 471
Individual, and culture, see Culture and society, 523
    wholeness of, 2
Individual differences, and defense of self, 430
    remembering, 249–250, 253–254
    sensitiveness, 307–308
Individualism—*Practice of exalting the interests of the individual:* 542–543
Individuality, and dreaming, 284–285
    and evolution, 8–12
    development, 38–45
    in thinking, 300–304
    life and adjustment, 12–15
    perceiving, 204
Individuation, 41, 49
        See also Differentiation
Industrial Revolution, 542–543, 545

Inferiority, compensation for, 434–437
Inhibition—*The stopping or restraining of a process from starting or continuing:* glandular, 63
    retroactive—*The blocking of the recall of already learned material as a result of the subsequent learning of new material:* 232, 262
Inkblot tests, Rorschach, 463–469
Insecurity, 452–453
Insight—*Realization of the meaning or use of an object or situation:* 233–234, 295–296, 315
Inspiration, 318
Inspiration-expiration ratio, 94
Instability, emotional, 63
Institution—*A social arrangement possessing a high degree of organization so embodied in rules, customs, rituals, or laws as to persist relatively independently of the individual members:* 522
Integration—*Process of bringing together and unifying parts into a whole:* 151, 230, 389, 532
    and creating, 312–313
    and thinking, 296–298
Intelligence—*Ability to profit from experience:* and environment, 34, 347–358
    defined, 333–335
    distribution, 344–347
    general, 322, 358–361
    genetic and environmental background, 347–358
    tests, see Tests
    theory of, 358–364
    variations, 330–333
Intelligence quotient (I.Q.)—*Mental age determined by a specific test, divided by the chronological age:* 338–342, 349–350, 352 ff., 360–364
Intensity, sound, 186
Interaction, 3, 12, 17, 18, 49, 276
    brain and body, 106–107
    endocrine glands, 57–58, 64
    heredity and environment, 32, 36–37, 205
    senses, 202
Interdependence of parts, 12–13
Interest—(1) *The attitude with which one attends to anything; the feeling accompanying attention.* (2) (*Especially in the plural*) *dispositions defined in terms of objects*

Interest—(Continued)
which one easily and freely attends to or regards as making a difference to oneself: 5, 372, 466
Interest tests, 5, 372, 373, 446–447
Interference, 231–232, 234, 263–264, 274
  response to, 90–91, 109
Interpretation, 297
Intersensory effects—*Qualities of sensation which belong to more than one sensory field:* 202
Interview methods, 443, 490–491
Intoxication, 70–71
Introjection—*The results of reacting to external events and persons as though they were within oneself:* 425
Intropunitive reaction, 126, 471
Introversion—*The tendency of an individual to direct his energies inward and to be absorbed in the things and activities of his own world:* 430–434, 509
Intuition questionnaire, 476–477
Inventors, 316, 318
Irving, Washington, 544
Isherwood, Christopher, 281–282
Italians, traditional and assimilated, 535–537

Jack, Lois, 431
Jackson, Andrew, 544
Jackson, Roscoe B., Laboratories, 23
Jacobson, Edmund, 113, 200, 277
James, William, 107, 131, 133, 134, 273, 279, 388, 532
James-Lange theory, 107–108
Janet, Pierre, 211
Janis, I. L., 298–299
Jean-Christophe, 396–397
Jefferson, Thomas, 544
Jews, traditional and assimilated, 535–537
Jones, Ernest, 423
Jones, M. C., 216, 220
Joyce, James, 436–437
Judgment, moral, 402–404
Jung, Carl, 430–431
Just noticeable difference, 140
  See also Threshold
Juxtaposition, 297–298

Kent-Rosanoff Free Association List, 98
Kidd, Joseph, 395–396
Kinder, E. F., 330–331

Kinesthesis—*Sensation resulting from activity of striped muscles (or tendons or joints):* 198–200
  and organic process, 201–202
Kinsey Report, 68, 443
Klein, D. B., 280–281
Klineberg, O., 354–355
Knighthood, 539, 540–541
Köhler, W., 233
Köhler cross, 143–144, 164, 178
Kuder Preference Record, 372–373
Kwakiutl Indians, 411, 519–520

Labeling, 256–257, 291
Laboratory, psychological, 3
Labyrinth experiment, 209
Ladd, H., 301–302
Lang, Josef, 424–425
Lange, Carl, 107
Language—*The symbolic use of words or other expressive symbols:* 289
Language responses, 234–235
Lasswell, H., 425
Latent dream, 284
Leahy, M., 34, 36, 351–352
Learning—*The process by which the organism becomes able to respond more adequately to a given situation in consequence of experience in responding to it:* 2, 9, 10, 20
  competition between responses, 214–224
  efficiency, 235–244
  elimination of useless movements, 205–209
  simplest types, 209–214
  skill acquisition, 224–228
  theory, 244–248
  transfer, 228–235, 240
Learning curve, 225–227
Leeds, M., 268
Lefford, A., 299
Leopold II, 422–423
Lerner, Eugene, 176
Level, intellectual, 334, 336–337
Levine, Robert, 169–170, 172–173, 175
Levinger, Leah, 121
Levy, David, 76
Lewin, Kurt, 124
Libido, 421 n.
Lie detector tests—*Tests made with an instrument that records respiratory changes, or pulse, or blood pressure, or the galvanic skin reflex, or any combination of these, as a*

GLOSSARY AND INDEX

Lie detector tests—(*Continued*)
 clue to physiological changes during deception: 95–100
Life-history methods, 441–443, 490–491
Light, response to, 214, 230
Limit, physiological, 226, 385–386
Linton, Ralph, 521–522
Localized acts, 41
Longitudinal studies, 503
 See also Cross-sectional studies
Loudness, 185
Love—*Positive response to another person (or idea or object):* 77, 117
Lovelace, Richard, 542
Lower centers, 48
Lukomnik, Mary, 212
Lynd, Robert and Helen, 545–548

McDougall, William, 132–133, 134, 426
McGranahan, D., 423
McGraw, Myrtle, 20–22
Madagascar, 521–522
Maier, Norman, 118–119
Maladaptive fixations, 242–243
Maladjustment, 444–445
Manifest dream, 284
Manipulative tests, 371–372
Manor house system, 540
Manus tribe, 520–521, 541
Market system, 541
Marquis, D. P., 213
Mass reactions—*Diffuse (random) movements of nearly all skeletal muscles, especially characteristic of embryos and infants; develop into or are replaced by more adaptive reactions:* 41, 137–138
Masserman, J., 105, 106, 109
Maternal drive, 74–76
Maturation—*Development of a trait (especially during growth after birth) so far as it is dependent upon orderly interaction of inner and outer factors, and more or less uniform for the species:* 42–45, 68, 88
 and nervous system, 49, 100
Maugham, W. Somerset, 413
May, M. A., 451
Mazes, 209, 334
 stylus, 223–224
Mead, Margaret, 520, 527
Mean, 375
Median, 375
Medieval system, 540–541

Memorizing, 238–239
Memory, see Remembering
Memory images, 249–257
Menstruation, 58
Mental defectives, 135
Menzies, R., 134
Mesomorphy, 510–512
Metabolism—*The processes concerned in building up and breaking down living matter:* 53, 142
Methods, psychological, 3–7
Michigan, University of, 492
Micropsia, 178
Middle class, 546
Middletown, 512, 545–548
Mill, J. S., 323
Milton, John, 312, 542
Miniature life toys, 462
Minkowski, M., 41
Minnesota, University of, 514
Minnesota Multiphasic Personality Inventory, 445
Minnesota Rate of Manipulation Test, 371–372
Minnesota Spatial Relations Test, 370–371
Mirror-drawing task, 209
Mittelmann, B., 55–56
Mode, 375
Monocular cues, 162, 163
Montessori schools, 357
Mood—*A relatively mild and enduring or recurrent state of feeling:* 111–112
Moore, Henry T., 187
Moral judgment, 402–404
Moral realism, see Realism
Morgan, J. J. B., 142, 276, 469
Mother, and self-love, 409
Motivation—*General name for the fact that an organism's acts are determined partly by its own nature or internal structure:* 25, 151, 175–176, 275, 297
 and recall, 262–264, 267
 in learning, 236–237, 240, 244
Motives, see Drives
Motor development, 45
Motor neurons, 47
Motor response, 472
Movements, restless, 205–209
Mowrer, O. H., 208
Mozart, W. A., 310, 314–315
Müller-Lyer illusion, 164–165
Munroe, R. L., 467, 474
Murphy, L. B., 301–302

Murray, Gilbert, 538
Murray, H. A., 276, 469
Muscular activity, 79–82
Muscular coördination, 45, 49, 72
Music, 186–188
Myers, Frederic, 317
Myxedema, juvenile—*A disease due to failure of the thyroid function during the childhood period:* 55

Narcissus, 408–409
Narcotic drugs, 160–161
Nash, Ogden, 410
Natural clusters, 384
Nature and nurture, 16, 18, 36–37, 76, 347, 356–357
Need persistence, 126
Needs, *see* Drives
Negroes, and environment, 29–30, 33, 354
   attitudes toward, 267, 483, 485–486
Nerve cells, 45–48, 70, 335
Nervous system, 9, 14
   and intelligence, 333
   and maturation, 49
   autonomic, and anger, 93–101
   development, 40–41, 42, 44–45
   nerve cell connections, 45–48
   nomenclature, 48
Neurons—*Individual nerve cells:* 45–48
Neurosis, experimental, 119
Neurotic tendency tests, 444–445
New Deal, 548
New Guinea, 412, 520–521, 552
Newman, H. H., 19, 347
Newton, Sir Isaac, 309, 552
Nietzsche, Friedrich, 423, 525
Nightmare, 283–284
Nondirective therapy—*A relatively short therapeutic method that involves a minimum of comment by the counselor. It is designed to enable the client to perceive his problems more clearly and with less emotion by allowing him to talk about his preoccupations in a permissive atmosphere:* 128–129, 438
Normal frequency curve, 345–347, 350–351, 375, 508, 509
North African campaign, 90
Nursery school, 460, 462

Oberholzer, Emil, 468
Object constancy, 166
Object dominance, 126
Object recognition, 148–149, 389

Odd-even reliability, test, 381
Odors, 193, 311
Office of Strategic Services, 453–455
Open-ended interview, 443, 492
Opinion sampling, 492–494
Organic sensitivity, 200–203
Organic traits, 496, 504
Organisms, and learning, 244–248
   stability of, 13–14
Organization, 177–178, 232–233
Otis Self-Administering Test of Mental Ability, 369–370, 373
Out-groups, 484, 488
Overtones, 185
Oxygen deficit, 70–72
Oxygen utilization, 53–54

Pain, 197–198
Painting, adult, 472, 474
   brush, 460
   finger, 308, 309, 459–460
Paradoxical cold, 196
Parallax, 163
Paramnesia, 268
Parasympathetic nervous system—*The part of the autonomic nervous system which is made up of two groups of nerves arising in the cranial and sacral regions, respectively, and their auxiliaries, and which has among its functions the constricting of the pupils, dilating of blood vessels, slowing of the heart, and increasing the activity of the glands and digestive and reproductive organs:* 48, 93–94
Parathyroid glands—*Small endocrine bodies in the neck near the thyroid:* 63
Participation—*Process of projecting one's inner thoughts upon the outer world so that the outer world mirrors one's thoughts; the breakdown of the distinction between reality and imagination (Piaget):* 400
Parts, interdependence of, 12–13
Past experience, dreaming, 278–279
   hearing, 185–189
   perceiving, 146, 151
   seeing, 162–168, 177
Patrick, C., 321–322
Pattern of abilities, 365–374
Patterning, 146
Pavlov, I. P., 213, 234
Pearson product-moment method, 375, 376–380

Perceiving, *see* Sensing and perceiving
Perception—*Interpretation of a stimulus:* extrasensory, 204 n.
  factorial analysis, 385
  visual, *see* Seeing
Performance tests, 343–344
Peripheral learning theory—*An interpretation of learning in terms of what the organism can be observed to do as it learns:* 108, 245–248
Peripheral nervous system—*Nervous system composed of all the neurons lying wholly or largely outside the brain and cord. These may be classified as afferent or efferent:* 48
Perky, C. W., 251
Perrin, A. C., 223–224
Persecution, delusions of, 424–425
Perseveration—*(1) Tendency of an idea to return without apparent associative stimulus. (2) More generally, tendency to continue any activity once begun:* 162
Personality—*(1) All the qualities, modes of reaction, etc., which set off an individual as distinct from all others. (2) The integration of these qualities in a unified system:* 3
  and attitudes, 487–492, 529
  and culture, *see* Culture
  and elimination habits, 72
  and endocrine system, 55, 57, 59–61, 64
  and oxygen deficit, 71–72
  and thinking, 300–304
  feminine, 550–551
  measurement, *see* Behavior tests; Projective tests; Verbal report methods
  patterns, 498–501; continuity and interrelations of traits, 502–507; sizing people up, 501–502, 563
  types, 507–512; need for, 512–517
Perspective, 237–238
  social, and self, 397–407
Phantasy, *see* Fantasy
Photographic reproduction, 256
Physical attributes, 410
Physical typing, 508–512
Physiological limit—*The stage of performance at which it is assumed that the subject has reached the maximum efficiency of which he is capable. It has been amply demonstrated that no such fixed point ex-*

Physiological limit—*(Continued) ists except for an arbitrarily defined condition of stimulation, motivation, etc.:* 226, 385–386
Piaget, J., 148, 297, 389, 398–404, 415
Picture tests, 276–277, 395–396, 469–472
Pilagá Indians, 526
Pintner-Paterson Performance Scale, 344
Pitch—*The quality of a musical tone which is determined by the frequency of the vibration of the sound waves as they strike the ear:* 182–185
Pituitary gland—*Endocrine gland located at the base of the brain:* 57, 62, 63
Plains Indians, 524–525, 526
Plateaus, learning—*Periods of apparent lack of progress during the learning process. So called from the graphic representation of learning in which this period is shown as a flat stretch:* 225–226
Pleasantness, 246
Plimsoll mark, individual, 90
Plutarch, 441
Poetzl, O., 284
Poggendorf figure, 165
Poincaré, J. H., 315
Polonius, 393
Polygraph, 98
Possessions, 410–411
Postman, L., 173
Posture, 101
  and attitude, 480, 481
Power motive—*The need to possess controlling influence over others:* 84–85, 274, 411
Powers, E., 473
Practice, distributed, 239
Predatory role, 530
Prejudice, 485–487, 488–489
Pressure, sense of, 194
Prestige motive—*The need to be highly regarded by one's associates:* 84–85, 274, 411, 519–520
Primary reinforcement, law of, 246
Probability, theory of, 494
Problem attitude, 297, 314
Problem situations, 222
Product-moment method, 375, 376–380
Projection—*(1) Process of attributing one's own qualities to others (Piaget). (2) Process of attributing*

Projection—(*Continued*)
one's own or baser qualities to others as a defense against acknowledging them as one's own (Freud): 131, 424–425, 457, 488, 515, 556
Projective tests—*Tests which use projection in experimental situations for the purpose of studying personality:* 555
  adults, 463–469
  children, 458–463
  defined, 457–458
  handwriting, 472–473, 474
  interpretation, 473–478
  picture, 469–472
  preliterate peoples, 526–527
Propaganda study, 235
Protest attitude, 72
Protestantism, 541
Pseudophone, 189
Psychoanalysis—(1) *Technique for investigating the mental life of a person by means of an analysis of his dreams, his free associations, and his blunders.* (2) *Body of doctrine based (largely) upon this technique. The essential tenet of this school is the part played in consciousness and behavior by motivations which are not open to conscious inspection by the person himself, though these motivations are of the same order as the wishes and desires of actual experience, and in some cases were formed in past experience. These motivations are designated by the term unconscious wishes or desires. They are kept unconscious, according to this view, because of conflict with other more advantageously situated or powerful desires. But through consciousness or behavior certain symbolic representations of themselves and in other ways give evidence of their existence:* 114, 129, 274, 313, 421 n., 438, 461
Psychology, and creating, 329
  and history, 537–554
  and learning, 237, 240
  and thinking, 300
  defined, 2
  methods, 3–7
Psychomotor functions, 371
Psychosis—*A relatively severe mental disease, i.e., one in which there is*
Psychosis—(*Continued*)
a loss of or disorder in mental processes: 130–131, 135
Psychosomatic—(1) *Pertaining to the relations between the visible organic structure and mental phenomena however defined.* (2) *Being both mental and bodily; having attributes similar to those attributed to both mind and body:* 56
Psychosomatic conditions, 56, 94
Psychotherapy—*The treatment of psychological difficulties by nonphysical means:* 127
  group, 438–439
Puberty—*Period during which the reproductive organs become capable of functioning and the person takes on the secondary sex characters:* 58–59, 62, 76
Public opinion research, 492–494
Pulse, 68
Punishments, 171–172
Pupillometer, 133
Puzzle experiments, 294–296, 303

Qualities perceiving, 146
Quartiles, 367
Questionnaire methods, 444–447, 476–477, 490–491

Rage, 90–93, 106, 110–111, 123
Rank-difference method, 375–376
Rarefaction regions, 181–182
Rasmussen, K., 273
Rating method, 447–451
Rationalism, 542
Rationalization—*Process of finding plausible reasons to account for one's practices or beliefs:* 422–423, 496, 515
Razran, G., 218–220, 230–231
Reaction formation—*Development in behavior of a trend directly opposed to one in the unconscious (psychoanalysis):* 425, 496
Reactions, frustration, 124–126, 471
  mass, 41, 137–138
Realism—*Tendency to accept what is experienced as real (Piaget):* 398–400
  moral, 402, 404
Reality, 434
  clues to 173

GLOSSARY AND INDEX

Reasoning test, 299
Recall—*Reproduction of specific previously learned material:* 260–266, 298, 416
Receptors—*Organs whose function is the receiving and translating of stimuli into neural activity:* 203
  pain, 197–198
  temperature, 196–197
  touch, 194
Reciprocity, 403
Recognition—*The identification of objects as those to which one has previously responded:* 266–268, 416, 433
  object, 148–149, 389
Recovery, spontaneous, 214
Reëducation, emotional, 114–115
Reflex, galvanic skin, *see* Galvanic skin reflex
Reflex activities, 66–68
Reflex arcs—*Neural pathways conducting from a sense organ to a muscle or gland:* 47
Regression—*A falling back to an earlier level of adjustment:* 425–426
Reik, Theodor, 258
Reinforced response, 213–214
Reinforcement—*The presentation of the unconditioned stimulus along with the conditioned stimulus so as to strengthen the conditioned response:* 214
Relationships, 309
Reliability—*The consistency of performance from one task to another or in the same task at different times:* 380
Religion, 539, 541–542
Remembering—*Function whereby past experience is revived or relived with a more or less definite realization that the present experience is a revival:* association, 257–260, 262, 268
  imagery, 249–257
  recall, 260–266
  recognition, 266, 268
Repetition, 227
  spaced, 239
Repression—*The process of excluding repugnant mental contents from access to consciousness:* 423–424, 430
Residual tension, 79, 200

Responses, 2, 41, 66, 80–81, 137–138
  conditioned, *see* Conditioned response
  extinguished, 213–214
    See also Emotions
Rest motive, 72–74
Restless movements, 205–209
Restlessness, 66, 67, 70
Retest reliability, 339, 380–381
Retina—*The inner coat of the eye which receives the light:* 156, 158 ff., 164, 184–185
Retinal rivalry, 163–164
Retroactive inhibition, 232, 262
Revised Minnesota Paper Form Board, 371
Revolutionary, 553
Rewards, 171–172, 175
Rhythm patterns, 80–81
Rhythmical structure, 188
Rigidity—*Inability to change a response preventing adaptation to a situation:* 488
Rigidity tests, 488–489
Rods, 156, 159
Rogers, C., 394–395, 438, 515
Role—*A social task or function carried out by the individual:* social, 529–532
Rolland, Romain, 327, 396, 417–418
Roman Catholic Church, 539, 541
Roman civilization, 538
Roosevelt, Theodore, 422–423
Rorschach, Hermann, inkblot test, 463–469, 472, 474, 475, 526–527
Rosenbaum, M., 531
Rosenzweig, S., 190, 430
Rosenzweig Picture-Frustration Test, 124–126, 470–471
Rossman, J. J., 316, 318
Ruger, H. A., 294–296, 297
Rural environment, 28

Salient traits, 450
Salivary responses, 213, 218–220, 230–231, 234
Sampling, 492–494
Sarah Lawrence College, 467
  Nursery School, 460
Sarason, S. B., 276–277, 430
Saturation—*The degree of purity of a hue; its degree of freedom of admixture from black, gray, or white:* 157
Scale, traits, 447–448
Schafer, Roy, 170–172, 175

Schroeder, R. W., 70
Schumann, Robert, 328
Screening procedure, military assignments, 453–455
Sears, Robert, 122
Seeing, 156–157
  and touch, 196
  past experience, 162–168, 177
  set, 169–173, 177
  social sharing of visual perception, 173–180
  visual quality, 157–162
Séguin, Édouard, 335
Self—*The individual as known to the individual*: 504–557
  and social perspective, 397–407; animism, 401; dreaming, 401–402; moral judgment, 402–404; realism, 398–400; identity, 405–406
  assertion of, 408–410; goals, 410–412; means, 412–420
  awareness of, 85
  defense of, compensation for inferiority, 434–437; education and therapy, 437–439; extroversion and introversion, 430–434; individual differences, 430; mechanisms, 421–426; super-ego, 427–429
  discontinuity of, 513–515
  discovery of, 388–397
Self-actualization, 560
Self-deception, 3, 417, 438, 558
Self-interest, 491–492
Self-love, 83–85, 408–409
Self-perception, 557–558
Self-regarding sentiment, 133
Self-reproach, 326
Self-respect, 133, 135
Self-understanding, 555–564
  education, 559–562
  suggestions, 556–557
  understanding others, 562–564
Sense-organ defects, 343–344
    See also Receptors
Sensing and perceiving, 504
  and thinking, 287, 292–293
  attention, 140–145
  defined, 137–138
  perception aspects, 145–148
  perception development, 148–154, 204
  thresholds, 138–140
Sensitiveness, 307–310
Sensitivity, organic, 200–203
  static, 199–200

Sensitivity factor, perceiving, 145–146, 151
Sensory apparatus, 181–185, 198
Sensory conditioning, 259
Sensory drives—*Drives manifested in a need for specific sensory experiences*: 82–83, 325
Sensory neurons, 47
Sensory toys, 460
Set—(1) *Tendency toward a particular direction of activity or association.* (2) *Readiness to respond in a particular way*: 214, 278, 336
  arts, 168
  attitudes, 480–482
  creating, 312, 314
  defined, 68–69
  hearing, 189–190
  imagining, 273
  perceiving, 146
  seeing, 169–173
  thinking, 292–300
Sex motive, 76–79
Sexual development, 57–63
Sexual responses, 68
Shakespeare, William, 422, 540
Shakow, D., 190
Shame, 436–437
Sheldon, W. H., 510–512
Shelley, Percy B., 275
Sherif, M., 173–176
Sheriff, Alex, 476
Sherman, M. and I. C., 43–44
Sherrington, C. S., 108
Shinn, M. W., 208, 289
Shirley, Mary, 25
Sigma (standard deviation), 350–351
  defined, 377–380
Significance, test, 383–384
Sioux Indians, 525–526
Size constancy, 166
Sizing up, 501–502, 563
Skewed curve, 347, 375
Skewers ordeal of, 525
Skill, acquisition of, 224–228
  creative, 310–316
Skinner, B. F., 189, 248
Sleep, and remembering, 264
  dreaming, 278–285
Sleep motive, 72–74
Smell, 191–194, 311
Social attitudes, *see* Attitudes
Social distance test, 484
Social drives, 84–85, 274
Social growth, 34–36
Social handicaps, 354–356

GLOSSARY AND INDEX

Social perspective, and self, 397–407
Social science method, 3, 4
Socio-economic status, scale of, 349–350
Sociology, 28
Socrates, 555
Sound, localization of, 185–189
Southwest Indians, 524 ff.
Space arts, 188
Spaced repetition, see Distributed practice
Spatial aptitude tests, 370–371
Spearman, Charles, 359
Spearman rank-difference method, 375–376
Specific energy of the brain—*The fact that the sensory quality called forth by excitation of a sense organ is independent of the stimulus. An "inadequate" stimulus like heat applied to the receptors for cold evokes cold, not warmth:* 197, 203
Specific gifts, 322
Spitz, René, 35, 36
Spohn, Herbert, 190
Spontaneous recovery, 214
Spranger, E., 446, 509
Staal, Murray, 172
Stability, environmental, 13–15
Stamping-in effect, 246
Stanford-Binet Scale, 338, 360
Stanford University, 319, 322, 327
Startle pattern, 89–90, 109
Static sensitivity, 199–200
Statistical concepts, test scores, see Tests
Status—*Degree of acceptance and honor accorded a person:* 84, 411, 529
Status anxiety, 547
Status competition, 412, 549–552
Stein, Leo, 147
Stereoscope—*Instrument which presents to the two eyes slightly different aspects of the same view, thus giving the impression of depth:* 163
Stern, William, 270–271, 337–338, 390
Stevenson, R. L., 278, 285
Stimulation, 47, 49, 66, 81, 87–88, 352–354
  sensory, 82–83, 139–140, 202–203
Stimulus—*Anything that excites a receptor: conditioned and unconditioned,* 213–214
Stock and environmental variations, 32–33

Stone, L. J., 197 n., 462
Storytelling, 462–463
Strachey, Lytton, 505
Striped-muscle response, 94, 100
Striped muscles—*Muscles which are attached to the bones and hence move the organism in the external environment:* 94
Stupidity, emotional, 243
Stylus maze, 223–224
Subject matter, 237–240, 381
Subliminal—*Below the threshold of consciousness:* 317
Summator, verbal, 189–190
Sun Dance, Wyo., 525
Super-ego—*The process by which in early childhood the individual strongly identifies with his parents as authority figures. The tendency to judge one's behavior by the same standards as those of important identification figures (Freud):* 427–429, 506
Suppression—*Conscious rejection of ideas or impulses:* 423
Sweat glands, 51–52, 87
Syllogisms, 298–299
Sylvester, E., 418–420
Symbols, 277, 462, 504
  acquisition of, 224–225
  conflict, 120–121, 133
  dreaming, 281–283
Sympathetic nervous system—*The division of the autonomic nervous system which controls the "emergency" functions, such as increased heartbeat, cessation of movements of the digestive system, and adrenal secretions during times of stress:* 48, 93–94
Sympathetic vibration, 183–184
Sympathy—*Demonstrated feeling or emotion:* 80
  See also Empathy
Synapse—*The region of contact between processes of two adjacent neurons where a nervous impulse is transmitted from one neuron to another:* 47
Synergy—*The exerting of force together. Synergic muscles act together to move a member:* 49

Tachistoscopic study, 151–154
Talent, 329
Taste, 191–194, 512

Tautophone (verbal summator), 189–190
Tear ducts, 52, 87
Telegraphic language, 225
Temperament—*The more or less characteristic, persistent emotional disposition of an individual, probably having a constitutional basis:* 111–112
  and genes, 23–26
Temperature receptors, 196–197
Tempo, 188
Temporal region, 184
Tensions—*Energies concentrated in various parts of the body:* and emotions, 87–88, 102–103, 113–114, 200
  and frustration, 123
  and motives, 66, 68, 72, 79, 205
  rating, 477
  reducing, 208, 241, 246
Terman, L. M., 338
Test differentiation, 444
Testimony, psychology of, 249
Testing method, 3, 5
Tests, ability pattern, 365–374
  art judgment, 168
  attitude, *see* Attitudes
  chain association, 274, 279
  intelligence, 331, 333–334, 360; adult, 340–342; group, 342–343; individual, 335–342, 369–370; performance, 343–344
  lie detector, 95–100
  neurotic tendency, 444–445
  personality, *see* Behavior tests; Projective tests; Verbal report methods
  reasoning, 299
  statistical concepts, 374–387; correlation coefficient, 351, 380–382; factor analysis, 359, 384–386; product-moment method, 376–380; rank-difference method, 376–380; significance, 383–384; validation, 382–383
Vigotsky, 291–292
Thema, 276
Thematic Apperception Test (TAT), 276–277, 395–396, 469–470, 487, 488
Theophrastus, 508
Therapy, 128–129, 437–439, 514–515
Thinking—*The processes by which the answer to a question is found:* 286–288
Thinking—(*Continued*)
  concepts, 289–300
  individuality, 300–303
Thirst motive, 69–70
Thompson, J., 44
Thomson, George, 306–307
Thorndike, R. L., 229, 246
  CAVD test, 343
Threshold—*The amount of stimulation required to elicit a response:* 66–68, 74, 76, 504
  and sensations, 138–140
  for discrimination—*The smallest difference between two stimuli (or changes in two successive presentations of one stimulus) which can be discriminated:* 140
  pain, 197–198
  two-point, 140
Thurstone, L. L., 384–385
Thymus—*Endocrine gland in the upper thorax which plays an important part in normal growth before puberty:* 57
Thyroid—*Ductless gland lying on each side of the upper windpipe. It secretes thyroxin, which helps to control the metabolic rate:* 53–57, 63
Thyroxin, 54
Timbre—*The quality of a tone which characterizes the instrument producing it. Timbre is determined by the number and relative intensity of the overtones produced in the sounding body:* 185
Time arts, 188
Tissues, 26
Titchener, E. P., 252–253
Tocqueville, Alexis de, 545
Tone, 184, 185, 186–188, 202, 230, 234, 259
Touch, 181, 194–196
Toys, miniature, 462
  sensory, 460
Traits—*Means of distinguishing one person from another:* 448–450
  and attitudes, 488–489
  continuity, 502–507
  interrelationship, 496–501
  sizing up, 501–502
  See also Attributes
Transfer—*Effect of training in one function on performance in another function or on performance of the same function in another*

GLOSSARY AND INDEX 583

Transfer—(*Continued*)
  part of the body: 228–235, 240, 288, 289, 295, 455, 557
Tryon, R. C., 24
Turner, W. D., 159
Turning away, 423, 432
Twain, Mark, 545
Twins, 20–22
  identical, 16, 18–20, 347–348
Two-class system, 546–548
Two-point threshold, 140
Typing, physical, 508–512

Ulcerations, 103–104
Unconditioned stimulus—*A stimulus biologically adequate to arouse a response:* 213–214
Unconscious mind—*In Freudian psychoanalysis, the entire mass of psychic processes which is unable to enter consciousness:* 263
Understanding, *see* Self-understanding
Undirected energy, 91
Undoing, 423
Units, higher, 225, 296, 311–312, 326
Unstriped muscles—*Muscles which chiefly provide internal adjustments:* 94
Urban environment, 28–29
Useless movements, 206–209

Validity—*The degree to which an instrument measures what it is supposed to measure; i.e., the degree to which performance on a psychological test corresponds to performance in a life situation:* test, 382–383, 444, 445
Value—*That which makes objects desired or desirable or to be sought after; worth:* 446
Values, tests of, 5, 446–447
Vancouver Island, 519–520
Varendonck, J., 272
Variation, 8–10
Veblen, Thorstein, 411
Verbal comprehension items, 381
Verbal report methods, 440–451, 490–491
  combined with behavior tests, 453–456
  interview, 443
  life history, 441–443
  questionnaire, 444–447, 476–477
  ratings, 447–451

Verbal summator, 189–190
Vernon, P. E., 497–498
Vibration, sympathetic, 183–184
Vigotsky test, 291–292
Vinci, Leonardo da, 508
Viscera, and emotion, 108
Visceral drives—*Drives which depend directly on varying visceral conditions:* 74, 273
Visual images, 252–255
Visual perception, *see* Seeing
Vocational guidance, 366, 368–374
Voluntary factors, 133–134, 143

Waehner, T. S., 472
Wallach, H., 166
Warmth, 196–197
Washburn, Ruth, 25–26
Washington, George, 542
Water deficits, 69–70
Wave of compression, 182
Wechsler-Bellevue test, 341–342, 360
Wellman, B. L., 34, 36
Wells, F. L., 95
Wenger, M. A., 79, 200
Werner, H., 149
Wertheimer, Max, 127–128, 297
Whitman, Walt, 307
Wickes, Frances G., 271
Will—*Regulation of behavior by internal symbols:* 131–136
Wilson, E. B., 12
Wish fulfillment, 283–284
Withdrawal, 527–529
Witkin, H. A., 167–168
Wolfe, Thomas, 227–228, 307–308
Wolff, Harold, 103
Wolff, Werner, 265–266
Woodworth, R. S., 229
Words, and remembering, 254–255
Working class, 546–548
World War I, 342, 426
World War II, 65, 90, 212, 273, 342, 382–383, 453–455, 492
Wright, H. F., 121
Writing, 207–208

X-rays, 11

Yale Psychological Clinic, 19–20, 45
Young, P. T., 189, 212

Zeigarnik, B., 416
Zuñi Indians, 520